REAGAN

REAGAN

THE MAN AND HIS PRESIDENCY

DEBORAH HART STROBER
AND GERALD S. STROBER

HOUGHTON MIFFLIN COMPANY

BOSTON · NEW YORK · 1998

For information about permission to reproduce selections from
this book, write to Permissions, Houghton Mifflin Company,
215 Park Avenue South, New York, New York 10003.

Library of Congress Cataloging-in-Publication Data
Strober, Deborah H. (Deborah Hart), date.
    Reagan : the man and his presidency / Deborah Hart Strober
and Gerald S. Strober.
        p.   cm.
    Includes bibliographical references (p.   ) and index.
    ISBN 0-395-77193-5
    1. Reagan, Ronald. 2. United States — Politics and
government — 1981–1989. 3. Reagan, ronald — Friends and
associates — Interviews. 4. Oral history.   I. Strober, Gerald S.
II. Title.
E876.S775   1998
973.927'092 — DC21   97-53059
                            CIP

Printed in the United States of America

QUM 10 9 8 7 6 5 4 3 2 1

With deep affection and
appreciation to our family
Judith and Mortimer Civan
Joseph Hochstein
Ruth Hockstein
Muriel and Myron Strober

And
in loving memory of
Philip Hochstein

Contents

Foreword

Since 1989 we have been engaged in the exploration and chronicling of the presidencies of the three men we believe will one day be regarded as the major American political figures of the last third of the twentieth century: John Fitzgerald Kennedy, Richard Milhous Nixon, and Ronald Wilson Reagan.

While our book about Kennedy was begun nearly thirty years after his assassination, and our Nixon volume was completed nearly twenty years after his forced resignation in the wake of the Watergate scandal, the present book on Ronald Reagan was researched and written, based on interviews with 108 of his political associates and contemporaries, less than ten years after he completed the second term of his presidency.

As we embarked on this project, we wondered whether Reagan administration insiders, as well as foreign leaders and personal friends, would be willing to speak with us on the record, and if so, whether they would be candid in recollecting the issues of the 1980s — issues that, we believe, have altered the course of world history.

As it happened, not only were they willing to cooperate with us, but many of them voiced their support for an oral history of the Reagan presidency; such an approach, they felt, would accurately portray not only the man and the presidency but also themselves.

Through the recollections and observations of our interviewees for these three books — more than three hundred of the leading political figures of our era — we have had the privilege of being witnesses to the events of what we believe historians will judge to be the most dynamic four decades of the twentieth century.

Deborah Hart Strober
Gerald S. Strober

Acknowledgments

Reagan: The Man and His Presidency could not have been written without the cooperation of our interviewees, all of whom received us with courtesy and responded to our inquiries with sincere efforts to help explicate the complex issues and events of the two terms of the Reagan presidency.

We were assisted along the way by our friend and colleague Martin Wenick, a specialist on the former Soviet Union; by the Israeli journalist Ze'ev Shiff, who provided us with extensive background information on a variety of Middle East issues; and by Maria Nicola, who translated the Spanish-language portions of our interview with Manuel Noriega.

One cannot bring a literary project to fruition without the support and professional expertise of one's agent and editor. In both cases, we are truly blessed. Chris Carduff, our editor at Houghton Mifflin, never flinched when presented with our massive manuscript, which he pared with consummate skill and tact; and our agent, Mitchell Rose, was there for us at every step of the way, enduring seemingly endless telephone calls, not to mention many visits by us to his office. At Houghton Mifflin, we also appreciate the efforts of Becky Saikia-Wilson, the manuscript editing and composition manager, and Cindy Buck, the copyeditor of our manuscript. And how could we have completed our manuscript without Vincent Joseph, who brought us to a state of computer literacy sufficient to enter the manuscript into our laptop.

We also want to express our gratitude to Bonnie Cutler and Mark Heutlinger; Evelyn and Raphael Rothstein; Marcia and Rabbi A. James Rudin; Florence and Harry Taubenfeld; Bronka and Jacob Weintraub; Betty and Morton Yarmon; Elaine and Martin Zuckerbrod; and Sheila and Herbert Zweibon, for their interest and support.

We want to express our thanks to our friends Michelle Meyers and Dorrit and Meir Nocham, the parents of our son Jeremy Benjamin's wife, Gabi, for extending to us their hospitality during our research visits to the Middle East. And we owe special gratitude to Gabi, Jeremy, and his siblings, Lori, Jonathan, and Robin Strober, for their love and for their faith in this, our most challenging project to date.

What I'd really like to do is go down in history as the president who made Americans believe in themselves again.

RONALD REAGAN, 1981

PART ONE

THE FIRST TERM

1

Reagan Is Elected President

Ronald Reagan was elected the fortieth president of the United States on November 4, 1980. He won by a landslide, garnering 43,901,812 votes, 51 percent of the popular total. The Democratic Party candidate, incumbent President Jimmy Carter, received 35,483,820 votes, a mere 41 percent of the votes cast.

Despite the Republican candidate's personal charm and enunciation of an optimistic vision and faith in the American way of life, Reagan's election was hardly a sure thing when he declared his candidacy for the presidency during a speech on November 13, 1979, in New York City.

Reagan's campaign would be marked by staffing problems, by the emergence of an unusually strong third-party candidate, John Anderson (who ran as an independent in some states and as the candidate of the National Unity Party in others), and by concern over his age: Reagan was born on February 6, 1911, and would be almost seventy years old upon taking office as president.

Further, his background as an actor, coupled with his status as a Washington outsider who, despite having served two terms as governor of California, was perceived by critics to have a shaky foundation in civics, created image problems for his advisers, some of whom attempted to keep "Reagan from being Reagan."

THE PRELUDE

Michael Reagan, son of Ronald Reagan   I started living with Dad [in 1959] when I was fourteen. At the time, he was giving speeches for General Electric. The bedroom had a sitting area in front of a large rockstone fireplace, and past that there were sliding windows. He would sit at his desk and write his speeches on three-by-five cards, and if you opened up the second drawer of that desk, there were piles and piles of these cards, wrapped with rubber bands.

I knew that he was getting very political when I would go back there and he would be sitting there, with his reading glasses on, writing speeches on these cards. The speech that really launched him, of course, was "A Time for Choosing," the one he gave at the 1964 Republican convention for Barry Goldwater. That speech really launched him because Goldwater lost, and they had already found the next conservative leader.

Lyn Nofziger, White House political director   When he was campaigning for governor, I said to Bill Roberts, who was running the day-to-day campaign, "You know, there is something out there, something between him and the people. He is going to be elected governor, and someday he might even be president."

It was not that I felt he was a genius, or a savior of the country. But there's no sense in being the most able man around if you can't get elected. And there was something very electable about Ronald Reagan; you could sense that people liked him, respected him, and felt that he was one of them. The main thing was — and I hate the word — this charisma he had that drew people to him.

Martin Anderson, campaign aide; domestic policy coordinator   I had first met Ronald Reagan when I was on President Nixon's staff; we had a cabinet meeting in California, and Reagan came to the meeting.

The first time I really began to get involved with him was in the late summer of 1975. I had been asked to dinner by [Reagan's campaign manager] John Sears and Lyn Nofziger, and they came right to the point: they said, "We're going to do it again; we're going to launch someone else for the presidency. We would like you to help us out with Reagan."

Joan Quigley, astrologer to the first lady   In 1980 I decided that Reagan was going to win, from his horoscope and from Nancy's horoscope. So I called Nancy and said, "I'd like to send you a written account of what to be careful of, and what to look out for in the last three months before the election. Would you like it?" She said, "I'd love it," so I sent it to her.

George P. Shultz, secretary of state   I had met him on a number of occasions when I was in the Nixon cabinet, but the time that registered the most with me was after I left the job of secretary of the Treasury, in 1974, and moved out to California. He was governor then, and he asked me to come to Sacramento for lunch.

I found myself spending about three hours in a nice, but probing, interrogation about how the federal government worked: How did the budget work? What was the interaction among the various departments and the White House? How did the cabinet work? All kinds of operational things.

I came away with the feeling that this man was preoccupied not so much with becoming president but with how to do the job effectively: he had an agenda, and what he wanted to learn from me was whatever he could about how to make that agenda come to pass. And I was very impressed.

Cal Thomas, vice president of the Moral Majority, 1980–85; columnist for the Los Angeles Times Syndicate   Things came to a head when Jerry Falwell, Howard Phillips, and Paul Weyrich had a meeting in Lynchburg [Virginia] in 1979 and discussed how they could mesh the growing political movement born in the Goldwater year of 1964, which knew it could not deliver the presidency on its own, and the growing religious movement, in order to turn the country around, morally and culturally. And out of that was born the Moral Majority.

The reaction was instantaneous. It was like nitroglycerin; it was what everybody had been waiting for. The Republicans found their ticket to the White House, and they had a candidate in Ronald Reagan, who could talk the language and engender great faith in these people to deliver this package of spiritual, moral, and cultural goodies that everybody longed for. Everybody wants safe streets and good schools and stable families; you don't campaign openly against those things. So all of these rivers came together in this major stream.

Martin Anderson   When he lost the nomination to Ford [in 1976], the next day, in the plane going back, he was talking about how the dream was still with us. That was the first day we started moving toward 1980.

BACKWARD GLANCES

Reagan, the Governor of California

Born, raised, and educated in small-town Illinois, Reagan first came to California in 1935, when he was twenty-four. A traveling sportscaster for a radio station in Des Moines, Iowa, he was on assignment near Los Angeles when an agent from Warner Bros. Studios hired him to star in a romantic comedy about a radio announcer called Love Is on the Air. *So began Reagan's Holly-*

wood career, spanning twenty-seven years and some fifty feature films, including Knute Rockne, All American *(1940) and* Kings Row *(1942). During World War II he served his country as the star of dozens of army training films. In 1940 he married the actress Jane Wyman, with whom he had a daughter, Maureen (born in 1941), and adopted a son, Michael (1945). Reagan and Wyman divorced in 1949.*

In 1947 Reagan was elected president of the Screen Actors Guild, a Hollywood union affiliated with the American Federation of Labor (AFL). He served five consecutive one-year terms, through 1952, and then again for a year in 1959–60. He began his service as a self-described "hemophiliac" liberal, a true child of the New Deal, but took a sharp turn to the right when exposed to the rule-or-ruin tactics of Communist union members. He cooperated with the Hollywood blacklist of suspected Communists, and though he appeared before the House Un-American Activities Committee (HUAC), he was wary in his testimony and refused to name names.

On March 4, 1952, Reagan married his second wife, the actress Nancy Davis, with whom he had a daughter, Patricia (born in October 1952), and a son, Ronald Jr. (born in 1958). In 1954 he moved from film to television as the host of a weekly dramatic series, General Electric Theatre. *For the next eight years he also toured the country as a public relations spokesman for General Electric, giving pro–free enterprise speeches with titles such as "Encroaching Controls" and "Eroding Our Freedoms."*

A Democrat who had supported Dwight D. Eisenhower and Richard Nixon, Reagan joined the Republican Party in 1962. He assumed the national political stage for the first time two years later with his nationally televised speech "A Time for Choosing," his endorsement of the presidential candidacy of Barry Goldwater at the 1964 Republican National Convention. Within days of this well-received speech, California's Republican leadership approached Reagan about running for governor of the state in 1966.

Reagan easily captured the party's nomination. His opponent for the governorship was the Democratic incumbent, Edmund G. "Pat" Brown.

Brown, who four years earlier had defeated Richard M. Nixon for governor, at first did not take Reagan seriously and worked to hurt Reagan's principal primary opponent, George Christopher, a former mayor of San Francisco. Throughout the campaign Brown made the mistake of concentrating on Reagan's career as an actor, failing to recognize that in 1964, when Lyndon Johnson had carried California by one million votes, the former actor George Murphy had been elected to the Senate as a Republican.

Reagan was elected governor with a plurality of almost one million votes, or 58 percent of the vote.

Craig Fuller, assistant to the president for cabinet affairs; chief of staff to Vice President George Bush When I was a student at UCLA, back in 1971, I met Ronald Reagan, who was the governor, and the people around him, including Mike Deaver and Ed Meese.

Although history records that he was unpopular with a lot of students, my reaction to him was that he was larger than life. There was a certain starlike quality. You would find young people — those who you thought might be protesting against him if they had a chance — standing in the halls of the capitol, hoping to photograph him or get an autograph.

Alexander M. Haig Jr., secretary of state I knew Ronald Reagan when he was governor of California and I was working in the Nixon White House. Reagan was a strong supporter of the administration and an advocate for a more robust conduct of the Vietnam conflict. I felt his support was very valuable; it was close to my own thinking at the time.

I had additional contacts with him during the period when I was White House chief of staff. At that time, during the Watergate crisis, Governor Reagan was a strong supporter of the institution of the presidency, and an opponent of the more emotionalized attitudes that existed about the crisis in some circles. There were elements in the Congress who were seeking to bypass due process — the impeachment solution — to force the president's resignation.

I felt that this could have been a major, major challenge to the American system of government, as visualized by our founding fathers. So in that context I viewed the then-Governor Reagan as an important stabilizing force in support of the system of due process.

Caspar "Cap" Weinberger, secretary of defense I first met him in a hotel in San Francisco when he came there to address a group of political people, a year or so before he gave the Goldwater speech.

After he was elected governor, it became clear that he chose very good people and had a firm philosophical rudder that guided him, rather than just paying attention to the polls. It seemed to me that this was a man we needed very much, in almost any position, in the United States.

Ronald Reagan's entrance into elective politics and his later political career were encouraged and abetted by a group of business leaders active in Republican politics. This group, known as "the kitchen cabinet," included Alfred Bloomingdale, Joseph Coors, Justin Dart, Leonard Firestone, Earle Jorgensen, Henry Salvatori, and Holmes Tuttle. These businessmen played an important

role in developing the financial resources for Reagan's campaigns and often
acted as advisers on policy and personnel.

Lyn Nofziger When they picked Reagan to run for governor, they went
against the old liberal party establishment that had controlled the [Re-
publican] party almost up until the Goldwater period.

[The kitchen cabinet] had a double role: they raised money, and they
gave advice, but didn't meddle very much. After he was elected, they set
out to help pick his cabinet-level people. They cared about things like
putting some of their friends on as delegates to the convention or putting
them on a commission, like the Horse Racing Commission, which were
prestigious assignments but had little to do with how you run the state.
Reagan would listen to them and then go about his business.

Stuart Spencer, campaign aide; political adviser I got to know him
quite well, politically and personally. I first met him in 1965, when he
was considering running for governor. I ended up working for him; my
partner, Bill Roberts, and I were his campaign managers in the 1966
and 1970 races. In 1976 I ran President Ford's campaign against Reagan,
and in 1980 I was Reagan's senior political adviser when he ran for the
presidency.

Bill Roberts and I had been asked by Reagan and his major primary
opponent, Mayor George Christopher, the establishment candidate, to
help their campaigns. At first I didn't know if he was for real, politically;
he was a charming fellow, and he was an ideologue. In those days the
John Birch Society was quite prominent, and a right-wing movement
emerged in the Republican Party, vis-à-vis the Goldwater candidacy of
1964. In the context of all that, we didn't know where Reagan was coming from.

Reagan called us and asked, "When are you guys going to make a decision?" I said, "You might be a right-wing nut; we don't know yet." He
said, "Come up to the house for dinner tonight." I'll never forget it. We
walked into the house, and he was wearing those red socks — a sort of
demonstration of his humor. It was his way of saying, I'm not a pinko.

On the Gubernatorial Campaign Trail

Stuart Spencer He developed a twenty-minute speech; he wrote all of
his own speeches. After the speech, he would do a Q-and-A, and he did
fabulously: if he didn't know the answer to a question, he was honest
enough to say so. People appreciated that.

Michael Deaver, White House deputy chief of staff People over the years tried to make him into something, whether they were working for or against him. But it was the sheer force of his personality and his beliefs that came through all of that during the over twenty years of his public life.

Frank Carlucci, deputy secretary of defense; national security adviser; secretary of defense In 1967 I was in Rio de Janeiro, and ex-governor Pat Brown came, and we had dinner at the Copacabana Palace Hotel, and the subject of Ronald Reagan came up. I made a disparaging remark about him, having to do with his having been an actor. Pat Brown said, "Don't sell him short."

What Ronald Reagan had, in addition to his ability to communicate and relate to people and to have convictions, was extraordinary intuition. He always seemed to have the right instincts.

A FIRST BID FOR
THE PRESIDENCY IN 1976

Reagan's second term as governor of California ended in 1974. For the next year and a half, while Gerald Ford occupied the Oval Office in the wake of the Watergate scandal, Reagan was urged by some Republican leaders to challenge Ford for the 1976 presidential nomination.

In the initial primaries Reagan fared badly, losing in New Hampshire by a close margin and then suffering defeats in Florida and Illinois. Then, in late March, Reagan confounded the experts by winning the North Carolina primary. He followed this victory by winning in Texas, California, and several other states.

At the convention in Kansas City, Reagan lost to Ford but received offers to join Ford on the ticket.

Michael Reagan At Kansas City the family was saying to him, "Take the VP spot." We thought, he is a little old, he may never get another chance at this. And to come this far and then not accept the vice presidential nomination . . . Our feeling was, don't be stupid, take it. Then you might automatically get the presidential nomination the next time around.

It was beside the point, because Gerald Ford never asked the question. Dad said to me, "You know, Michael, what I really wanted was to get the presidential nomination and then win the presidency in November because I was looking forward to negotiating the SALT Treaty with

[Soviet President Leonid] Brezhnev. It has been a long time since an American president has stood up to the Soviet Union. It seems that every time we get into negotiations, the Soviets are telling us what we are going to have to give up in order for us to get along with them, and we forget who we are. I wanted to become president of the United States so I could sit down with Brezhnev. And I was going to let him pick out the size of the table, and I was going to listen to him tell me, the American president, what we were going to have to give up. And I was going to listen to him for maybe twenty minutes, and then I was going to get up from my side of the table, walk around to the other side, and lean over and whisper in his ear, 'Nyet.' It's been a long time since they've heard 'nyet' from an American president."

That is what he told me that night in 1976, and it is interesting that almost to the date, ten years later, my dad met with General Secretary Mikhail Gorbachev, and Gorbachev said what every Russian leader had said before: "Here is what you are going to have to give up for us to get along with you." And what he wanted Ronald Reagan to give up was SDI [Strategic Defense Initiative]. And Ronald Reagan said, "Nyet." He got to say "nyet."

Gerald R. Ford, former president of the United States   I had been advised by one or two of his top people that if we won and he lost, I should not ask him to go on the ticket.

I was disappointed, because I felt that if I won, I ought to have the option.

Michael Reagan   I've seen Nancy vulnerable twice in her life. The last time was at the 1996 Republican convention in San Diego.* The other time was the night we knew that we were going over to the convention hall in Kansas City in 1976 and Dad was not going to get the nomination.

We had this private family dinner, and Nancy more or less, in a little toast, asked Dad to kind of forgive her, as if she wanted to take something off his shoulders: you didn't win, but I've been there with you, I've been pushing you, let me take some of that burden from you as you go down tonight to the convention hall. And let me ask your forgiveness for maybe pushing you through this situation. Maybe you did it because you thought I wanted it.

---

* Nancy Reagan gave a tribute to her husband, who was unable to attend owing to the effects of Alzheimer's disease.

She was very vulnerable and teary-eyed. By the time she got to the end of it, we were all in tears. It was the first time I had ever seen her vulnerable.

Joan Quigley I knew he wouldn't succeed, because he had something in his horoscope under which people just don't succeed. But I did give them some time during the try for the nomination. At that time, I met Nancy in person, because she came up to San Francisco for a fund-raiser on a houseboat out on the bay. She had always said she wanted to meet me, so we met.

Michael Reagan When we got to the convention hall the night Ford was nominated, we never thought Dad would be speaking. Afterwards, a lot of people said, oh, he had this whole thing written out, this was the speech he would have given if he had won.

But he didn't know he was going to speak. We were up there in a booth above the floor, and a man who was drunk comes up to the booth. He knocks on the door, walks in in a drunken stupor, and says, "Let me tell you, I'm in the pool, and here's what's going to happen. The president of the United States is going to come in, and he will give a speech, and when he is done, he is going to look up at this booth and say, 'Hey, Ron, come on down and bring your lovely wife, Nancy, and say a few words.'"

Then the man left the booth. Most of us did not take this very seriously, and we returned to the hotel. We left during the Ford speech so we could beat the rush out of the hall. I was watching the speech back at the hotel with my wife, Colleen, and my sister, Maureen, and at the end of it Ford looks up and says, "Ron, why don't you come down and say a few words?"

We looked at each other and said, "Who was that guy?" Nobody had told Dad what he had said because he was so drunk that there was no chance it would ever happen.

Gerald R. Ford I was thinking that it would be a nice gesture to invite him to come down to the convention floor and be seen on national television as a good loser. I was hoping he would react favorably to the invitation because, although we had had a very contentious primary campaign, there was nothing personal in it.

I was a bit disappointed when he and Mrs. Reagan didn't volunteer to come down. They hesitated a bit; there was no question about it. But then he did come down, and we had a joint appearance on national television.

I think it was the pressure of the crowd of delegates that was persuasive in getting Governor Reagan and his wife to come down and be on the podium with us.

Joan Quigley At the time Ford was running against Carter, I was on *The Merv Griffin Show*, and I said the one thing I could see was that Gerald Ford would misspeak himself and cause himself to lose the election. Well, that happened; he did make that misstatement about the happy people behind the Iron Curtain, and it did lose him the election.

At that time, I thought how helpful an astrologer could be to a political person by warning him that this was not a good night to hold a debate — that he could misspeak himself — and that he should hold the debate at a better time.

THE 1980 PRESIDENTIAL CAMPAIGN

Charles Z. Wick, director of the U.S. Information Agency In the spring of 1979 Reagan was working out of an office near the airport. My wife and I decided to help raise funds for this operation. We hosted a fund-raiser at our home on June 29 and raised about eighty thousand dollars. This event was later replicated in several other places in southern California.

In August the Reagans spent a weekend with us at our home on the beach. One afternoon, as we were walking along the beach, I said to Ronnie, "You need to get the attention of the media." At that time, he was way down in the polls among the many other potential Republican presidential candidates. "We should organize a ground-floor function in New York."

Shortly afterwards, Mike Deaver and John Sears took me to lunch and asked me to organize a New York function. Through a friend, I put a hold on the New York Hilton ballroom for November 9. In September, Bill Casey [New York attorney and longtime Republican Party supporter] took Mike and me to lunch at the Pan Am Building. We decided to go ahead. Mary Jane and I took a three-bedroom suite at the Mayfair House, which became our "boiler room," and began to organize what we called the Ground-Floor Committee.

Casey recruited Ray Donovan° and other important Republicans,

---

° Raymond Donovan served as secretary of labor in the first Reagan cabinet and became the first sitting member of a cabinet to be indicted on charges of fraud and grand larceny. Donovan and several other executives in his New Jersey construction firm were acquitted in 1987.

and we would meet every afternoon at five o'clock in our suite. We had originally aimed for 250 people. Then, little by little, we thought, 300, then 400. Well, it was one of the major thrills of my life when, on the evening of November 9, we had about 1,850 people in the Hilton ballroom. During the evening, Deaver and I went up to the mezzanine, where over 200 of the world press were gathered to cover the event. It was the giant impetus that set everything going.

Ford Decides Not to Run Again

Gerald R. Ford When Reagan announced early in 1980 that he would be a candidate, I assumed that if I didn't run, he would be the nominee. I was urged by many people all over the country to become a candidate. If I had been, there is no question that there would have been a head-to-head confrontation again.

I thought about it, and to be honest, I had lost my enthusiasm to have a national campaign, where I had to raise fifteen or twenty million dollars. And I said to myself, if we have another Reagan-Ford campaign, it will probably enhance Jimmy Carter's getting reelected, so when I looked at the overall picture, I thought it was best for the party, myself, and the country not to do it.

Stuart Spencer Mrs. Reagan was the personnel director; she screened all of us, looking for hidden agendas. And she was tough and pretty good at it. He had never fired anybody in his life.

The actor thing was a plus and a minus: he was well known, he didn't have a name ID problem. His support among women was in the 92 percent bracket. He was very sound ideologically; he had a value system of his own that never left him in all his years in politics.

Nancy was mad as hell with me in 1976. In 1976 I went with Ford because I believed a party should run with its incumbent. Also, in the last years of Reagan's governorship, there had been a lot of problems and infighting, so we would never have been asked in 1976. They wouldn't have been happy with me.

I understood Reagan's dilemma at the time. Here comes this guy out of Michigan, from nowhere. In the normal process, it would have been Reagan, he would have been the heir apparent. Then Nixon gets into trouble, and he's out of there. And Ford is elevated to the presidency, and he likes the job. So all of a sudden, you have two gorillas: the guy who is president, and the guy who, in the minds of a lot of the Republican electorate, is the heir apparent.

I have always maintained — and a lot of his right-wing friends think I am nuts — that Reagan was lucky he got beaten in the 1976 primaries. He would not have won that race: Jimmy Carter was going to carry the South, and without the South, Reagan could not have won in 1976. But come 1980, after Carter had basically had a bad presidency, Reagan was the beneficiary. He has always been a lucky politician.

Gerald R. Ford   There was no doubt in my mind that if I were to be the candidate in 1980, I would beat Jimmy Carter, period. President Carter was very vulnerable, more vulnerable to me, I felt, than to Reagan. I thought I could do a better job than Reagan; I thought I knew more about the federal government, domestically and foreign policy–wise, and therefore I thought I could do a better job than either Carter or Reagan. And I still believe so today.

Staffing the Campaign

Stuart Spencer   Nancy Reagan came around in 1980. This is one of the reasons he was elected president: she realized they needed some help. No matter how mad she was at me, she respected me politically. If there was a political question, they would ask, "Where's Stu?" I was the first person they would talk to.

When I joined the campaign, I saw that there were two campaigns: one was at headquarters, in Arlington, Virginia; the other was on the plane. In most campaigns whoever owns the body owns the campaign, so I put good people on the plane.

I had enough ideologues so I couldn't get off-base. I had guys who could deal with the press, like Jim Brady. And Deaver was there; he was probably the person closest to the Reagans. And when I say "the Reagans," that is important, because they are a team; he would never have been president of the United States without Nancy Reagan.

John Sears

John Sears served as Reagan's campaign manager in the 1976 race against Gerald Ford. Sears, who had worked in the Nixon White House, was brought into the Reagan camp because the team led by Stuart Spencer and Bill Roberts, who had managed Reagan's gubernatorial campaigns, had committed to work for Ford.

In 1980 Reagan initially turned again to Sears.

Martin Anderson If it had not been for John Sears, Ronald Reagan would never have been president of the United States. He was the guy who got it going. Then, as the campaign developed, he transformed and acted like a megalomaniac.

Edwin Meese III, counselor to the president; attorney general of the United States Sears had headed up the campaign in 1976. And in 1979 he was brought in to head it up again. At the end of 1979 he had edged Lyn Nofziger, one of the governor's oldest supporters, out of the campaign. In November he had created a situation in which Mike Deaver felt compelled to leave, essentially because Sears and his associates, Jim Lake and Charles Black, had said that it was Deaver or them, and Mike didn't want to put the governor in the position of having to choose.

Also, Sears was directing the campaign to political leaders, and Reagan wanted to get down and meet with the people; that was how he had campaigned in California. There were also personality differences: it seemed hard for Sears to communicate with the candidate.

Lyn Nofziger John Sears is a strange kind of person. He likes very much to control things. He controls by dealing with people one-on-one; he does not accept advice. He apparently believed that the old people around Reagan were a danger to him in his ability to control the campaign, so he set out to get us, one by one, and I think I was the first to go. Then they got Martin Anderson, and then Deaver, who had been Sears's instrument for getting other people.

The funny thing is that after the 1976 campaign, a lot of us old people had decided that Sears was a negative, but Deaver convinced Reagan that he could not win without John Sears. Let me tell you, Reagan could win if *you* were running his campaign. I guarantee that.

Michael Deaver The problem with John Sears and the people around him was that they didn't understand Reagan. They tried to make him into something they wanted him to be, just as the right wing wanted him to be something he wasn't. He was different from all those people; he was, simply, Ronald Reagan.

Edwin Meese III At the end of January, after the Iowa caucuses, it was clear that two things had happened: the Sears campaign organization had spent an awful lot of money (and because of the limits on spending, that was a serious matter), and Sears had a strategy of, I've won this thing, we're just biding our time until we get crowned at the convention. He had recommended that the governor make very few trips into Iowa, and we lost the caucuses [to George Bush].

Finally, in February, in New Hampshire, Sears and his group were closeted most of the time, and there was very little communication. Along the way, with these difficulties, I had been meeting with Reagan's kitchen cabinet. And in the course of this, Bill Casey, who met with the group, volunteered to help out on issues and other matters, so I got to know Bill and was impressed with his knowledge and management skills. I felt he was someone with whom the governor should talk.

The New Hampshire Primary

On February 26, 1980, Reagan advanced his campaign considerably by win-ning the New Hampshire primary. The first such contest in the presidential election year, the New Hampshire primary is regarded as an indicator of a candidate's prospects for victory in November.

Max Hugel, a Nashua, New Hampshire, businessman and friend of the soon-to-be Reagan campaign director William Casey, was responsible for turning the city of Nashua out for Reagan in this pivotal primary.

Max Hugel, campaign aide; deputy director for operations, Central Intel-ligence Agency (CIA)   When Reagan lost in Iowa, we were in trouble. We realized that we needed to have him spend a maximum amount of time in New Hampshire, and we got through to him through Nancy, who was close to Bill Loeb [publisher of the influential *Manchester Union Leader*].

[Nancy] was politically smart; she was the one who overrode every-body to get him to campaign in New Hampshire. There are a lot of mis-conceptions about her, but she protected her husband.

So Reagan came in, and it was amazing how we beat Bush in every ward in Nashua, a town that was normally a liberal stronghold. From my perspective, the presidency was won in New Hampshire.

Sears Is Fired

Edwin Meese III   Finally, Reagan decided he couldn't go on this way. He wasn't comfortable, he didn't think John was comfortable, and cer-tainly the campaign was not going well. So he asked Casey to come in, and he asked me to work with Bill, and he had the two of us kind of take over the campaign. It was decided that Reagan would meet with Sears on the day of the New Hampshire primary.

Martin Anderson I quit the campaign in late 1979 and walked away; Deaver walked away; Nofziger walked away. The whole thing simmered, and then, just hours before the New Hampshire primary, Reagan did something he would not normally do in terms of staff matters: he stepped in and did something that, I am sure, stunned these people.

Sears, with Jim Lake and Charlie Black, had gone to the governor just before the primary and said, "Get rid of Meese, or we're out of here." That's like making an offer no one can refuse, given the stakes and what was happening. Reagan called them into a room and said, "Here. Put out this press release." That press release said they were fired.

Lyn Nofziger Up in New Hampshire, Sears tried to get rid of Ed Meese. About two days before the primary, I had a call from [the long-time Reagan political associate and pollster] Dick Wirthlin. He said, "If Sears goes, would you come back?" I said I would have to wait until before the California primary.

Reagan is terrible on personnel. His problem is that he thinks that if you work for him, you are going to be loyal to him. He finally figured out that Sears was trying to control him. In Iowa, which Reagan lost and should not have lost, Sears was acting more like the candidate. And Reagan, who never really liked Sears, said, "He never looks me in the eye; he looks me in the tie."

It finally reached the point where Reagan and Nancy understood that Sears was just destroying the campaign. So they summoned Sears and his associates in and said, "Here's your resignation announcement."

Martin Anderson And they never came back; there was no forgiveness. [Reagan] was not mean, or bitter, about it. But he never saw them again. And within a matter of months, Lyn, Mike, and I came back. There were no big speeches; it was as if no time had passed at all.

Michael Reagan I will tell you exactly what happened. I will take credit for it, 100 percent credit. Between Christmas and New Year's in 1979, I got a call from the campaign, asking me to campaign for my father in Iowa. I spent five days going all over the state, talking to people, and I noticed that there was one thing missing in Iowa: Ronald Reagan.

John Sears had set himself up to be on television more than anybody else; every time he was on television he was smoking that stupid cigarette of his. They were turning down events for Ronald Reagan; they were running the campaign as if he were already the president of the United States. They would not allow Ronald Reagan to be Ronald Reagan.

So I picked up the phone and called my father. I said, "Dad, you are going to get beaten in Iowa." He said, "Why do you say that?" I answered, "Because I have been all over the state; I've talked to a lot of people. Bush is on the ground here every single day. You're not here. The people think you're above them. You are going to lose Iowa."

He said, "I just got off the phone with John and Charlie, and they say we are looking good." I said, "They are lying to you. It's looking good to them because they are getting paychecks." And as a father would do, he says, "Michael, thank you very much. I appreciate the information, but I think we have a good team." I said, "Okay. But just remember where you heard it." Needless to say, he lost Iowa.

We now go fast-forward to New Hampshire. The phone rings at six-thirty in the morning in my house. My dad never calls me; the only time he calls me is when I've done something wrong. Dad says, "I'm calling you because I am about ready to issue a press release, and I would like to have your okay before I give it to the national press."

I said, "Why are you reading it to me?" He said, "Because you, above anybody, would understand it." It was the press release firing Sears and Black and that whole group.

I said, "Dad, of course you have my permission." Then I said, "Are you going to win New Hampshire?" He says, "Oh yeah. We're going to win. Don't worry about it."

Casey Replaces Sears

Bernadette Casey Smith, daughter of William Casey (CIA director) Dad had left Washington in 1977 saying he would never go back. They had a wonderful house there, but he said, "Let's sell it. I'm never going back."

My aunt, who has since passed away, told of how Mom and Dad were in Florida in February [1980], when Reagan asked Dad to take over the campaign. My aunt was serving Dad dinner, and he said, "I just have to do it." He thought the country was going in the wrong way and that Reagan could straighten it out.

There were questions as to whether the Californians would follow a northeasterner who was running Reagan's campaign, but he fit in beautifully with them.

Lyn Nofziger Casey was a very smart and tough guy. He did what had to be done. He had to save the campaign financially, so he went around and fired everybody, although when the money began to come in, some were hired back. He and Reagan became very good friends.

Gerald R. Ford I have to be honest. Whatever I say about his participation in the campaign is prejudiced because of my personal adverse feeling toward him. Bill Casey was not one of my favorite people. He wasn't during the campaign, and he certainly wasn't as the head of the CIA.

Reagan probably would have been better off if Casey hadn't been his campaign manager.

Max Hugel After the New Hampshire primary, Bill Casey, whom I had known on Long Island, although I had not supported him for Congress, asked me to join the campaign and to work on organization nationally, along the lines of what I had done in Nashua.

Casey gave me two fat books, which were a critique of the 1976 Ford campaign for the presidency. He said, "Read this, and don't you dare do anything like it." I read the material and realized that Ford could have won. In the last days there was three million dollars available, which they could have used in Ohio. So I could see what Casey was trying to get at.

Jim Baker [Ford's campaign manager] is the biggest phony who ever lived. Casey brought him into the campaign. He had been with Bush. The next thing I know, he is sitting next to Casey, where I had been.

One day we were in a budget meeting, and I said, "I need three million dollars for my voter groups." Baker turned to me and asked, "Why do you need all that money?" I said, "I'll tell you why. I studied the campaign you ran for Ford in 1976, and if you had used the three million you had left wisely, you would have won."

THE 1980 REPUBLICAN
NATIONAL CONVENTION

Selecting the Vice Presidential Candidate

Edwin Meese III In the spring of 1980, Casey and I talked with the governor, and Bill suggested that we have someone do a background check on about twelve people who were potential vice presidential candidates, and this was carried out.

Martin Anderson If Reagan could have had his own choice — forget about the polls — it would have been Paul Laxalt.* He liked Paul; they

---

*Laxalt, a Republican senator from Nevada, had been involved in Reagan's 1976 campaign for the Republican presidential nomination and played an important role in the development of Reagan's 1980 campaign, serving as its national chairman.

were extremely compatible on the issues. People forget that in 1976 Paul had been one of the few politicians who had supported Reagan early on.

Lyn Nofziger I often wonder how the hell we could have been so dumb. I don't mean in picking Bush. By the first of June, by the time I got back to the campaign, Reagan had [the nomination] wrapped up, so we had at least two months to find ourselves a vice president.

We didn't do diddly. Reagan really wanted Paul Laxalt, but there were problems there that had nothing to do with Laxalt as a person. He comes from Nevada — which gives him no base, which is in the same geographical part of the country [as Reagan comes from], which has legalized prostitution, and which used to have many residents who were part of organized crime. So it seemed to a lot of us there were problems there which would mean spending the whole campaign on the defensive.

The Dream Ticket

Edwin Meese III The week before the convention there had been a lot of talk among the political leaders in the Republican Party about the so-called dream ticket that would include Reagan and Ford, who would be asked to come back as vice president. Some of the people from the East apparently were not sure that this guy from California could do the job. One of the things about Reagan during his entire political career was that he was consistently underestimated.

Michael Deaver I'm not sure where the Ford idea started. It was an option. I don't think Reagan was very comfortable with it, but he became convinced it might work.

Martin Anderson There is a story that has never been told accurately. There was a big internal discussion about who should be the vice president. Dick Wirthlin's polls were driving it: they matched up Reagan and x, Reagan and y, and Reagan and z, to see how he did. The only matchup that showed Reagan winning — people think that this is impossible, but we were way behind — was Reagan-Ford. It didn't seem reasonable, because he had already been president.

Lyn Nofziger We came into Detroit, and Wirthlin said, "Here's my poll. There are three people who can help you for vice president: Gerald

Ford, George Bush, and Howard Baker."* Well, Reagan didn't want any of them; he thought Ford had stolen the nomination from him in 1976, which he had not. After the debate in New Hampshire, he thought Bush was a wimp, and he hated Howard Baker because Baker had been on the side of giving away the Panama Canal.

Dick's poll said that Ford would help us the most. I must tell you, that would have been the worst decision we had ever made — a total disaster. The American people would have thought, Reagan doesn't think he is up to being president, so he's brought in this guy.

Gerald R. Ford   Sometime in March 1980, I announced I would not be a candidate. My wife and I went to the convention in Detroit. We had not identified whom we would urge as the vice presidential candidate. As soon as we got to our hotel, we got word that Governor and Mrs. Reagan wanted to see us.

Governor and Mrs. Reagan walk into our suite, and he hands me an Indian peace pipe, which was a very nice gesture. And almost immediately he says that he and Nancy — and she's right there — have concluded that if I were to be on the ticket as vice president, it would be more certain that we could beat Jimmy Carter.

I was shocked, because I had had no forewarning. My wife was equally shocked, because she thought we were out of politics. We talked about it. I said, "I can't make a snap decision. Before I would consider it, I want on paper what my responsibilities would be if we won."

We agreed that I would appoint three or four people to represent me — I appointed Kissinger, Greenspan, and Bob Barrett† — and Reagan, in turn, would pick three or four people, and that those people, in the next twenty-four to forty-eight hours, would try to come up with some kind of a statement that would put in writing the relationship of the vice president to the president. That group met to try to come up with some sort of a document.

---

* Baker, a Republican senator from Tennessee, had served as Senate minority leader and had been the ranking minority member of the Senate Watergate Committee. In 1987 he would become the White House chief of staff.
† Henry A. Kissinger served as national security adviser, and then as secretary of state, in the Nixon administration, and as secretary of state in the Ford administration; Alan Greenspan was an economic adviser to President Reagan and became chairman of the Federal Reserve Board in 1987; Robert Barrett was an adviser to Gerald Ford.

Martin Anderson The Ford people were aware of the polls and realized that Reagan needed Ford. I think that Ford was reluctant to do it. He had been president; why would he want to be vice president? So they tried to work out something that might be attractive to Ford, and to them.

Gerald R. Ford My people came back to me and said it wasn't possible. So I met with Reagan, and I said, "Under these circumstances, it doesn't seem feasible. If I'm going to be on the ticket, I want some impact as to who you are going to have in your cabinet. I would strongly recommend that you have Henry Kissinger, so that you have continuity in foreign policy." I don't think he reacted favorably to that. Why, I don't know.

As a member of the team exploring the dream ticket possibilities, Henry Kissinger played a role in the drumbeating for that option. Thus, there is some irony in the situation: in August 1974, as President Richard Nixon was preparing to resign, there was concern in some quarters that Vice President Ford might not be up to the complex challenge of dealing with foreign affairs.

  According to Ford, whom we interviewed for our book Nixon: An Oral History of His Presidency,* *Nixon sought assurance from Ford that Kissinger would continue to serve as secretary of state in the Ford administration.*

Edwin Meese III It had been pushed on the governor by a lot of the party leaders. But there were many practical problems. The average voter might think that if Reagan brought back a former president, it would look as if Reagan didn't feel he could do the job himself. Also, if you have someone who has been president, isn't it a slap in the face to him to play a secondary role?

  We didn't see that the benefits outweighed the problems. But out of fairness, Reagan had to try to see if it could work.

Lyn Nofziger Of course, Ford exacerbated it by the co-presidency idea, and by demanding that he have the role of chief of staff; he, Ford, would pick the secretary of state and secretary of defense.

---

* Deborah Hart Strober and Gerald S. Strober, *Nixon: An Oral History of His Presidency* (New York: HarperCollins, 1994), 477. Ford, recalling his Oval Office meeting with President Nixon immediately after the departure of Senator Hugh Scott (R-Penn.), who had told the president he must resign, told us that Nixon "urged me to retain Henry Kissinger. I told him that I had worked with Kissinger for a long time. I was a strong advocate of his policies, and, therefore, it was my intention — if and when I became president — to retain him, which I did."

Ed Meese came down from one of the negotiating sessions and showed me this, and I said, "Ed, they are trying to steal the government." And Ed said, "Yes. But they are not going to get away with it." After two days everybody came to the same conclusion, Ford included, that this was a dumb thing.

Gerald R. Ford Under no circumstances was it anticipated that it would be a co-presidency. I did make the suggestion — and my negotiators tried to promote it — that, if elected, as vice president I would be the chief of staff and do the management instead of just hanging out there in photo ops. I'm not sure that Reagan wanted to have a vice president who was chief of staff. I still think it would be a good idea.

Why Ford Was Ruled Out

Stuart Spencer It wasn't serious at all, in my judgment. There were people around Ford who wanted to keep their finger in government; they wanted some leverage. The idea was ludicrous for anybody who understood the political process and understood government.

How serious the Reagan side was, I don't know. I can see the courtesy of it. But to take it seriously?

Gerald R. Ford The only way, under any circumstances, that I would have done it was if I had been convinced that my presence on the ticket would guarantee that Reagan would win. And secondly, if we won, if I was assured that I would have some defined responsibilities.

James A. Baker III, White House chief of staff; secretary of the Treasury There were a lot of negotiations about exactly how it was going to work — I mean detailed discussions about how President Ford would be in charge of the White House staff. This would have been very hard to work out. A president has to have his own staff. Many times the differences that sometimes crop up between presidents and vice presidents occur because of the protective nature of the president's staff and the fact that decisions with respect to the president have to be made with only one thing in mind: what is in the president's best interests.

That's why George Bush, in my opinion, was the perfect vice president for President Reagan: he understood that the job was one of deference. George Bush was very careful to make sure there was never any suggestion that he had an independent agenda on any items, or that his staff was somehow supporting an independent course of action.

That was the case until 1988, when it was obvious that he was going to be the nominee, or at least was the leading candidate for the nomination. And then there were a couple of instances when he broke with President Reagan on policy, one of them being Noriega.* I remember a long series of discussions on that.

Edwin Meese III   The governor felt he owed it to all the people who were suggesting the Ford option to try it out, and he felt he owed it to Ford to see if it could work — if Ford was interested.

Each one of them set up a team to see how this might work out. The Ford team included Alan Greenspan, Dick Cheney, and Henry Kissinger; the Reagan team was Bill Casey, Dick Wirthlin, and myself.

We met for several hours at a time over that week. On Tuesday night Ford talked with Walter Cronkite and in the course of the discussion made it seem that it was imminent.

Michael Deaver   When Ford, in his television interview with Cronkite, made his comments about a co-presidency, I was having dinner with Ronald and Nancy Reagan in their suite. When Reagan heard what Ford said, he exploded and said to me, "Go get Jerry Ford. I want to talk to him."

So I went upstairs to Ford's suite and talked my way past the Secret Service. Meese and Wirthlin were very unhappy that I had come up. They said, "This is all going to work out, so don't interfere." And I said, "All I know is that the governor wants to see Ford. It isn't going to work."

Kissinger — or one of the other Ford people — said to me, "You can't see him, he's gone to bed." It was only about eight-thirty, so I said, "Somebody is going to have to get him, or Ronald Reagan is going to go on television and pull the plug on this."

Jerry Ford came down to see Reagan, and they went into a room and talked for about five minutes. Then they came out, exchanged a few words, and Ford left. Reagan then came into the living room — there were five or six of us there, waiting to find out what had happened — and said, "It's off. Jerry said it's a bad idea, it won't work. He's with us all the way, and he'll campaign for us."

Martin Anderson   It all came to a head when we were in a suite at the convention with the governor. We were watching television, and on came Walter Cronkite, interviewing Ford. They started talking about co-presidency,

---

* General Manuel Antonio Noriega, the leader of Panama from 1983 to 1989, maintained a close relationship with the CIA and other sectors of the U.S. government.

and Reagan was stunned. He said, "That's it. No way." So he sent the-word up: "No co-presidency. If he wants to be vice president, fine." The word came back that Ford wanted to think about it. Reagan said, "No. You have an hour. If you don't accept in an hour, the offer's off the table." A short time later, down comes Ford. He and Reagan walked over to one side of the suite. They went behind the kitchen/bar and talked. We couldn't hear a thing. They were laughing and joking. Then they smiled and shook hands, and Ford left. We asked Reagan, "What happened?" Reagan answered, "We both agreed that this wasn't going to work. It's simply not the right thing to do."

Then, within minutes — maybe seconds — he turned to Deaver and said, "Get Bush on the phone." Just like that. We found out later that over in Bush headquarters they were beaten; they had taken their ties off, and they were drinking and having a good time. And suddenly it was like raising Lazarus from the dead. Reagan reached out and said, "Hi, I'd like you to be my vice president."

Gerald R. Ford We said, "Let's not make a final decision at this time." It was agreed that we would be back in touch. A few hours later, after talking with my wife and talking with the group that represented me, I called Governor Reagan and said, "It's off. I think you ought to find another vice president."

Within about thirty to sixty minutes, he announced that he was picking George Bush. To be honest, that was fine with me. I was a great admirer of Bush: I had sent him to China as ambassador; I brought him back and made him the head of my CIA. That is the precise way the situation developed — and how it ended.

Enter George Bush

George Bush, vice president of the United States I was sitting in my hotel suite, convinced that Reagan had already selected Gerald Ford, when the phone rang.

It was Ronald Reagan, and he asked me to go on the ticket with him.

Martin Anderson Reagan sent me and Richard Allen over to personally convey the thing to Bush. It was like walking into a fraternity house at about two o'clock on a Sunday morning, after a big party.

We had been fighting these people, but Reagan did not have animosity toward Bush. Suddenly they were blissfully happy. Some of them might have been drunk, but they were happy.

James A. Baker III   Governor Reagan asked Bush only one question when he called to ask him to be on the ticket: "Will you support my position on abortion?" And Mr. Bush said, "Yes, I will. I can support your position, you're the nominee." Even though, perhaps, it didn't comport exactly with his position at the time.

Jerry Falwell, president of the Moral Majority   As the thing was winding up, I was in Houston, preaching, and I got a call from Billy Graham at my hotel. He asked if I was pleased with the convention. I said I was very pleased with the way Mr. Reagan handled it. He asked if I was upset over the Bush nomination. I replied, "Billy, I'll just pray that God will give Ronald Reagan eight years of wonderful health."

I asked, "Who are you with?" He said, "Mr. Reagan." So I called Mr. Reagan. I said, "Mr. Reagan, you know I will support you." He said, "Why don't you talk to George about these things that bother you."* I said, "I will be happy to," and Mr. Reagan set up my first meeting with George Bush.

We had a long discussion of the issues, and I've never found a more open and reasonable person than George Bush. I am not sure whether I influenced him, or whether he came to these conclusions himself, but he very soon became a clone, philosophically, of Mr. Reagan on both social and fiscal issues. And Mr. Bush and I became even closer friends than Mr. Reagan and I had been — and are — to this day.

Stuart Spencer   When I first came into the campaign in 1980, I was flying with Reagan to Detroit and he started talking about the vice presidency. I listened to him, and when he got through, I said, "Well, you're going to pick George Bush."

He was mad at Bush then; he had said these terrible things about him. I said, "The platform committee is going to come up with a right-wing document. You have to have somebody on the ticket who is perceived to be more moderate." I wasn't pushing Bush, I was just making an observation.

He says, "Hmm." And sometime during the convention he asked me if I still felt the same way about Bush, and I said yes. The selection of Bush shows you the pragmatism of Ronald Reagan.

---

* Bush had worked for passage of the Equal Rights Amendment and was pro-choice on abortion.

Edwin Meese III He had been impressed that George had been a real gentleman even in the primary campaign. He felt Bush would be a team player, and he also felt that George would provide good balance because he came from the East.*

As far as the Bush theme of "voodoo economics" [his characterization in the primary campaign of Reagan's supply-side theory of economics] was concerned, when that would come up in the campaign, I would always say, "Well, he had his exorcism in Detroit."

James A. Baker III On "voodoo economics," the Bush campaign was wrong and Reagan was correct. I said that in many speeches after I became secretary of the Treasury and saw supply-side economics work. I used to say, "I'm a reformed drunk when it comes to supply-side economics."

Lyn Nofziger One of the many things about Reagan is that he is an in-cluder. The morning after Bush was picked, Reagan had George and Barbara in for breakfast, and he said, "We are all one team." When Bush became vice president, Reagan said, "You are welcome to sit in on any meeting I have." They had lunch once a week when both were in town.

I will say this for George Bush: he was a loyal vice president. He never leaked; he wouldn't speak up in meetings. He said, "Anything I have to say to the president I will say privately."

George Bush My relationship to [Reagan] was a very close one; we be-came friends, very good friends. He was unfailingly considerate to me. My brief was to support the president. He knew that I was loyal and would never compromise that loyalty.

Craig Fuller It is a remarkable relationship. George Bush, who was full of ideas and active and aggressive, and Barbara Bush, who is person-able — they were active in Washington and had many friends there — came to the conclusion, as Bush became vice president, that Ronald Reagan had to be the person onstage, and that they were playing a sec-ondary and supportive role.

I don't think that Bush did it because he made some calculation that

---

* While identified in recent years with the state of Texas, Bush was raised in Con-necticut and educated on the East Coast. His father, Prescott Bush, represented Connecticut in the U.S. Senate.

this was the best way to get himself elected president. He did it because he thought it was the right thing to do. He made up his mind about how he was going to conduct himself, even though it was quite contradictory to the way he normally conducted himself. He was extremely careful not to divulge what he shared with the president; he played a very supportive role.

I know that he admired Ronald Reagan. He told me when he asked me to be his chief of staff, "If I am going to have a chance in the next term to position myself to run for president, I have to be more like Ronald Reagan." This was my first really clear sense that he really appreciated, and respected, the qualities that Ronald Reagan brought to the White House.

Reagan was very happy to have Bush. Members of the cabinet could confide in him and feel that their confidence was never going to be betrayed; world leaders could confide in George Bush. It was really quite valuable for Reagan to have a partner in whom heads of state had such confidence.

ON THE CAMPAIGN TRAIL

Gerald R. Ford   Almost immediately after the convention they asked me to participate in the campaign. They worked out a schedule. I went with Governor and Mrs. Reagan to Michigan, where we spent a full day. I also went to Ohio and did several other joint appearances. When it looked like the election was going to depend on California, they got Charlton Heston and me to spend a whole day campaigning all over the state.

When I look back on it, I campaigned very hard, and effectively, because I could point out the disaster of the Carter administration. Reagan at that time was not really up to speed about how badly Carter had been running the country domestically.

Ronald Godwin, executive vice president of the Moral Majority   Carter was religiously incorrect to many fundamentalists. He should have known better; he was close enough to the truth to not have missed it. I very clearly remember hearing people say, Jimmy Carter is just another one of those liberal Southern Baptists.

They had no expectations of Reagan. But then he would give these tremendously inspiring speeches that had all the right rhetoric, that articulated the dreams, aspirations, and values they cherished. If you don't have expectations and you hear all the right things being enunciated, it's like getting a Christmas present. Whereas, no matter what Carter said, he should have said it better — and more correctly.

James A. Baker III   There had been a fair amount of resistance to my joining the Reagan campaign after the Bush campaign folded, even though I was the only Republican who had run a national presidential campaign, except for John Mitchell — who had gone to jail.

I think Bill Casey wanted me to come in, but there was some resistance on Ed Meese's part. I can understand that. Bill wanted me to be his deputy. Ed Meese, I think, was his deputy, and he didn't think there ought to be an equivalent position or rank there.

They offered me the job of field director for the general election, and I said I wouldn't do that, having run the prior Republican general election campaign. Then we settled on the rather amorphous title of "senior adviser," which is what I was, and I ended up doing the debate discussions and negotiations.

Jerry Falwell   We were careful in those days to say we could not endorse or support a candidate under federal law, so we said, "Just vote for the Reagan of your choice." We got the feds shook up; we were getting phone calls and audits.

We planned a big meeting in Dallas in the summer of 1980. We called it a "national affairs briefing." We had twenty thousand people there, most of them pastors.

Reagan came. We met with him ahead of time. I told him, "We can't legally endorse you, but you can endorse us." So that night, those were the words with which he started his speech. He said, "I know that you cannot legally endorse me, but I endorse you." The place went wild. It gave credentials to the evangelicals, who were a disenfranchised generation. I compare them to the black churches in the civil rights days: not registered to vote, they were on the outside, and Martin Luther King brought them in; they became the base for the civil rights movement.

Ronald Godwin   The most important point to realize is that in 1980 the vast majority of fundamentalist Protestants were a very insulated, provincial subculture. They believed strongly in God, in family, and in raising their children in their religious faith and practice, and they believed that if they got all that done, they had largely carried out the will of God.

They weren't taught by their leaders that fulfilling the will of God for themselves and their families involved political activism. In fact, there was a pervasive impression that Christians who were really fundamental in their faith and practice really had no business consorting with secular political types, or with political types of other religions.

Dr. Falwell, a leader of that movement, did something that required vertical thinking on his part, that required him to behave in a totally atypical manner. This man, a product of his subculture, decided to reach beyond fundamentalists — to Southern Baptists, to evangelicals, to people of other Protestant denominations, to Roman Catholics, to the Jewish community. For him to do this was roughly the equivalent of my deciding to walk from Baltimore to Miami on water. He was a pioneer — very courageous.

We often talked about how he was at great risk because he was so far out in front of his troops that he risked breaking the bond and becoming a casualty of the campaign he was actively leading.

It is important to understand how he galvanized his base to follow him in this radical reaching out. He would tell pastors, "When you go to your doctor, you don't ask him what church he goes to. When you cooperate at the school board level, you don't ask them to pass a religious litmus test. So, when you are a citizen working on a political issue, there is no requirement for you to do that either." He taught fundamentalists that it was religiously okay to become an active citizen.

A phenomenal number of American Jews were interested in his positions. And I myself, as an administrator of the Moral Majority, was constantly asked to speak in synagogues to explain Dr. Falwell's position toward Israel and American Jewish interests. Dr. Falwell engaged in countless numbers of these meetings as well.

Candidate Reagan

Constantine Menges, campaign aide; national CIA intelligence officer for Latin America; special assistant to the president for national security affairs   I was asked to join the Reagan team by Richard Allen and [Undersecretary of Defense] Fred Ikle. In the campaign, I served on three committees: the committees for the Soviet Union, Europe, and Latin America. We issued papers and proposals for statements by the candidate.

I thought that Mr. Reagan had a great sense of realism about the situation the United States faced internationally. I was taken by how insightful he was on a number of issues. He brought up issues that none of his foreign policy advisers had brought up. He suggested that we try to settle the Greek-Turkish problem; none of us had brought that up.

Martin Anderson   He was a tremendous writer. In the early days of the campaign, he wrote all his own speeches. He shared one trait with Nixon: he liked to write on long yellow legal pads. He wrote in black ink.

I remember once coming across a speech draft that had been written a third by him, a third by a speechwriter, and a third by me. That night, I got home and read it out loud, and when I got to what he had written, it sounded good. He had a way of making complicated, serious things perfectly clear.

The reason people liked him so much was what you saw on the street in Kokomo was what you saw on the plane and what you saw at night. He was unlike other politicians in the sense that he didn't spend a lot of time at the end of the day going around, sitting with the staff, having a drink, and making small talk.

At the end of the day he would say, "Good night, fellows," and go to bed. Later we would discover that he was doing his exercises. He was a doctor's dream: he did exactly what he was supposed to do.

Jerry Falwell   My first time alone with him for an extended period was in New Orleans during the campaign. I met him at the New Orleans airport. I was ushered over to his limousine after he arrived and got into the backseat with the governor. We drove from there to the hall where he was holding a meeting.

He knew of me because I had corresponded with him and had called him on a couple of occasions. His interest then was to assure me, as the founder of Moral Majority and as an evangelical leader, of his views on things that were important to us. During that ride he said some very profound things that impressed me indelibly. He said, "Reverend, sometimes I think that we are approaching Armageddon. The horrible arms buildup and the seemingly hopeless dilemma the nations of the world face today can certainly make one wonder if it can be reversed. My number-one responsibility, if I am elected president, is to attempt that reversal."

"I do believe the Bible," he said, "and that there will one day be a final war. I must admit that I have some personal concerns that we, in fact, may be heading toward that — maybe not in my lifetime or yours, but in the near future."

We also talked about family issues, about the moral breakdown in the country. He told me that in his earlier life he had not always lived by the values that are precious to him today. He said, "I have had some sadness in my life, and I am not approaching the presidency as a pharisee, with the idea that I have all the answers. Much of what I have learned has been by trial and error — sometimes more by error than by trial. But I want to assure you and all God-fearing Americans that I am sincere." He wasn't really appealing for a vote or a campaign worker; he was more or less trying to communicate heart-to-heart, and he did it very well.

When we got to the meeting place, we were sitting in the holding room, and a reporter who was there from *Time* magazine with a camera asked me, "Would you and the governor have a prayer together maybe?" Well, Mr. Reagan immediately picked that up as a setup. He said, "The Reverend does his praying in the appropriate place and time, and so do I. We are here discussing issues, not holding a prayer meeting." I picked up instantly that he was very skilled — no pushover or dummy. So my first impression from this first meeting was of his very deep faith and his sincere approach to the presidency.

The Rise and Success of the Moral Majority

Ronald Godwin   Dr. Falwell had experienced a surge of interest, as a fundamentalist Christian, in becoming more active politically. So he came to Washington and met with well-known conservative activists.

There was a brainstorming session, and one of the participants said, "Most Americans are morally concerned people. In fact, it is safe to say that the majority of Americans are morally concerned, responsible citizens." And somebody said, "That's a great phrase — the Moral Majority." That was the genesis of the name.

Jerry Falwell   We couldn't have done it without Jimmy Carter. He's the only person who will profit from the Clinton presidency: he'll no longer be known as our worst president. Carter was a disaster — a good man, but just incompetent, and influenced by whoever left his office last. He had brought the Christians out in 1976 as a result of his profession of being born again. Then, after two years, they all felt defrauded.

In 1979 several evangelical leaders met with me in Lynchburg, and we decided to organize a group. We named it the Moral Majority. We did not know how right the time was. I had the national television program [*The Old Time Gospel Hour*, broadcast weekly from Falwell's Thomas Road Baptist Church], and I began talking out loud about what needed to happen, and it just struck fire. We had unbelievable support from conservative Catholics, priests, and mainline Protestant people who were conservative, and, of course, the evangelicals and charismatics. Within twelve months we went from half a dozen of us in a room to several million people. Nothing like that had ever happened before.

When we formed the Moral Majority, we had to break down the psychological barrier in the minds of most of the pastors that it is not wrong or unspiritual to be politically involved. We then had to register them to vote. We organized big campaigns and registered over eight million voters; we mobilized millions more who, although registered, were not voting. Eventually, in 1980, about 20 percent of the voters were Moral Majoritarians, and they voted for Reagan.

Eventually, about two hundred organizations were spun off the Moral Majority, including the Christian Coalition. We were there at the right time, at the right place. Moral Majority had four tenets: pro-family, pro-life, pro–strong national defense, and pro-Israel. It didn't matter who you were, or where you went to church, or if you went to church or not. If you could say yes to the four tenets, you could be a part of it. There were millions out there who were ready for that; the Soviet Union then looked like an unstoppable force.

Cal Thomas   The problem with the Moral Majority, as we later discovered, was that it was sort of spiritual shoplifting. We went in and promised people almost instantaneous results; the suggestion was either implicit or explicit that what ailed America was political, economic, and cultural, and was not a matter of the heart and of the spirit — what I later called "trickle-down morality." That if we got the right people in the White House, on the Supreme Court, and into the Congress, people would love their wives or husbands, they'd be parents to their children, they wouldn't engage in promiscuous sex, they wouldn't take drugs, they wouldn't look at dirty movies, and they wouldn't buy *Playboy* magazine and shove it under the pillow at night. That was implicit in all of this.

And you saw in Reagan's first term a lot of these people, who had been energized, who went out and did the old-fashioned political work, banging on doors and stuffing envelopes, saying: Well, the Messiah has arrived — Ronald Reagan was the Messiah to a lot of people — now we can sit back and get on with our lives.

The Moral Majority and Ronald Reagan

Ronald Godwin   Reagan was not doing too well until he went into the Carolinas. With the help of the then-fledgling, almost totally unknown Moral Majority — Jerry Falwell's network of pastors — his candidacy sort of caught fire.

Dr. Falwell was invited to meet with the then-candidate Reagan at various places around the country. Some of the meetings took place in the backseat of Mr. Reagan's limousine, or in a holding room prior to or after a campaign speech — always out of sight of the general public and carefully handled so as not to be public meetings.

In those sessions Falwell and Reagan achieved a certain degree of understanding and comfort with one another, but not, in fact, a public accommodation of any significance. It was done this way because Dr. Falwell represented fundamentalists, independents — not even Southern Baptists — and while he seemed to be the leader of a burgeoning movement, he was a somewhat controversial, unknown figure, and Reagan's handlers were being very, very careful.

I think that in the second half of the campaign Reagan realized what was very obvious to anyone not living in a cave: that there were a surprising number of conservative, fundamentalist Christians becoming interested and involved in the political outcome of that campaign — a group that had not appeared on the political landscape in anybody's lifetime. This was a radical event: conservative Protestant Christians had suddenly become politically active.

In 1980 the country was ready for a paternalistic, positive, inspirational personality like Reagan. Looking back, you could say a lot of things about him, but in 1980, would the country have responded to a George Bush anywhere nearly like they responded to Reagan?

The Astrologer Joan Quigley
Offers Advice to the Campaign

Joan Quigley [In 1971] when I was working on my first book, I was on a late night radio show in New York with Long John Nebel. Long John was a real skeptic, and there were three or four other skeptics on the show, and they gave me a very bad time. I happened to have Long John's horoscope, and I said, "You had a very bad sore throat this week." He said, "Yes," and from then on they were just angels.

A reporter from Wilmington heard this, and he called me and asked, "Will you predict our elections?" I said, "Yes. I want to know who's running against whom, and I just want their time and place of birth." He gave me that information, and I did predict that election. And they had the whole front page of the paper devoted to it.

Reagan had been the governor of California, but he was perceived to be weak in foreign policy. I had put my report in on the very day that he said he would recognize the Republic of Taiwan instead of China: "Do not make any foreign policy pronouncements on this particular day."

Well, they began to look at it; someone noticed that I'd said that. Then Nancy was on the phone two or three times a day.

The Third-Party Candidate

John Bayard Anderson III, of Rockford, Illinois, a fifty-eight-year-old, ten-term Republican member of the House of Representatives, dropped out of the race for the Republican Party's presidential nomination in April 1980. He then ran as an independent, with Patrick J. Lucey, a Democrat and the governor of Wisconsin, as his running mate.

In late September, Anderson engaged in a one-on-one debate with Reagan in Baltimore. On November 4, 1980, Anderson received 7 percent of the popular vote (5.1 million votes).

Lyn Nofziger The only scary thing about Anderson was that Reagan, all on his own, agreed to debate him. I didn't worry about Reagan, but you do think: this is a chance where a guy can make a mistake. Also, we didn't have to treat John Anderson as an equal.

But Reagan held his own — and that was all he had to do.

Joan Quigley I picked the time that they left Washington for the Anderson debate. I saw that there would be a mechanical difficulty, but I knew it didn't have anything to do with the plane, so I said, "Nancy, the only other mechanical thing I can think of is the microphone. It could be turned down just before Ronnie goes on, so please check it at the very last minute." And Nancy called me and said that, sure enough, it had been turned way down.

This was his first really big public appearance, and if his voice had come across as weak — and therefore old — it would have been very negative for them.

The Reagan-Carter Debate

On October 28, Governor Reagan debated President Carter in Cleveland. Reagan was widely perceived to be the winner, owing in part to Carter's mention that, when he had asked his then-thirteen-year-old daughter, Amy, what she considered the most important issue, she had responded, "Nuclear weaponry and the control of nuclear arms."

In another instance, Reagan deflected a potentially harmful comment by Carter regarding Medicare by saying, "There you go again."

Joan Quigley   Nancy had very good political instincts. She kept saying, "They've got to debate." It was the biggest gamble they could take: if things went wrong, they would not have time to recover.

I must say, Reagan was a superb debater. But on the other hand, I take the credit for the fact that Carter lost: what I did was pick a time when Carter could get careless and misspeak himself.

He did exactly what I expected him to: he made that remark about consulting Amy, his daughter, about nuclear issues. And, of course, that put the ball in Reagan's court, and he just batted it over the net.

Lyn Nofziger   We had pretty much decided that we were not going to debate Carter. I got up one morning in Sioux Falls, South Dakota, and said to myself, We are going to have to debate, the campaign is just dead out here. I walked down the hall to tell Stu Spencer what I thought. Before I could open my mouth, he looked at me and said, "You know, we are going to have to debate." I said, "Damn you. I came down here to tell you that."

That morning on the way to the airplane, I, for no particular reason, rode out with Reagan. He looked over at me and said, "You know, Lynwood, we are going to have to debate." I said, "Damn you. Stu, Deaver, and I agreed that we would talk to you when we got on the plane, and now they are going to say I talked to you in advance, so you have to do me a favor: when we get on the plane, you have to act as if we never talked about this."

Stuart Spencer   We knew two things: we had to debate Carter — in those times, and now, you couldn't run for president without debating — and I knew that with the right kind of preparation with Reagan, he would do fine. It was not a question of winning the debate; it was a question of not losing the debate.

Martin Anderson   He disagreed with Carter's policies. His criticism was that Carter meant well, but he was trying to do everything at once, and you couldn't do that. There had to be priorities.

Lyn Nofziger   We didn't have to wait for the debate to end. As soon as Jimmy Carter said that he'd consulted Amy on nuclear issues, I said, "We've won it!" Then, of course, when Carter kept needling Reagan on past remarks, Reagan said, "There you go again." Everybody in the room knew we had won. It wasn't so much that Reagan had won, but that Carter had lost.

The Purloined Briefing Books, or "Papergate"

In the days prior to the debate on October 28, 1980, the Reagan camp had come into possession of briefing materials used by President Carter in his own preparation. Following the revelation of this in June 1983, two key Reagan campaign aides who occupied major positions in his administration, White House Chief of Staff James Baker and Director of Central Intelligence William Casey, accused each other of being responsible for the incident.

One of our interviewees told us, off the record, that while Baker pointed the finger at Casey, if anyone was responsible for the theft, it was Baker and David Gergen, a campaign aide and future communications director in the Reagan White House.

Our source also speculated that the briefing books may have been obtained by the Reagan aides through someone within the Carter camp who did not want the incumbent to be reelected.

Alexander M. Haig Jr.   Baker got a great deal of entrée during the last part of the campaign, when he brought the briefing books from the Carter White House. He claims that it was Casey. But that's not true; it was Baker who brought them, and who then became part of the coaching team to prepare Ronald Reagan for the debate.

Sophia Casey, widow of CIA Director William Casey   Jim Baker was against Casey. You recall the situation with the briefing book. Bill said to me, "I wouldn't touch that with a ten-foot pole." When the issue became public, Bill wouldn't say anything, but Baker said that he was a liar.

Was There a Danger of an "October Surprise"?

During the last two weeks of the campaign, Reagan's staff worried that if Iran were to release the remaining fifty-two of the sixty-six Americans taken hostage in Tehran on November 14, 1979, prior to election day, Carter would receive the credit for the release, hence an "October Surprise."

The hostages were released on January 20, the day of Reagan's inauguration.

Donald Gregg, staff member of the National Security Council (seconded from the CIA), with responsibility for intelligence, and later for Asia; national security adviser to Vice President George Bush   I was in the Carter White House almost the entire time of the captivity of the hostages. I knew a couple of them personally. It was just a heavy cloud over the Carter White House.

I was there when the frustration level reached a point where the mission to rescue them was planned, and I was privy to some of the planning. It was a case of micromanagement — not letting the military do the job as they felt it ought to be done — and it failed, disastrously.

Stuart Spencer   On the campaign plane we really didn't worry that much. If it happened, what could we do about it? I don't think it would have made a difference in the election. Reagan would have been very happy to see those hostages come home. Carter would have gotten some Brownie points for doing it, but people would have asked, What happened during the other 365 days? Where were you?

Donald Gregg   I was also later part of the "October Surprise" theory and was accused of having traveled to Paris in the fall of 1980 with Bill Casey and George Bush to negotiate with the Iranians not to release the hostages until after the election.

That is an absolutely ridiculous assertion, but it gained some currency in the rather fetid atmosphere that accompanied the end of the Reagan presidency.

But there certainly was a sense of deep disappointment in the Carter White House when they were unable to get the hostages out, and there was a tremendous sense of elation in the Reagan White House when they were released. It was a sense of a chapter having been closed, and a sense of Iran having recognized that it was in their best interests to release these hostages rather than having to face what Ronald Reagan would do about it.

The Mood in the Campaign
Just Before November 4

Martin Anderson   Up until two or three days before the election, we weren't ahead; the polls were not good. He may have known, however, that the situation was changing.

I changed my view a day or two before the election, when Wirthlin got on the plane and, instead of looking concerned and harried, he looked relaxed and happy.

Stuart Spencer   I remember telling him one night before the election, "You know you are going to win this thing." He hated to hear that; he was superstitious.

ELECTION NIGHT

Michael Reagan   Every election night the family and friends would get together for a private dinner before we went to the headquarters hotel. And there was Dad, at five o'clock in the afternoon, in the shower, getting a call from Jimmy Carter. Nancy says, "Honey, the president is on the phone." Dad says, "Can you tell him I'm in the shower?" She says, "I told him, but he needs to talk to you."

So, you've spent all these years running for president, and you have won, and you're standing with a towel wrapped around you, saying, "Yes, Mr. President." I don't think this was quite the image Ronald Reagan had of finding out that he had won the presidency.

Charles Z. Wick   On election night, the kitchen cabinet members went up to the Jorgensens' home for dinner. We arrived early, at about five o'clock — when we got there, Ronnie was in the shower — to watch the election returns. All of a sudden, just after five, California time, he was announced the winner by all the pundits. We had to get him out of the shower.

When he came out of the shower, he had this typical half-smile on his face — "Well, I'll be . . ." He was probably one of the most humble men I've ever known, with a remarkable nondilution of steely resolve and firmness and adherence to principles.

Later that night there was a victory celebration in Los Angeles, and we traveled there in a caravan of cars, snaking down from the Jorgensens' to the hotel. There was a portable television in our car, and it was thrilling: there we were, coming down from the microcosm of the Jorgensen house and exploding into a universal scene by virtue of being participants in this election of a new world leader.

Cal Thomas   There was a rally in Lynchburg the day after the election, and a bunch of us were sitting on the platform. The place was jammed, with every camera from every network, every newspaper, wire service photographers, and reporters, the top guys, and Falwell comes in, and the band plays "Hail to the Chief."

Right then I knew something significant had happened. The mentality was: We did it, we put Reagan over the top, and we are going to get the respect that has been denied us for so long. It was electrifying, an amazing moment.

Jerry Falwell A couple of mornings after he was elected in 1980, [Reagan] held a press conference in California. One question was, "Are you going to be listening to the Moral Majority?"

He answered, "I'll be listening very closely to the people who got me this job." A lot of politicians would have hedged on that one. And from that day, he never turned down a phone call; there was not a stiff-arm from that day until he walked out of office.

James Watt, secretary of the interior One of the problems the conservatives then had was that once Ronald Reagan got the nomination and won the election, they attributed to him their rock-ribbed philosophical views. They thought that since they had supported him, he supported them. In politics, loyalty flows up and down, and they could never comprehend that concept.

INAUGURATION DAY

Charles Z. Wick The day of the inauguration, about thirty of us were invited to tea by the Carters. I remember walking around the room, looking out over the south driveway, and seeing a station wagon. And there was Amy Carter, in blue jeans, shoveling some of her stuff into the back of the station wagon. It was a symbol of the transfer of power.

Michael Reagan Colleen and I were the hosts of the very first ball my father was going to attend on the night of the inauguration in 1981.

Dad and Nancy joined us in the holding room at the Washington Hilton. Dad turns to a mirror — he's looking in the mirror, straightening out his white tie — and he stops for a moment and just looks. And then he cocks his head and gets that little twinkle in his eye that he gets whenever he is going to do something dynamic, and Dad turns around, and he jumps straight up in the air, with his hands on his tie, clicks his heels together, and says, "I'm the president of the United States of America!"

2

Reagan's Personality, Character, and Relationship with Nancy

FIRST IMPRESSIONS

George Bush I first met Ronald Reagan in 1973, when I was chairman of the Republican National Committee. I did not know him well back then. However, I was very favorably impressed with him.

Gerald R. Ford The first time I met him was when he came to Washington to meet with Republican members of Congress. He had an excellent personality. He was as attractive in person as he was on his programs for General Electric.

Martin Anderson The first impression you get is that he is very big; it's like meeting a football tackle on the San Diego Chargers. The second thing that strikes you is that when he's with you, he's interested in you.

Edwin Meese III I met him for the first time in 1966, after he had been elected governor but before he had taken office. I spent about half an hour with him, talking about criminal justice and law enforcement. And my first impression was of literal amazement at his alacrity of understanding of concepts that I had spent my whole professional life working on. He was able to assimilate the information, mix it with his own ideas — which I found very challenging — and then come out with ideas of where he wanted the state to go in regard to law enforcement.

Geoffrey Howe, chancellor of the Exchequer; British foreign secretary
The first time I met him was when he was on the trail for the presidential nomination. He came to London in 1976, to a small meeting in the House of Commons, to discuss economic policy. He had only one aide, who was a bag-carrier rather than an economic adviser.

There were three of us present; we all had a background in economics. I've never been one of those who subscribed to the view that Ronald Reagan was of limited political capacity; many commentators would have said that it was a gathering in which Ronald Reagan would have been out of his depth.

And he wasn't, in any sense. We had a discussion that lasted two hours, and we were learning from him the lessons of political management that he had learned during his governorship of California. We were very impressed by his grasp of the realities of political decision-making.

Jeane J. Kirkpatrick, permanent representative of the United States to the United Nations, with the rank of ambassador I had been a lifelong Democrat. I wrote an article that appeared in the December 1979 *Commentary* ["Dictatorships and Double Standards," in which she distinguishes between anti-American, totalitarian Communist regimes and pro-American, authoritarian regimes]. Richard Allen told me he had handed the article to Reagan when he was in Washington on a brief trip. Reagan later told me himself that three people had given him the article.

Allen told me that Reagan — who was on a trip — got off the plane in Chicago and called him and asked, "Who is he?" Allen replied, "Who is who?" Reagan said, "Who is this Jeane Kirkpatrick? Who is he?" Allen said, "Well, first, he's a she." Reagan wrote to me and suggested we meet because the article discussed issues that were of great concern to him. That is how I came to meet him. A few minutes after I agreed to meet him, the phone rang. It was the White House; the call was from Bernie Aronson, a White House aide, who said that the president [Jimmy Carter] was concerned that the position of the Coalition for a Democratic Majority be represented in the Democratic Party platform committee hearings that were being held around the country.

The president wanted to know if I could attend the hearing in Baltimore. The hearing was to be held at the time I had agreed to meet with Reagan. I said to Bernie, "It is too late; I have just made another date." It was a turning point in my life.

Hans Dietrich Genscher, foreign minister, Federal Republic of Germany Chancellor [Helmut] Schmidt and I spent time in Washington in November 1980. We met for one hour with the incoming president. He carefully explained his program for the American economy. I was impressed by his clear approach.

The man was bright — without any discussion of foreign relations. I fully understood this; it was better than to give us ideas that would be binding. He had a strong personality and was convincing. He had the right feeling for tendencies, and for substance. He never did focus on the details; maybe that was his success.

Yitzhak Shamir, Israeli foreign minister; prime minister   I met him for the first time when I was foreign minister and I came to Washington with Prime Minister [Menachem] Begin. My impression of Reagan was wonderful; I saw immediately that he was a very good friend of ours. It was instinctive, you could see it.

THE REAGAN PERSONALITY

Stuart Spencer   First, he was a very decent human being, a decent person. That's the essential Reagan. What the American people saw, what all of us saw, was what you got. There wasn't a secret Ronald Reagan, a different Ronald Reagan. That's not true of most public figures.

Shimon Peres, Israeli prime minister; foreign minister   I was always impressed by his friendliness; he gave the impression that he was interested in you. There was always an air of modesty about him; if you didn't know who he was, you would not know he was the president. I liked him tremendously. He was a very likable person, not an egocentric, unlike others in power positions.

Michael Reagan   Dad never talked down to, or was negative to, anybody. I think that was the magic of Ronald Reagan: he gave everybody time, and talked at whatever level you were at. That's where he was at: he could talk to a world leader and then talk to somebody on the street.

He was always able to put people very much at ease and never get so full of himself that he thought he was better than you. That's the warmth of Ronald Reagan: he was one of us. We looked up to him, but he never looked down.

Margaret Wright, wife of Sir Oliver Wright (British ambassador to the Federal Republic of Germany and to the United States)   President Reagan was just this warm, caring, very amusing human being. He was one of the best raconteurs I've ever met, but his stories were always very warm and loving; he wasn't making fun of people.

He could identify with the American people, and it was genuine, not an act. I am an actress, and I know that he was genuine. I've sat by a lot of great men, and their eye contact is above your head while they are talking to you. He was different.

Michael Reagan Dad picked up a lot from his mother, Nellie, who had a warmth and a love of people, who never said anything mean about anybody. Perhaps his outlook and personality came from his mom. She was a volunteer; she used to go to the hospital every weekend to visit the children who had TB. She had a loving heart for people.

She mainly raised the family. Dad's father was an alcoholic. She also had Alzheimer's, yet in the early stages of it she would still find her way out to the hospital on weekends to visit the children.

Langhorne Motley, ambassador to Brazil; assistant secretary of state for inter-American affairs He didn't have a mean bone in his body. I saw occasions where he was very disappointed with someone's performance. He wouldn't get mad; he'd get sad.

John Poindexter, deputy national security adviser; national security adviser The president had few personal relationships. People have asked me who his closest personal friends were, and I am always hard put to identify somebody. Most people view Reagan as an extrovert; in my opinion, he's much more of an introvert.

Lyn Nofziger He is a very amiable person. There was, at the same time — and I always felt it — a kind of veil between him and the rest of the world; there was that final bit that you couldn't penetrate. Even Nancy mentioned this one time.

There was a protective mechanism, perhaps because of his father or his mother, or because, as a movie star, people are on you all the time and you have to hold back something. But I never felt that you got clear inside Ronald Reagan, which, maybe, was fine.

Michael Deaver My theory is that at some point in his life, he was terribly hurt. If you ever started to talk to him about something he didn't want to discuss, you could just see this curtain come down.

On two or three occasions when that happened, I wouldn't let it happen. I would say, "Don't do that to me. I'm telling you this for your own good."

Michael Reagan Once, very early on in the administration, we were at the Beverly Wilshire Hotel, and I asked him, "What is the hardest part about being president?" And he said, "The hardest part is that I wish I could walk right out the door of this room, go down on the elevator, and just walk down Wilshire Boulevard like I used to, and have nobody stop me, nobody approach me, no Secret Service, and just window-shop. That has been taken away from me for the rest of my life."

Martin Anderson   The problem people have in understanding Reagan is that they compare him to something in their own lives. That doesn't work, because he was unique, he was different. He had a style I had never seen before and have never seen since.

He was the most warmly ruthless man I've ever seen. When he was going to get something done, you did not want to be in his way. He didn't take any pleasure in hurting people, but you were gone if you were in his way.

He was perfectly happy to be by himself. It wasn't that he didn't like people, because he was very friendly. It was that he didn't need people. But he needed Nancy.

The president's need for Mrs. Reagan was demonstrated when on Friday, July 12, 1985, during a routine medical checkup at the Bethesda Naval Medical Center, doctors discovered a polyp, which they removed. But nearby was another, large growth, which merited further examination.

Colonel John Hutton, assistant White House physician; White House physician   After completing the colonoscopy — and seeing this enormous mountain of a tumor — and after the biopsy, we went in to see Mrs. Reagan. I said, "Clinically, it's cancer to me, and we had better move with it."

The question was, the president of China was coming in ten days. Could we delay this? I said, "If it were me, I'd want someone to do it tonight. Would you settle for tomorrow, because I have everything ready to go?"

With great aplomb, Mrs. Reagan said, "Let's do it tomorrow. I'll call Don Regan." And she picks up the phone, and I hear her end of the conversation. She says, "Don, the doctors have found something, and they think they probably ought to — if everything is all right around the world — they think they ought to operate tomorrow. I agree with this."

I could sense he was asking, "Is there something you can't tell me?" She didn't want to use the word *cancer*. Number one, we hadn't made a definitive diagnosis; number two, she wasn't quite sure of the security of the telephone line. So she said, "I'll call you later, but we're going to make plans to do it tomorrow." We had discussed with [White House counsel] Fred Fielding the Twenty-fifth Amendment procedures, and a letter was written, turning the power over to Vice President Bush.

The interesting thing about this was that at no time did she even think of calling this astrologer. I was there; she never called Joan Quigley. In her book, she says, "I delayed the president's cancer operation by three days, so it would come under the right time."[*] Any fool could read the newspaper and realize that we had discovered it on Friday afternoon, and by eleven o'clock the next morning we had our hands on this thing.

When we went to tell the president, it was a beautiful scene. Mrs. Reagan said, "Let me be the one to tell him." She sat on the side of his bed in this little recovery room, she put her arms around him, and the president said, "Why is everybody so quiet?" as if we had some ominous news.

She said, "The doctors have found something in there that they can't get out through the instrument, and they think they had better operate tomorrow." And he says, "You mean that the bad news is that I don't get to eat supper tonight?"

With that, we could all laugh and have absolutely no problem telling him that we would get a CAT scan to make sure his liver was all right, and do this and that, and prepare his bowel for the operation. It was almost as if it were a non-event.

The next morning, at about ten-forty, we took him to the operating room. The president joked when we put him to sleep, and he joked when we woke him up. It was amazing. He was such a perfect patient, and his postoperative course was absolutely perfect. He would entertain us by the hour.

He felt guilty that he was keeping us; he would say, "You don't have to sit here all night." I said, "Mr. President, on every ward in the hospital there's a nurse sitting there, watching after the patients." Then he'd get to talking about old movies. He loved to tell stories — the humorous aspects of his past life — and I'd sit there by the bedside, and we'd while away the hours.

NANCY REAGAN

Nancy Reagan, who first met her future husband when he was involved in vetting the anti-Communist credentials of Hollywood actors, remains a controversial figure. Her admirers describe her as fiercely loyal to and protective

---

[*] *What Does Joan Say?* (New York: Birch Lane Press, 1990), 12.

of Ronald Reagan, while her critics maintain that she is overbearingly ma-
nipulative of her seemingly docile and malleable mate.

Mrs. Reagan was criticized when she replaced chipped White House
china with costly new dinnerware, castigated for being a dysfunctional par-
ent, and pilloried by her critics when it was revealed that she had been
advised by an astrologer on White House matters.

While first lady, Mrs. Reagan instituted the "Just Say No to Drugs" cam-
paign, endured her husband's hospitalization following an assassination at-
tempt, as well as his numerous surgical procedures and her own surgery for
breast cancer, following which she was assailed by proponents of lumpec-
tomy when she elected to have a radical mastectomy.

John Hutton   Talk about aplomb. [In October 1987] I went in to show
Mrs. Reagan that the films indicated, until you could prove otherwise,
cancer of the breast.

She said, "Well, I guess it's my turn." That's exactly what she said. I
said, "When we get back to the White House, I will explain the options
to you. We'll talk about doing a lumpectomy, or a quadrupectomy, or a
mastectomy."

I must say, it was a silent drive back there. She said, "John, you're going to have to tell him." So I walked into the Oval Office, and I tried to explain to the president that we had discovered a cancer in his wife's breast.

He took it with absolute denial, and sort of summarily said, "I know
that you doctors will take care of it." It was more than he could handle.
Afterwards, I went to Mrs. Reagan, and she said, "How did he respond?"
I said, "I might as well have hit him with a baseball bat."

I was up there when he came in that night, and he tried to over-
compensate by being cheerful, but he couldn't talk about it until a day or
two later. The next morning, he said to me, "John, I wished you had
stayed up there and given me a good kick. I just couldn't address it." Being shot was nothing compared to hearing that his Nancy was now going
to have to wrestle with cancer of the breast.

Because they had several friends in the theatrical world who had not
done well with it, Nancy wanted to have a mastectomy. She said, "I don't
want radiation, or chemotherapy; let's just be done with it. I've got too
much to do."

The First Lady's Image

Joan Quigley   She wanted to do a good job. She had many good points:
she worked much harder than Jackie [Kennedy]; she was an extremely

capable person; she was a wonderful hostess; she supervised everything that went on in the White House; she knew who her husband's true friends were and who was just taking advantage of him. She was a wonderful wife for a president.

Stuart Spencer   She is a tough lady, with willpower. She wasn't passive; she was active. Ronald Reagan wanted her to play the role. They were a team; they went into this thing together in 1965.

She was in every discussion with us. Early on she did a lot of listening. Over time the longer she was there, she did more talking. They were a team, but on the other hand, I have heard him say to her, "That's enough." Of course, she could find another way of getting around him, but I have heard him say, many times, "Nancy, that's it."

Martin Anderson   She did have influence. She was very smart and very shrewd, and there was one way in which she differed from President Reagan: his weak point was that he believed people — he is a very accepting, trusting person — and he couldn't believe that someone would lie to him; Nancy was very skeptical of what people said, so she acted as a check.

Michael Deaver   I don't think Reagan would have been governor, let alone president, without Nancy Reagan. He would still be agreeing to give speeches in Lompoc, and driving there.*

He was the world's nicest man. She understood that, and knew how to prioritize his time, and how to get people to help her achieve that; that's what I did basically.

She and I knew Ronald Reagan's main reason for wanting to be president: he believed in destiny; he believed he was destined to get the Soviets to the table. I think that is one of the reasons that, after a year and a half, he finally said to Jim Baker, "Screw it. I'm not going to spend any more time trying to get a budget out of this Congress; I am going to continue to build up the Department of Defense, so we can get the Soviets to the table. And we will take the blame for these deficits." And he just forgot about it in the next six and a half years. Of course, there were other issues he did get into, but the Soviets were his main concern.

---

* Mr. Reagan early in his public career hated to fly and therefore planned all engagements so that he would be able to use other forms of transportation.

Oliver Wright, British ambassador to the Federal Republic of Germany and to the United States   I believe that she was predominantly concerned, as consort to the head of state, with his role as head of state. And she carried out these duties beautifully; I believe that she supported him to the hilt in his role as peacemaker.

I am convinced that Reagan's first term was devoted to making America strong again, and his second term to using that strength to talk peace with the Russians, with very considerable success. And I'm quite sure that Nancy wanted Ronald to go down in history as a peacemaker.

Jack Matlock, special assistant to the president; ambassador to the Soviet Union   As far as I know, she never advised on specific agreements. She did have very important influence in one respect: she wanted him to go down as a peace president. I think that one of the reasons he began to get more resistant to rhetoric like the "Evil Empire" was Mrs. Reagan: she did not want him to sound bellicose in presenting issues to the public.

Hans Dietrich Genscher   Nancy's influence was very strong. Reagan told me that when the Gromykos left the private dinner at the White House — the Reagans accompanied the Gromykos to the door, which was exceptional — Mrs. Reagan whispered the word "peace" in Gromyko's ear, and Gromyko said, "Tell that to your husband tonight in your bedroom."

Jerry Falwell   I don't think Nancy always agreed with him on the issues that were important to him. To her credit, she stayed in the background, like Mrs. Bush. I don't think she ever held to the pro-life position. I'm not sure that Nancy liked all the people who helped put her husband in.

James A. Baker III   I don't think Nancy was manipulative. My wife has a lot of influence on me. Nancy Reagan sure as hell didn't do what this first lady [Hillary Rodham Clinton] is doing, sticking her nose into the details of policy.

Nancy looked at the big picture. She thought an arms control agreement was good for the country — and good for his presidency — and it was. That's where you could see her influence.

Lyn Nofziger   [Her influence] became more pronounced in the latter years of his presidency. When he was governor, she would get mad at someone; she tried to have me fired half a dozen times. She has a strong protective feeling about her husband. She has good political judgment.

She is probably smarter than her husband, if you give the IQ tests.

She sat in on the meetings where he would decide whether to run, and how to run. But she seldom interfered; she was not a domineering wife at all. She probably was the deciding force on the appointment of Jim Baker, instead of Ed Meese, as the first chief of staff. Nancy likes people who are well educated, well-spoken, well dressed — who can move about easily in polite society. Some of us didn't quite fit those criteria.

Those who say his wife ran him, or Deaver or Jim Baker ran him — no. Ronald Reagan didn't care about most of the things in government — properly so, I might add. On the things he cared about, the things he thought were important to the state, and then to the nation, he listened and he made his own decisions.

Alexander M. Haig Jr.   The first session I had with Reagan in California when I was still at NATO was very unsatisfactory. Mrs. Reagan ran the show, so the second time I was asked to see him, I said, "Please, I would like to meet alone with him." She didn't like that; I got off to a bad start with her.

Oliver Wright   Woe betide anybody who even by so much as a hint, or a wink, demonstrated what she considered to be lack of loyalty to Ron. No one lasted five minutes in the White House unless they gave 100 percent loyalty to her husband.

Michael Reagan   Nancy is not an issues person, she is a people person. She has the sense of what is good for Ronald Reagan and what is bad for him. She is usually not far off. Sometimes that got her into a lot of trouble; it doesn't play very well with the egos in politics: "I have to go through whom to get to the president? Are you nuts?"

She got a bad rap in a lot of ways. In some ways she probably deserved some of it, because she gets overbearing sometimes. But, again, it is all done to really protect Dad. Dad looks at half a glass of water and says: Look at this! It's half full! Nancy is always trying to figure out: Who stole the other half from my husband? Ronald Reagan wouldn't have been president being married to Jane Wyman. He needed a Nancy, who was willing to give up her career to be there, by his side.

Joan Quigley   She said, "Well, I have two problems: I want to keep Ronnie safe, and I'm having terrible trouble with my image." Nancy was getting a terrible drubbing in the press. I knew exactly what to do.

When the Reagans went to Washington, he was a very popular person in the beginning. She had been responsible for a lot of his success, manipulating people and being a devoted wife. In 1988 she attributed all this to Mike Deaver. Well, Mike Deaver had been in charge from the time they went into office until the time I took over, and he didn't do anything. When her image began to get better, she attributed it to someone on her staff, who was inconsequential. She really never gave me the credit for that.

Nancy was the most glamorous woman since Jackie to occupy the position of first lady. She expected to be treated like a fashion symbol — as Jackie had been — but the situation in the United States was very different from what it had been when the Kennedys were in office. At that time, people had wanted royalty figures; by the time the Reagans had come to Washington, we had double-digit inflation and the country was rather dispirited as a result of the hostage situation.

Things like getting extra china, though it was being donated privately, seemed extravagant, and her social connections, her playing that up, was not sympathetic to the average person. Also, being a fashion plate wasn't appropriate at the time.

So I said to Nancy, "No fashion magazines. You can go to parties if you want to, but the only things that should be talked about should be official functions. In order to be more sympathetic, you must play up children in trouble, and small people."

I knew that any woman in Nancy's position would have some pet project. I said to her, "What are your projects?" She replied, "The anti-drug crusade and the foster grandparents thing." I said, "After this, that's what you talk about; you don't talk about anything else. That's your crusade, that's your campaign. We're not going to give out any interviews for a while."

And I made a month, or six weeks, between the time of the bad image and the time we were going to start in on the good image. Then I cautiously tested the waters, and only let her give interviews at the most propitious times.

She did that, and gradually her image improved. And by 1983 or 1984 she was on the top of the list of the most liked women; she was getting all sorts of honors and awards. It did work out.

The Astrologer Joan Quigley

Stuart Spencer   I knew that Nancy was involved with astrology in 1965. I didn't know about Joan Quigley. It was nothing earthshaking. There was another one before her, several in fact.

Deaver and I were about the only ones who knew about it. The president knew about it, but this was something that Nancy wanted. The first thing he read in the morning was the funny papers, never the first page. The first thing she probably read was the astrology section.

Joan Quigley   I first met Nancy Reagan as a result of being on *The Merv Griffin Show*, which was the most popular afternoon show in the country during the 1970s. Merv said that I was the only astrologer or psychic who had ever been on the show who'd told him things about himself that actually happened, so he was quite convinced that I knew what I was doing.

He and Nancy shared a birthday, and an interest in astrology. At that time, she was the wife of the governor of California. Merv knew that I would only take people I wanted to take. He asked if Nancy could call, and I said yes, and she did call. I told her things about herself, and she was impressed with that.

But I really didn't do her very much — maybe once every six months, or a year — until in 1976, when Reagan tried to get the Republican nomination.

From my standpoint, it was ideal. Nancy was very nice to work with: she was extremely polite and cooperative, and she combined what she knew about the situation with what I knew about astrology. You see, for an astrologer to have an ideal client, you must have someone who cooperates and who describes what they need, and describes enough about the situation that you can look into the astrological chart and give them what they need as far as timing is concerned.

Another way in which the Reagans were dream clients was that they could command the time they did anything, except for a few occasions, like the inauguration. There were very few things that were restricted; I could do anything I wanted.

Michael Reagan   Nancy felt terribly guilty that she hadn't been with Dad when the assassination attempt happened. She thought somehow that if she had been there, it never would have happened. So she reached out to try to find any way that she could stop this from happening again.

Alexander M. Haig Jr.   It explains a lot of things. For example, when Sadat was assassinated,* I thought it was very important for Reagan to go

---

* President Anwar Sadat of Egypt was assassinated on October 6, 1981, in Cairo by Muslim fanatics who were opposed to his having signed a peace treaty with Israel. President Reagan did not attend Sadat's funeral.

to that funeral. As a matter of fact, Nixon called me and said, "I'm going, with or without the president, if I have to take a commercial airliner." That embarrassed the White House into inviting all the other former presidents.

Reagan was anything but a coward — anything but a man who would have avoided danger — so it had to be something very extraordinary that he wouldn't go. And I understood it later.

Jack Matlock Mrs. Reagan did watch the tone of the administration, the timing of events, and his schedule in terms of his health. She insisted that he not be overworked; we could not schedule him twelve hours a day. Anyone who did would have to answer to her. That was quite proper, because she understood what he could take.

Joan Quigley If he was going someplace, I'd have to look at all the location charts — the chart of the country, or the chart of the premier of the country. I had to look at Reagan's charts; I did more than fifty or sixty charts for him every year.

We had agreed in the beginning that it was absolutely essential that what I was doing be kept secret. I agreed with that because I was not only ahead of my time in possession of knowledge of when Reagan would do things, but I was actually setting the times for these movements. I was timing the takeoffs and landings of Air Force One; I timed all the press conferences.

To keep it secret, I switched over from doing astrology by hand to having it done by computer. The Reagans' own charts, the technical charts, I had done from Washington. When something had to be in Santa Barbara, or Tokyo, or wherever he was going, I had to do that myself, by hand. It was a tremendous amount of work; it should have been done by a team. But I've always worked alone.

Robert C. "Bud" McFarlane, counselor, Department of State; deputy national security adviser; national security adviser I was never aware of the relationship. I have enormous respect for Mrs. Reagan. She and I would talk often. She would come up with ideas about ways in which a foreign undertaking, a trip, a letter, or a public position would benefit the president domestically.

In 1984, an election year, she was nudging that his dialogue with the Russians go a little faster; that we try to make more concessions; that we send George Bush to the funeral [of Soviet President Yuri Andropov]; that we make visible signs of reaching out to the Soviet Union.

But when George Shultz or I would say, "The downside of that is that you risk being overanxious; of course, the president was saying he was in no hurry anyway," she would always say okay. She was never unreasonable, or invoking these other influences at all.

Joan Quigley She was nice to deal with as long as I was helping her out. They came to me for the most pragmatic reasons. They kept me on for seven years, because I was producing what they wanted. As Nancy said to me in 1987, "Joan, you have been a very important part of this administration." I gave a great deal of advice on the relationship between the superpowers.

Donald T. Regan, secretary of the Treasury; White House chief of staff I was aghast to think that the wife of the president of the United States was using a public telephone to discuss the movements of the president of the United States with a party who had never been cleared by the Secret Service, or anybody else. It was wrong. And I don't care what others say of my conduct in reporting this, but I think it had to be out of bounds.

Nancy Reagan's Relationship with Joan Quigley Following the Disclosure

Joan Quigley When the news broke, my name was being rocketed around the world. For at least three weeks I refused to go on any talk shows. Nancy didn't want me to do anything. She said, "Just hold your hands up, like the president does, and refuse to talk to reporters." I said, "Nancy, I'm not the president. I'm not going to injure you in any way, but I will deal with the main news shows."

She did some things to me that were rather cruel after the story broke. She had promised me things that she reneged on: she promised me that when they got out of office, they would say that I had been their astrologer. That would have been helpful, because I had a book that Nancy had read and liked very much; she said it was fascinating.

Nancy knew how helpful my counsel had been to her through astrology. She believed in astrology; she knew it worked. Nancy was very careful with her money, and she was spending her own money on this. That lady wouldn't be paying anybody for seven years unless she was getting her money's worth, and yet she didn't want [my] book, that would help other people, to be published.

I knew Nancy so intimately. I knew Ronnie from his horoscope and from what he did, and what Nancy said about him. I don't think I would say that he was as ambitious as she was.

Even though you have someone's horoscope, and you've talked to them a great deal on the telephone, there is an added dimension when you are in the same room with them. Nancy embraced me and said good-bye very warmly, but I had a feeling of such ruthlessness. She had to be that way; people who get into these positions of power have an element of ruthlessness.

I felt rather disillusioned about the whole thing. I think that she had always planned not to say anything. She made the promise merely to encourage me to do all the things she wanted me to do. I think she valued me very much, but I think she wanted me to disappear. I don't think she ever wanted it to be known what I had done.

What really broke me up was when the president said he read his signs in the sun sign columns — after these hours of technical work and effort that I put into it, and for so little money, and sacrificing my whole career.

The kind of astrology I do has nothing to do with those stupid columns. It trivialized what I had done, and it trivialized astrology.

REAGAN'S RELIGIOUS FAITH

Charles Z. Wick   Reagan has a marvelous intuitive feeling. He is very tolerant; he is deeply religious.

Edwin Meese III   He had a very strong personal faith, which came up as a natural thing in private conversation. The president was able to talk about religion in a comfortable way, better than almost any person I've ever met. He did not want to parade it before the public, where people would think he was using it for political purposes or to try to engender the idea that he was a religious man. He didn't feel that he ought to hold church services in the White House, as Nixon did; he felt that was ostentatious. Also, he felt that if he went out to a regular church service, he would disrupt it. As soon as he left the presidency, he became a regular churchgoer.

Joan Quigley   I said to Nancy, "I would like to come to Washington one time during your administration." Just before that, in March 1985, Gorbachev was made secretary general of the USSR. I did not have very much information on him; I had his date of birth and place of birth. Somehow it was like a scientific discovery: you go from not knowing, to knowing — a giant leap, in a flash. That's what happened with Gorbachev's horoscope, and it was absolutely accurate.

I rectified his chart before I went to Washington, and I saw how fantastically well it went with Reagan's chart, and how they could share a vision. I went to the state dinner and to the festivities beforehand on the East Lawn. Everybody was curious about who I was — particularly Nancy's social secretary, because I would occasionally call her and ask her to "have Nancy call Joan." I always assiduously avoided the White House switchboard.

I sat at George Bush's table at the state dinner, and we talked quite a bit. I had gone through the receiving line, and the president leaned down and kissed me, because he knew who I was and what I had been doing. He said, "Hello, Joan." I said, "Mr. President, I think you've been chosen to bring peace." He smiled, and when I got to Nancy in the receiving line, she asked, "What did you say to Ronnie, that he smiled?" And I said, "I'll tell you later."

Afterwards, the president came up to me and said, "You know, I think I've been given a mission in the world, and I believe that God gives me my strength." It was so amazing, because he has his Jupiter in Scorpio; the description of Jupiter and Scorpio is so very much the confidence that people have in themselves because they feel their powers come from God, and that their mission comes through God. He had that kind of confidence in himself.

Miguel D'Escoto, Nicaraguan foreign minister; Maryknoll priest Reagan would end his speeches by saying, "God bless you." He was pontificating. From my perspective, he is not a person who gives a hoot about religion. The religious dimension was not there, and God became someone to manipulate and to use for the advancement of Reagan's purposes. He used God, playing with the hearts of the American people, touching chords that would produce the effect that he was looking for.

REAGAN'S EMOTIONAL LIFE

Edwin Meese III He had a great sense of humor. He would tend to leaven his conversation with stories about Hollywood, or with jokes, and a lot of people took that as a lack of seriousness, whereas for him it was a way of putting people at ease. He took his job seriously, but he didn't take himself seriously.

Shimon Peres   He was extremely pleasant, with a good sense of humor. He liked to tell stories, usually anti-Russian.

Once, when I was visiting him in the Oval Office, he told a story about Stalin and Churchill. One night [at Yalta] Stalin and Churchill get very drunk. The next morning, Churchill says, "We were very drunk last night. Who knows what we talked about?" Stalin replies, "Yes, Comrade Churchill. The bad news is that we said all sorts of secret things, and the interpreter was present. The good news is that we shot the interpreter early this morning."

Nimrod Novick, senior political adviser to Prime Minister and Foreign Minister Shimon Peres of Israel   The prime minister and Reagan would swap Soviet jokes. One that the president told was about Gorbachev. He said, "Gorbachev says to his driver, 'Step on it. We have to be at the airport in twenty minutes.' The driver says, 'But Mr. Secretary General, you have issued a decree that limousines must abide by the speed limit.' Gorbachev says, 'Look, we have to be at the airport.' And the driver says, 'What about your decree?' Gorbachev is furious. He tells the driver to sit in the back, and says, 'I will drive.' He proceeds to zoom through Moscow at a high speed. He turns a corner, and a policeman goes after him. Ten minutes later the policeman comes back to his post, and his partner says, 'Did you give him a ticket?' He says, 'No. It was a very important person. I don't know who he was, but Gorbachev was his driver.'"

Martin Anderson   He would tell wonderful, funny stories. He could be an incredible actor; he could put on facial expressions, and act out stories, and have the staff in stitches. He was fun.

But he was different. People kept [misinterpreting him], because he was so friendly and genial. It was like seeing a beautiful, soft satin pillow, but what you didn't know was that there was a stainless steel bar, right down the middle, about two inches thick.

He had a strong temper when he was crossed; you did not want to cross him. It didn't happen frequently, but it was there.

Edwin Meese III   He showed flashes of anger more rarely than any other person I've ever met, in a job that has natural tensions. I can remember, in the gubernatorial days, the only times he showed anger were in two types of situations. When he was overscheduled — he was a very polite person and he never liked to have to usher somebody out of his office abruptly, but he didn't want to be late for his next appointment, and that created tension. He used to throw his glasses across the desk; that was a sign he was exasperated.

And the other thing — this only happened once or twice — was when the capitol was invaded by people, demonstrators and protesters. We insisted on leading him around the back way, and he wanted to go right through and confront these people.

Craig Fuller   The only time I would see him snap at meetings was when people would try to get him to think about what was politically right for him. He would say, "Look, we are going to do what we think is right and let the politics take care of themselves."

The truth is that in private meetings he would become frustrated at times, but you didn't see displays of anger. He's an optimist; he looks for the positive side in everything.

Martin Anderson   I have never seen Reagan depressed, or down, in the sense that something is not going to work. He used to tell a story about a family with two children. One was very pessimistic about everything; the other child saw everything as being bright and happy. So the parents took the children to a psychiatrist.

He put the children in separate rooms. The pessimist was in a room filled with brand-new toys; the optimist was put in a room filled with horse manure. And after a few hours the doctor took the parents to each room. They found the pessimistic child crying and complaining that this or that toy wouldn't work.

When they opened the door to the room where the other child was, they found him laughing and moving the manure around. So they said, "What are you doing?" and the child said, "Well, there must be a pony in here somewhere."

3

Staffing the Administration

Martin Anderson There were academic studies done on the transition. The way it was set up was interesting; it had never been done that systematically before. Meese had the overall charge. We had groups dealing with policy issues, personnel, and management. We had all these policy issues. The question was: How do we get all of them done? We weren't developing policy; we were trying to figure out how to implement policy. That was the whole key.

We put together four-inch-thick briefing books, in which we had everything Reagan had said on specific issues. So when Don Regan came in to be secretary of the Treasury, he first talked to the people in personnel and was given lists of people who would be good undersecretaries and deputies, and then he talked to people in the organizational structure, who told him where all the buildings were — everything you needed to know to take over.

Then the thing went over to another group that got this book saying: This is what your president believes. So later on, when Don Regan wrote a book and said, I never knew what the president wanted, that was absolute nonsense. He knew clearly what Reagan wanted.

George Bush I was included in all the transition meetings with President-elect Reagan. But it was his cabinet, and his selections. I did give him advice on some of the names.

Max Hugel I was in the transition. I said to Casey, "Bill, this is ridiculous. We've got three thousand guys, presidential appointees from the Carter administration, and we have to fire them. If we don't, they are going to dig themselves into the government, and we're trying to get our agenda through."

He says, "Well, call Weinberger." So I call him out in California. I said, "Mr. Weinberger, we have to fire all these people." He said, "Are you crazy? Who's going to run the government?" I said, "About three million other people that we have out there."

SELECTING THE CHIEF OF STAFF

The longtime key aide and Reagan loyalist Edwin Meese, who had served for six years as Reagan's chief of staff in Sacramento, was expected to receive the post of White House chief of staff. But in the weeks before the election, other influential Reagan aides convinced the president-elect that Meese did not have the requisite administrative skills and Washington background for that position.

This decision—one not without its element of intrigue—would have major ramifications for the Reagan presidency in the ascendancy of James Baker.

Craig Fuller I believe that when those around Reagan began to contemplate that, in all likelihood, he was going to be elected, they were somewhat in awe of what they were about to do. California is a remarkable training ground in many ways — it is a nation unto itself — yet the people who had spent six to eight years with Governor Reagan realized that Washington was one very large, difficult place to come in to and be successful in.

Some thought that, as outsiders, they could come in and take the place by storm. Others, probably more level-headed, recognized that they really needed somebody who understood Washington and its ways and could help to balance the California group, the people who had been around Reagan, in a way that they could get things done. I really give a lot of credit to Mike Deaver. Mike saw this better and more clearly than anyone else.

Michael Deaver Three or four weeks before the election, I said, "You need to start thinking about putting a team together."

He said, "I've given some thought to my national security adviser." I said, "That's great, but I'm talking about chief of staff. I'm not sure Ed is the guy." He said, "You're right." And I broached the idea of Jim Baker. He thought that was a good idea.

One of our interviewees told us, off the record, that Casey had told him that he had gotten Baker his job as chief of staff and that it was the biggest mistake he ever made.

Michael Deaver   I knew it was going to be difficult. I talked to Stu Spencer and Bill Clark. It was Clark's idea that Ed be given the title of counselor to the president. Ed never forgave me, but he was not an administrator, and I really did think we needed someone who knew his way around Washington. And I was right.

It was devastating to Ed. I sat in on the session where Reagan told him. But on my part, and on Nancy's part, we wanted to be sure we were going into this thing not only with people who were loyal, but with people who understood how Congress worked, who understood the Beltway media and understood all of the ethical and legal problems that could come up. And it worked extremely well.

Stuart Spencer   It was sort of an heir apparent situation in everyone's mind. I knew that Ed Meese would be a lousy chief of staff for Ronald Reagan. When Ed was counselor in the White House, the paper in his office started on the floor and went up to here and crossed his desk; everything went in, and nothing went out, and expediting paper is the biggest job a chief of staff has to do.

About four weeks before the election, I said to the Reagans at dinner in Dallas, "Why don't you make Ed attorney general?" They both said, "He won't be chief of staff." They understood Ed's weaknesses. They weren't being negative about him; they understood what a lot of us did. Deaver did too. In that discussion, I suggested Baker, whom the president didn't really know.

That meeting in Dallas was the first indicator I had that it wasn't going to be Meese. We were all typecast: I was the pol, Deaver was the gatekeeper. We all had our roles. None of us was considered chief-of-staff material.

Craig Fuller   I first became aware of these discussions during the preparation for the Carter-Reagan debate. The Reagans were at a house in Virginia, and Mike Deaver invited me to come out.

I watched the rehearsals and preparation and participated in some of the discussion. And then, during the evening, I realized that Deaver and others were trying to figure out how to structure the White House. They were looking at the realistic needs of a new administration. At the same time, Ed Meese — whom I have a tremendously high regard for and who, in many ways, was the policy conscience of Ronald Reagan — was working on the "take Washington by storm" approach. He was working on a plan with respect to both policy and people.

This was different from what Mike was doing. Mike at all times moved in the direction he thought best for Ronald Reagan, but it wasn't always in the same direction. Mike was a little more pragmatic; he saw the need for somebody with real expertise.

Lyn Nofziger   Mike Deaver is very close to Nancy. He had taken care of them most of the years in Sacramento and had stayed close during the out years. Deaver falls in love with people who are above him socially and who are richer than he is.

Baker is everything that Deaver would like to be. He is tall, handsome, and rich; he went to Princeton instead of San Jose State. And Baker is a very impressive man till you get to know him. If you think I am letting my feelings through, you are absolutely right.

What apparently happened was that Stu Spencer and Deaver went to Nancy and said, you can't pick Ed Meese. He never gets anything done; he is disorganized. You need to have Ronnie pick Baker. So they convinced Reagan.

James A. Baker III   It was really only a few days before the election that I got any wind whatsoever that there was some thought being given to putting me in the Reagan White House. And even then, I didn't know it was as chief of staff; I just assumed that Ed Meese was going to be the chief of staff. Most people assumed that. I think, frankly, that Ed assumed that.

Ed had a chart drawn up. But Deaver and Spencer, and the first lady particularly, had had experience with Ed's organizational efforts in California — and by the way, he is a wonderful person, and a wonderful man to work with, notwithstanding the fact that we were always juxtaposed as being opposed to each other. We really weren't.

I don't think we would have had a successful first term without Ed Meese in there, running the policy apparatus. But he was not a "cross your t's and dot your i's" type of person; he liked to think and ruminate and philosophize. He is extraordinarily bright and competent in that regard, but he's not a "make the trains run on time" person. I think anybody would tell you that, and maybe even Ed would.

Anyway, that's why they came to me. I knew the Washington scene. I had been here, and I had worked with the Ford White House, even though I had not been in the Ford White House. I knew the power centers here, and I knew a little bit about what you had to do to get along in Washington. But it was a Spencer–Deaver–first lady idea.

Lyn Nofziger   Reagan calls in Meese — who thought he was going to be chief of staff — and he says, "Jim Baker is going to be chief of staff, and you can have any other job you want." So Ed sat down and wrote out a list, and he had taken everything, but he didn't follow through on it.

James A. Baker III   When the governor asked me to do it, he said, "I want you to work with Ed; you might want to talk to him." I went to Ed. I invited him to have breakfast, and we talked about it. And I think it was my suggestion that he be a counselor with cabinet rank.

I remember thinking to myself that there would be one way where it might work — if I didn't take cabinet rank. And I didn't. In the White House cabinet rank doesn't mean a thing because you have the power whether you have the rank or not.

I had the political, public affairs, press, communications, and legislative aspects, and Ed had policy development; he supervised the NSC [National Security Council] and the Domestic Policy Council. It worked, notwithstanding some of the tensions that would accrue from time to time. We had an extraordinarily successful first term in terms of the way the White House operated. We didn't have any Iran-contras, and we got a lot done.

Lyn Nofziger   You can talk about the troika all you want, but the fact is that we wound up with a divided White House, with the Baker-Deaver people on one side and the Meese people on the other side — the Reagan loyalists versus the Baker loyalists.

Martin Anderson   My understanding was that Meese was scheduled to be chief of staff, but Deaver said he would never work for Ed Meese.

Well, that was a problem, because Reagan wanted Deaver in the White House, and so did Nancy. How about Ed working for Michael? No way. So we had a nice stalemate, and I think it was Michael who said, "Jimmy Baker." And the Reagans said, "Okay, he's a smart fellow, we can work with him." So they set up this troika. It worked brilliantly — for a while.

Craig Fuller   Stu Spencer was definitely counseling that if the president was going to be successful — and was going to lay the groundwork for re-election — he needed somebody like Jim Baker, who could translate your policy preferences into action.

Somewhere in the mix of Deaver and Spencer emerged the notion that it would be smart to turn over some of the levers of power in the White House to somebody who really knew Washington a lot better. And that was Jim Baker.

It helped in another way, which I don't know that they thought much about: it helped enormously to create a comfort factor with George Bush, who was a very valuable vice president and a true partner with Ronald Reagan. It created an element of trust and a line of absolutely confidential communication between the chief of staff, the vice president, and the president. There was no one else in the White House who could have done that. Bush wouldn't have trusted anyone else, so Baker was a perfect fit.

For the most part, it was a pretty effective team for the first two years. It certainly began to fray, but it held together pretty effectively over that first term.

James A. Baker III   My wife dissolved in tears when she heard the news. I told that to President Reagan, and — Reagan is so terrific — he went to see Susan, and he said, "Don't worry. Your husband is going to be home at seven-thirty; I quit at five-thirty." Well, of course, I got home at eleven o'clock most nights.

I told President Reagan, "I'll be glad to do it, but I think it's best done in two-year increments. A chief of staff gets worn out; you burn up your chits very quickly. You're a target: when people can't take their frustrations out on the president, they take them out on the chief of staff." I went into the job thinking I'd be there for two years. Four years later I was still there.

The Troika

Alexander M. Haig Jr.   There was a lot of self-serving going on. It was a real struggle with the triumvirate, between Jim Baker, who was the master of them all, Ed Meese, who is, in my view, a very honest, dedicated servant of the president, and Mike Deaver, who had no qualifications whatsoever for being an executive in the central office of our executive branch. He had other, very important talents, and he had a very unusual rapport with the first lady.

Jerry Falwell   Ed Meese was my buddy. Jim Baker was a good friend, but he was a pragmatist par excellence. He was a peacemaker; he didn't have a philosophy. His thing was to make Mr. Reagan successful, but he didn't have an opinion on anything.

Ed Meese was opinionated; he was our man there. Michael Deaver was just the PR guy, the noisemaker and protector. But in the early days he exerted more authority than Meese or Baker. If he didn't want to let you in, you wouldn't get in.

Now and then, he would talk off the record to the *Washington Post* and others. I think he made the president look bad at times. He made a comment once to the *Post* that the Religious Right and the ultraconservatives have to come through the back door of the White House — he was talking about guys like me.

CABINET-LEVEL APPOINTMENTS

Edwin Meese III   The way the cabinet selection process worked was that the governor asked that a kind of kitchen cabinet group be set up that would include a lot of the old California kitchen cabinet, augmented by some of the people who had worked in the campaign in leadership positions. About twenty of us were involved. All of us came up with lists — perhaps a dozen or more candidates for each position.

Secretary of State

Hans Dietrich Genscher   Our first question was, Who will his foreign secretary be? Schmidt thought it would be Shultz. I thought it would be Herr Haig; I knew him from his time [as NATO commander] in Brussels.

Michael Deaver   When Al Haig was thinking of running for president, he came to see Reagan at the ranch; he had lunch with the former governor. I was in Los Angeles, and at about two o'clock I got a call from Reagan. He said, "We had a great time. I really like this guy. If we ever get to Washington, I'd like to have him in the cabinet." So that stuck in Reagan's mind.

Edwin Meese III   Nixon had suggested Haig. People were impressed with him because they felt he had done a good job in the Nixon years. The group also wanted somebody who was clearly a foreign policy expert.

The president was concerned: he didn't want somebody in that job who would use this post as a jumping-off point for running for president, so a couple of us were deputized to meet with Al Haig. We did, and we had a full and frank discussion on his plans. We were satisfied that he didn't have another agenda — at least at that time.

Gerald R. Ford   I like and admire Al Haig. Based on his experience in the Nixon White IIouse and as a commander of NATO, Haig was certainly qualified to be secretary of state. I think he got a little ambitious of something beyond secretary of state.

If he had wanted to run for president, he should have concentrated on being the best secretary of state instead of acting like "I really want to be president sometime." He did a good job, but it was undercut to some extent by his own personal ambition.

Alexander M. Haig Jr.   I didn't want the job; I wasn't seeking it. First, let me say that my relationship with Reagan went back to the early 1970s. Later, after I became NATO commander, I was asked by Dick Allen, who was working for the then-retired governor, to visit California to meet with Reagan during one of my trips to the United States. That was followed by a second request, after I retired, asking me to join the Reagan team, which I declined to do for a host of reasons, one of which was that I wasn't certain as to what I wanted to do in the future.

Having said all that, in December 1980, after a number of other key appointments had been made, I received a call from the president-elect, asking me to accept the position of secretary of state. I had been alerted to the possibility of such a call — first for Defense — by Bill Simon,* an old friend from the Nixon years.

I told Bill that I didn't think that it was an appropriate job for a military person, and that it required congressional exemption. Later, at the Republican convention, Justin Dart, who was a member of the kitchen cabinet, said to me — much to my surprise — that I would probably be Reagan's choice for secretary of state.

I had just completed my first year as president and chief operating officer of United Technologies, which was a position of some promise for me, with millions of dollars in stock options, to say nothing of a level of compensation I wasn't accustomed to as a former soldier, plus a great deal of respect for the then-chairman, whom I was scheduled to replace someday.

So when the president-elect called, I said it would require a great deal of sacrifice on my part, but that it was a great honor, and that I would want to know two things. First, how my chairman [Harry Gray] felt, because I owed him that. And secondly, having been involved in the executive branch with a number of presidents and having seen good arrangements and less-good arrangements, I wanted to know if Mr. Rea-

---

* William Simon, secretary of the Treasury in the Nixon administration.

gan, in fact, wanted a secretary of state. That would mean that the individual would be the primary deputy to the president for the conduct of America's foreign affairs. I used the term "vicar"; that became a dirty word when I used it, but the proper interpretation of "vicar" is a deputy.

He assured me that that would be the case and that I would be *the* spokesman for the U.S. government. Having lived through the Nixon-Kissinger debacle, I was convinced that I didn't want to be part of an administration that had some uncertainty about lines of authority — not because I am that arrogant, but because I don't think it works, and it doesn't serve the American people.

So Reagan reassured me on that, and I talked to Harry Gray, and he said, "If the president asks, you have to do it, as painful as it is to both of us." So I did it. And it *was* very painful, because it meant a dramatic change for my family and myself.

William Casey's Desire to Be Secretary of State

Edwin Meese III   Casey would have liked to have been secretary of state, but the president, right from the start, had Bill in mind for director of central intelligence because of Casey's background in the OSS [Office of Strategic Services] during the Second World War.

Lyn Nofziger   It is true that Casey wanted State. But there is a little bit of Casey that did not fit into the striped-suit bunch. He wasn't quite suave enough: when he talked, he chewed on the end of his tie; food would get caught in his teeth, and in the middle of the meal he'd reach around and get it out. But he was a very able man, and probably the best CIA head we've ever had.

Martin Anderson   He not only wanted to be secretary of state, he thought he deserved the position. He had come in and taken over this campaign when it was in deep trouble, had become the chairman, and did a brilliant job of reorganizing, structuring, and driving it. And winning it.

He had the background. In retrospect, it was one of Reagan's mistakes, because when he put Haig in as secretary of state, that didn't work; he didn't know Haig. That was a bad play. Casey would have been a really good secretary of state. He might not have been as photogenic, he might have mumbled a few words, but he was smart and shrewd.

It was a double mistake, because he put an embittered, brilliant Casey in charge of the CIA, and that led to problems. And to a certain extent, Casey set up his own State Department and had a wonderful time.

Bernadette Casey Smith I don't think he ever wanted the State Department. After Dad died, I found a letter that he had written to Nixon in 1968, asking him for the CIA. And, of course, he got the SEC [Securities and Exchange Commission].

I guess anyone would like to be asked to be secretary of state, but I never heard him ask about it, or talk about it, and I know that he was thrilled when he got the CIA. He had come full circle: he started in the OSS at the age of thirty. From Nixon on, anytime there was a commission, or an intelligence committee in the government, he was always on it. So, since the Second World War, when he headed OSS operations in the European theater, he had kept in touch with his friends who went into the CIA when it was formed. And he was on intelligence boards, so he kept up with it for thirty years.

He often said to Mom that he had the best job in Washington. The quality of the people who worked at the CIA was extraordinary. He loved it.

Reagan's View of Shultz as Secretary of State

A source who preferred to speak off the record told us that Casey said that George Shultz was being considered for secretary of state at the very beginning of the Reagan administration, and that Reagan had asked Casey to see whether Shultz would be interested.

According to our source, Shultz was not offered the position. Reportedly, Shultz told Casey that he would not be interested for three reasons: he had made a commitment to Bechtel; it was useful for him to stay on there because he was making money for the first time in his life; and he believed he did not know enough about foreign policy to be secretary of state.

Our source added that Shultz has denied that this conversation ever took place. But our source, a close friend of Casey's, expressed "perfect confidence" in Casey's information.

Michael Deaver His first choice for secretary of state was Shultz. I think Shultz would have been secretary of state except for the way Reagan handled it.

We had decided that Shultz would be the first choice. Reagan called George, and the conversation went something like this: "Well, George, I'm here with some of the fellows, and I'm calling to see if you'd like to come back to Washington with me."

He never mentioned the position of secretary of state. Shultz — thinking, I'm sure, he wants me to be secretary of the Treasury — says, "O'Bie [the late Helena O'Brien Shultz] and I have had enough of Washington." Reagan says, "Thank you very much."

If Reagan had said, I want you to be secretary of state; I know this is a sacrifice; you've done all these other things, but you're the best guy; here's what I want to do as president: I want to get the Soviets to the table — I think Shultz would have signed up right there. So we go to the second list of names, and Haig's is at the top.

Alexander M. Haig Jr. I came down to Washington with mixed emotions, although I felt that my experience and background suggested that I could make a real contribution. I didn't know who the competitors were, but I knew that because of the delay in making the call, there must have been a lot of pulling and tugging in the Reagan family as to who should get the job. I'm sure that George Shultz was an important front-runner. Not Casey, who, on the surface, was not qualified for the job.

Secretary of Defense

Caspar Weinberger There were discussions for a number of different posts: secretary of the Treasury, the Office of Management and Budget, and secretary of state. But the president was anxious to have the kind of work I had done for him in California, and elsewhere, at the Defense Department. He wanted to have a strong defense, and he knew that I supported that very strongly.

Ultimately, he just telephoned me and said, "We know you have a very full and a very rich life, and I want to spoil the whole thing now and ask if you would be secretary of defense." I told him that I wanted to talk it over at home, and I did. And I accepted because, having worked very hard for him to be president, I wanted to do all I could to help him succeed.

Attorney General

Michael Deaver In the first session we had to discuss the cabinet, Reagan came into the room — there were five or six of us sitting there — and he said, "Now listen, before we get started, Bill Smith* is going to be my attorney general."

Somebody said, "Have you thought about the fact that he has had no experience?" And the governor said, "Let me just tell you something, fellows. I have made a decision: he is going to be my attorney general."

---

* William French Smith, Reagan's attorney and the head of the Transition Advisory Committee, a group that included many members of the kitchen cabinet.

In a way, that was very unlike Reagan. It was much the same way with the Casey appointment.

Secretary of the Interior

James Watt   I had never known Reagan; I had never shaken his hand prior to being asked to be a member of his cabinet. The president and his people had selected former Senator [Clifford] Hansen, from Wyoming, to be secretary of the interior. He is a dear friend and neighbor of mine. After doing background checks, they determined he would have to surrender some significantly valuable grazing permits.

In December he told them no, and they were hustling to put their team together. Senator Laxalt had played a major role in the campaign and had personally gained two commitments from Reagan: one, that he would be given the privilege of playing tennis on the White House courts; and second, that he could pick the secretary of the interior.

So a group of senators got together. Jim McClure, the senator from Idaho — and the man who was going to become chairman of the Interior Committee — threw my name out because of the work I had done at the Mountain States Legal Foundation.

I was interviewed by Laxalt; I had lunch with him and Senator Malcolm Wallop [of Wyoming]. They grilled me on every conceivable subject. The breadth and depth of the Department of the Interior is way beyond the comprehension of most people. I had views on everything, and I had predetermined that I was not going to flavor anything.

Laxalt then called Ed Meese, who was working in the transition office, and Laxalt said, "Ed, we have our new secretary of the interior." The next day they introduced me to Reagan, and he and I had a long and, from my perspective, extremely important interview.

There were two or three things that fascinated me. He understood the Department of the Interior and the responsibilities that I would be carrying out; as governor of California, he had worked closely with the then–secretary of the interior. The second thing that impressed me was the compassion that man had in his eyes.

The reason that the interview was so significant was that I had a five- or six-point agenda — we went through these points in specific detail — and in every instance he had comments, discussed it with understanding, and sometimes added to it.

When we got through the five or six agenda items, he looked deep into my soul, in effect, and said, "Are you and your wife willing to take some of the abuse that will be necessary to accomplish the objectives we've discussed?"

At the time, I thought it was a very sensitive and perceptive question. With hindsight, it was hugely perceptive. Being then much more naive than I am now, I quickly smiled and said, "Yes, we are willing to take the abuse." I then said, "Governor, if you select me, you'll need to back me, and back me, and when you can no longer do this, you'll have to fire me." He smiled with his eyes, and with his face, and said, "I will." And we laughed.

Ambassador to the United Nations

Jeane J. Kirkpatrick I had checked Reagan out, mainly with some Democratic friends of mine who were active in California politics. I asked political science–type questions about whether he could govern. I checked his capacity to compromise, which you have to do if you are going to govern.

I satisfied myself that he was a credible and a feasible candidate. Every time I saw him, I liked him. After his election, he appointed me to his senior foreign policy task force. I was the only person on it who was not a Republican, a former cabinet member, or a very distinguished Democrat. Then, in December, he called and asked if I would serve as his representative at the United Nations and be a member of his cabinet.

I said, "I am not sure I can do that. Do you want an answer now?" He said he did. I said, "I've never done anything like that." He replied, "I feel that you will do just the job I want done." So I said, "Okay, Mr. President, if you think I can do it, I'll give it my best try." He said, "Jeane, you've made my day."

SUB-CABINET-LEVEL APPOINTMENTS

Director of Central Intelligence

David Abshire, ambassador to NATO; special adviser to the president The president had great affection for Casey, so if he wasn't going to make him his secretary of state, he would make him DCI [director of central intelligence]. After all, Casey had served in the OSS.

Max Hugel Casey actually wanted to leave after the election. He was disgusted that the kitchen cabinet was going to make the decisions on key personnel when he was the one who had truly elected Reagan.

He told me that there were three important cabinet offices: Defense, State, and Treasury. He wasn't disappointed with the CIA job. He told me, "It's the one area where you can really do things for the country, things that you can do privately, and secretly, and no one will bother you, so you can get things done." And he got a cabinet post with it, which was part of the deal.

Constantine Menges   I worked very closely with Bill Casey. I came to the CIA as one of the very few outsiders who were brought in, explicitly by Bill Casey, because he felt it needed some outsiders in senior positions to do some fresh thinking.

Generally, the morale at CIA was positive because Casey was seen as a person who was close to the president, and as a pro-active person who wanted to make the institution relevant in a dangerous world, and who was also very brilliant and had very interesting ideas.

Bernadette Casey Smith   Dad was very loyal, and loyalty and integrity were two qualities that were very important to him. Intelligence was the third thing, but if you didn't have integrity and loyalty, it didn't matter how smart you were.

Gerald R. Ford   I was absolutely surprised when President Reagan selected Casey to be his DCI. He was not qualified to be the head of the CIA. And his performance justifies my statement.

Bernadette Casey Smith   He was probably investigated more than any politico. He used to say, "I've been confirmed six times, five by the Congress and once by the bishop." It didn't affect him; he knew it was smoke and mirrors.

Dad had a completely optimistic personality. He woke up every day saying, "This is a great day; we're going to learn something new," or, "We're going to accomplish something."

He would work very hard, but it was a joy to him. He was one of the most-traveled CIA directors; he went to every station, talked to all the heads of station. He loved his people; he thought they were terrific.

He had a photographic memory. He could be in everything and never look like he was working. He was working all the time, but he could drop everything and go to a movie.

Michael Reagan   Dad was fond of Casey. During the 1980 campaign Casey always used to lose his Secret Service pins; the Secret Service always had to keep a pocketful of them for him. Then, when my dad said this guy is the head of the CIA, Colleen and I looked at each other and said, "This guy can't keep a Secret Service pin!"

Donald Gregg   Certainly, Admiral [Stansfield] Turner [DCI in the Carter administration] was extremely unpopular. In fact, I told one of his people, "The DO [directorate of operations] is like a combat brigade: there is a spirit to it, and we feel we are taking casualties from friendly fire — from the director."

That didn't do my career any good, but I felt it really had to be said. Turner was never really comfortable with people like me; I had been in operations, and he thought that people like me got the Agency in trouble, that a lot of modern espionage could be done through satellites and electronic surveillance.

He was wrong. So when Casey came in, there was a sense that here was an old pro, somebody who really understands this — a sense of relief. The problem with Casey was that he was a swashbuckler. I don't think he learned much from the days at OSS. The CIA into which I went in 1951 really was a stepchild of MI6 [the British equivalent of OSS] and OSS.

We had a great image, but we had practically zero capability. The training that we received, which was based on what had been given to people during World War II, really wasn't very appropriate for dealing with the Soviets. So, whereas Casey was welcomed when he first came, his directorship was mixed, at best.

Duane "Dewey" Clarridge, chief of the CIA's Latin American Division; chief of the CIA's European Division; chief of the CIA's Counterterrorism Center   I wasn't there; I was in Rome. That was kind of far away. Nobody knew who he was.

Casey came to Rome in March, or perhaps April, of 1981. It was a typical thing that directors do; they usually come to Europe first. I had never met him. He was a man who played things very close to the vest. He was probably more connected with the intelligence business — not unexpectedly, because he had had experience with the OSS, although a long time ago. So he seemed to understand all of that part of it, and he already knew a lot of people in Italy in terms of a station.

He would ask penetrating questions; he was obviously an intelligent fellow. Had he done any homework beforehand? I don't think so. But the purpose of the trip was to do his homework on the ground. He went around and saw the various people that we, as the CIA, dealt with. He was looking for information to make himself up-to-date, and he was also interested in what the station was doing.

Bernadette Casey Smith If he saw a report that he liked, he used to go down and talk to the person, because he was so fascinated by what they were saying that he wanted to hear it firsthand. He was probably one of the first directors who would go down into the bowels of the CIA and look for people and ask questions.

He read everything. Everything. There were books all over the house. He could tell you what was in each book; he had read them all.

Casey's OSS Mentality

According to a high-ranking adviser to the president and colleague of William Casey's who preferred to speak off the record, Casey had a problem with what our source described as "the culture of OSS." Casey's colleague added that Casey never fully made the transition from the OSS period to the 1980s and thus was hurt, as were others in Washington who could not adapt to the contemporary culture.

Duane Clarridge You have to understand where Casey came from: he had a lot of contempt — maybe that's too strong a word, maybe it's not — for the congressional bodies. He felt that they were self-serving, that they tended to be focused on their own, parochial issues, and that they would use certain things to beat up on the administration.

To say that he didn't realize that oversight was there is ridiculous. The case was that he wasn't going to stomach any more than he had to.

Bernadette Casey Smith Dad made very few mistakes. The one mistake he did make was that before he went into the CIA, he wrote his memoirs on the Second World War and didn't complete them. They were almost complete, but he said, "I really shouldn't publish them until after I'm out of government."

If he had published them, people would have realized that he had this background, because he was always written off as a Wall Street lawyer. That was one of the hats he wore, but he could wear many hats.

Sophia Casey He worked on the memoirs for ten years. I would see him walking up and down, and saying, "I don't know what I should do about this book. The publisher wants me to send it in, but I don't know if it would be good, because people will say it's self-serving." I said to him,

"Bill, I think you do it pretty well, and gracefully." But he said no; he knew how people treated him.

National Security Advisers and Staff

During the two terms of the Reagan presidency there were no fewer than six national security advisers. The first one, Richard Allen, had served as the 1980 campaign's foreign policy adviser. Once in the White House, Allen was denied direct access to the president and remained in the position for less than one year, being forced to resign when it was disclosed that he had accepted the gift of an expensive watch from a Japanese businessman.

Allen was succeeded by Judge William P. Clark, who had served as chief of staff to the then-Governor Reagan and was a close personal friend. Judge Clark was subsequently appointed by Reagan to the California Supreme Court.

In the fall of 1983, Judge Clark left the White House, to be succeeded by his deputy, Robert C. McFarlane. McFarlane, in turn, would be succeeded, in December 1985, by his deputy, Admiral John Poindexter, who would be forced to resign in the immediate aftermath of the Iran-contra revelations.

Reagan's fifth national security adviser, Frank Carlucci, prior to becoming secretary of defense, would reorganize the NSC staff, with the help of his deputy, Lieutenant General Colin Powell.

General Powell would assume the national security adviser post in 1988, setting the stage for his appointment, during the Bush administration, as chairman of the Joint Chiefs of Staff.

In what would turn out to be a fateful appointment, Major Oliver North, a marine and a Vietnam veteran, joined the NSC staff in 1981.

Edwin Meese III As to who ought to have the job, I think that Casey pressed for Kirkpatrick. But among the players on the National Security Council and in the foreign policy field, there were some differences of opinion as to how we ought to handle Central America and the situation in Nicaragua — the State Department being of one mind, and Casey, and perhaps Cap, being of another — and as to how intensively we should support the freedom fighters, and what actions we should take as a government. Jeane was very strongly involved in that because of her interest in Latin America.

It was thought that what you wanted to have in the national security adviser role — which is really a senior staff role rather than a player role — was someone who would be like Bill Clark was, an honest broker who was not a major propagandist in the debate on one side or the other. That was how the president felt about McFarlane — that he would be more of a staff resource than one of the major players.

Robert C. McFarlane   I had served in the marines for twenty years, nine of them on assignment to the White House in the Nixon and Ford administrations. I worked on foreign policy matters during the Reagan campaign, and once he was elected, I was asked by Al Haig to be his counselor at the State Department. I then went to the White House to be the deputy to Judge Clark when he became national security adviser, and then, two years later, when he became secretary of the interior, I became national security adviser.

Reagan seemed to me to be unique, in my experience with other presidents, in his unshakable commitment to a few principles. He would not equivocate. He was committed to policies I considered to be sound — a strong military. I wanted to join his team because he was concerned about the growth of nuclear weapons, on both sides. I believed I had come up with a strategy that might help turn it around, and I thought that Ronald Reagan was the kind of person who would be able to build popular support for that strategy.

John Poindexter   In the period following the assassination attempt, there was concern in the White House over the operation of the Situation Room, which is the national security area, a sort of nerve center of communications — [concern over] not the actual transmission, the electronics part of it, but the handling of the messages. There was concern on the part of Allen, and others, that they didn't have a good handle on what role the Situation Room should play in a crisis. So Allen was looking for a military assistant who would look into the question. I was suggested for this position, and at the end of May 1981 I came to the White House.

Oliver North, director of the NSC's Military-Political Office   I joined reluctantly; I was ordered there. I was a student at the Naval War College in Newport, Rhode Island. I had come from the Fleet Marine Force. I wanted to go back there. The gifts the good Lord lent me are in motivating young people to do difficult, and sometimes dangerous, things. I had been very, very good at it. I had been promoted early, two times, and, without any hubris intended, had done remarkably well at it. This was rather an unprecedented series of promotions and accolades for my service, and I believed that that was where my talents could best be put to use. On top of that, I enjoyed being with marines. I had had a head-quarters assignment several years before. I thought that for the good of the corps and for the good of my own sense of accomplishment, I'd be best off back in the fleet. But the Marine Corps, in its infinite wisdom, decided that I would be one of the three or four candidates they would submit to the White House.

I picked up the phone and called my monitor — the assignment offi-cer in the marines who handles your rank — and complained. I said I didn't want a staff job; I wanted to go back to the infantry. He said, "Carry out your orders." So I came down for the interview. I spoke to the deputy chief of staff for manpower, who had at one point been my divi-sion commander. He told me, "Carry out your orders."

I told John Lehman, the secretary of the navy, the same thing. He sent me over to the White House, where I told Dick Allen, the national security adviser, the same thing. He said, "Fine. That's the kind of person we want here: someone who doesn't want to be here."

So my last gasp was with the commandant of the Marine Corps, Gen-eral Robert Barrow. I told him, "I really don't want this assignment; I want to go back to the Fleet Marine Force." And the general, who was a wonderful southern gentleman, stood up behind his desk and said, "Brother North, it isn't like us to whine. Carry out your orders." So I re-luctantly went to the White House.

Fawn Hall, secretary to Oliver North in the NSC's Military-Political Of-fice I went to work for Colonel North in 1983. Prior to that, I worked for the Department of the Navy at the Pentagon, in the office of the chief of naval operations. I had been working for the navy since I was sixteen. Two of my biggest assets — of which I was very proud — were that I took dictation and I was a workaholic.

I interviewed with Colonel North. I said, "I like to work long hours. I'm not married; I don't have children. I have a car. I take shorthand." These were things he was looking for. When I'm interested, I throw my-self into things; it makes me feel good. One of the things I think about in being a secretary is that I really enjoy making someone look their best and assisting in any way I can. So I really enjoyed it.

Jack Matlock I was asked to come to Washington to meet with Bill Clark in the spring of 1983 concerning a senior position on the National Security Council staff involving Soviet policy. I had breakfast with Judge Clark and his deputies, Bud McFarlane and John Poindexter, and it was explained to me that the president had decided it was time to develop a negotiating plan for the Soviet Union. They realized they had no one on the staff with direct experience, and they wanted me to come on board to devise the negotiating plan. I couldn't turn down this offer.

Chairman of the Joint Chiefs of Staff

John W. Vessey, vice chief of the army; chairman of the Joint Chiefs of Staff I had no idea I was in line to be chairman of the Joint Chiefs. Three years earlier I had been sent over to see President Carter concerning the job of chief of staff of the army, and I had failed my orals with him.

I was on a trip to South America; my retirement papers were in hand. And I got a call from Mr. Weinberger, on a Saturday, when I was in Punta del Este, Uruguay. He wanted to speak on a secure phone, but none was available, so we agreed that I would call him when I returned to Washington late the next evening.

The call bothered me because I couldn't figure out why he had called. I went over to see him at eight o'clock on a Monday morning. He said, "We have an appointment with the president in a few minutes." In the elevator going down to the secretary's car, he told me that the president wanted me to be the next chairman.

I said, "I have my retirement papers in. We are building a house in Minnesota that is draining us dry; I just can't afford to stay." Weinberger replied, "Well, you'll just have to explain that to the president."

I met with the president for about an hour, discussing military matters. But he didn't mention the chairmanship, so I thought: I've failed my orals again. Then, at the last minute, Weinberger and Judge Clark came in, and the president said, "I was just getting ready to ask General Vessey to be the next chairman."

We went back to the Pentagon, and I said to Mr. Weinberger, "I have a few conditions. I have studied the chairman's job, and the law says that the president's chief military advisers are the Joint Chiefs of Staff. I realize that presidents have gotten military advice from all sorts of places, but I believe that — having watched other presidents who worked, or failed to work, with the Joint Chiefs — the president should meet regularly with the Chiefs." So we met quarterly with the president on strategic issues. Of course, as chairman, you probably meet with him three times a week.

President Reagan took a great deal of interest and pride in those meetings with the Joint Chiefs. He came to the meetings prepared; he helped set the agenda for those meetings.

A DEARTH OF JEWS IN
HIGH-LEVEL POSITIONS

Abraham Sofaer, counselor to the Department of State   I felt that there
were no Jews at the top levels of the administration. The deputy attorney
general under Ed Meese was Jewish. Richard Perle was extremely influential; I think there were a large number of Jewish people who had significant influence.

I believe that the problem was that in Republican circles, if you were
Jewish, you suddenly heard about guys in your own party attacking you
privately, or quietly, for being a Zionist.

It was amazing; there was quite a bit of that. I remember when the
FBI directorship opened up, someone suggested my name to a person
high up in the administration, and that high official said, "But he's Jewish,
isn't he?"

If you put a Jewish name in front of Ronald Reagan, I don't think he
would have hesitated, because I don't think he had an anti-Semitic bone
in his body, but there were a lot of people around who were not very comfortable with the notion of trusting Jews in the national security positions.

OTHER ADMINISTRATION POSITIONS

C. Everett Koop, U.S. surgeon general   No one really knows how I was
appointed. I had three telephone calls in August 1980, all in the same
week: one from a staff member of Jesse Helms, one from the Heritage
Foundation, and one from a former congressman. They all asked me the
same question: Don't you think it's time that the surgeon general is a
surgeon?

The reason for that is that most surgeon generals have been pediatri-
cians, or public health officials, or something like that. I told them all that
serving in government had never entered my mind, but that I'd think
about it.

On election night, the night of the Reagan victory, my wife reminded
me that I was coming to the end of my tenure at the [Philadelphia] Children's Hospital: I would reach the retirement age at the University of
Pennsylvania the next year. She reminded me that I'd be pretty misera-
ble after being the chief for thirty-seven years. She said, "Why don't you
consider those offers you had for surgeon general?" So I called all three
men and told them that I was now enthusiastically seeking that position.

I was surprised at the length and vehemence of the confirmation process; if I had known that, I never would have come to Washington. The issue, without question, was abortion, in spite of the fact that on the third day I was in Washington I said that I did not intend to make abortion a major issue of the surgeon general's office. Indeed, it does not belong there.

Nevertheless, that is what people went after me about. There was a tremendous coalition of organizations, such as the National Organization for Women [NOW], the pro-abortion forces in some of the churches, the National Abortion Rights Action League [NARAL], and the American Public Health Association, which was very pro-abortion for population control. They did their best to sink my ship, but they never said it openly. They said I was incompetent, I was too old, that I didn't understand public health. They couldn't find any scandals in my life, so they just stuck to incompetence.

It was by steady perseverance, the president's confidence in me, but especially the efforts of Richard Schweiker, who was secretary of health and human services, and Orrin Hatch [R-Utah], who was the chairman of the Labor and Human Resources Committee of the Senate, that I was confirmed.

Major General Richard Secord, director of U.S. Air Force international programs; deputy assistant secretary of defense for the Near East, South Asia, and Africa   There was a dispute over a middle-level job in the office of the secretary of defense, that of the deputy assistant secretary for the Near East, South Asia, and Africa. The supporters of Israel had their boys that they were pushing, and the nonsupporters of Israel were pushing the other way, so Weinberger and Carlucci decided that they would appoint a military officer — by definition a political person.

Carlucci told me that they were going to appoint me. That was not what I had in mind, because it was a death knell for a military officer.

So I had two commissions: one as a military officer and one as a political appointee. It wasn't the first time in history that it happened, but it seldom does happen. I held this job from 1981 until the summer of 1983, when I retired.

Craig Fuller   In 1977 I joined the firm of Deaver and Hanneford. Reagan had an office there and would come in regularly. He would tell stories and jokes and enjoy talking to people. He was somebody I enjoyed getting to know. Later it was a wonderful advantage for me to have really gotten to know him well in the interim between his being governor and president.

When Ronald Reagan sought the presidency, Deaver, Meese, and Jim Baker urged me to come to Washington. I was twenty-nine years old when Reagan was elected. I said I would be happy to come and do whatever they thought would be useful. Late in the transition, in a fifteen-minute meeting in January 1981, Ed Meese said, "If you really are willing to take on anything, how about taking on the cabinet affairs position?"

We flew back to California together, and I packed over the weekend and came back to Washington on January 13.

Lyn Nofziger   I had said before the campaign was over that I did not want to be the president's press secretary. I really didn't want to be in the administration. I was going home.

Shortly before my wife, Bonnie, and I left to drive across the country, Jim Baker — who by this time had been picked as chief of staff — said, "I have a job that you might be interested in, a political job." At first I said no. Then I talked to Ed Meese and others. I said to Jim, "Don't take the 'no' permanently. I'll call you when I get back to California."

We got home just before Christmas, and I called Baker and said I would take the job. I figured out that the reason Jim asked me to do this job was not because of love or admiration for my talents. He needed to be able to say, I have brought some conservatives into this administration. He brought a number of people into the White House who were not his and Reagan's people.

Charles Hill, executive assistant to the secretary of state   I was in charge of the operations-center end of the contact with Phil Habib, who in 1982 was conducting diplomacy in Lebanon. My duties required me to stay in the operations center almost all the time.

I had the only line open to Habib. All other communications were down; no one else could talk to him. When Shultz came into the building on a Sunday afternoon, I was there. We met, and he took me on as his executive assistant as a result of that one contact.

STAFF RESPONSIBILITIES

James A. Baker III   The days were long. They would start at six o'clock in the morning, when I would wake up. I would usually get there by about seven. I would have a meeting with Meese and Deaver, and then we would have the senior staff meeting.

It's the worst job in government except for being vice president: you are right at the heart of the political centrifuge. And you are the target; you catch the spears that are aimed at the boss. There was a lot of stress, particularly because of the Californian/non-Californian element.

Edwin Meese III   There was no question that I would be the senior member of the White House staff — the only member of the cabinet from the White House — and that the role of counselor would be one in which I could concentrate on the policy aspects and the government aspects, whereas the political and legislative liaison and the press would be handled by the chief of staff, and Mike Deaver would then concentrate on the personal things for the president.

I was very satisfied, and the president eventually let me lay out the division of responsibilities. The other thing that I thought was good about having Jim Baker there was that we were from California. We knew a lot about campaigning year after year; we knew what we wanted to get done, but we didn't have anyone in the inner circle who had been in Washington before, in the White House, who knew the process of how to do it. So this was a good way to accomplish that.

Michael Deaver   I always thought my role was to fill up the space around the president. And I say that because of television: I wanted to be sure that his head was in the best space it could be. I didn't concern myself a lot with what came out of his head, unless it was going to be a problem. Then I would get into it.

From the very first, there was a symbiosis between me and Ronald Reagan. I can't explain it. I knew instinctively what was right for him. And he trusted me completely. So it was very much a team, as long as I was there. I wish in many ways that I had gone in earlier to recover from my alcoholism and had stayed on. But you can't rewrite history.

Caspar Weinberger   My brief was to regain our military and defensive strength. The president had said many times — on the stump and many times to me personally — that if it ever came down to a question of a balanced budget or a strong military, he would always choose a strong military, that the only way we could achieve peace, or secure freedom with peace, was to have a strong military. We had let ours go very badly, in what he called "a decade of neglect." The Soviets were in their third decade of expansion, and a dangerous gap was opening.

He and I agreed that we had to do something about that as quickly as we possibly could. Until we could start to close the gap, it was a dangerous period. We never wanted superiority; we simply wanted to have a deterrent capability.

Frank Carlucci   The Department of Defense was, in Cap's and my view, a starved institution in need of nourishment, tender loving care, and rebuilding. Cap and I decided on a strange division of labor: he focused on foreign affairs and operations; I focused on the budget and the procurement side.

John Poindexter   At the beginning of the Reagan administration, Ed Meese, as counselor to the president, would handle most domestic and foreign policy issues and integrate the two, to present the president with an integrated look at the two issues.

Under Ed Meese were Dick Allen on the national security foreign policy side, and Martin Anderson on the domestic policy side. So Dick, although an assistant to the president for national security affairs, was never referred to as the national security adviser.

Oliver North   My actual first assignment, while Dick Allen was still there — then subsequently with Bill Clark, Bud McFarlane, and John Poindexter — was to work on a very sensitive project involving the survival of the presidency. It was designed to ensure that we would always have control over the military; that we would never be disconnected; that the military would never be without civilian command and control. I derived a great deal of satisfaction from it; it's something I believe in.

I worked on that for two years, from August 1981, when I arrived at the White House, until the middle of 1983, which was when I was redirected into working on counterterrorism and crisis planning. It just happened that the first major crisis that occurred was the deployment of the marines to Beirut and, ultimately, the October events: both the planning for Grenada and the terrible tragedy in Beirut.

Michael Ledeen, special adviser to the secretary of state; consultant to the NSC   I was a kind of intelligence courier for the White House: I would go and talk to various people in Europe. There are certain kinds of conversations that an American president will want to carry on outside of official channels. I carried some of those private messages.

My other responsibility was that I worked with North on counterterrorism. I read all the intelligence on terrorism, and North and I would discuss it.

John C. Whitehead, deputy secretary of state   One of my assignments, after the appointment of George Shultz as secretary of state, was to be Shultz's alter ego. That meant that when he was out of Washington, I was the acting secretary; that it was up to me to handle anything that came up on my watch as if I were the secretary. It was up to me to carry through on that project even after he came back.

He had more than enough to do. He wanted me to be a separate force rather than an assistant. He didn't want to split it up and say, You be the inside man and I'll be the outside man, as some secretaries had done. He wanted somebody who could take a chunk of the problems off his plate so that he could concentrate — particularly on the Soviet Union situation, which was his main job all the time he was in office.

C. Everett Koop   No one ever knows what his job is in Washington. No one ever tells you. No one ever said, This is what the surgeon general does, this is what he used to do, and this is the way we plan to clip his wings in the future. Even after I arrived in Washington, no one ever told me what my job description was.

The reason that I was a successful surgeon general is that it took me eleven months to be confirmed, and I looked at all the issues, and by the time I was confirmed I had an agenda.

Smoking is on the surgeon general's plate when he comes into office, and it remains there. There is a principle in public health that you put your money where the greatest morbidity and mortality is. Smoking is the single preventable cause of death, and it behooves somebody to be talking about it.

The second behavioral problem in the country is obesity. Twenty-five percent of Americans were obese when I was in office; now it's thirty-three. Those people account for three hundred thousand deaths a year. I never tackled obesity while I was in office, but I did after I left, and I run a national program now called Shape Up America.

The third behavioral problem is alcohol, and I went after that as well as I could. I especially emphasized drunk driving.

I was very involved with the problems of the aged, not only because I was a senior citizen, but because with that burgeoning population, we had a tremendous number of things to look at and plan for.

As I was in my former life a pediatric surgeon, maternal and child health programs are very high on my agenda. Some of the things I am proudest of are the things we accomplished in providing comprehensive, coordinated, family-centered, community-based care for children who have "special needs" — what some people call the "handicapped."

Those were the major things I dealt with day by day. If you look at the public health law and see what it demands of the surgeon general, it isn't much. He's an educator: he tells people what they can do to avoid disease and to promote good health. He has no power, and no budget, but he has a tremendous amount of moral suasion, and it's an office that lends itself to public confidence.

AN APPOINTMENT TO
THE SUPREME COURT

In February 1981, Justice Potter Stewart declared his intention to resign from the Supreme Court. Following up on a campaign pledge to put a woman on the Court, President Reagan on July 7 nominated the Arizona Appeals Court judge and former state senator Sandra Day O'Connor to fill the position.

While Judge O'Connor had the support of the Reagan adviser Paul Laxalt and other prominent Republicans, including Barry Goldwater and Justice William Rehnquist, her nomination was opposed by leaders of the conservative movement.

President Reagan, however, declined to interview any other candidate for the Court, and Justice O'Connor was quickly confirmed by the Senate, becoming the first woman to be appointed to the Supreme Court.

Jerry Falwell I was at Myrtle Beach [South Carolina]. The president called me and said, "Jerry, I am going to put forth a lady on the [Supreme] Court. You don't know anything about her. Nobody does, but I want you to trust my judgment on this one."

I said, "I'll do that." The next day he announced the nomination of Sandra Day O'Connor. About two weeks later he called me again and said, "Jerry, I've had a chance to talk to her, and my people have, and I can tell you that her views will not disappoint you, and I hope you can help me bring the troops in." So I began calling conservatives, asking them to back off.

I think she has done well; she broke the [all-male] tradition in a dignified way. The president knew that I would be concerned, and that the Religious Right would be upset, but I believed in and trusted him. And I haven't been sorry I did.

STAFF CHANGES

Haig Resigns

Martin Anderson   It didn't work, fundamentally, because Haig did not understand Reagan and how he worked. Reagan would have a cabinet meeting, and if you were talking about economic policy, he didn't mind if the secretary of state made a comment, or vice versa.

There were some people — Haig, for example — who didn't like this approach; he thought that foreign policy was his. Early on there was a presidential trip to Canada, and a meeting was called in the Cabinet Room to prepare and discuss the trip. I was invited because there were some domestic issues involved. I went in there a few minutes early, and Haig was there. He looked up, looked me straight in the eye, and said, "What the —— are you doing in my meeting, Anderson?" I looked at him and said, "Hey, anytime I get a chance to brighten your day, I take it."

There was this hostility all the time. He could do it to me, but Meese and Baker wouldn't put up with this stuff, and he was just finally fired. It wasn't that he was so bad on policy. If he had come in and said, Let's see how the president likes to work, and then had cooperated, I think he might have been very successful.

Donald Gregg   I used to describe Al Haig as "a cobra among garter snakes." At the cabinet meetings, whereas everybody else would be sort of slithering happily around the table, he was up there, with his lips spread, looking for somebody to bite.

He never really was at ease in the White House. I finally came to realize that he realized what he and Kissinger had done to Rogers as secretary of state;* he was afraid that Dick Allen and company were trying to do the same to him, as secretary of state.

Alexander M. Haig Jr.   The situation led me to believe over time that the best thing I could do would be to leave. I told my wife after two months that I would not stay on more than one year because I couldn't work in that environment.

I stayed on a little longer because we had two crises that were rivet-

---

* William Rogers, the first secretary of state during the Nixon presidency, was undercut on countless occasions by National Security Adviser Henry Kissinger. Haig served at the time on the National Security Council staff.

ing in importance, the first being the Falklands War, and the second being the Middle East crisis and the war in Lebanon.

Shultz Is Selected to Replace Haig as Secretary of State

Craig Johnstone, director for Central American affairs, Department of State; deputy assistant secretary of inter-American affairs; ambassador to Algeria We were enormously encouraged by the Shultz nomination to State. Haig had his own charm — he is very intelligent and perceptive — but he is also very impetuous; his gaffes had compromised the department's ability to influence policy. So someone like Shultz, with his stature, was a welcome relief.

Nicholas Platt, deputy assistant secretary of state for international organization affairs; acting assistant secretary of state for international organization affairs; ambassador to Zambia; executive secretary, Department of State; special assistant to the secretary of state; ambassador to the Philippines We were sorry to see Haig go. None of us were particularly surprised when this happened. But we liked the idea of Shultz very much, and we thought he would be successful. The thing that impressed us about Shultz was that he was willing, right from the beginning, to use the institution and its machinery.

I heard that the day he arrived to take up the job he came accompanied only by a beat-up, old leather briefcase — he didn't even bring a secretary with him — and he said, Okay, let's get to work. In no time he had the complete support of the department.

George P. Shultz I had a pretty good idea of what kind of person Ronald Reagan was. I had worked with him during the campaign. I was the chairman of an economic policy group that gave advice before the inauguration, and then it was brought back into being after the inauguration, and we had lots of meetings with him. I had appeared as sort of his spokesman on *Meet the Press*, and I met with him a long while before I went to Washington and made that appearance. So I felt, I understand him, we are on the same wavelength, I can work with him.

Gerald R. Ford George Shultz is one of my favorite people. He has done a first-class job in every position he has held.

Jerry Falwell I thought the appointment was a step backward. He is a good man, and a principled person, but I felt that he was pretty much controlled by the oil interests.

Barry Schweid, Associated Press diplomatic correspondent Shultz and Weinberger were "the boys from Bechtel" to me.

An Unfortunate Remark and
Watt Is Forced to Resign

On September 21, 1983, in an address to the U.S. Chamber of Commerce, James Watt referred to an Interior Department commission as follows: "We have every kind of mix you can have. I have a black, I have a woman, two Jews, and a cripple. And we have talent."

James Watt I am concerned over the huge injustice that has been done to me, personally, and to those of us in the Reagan camp, by the Eastern Establishment, particularly the press. It's been a cruel experience.

The Baker and Deaver Proposal

In October 1983, in the wake of William Clark's departure from the post of national security adviser to become secretary of the interior following the resignation of Watt, Baker and Deaver hatched a plan: Baker would succeed Clark, and Deaver would become chief of staff.
    The plan was strongly opposed by many of President Reagan's advisers.

James A. Baker III Bill Clark was just not comfortable with a lot of the subjects in the job. When he would come in to brief the president in the morning, he would have the briefing done by an expert in a particular area. And he got caught up in the idea — which I think is baloney — that Shultz and the State Department were not carrying out the Reagan agenda.

Craig Fuller There is always change in the White House. After the first year, a photograph was taken that showed that only three or four of us senior staff members were still there from the twenty or so who had been there at the beginning of the administration. People moved around a lot. They went off into the departments; they went to foreign posts. It is not unusual that people in these very intense jobs think that they would like to try something else.
    This hasn't been reported before, but I knew about the Baker-Deaver

shift the morning of the non-event. Mike asked me to come to his office and told me this was going to happen during the course of the day, and that he would like me to take charge of policy, but that I couldn't discuss this with anybody.

So I went back to my office. And in about an hour the whole thing had been literally undone. I was almost involved, but it didn't happen. And, of course, making the attempt frays relationships.

Jeane J. Kirkpatrick Mike Deaver moved Clark out of the national security adviser job. He did it very suddenly, and very clearly, with a plan in place to appoint Baker as his replacement.

There was then a kind of cabal — Baker, Deaver, and Shultz. Well, not a cabal. An alliance — one based on something other than views on issues. Casey and Cap were not able to persuade the president that he must not appoint Jim Baker. That occurred in a meeting in Bill Clark's office at the NSC.

I know that, because I arrived before it was finished and went into the room where the NSPG [National Security Planning Group] normally met, and nobody was there. I didn't know where everybody was, but I learned that they were in Clark's office. That was where the case was being made to the president that he should not appoint Baker.

Michael Deaver It was a tactical mistake. Baker had decided that he wanted to do this. He convinced me that I could be chief of staff — that it would all work — and he prepared a press release. Then we both decided, at Baker's suggestion, not to go to the meeting of the National Security Council, that it would be better if he went down there.

Evidently, on the way in, he handed the release to Meese, who got Clark and Weinberger out of the room. Clark and Meese and Weinberger just went crazy. Casey hated Baker because of "papergate," and Meese and Clark didn't want Baker mucking around in foreign policy. And whatever they would have said would have convinced Cap.

So here the president had three of his oldest and most trusted people saying, "You cannot do this." And they may have been opposed to me, saying, Deaver can't handle this. All I know is that when Reagan came back, he called me on the intercom and said, "You'd better come in here." He started to tell me this, and I said, "Wait a minute. Let's go to Baker."

Jeane J. Kirkpatrick When the president told Deaver he was not going to make the appointment, Mike had a temper tantrum and shouted at the president — something, I was told, the president never forgot. Everybody I know who dealt with Ronald Reagan treated him with respect — and was expected to.

Michael Deaver   There was a book that stated that I had this outburst and said, "Goddamn you! This is the second time you've done this to me!" But it was only me and Jimmy Baker and Ronald Reagan in the room. I most certainly didn't say that, I would never say that. I may have been thinking it, but I wouldn't have said it. Reagan was sitting there, saying, "I am going to have to think about this now."

And I was standing just a little behind Baker when I realized he was saying to the president, "Don't worry about it, Mr. President. I came here to serve you and whatever you want me to do, I'll do."

And I'm thinking to myself: Here I am, a jerk, and here's this guy, who's a nice guy, and I should be thinking this, and not what I'm thinking. We went back into my office, and I said that to Baker. He then went and said that to [Richard] Darman [a Baker aide]. Maybe Baker said it himself, to Hedrick Smith.* But I didn't say that to the president.

William P. Clark, deputy secretary of state; national security adviser; secretary of the interior   Deaver and Baker convinced the president that they could handle the government by Deaver's assuming the position of chief of staff and Baker, and then Darman, would assume the responsibilities of national security adviser.

I had to go up to get the president to come down to a national security briefing. He told me that he was determined to go forward with the staff changes. I told him that I felt he owed it to Weinberger, Casey, Meese, and others who were waiting for him in the Situation Room to talk to them, individually, before announcing it as an accomplished fact.

I pleaded with him to roundtable — his favorite term — that decision, realizing that there were strong feelings in policy and philosophy between Mr. Baker, Mr. Deaver, and Mr. Darman on the one hand, and the key principals in the National Security Council, and that he should get their counsel on compatibility before I moved on to Interior. So he did not announce the decision in the Situation Room, but rather, he met

---

* Hedrick Smith (*New York Times* correspondent), *The Power Game: How Washington Works* (New York: Random House, 1988), 324. Deaver is reported to have yelled at the president: "You don't have enough confidence in me to make me chief of staff."

in my own office with these individuals and decided against it. The press conference to announce the change was canceled.

James A. Baker III   It would have been a good thing, because the truth of the matter is that the one area we did not have a crisp operation in was the national security area; the process did not work the way it was supposed to work.

There was constant fighting throughout both Reagan terms, throughout six national security advisers. You never had a day when the secretary of state and the secretary of defense weren't at each other's throats, or when the national security adviser and the secretary of state were not at each other's throats, or when the national security adviser wouldn't walk in and say, "Mr. President, I think we ought to send Jeane Kirkpatrick on a mission to Latin America," and the secretary of state didn't even know about it. And it was up to me, the chief of staff, to say, "Mr. President, do you really think you ought to do that without the approval of your secretary of state?"

Those were the kinds of things that were going on, so Mike and I and the first lady felt that we somehow needed to bring the operation of the NSC within the orbit of the rest of the White House, so that there would be some supervision that would operate in the president's best interests.

You have to run a presidency like you run a campaign: it's a constant, day-to-day thing. What are you going to concentrate on on this day? On that day? What should be the focus of the news?

We were never able to get control of the national security side of that in a way that it could be run in a coordinated and effective way, so that was the reason for the idea that I would become the national security adviser and Deaver would become the chief of staff.

Craig Fuller   Reagan always knew that the people who worked for him were going to be at odds with one another at times. He just stayed above it. I'm not sure that that was true of Nancy Reagan, but it was true of President Reagan, so his antennae weren't picking up some of the trouble signals that people may have been sending over this realignment.

He likes to achieve consensus. He had to know, based on what he had been told, that not everybody was going to be supportive of this. When he got close to doing it, he realized it wasn't going to fly. When he found out the extent of the opposition, and the level of the concern, he simply backed away from it. He realized it would be detrimental to going forward.

James A. Baker III   It was all wired; the president had agreed to it. And then we went into the NSC meeting. The president had told Clark about it. Clark passed notes to Weinberger and Casey. The people who shot it down were Casey, Weinberger, Meese, and, maybe, Kirkpatrick.

The president said to me, "There is an objection. I want to think about it. I'm going to Camp David." I said, "I don't want to put you in a position like that if the objections are that vehement. You should just forget about it."

Deaver didn't react quite that way. He got mad and went in and said, "How could you do this? You told us you were going to okay it."

The president went up to Camp David and decided it was not something he wanted to do. And I said, "I certainly understand." But I continue to think, to this day, that it would have been a healthy thing. If it had happened, we wouldn't have had an Iran-contra.

Geoffrey Kemp, NSC senior director for the Near East and South Asia; special assistant to the president for national security affairs   Judge Clark left because he was having increasing fights with James Baker and Deaver and Nancy Reagan. It was clear that while Clark had been much more assertive than Richard Allen, because of his intimacy with Reagan, even he was running into real trouble.

At the time Clark said he wanted to leave, there was a flurry of speculation that two other candidates were in the wings: Jim Baker and Jeane Kirkpatrick. Now there was absolutely no way that Baker was going to allow Kirkpatrick to have that job, no way at all. Similarly, he was not able to orchestrate it for himself either.

William P. Clark   As far as the possibility that Jeane Kirkpatrick would succeed me, my understanding is that Shultz threatened to resign. Mrs. Kirkpatrick had great respect for the State Department. She had to report most of the time, and through Shultz, from her New York position.

Jeane J. Kirkpatrick   I was very sorry that Dick Allen left. I believe that he was a victim of the media — actually a combination of some White House mischief-making and some media mischief-making.

It never occurred to me that I was being considered. I just wasn't that deeply involved in Reagan's inner circle at that time. I was really quite new to this scene.

One of our interviewees told us, on the condition that he not be quoted directly, that some of Shultz's staff said that the secretary of state's position on the national security adviser post—and on certain ambassadorial appointments—was "a question of manhood."

In addition, the interviewee said, Henry Kissinger stated that no secretary of state was more ruled by, or captive to, the department itself than Shultz was, and that the feeling was that Jeane Kirkpatrick should not become the national security adviser.

Jeane J. Kirkpatrick I was never an active candidate; I never said to Reagan that I would like any job. I know that there were some people who were trying to promote me for the job, who were talking to the president about it. I came to know that later because some very close friends of the president called and told me they had talked to the president.

I was actually at home with the flu during about the five days that the affair was at its height. When it was all over, a week or two later, I sought an appointment with the president, because there were headlines in the newspapers saying: "Kirkpatrick Threatens to Resign." This was pure, absolute fiction, so I thought I'd better tell that to the president.

I told the president that I would really like to leave. I had a couple of reasons. At the time I had accepted the appointment I had made a commitment to myself, and to the president, to stay for two years. Georgetown University had given me a leave from my chair; I didn't feel that it was right to keep the chair tied up indefinitely. Also, beginning in about my third year [as UN ambassador], my husband's health began to deteriorate. By the time I finally left that was really the reason for leaving.

The president asked me to stay one more year, and I agreed. Then he asked me to stay one *more* year, and he gave me his word that he wouldn't ask me to stay any longer.

After our interview with Ambassador Kirkpatrick, we left her office and were in the reception area, preparing to depart, when her assistant appeared and said, "Could you return to her office? She has something else she wants to tell you." We did so and were told the following:

Jeane J. Kirkpatrick Several people told me that at the time Baker had been turned down for national security adviser, a number of the president's old friends, personal friends, called to tell him that I would be the right person. The president said that he would be happy to appoint me but that George Shultz had told him he didn't feel that he could work with me, and that he would not be able to stay on if he were to appoint me.

I was told that by two or three people who had spoken directly to the president. George Shultz denied this when he was asked about it; this story was around town.

Geoffrey Kemp   Once it was decided that the job would not go to a Baker, or a Kirkpatrick, Bud McFarlane was the natural choice. He was low-keyed and got along with everybody — and he was a professional.

4

Administrative Style and Surviving an Assassination Attempt

REAGAN'S ATTITUDE TOWARD THE PRESIDENCY

Craig Fuller For the most part, it was something he relished and thoroughly enjoyed. He was profoundly moved by the opportunity and the responsibility.

The beauty of it was that he had such a clear view of the fundamentals of his presidency that every day he looked for opportunities to make a difference in the areas he thought to be important.

Most days for him promised an adventure that he pretty much lived for. Even in the latter part of the second term he was quite enthusiastic. I've really met no one like him in terms of their constant focus on what is right.

Max Hugel He wanted to turn the country around. He wanted to change it from a federal government–based operation back to the states. All the things you see today that the conservatives have won were Reagan's agenda.

And Reagan's agenda — strong defense, less taxes, less government interference in our lives, and stop the Russians — was right for the times.

PRESIDENT REAGAN'S ADMINISTRATIVE STYLE

Jeane J. Kirkpatrick Reagan liked to approach issues by hearing the differing views of advisers. I don't think he sought agreement among them. Whether he deliberately sought disagreement is another matter. I doubt that he did.

Reagan personally chaired all the NSPG [National Security Planning Group] meetings. He was the one who sought out the opinions of the different advisers around the table. It didn't bother him that some advisers had different opinions; it bothered some of the advisers. It interested the president.

James A. Baker III   He was used to having a script for the day. That's why we could do things the way we did them in the first term, because we could say, "Mr. President, if you agree, we think we ought to concentrate on your economic agenda, to the exclusion of everything else, for the first three months of your administration." And that's what we would do. He would expect us to come to him every day and say, "Here's what the day looks like." And if he approved it, that's what we would do.

It enabled us to beat back efforts by Haig, in the first couple of months, to go to the source in Cuba, to bomb Cuba. It was like the guys in the military: you have a hundred days to make your mark; you'd better have a good hundred-day plan. We had a good hundred-day plan, and we stuck with it. That was the president's management style.

Colin L. Powell, military aide to the deputy secretary of defense; military aide to the secretary of defense; deputy national security adviser; national security adviser   When I first met him, I was a two-star general [major general], as military assistant to Cap Weinberger, and I was not in the inner sanctum or sitting around in policy meetings.

If the issue under discussion was one of his core issues, he would get deeply engaged and would be very firm. There was no question that he had thought it through and was willing to take risks. Below that threshold, he was quite willing to delegate to others. And having delegated it to you, he really didn't see why he had to spend so much time worrying about it. Otherwise, why did he hire you?

Donald Gregg   The president was not a detail person; he had broad concepts. I would watch him, in meeting after meeting, and I would think to myself, Is he awake? Does he understand what's going on? Is he listening?

And then, at the end of the meeting, he would focus, and he would draw on some of these deeply felt concepts that he had, and that would get the meeting back on track. He had two or three themes that were absolutely fundamental. He just never wavered from them.

Nimrod Novick   [Israeli Prime Minister Shimon Peres] felt that Reagan was a very careful man to appoint people more capable than himself in the specific areas of his responsibility, that Reagan set the broad guidelines and the professionals were expected to carry them into action.

Peres was very much impressed with the fact that the secretaries were so careful not to do anything, not to make a commitment, unless authorized by the president; it was clear that the secretaries took him very seriously. We have seen administrations — and we have seen other countries — where ministers dismiss the boss very easily and go in any direction.

Robert C. McFarlane   Reagan believed that strength is better than weakness; that ideology and ideas are important; that he was selling the rightness of our institutions and our system, not a given outcome that might enhance his domestic political standing. Every day he picked up on the big things. The little things might escape him, but that's what I was paid for — not him.

George P. Shultz   In the intensive period of six and a half years that I served as secretary of state, we had lots of meetings with large and small groups, and I saw him in the process of major international events of one kind or another.

We covered everything you could imagine. I wanted to hear his ideas, of course, but I wanted to tell him what I thought was going on, and to get his reactions and therefore be on his wavelength and be doing things that I could instinctively feel were what he wanted.

I found him very good to work with. He asked lots of questions; he contributed ideas. But the main thing he contributed was a strong thread that guided him. And he knew what it was, and he knew when we were getting off that beat, and he would get us back on it again.

Martin Anderson   He was a loner. He had, in a sense, the personality of a professor: he liked to get to his briefcase and work on those papers. The great myth is that he didn't work; he worked all the time. The myth was that he napped on the plane; I never saw him take a single nap.

When he got on the plane, he sat down and opened up his briefcase. When we traveled alone with him, he would get the inside seat, the staff person the outside. This was to protect him. If someone came up to him, he would stop and talk to him, so we tried to discourage people.

Michael Deaver   He never pretended to be a great administrator. It was his force and style that moved the governorship and the presidency. Somehow you never expected him to bark orders, or to be very concerned about how things worked. He was the center of what made things work, what moved things. That has been largely misunderstood about him; [the myth is] that he slept in meetings, that he wasn't intellectual, that he didn't read.

AN AMIABLE DUNCE?

His critics maintained that Reagan's grasp of the issues was somewhat lim-ited, and some went as far as to characterize him as "an amiable dunce"—al-beit a caring individual—whose fuzzy grasp of issues necessitated detailed "scripting" by key staff.

Lyn Nofziger   May I point out that the "amiable dunce" was governor of California twice and president of the United States twice? So being an amiable dunce isn't all that bad. The rumor was passed along very early that this guy is an actor and you have to give him his lines. This made him mad.

Stuart Spencer   [Sometimes] he'd break the mold; he would go out and do something that was his idea. The media didn't believe he could do that, so it would be either Stu Spencer's fault, or Jim Baker's fault. It couldn't be Ronald Reagan who took this position.

Oliver Wright   The idea that he was scripted is a common view in Eu-rope. I've always thought that Ronald Reagan was greatly undervalued in Europe. I believe that there are two reasons. One is that most of our scribblers are left-of-center in politics and therefore were politically op-posed to him. And secondly, they are all intellectual snobs, and the presi-dent was not an intellectual, so these people couldn't face the fact that he turned out to be a great president.

Martin Anderson   The great myth was that he had these little three-by-five cards and that he nervously looked at them and what the staff had written. The cards were four-by-six inches — a critical difference — and he deliberately chose that size because three-by-five was too small and five-by-seven was too big; they wouldn't fit in his pocket.

After he wrote out a speech in longhand, he would "card" it. He had invented his own shorthand. When I asked him why he did that, he replied, "Well, the audiences hate for you to read a speech; they get bored. On the other hand, you can't give a serious policy speech unless you write it out and read it."

Edwin Meese III   Sometimes people would try to overprogram him with cards. I saw one card — I think it had been prepared by the State Department — that said, "Good Morning, Mr. President," to some head of state.

Howard Teicher, policy analyst, office of the secretary of defense; staff assistant to the State Department counselor; NSC senior director for political-military affairs   Many in the media — and the public in general — have been very unfair to Reagan with regard to his intellectual capacity. I'm not trying to suggest he was a rocket scientist, and I am not suggesting that he at times did not get things confused or wrong. But he did have a very good grasp of the basic issues I was working on.

On a number of occasions he asked what I thought were extremely succinct questions about Israeli and Arab politics that were not necessarily rooted in a career of study but in an understanding of human nature.

Oliver North   He had the old-style TelePrompTer, and in the speech of April 1986, on Libya, I watched as he literally took out the words — scratched them out, as it were — on the TelePrompTer that all our aircraft had returned safely, because we knew we had lost an F-111.

Abraham Sofaer   People who say he drifted off were just wrong. He would drift off — after he heard what you had to say. When he became convinced that you had nothing further to say to him, that he couldn't learn anything further from you, he did drift off. I have seen him do that in big meetings.

Lyn Nofziger   Reagan is probably the most underestimated politician of the post–World War II era. All those guys yearned to run against him — George Christopher in the primary; Pat Brown in the election; Jimmy Carter wanted to go against this dumb actor and this dumb actor clobbered him — because they always assumed that Ronald Reagan is not a genius.

But he is smart, quick-witted. He has a good retentive memory for everything except names and faces. I used to say that if he was gone for two or three days, we would have to introduce him to his wife again. The caricature of him painted by the Democrats was one they wanted to perceive; it was not something that was there.

Martin Anderson   I find it amazing that so many people accept this version: that he is kind of slow; that he was not very smart; that he didn't work very hard; that he took naps all the time. It simply does not jibe with all that he accomplished.

We are talking about a highly intelligent person, probably a genius mentality in a fascinating way: you could talk to him about a very complicated issue and he'd absorb the whole thing, just like that. Then weeks, or months, later, he would take that issue, analyze it, put it in his own way, and put it out so that it would sound like poetry.

Shimon Peres   I was surprised by his sharpness of judgment. He had a much better memory than one thought. Of course, he did not know everything, but what he knew, he knew well.

He had the capacity to address the heart of the issue. He was interested in the subject matter rather than in the details. And on those issues on which he had an opinion, his opinion was unshakable.

Jeane J. Kirkpatrick   He was not an intellectual, not a professor, [and] not a journalist — but he was a person who communicated. Ronald Reagan is a very intelligent man. He was particularly concerned with the big picture. But when the big picture depended on details, he could follow the details as well. What made him an effective president — an effective executive — was that he never lost sight of what he was going to accomplish.

DEALING WITH THE CABINET

Donald T. Regan   The initial promise of Baker, Deaver, and Meese was that this would be a full-cabinet government. That was BS. It was no more a full-cabinet government than in any other presidency. But the cabinet did have to get together on occasion to see how things were going, and also so the president could at least stay in touch with his cabinet members.

When there was a full-cabinet meeting, we used to call it "show and tell," because it would be called in order to let some cabinet department explain its problems, or what it intended to do in a certain area. Or, at the end of a meeting that was called for a different purpose, the president would go around the table and ask if anyone had something he or she wanted to bring up.

Then some cabinet member — like a good little kid in school — would raise his or her hand and proceed to say, What a good boy I am (or, What a good girl I am), look what I've done recently!

Craig Fuller   In the beginning [the cabinet] was tremendously valuable. The cabinet as a whole became a forum for sharing ideas and comparing notes on what was working and what was not working. It was a way of linking together the senior people in the administration so that we could more effectively speak with one voice.

Edwin Meese III   Reagan liked the cabinet system. What he didn't like was what he had seen in the Nixon administration, where White House staff people were telling cabinet members what their orders were.

He had used the cabinet extensively in California; out there his cabinet was the focal point of decision-making. In Washington he adapted the system he had used in Sacramento by developing cabinet councils. In this system, a portion of the cabinet would come together on a subject-matter basis.

Craig Fuller   The cabinet councils themselves became vehicles for formulating ideas across departmental lines. The cabinet councils, because they met so frequently, brought the members of the White House staff and cabinet together regularly, so you didn't have some of the conflicts that had plagued other administrations.

Donald T. Regan   In the first administration there was the cabinet council on this, the cabinet council on that; there were six or seven of them. The one I headed up, in economic affairs, definitely overlapped with the cabinet council on economics. It became quite unusual for cabinet officers to get their points of view directly to the president; they had to go through these cabinet councils.

There are good and bad points to this system, and I think there were more good than bad ones. Having been a chief executive officer — and having been one for ten years in a large organization — taught me that you cannot take up the chief executive's time with a lot of minutiae and debris-clearing; you have to clear the area out so he can see where the trees are and the land lies, and what the big picture is. The cabinet council system served to do that.

Craig Fuller We maintained lists that tracked all these issues as they were moving through [the cabinet councils]. I would say to people, "Give me an issue, and I can go to this book we have, and I can show you the path it took to be decided by the president." It was pretty hard to find an issue that hadn't gone through the path, which is a pretty remarkable thing. In some cases — enterprise zones, for example — we might have had fifteen different discussions within a cabinet council as the issue was developed, shaped, and crafted.

Edwin Meese III The cabinet councils covered major issue areas, including the National Security Council, which already existed by statute. By the beginning of the second term the system was streamlined and the number reduced to three: the National Security Council, the Economic Policy Council, and the Domestic Policy Council.

The president was the chairman of all the cabinet councils. He spent an awful lot of time in working the cabinet system — perhaps four to six times a week in some kind of cabinet activity.

THE NATIONAL SECURITY COUNCIL

The NSC Structure

Donald Gregg The Reagan people were very much against people from the State Department; they didn't have a single person from the State Department on the NSC staff. And once I had been confirmed as staying on, I began to agitate to get someone on the NSC staff from State, and the first person they brought in was Jack Matlock, who later became the ambassador to the Soviet Union.

But the Reagan attitude was that State was too bureaucratic — their people are late for meetings, they are late with their papers — so we will try to get along without them. And you really can't.

Constantine Menges What was very important in his decision-making style was the regularity of the National Security Council meetings. There were roughly 149 in the first Reagan term, compared to 45 in Carter's four years.

Due to the regularity of the meetings, all the advisers could get together and offer their judgments on particular issues. And President Reagan would follow the issues over time. Many issues were unfolding and developing in international politics; the discipline he applied kept him informed about the most important questions, and he could turn his attention to those questions when there was a need to. So he focused on the major issues in a continuous, systematic way.

Geoffrey Kemp Richard Allen was told to report to the president through Meese, which was a unique downgrading. And when you downgrade the NSC adviser, you downgrade his staff, so all of us were downgraded.

The problem for State was that Haig didn't have this direct line to the president and Caspar Weinberger did. And then you had a third, very powerful player, William Casey. The net result in the first year was that the three heavy hitters in the foreign policy establishment — Haig, Weinberger, and Casey — all neutralized each other, and the NSC was unable to crack the whip.

Everyone realized that the situation could not go on. When Allen finally left at the end of the first year, and Uncle Bill [Clark] came over from the State Department, things changed dramatically.

The irony is that Dick Allen was — and is — a specialist on international affairs and really knew the field extremely well, and Bill Clark was a complete novice — and admitted it.

And suddenly, overnight, the power of the NSC changed, because Clark had been Reagan's chief of staff in Sacramento and knew how to handle the president, and he was on an equal par with Deaver, Baker, and Meese. And therefore the whole structure of the staff rose, in parallel.

In the wake of Iran-contra, there was talk of downgrading the NSC, or making the adviser subject to confirmation. It didn't get anywhere because everybody understands the realities of Washington. In this day and age, efforts to sidetrack the National Security Council never work because the power of the president and the immediacy of the events — be they bureaucratic or crisis-oriented — force decisions into the White House. So if you don't have an NSC, you have to create one.

Jeane J. Kirkpatrick There were some splits in the Reagan National Security Council. The principals, with few exceptions, were more civilized in managing those differences than a lot of the people who tried to describe them.

There were a lot of differences on cold war issues, about how much capital the administration should spend in trying to get support for some Central American issues, or some Soviet issues. Some of us were more enthusiastic about the Reagan Doctrine than others. Some of us were more committed to the proposition that our job was to uphold Ronald Reagan's policies and perspectives, that he should decide, and that we should faithfully seek to execute his views.

William J. Crowe Jr., commander in chief, NATO forces, Europe (1980–82); commander in chief, the Pacific (1983–85); chairman of the Joint Chiefs of Staff Shultz and Weinberger clashed over me. By legislation, the chairman of the Joint Chiefs was made the defense adviser, not only for the secretary of defense but for the National Security Council and the president.

And Shultz felt that, being on the National Security Council, he should have access to my military advice anytime he wanted it. Weinberger didn't like that. He said, "Sure, you can have it, as long as I'm there."

And Shultz disagreed. He said, "The legislation does not mention the presence of the secretary of defense." They had a huge argument; Weinberger got mad as hell.

I did brief Shultz, but I would always tell Weinberger first.

CONTINUING CONTACTS WITH
THE MORAL MAJORITY

Ronald Godwin There were numerous meetings and — I am speaking symbolically — all of them through the side or back door of the White House.

I attended several dozen meetings, some with Dr. Falwell, and some as his Washington representative. I met with President Reagan a number of times; we met with Ed Meese and were treated very kindly; we met with Mr. Baker and were treated carefully. Reagan went out of his way to keep these constituencies involved.

There was great controversy during this time that we were like Indians representing tribes of potentially dangerous warriors. Therefore, they would occasionally bring us in and give us beads and mirrors and shells; these were largely gestures meant to satisfy egos and placate frustration. They cost the administration very little in terms of public commitment. Nevertheless, those types of meetings were fairly frequent during the first term.

There seemed to be a genuine chemistry between the president and Dr. Falwell. I didn't sense that it extended to Mrs. Reagan. I got the feeling that President Reagan and Dr. Falwell got along famously, and that Mrs. Reagan was not that pleased about it.

Activities would be planned and then at times would be mysteriously canceled. Often what was agreed upon in meetings would be rather significantly altered. We had some back-channel sources in the White House among the Secret Service. We were able to pick up certain information that Nancy was involved in these changes. Mrs. Reagan was always very protective of her husband in his public relations.

Dr. Falwell and the Moral Majority went through a transformation. Early in their coming out, they were treated by the press as a rather colorful, peripheral issue in an otherwise not exciting campaign; they were treated as a curiosity. Then, as important liberal candidates began to fall by the wayside, the Moral Majority's power — and perceived influence — went from being underappreciated to, in fact, being overestimated. Dr. Falwell was respected for the number of troops they perceived he represented; he was somewhat feared for the controversy that seemed to swirl around him. Falwell's power and his flair for confrontation with liberals alarmed the protectionists in the White House, among them Deaver, Baker, and Mrs. Reagan.

The press came back with a vengeance and began to attack in a most unfair and vitriolic manner, so Dr. Falwell was a controversial and much-maligned figure. I am sure that Mrs. Reagan was concerned that the president would be tarred by too public an association.

It's fair to say that Dr. Falwell was contacted on certain issues by the president's representatives. Dr. Falwell would also call the White House concerning specific issues — school prayer, for example.

On issues like relations with the Soviet Union, Dr. Falwell became an unofficial apologist to evangelical and fundamentalist leaders for the president's positions. I was always struck by how hard he worked at being a faithful friend to the president. But I didn't always feel that the president had been that loyal in return. I used to say, "Dr. Falwell, you don't ever cash in your chips; you keep giving and giving, and you don't ever call in your chips. In Washington they don't respect you for this."

REAGAN'S RELATIONS WITH THE STAFF

Edwin Meese III The president, unlike some of his predecessors, didn't like to telephone people at night. He felt that after working hours, matters could probably wait until the next morning. We tried not to bother him at night; I would rarely call him at night.

Stuart Spencer Reagan thought that the whole ritual that developed during the Nixon era — of everybody working sixteen hours a day, being on top of everything, crisis, crisis, crisis — was a joke. And he was right — it was a joke. People were all staying there to be the last guy in the office so somebody couldn't do something to them.

He was never part of that culture; he couldn't understand why someone would stay fourteen hours a day. He went out of his way to tell them, "Go home. See your family." Although a lot of his staff became part of that culture.

Reagan didn't play people off against each other. The worst thing in the world for Reagan was to have some of his people come into the Oval Office and get into a big argument. Reagan's view was, Go outside, settle it, and come back. That was his style. I don't care what anybody tells you, he didn't like confrontation.

James A. Baker III   President Reagan was a remarkable person. He would referee these nasty fights in the White House — and there were a lot of them — and he would make a decision, and everybody would leave feeling that they hadn't been trashed, and that they hadn't lost, even though the losers had lost.

Edwin Meese III   He didn't like to fire people. That went back to his own experience as a young boy, when his father got fired on Christmas Eve. This was during the Depression days. When I was chief of staff [in Sacramento to then-Governor Reagan], it was necessary on a few occasions to fire people, and he was good in backing me up.

He would much prefer to handle a situation. One example is Dave Stockman, who showed such poor judgment that I felt he should have been fired in 1982. There were some among the advisers who thought otherwise, and that was enough for the president to say, "Let's give him a second chance."

As it turned out, Dave Stockman repaid the president by a very bitter and vitriolic book, plus some things he did while he was still in the administration.

Uri Simhoni, major general, Israel Defense Forces; military attaché for the United States and Canada, August 1983–August 1986   I am not impressed by people who work twenty hours a day. When I read in the newspaper that Peres sleeps only four hours a night, it worries me, it frightens me. I would like him to sleep ten hours a night so he would make fewer mistakes and be more relaxed. I don't want a leader to work around the clock.

I attended many meetings with President Reagan. When you came into the meeting, the first message you received was to relax. The jelly beans would be passed out, and since I was the last person to receive them, I would have the most.

He was very relaxed. He listened. I always sat in the last row, so I could see how he looked at his cards while he talked to people. I said to myself, This is a good idea, at least he has consulted his people. He is not supposed to know everything.

DECISION-MAKING

Langhorne Motley   In a crisis he was very quiet, very calm, and solicitous of opinions. That goes to his decision-making, which a lot of people don't understand. In my dealings with him — and I spent time with him because he was interested in Central America — he had several guiding principles. One was that democracy is better than communism; second, that capitalism is better than socialism; third, that government is too big.

Robert C. McFarlane   He faced a number of very hard decisions in his administrations. He would go about them methodically and come to a decision. After a meeting was over, he would never have second thoughts. And the next morning I'd say, "We are already getting a certain amount of criticism, Mr. President." And he would say, "Well, that's going to happen." He was quite self-assured.

Martin Anderson   In 1976 there was a point about whether or not we should announce the vice president before the nomination. He started to express himself as to whether you should or shouldn't.

Somebody on the staff said to me, "That's stupid, what he's doing. You'd better tell him." I said, "Hey, you tell him." So this guy goes in and tells him exactly why this is a dumb thing to do. You couldn't tell from Reagan's face whether he was in agreement.

The next day there was a press conference. The second question was on the issue of the vice presidential candidate. And before Reagan answered it, he looked around the room and looked this guy straight in the eye, and gave the wrong answer, according to what he had been told. He operated that way. It was subtle, and people missed it completely.

George P. Shultz   It was very clear that when he made his decision that the armed forces should go ahead [with the invasion of Grenada] and he told them what to do, that it was then going to be up to the admirals and the generals to direct that operation. He was not going to try to do it from the White House.

He had learned from the experiences of Jimmy Carter — when he tried to run that rescue mission out of the White House — that that was not the way to do it. The way to do it is to make the decisions that need to be made, and then rely on other people to do what they do. And you don't try to act like you're a general, or an admiral, because you aren't. He had that confidence, and that approach.

James A. Baker III　There were times when Clark was NSC adviser when we — meaning me and Deaver — did not know everything that was going on. There was the incident [in 1983] where there was a leak about a shelling incident, and Clark went in and got the president to agree to put everybody under a polygraph.

These kinds of things were used to solve political differences within a White House. That's a terrible misuse of investigatory power.

The minute I heard about it, I went to see the president. He was having lunch with Shultz, who said, "If you strap me up, I'm out of here." I said, "If you strap me up, I'm out of here. But what about the vice president" — he was in that meeting — "Mr. President? Are you going to strap him up too?"

And he said, quickly — that was the way he was — "Bill shouldn't have done that." He got on the phone and said, "Bill, I don't want to do that. You should not have brought that in here to me." That's a good example of Clark's appealing to the dark side of the man.

Lyn Nofziger　Baker is one of the great leakers of our time. He spends a lot of time with the press. You could tell every time something came out that was needling Meese, or me, or one of us. You knew exactly where it came from.

I had reached the conclusion that we needed a new national chairman of the party. I went in to see Baker, and he said, "Let's get Meese and Deaver in and we'll discuss it."

They said, "You have to go in and convince the president." So I went in to see him, and he said, "If you have to. But don't hurt Dick [Richards, the then-chairman of the Republican National Committee]."

Then Baker said, "What is said in this room remains here." Two days later there is an [Rowland] Evans and [Robert] Novak column saying that I was trying to get Richards. It came from Baker, because Deaver always leaked to [the *Washington Post* correspondent] Lou Cannon. That was a typical way Baker worked.

Geoffrey Kemp The public perception of Reagan was what Michael Deaver and company wanted it to be. The reality of Reagan as a decision-maker is that he made very few decisions.

There was concern, right from the beginning, that because Reagan was laid-back, he didn't need to be in on half of these meetings. That reached its first climax during the summer of 1981, when we shot down a couple of Libyan jets and Reagan slept through it. Ed Meese had said, quite correctly, "It was a successful operation; no Americans were killed. Why wake the president?"

And the perception was that he was not on top of the job. So from then on we had to wake him up every time. He would be dragooned into coming into NSC meetings on a Saturday, when he wanted to be chopping wood, so a picture could be released showing that he was presiding over an NSC meeting.

After the assassination attempt, he used to work out with weights every day; he had terrific biceps. He would come in with these jodhpurs and a tennis shirt on, looking incredibly macho, presiding over the NSC meeting. We used to roar with laughter at the comparison with what really went on in the meeting, where Weinberger and Shultz would be screaming at each other.

The president never came in and said, "Gentlemen, we have three tough decisions, a, b, and c." McFarlane or Poindexter or Meese would do that. Reagan would never sum up a meeting; Meese would do it for him. He was an extraordinarily passive participant. That is the reality.

TENSIONS

The President's Noninterference in Staff Disputes

Edwin Meese III There were some basic disagreements at cabinet and other meetings. In general, the president liked to have people discuss things in front of him and present different views, because he got a lot out of that.

He didn't like these discussions to become personal or vitriolic, and he didn't like at the end to have winners and losers, which is why he deferred his decisions to afterward, when he could not only think about them but also have a chance, ahead of time, to inform a person who was not taking his advice.

Jeane J. Kirkpatrick If I disagreed on a matter of conscience or principle, so that I couldn't in conscience represent that position, I thought that I had an obligation to resign. I am a very strict constructionist in the sense that I always followed the president's decision in as much meticulous detail as *I* possibly could.

There were a number of us who were almost always in agreement. A lot of interesting discussions were held in the NSPG discussions between Cap and Shultz. I was usually on Cap's side; Cap, Casey, Clark, and I were usually on the same side of the issues. We were also usually on the same side as the president.

Howard Teicher   We constantly had this high-level struggle going on, frequently in the presence of the president. The president could not have failed to understand what was going on between his advisers. He didn't want to have to intervene, and he chose not to. The net result was a pattern of policies that led to Iran-contra.

Lyn Nofziger   In the White House there were the Reagan people, those who wanted to do what Reagan wanted done. Then there were the other people, who wanted Reagan to do what they wanted done. Casey — along with Meese, Clark, myself, and Martin Anderson when he was there — was part of the first group.

The other group — the people who looked down their noses at Reagan and thought he was that dumb actor — were Baker, Darman, and Gergen. And unfortunately, Deaver got wrapped into that group.

Craig Fuller   There is an enormous amount of pressure in the White House. People imagined that Ed Meese and Jim Baker were at odds with each other when they weren't. At other times, they *were* at odds with each other, over what they thought was best for the president. And with a president who delegates so much, by not settling it sooner he allowed factions to form. So you had a Baker faction and a Meese faction.

James A. Baker III   In fact, there were more strains between Ed and Mike than there were between me and Ed. Deaver and I got along very well. Clark and I had some problems. Clark and Deaver had huge problems.

Craig Fuller   I did my level best; I told both [Baker and Meese] that I didn't want to participate in a strategy to outmaneuver and outfox the other, and I left the room at times when some of these discussions took place. I couldn't do my job and get caught up in a slightly paranoid conspiracy that might be going on.

Michael Deaver   After Bill Clark came to the White House, things got very bad. Either Reagan didn't see it, or he didn't want to see it. At one point, I went in to him and said, "You have a civil war on your hands." He replied, "It's a figment of the media." I said, "Not only is it not a figment of the media, but I'm not going to sit here and manage this thing. You have to get involved."

So we had a session, which was ridiculous. Reagan and the four of us [Meese, Baker, Clark, and Deaver] just sat there. I finally said, "Mr. President, I assume you want to do something about this." Of course, nothing happened until Clark went on to do something else.

A source close to the situation, who declined to speak for attribution, opined that Secretary of State Haig did not have a lot of respect for the president and believed that Reagan could not manage foreign policy—but that he, Haig, because of his experience during the Nixon administration, could.

Alexander M. Haig Jr.   I wouldn't call President Reagan a student of foreign affairs. On the other hand, Ronald Reagan was imbued with very deep convictions, which were held viscerally.

His strength was in not departing from assaults on those convictions. He wasn't called "Dutch" [Reagan's nickname since childhood] for nothing: he was a very stubborn man. It was a great strength for the office of the presidency to have that stubborn streak and his adherence to principles, which he carried in his intellect, and in his heart, and in his stomach.

John Poindexter   There was an underlying problem that surfaced in the early months of the administration and continued on for the first year. Who was going to be in charge of foreign policy?

George P. Shultz   I had read about the turmoil in the administration. There was a lot of tension between General Haig and the White House. I believe that that was in part because Haig thought he had a better idea of what American foreign policy should be than Ronald Reagan did. I think his phrase was that he wanted to be the "vicar" of foreign policy, so it would be the Haig policy.

I had a different idea — from my experience in government — of how the Constitution sets out what should be done. That is: I'm working for the president; he's the guy who got elected; he's the guy who will call the shots. My job is to help develop the right ammunition and make my suggestions. But the important calls must be the president's calls.

That was one reason that I wanted personal interaction with him. I could see that he gave you a long leash if he had confidence in you. But I wanted to use the long leash properly. That's the basic attitude I have, that the president must decide.

Alexander M. Haig Jr.   I didn't have trouble conveying to the president what I wanted to do. More often than not, my difficulty was with the staff around the president, who shielded him and made it impossible on most occasions to even have an intelligent dialogue with him. They were rushing in and out and calling his attention to other things. They never would permit one-on-one meetings.

I think that the president at that stage in his life was, on some occasions, less than in total command of an issue. And the people around him were quite rightly intent on protecting him and reinforcing him and being sure that he wasn't embarrassed.

But there was also an unusual measure of infighting. And having been a White House chief of staff, and having lived in the White House under great tension, you know the White House attracts extremely ambitious people. They are the most ambitious people I've run into anywhere. Those who get to the top are usually prepared to go to extraordinary lengths to get there, and to retain it, and to enhance it.

The Haig-Weinberger Relationship

Geoffrey Kemp   The relationship between Haig and Weinberger was extraordinarily adversarial. But, I would have to add, it was probably not as adversarial as was the relationship between Weinberger and Shultz, which occurred in the second part of the first term.

There were personality problems between Haig and Weinberger, but there were also very substantive questions as well. The Middle East became a capstone for much of this quarreling; the Pentagon had a much more pro-Arab position on issues such as arms sales and military aid.

The Shultz-Kirkpatrick Relationship

Jeane J. Kirkpatrick   Frankly, I never felt George Shultz was an enemy of mine. If he described me as an enemy of his, I'd be surprised. He and I had, and still have, a cordial relationship. I would be happy to have lunch with Shultz today.

I have a lot of respect for him. I felt that in the beginning he was not very well informed about the aspects of world affairs that it was important for a secretary of state to be knowledgeable about.

One of the things I respect about Shultz is that he did a very intensive job of informing himself. I think he did a serious job as secretary of state. I often thought that he assumed that I wasn't there.

The Shultz-Weinberger Relationship

A White House adviser who for a time had unlimited private access to the president believed that the enmity between Shultz and Weinberger was intolerable. He tried to point that out to the president, as he believed in "putting the house back together." The adviser said that Nancy Reagan recognized the problem the enmity created in the cabinet.

Frank Carlucci   George was basically a negotiator, and Cap was a position-taker. They always approached issues from very different perspectives. Cap came at issues from an ideological perspective — for Cap, everything had to fit into Reagan's philosophical mode — and with a lawyer's brief. George was much more of a pragmatist: How can we go for the long-range goal?

John W. Vessey   They were usually in basic agreement. But I swear that there were times when you could talk to them before a meeting and they were in agreement, and by the time they were in the room they were disagreeing.

Part of that is not just the two men; part of it is the sort of perpetual tension between State and Defense on issues of national security, so it's not unique to Weinberger and Shultz. I thought that President Reagan handled them quite masterfully.

William J. Crowe Jr.   John Poindexter told me, at a meeting of the National Security Planning Group, that everyone present, including Weinberger and Shultz, was in favor of putting another shuttle up. After the meeting Poindexter went in to talk to the president. He said, "Mr. President, I don't think we should spend that kind of money on another shuttle." And the president said, "John, I have to. It's the only thing that Shultz and Weinberger have agreed to since I've been here."

Colin L. Powell   The antagonism was real. They agreed on many things, but when they did disagree, they disagreed rather forcefully. I don't think that it ever devolved to personal animus, but certainly there was professional competition, with roots that went back to their business relationship at Bechtel and continued into the administration, with Weinberger believing that he had a larger role to play than just being the secretary of defense, that he could comment on how his defense policies were being integrated into broader foreign policy issues.

He was also an old friend of the president, he had worked for the president in California, he had been one of the kitchen cabinet, he had been with the president for a long ride — and therefore he deserved additional standing in the president's platoon of advisers.

And it was also carried on some layers below that. It was fought out in the Congress, between the hard-right and the not-so-hard-right and the moderate and left wings of the political spectrum. So it was not just Weinberger and Shultz. They represented many others, and there was legitimate debate and antagonism between them on these issues: principally on the amount of trust you could put into what the Soviets were doing; verification of arms control treaties; and the State Department's being a little too quick to find ways to go to battle stations, with the Pentagon being a little more reluctant and always asking to be pulled along.

Some of this is normal. Some of these tensions exist today between diplomats, who love to move armies around, and soldiers, who are the armies that are being moved around.

Charles Hill   It is almost impossible to re-create the temper of those times. To try to tell college students today about the cold war mentality and atmosphere is like trying to get them to believe in fairy tales; it is just beyond their comprehension.

Back then there were just two kinds of politics: high politics, which meant national security issues, and low politics, which was everything else. So all the focus was on national security. And the concern was that the country under Carter had essentially been terribly weakened in terms of its credibility and preparedness and international standing. And people were almost desperate, and the combination of real classic Republicans, like Reagan, and these ex-Democrats — the Scoop Jackson Democrats, the neoconservatives — felt something had to be done in a massive way, and Reagan led that movement into the White House.

The people who came in with him took that as their guideline, their mantra. They would not agree to anything that was not resolutely, confrontationally, anti-Soviet all the time. They would not agree to anything that would appear to be a conversation, or negotiation, or anything that would balance out the only priority, which was making the United States stronger and stronger and doing nothing else except confronting the Soviets everywhere.

Shultz believed from the very first moment that this was nonsense. You couldn't do that; you had to have diplomacy with strength. If you had only strength, you couldn't get American domestic support for what you wanted to do. This was true. The public and media were screaming bloody murder because they thought that the Reagan administration was leading the country into a confrontation that would mean nuclear war.

But you couldn't have just diplomacy, because there is no muscle in diplomacy. You had to put the two together. Every time Shultz tried to put the two together, the Reaganites would attack and undermine him because he was departing from the principle of strength and nothing else but strength.

Stuart Spencer The Shultz-Weinberger relationship probably ate him up alive. The worst I ever heard him say when there was an argument was, "You want to be president? You run for it." He didn't mind taking on Gorbachev and taking on Kohl. But he didn't like his staff arguing. Maybe some of those people took advantage of that.

The State Department

Robert C. McFarlane Reagan had one or two new directions in which he wanted the country's foreign policy to go. One of them, centered on the SDI strategy, took us dramatically away from what our NATO strategy had been for forty years: offensive deterrence.

State Department professionals — career people as well as Shultz and the appointees — saw Reagan's move to defensiveness as so disruptive of something that was, in their judgment, working that it led them to dismiss Reagan as not only superficial but dangerous.

It is disappointing that his own political appointees, who one would expect to be a little more loyal and original, weren't. Shultz resisted the SDI strategy quite firmly, as did the European and political-military bureaus.

Michael Deaver There was this incident where he drafted a letter to [Leonid] Brezhnev* while he was in the hospital. When he was back in the White House he met with Al Haig and Dick Allen and said, "Why

---

* Secretary general of the Soviet Union during part of President Reagan's first term. Brezhnev died in November 1982.

don't you look at this letter?" About three days later it came back to him. It had been rewritten by the Soviet experts at the State Department and was totally changed.

Reagan read it and said, "This isn't what I had written, but I suppose they are the experts." And he started to hand it back, and I said, "You know, Mr. President, those assholes have been running the Soviet business for the last forty years, and they haven't done a very good job of it. None of them ever got elected to anything; you got elected. Why don't you just tell them to stick it and send the goddamn letter?"

And Reagan said, "That's a good idea." And the meeting went on. And then they left, and he and I walked back into his study, and he was standing at his desk, and he turned to me and said, "Thank you" — he had probably not said that to me three times in twenty years — "you're right. The one thing I realize from this experience is that I need to follow my own instincts. And I'm going to."

PERSONALITIES

General Alexander Haig Jr.

Charles Hill Graduates of service academies have a very different attitude toward personal relations than others do: they regard every encounter as a personal confrontation that you have to win. Haig was that way. He came in at the beginning of an administration where everyone was scrambling for position and trying to wipe out everybody else. So when you throw Haig into the middle of this . . .

John Poindexter His tenure as secretary of state was very traumatic. About 50 percent of the problem was the result of the personalities involved; the other 50 percent was the way the White House was organized. The idea that Meese could handle both domestic and foreign policy was unworkable.

As a result of this constant tension that existed between the White House and the State Department about who was going to be responsible for national security and foreign policy, we got very little done in the national security and foreign policy areas during that first year. We didn't issue a single decision document during the first year because there was constant fighting over wording.

It came to a climax near the end of the year, when Allen left. By that time, there was a realization that the system wasn't working and that changes were needed. That was when Judge Clark came over. While he didn't have experience in national security, the big advantage he brought when he came over from the State Department as Haig's deputy was that he understood the president and had his confidence.

He came to the White House on the condition that he would report directly to the president, and not through Ed Meese. It would be a cabinet-level position, and he would be, as in previous administrations, the national security adviser. But the disagreements between the White House and the State Department continued until Bill Clark engineered Al Haig's departure and his replacement by George Shultz.

Jeane J. Kirkpatrick The relationship between a UN ambassador and secretary of state is usually somewhat difficult because the secretary of state would generally wish that the UN ambassador was not a member of the cabinet. But the truth is that the UN is a special kind of place, and it is very important to have a high-level person who can operate with authority for the president.

I had not known Haig. The media made a great deal more of the Haig-Kirkpatrick relationship than was ever warranted in fact. We simply didn't deal that much with each other. I think that there was some effective mischief-making at the White House. A good deal of the famous Kirkpatrick-Haig difficulties were a consequence of that.

An adviser to the president who wished to speak off the record said that Haig had a phobia—with some justification, the adviser said—about Chief of Staff James Baker being out to get him.

Robert C. McFarlane I believe that General Haig was victimized by the White House staff, specifically three persons, Meese, Baker, and Deaver, who saw him as detracting from and willfully taking away the spotlight from the president.

These three people saw Haig's ambition for the presidency as motivating him to grandstand and to be a headline stealer. That was misguided. Yes, he had been interested in the presidency in 1980, but Al is a soldier, and he was the most loyal cabinet officer the president had. He was also the president's most sound thinker in national security affairs and saw that he had a mandate from the president to lead in that area, never undermining the president.

Haig had been raised in a military tradition: you were given a mission and you accomplished it. He believed he had the president's trust, and I think he did.

But each day this triumvirate in the White House would undermine

Haig in the president's eyes. On a trip to Europe one or two incidents involving Haig were portrayed by the triumvirate as discourtesy to Nancy. One thing that really annoyed the president was the appearance of discourtesy to Mrs. Reagan. So the president came home with a source of angst about Haig. You could say that was trivial. Not to Ronald Reagan.

Charles Hill   My sense is that the White House just didn't like Haig as a person — period. And Haig — having been a guy in the military who knew what staff did, and how to run staff — recognized that instantly. He was determined not to let the White House staff get in his way, because that would destroy his secretary-of-state-ship. So they were totally at odds.

A friend of mine, who was then working with Haig as a staff assistant, described how the White House would deliberately try to leave Haig off helicopters [during official trips] in order to torment him. It was basically personal animosity and childish behavior.

Caspar Weinberger

One of our interviewees, who preferred to comment off the record, told us that Weinberger probably had one of the best retentive minds of anyone the interviewee had ever met. The interviewee also noted that Weinberger had a great sense of humor, which he was urged by a staff member to use in his speeches. Weinberger reportedly replied, "I'm not going to be the Henny Youngman of this administration."

Weinberger "carried around a lot of conservative luggage" and saw himself as the defender of the Right in the Reagan administration, approaching every problem by asking, Do I have a conservative interest in this question? The secret was to get in there before he made his mind up, our source said.

While Weinberger—being "terribly anti-Communist"—initially had wanted nothing to do with the Soviets, he was, according to our interviewee, "a very conscientious civil servant and very devoted and loyal to Mr. Reagan."

PRESIDENT REAGAN AND THE MEDIA

George P. Shultz   Everybody liked him; that was one of the reasons he was so effective. But the liberal media didn't like his policies, so they tried to tear him down in whatever way they could. But they weren't successful.

He was very content with himself; that was one of his great strengths. I worked very closely with both President Nixon and President Reagan, and one of the great contrasts between the two was the inner peace of Reagan as contrasted with the inner turmoil that you always felt with Nixon.

Craig Fuller   People mistook his willingness to delegate for either [lack of] interest or inattention to detail. One of the realities is that the working media, particularly in Washington, then and now didn't agree philosophically with Ronald Reagan.

They were in a state of disbelief that this man could achieve the popularity he did as governor or achieve the popularity and support he did as president. So they thought there must be something manipulative about the way he did it.

Now, to be sure, there were those around him — and I am one of them — who worked very hard to portray him as a strong, successful president. We did it with substance, but we also did it with imagery, trying to project the best story on the evening news every night. That was something Mike Deaver was brilliant at. And the press resented it because oftentimes we got the good story on the evening news.

So this debate began as to whether he had earned the support he got. Is he really as compassionate as a Kennedy? I might argue that he was even less manipulative than a Kennedy.

Most perceptions have a kernel of reality, and the reality is that Reagan delegated very effectively. He trusted people around him to get at the heart of issues, not because he was uninterested, but because he knew that he had to get through thousands of issues and that if he got too fascinated with any one of them, he couldn't attend to the others. But this was hard for a lot of people to accept, particularly for those who didn't agree with him philosophically.

Stuart Spencer   Reagan had a value system. That system bothered a lot of liberal Americans from day one. They never accepted that he had an intellectual capacity, but Reagan understood what the majority of Americans wanted. I used to take media people into ethnic bars in Chicago when he was on television. Reagan would be talking, and the guy at the bar would be shaking his head, saying, "You're goddamn right." That was where his base was; that was where his support was. It was never in Georgetown. Never up on Nob Hill in San Francisco.

THE ASSASSINATION ATTEMPT

On March 30, 1981, two months and ten days into his first term, President Reagan had just concluded an address to a group of union officials at the Washington Hilton Hotel when he was shot outside the hotel's ballroom entrance as he was about to enter his car.

The would-be assassin, John Warnock Hinckley Jr., a disturbed twenty-five-year-old with fantasies about impressing the film actress Jodie Foster, had fired a total of six explosive bullets, hitting the president in the chest, critically wounding the presidential press secretary, James Scott Brady, in the head, and also injuring a Secret Service agent, Timothy J. McCarthy, and Thomas K. Delahanty, a member of the Washington, D.C., police force.

Michael Deaver Hinckley was shooting over my right shoulder. When we got to the hospital, they didn't find the bullet hole for twenty minutes or so. When Nancy arrived, she asked me, "What is happening?" I said, "He hasn't been shot." About five minutes later the doctors come into the little room where I am sitting with her, and say, "He's been shot." Nancy turns to me and says, "I thought you said he hadn't been shot." I replied, "It's news to me."

The Severity of the President's Wounds

While it was not originally thought that the president had even been wounded, the explosive bullets had done extensive damage internally. Rushed to nearby George Washington University Hospital, the president soon underwent surgery to remove a bullet from his left lung.

The president did recover fully from his wounds. But the process was extremely painful. In fact, the public was not aware at the time that, owing to the severity of his wound, the president's life hung in the balance during the first critical hours after the shooting.

John Hutton He wasn't in incredible pain, but his lung was filling up; the space between the lung and the ribs was filling up very rapidly with blood, which was making it difficult for him to breathe. As they examined him, the doctors noticed this little defect in his skin. It was almost imperceptible, but on examination it was obvious that there was something wrong with his lung, so they placed a chest tube in, and immediately out came about twelve hundred cubic centimeters of blood.

So there was no time to fool around. They determined he needed an operation. They removed the bullet — called a Devastator — that no-body had had any experience with, a bullet with a hole drilled in the top and filled with a compound called lead azide, and a percussion cap on top of that. It is supposed to explode when it impacts on its target.

Stuart Spencer   He came very, very close to dying. I was at a golf club when someone gave me the news. I went home. I didn't call anybody. I knew they were all busy.

Alexander M. Haig Jr.   I was shocked when I saw him. It was ten days af-ter the assassination attempt. He was a shell of his old self, but I was equally impressed by the character of the man — which was exuberant — [and] with [his] optimism, his willingness to go back and lift weights and all the things associated with turning himself into something that was better than before he was shot.

I don't think he was psychologically damaged. I think she was. I don't mean to say damaged; I mean affected. I am sure that it was the worst thing that ever happened to Mrs. Reagan. I don't blame her. I would have been too. Who wouldn't be?

Lyn Nofziger   You could probably find a dozen psychologists and psychia-trists who would tell you that the assassination attempt had a major effect upon Reagan. I don't think it did; I don't think that he changed much. You can't say that as a result of being shot he turned more authority over to underlings, because he always turned authority over to underlings. I could see that Nancy became more protective.

Michael Reagan   He came very close to dying. It was the difference from the car making a left turn, to the White House, or a right turn, to the hospital.

After he was shot, I saw my dad in the hospital, and he said, "Michael, I'm going to give you advice. If you are ever going to be in a position to be shot, don't be wearing a new suit. That suit I had on, it was the first time I had worn it, it was a brand-new blue suit. Do you know how they take your suit off in a hospital? They don't hang it up. The last time I saw it, it was in a corner, in shreds; they cut it off me. I understand the par-ents of the young man who shot me are in the oil business. Do you think just maybe they'd buy me a new suit?"

Michael Deaver   Nancy called me about ten days after the assassination attempt and said she had talked to this woman who had seen it in her charts. The woman said she would be glad to give Nancy advice. I said, "Fine, anything that works." So Nancy said, "I want to talk to her about the schedule."

I don't think that Joan Quigley had anything to do with substance, but she did give Nancy advice on the schedule. There were times when he should not be making public statements, or should not be in large crowds; the stars were not right.

I do remember changing things a couple of times. Nancy would call and say, "I just received the three-month schedule, and April 7–9 is a very bad time." But other than that, I don't think it was a major factor.

Joan Quigley They won the election. I had donated my time, and I thought my work was over. Then the assassination attempt occurred.

After that Nancy called me, and she said, "Could you have told about the assassination attempt?" I could have told of it. I said to her, "Yes. If I had been looking, I could have told."

I did some pretty hard thinking. She had said, "I'm willing to pay you." I knew that Ronald Reagan had been elected in a year ending in zero, and that every president since William Henry Harrison (in 1840) who had been elected in a year ending in zero — and also every Aquarian president — had died in office.

This sounds like superstition. It had to do with the Jupiter star in conjunction; it's called the Great Mutation. At the time Reagan was elected, it fell in Libra. While I felt it was dangerous — and Reagan's own chart showed danger to that type of thing, rather like Lincoln's — I thought I could do it, that if I really concentrated, I could keep him safe.

Michael Deaver He was severely hurt. The staph infection he got within twenty-four hours was even more serious. Two days after the shooting I came home at night and totally broke down. I had seen him that evening and he looked awful.

It was at that time that the so-called triumvirate was thrust into it. It was the first time in my life that my public exposure went up. The three of us would meet at the hospital every morning. When we would come out of the building, the media would be right there. They were saying, "These are the three guys who are running the government." It was never the same with us after that.

Deciding Not to Invoke the
Twenty-fifth Amendment

James A. Baker III   We made a decision in the hospital — in a closet — that we wouldn't go to the cabinet to invoke the Twenty-fifth Amendment,* even though the president was going under anesthesia, because there was no indication that it wouldn't be just a very short-term thing and then he would regain his ability to make decisions. If something came up that required a decision while he was under anesthesia, you could always do the Twenty-fifth Amendment.

We were talking to the vice president on the phone as he flew back to Washington. We told him, "We don't plan to do this." It wasn't really the staff's job, but that's the way things work in Washington. Who is going to challenge it if Jim Baker, Ed Meese, and Mike Deaver say, "We're not going to do this"? The cabinet isn't going to rise up and say, "Oh yes you are."

I think it was the right thing to do; I don't think we should have invoked it at the time. Some critics suggested that we should have. But the way things work, you are never going to have a situation when a president is going to take it on himself, when he's removed from the scene, to overrule the president's closest advisers. The cabinet is not in a position to know. They weren't there in the hospital; they weren't involved in what was going on.

The Vice President's Performance

James Watt   I was critical of Reagan's selection of George Bush. He had never demonstrated to me a commitment to the philosophy of Reagan, so I was probably improperly skeptical of the selection.

Then an unusual set of circumstances unfolded that put me in the Situation Room of the White House when the president was shot. Bush was out of town; he came back and presided over a meeting that I sat in on. He moved with loyalty to the president — and with a measure of confidence — and in that evening he won my confidence, loyalty, and respect. He was a fine man to work with, and I enjoyed personal times with him.

---

* The Twenty-fifth Amendment, ratified in 1967, spells out the procedures to be followed when the president is incapacitated.

The Atmosphere in the Situation Room

James Watt   Had you been there and watched Cap Weinberger and Bill Casey report on what was going on, you would have been proud of several things: of those men personally, and of our intelligence network, and of our armed forces. It was not a country let loose to founder; there were people in charge. It was a magnificent display of democracy.

Haig's Post–Assassination Attempt Statement

In the confusion after the assassination attempt—and in the absence of Vice President Bush, who had been airborne at the time of the shooting, on a speaking trip to Texas—Secretary of State Haig, in an attempt to clarify the situation, uttered three words that would haunt him.

Charles Hill   The statement was a trick, a trap sprung by the media. The media was screaming, shrieking, "Who's in charge? Who's in charge? There's nobody in charge!" And Haig said, "I'm in charge." And bang! They got him on that and went after him.

Michael Ledeen   As Haig told me, the cabinet was in the room, and Larry Speakes came in and said, "Everybody is going crazy. Who's running things?" Bush is on an airplane; Reagan is in the hospital. And they all said to Haig, "You're the ranking cabinet officer. Go up there and explain to the media — and the Russians and our allies — that there's a normal process."

So here is a man, who's had bypass surgery and was still smoking two packs of cigarettes a day, who comes running up two flights of stairs from the Situation Room and bursts into the press room without thinking through exactly what he's going to say. So instead of saying, "There's a constitutional order of government; I'm the ranking cabinet officer; everything is proceeding normally," he came in and said, "I'm in charge." And it sounded as if he might have meant the order of succession. And they all jumped on it.

Lyn Nofziger   That is going to be the third paragraph in his obit. Al is a very aggressive guy. When he was first named secretary of state, he went in to Reagan with a paper he wanted him to sign which would have given Haig complete control over foreign policy. Of course, Reagan didn't sign it; he was not quite as dumb as a lot of people thought he was.

The post–assassination attempt comment hurt Haig because it made a laughingstock out of him. That's the one thing that's hard to overcome in this business. But Al was never quite comfortable in that job, because he wanted more than Reagan was willing to give him.

James A. Baker III   Haig got into trouble because he was too tense. It looked like he was afraid of something; he was sweating profusely, and he got the succession wrong. He said, "I'm in control here at the White House." What he should have said was, "The president is going to be all right, things are going to function normally. And while this is a tragedy, it's something we are going to overcome."

But there wasn't anything wrong with going on the tube and saying, particularly to foreign countries, "Hey. Don't get any ideas. We've got everything under control."

Alexander M. Haig Jr.   Jim Baker was the biggest leaker in the Reagan and the Bush administrations. And when you feed the animals, the animals are grateful, until you can no longer feed them. Believe me, anybody who deals with the American press and loses sight of that . . . if he thinks he's loved by the *New York Times* because they love him, he's kidding himself.

He was their main source. I happen to know that they triggered a television assault on me on one of the major networks. Only a very fine, educated hand could do that. This was a very dangerous period in American history, and how it could have been turned into what it became is beyond me.

In the first place, they were wrong. In the cabinet meeting, the White House lawyer said, "We have to deal with the matter of transition of power." I said, "No way! The president is not in extremis." What I was talking about was the pecking order within the executive branch of the government.

To this day it's been distorted to say that I was talking about the transition. That could only have come from a persistent leak to that effect. Weinberger was also involved, because he had alerted our nuclear forces without discussing it with the cabinet and sending the message to the Russians that we believed they had tried to kill Reagan.

What could have been more dangerous? That's why I went into that press room . . . to tell the Russians, "Hey! Look. We've got a functioning government."

Incidentally, nobody had called George Bush. I got to the White House, and the only thing moving was the curtains. They were all over at the hospital.

I asked, "Who called the vice president?" Nobody had. I called him on an open line and said, "I am sending you a classified message: turn your airplane around and come back here."

The Post–Assassination Attempt Atmosphere in the White House

Edwin Meese III   The president's objective was that the general tone and tempo of the White House not be affected. In terms of the White House, it didn't change the atmosphere. But obviously, as a result, a lot more precautions were taken.

Craig Fuller   Like many of us, he thought of himself as invincible. Anyone who charges over the mountains in California on horseback doesn't see himself as somebody who is going to be hit by something, or hit by something he couldn't survive.

The Media and Reagan After the Assassination Attempt

Michael Deaver   The media is basically lazy, so for years it was, "Ronald Reagan, the former actor, the right-wing governor of California." That's what started every sentence. It took eight years in Sacramento for the media to drop the "actor" part of it. Then it became "the former right-wing governor of California."

It really took the shooting incident to soften his image. The media dropped the "right-wing" description of Reagan after that happened. There was something about what the people understood about him that changed that.

PART TWO

THE ISSUES:
THE FIRST TERM

5

Domestic Issues and
the Emerging AIDS Crisis

President Reagan's vision for the economic restructuring of the U.S. government—what came to be called "Reaganomics"—was articulated in a message to Congress on February 18, 1981. Entitled "America's New Beginning: A Program for Economic Recovery," his plan included proposals for the deregulation of business, tax cuts, and increased spending to strengthen the military.

These proposals generated both optimism and controversy. While economic growth was spurred for a time, rising unemployment and other factors led to the stock market crash of October 1987.

Alexander M. Haig Jr. In the early part of the administration, Baker and Meese believed that the president had to set aside international affairs and straighten out the domestic mess. That was a mistake: there is no way for a president to be successful at home if he fails abroad, any more than he can be successful abroad if he fails at home. These are balanced constituencies that demand concurrent priority. They didn't understand that.

Donald T. Regan In the domestic area, his main theme was a strong defense. He wanted to build up the armed forces, which, he felt very keenly, the Carter administration had let go too far down, as he said in a debate during the campaign.

It was bad enough under Nixon and Ford. While we had stabilized the size of our armed forces some, under the Carter administration, [the armed forces] had been cut and weakened; we did not have a real dominant type of force, which, he firmly believed, would be necessary to overcome communism. Reagan's attitude was, If they want it and they need it, let them have it. [Overcoming communism], hopefully, would be achieved by peaceful negotiations — but, in point of fact, maybe by armed conflict.

That was his priority. And whatever it took, he wanted to do it. Cap Weinberger carried that out to a tee.

Donald Gregg I am very close to the military. The military would say to me, "There is absolute day and night between dealing with the Carter White House and dealing with the Reagan White House."

The Reagan White House would say, "Boys, this is what we want you to do, and you do it." That was it. There was no micromanagement. The military just blossomed during Reagan's presidency.

John W. Vessey President Reagan liked the military services. He had a good understanding of their tie to the American body politic. He took genuine pride in his association with the military services.

The budgets of the military service — from the last of the Nixon administration on down to the Ford and Carter administrations — had been cut quite steadily. We had been recovering from the withdrawal from Vietnam, and things were not in good shape by the tail end of the Carter administration. As a matter of fact, they were in poor shape.

When President Reagan came into office, he immediately made it clear that he believed he had a clear mandate to raise the strength and quality of the military forces.

James Watt He understood that if we were going to rearm America and meet the consumer's needs, we had to have significant energy resources, and that the secretary of energy and the secretary of the interior really control energy policy in America.

He saw the big picture in an unusual way: you can't have military might if you don't have energy. Milk doesn't come out of a carton; energy doesn't come out of a pump, it comes out of the ground.

Few members of Congress had any understanding of these concepts. He did. When I talked to him about water or energy or resources or parks or the environment, I felt that the man understood what I was saying and contributed to the specifics of what I was doing.

THE ECONOMY

The Federal Budget

Gerald R. Ford Another area where the administration promised action and didn't produce was in the federal budget. In eight years, President Reagan never submitted a balanced budget — never to the Congress and never to the American people. For six years, they had a majority in the Senate; they couldn't say it was an all-Democratic Congress.

That was a promise made in the campaign, so the Reagan action on the federal budget does not get high marks. I was personally disappointed in the administration's budgetary record.

Tax Cuts

James A. Baker III   He held some views very, very strongly, principles that made him a great president. Everybody knew where he stood on a strong defense, peace through strength, free-market economics, supply-side economics, opportunity, and so forth. He'd get mad at you when you'd come to him with something that violated those macro-principles.

Sometimes we did. We cut taxes more than we'd committed to in the first term. In the campaign we had said a five-hundred-billion-dollar tax reduction; we reduced it [by] seven hundred and fifty billion dollars.

Donald T. Regan   Reagan firmly believed that America needed a tax cut. He once told a story of how he first realized what taxes were doing to the American ethic. When he was in Hollywood, he would make about three or four hundred thousand dollars per picture. It took about three months to complete a picture. Reagan would work for three months, and loaf for three months, so he was making between six and seven hundred thousand dollars per year. Between Uncle Sam and the state of California, over 91 percent of that was going in taxes. His question, asked rhetorically, was: "Why should I have done a third picture, even if it was *Gone with the Wind*? What good would it have done me?"

So he loafed for a part of the year. And he said the same thing was happening throughout America. People would reach a certain peak, and then they weren't willing to do the extra effort that was needed to keep us a first-class nation.

He thought we should cut taxes; at that point we were in the 70 percent federal bracket. This was a priority of his; he got it passed in the first year. But I'm sorry to say that Bob Dole and others in the Congress, under the lashing of the Democrats, kept whittling away at it as they saw the deficits increasing.

Rather than cut spending, they wanted to take back some of the tax cuts. Reagan was adamant on that; only as a very reluctant last resort, when he was convinced that the Congress would go nowhere else, would he then agree to some tax increase in return for spending cuts. And he never got the spending cuts; he always got the tax increases.

Craig Fuller   If you look at the achievements in the first six or seven months, with the tax reduction act and the spending reduction act — huge, comprehensive pieces of legislation that were actually conceived, developed, and pushed through, and then signed at his ranch in the summer of 1981 — it was really an enormous accomplishment.

James A. Baker III   We had seven and a half years of sustained, noninflationary growth; we took six million poor Americans off the tax rolls; it was the longest peacetime expansion in the history of this country. Why? Because of supply-side economics.

People say, "Well, yes, instead of tax and spend, it was borrow and spend." My answer to them is, Baloney! We were dealing with a Democratic Congress. Given half a chance, we could have made significantly more spending cuts than we made, even though we did do some cutting, particularly in the first term.

David Stockman

David Stockman, a Republican member of the House of Representatives from Michigan, was appointed director of the Office of Management and Budget (OMB) largely on the basis of his effective performance in preparing Reagan for his debates with John Anderson and Jimmy Carter during the 1980 campaign.

Stockman's tenure at OMB was marked by frequent clashes with Reagan's other key economic advisers, and with the president himself, over taxes and the size of the federal budget.

After he left the administration, Stockman criticized Reagan's policy in a controversial book, The Triumph of Politics: How the Reagan Revolution Failed *(New York: Harper & Row, 1986).*

Donald T. Regan   David Stockman was a former congressman. He knew more about the budget — at least in the first year of the Reagan administration — than most of the others in the administration. He had been intimately connected with it as a congressman and had a lot of friends on the Hill who were furnishing him with information. The professionals at OMB also filled him in on where the budget was going wrong, and where we were spending more than we were taking in.

Stockman, being a congressman — and most of them, once they are there, get the idea, okay, I can't have black, and I can't have white, I've got to go for some shade of gray (that's politics for you) — Stockman's whole idea was, Which shade of gray do we go for?

I couldn't stand it; I was a black-and-white guy. If the president wanted a tax cut of 10 percent, I was for 10, not 7. Stockman wouldn't do that in the budget. If we had thirteen billion for a certain department and the Congress said, "No, we want fifteen billion," Stockman would come in with fourteen billion, even though Reagan wanted only thirteen billion.

Jerry Falwell Ed Meese told me that in 1981 David Stockman was saying, "We have to increase taxes." Reagan had promised he wouldn't do that. Stockman then received an assurance from Don Regan that he would support him. In the ensuing cabinet meeting, Stockman told the president why there had to be a tax increase. He then looked at Regan to give his view. But Regan had read the president's face, and he let David stay by himself. Then the president said, "David, if you believe what you just said, what in hell are you doing in here?"

Donald T. Regan Dave was a wunderkind. He was one of the bright, young stars of the administration. He knew how to get along on the Hill. He had a lot of friends. He knew all the answers.

He always controlled the paper flow; that's where he controlled the direction the debate would take. He had the papers, and whenever there was a meeting, he brought the new figures to the table so that everybody was working off his figures. It used to drive my people at Treasury up the wall when I would come back with a new set of figures, and they'd say, "Don, he's wrong on this, he's wrong on that." I'd say, "Wait a minute, guys. You didn't give me any paper to take over there."

James A. Baker III We didn't fire Stockman. We went to the president and, in effect, talked him out of it. It was probably a mistake in both instances, but the president was a softy; he didn't like to fire anybody.

I felt that we needed Stockman to continue the main thrust of the first term, which was to get those tax and spending cuts. He wasn't fired, and I don't think it was a mistake not to fire him; we did need him.

OTHER DOMESTIC ISSUES

Social Security

Donald T. Regan Early on we were told that social security was going broke, that it had to have a major fix. And in 1983 we did have a major fix of that problem. It was handled mainly by the Department of Health and Human Services and by its head, Richard Schweiker.

A Social Net

Donald T. Regan   He believed in a social net, but he did not believe in a social net that was as strong as what the Democrats wanted, so he was constantly having a fight over the social programs: welfare, Medicare, and Medicaid. These social issues were quite high on his domestic agenda, but not as high as a strong defense and tax cuts.

The Air Traffic Controllers' Strike

President Reagan met the 1981 air traffic controllers' strike with a policy of noncompromise, leading to the decertification of the striking workers as well as to major changes in the nation's system of air traffic control.

Bernard Ingham, press secretary to British Prime Minister Margaret Thatcher   In this country, Reagan rapidly became a folk hero because he fired the striking air traffic controllers. There were a very large number of people in this country, who had put up with an extremely large number of strikes, who thought that it was about time that somebody did something like that here.

They admired his determination, guts, and decisiveness, so people here began to sit up and take notice of this man.

The Environment

Secretary of the Interior James Watt and environmentalists crossed swords on a number of occasions prior to Watt's resignation over his controversial remarks about minority group members and the disabled.

According to a source close to the situation, under Watt's administration the Department of the Interior was not accessible to environmentalists for their comments and recommendations.

In addition, the department had image problems, both internally and with the media, over such incidents as the banning of the Beach Boys, a popular musical group, from a government-sponsored event and the decision not to build a Vietnam veterans' memorial.

Stuart Spencer   There was vision; there was understanding of issues that he was interested in. He had no interest in reforestation programs in this country; he had no interest in dams being built; he didn't have any major interest in the infrastructure of the country, which was the whole basis, to a degree, of Lyndon Johnson's and Eisenhower's presidencies.

His concern was, government is too big. We have to get it off our backs.

THE AIDS CRISIS

When Reagan took office, the AIDS crisis was in its infancy. Advocates for those afflicted with the incurable disease pushed for major governmental action, including federal funding for AIDS research, to combat the spread of the disease. Many of them were disappointed in what they perceived as the administration's lukewarm response.

C. Everett Koop Gary Bauer [Reagan's domestic policy adviser] was number one. He presented the president with all of the downsides of things. The thing that bothered me about it was that it made the president look noncaring; it made him look stupid, because he appeared as though he didn't care.

Larry Kramer, writer; film producer; cofounder of Gay Men's Health Crisis; founder of Act Up My first incursion into the White House was to see Gary Bauer in an interview that was set up for me by a journalist friend in Washington. This is a man who makes no secret about his loathing of homosexuals. It was one of the scariest interviews I have ever had in my life.

He reiterated what Reagan had already said publicly, which was that he would not in any way support, or lend his name to, anything that could be construed as an endorsement of homosexuality, i.e., helping AIDS [patients] in any way.

Bauer was so misinformed that he called AZT, which was the drug we were trying to get released at the time, ACT. The only thing that seemed to interest him was whether straight men could get the disease from heterosexual transmission with women. In those days we didn't know. He took as reassuring the fact that we didn't know. The man is still hateful on all of these issues.

C. Everett Koop I was told that I had so much on my plate that AIDS would not be expected to be under my purview, and that I was to keep out of that, and that other people would handle it.

I don't know to this day what the motivation of that was. Certainly no one knew how I would react to AIDS. I have a feeling that they knew I was a "pick up the ball and run with it" kind of person. And the people who surrounded Reagan didn't want anybody picking that ball up and running with it because they didn't like it.

Larry Kramer   Koop, very courageously, put out a report that, according to Bauer, Reagan never read.

John Hutton   The president was an avid reader of newspapers and news magazines. If he read anything concerning a medical matter, he would usually ask me about it, so he was aware of the AIDS situation.

The AIDS issue really came into focus in his mind after he heard that Rock Hudson had gone to Europe, presumably for treatment. The Reagans called him and asked if they could do anything. He said no, that he was all right at that point.

The president then asked me for a full rundown on AIDS. And when I shared the information with the president, he was appalled. He said, "This sounds worse than a thermonuclear explosion."

C. Everett Koop   I know that he is a realist. I know that if you give him facts, he can work with them. I know that he is an extraordinarily compassionate man.

I suspect that he was told, "AIDS is something you don't have to worry about, Mr. President, because, after all, it affects homosexuals, it affects drug abusers, it affects sexually promiscuous people, Mr. President. And these are not your people."

I wasn't there to hear that, but that is what I suspect, because I know that that is what a lot of the people around him felt. And he was also surrounded by a lot of people who thought that sex education was the worst thing that could ever happen to America. And some of them actually told me, to my face, that I was leading the children of America down the garden path to immorality.

It was a discouraging time. Occasionally when I went for meetings in the White House where AIDS was discussed at a lower level — or at several cabinet meetings where it was discussed — the reaction of the people around the table was not modern, was not scientific, was not compassionate, and was not realistic.

Larry Kramer   Ronald Reagan made me an AIDS activist. On this issue, and on anything having to do with homosexuality, Reagan was just dreadful. I have no doubt that there are very specific reasons. One was, I think, that there was a great deal of self-consciousness on the part of both parents about the son. He was at that time launched on a career as a ballet dancer with the Joffrey, and there was a great deal of scuttlebutt within the gay community, and even the Yale community, where he had been a student, that he had more than experimented with homosexuality.

Reagan was awful on the gay stuff — gay rights and antidiscrimination stuff. Again, I'm sure it was because of Ron Jr., probably even more so than AIDS, because he was perceived as a gay kid. He actually wrote me a letter at one point and asked me to stop calling him gay, that his wife found it very distasteful and uncomfortable.

C. Everett Koop I discussed AIDS with Mrs. Reagan only one time, at a social affair, and I had a feeling that she was approving of what I did. And in several letters I have received from her since that time she expressed appreciation and approval of what I did for the country during the AIDS epidemic.

And I thought she understood it rather completely, in the terms that any layman could. I don't think she was ever in opposition to what we were trying to do.

Edwin Meese III The administration, from the president on down, reacted quickly and intensively. I don't think there was any topic on which more time was spent in the cabinet council on human resources. I can remember innumerable planning sessions and meetings.

C. Everett Koop I found it extraordinarily difficult to get close to President Reagan. I don't think it was the president's doing, but he was surrounded by people who really didn't want him to know an awful lot; he was surrounded by people who didn't want him to know anything about AIDS; and he was surrounded by people who didn't want him to talk to me, because I would have told him the situation like it is, and I would not have succumbed to political pressure from some of his advisers.

So it was almost impossible for me to ever get to the president. I did it by subterfuge. I delivered messages to the desk in the Oval Office through a co-conspirator who handled the president's mail, and the president would call me. I had several people I was able to talk to who had the president's ear.

But my access to President Clinton, in a Democratic White House — with me as a Republican — is at least a hundred times easier, and more frequent, than it was in the Reagan White House. My opportunities to be with the president took a tremendous amount of effort [and] contrivance

on my part to be at a place where I would cross his path or catch him after a cabinet meeting before he was swamped by all those people who
were trying to do the same thing.

So it was, all in all — not by his desire or mine — a very unsatisfactory personal relationship. But I can say that I never saw the president in
a situation where he was handed something that was new to him that he
didn't react in a way that I thought was admirable, and didn't act sharp,
and handle the situation with dispatch.

I was frequently annoyed the next day when the press reported his
reaction to things. It reflected the massage of his handlers, and it was not
what he himself felt. There are innumerable examples that I and others
can tell you about how he made up his mind to do something, it would go
to a staff meeting, and then he would be talked out of it. And what the
press reported was what the staff wanted to do, and not what the president wanted to do. It's my opinion that the people who surrounded the
president did not serve him well.

Donald T. Regan   The Reagan administration realized that there was
an AIDS crisis, but that it was being caused by immoral practices.
And how far do you want to go to make the world safe for immoral
practices?

C. Everett Koop   I'm sure that there was homophobia. It's a bad word, because homophobia means fear. And they weren't afraid; they hated [gays].

I spoke to the National Religious Broadcasters. I talked to them specifically about their attitude toward homosexuality. My message was,
"If you, as members of a large group of Christians, believe that homosexuality is a sin, then I know that wherever you learned that, you also
learned that the Christian is to separate the sin from the sinner. You may
not like the action, but you are not to condemn the person."

My whole plea to the religious world from the first part of 1985 — for
six weeks I spoke only to religious groups, trying to get them to turn their
eyes around about homosexuality, and I expressed it in my report — was
that we are fighting a disease, and not the people who have it.

Slowly, I think, it began to have effect. Today most Christian
churches have a ministry toward people who have AIDS, and toward
their families, who are devastated by the AIDS epidemic.

Larry Kramer   We wanted to get information out there. Something is
happening; it's contagious; here is the information. We were recom-

mending to people to stop having sex — or, certainly, to stop having promiscuous sex — and to use condoms. To this day you do not see condoms being promulgated by the government as a tool of safety.

Early on our primary focus was trying to stop the spread of a virus. The comparison was with the Tylenol scare, in which all the forces of government and the media were so harnessed that practically overnight in this country practically everybody stopped taking Tylenol.

We were unable to make this case with Reagan.

C. Everett Koop I think that they truly believed that if you ignored it, it could go away. I don't think the people around Reagan ever understood the seriousness of the epidemic, and I don't know whether they have yet caught on as to how many people have died in this country, how many are infected, and what the world situation is — which is an absolute, ghastly tragedy.

After a while I began to take a lot of flack for the president, who had not yet said a word about AIDS. Then, toward the end of the first Reagan term, as people began to pack up and leave — knowing they would not be reappointed, or not wanting to be reappointed — a vacuum developed in the power in the Reagan administration.

The crying need was for somebody to inform the public. If ever there was a disease that was made for a surgeon general, it was AIDS. And so, in the last year of Reagan's first term — without anybody asking me, and without asking any permission — I slowly began to assume a role of spokesperson for the Reagan administration. I began to speak out, and the people around the president began to realize what I was saying.

They would really have liked to have stifled me if they could have. But by that time I had gained a lot of respect from the press — they listened to me, they knew I was a no-nonsense guy, they knew that I thought that health was nonpartisan, and they knew that I did not respond to political pressure — and I began to be heard.

And I think that the people around the president were a little hesitant to slap me down as hard as they had the power to do, because I had become popular, and because the country was really eager for some information, which they were not getting.

So AIDS did affect my tenure. If AIDS hadn't come along, would I have been as popular a surgeon general? I can't tell you. It certainly was a very important event in molding my career, and in having me stake out a claim for the health of the nation in reference to that disease.

Donald T. Regan   Reagan was not inclined to be too sympathetic. He recognized that we couldn't let this epidemic get out of hand, but on the other hand, he was not inclined to rush in and throw money at the problem just because the gay community was insisting upon it.

You have to remember, you are talking about a very conservative president, who believes in family, God, and the Bible. And aid to that group is anathema. AIDS is nothing but a disease that is primarily spread by sexual practices, although they now claim that a lot of it is exchange of needles. But 90 percent of it is not done by needles; it's done by sexual practices. How much of the taxpayers' money do you want to spend to make that a safe practice?

C. Everett Koop   I made it a point — and I never failed when I talked to the public — to talk about abstinence for young people, mutually faithful monogamy for older people, and condoms. Yet the headlines would say, "Koop is for condoms," as though there were no other way to attack this disease.

It was the only place where I felt that the press let me down, because they were really on my side during the whole AIDS campaign, and I believe that they did an absolutely outstanding job in keeping the public informed of what little we knew, and in such a way as not to scare them.

Edwin Meese III   The reason some people are critical is because of the approach the AIDS advocates wanted, which was — from the homosexual community, primarily — a political approach rather than a public health approach.

If you have a communicable disease, the public health approach is to confine the disease, to determine who is afflicted with the disease, to take the necessary quarantine provisions, and to handle it as you would any other public health problem.

Here they had a political agenda that went beyond dealing with the disease itself. I think they used that agenda's support to promote their lifestyle, and not to have restrictions on their lifestyle that good public health practices would have required: the closing of bathhouses, trying to stop this promiscuous behavior, and all the rest of it.

C. Everett Koop   The president never said one word to me at any time that he didn't like what I was doing. He did, in a couple of private conversations, thank me for what I had done in assuming the burden of AIDS. And after I retired there was a celebration, and he prepared a videotape in which he was very outspoken about his confidence in me and about his pleasure at what I had done.

But he was fighting an uphill battle, as I was. When I put out the first surgeon general's report on acquired immunodeficiency syndrome, at his request — everything in that report about the transmission is still true, in spite of the fact that it was written in 1986 — within three weeks I was approached by Gary Bauer and another member of the domestic policy staff to ask if I didn't think it was time for a second edition.

I said, "Why would I possibly want a second edition when this one has not yet been used up?" They said, "We thought you'd like to make some changes." I said, "Like what?" They said, "Well, like taking out of it certain words, like *condom* and *penis* and *vagina* and *rectum.*"

And I said, "That's not negotiable from a public health officer. And as long as I'm here, the public will know what the problems are with AIDS, and they will know all the facts — in as delicate a way as I can present them — so that they can protect themselves and their families from this virus." And that's the way it went, all the time.

Larry Kramer   All you have to do is to compare what happened in this country to what happened in England. There have been very few cases of AIDS in England to this day because, initially, immediately, and amazingly, under Margaret Thatcher, there was an unbelievable government campaign to spread information. It worked. The government took major ads, weekly, in every single British newspaper: "Stop having sex, because something is out there. Use a condom." That country was brainwashed in the right way.

C. Everett Koop   When Nancy Reagan was about to announce her "Just Say No" program, I tried to get to the president. My plea was that he could do an awful lot for himself, and for the country, if, when Nancy announced the "Just Say No" program, he would say, "This includes 'just say no to intravenous heroin' as well," because not only will we be cutting down on the heroin problem, but we will be cutting down on the transmission of AIDS, the virus being transmitted when people share the works of intravenous drug abuse.

The response I got from the White House that night was very encouraging. The president had seven questions — and those questions were very pertinent — that led me to believe that he knew something about AIDS but not enough, and that he was eager to know more.

The rest is hearsay, because I wasn't there. But I am told that he came into the staff meeting the next morning, told the usual joke, and then said, "I have decided to include intravenous drug use [in Nancy Reagan's program] and to mention AIDS at the same time."

And the response was unanimous: "Oh, Mr. President, you can't do that. That is a lose-lose situation, Mr. President. What you want is win-win, and you just say no and never mention AIDS, because that's lose-lose."

So once again his massagers talked him out of what he really wanted to do. It would have put him in the position of letting the public know that he understood AIDS, that he was sympathetic to the needle problem and knew that the transmission of AIDS could be cut down by getting into the needle problem. But, once again, his handlers made that impossible.

The President Decides to Take Action

C. Everett Koop I was reduced in 1984 and 1985 to defending the president in the following way. When it was asked why had the president not talked about AIDS, I would say, "Well, I'm the person who's talking about AIDS. I am the president's surgeon general, and I am your surgeon general. I know what AIDS is all about. Ask me any questions, and assume that the president is backing me."

John Hutton The president decided to form a commission on AIDS. He also wanted to demonstrate to the American people that the disease was not communicable, so in the fall of 1985, two months after his cancer surgery, he went out to visit the children's ward at the National Institutes of Health [NIH], in Bethesda, a trip that made some of his staff uneasy. He met the children [with AIDS] and picked some of them up. He was very moved by that experience.

Larry Kramer That kind of business is, in essence, a slap in the face to everyone else except the babies, because of all this business about the babies being the innocent victims and everyone else being not innocent but guilty victims. That's all that he did, and it didn't get much press.

C. Everett Koop We were there [in Bethesda] together. That was one of the funniest days of my life. I was asked to go along as sort of window dressing. When the president got to the place where he was with patients, I was so far in the background that I couldn't see him.

Then, all of a sudden, there was a security scare, and the president and I, alone, were shoved into a closet, with the door closed. And that was where the best talk I ever had with him about AIDS took place. I thanked him for the support he had given me — which really meant, Thank you for not letting your handlers go after me — and I told him where we were in the epidemic, and what I thought the future was. And that's probably the best briefing he ever got on AIDS in his whole term.

I'm sure that there were people on the White House staff who didn't want him to go. He was right to do it. Every time I went to the NIH, I would sit on the beds with the AIDS patients, and put my arms around them, and hold their hands, and talk to them, and hope that the press would take pictures to show that the surgeon general wasn't afraid of getting AIDS by having close contact with people who were dying of AIDS.

This is what monarchs have often done. They'd go out in the days of the plague and show that they were not afraid. It's one of the things that's expected.

Larry Kramer   Nobody would confront the man. I don't know what there was about him and Nancy — as if they were some kind of holy royalty — that people were terrified of doing anything but kissing their rings.

C. Everett Koop   I think that [his] total silence was what bothered the people; the president barely spoke about AIDS in public. The night he spoke most about AIDS was when he and Elizabeth Taylor gave me an award, in Georgetown. But that was never well reported in the press. That is the only time I ever heard the president speak forcefully about AIDS.

Larry Kramer   This is a puritan country, where hypocritical morality rules the day — and to our detriment. Ronald Reagan did not say the word *AIDS* until 1987. There was a fund-raiser in Washington for the American Foundation for AIDS Research, and he made a speech, and he didn't say the word *AIDS*; he didn't say the word *gay*. It was a hideous speech, and he was booed — I was there, and I was one of the booers — and he didn't like it.

This was a plague that didn't have to happen. It's simply because Reagan and the politicians of this country, for whatever ideological reasons, had to look the other way.

6

Foreign Affairs

In the years since Ronald Reagan's presidency, his impact has been felt on many foreign policy issues, especially in relation to the former Soviet Union, Central America, and the Middle East.

President Reagan characterized the then–Soviet Union as the Evil Empire. His deep concern about arms control, reinforced by the Chernobyl nuclear reactor catastrophe, led him to adopt a two-track approach: development of the Strategic Defense Initiative (SDI) and the reduction of both U.S. and Soviet nuclear arsenals—the latter accomplished through U.S.-Soviet summitry.

In Central America he sought to contain the Communist threat to the Western Hemisphere through aid to the contra forces in Nicaragua and support of the government in El Salvador against insurgent forces. In a perhaps related action, President Reagan responded to the request for assistance in curbing the excesses of a Marxist regime in Grenada.

In the Middle East President Reagan aroused controversy early in his first term with the AWACS sale to Saudi Arabia, and he resuscitated the Nixon-era Rogers Plan as the Reagan Plan, angering both the American Jewish community and the Israeli government. He also grappled with the ramifications of Israel's 1982 invasion of Lebanon—including the October 1983 bombing of the U.S. Marine barracks at the Beirut airport.

In what many regard as the most controversial action of his presidency, President Reagan authorized the trading of arms for hostages with Iran in an attempt to liberate American citizens held in Lebanon—or, as some believe, to forge a strategic relationship with perceived moderates in the Iranian government. This action, coupled with the diversion of profits from the arms sales, would threaten the survival of the Reagan presidency.

PRESIDENT REAGAN'S WORLDVIEW

Frank Carlucci He once said, "An American ought to be able to walk safely down any street in the world." That, of course, is a stunning statement, but that was his view of the world.

Elliott Abrams, assistant secretary of state for international organization affairs, human rights, and humanitarian affairs; assistant secretary of state for inter-American affairs Reagan was not a realpolitik type. He had been critical of Ford foreign policy; he had criticized Ford for not receiving [the Russian novelist Aleksandr] Solzhenitsyn in the White House. Reagan was an idealist, and therefore human rights policy, redefined in a Republican manner, was extremely attractive to him.

When you think of his great speeches on foreign policy, it's always "this city on a hill," it's never a somber speech about American responsibility and power. His speeches are more reminiscent of President Kennedy than they are of Nixon or Ford.

Rozanne L. Ridgway, counselor, Department of State; special assistant to the secretary of state for negotiation; ambassador to the German Democratic Republic; assistant secretary of state for European and Canadian affairs The language was very strong. It was provocative, hard-line, and robust. The language of his speechwriters gave him the "Evil Empire" themes, [and] I saw that as consistent with what he had said about the Soviet Union throughout the period of his candidacies and during his campaign.

There was a war going on throughout the period of the Reagan administration — an ideological war as to whether or not it was in the American interest to find a way to talk to the Soviet Union on an agenda of common topics, or whether to go to war with them. I am convinced that, even in 1996, there are people who would like to plow Russia under and salt the earth.

Constantine Menges He was especially interested in the U.S.-Soviet relationship and its future. He was very concerned with the dark and negative things that had happened between 1975 and 1979. There was a sense that the Soviet Union was on the move during that period and that the U.S. was at great risk if the momentum continued. Reagan felt that and communicated it.

John W. Vessey He clearly had a view that the Soviet Union was not a permanent institution — that communism was not a permanent institution. We had lived in an era when we had been told by the intellectuals of this country, "They are here to stay, and it's something we have to deal with." President Reagan didn't accept that view.

Nimrod Novick Peres felt that Reagan had a very clear worldview. He felt he was an emotional person who was emotionally involved in what he was doing; he felt he was an honest man who said it as he saw it.

Abraham Sofaer He liked Jews. He had a warmth and generosity of spirit toward everybody. I suggested to him that he join in commemorating the fiftieth anniversary of Kristalnacht. He immediately agreed; he was so moved by the Holocaust.

Yitzhak Shamir He was a decent man, not a tricky man. From time to time he tried to explain to us that he was influenced by what he saw during the Second World War, the Holocaust and all that. He kept it in his memory.

For Reagan, the world was divided into black and white; we [Israel] belonged to the white. It was clear that he liked us. Of course, among friends, there are from time to time differences; the Americans do not have to feel that we will always accept their positions. It is not good; if you want to have an ally, you want a serious ally, not a slave.

We knew that he doesn't like the Arabs especially. His position on the Soviets was clear to us — that he was against them. And, of course, the Soviets had been against us all the time.

King Hussein, Hashemite Kingdom of Jordan He had many responsibilities throughout the world. His focus on this area was not as acute as it could have been. But he was always available to me, always a friend. We kept in touch throughout his presidency.

William P. Clark In the cases of Iran and Libya, we went so far as to say that we would normalize relations, "subject to the following conditions."

This happened with Castro too, in a way, and with [Maurice] Bishop [in Grenada]. In each case where we had a belligerent — a maverick — we said we would go forward, but that we had to have some assurance of their substantial compliance with our conditions. As in summits with the Soviets, the president was always willing to lay out the conditions of normalcy.

Frank Carlucci   He'd talk about Armageddon quite frequently, and wormwood — in Russian, "Chernobyl" means wormwood. It was not religion in terms of his being a particularly religious person; it was religion in a historical sense.

Stuart Spencer   He was absolutely obsessed with the threat from Russia; the whole nuclear picture revolved around that threat. He used to talk about Armageddon. To my mind, Armageddon tied into his concern about the nuclear chaos that he knew about as president, from the information he would get in his national security and other briefings. These were the things he worried about. He had a vision about them; he read about them, thought about them, and talked to a lot of people about them.

Martin Anderson   If you look at the "Evil Empire" speech, he described the conflict with the Soviet Union as an apocalyptic struggle between right and wrong, and good and evil. He really did believe, given the enormous nuclear weaponry of the Soviet Union and the United States, that you could have a conflict that would be the equivalent of Armageddon, so he was concerned as to how to avoid this modern-day Armageddon.

When he went out to NORAD [North American Air Defense Command] headquarters, it was made crystal clear to him that a president has only two choices if, for any reason, missiles are launched at the United States. You can sit back and let them come in and wipe out a city or two, or you can retaliate.

He said, "Both choices are wrong. There has to be a third choice." He was driven by that; he kept trying to work on that. I don't think he believed literally in Armageddon, but he used it as a metaphor for what we were facing, and for why he went to such extraordinary lengths to negotiate secretly with Andropov, and to meet with Gorbachev.

Jerry Falwell   Many thought he was a hawk, but I never saw him that way at all. I think his "peace through strength" initiative was just the opposite. And it turned out to be correct: it brought the Berlin Wall down; it brought Soviet communism to an end. He knew that they could not match us. He broke their back militarily and economically. I believe that this was his goal upon taking office.

Victor Hugo Tinoco, Nicaraguan vice minister of foreign affairs   The Reagan administration was not concerned with democracy in Central America. The revolution in Nicaragua occurred because there was a dictatorship here; we had no democracy. It was a dictatorship supported by the U.S., as was true all over Latin America, where there were many dictatorships. What was important at that time for the Reagan administration was the confrontation with the Soviet Union.

Desima Williams, permanent representative of Grenada to the Organization of American States (OAS); deputy governor of the World Bank from Grenada; UN delegate with ambassadorial rank; ambassador-designate of Grenada to the United States°   The Reagan worldview was centered in a very ideological — rather than a geographic — focus. The [Caribbean] region had always been very important in the attainment of the American dream at the global level. Any way in which this region could be brought under the power of the United States was important for the political and psychological continuity of the U.S. power elite. This hemisphere had to be continuously accessible to these individuals in power.

Richard Schifter, assistant secretary of state for human rights and humanitarian affairs   He had these instincts, based on personal experiences. He had lived through all of this in Hollywood, particularly when he, as a liberal Democrat, became head of the Screen Actors Guild and he did battle with the Communists.

He didn't read any books on the subject; I don't think he was a theoretical student of communism. He had become well aware of what the difference was between a believer in Leninist-Stalinism and somebody who might have left-of-center political ideas.

He didn't have to read a lot of books. He didn't have to read a book about Gorbachev. He began to see that this guy was different from those with whom he did battle. He saw that there was a basic change. It was clear that they were really repudiating Leninism, not just getting away from Stalinism, but repudiating basic doctrines of Lenin.

Giandomenico Picco, UN official; hostage negotiator   The Reagan administration wanted to totally destroy the United Nations — not President Reagan, who was probably unaware of it, but the people who were managing this particular relationship. It should finally be said: they did not want to reform the United Nations; they wanted to destroy the organization, because they didn't know how to use it. That's what happened with Madame Kirkpatrick.

° Her nomination to that post was refused by the United States.

Ambassador Kirkpatrick was a professor totally ignorant of the world — except from books — who comes onto the scene never having lived in a foreign country and having a very vague idea of the United Nations; who forbade her own diplomats from coming to the United Nations to talk to people; who severs all kinds of continuous daily relationships in the United Nations.

And then, of course, she uses the most banal propaganda statements that only Stalin in the 1950s could be accused of. You have this kind of violent attack, and simply because they did not make the effort to understand the United Nations better and, therefore, to use it better.

PRESIDENT REAGAN'S RELATIONSHIPS
WITH WORLD LEADERS

Edwin Meese III I can't think of any foreign leaders he *didn't* like, in the sense of having a personal animosity. He really liked Margaret Thatcher; that was a very close relationship. He was particularly fond of [Canadian Prime Minister] Brian Mulroney. He was much more formal with some other leaders — [former Canadian Prime Minister] Pierre Trudeau and [French President François] Mitterrand — because they were formal too. He and [German Chancellor] Helmut Kohl were more personal. He had a very high regard for Prime Minister [Eugenia] Charles of Dominica.

Margaret Thatcher

Sir Charles Powell, deputy head of mission to the European communities, Brussels; private secretary to British Prime Minister Margaret Thatcher There is no doubt at all that the personal relationship was extraordinarily strong. It dated from his visit to London shortly after she became the leader of the opposition, in 1975.

They found immediately that they were instinctively on the same wavelength, that they believed in the same basic, quite simple propositions: [they believed] that communism was evil and had to be destroyed; they believed in the free market and low taxes.

The fact that they were then together in power was a very happy coincidence. It meant that they could both pursue their very similar agendas, more or less in tandem, so this gave enormous strength to the whole Western alliance.

On a personal level, she was enormously respectful. First of all, she is — and always was — very respectful of the office of the president of the United States. She is a great believer in the United States; she sees it as the great pillar of the free world, so the president of the United States was the most important man in the world.

Even though she was a close friend of the president, she almost invariably called him Mr. President, rather than Ron or anything like that. She had great affection and huge admiration for him, and that really persisted and still does persist.

And time and time again that personal relationship enabled her to make an end run around the American bureaucracy — around the State Department and the Pentagon — and get to the president, and get her ideas accepted. He was a tremendous friend and ally.

Bernard Ingham It was perfectly clear that Margaret Thatcher and Reagan were political soulmates from a long way back.

Mrs. Thatcher was not only delighted to see a political soulmate in office, she was also delighted to see there a man she felt happy with politically as the leader of the Western world.

I don't think that President Reagan had much in common with Margaret Thatcher as a personality. He frequently looked pretty vacant at meetings; he didn't give the impression that he was on top of the argument. He delegated, almost to a fault; Mrs. Thatcher would never have delegated the way he did. He was no debater. He was quite laconic in his approach. He had an endless number of stories, and Mrs. Thatcher has never told an anecdote in her life!

They were not the same kind of people, but they did get on like a house on fire.

Geoffrey Howe Ronald Reagan was one of the three people whom Margaret Thatcher treated with deference — the others being King Hussein and Mikhail Gorbachev. She had respect for Reagan as a successful president of the United States.

Their relationship went beyond that: they had a mutual respect for the ability to communicate simple truths. They both had the ability to identify with the instinctive reactions of their people. They both had a tenacity and a determination, which they respected each other for.

Middle East Leaders

Geoffrey Kemp Begin and Shamir had similar qualities: both out of Poland, both extremely polite (unlike most Israeli leaders), both immaculately tailored, very rarely raising their voices, but hard-nosed.

I would say that Reagan got on with both of them rather well. In the case of Begin, it was quite an effort to have Reagan focus on him, because his first real encounter with a Middle East leader was with [Egyptian President Anwar] Sadat, who was glamorous, effusive, and outgoing. He liked to ride horses. Deaver arranged for Reagan and Sadat to go riding in Quantico on beautiful national park horses.

Then the question came up: Begin is coming to Washington next month; what *on earth* are we going to do? We can't see him on a horse. Let's have him to tea. So there was this great effort to sort of equalize things.

What helped was an extraordinary video that the CIA took the initiative for — and that we all commented on and helped to edit — that was shown to Reagan just before the Begin visit. The first seconds were of bulldozers at a Nazi concentration camp, pushing bodies into mass graves — we knew that Reagan had seen this imagery in his World War II days — and we overlaid on it photographs of Menachem Begin speaking, saying, "Never again! Never again!" Then the video said, "To understand this man, this is all you need to know."

Yehiel Kadishai, senior aide to Israeli Prime Minister Menachem Begin Begin liked Reagan very much as an open person. Reagan showed his sympathy to the state of Israel. He even mentioned that he had been in the milieu of Jewish people almost all the time in the film industry.

Nimrod Novick   The chemistry between Peres and Reagan was excellent from day one. I remember the first meeting between them, which was just as Mr. Peres became prime minister [in September 1984]. We went to Washington in October. By the time the tête-à-tête that was the first session of the visit was over, these two gentlemen were very comfortable with each other.

Geoffrey Kemp   He was very sensitive to the human factor in relations with both foreign leaders and with our own politicians. He was very concerned that we treat King Hussein with great respect.

Hussein is one of those leaders whom every politician in America has met at some point. Reagan knew that this was a remarkable man in his survival capacity. He was basically pro-American — married to a beautiful American girl — so he was somebody we should nurture, even though there were a lot of tricky issues between us.

George P. Shultz   He liked King Hussein as a person, and he was much more patient with him [than I was] because he recognized that Hussein had a rather weak hand and he had to play it with caution, so he tended to calm me down. I remember that on one occasion, when I was complaining to him about King Hussein, the president said, "Look, George, you have to remember, he's a king."

Geoffrey Kemp There were occasions when he had a better sense of foreign leaders than others did. One of the most difficult leaders we ever had to deal with was Mrs. Gandhi* — an uptight, mean, awkward, extremely difficult woman to talk to and deal with.

The issues were very testy. But Reagan met her for the first time and absolutely charmed her. He told us all later, "Well, I went for a walk with her in the garden, and we discussed grandchildren. You know, she's terribly shy." And that meeting enabled us to have some serious discussions with Mrs. Gandhi at a later point, so there were areas where Reagan's laid-back charm actually had substantive importance to foreign policy, far more than did his wisdom on details.

Soviet Leaders

Jack Matlock What Reagan's critics missed was that although he berated the [Soviet] system and the ideology, he never berated the individual; he did not answer in kind. They were denigrating him all the time as an individual, as a person. On that, he simply turned the other cheek.

He kept trying to convey, first in private and increasingly in public, "I want to talk, and I am going to be reasonable." The key speech was delivered on January 16, 1984, when he laid the foundation of his policy toward the Soviet Union. That was over a year before Gorbachev came into office, so anyone who says that Gorbachev started the process is simply ignorant of history.

But neither [Yuri] Andropov nor [Konstantin] Chernenko recognized that the system was in trouble, or had the intellectual acuity or the political guts to push for new policies. Gorbachev did engage us. He had to come to terms with us in order to have a free hand for reform. He didn't do it to please us. I very much doubt that Andropov would have gone for these reforms.

---

* Indian Prime Minister Indira Gandhi, the daughter of the late prime minister Jawaharlal Nehru. Mrs. Gandhi was assassinated on October 31, 1984, by members of her own security detail as she walked in the garden of her residence.

CENTRAL AMERICA

Craig Johnstone   In the beginning of the Reagan administration, the basic CIA analysis was that Nicaragua had fallen, that El Salvador would not last six months, that Guatemala would come right after it, and that you were going to have at least four, or maybe five, states in Central America that would be tied to Cuba and have a strong Soviet influence.

In the context of the cold war, that was viewed by Reagan as absolutely unacceptable. It was not going to happen. It was not an unfair characterization, [but] you could argue that it was overdone. In the wake of the end of the cold war, all of this seems less real than it was at the time.

George P. Shultz   It was important to put a stop to a Communist movement that was entrenched in Nicaragua and was actively trying to spread itself. There wasn't any doubt about that: they had a military buildup that was very disproportionate, in Central American terms.

From our standpoint, the threat was that you had big Soviet bases in Cuba that provided a major intelligence platform — a place from which they could fly missions all along our Atlantic coast.

If you had a similar arrangement in Nicaragua — and if they were successful and propelled themselves up the isthmus, toward Mexico, which was a very flaky place for a while — you could have a similar situation having to do with our Pacific coast. So it was a serious matter. It was important to counter the Sandinistas.

Harry Shlaudeman, ambassador to Argentina; executive director of the Kissinger Commission; special U.S. envoy in charge of Central American negotiations; ambassador to Brazil   The president certainly could grasp the concepts. It was really his reading of Jeane Kirkpatrick's essay "Dictatorships and Double Standards" [*Commentary*, December 1979] that set the tone for policy in Latin America during his administration.

I don't think that his responses were automatic by any means. I think that he thought about these things. How much did he really understand about Central America? Probably not very much. About the reality on the ground, probably not very much. He was inclined to see things in a black-and-white way. I don't think he really understood what wretched places these are.

I had read Jeane Kirkpatrick's famous article, and I did expect that the Reagan administration would adopt a somewhat different, less confrontational attitude toward these military governments over the question of human rights.

Initially that was certainly true. That changed, particularly as the Central American problem became more acute. The administration became more enamored of the idea of democracy — not so much human rights [but] democracy. It was in the platform. Everybody knew that we were going to take a very hard line on Central America, particularly on Nicaragua.

Langhorne Motley   He had a better sense of the subtleties of the issues than many people gave him credit for. Kennedy viewed Latin American policies from an altruistic, goodness approach in line with his speeches. If not us, who? If not now, when? Johnson took a Tex-Mex approach, a patronizing approach. Nixon saw everything in East-West terms. How did it affect the balance between the United States and the Soviet Union? Carter saw it as one or two single-issue policies that had a "holier than thou" connotation. He didn't want to get involved in all the nitty-gritties that make any kind of relationship a two-way street.

Reagan brought a different perspective, a California perspective. If you look at Spanish-American history, you know that the Spanish who went to California were totally different from the Texas-Mexico-Arizona-border type of thing: a part of their culture [was] at a high level in California, as opposed to a lower level in the Texas-Arizona area.

Reagan wasn't a great student of Latin American politics, but he had instincts — the proper instincts — to look at it on a more mature level. He was attuned to their cultural needs and differences. He would be able to appreciate some of the things around him that his advisers wouldn't.

For example, in the case of [President José Napoleón] Duarte in El Salvador, he could relate to what they were trying to do under the circumstances of what they were doing, as opposed to whether they were following a checklist we wanted them to follow, as suggested by some of Reagan's advisers.

Harry Shlaudeman   I got to know Duarte very well. He had the best of intentions, but he just couldn't do it. He basically couldn't hack it because he couldn't get out from under the military; he couldn't get the country going again, the economy kept deteriorating, and the war kept getting worse. It was one of these ironic things — that the answer was on the right, not in the middle. We kept it going. That's about all we could do.

Duane Clarridge   To ignore Salvador would have been a mistake, because the pressure we put on Salvador — the efforts there — were rather significant. One, to get Duarte elected there; then the suppression of the rightists, in which Casey played a very large role.

Nicaragua was more sexy in some ways, but certainly Salvador was a key element — and one of the administration's major problems.

Nicaragua

On July 17, 1979, the forty-three-year reign of the Somoza dynasty in Nicaragua ended when President Anastasio Somoza Debayle and his family were forced to leave the country.

Opposition to the Somoza regime had been building since the founding in 1961 of the National Liberation Front (FSLN), a group popularly known as the Sandinistas, named for General Augusto César Sandino, an opponent of U.S. policy in Nicaragua who was assassinated in 1934.

In the 1970s—and particularly after an earthquake devastated the capital city of Managua in 1972—opposition to Somoza's rule intensified, reaching a crescendo with the assassination in January 1978 of Pedro Joaquín Chamorro, the editor of La Prensa, *Nicaragua's leading daily newspaper.*

Chamorro's assassination led to the creation of an opposition front in which non-Marxist forces joined with the FSLN in the struggle against the Somoza regime. In February 1979, the U.S. government dealt the regime a mortal blow by suspending all economic and military aid.

The Provisional Government of National Reconstruction formed to replace the Somoza regime was headed by a five-member directorate, including Violetta Barrios de Chamorro, the widow of La Prensa's *slain editor, and Daniel Ortega Saavedra.*

Although the Sandinistas had expressed the desire to institute democratic reforms, they instituted instead a series of repressive measures, leading Mrs. Chamorro and another moderate member of the directorate to resign. The Sandinista Party then assumed control of the government and announced in September 1980 that national elections would be delayed until 1985.

Concern within the U.S. government over events in Nicaragua was heightened when it was learned that military equipment sent by Cuba to aid rebel forces in El Salvador was being shipped through Nicaragua. This concern only grew in 1980 and 1981, when Nicaragua signed agreements with the Soviet Union and East-bloc governments, providing for military and intelligence assistance, while at the same time increasing the number of Cuban advisers in Nicaragua.

The Fall of Somoza and the Rise of the Sandinistas

Arturo Cruz Sr., member of the Revolutionary Junta; ambassador of Nicaragua to the United States; leader of the opposition Most Nicaraguans were eager to get rid of the Somoza rule. Unfortunately, we did not know how to get rid of Somoza. We should have been more careful of what would follow.

We were so fed up with Somoza that we were willing to support the Sandinistas, who during the years of 1978 and 1979 had shown courage in the struggle against Somoza. The whole nation was moved by this romantic feeling: here are these young men who are bravely fighting against this corrupt government.

And we practically gave them a blank check. But in the end we lost it because what resulted was the installation of a more corrupt, inefficient, ruthless government; that's what the Sandinistas were. Not only were the Nicaraguans enchanted with the Sandinistas, there was a great deal of sympathy throughout the world, in the same way that Castro aroused so much admiration throughout the world. And then, the disenchantment began.

Adolfo Calero, head of the Nicaraguan Democratic Force (FDN) I did not like them [the Sandinistas]. I knew them for what they were. I knew that they were Communists; that they were pro–Soviet Union; that they were pro-Castro; and that what they wanted was to establish in Nicaragua just what they did.

They came like heroes here. They had a tremendous opportunity to do good for this country. Within the first year they lost tremendous sympathy because of all the decrees and all the denial of freedoms — the denial of democracy and all the things they had supposedly worked for.

Arturo Cruz Sr. The story throughout the world was that it was a bloodless revolution, that nobody was wrongly killed. That is a lie; it is totally untrue. In my hometown they killed people for silly reasons, like the fact that a businessman's name appeared in the logbook of the National Guard commander, who had fled. The man could have gone there to complain about something. They executed him.

They executed lots of people, in Managua and everywhere. The world said, "No, the Sandinista revolution was bloodless." No. It was bloody. There were executions; there were tremendous atrocities committed.

Victor Hugo Tinoco There were three main sources for the Sandinista Front's principles. The first was Marxism — the ideas of socialism, defined as the search to find social justice, not necessarily a model of the organization of the state. Second was Christian ideas; I have no doubt that Christianity was important in the FSLN. And the third source was Sandino's ideas, [which were] basically nationalist — independence and nationality.

Duane Clarridge They had the capacity, and they proved it when they kept the Salvadoran thing going for ten years. Their intention was to first knock over Salvador and then go on from there.

I don't think anybody disputes that. What most people don't understand is that Carter signed more presidential findings than any other president in the history of the United States. By 1980 he finally recognized that the Sandinistas were a bad crowd.

The findings he signed and implemented — and that would continue to be implemented under the Reagan administration — were largely in the political action area: in Nicaragua's supporting the church, the democratic parties, the industrial organization, and the farmers' cooperatives.

That was continued. The same thing in Salvador — the idea in Salvador was that eventually some sort of reasonable, democratic government would come to power. That was the political action part of it. The second part of it was major support to the security services of Salvador, Guatemala, and Honduras, to bolster their ability to deal with subversion, which was being supported from Nicaragua, and to try to interdict the arms supplies that were coming, through various means, to Salvador and, to a lesser extent, to Honduras and to Guatemala.

Victor Hugo Tinoco When Reagan was elected, we weren't happy with the change in the U.S. We thought that in U.S. society there was an upsurge of a very conservative movement. So we knew that the relationship we would have with the U.S. government would be based not only on what we were doing in Nicaragua but also on a new political fate that was growing in the U.S. So we had some feeling that they would do something against us. But, of course, at first we didn't have a clear idea of what would happen.

The U.S. had the view that the Soviet Union was supporting revolutionary movements in Latin America and other parts of the world. Therefore, the U.S. had to oppose those movements.

The U.S. did not take into account nationalism, social justice, and the real reasons for insurgency. The feeling was, "Those are Soviet Union–organized plots, so we will have to oppose them." They totally neglected that, in many respects, national ideas and local ideas, and poverty and injustice, were the causes of those changes taking place in different revolutions. In the case of Nicaragua, the FSLN never had, practically, a relationship with the Soviet Union. The role played by Cuba was different. At that time Cuba had differences with the Soviet Union on how to deal with revolutions in the area.

Sergei Tarasenko, deputy director of the U.S. desk, Soviet Foreign Ministry; private assistant to Soviet Foreign Minister Eduard Shevardnadze; chief of staff to Shevardnadze Our intention was to persuade the Sandinistas to lie low, not to speak about any socialism, any confrontation with the United States, because it was really a burden on our side. We couldn't possibly gain anything from this situation.

I would admit that there were some people on our side who were interested in promoting and encouraging this conflict, maybe in the military or special services. But at least on the level of the Foreign Ministry, reasonable people did not believe that we could have any chance to have a foothold in Latin America and Central America. We knew our lesson from the Cuban crisis of 1962.

Reasonable people were not interested in fostering some kind of anti-American activities in this area. But the Foreign Ministry was not the only participant on the scene. There were other agencies and forces that might act contrary to what we thought at the time, politically, was necessary.

Miguel D'Escoto I think that Reagan was sick, totally sick. The man had a great obsession; obsessions are always pathological.

I think he knew perfectly well that the Communist scare was not a possibility. The real problem was the total commitment, in his gospel, of free enterprise, and the willingness to sacrifice anyone and everyone who dared present a different alternative for this method of development.

I don't know what angered him so much about Nicaragua, except the possibility of what he was saying — that it could have the domino effect in the rest of Central America, and then go to Mexico. Maybe that was it. But he really oversold the American people on his idea that Nicaragua could become a threat.

You don't have to be too intelligent to understand that if Nicaragua really were of a mind to invade, say, Costa Rica, how long could we hold it? For two hours? Three hours? Half a day — no more than that. And to what avail? If we were such a menace, allow us to do something wrong, and then immediately they could have reversed that situation.

They were also concerned about the fact that the United States is not loved in Latin America; it's feared. I think the idea was, make sure they continue to fear us, not look up to us as an example to emulate.

The United States did not want to lose its credibility as a nation that carries out its threats. It wants to be feared. The U.S. feared the development of a model here that could ignite a spark of hope in Latin American countries.

Arturo Cruz Sr.   In 1979 the Sandinistas had a strong mandate; they would have won an election with perhaps 85 to 90 percent of the vote.

People came from all over Nicaragua to greet the Sandinistas the day they arrived in Managua, but you should have seen the reaction of the people the next day. Everybody was worried, including the mother of the foreign minister. So the support of the Sandinistas began to decrease and decrease. It kept dropping through the early to mid 1980s.

Even the war worked against them, because they established compulsory military service. Since they had a totalitarian impression of things, they said, "We are the country. We are calling your children to help fight the contras, to defend the fatherland." But the families said, "No. They are not defending the fatherland. They are defending a political party."

Manuel Antonio Noriega, leader of Panama   There was an overreaction by the United States to the Sandinista government. The U.S. made a big mistake in its analysis.

The Contras

The activities of the Sandinistas led to the development of an opposition movement commonly known as the "contras." The contras consisted of three elements: former members of the National Guard and right-wingers who had fought with Somoza against the revolution; individuals who had backed the revolution but now opposed the Sandinistas; and other citizens who, while not involved in the revolution, were concerned with the character of the Sandinistas' rule.

The largest of the contra groups was the Nicaraguan Democratic Force (FDN), headed by Adolfo Calero Portocarrero, a businessman who had been active in the effort against Somoza. Other contra leaders included Alfonso Robelo Callejas and Arturo Cruz Sr., who served in the early 1980s as Nicaragua's ambassador to the United States.

Other resistance groups included the Indians who lived along Nicaragua's Atlantic coast and a group led by Edén Pastora, a former Sandinista guerrilla leader whose forces were based on Nicaragua's southern border, adjacent to Costa Rica.

Arturo Cruz Sr.   My father, who died in 1980, hated the Sandinistas. Shortly before he died, in the summer of that year, he said to me, "Son, here comes the man who will finish them. He will be the next president, and he will defeat them." In that way my father was a good prophet, because Mr. Reagan was right in the overall strategy.

Adolfo Calero   We were totally anti-Communist; we [the contras] were against Fidel Castro. We thought that the way Carter had handled Nicaragua was a disaster — his administration's lack of decision had just fouled up the whole effort to get Somoza out on time in 1978, rather than three months later — and that the way he handled Iran was another disaster. And that Reagan meant business.

Our movement did not exist when President Reagan was elected. We had great expectations that Reagan would do a lot better than Carter. When he started his presidency, Reagan showed courage, decision, and another type of leadership.

I had read Jeane Kirkpatrick's article in *Commentary*, and we were so happy that she was going to be taken into consideration by the Reagan administration. We knew we had a friend there. We were full of hope.

Reagan Administration Support of the Contras

In the early months of the Reagan administration, a determination was made to work for the overthrow of the Sandinista government. This decision was given official sanction when, on December 1, 1981, President Reagan signed a finding authorizing the CIA to conduct a covert action program to "support and conduct . . . paramilitary operations against . . . Nicaragua." The authorization provided $19.95 million to organize, train, and arm a force of Nicaraguan exiles—the contras.

In presenting the finding to the congressional intelligence committees, CIA Director William Casey stated that the operation's main military purpose was to stop the flow of weapons allegedly moving from Cuba to Nicaragua to leftist rebels in El Salvador.

Richard Secord   The thing evolved; it wasn't all written out in an op[erational] plan. It evolved for far too long.

Miguel D'Escoto   U.S. policy took a few years to shape. When Reagan decided to move militarily, he actually thought that the overthrow of the Sandinista government would be done in three months at the most.

Washington — after a lot of reluctance by Honduras — was able to secure their collaboration. The U.S. had said, "This is only for a month." They asked Honduras to do something that is totally unprecedented in the history of Latin America: using one country in Latin America as a base of aggression against a weak neighbor. The same happened with Costa Rica later on.

Remember, this is Central America. I was also talking to people from Honduras; there was always someone we could talk to. The U.S. plan was to seize territory in the northern part of Nicaragua. They would establish a government there; the U.S. would recognize it officially and would get other countries who are more permeable to Washington's pressure to also do the same.

And having so established there a "Nicaraguan government," they could provide logistical support directly there, not just from the territory of another country. Then they would push down and take the whole of the country.

Finally they told Honduras it would not take more than three months. As time went on and on, when Reagan was in office about fifteen months, he changed policy. In this case, he was persuaded by his advisers that the objective of military overthrow was no longer feasible.

But he was also persuaded to — or he himself wanted to — maintain the contras. But now the contras were an important component of an overall policy [whose] purpose was to bring about the economic destruction of Nicaragua, because by this time he believed that if you destroy the economy — people understood clearly where the United States was — through embargo and other methods, then the people would eventually cry uncle.

It has been estimated that, in the overall effort to destroy the Nicaraguan economy and isolate and then bring down the Sandinistas, the United States spent more than ten billion dollars.

Duane Clarridge The whole thing started in the fall of 1981. There was already a political organization of sorts [in Nicaragua]. There is a myth that the U.S. government forced this fusion of the political leadership and the military — these five hundred people. This is not true; they did it on their own, and then they changed the name to the FDN [Nicaraguan Democratic Force].

When we approached this group, they had been working with the Hondurans and the Argentineans. When we first lined up with them, it was mainly with the military side, if you can call it that. It was basically led by [Enrique] Bermúdez.*

---

* Bermúdez, a former colonel in the Nicaraguan National Guard, played a role in the formation of the contra forces.

The Chamorro brothers [Edgar and Pedro Joaquín, the sons of the assassinated editor of *La Prensa*] approached us and wanted us to anoint them to take control of the whole thing. Well, we weren't going to do that. They didn't have the political clout that was required. We needed a larger, stronger political base.

There are people who will say, correctly, that I delayed quite some time in putting together a political apparatus, and that I emphasized the military. In my own defense, I had problems, in that I had to make a mark in Nicaragua rather quickly — to tell the Nicaraguans that we were coming after them. So I had to get the military thing off the ground rather quickly.

By the summer of 1982 we had put together a new political apparatus. Now, did these people come from underneath? No. They were people we saw as basically representative of the Nicaraguan population, who had been anti-Somoza, and who had a certain standing.

The troops at that time had no political consciousness whatsoever. In the end their representative, Bermúdez, was made part of the political directorate.

Craig Johnstone   There were a lot of people who thought we should use combat forces in Central America. And every time things turned sour, these people would have a platform to try to advance the notion that we ought to move a brigade of troops.

There was a great deal of tension concerning the contras. Not about whether it was useful to maintain a contra force; there was a fair amount of consensus about the need to maintain some kind of a mechanism for being able to act as a quid pro quo with the Nicaraguans for their support of the guerrillas in El Salvador. And if you didn't have some kind of offsetting force, there was very little prospect of ever succeeding in El Salvador.

In the final analysis, people were always bedeviled by what would happen to the contras. Some thought that the contras should be supported to the point of winning, while others saw them as a negotiating chip. Whether to maintain a negotiating track with the Sandinistas was the single most controversial issue of the administration.

Those of us who advocated maintaining a constant negotiating track — putting proposals to them and essentially looking for a way out of the dilemma — were under a constant state of siege from people in the NSC who strongly opposed that view, and from those who believed that the ultimate victory of the contras was the only way out of the situation.

American Public Opinion of the
Administration's Support of the Contras

Langhorne Motley   Central American policy ran between two goalposts, the goalposts being the limits that America would stand. What America would not stand for was a Cuba on the mainland where they lived. On the other hand, what they didn't want was another Vietnam; they didn't want to commit any American troops. So you had to run a policy between these two posts.

Now the heavy breathers — that's what I call our hard-liners — didn't see this second post. Congress had read the American people fairly well, but there was no other option. We had to run between the two goalposts.

Adolfo Calero   In the U.S., the liberals were very tolerant of leftist and socialist governments; the Catholic Church, with its liberation theology, was even pro-Communist. People in the United States knew very little about Central America, and very little about Nicaragua. There was a tremendous network of Communist sympathizers, or liberals, or whatever. There had been tremendous propaganda against Somoza.

Besides this, the leftist network of propaganda was tremendous. I have been at the Honduran border, under grenade fire, but the time I was the most afraid was when I was at Northwestern University, when a professor there who had lost tenure mounted a very aggressive student protest against my presence there. I was beginning to lecture, and they threw butcher blood at me, and we were attacked. If it hadn't been for the police . . . we were led down into a basement. It was terrible.

The Boland Amendment

As the contras conducted a military campaign within Nicaragua, their efforts did not go unnoticed in the United States, as major media revealed details of their activities.

These revelations caused increasing concern in the Congress, leading in December 1982 to the passage of the first Boland Amendment, named for Edward P. Boland (D-Mass.), chairman of the House Intelligence Committee. The amendment prohibited the CIA and the Department of Defense from furnishing "military equipment, military training or advice, or other support for military activities, to any group or individual not part of a country's armed forces, for the purpose of overthrowing the government of Nicaragua or provoking a military exchange between Nicaragua and Honduras."

Miguel D'Escoto   The Boland Amendment was the successful work of many people who did have a conscience, who could not be intimidated.

I remember spending nights in my house, here in Nicaragua, with U.S. senators and legislators. I remember witnessing the clear sense of weakness and ineptitude — of powerlessness — vis-à-vis President Reagan. People were really afraid to stand up; they thought that whoever Reagan fingered would be politically destroyed.

Richard Secord   The Boland Amendment is vastly misunderstood. It is an anti-appropriations measure and a much-debated and compromised measure.

Boland and his supporters wanted a much stronger bill, one that would bar assistance of any kind by any Americans, at any time and place, for the contras. But they couldn't get anything like that, so what they got was a piece of Swiss cheese, which said that intelligence agencies were barred from providing aid. Then that was modified.

Of course, when it was discussed up on the Hill, especially during the televised hearings, you would have thought it was holy writ, and akin to federal murder legislation. But it was a piece of Swiss cheese.

The CIA, Manuel Noriega, and Oliver North

Manuel Antonio Noriega   During the Torrijos government, I was the liaison between the CIA and the government of Panama. We used this channel to communicate with the United States and Cuba. The United States used this channel in many opportunities, to its own benefit. Never was this communication relationship undercover, or for spying. If the United States needed some communication — some message to Cuba, or to Fidel Castro — we would call to Havana, or go to the diplomatic mission in Panama and communicate with Cuba.

We continued in the relationship in this form in the Reagan administration. He accepted to continue this relationship because of the benefits to the United States.

During the Reagan administration, we maintained some levels of cooperation with the CIA. We knew Bush when he was director of the CIA. When he became vice president, we continued this communication. And meeting with him was normal — within the limit of the parameters of the diplomatic relation and military communication, and official communication. All was very good; there were no problems.

Under Reagan, there was more attention, and more communication, on Latin America, but the situation was different. There had been a change in Nicaragua with the Sandinista government; there was an increase in guerrilla activity in the area; and there were other types of problems.

There was more attention because the United States had more interest in the penetration and control of the CIA and the problem of the guerrillas.

Mr. Casey was different from other directors of the CIA. He was more active, he visited more Latin American countries, and he communicated more with friends in the area and discussed the problems face to face. He had more knowledge of the problems.

Duane Clarridge   A couple of days after I got to Langley, Casey said, "Take off a month or two and basically figure out what to do about Central America." That was the sum total of his approach. And it didn't take rocket science to understand what needed to be done.

But you just don't go back in a couple of days and say, "I figured it out." The Latin American Division had been badly beaten up in the 1970s by the Church and Pike stuff* and all the investigations, so it was shell-shocked, to say the least. I knew that I was a new boy; I had never served in the division. And the Latin American Division had always been an isolated division within the agency; it was almost like a little barony.

So the main thing was to carry the division with me. After a couple of weeks I went back up and told Casey, "This is what we ought to do. Why don't we take the war to Nicaragua and put pressure on them so they will reduce their capacity to ship arms and advice to El Salvador and other places in Latin America? We have to build a backfire over them."

This was exactly what Casey wanted to hear, and he said, "Okay, go ahead and do it." Then something happened — or continued to happen — that made a lot of the Agency's upper echelon uncomfortable: Casey [dealing] directly with me rather than going through the chain of command.

Michael Deaver   Jim Baker didn't want Casey to see Reagan alone; he was always bugging me about going in there when Casey was in Reagan's office. I understood that, under federal statute, there were two officials who could see the president alone at any time, by request: the CIA director and the attorney general.

Baker was convinced from day one that the hard-right people —

---

* Senator Frank Church (D-Idaho) and Representative Otis Pike (D-N.Y.) in 1975 co-chaired hearings in the Senate and House of Representatives that resulted in the sharp curtailment of the CIA's ability to carry out covert activities in Central America.

Casey, Clark, and Haig — would try to move the president into some kind of military action in Central America and would destroy his presidency.

So he would use me, because I could go into a meeting since I wasn't thought of as a player, as far as policy was concerned. I did that a couple of times, but I didn't think Baker had to worry about Casey. Reagan couldn't understand Casey most of the time.

Donald T. Regan   In the foreign field, anything that could be done to oppose communism, whether overtly or covertly, was where Bill Casey got quite a free hand to do whatever he could to disrupt communism and also ferret out whatever they were trying to do to disrupt us or spy on us.

Adolfo Calero   I believe in the sincerity of President Reagan and all the CIA people — Dewey Clarridge and the others. They were all out for us. So were people like Jack Kemp and congressmen who went out of their way to help us, at least during the Reagan presidency.

There were stages. When I first arrived, the CIA was financing the whole thing. Then the CIA had to pull out, and we began to get money from other countries. I didn't know where the money was coming from, and the one who notified me about that was Ollie [North].

Manuel Antonio Noriega   I knew Oliver North because he wanted to know me. In this moment, he had the problem of the contras in Nicaragua, and they were working on the United States' plan with the contras and Iran, and they wanted Panama's help in this plan to help the contras.

I was in communication with, and meeting with, North because Casey certified that North was on an assignment by President Reagan and Bush in this operation. And in this way I received the request about this requirement, because he wanted to produce in Nicaragua ammunition and incursion of Panamanian troops inside Nicaragua, because the contras did not have the capacity to fight.

I did not give the permission of Panama to participate in this type of scheme, in this type of help: they requested that I help North, that Panama's troops should go to Nicaragua. In the first meeting Poindexter showed me where they wanted troops, and I said no. And North insisted, and I said no.

I was opposed to this plan because it was an interference and violation of the dignity and sovereignty of another country.

Adolfo Calero   The first time I met Ollie was in Honduras. I had been lobbying Congress through 1983 — I had spent a lot of time in Washington, trying to get the swing votes and talking to those who wanted to help — so I met North in Honduras, and I knew then and there that something was happening.

The next time around it was in a restaurant in Virginia when the CIA said to me, "We are not going to see you anymore. This operation is going to be handled by Colonel North. He is going to be your contact."

I was very, very positively, favorably impressed by Ollie. He came through as an honest man, very sincere, and devoted; I thought he was very patriotic. He told me about his efforts in Vietnam — how he had worked with this tribe — in a very casual way, not trying to impress me, just telling each other of our pasts. We used to talk about Navy–Notre Dame games — I went to Notre Dame, and he is a graduate of the Naval Academy — so we became friends.

He is a workaholic; he worked at all hours — very sober, very austere, very religious. I felt he was as much of a conservative as I was, a family man, raised in a Christian family. When things were going wrong for us, or when we were not having enough support, you could tell that he was moved by that. If it had not been for him, things that were already difficult would have been a lot more difficult.

You could tell that he was very important. A lot of people in government, and wealthy people in the United States, had great respect and admiration for Ollie. He was right in the Executive Office Building, and he used to talk a lot to the national security adviser. He had immediate access to McFarlane, who had been a marine colonel, [and] he also had access to Bill Casey; so I had all the indications that he was the right man to be dealing with. And he came through.

I visited with Ollie some fifty-odd times. I didn't keep count, but the independent counsel told me that. I used to see Ollie: we were getting the money, it was coming to a bank account and was used to take care of all our operations, we had to buy weapons and the ammunition, and we had to find who would do it. And then came General Secord, and he got us weapons from China and from Portugal.

I began to have another impression when Bush came in. I thought they were trying to get rid of a hot potato.

I never thought that it was wrong for us to get support from the United States; I thought it was the right thing to do. I thought it was in their interest — in a way it was their obligation — because they were the ones who had bungled and mishandled things in supporting Somoza for so many years and not making a clear decision for Somoza to leave.

Duane Clarridge   At some point — I think it was in 1983 — I needed a training area for Pastora, so I went down and talked to Noriega about it, and he gave me an island. We never actually trained anyone there; Noriega was getting ready to run for president. He told me we couldn't go in. I always suspected it was Cuban pressure; Noriega said it was due to the presidential election.

Adolfo Calero   I met many Central and South American presidents, but for some reason I never met Noriega. We had the doors open in Panama; we had meetings there that we couldn't have had in other countries. He provided protection for us whenever we were there.

We in the FDN never had any people training in Panama. Pastora, on the other hand, was closer to Panama; they were operating in Costa Rica, so there was more contact. But we never got anything from Panama.

I heard at some point that Noriega would send in agents — I heard this from a Cuban — that Noriega was going to send people in here to do sabotage. But it never did materialize.

We never did sabotage. We were very careful to treat the civilians right — to buy food from them, besides what they gave to our people. Their people were the ones fighting. These people had relatives in different places. Some had little farms. This was really like armed citizens; they were not ordinary soldiers, much less "mercenaries," as our opponents called them.

Elliott Abrams   Noriega had no role with respect to the contras. He offered to have a role; that was rejected by Shultz. When North met with Noriega, he made that offer. North then came to me and said, "He can be really helpful."

I told North that this was above my pay grade, and I took it to Shultz, who said, "Tell him [Noriega] to clean up his act, which will help him a lot. But we don't want him to do anything for the contras."

Manuel Antonio Noriega   North requested this. No contras trained in Panama. Never. Not at any time. There was an area in Panama where there were many forts for training for the United States; the United States has jurisdiction in this area. But in the Panamanian area the contras never received training.

North's claim that we would assassinate the top Sandinista leadership is stupid; it does not make any sense. In August they wanted to talk with me, and I was in England — I was in London — and they came from

Iran to see me, with the necessity to talk to me. And this time they insisted on the plan involving the PDF [Panamian Defense Forces] in this action, because they have a problem with the Congress to obtain money, because they did not have good results from the contra operation.

I said, "I only came to see you this morning because I was continuing my visit." This was in the morning, in the Hotel Victoria, and I spoke with them in one corner of the big lobby of the hotel.

They didn't tell me what they had done in Iran; they didn't tell me they had been in Iran. But I know the game; I knew it from international intelligence contacts. I knew about the arms sales to Iran. It was a very big problem; it involved not only the United States but it was an international problem. I was not surprised that the United States was doing this.

The CIA Manual

In a controversial move reminiscent of its activity in Vietnam, the CIA prepared a manual for use by the contras.

Adolfo Calero   The book was translated into Spanish. Apparently notions in the book were used by the CIA in other places.

They [the CIA] showed the translation to me because I was the president of the FDN, the commander in chief, and I made two observations. There were two places where I said this could lead to a misinterpretation. One of them was the word *neutralize*. So I told Edgar Chamorro, who was our director in charge of propaganda, to take it out.

One page was replaced — something was taken out — but as for the other page, he thought it was too costly because they had already printed the manual. He said, "We have to get it out, and the word doesn't mean 'to kill.' " "But," I said, "it can be interpreted that way." It was something that could have been prevented. I remember telling him so clearly that it could lead us into trouble. But the page he took out was worse.

The people who were going to be instructed by this book were not very highly educated. This was so subtle, and they would not understand the subtleties. And Edgar Chamorro, the man who was responsible for it, was thrown out of our organization. He then went to the press to denounce us, although he was responsible for it.

Duane Clarridge   I wanted Casey to give me the reprimand. By this time Congress wanted me badly, but Reagan wouldn't do it. His approach was, "If I reprimand you, I reprimand myself."

The Mining of the Harbors and
the Second Boland Amendment

In September 1983, the president signed a finding allowing for a CIA program to put pressure on Sandinista attempts at subversion in Latin America and to promote democracy within Nicaragua.

One operational aspect of this effort resulted in the mining of Nicaraguan harbors by CIA contract agents. This activity and the increasing evidence of Reagan administration support for the contras led to the passage on October 10, 1984, of the second Boland Amendment, which banned further U.S. support for the contras during fiscal year 1985. In summarizing his amendment, Representative Boland said, "It clearly ends U.S. support for the war in Nicaragua."

Alexander M. Haig Jr.   I never knew before the fact that limpid mines had been put on Nicaraguan freighters. That was done around me, through some entrée to the president that was both against the law and wrongheaded in the extreme.

Langhorne Motley   Here's the interesting thing about Washington. If there were a dozen fathers of [the invasion of] Grenada, you could have filled every seat in RFK Stadium; if there were six fathers of the mining of the harbor, you could find room for them in a phone booth. I was involved in both; I am one of only two people who will admit to being involved in the second.

In a technical sense, the mining of the harbor did not fit other findings, so it required a special finding. There was agreement at my level to go ahead. Each of us briefed our secretaries. Shultz has told me that if I tell him that I briefed him on the mining, he accepts that as fact, but he doesn't remember. I know him well enough to know that he is not hiding on that.

We could not use conventional mines because they would blow up ships and kill people. We didn't want to hurt or kill anybody. We had small mines made in a garage in McLean, Virginia, that did exactly what needed to be done — which was to shut down Lloyd's of London as far as insurance went. That was the whole object of the exercise.

Lloyd's was goosey about the thing; if they would stop insuring, nobody would go in but the Russians. It worked from that point of view. Where it didn't work was when it became public.

Continued Support of the Contras

The Boland Amendments notwithstanding, the White House continued in its determination to aid the Nicaraguan opposition. The administration's efforts included the establishment in the Department of State of the Office of Public Diplomacy for Latin America and the implementation through this office of a program aimed at both building popular support for the contras—by depicting them as freedom fighters against the Marxist-oriented Sandinistas— and raising funds to further the contra cause.

The major portion of this fund-raising campaign was conducted through the National Endowment for the Preservation of Liberty (NEPL). The organization's efforts were enhanced by the participation of senior administration officials, who briefed prospective donors, and by the president himself, who met with several individuals who had each contributed at least three hundred thousand dollars.

Another major avenue of funding for the contras involved solicitations of other countries, most notably Saudi Arabia—which by April 1985 had contributed thirty-two million dollars—and from the world's reputedly richest man, Haji Hassaval Bolkiah Mu'izzadin Waddaulah, the sultan of Brunei, who contributed ten million dollars after a clandestine meeting in London between one of his representatives and Assistant Secretary of State Elliott Abrams.

This donation would prove to be a source of frustration to the Reagan administration when it was transferred by mistake to the account of a Swiss businessman, who apparently was not associated with the contra effort, rather than to the Credit Suisse account that was used to purchase arms for the contras. The commonly accepted explanation is that Oliver North's secretary, Fawn Hall, transposed numbers in the account of Lake Resources, a front company of the Enterprise (the name given by Iran-contra figures Richard Secord and Albert Hakim to various operations in which they were jointly involved). Roy Furmark, one of our interviewees and an associate of Adnan Khashoggi, suggested to us that the ten million dollars may have been deliberately deposited into the account of an individual with close ties to Israel.

Arturo Cruz Sr.   When I had to resign from the leadership of the contras two or three years later, whenever I said, "I'm going" — because there were pressures on me not to go — they would say, "Please give us three more months." I would say yes.

I decided to go on my own, unilaterally, to say, "This is a war that isn't just." I am a Roman Catholic, and I was taught that war is justifiable in three cases. One, if the cause is just. Second, [if] you have no other choice. And third, [if] you have a chance to win. If you don't have a chance to win, the war isn't correct.

And I felt pain. I said that publicly. I sent in my resignation to the *Miami Herald* and to a newspaper in Costa Rica, because I could see that the Afghanis were receiving from the American allies nothing less than Stinger missiles; they were bringing down Soviet planes like flies. Our kids were fighting with RPGs [rocket-propelled grenades]; there is no correlation. The Soviets gave the Sandinistas nothing less than the gunships and the Hind helicopters.

Richard Secord I became involved in late 1984. I had known Casey from the period when I was on active duty. North told me Casey asked him to bring me in. I didn't ever directly ask Bill Casey whether he had asked North to bring me in. Nobody hated seeing Casey die more than I did because he was my ace in the hole.

I was surprised when North first approached me because I didn't know anything about it, and because I had never worked in that region before. But they were looking for someone they could trust, someone who had special operations experience, so I was a logical candidate.

I didn't even know North. He says he knew me, that he had been in meetings in which I had participated at the Pentagon. But I didn't remember him. I checked him out with an officer who had worked for me and was, at the time, on the NSC staff. He told me that North was a good guy who was working on some very difficult issues.

Robert C. McFarlane Bear in mind that they only began to organize in the fall of 1981. When you look at how long other insurgent movements have taken to mature and develop, when you look at their performance in 1982 and 1983, there were no strategic victories. But it was absorbing more Sandinista effort to deal with them, which was diminishing the amount of resources they could put into other things.

I went to Calero in January 1985 and said: "We think you are right-minded, but for your movement to be viable, you need two things you don't have. One is political purpose — a platform, a program, a reason why people should rally to you that is more visible than it is right now. You and I talk about it; that's coffee shop stuff. You have to have people, politicians, credible figures who rally to you.

"The second thing is that you have to be militarily competent. There are a lot of potential supporters in the Congress who would vote for you but who come to me and say, 'Do you think they can win? I don't want to back a loser.' So in the next year two things have to happen or the Congress will bail out — and so will I. You have to win battles, and you have to have a political platform."

In 1985 they did that. They developed a peace proposal, as well as bringing in Arturo Cruz and one or two other credible political figures. In Miami they wrote down a doctrine, a constitution, and the trappings of governance. By 1987 they had fifty thousand troops in the field and, I think, would have begun to have a telling effect upon the ability of the Sandinistas to govern.

Victor Hugo Tinoco   I came to believe that the U.S. government was using the "democracy" argument as a rationale for trying to achieve other results in the East-West confrontation — that they were not exactly concerned with democracy itself, but as a means to achieve other results. I tried to imagine what the U.S. would have done if they had been able to overthrow the Sandinista government. Would they have organized a democratic state here?

Richard Secord   If we had gotten out when we wanted to, in the summer of 1986, there would have been only a few ripples instead of this great mess. The deal was that we would pull out our air operation, which was the single most important aspect. We had already bought up a bunch of ammunition and infantry-style weapons and had them in place, so we were cruising along pretty well, logistically.

The little tactical airlift operation we were running down there was a crucial part of our bridging operation to keep those troops in the field. Then the Boland Amendment was repealed, and the CIA in effect got its hunting license back. That was exactly how I characterized it to Casey in our last conversation; North was there. I told Casey, "You have to get your guys into the field now. This ragtag operation I have going is not going to hack it; we don't have the tools we need." But the CIA fiddled and faddled around trying to work out the perfect plan and was so scared because of the hassle over the Boland Amendment.

Could the Contras Have Succeeded
Militarily on Their Own?

One of the lingering questions concerning U.S. support for the contras is whether those forces had the potential to achieve a military victory over the Sandinistas.

Richard Secord   I didn't consider myself an expert on the contras' military capabilities; my expertise is not on Latin America. But I know something about guerrilla forces, and I evaluated the contras as being fairly rugged and capable of continuing to eat away at the ankles of the regime.

But in no way were they capable — nor did I ever see them becoming capable — of a military victory in the classic sense. They didn't have the numbers, or the money. But it was our hope to keep them in the field until the Boland Amendment issue could be taken care of. That was my mission as I saw it, and as I was asked by the White House: to try to keep them in the field, a bridging operation, a painful bridging operation. That is why we bought what we bought; we didn't buy what they wanted.

Colin L. Powell   I was convinced that the contras would never have enough power to be an army that would come storming out of the mountains, go down to the lowlands, defeat the Sandinista army in the field, and march triumphantly through Managua.

Once that was clear to me, I then said, "What other purpose do they serve?" The purpose they served was that they were a constant irritant as a guerrilla force, as an insurgency, against the Sandinistas; [they] would be a drain on them for a long period of time; and [they] were worthy of support. Who knows? There might be a time in the future when there would be a popular rallying behind their cause and they could gain more strength.

At the time we started to change our policy — and Congress said, "Enough of this!" — it looked to me as if the contras had reached their peak strength of somewhere around fifteen to seventeen thousand; that was probably as big as they were going to get.

Manuel Antonio Noriega   The contras never had the power to change the Sandinista government; they didn't have the tactical or operational potential. The activity was relevant when they had the support of mercenaries, or some CIA men, but never did the contras alone conquer anyplace in Nicaragua.

Duane Clarridge   They won. In the beginning we never expected them to. In 1981 there were five hundred people running around the Honduran border. Some were ex–National Guard soldiers, some were almost bandits, cattle rustlers, so there was never any great anticipation that it would grow into the largest peasant army ever assembled in Latin America.

It wasn't that we did it. The Sandinistas did it — through their own policies, their anti-Catholicism, their collective-farm, rudimentary efforts at confiscation. They basically handed it to us.

It eventually went from five hundred to twenty thousand. Very little of that was based on recruiting efforts. In fact, there were more people coming in to fight than we could arm, which was a constant problem.

Harry Shlaudeman   I learned afterwards that they came awfully close; that if they had had constant funding over those last few years, they would have done it; that they did have the capability.

By those last two years they, in effect, had carved a corridor from the Honduran border all the way down to the Costa Rican border, where they did as they liked. They really had the Sandinistas hurting; there is no question about that. They had a lot of support in the north, from the campesinos.

I'm not saying I would have picked this policy — it was the wrong policy for us in a number of ways because it got us involved in "Vietnam" all over again — but in military terms, given enough time, they would have done it.

Arturo Cruz Sr.   My misgivings — because I had serious misgivings about the leadership of the contras — was that I was afraid that we might be reestablishing in Nicaragua the powers of the former National Guardsmen. That was no solution.

But the fighters were campesinos. These kids who lost their sight, lost an arm, a leg, were campesinos — not our children, not the children of the gentry of Nicaragua. That is something we have to recognize.

If we can come to grips with reality, we have to say that we all made tremendous mistakes.

Victor Hugo Tinoco   Had it not been for the contras, we would today have a Sandinista government pursuing democratic goals and able to make gains in social justice. The situation of the people would be better than it is today.

We went through a difficult period as a movement. Some people on the contra side thought we would disappear. But since 1994 we have passed the survival stage and have now moved to the state of expectation.* We will continue to be a very important source for social justice in Nicaragua.

Oliver North   Without the military pressure that the contras brought to bear, there would not have been a political solution in Nicaragua. Even with the collapse of the Evil Empire, you would have had the Cuban-style Communist state fomenting rebellion all over Central America.

Was Shultz Too Preoccupied with the Middle East?

Richard Schifter   There were all kinds of criticisms directed against George Shultz which, I thought, were inappropriate. To the extent to which that problem in Central America was created by the Soviet Union, if you solved the problem with the Soviet Union, you would solve the problem in Central America. That's the way it turned out.

Harry Shlaudeman   There is no question that Shultz was interested in Central America. In late 1984 and most of 1985, he was very much involved. In June we went to El Salvador; then he went on to Nicaragua, which was a high-profile, by no means risk-free, exercise.

There was never any piece of paper that said, "This is what you are supposed to do." I think that they wanted sufficient diplomatic activity to persuade the Congress that we were interested in diplomatic solutions to these problems without getting in the way of the fundamental policy, which was to win those two wars. That seemed to me to be what it was all about.

There was a very sharp division within the administration as to how far we should go in testing the diplomatic waters. Shultz's inclination was to negotiate; Weinberger, Casey, Kirkpatrick, these people really didn't want to negotiate anything, and certainly Menges didn't.

Ultimately Shultz decided — and I would have in his place — that he had more important issues to deal with than that one. He pretty much let them have the field as far as policy issues were concerned.

Victor Hugo Tinoco   The State Department and Mr. Shultz were concentrating on European affairs, and the Central American problem was

---

* On October 20, 1996, the Sandinista presidential candidate, Daniel Ortega Saavedra, was defeated by the rightist candidate, Arnoldo Aleman, a former mayor of Managua who ran under the aegis of the Liberal Alliance, winning by an almost 10 percent margin over his opponent.

left to the CIA and other intelligence organizations dealing with that kind of problem. If the State Department had taken a more direct role in control of Central American policy — [having], for example, more profound negotiations — the results would have been different.

Charles Hill   He was certainly primarily interested in the Soviets. But in my experience — which goes back to working with Kissinger — he was unusually interested in all of the major issues, more so than any other secretary of state.

Central America was the most murderous of all the problems he had to deal with because the people on our side trying to get anything done were just cutting each other's throats, and those on the other side were very deftly making the very best of this, time after time. It was almost an intractable problem because of the Washington scene, because of the insanity of the Boland Amendment, which is incomprehensible.

We tried to do a study of the Boland Amendment; we had people working on it for eight months. It was a set of laws you could not abide by. To me, the only way to solve Central America was the way it was solved — that is, by the fall of the Soviet Union.

George P. Shultz   When I came into office here, Beirut was on our hands, and that was a very preoccupying matter. In that context, I helped the president develop his Middle East initiative.

Then there was this gigantic dispute over the Siberian pipeline. We had these negotiations going on, but we also had the deployment schedule of the INF [intermediate-range nuclear force] missiles.

So I didn't pay that much attention to Central America in the first four or five months of my time. And Bill Casey — he was totally preoccupied with Central America — got after me about that. He said, "What are you doing, paying attention to the Middle East and Europe and the Soviet Union? The real problem is in Central America." And we had an argument about that.

But, in fact, I paid a lot of attention to Central America. I testified a great deal; I went there a great deal. And I think I helped the administration's effort much more than did some of the people who considered themselves to be the hard-liners who were preoccupied with it.

In fact, a lot of what they did turned out to be counterproductive. It wasn't productive to mine the harbors; that backfired badly. We had the Congress on our side for a while; they appropriated a hundred million dollars. But the effort to go around them just blew it all away.

So I did pay a lot of attention to Central America, and I had a better view of it than many of the people who criticized me, like Bill Casey and Constantine Menges — who was a wild guy, who thought he was more important than he really was.

The Enders-Motley-Abrams Succession

During the Reagan administration three officials served in the post of assistant secretary of state for inter-American affairs: Thomas Enders, Langhorne Motley, and Elliott Abrams.

It could be inferred that the succession from Enders to Abrams represented the administration's determination to adopt a tougher policy on Central America.

Charles Hill   What you are seeing is the search for someone who would run the policy, who could minimally handle the far hard-line right. It [the succession of Enders, Motley, and Abrams] was more the choosing of people who appeared to be in better odor with the hard-liners [and] who, at the same time, were not going to drive the soft Congress crazy.

All three assistant secretaries tried to follow the Shultz point of view: that we had to really try to have serious negotiations. Over time the hard-line view began to emerge among people who, like me, were not hard-liners. I saw that the intent to carry out negotiations was not working because the other side, the Sandinistas, had enormous support on the American political scene, not only in Congress but in the mainline, mid-America churches. They were playing to that; it had worked before. I had gone through it on Vietnam. You couldn't get negotiations going with a Communist government who realized that they could get what they wanted — or at least prolong the situation to their advantage — by playing to an American audience that was not the administration.

Was the Use of U.S. Troops in Nicaragua Ever a Possibility?

Arturo Cruz Sr.   An American operation here would have only lasted a couple of hours, and it would have been over — two shots and run. I don't know why there was no such operation.

Richard Secord   It wasn't realistic to use U.S. troops in Nicaragua, but certainly, we should have used special forces; then it would have been a different story. They could have been used in conjunction with the contras. I fail to see the difference between the use of American special forces, acting as advisers and logisticians, and the use of American CIA paramilitary people, who are all ex–special forces, in that kind of situation.

Adolfo Calero I was told that it was possible for the U.S. to have a military operation here. As a matter of fact, a former classmate of mine who was in the Marine Corps, stationed at San Diego, was put on alert at times when the Sandinistas were going to bring in the MIGs [advanced Soviet jet combat aircraft].

It didn't happen because the Sandinistas were very careful not to mount a provocation that would have warranted intervention. They were very well counseled by Americans on U.S. policy.

Joseph Metcalf III, vice admiral, U.S. Navy; commander of the Grenada Invasion Force; deputy chief of Naval Operations We were ready to go into Nicaragua and El Salvador; we were ready to go into Panama. Left unattended, the Sandinistas would have taken over El Salvador. And Costa Rica was very vulnerable.

We did the right thing by containing them. We didn't put enough in to win; the president was inhibited by Congress. But left to their own devices, the Soviets would have continued to supply them.

The Contadora Process

In January 1983, Mexico—joined by Colombia, Venezuela, Panama, and five Central American nations, with the indirect participation of the United States and Cuba—began discussions on Contadora, an island located off the Pacific coast of Panama, toward a solution to the problems of the Central American region.

In September 1983, the process produced a document of objectives twenty-one points concerning the promotion of democracy, territorial integrity, arms control, and arms reduction.

The U.S. State Department began early in 1984 to seek ways to implement provisions of the document of objectives through diplomatic means. It began by condensing the twenty-one objectives to four: the exit from Nicaragua of Cuban and Soviet advisers; the cessation of Nicaraguan support for guerrillas operating in El Salvador; a regional agreement that would include the reduction of Nicaragua's large armed forces; and free elections in Nicaragua.

In return for the implementation of these objectives, the United States would agree to end its support for the contras and reduce its visibility in the region.

Constantine Menges I remember a chiefs-of-mission meeting in El Salvador with Secretary Shultz, where I said, "We have four Contadora countries and four Central American countries. Right now it's six on our side versus Mexico and Nicaragua. The aim, politically, will be to essentially make the other three Contadora countries join Nicaragua, and then draw Honduras and Guatemala in and, ultimately, isolate El Salvador." I said that this was the sensible plan for the Communist side to do.

Jeane J. Kirkpatrick I thought that they made a major turn in Central American policy with the Contadora accords. I was not very optimistic about them; nothing anybody had done had worked in the sense of producing desired effects.

I am a very pragmatic person. I never doubted that Shultz's goals were the same as my goals. But I wasn't optimistic, and I was concerned that the issue would be transferred to the UN at that stage. I thought it would be deadly, because the Soviets had a real hammerlock on lots of the process.

Constantine Menges The fundamental error of the Department of State's perspective on Central America was the belief that they could get a paper promise from the Sandinista regime that they would stop armed subversion. If they would stop, then the resistance movement could be disbanded and everybody would live happily ever after. [It was] basically a reprise of the Kennedy-Khrushchev agreement on the end of Cuba's armed subversion in the hemisphere — which, as we know, didn't work.

The Kissinger Commission

The Kissinger Commission, a bipartisan body headed by Dr. Henry Kissinger, was appointed by President Reagan in July 1983 in the wake of increasing concern over the destabilization of Central America owing to the threat of Communist expansion in the region, with Mexico being the ultimate target of that expansionism.

The commission reported to the president on January 11, 1984, that U.S. interests in Central America could be best served by aiding the region economically and politically—with aid to El Salvador specifically conditional on the cessation of the rightist death squads—and by advancing the cause of democracy in order to stem the Soviet Union's consolidation of its influence in the region.

In February 1984, President Reagan, using the commission's recommendations, proposed to the Congress the appropriation of eight billion dollars for aid to Central America over a five-year period, double the amount the Congress had already approved for 1984.

Harry Shlaudeman The commission grew out of a speech that Henry Jackson [D-Wash.] gave in the Senate. Jackson, along with many other people, was searching for some way to deal with this problem in a broader and more consensual context in terms of domestic U.S. politics. Jackson said, "Why can't we have a Marshall Plan° for Central America and a broad, bipartisan coalition?"

They brought Henry Kissinger in. They had given him several names of people who would be available to be executive director of the commission, and he picked me. I had been assistant secretary under Kissinger [in the Nixon administration].

I would say that the commission, like most commissions, had very little impact upon the Reagan administration. We never got the money we were hoping to get. The administration, quite frankly, was never really very interested in that aspect of it; they were much more interested in trying, through the commission, to get broader support for their overall policy, which, of course, involved the contras and support for the existing government in El Salvador.

The commission did have an interesting side effect in that some very prominent people who participated in the commission's work became educated on Central America — people like Jack Kemp [R-N.Y.] and Robert Strauss [the former chairman of the Democratic National Committee], who ordinarily would have paid no attention whatsoever to Central America.

The Manzanillo Process

Secretary of State Shultz planned to attend the inauguration of José Napoleón Duarte on June 1, 1984, in El Salvador. One week earlier, on May 23, during a planning session for a meeting of NATO foreign ministers at the end of the month at the historic Wye Plantation in Virginia, Shultz had raised with President Reagan the possibility of a meeting between himself and the Sandinista leader, Daniel Ortega, in Managua, following the Salvadorian ceremony.

On May 30, following consultations within the administration as well as with the leadership of the Core Four nations (El Salvador, Honduras, Costa Rica, and Guatemala), President Reagan approved the meeting, which took place at the Managua airport on the afternoon of June 1. The meeting would lead to the convening of the Manzanillo Process.

° The post–World War II aid plan for Europe developed by General George C. Marshall when he was secretary of state in the Truman administration.

Adolfo Calero   We visited with Shultz a number of times, especially when we began to deal with the Sandinistas. We were notified when he came down to Nicaragua to meet with Ortega so we wouldn't be caught by surprise. It was explained to us: we have to do this. And I understood that; it was part of a necessary game.

Victor Hugo Tinoco   Our expectation was that it could mean the beginning of negotiations, that they were willing to open the process. We weren't expecting a solution, but we were expecting that this new track would open negotiations.

Harry Shlaudeman   It was very cool and businesslike; there was no glad-handing. It was a meeting between adversaries. However, there was no screaming, no overt hostility.

I know Ortega quite well. He is a strange guy. He doesn't show much emotion, he's not very articulate, and he just kind of sits and looks at you. D'Escoto would talk all the time. And that's what happened that night.

The idea was that it was really time to see if we couldn't negotiate. We all felt that in the department. And then we got into the old problem about whether we had to add democracy or not, which was really the basic issue.

It's ironic that, in the end, we did. We weren't sure what was going to happen at the meeting in Managua, but I think we thought that they would accept negotiations. They kept saying that they would like to negotiate as long as it didn't involve their sovereignty.

Manzanillo, a resort city on Mexico's Pacific coast, was selected as the site for further talks between representatives of the United States and the Sandinistas. There was opposition, however, to the discussions from within the National Security Council.

Following an intense debate within the administration, with Secretary of State Shultz insisting on the efficacy of the meetings, the first session of the Manzanillo Process was convened on Monday, June 25, 1984, with Harry Shlaudeman and Victor Hugo Tinoco representing the United States and the Sandinista leadership, respectively.

Charles Hill   Manzanillo was a serious effort, and all the more serious because it was conducted against the screams of people who said we must not do that because any kind of negotiation is weakness. With all of that, it appeared that the hard-liners were right, because the other side was using it to their advantage rather than using it as a chance for negotiation.

Harry Shlaudeman   I remember vividly the meeting in the Situation Room right after the first Manzanillo session. I reported on the initial meeting; that one went all right. But the second meeting, the one in the Cabinet Room, turned into a donnybrook, where Shultz and Weinberger in particular were attacking one another.

Langhorne Motley   It caused us huge grief among the hard-liners. We were going to plumb their intentions, take it as far as we could. The meetings did get off to a fairly good start, but as Harry would report, they [the Sandinistas] couldn't go to the bathroom without checking with Managua.

It had two purposes. If it worked, fine. If it didn't, we had made the effort and the record. Shultz was serious about it; he wasn't going to waste that much political capital just for smoke. We had to fight some guys tooth and nail.

Harry Shlaudeman   I believe that he [Shultz] determined during the Manzanillo negotiations — and during these very acrimonious arguments within the administration — that things like the opening with the Soviets were a lot more important, and that he wasn't going to win that fight anyway.

And what was he going to win it with? One of the things that Manzanillo proved was that, at that point, there was really no negotiated deal that would have been even halfway acceptable to that administration.

Victor Hugo Tinoco   At the beginning we had some expectation that something positive could be produced there. But after four or five meetings we realized that they were not serious.

The idea of Manzanillo was accepted by the administration because of internal pressure in the United States. They felt it was important to make some gestures to diminish the criticism inside the U.S.

So while, at the time, we did hope that Manzanillo was a new beginning, I now feel it was a response to pressures, to circumstances. I don't think they were following a systematic process of negotiating; it was more a matter of tactics. I think they were looking for a military solution.

The Aftermath

Constantine Menges There were end runs from the State Department against the president because the Department of State officials decided that they knew better than the elected president — and that George Shultz agreed with them — that their approach was the better approach.

I think that the most shocking of all the end runs and maneuvers was the time of what I call the "election eve surprise," the pulling together, contrary to the president's decisions and orders, of a sixty-page treaty co-operating with the Central American leadership, starting with Ortega, in the UN meetings in September 1984, to actually present President Reagan with a fait accompli: that there are Central Americans who have signed this peace agreement. Isn't it great? We have to endorse it. And what a success this is for you on the eve of your election!

That was the combination of George Shultz, Michael Deaver, and the Department of State people. I thought it was totally misguided, totally wrong. It would have unraveled all of the pro-democratic forces in the region and would have led to enormously increased human suffering.

It represented a view in the Department of State that they knew what was best for the country and that what the elected president had ordered was irrelevant. Once I was talking to Assistant Secretary Motley, and I said, "The president has ordered so-and-so," and he answered, "But it's only the pres —" and he stopped halfway through the word *president*.

The 1984 Nicaraguan Elections

U.S. policy-makers were divided as to how to react to the announcement by the Sandinistas that elections would be held in the fall of 1984. The basic question was whether participation in the elections by a U.S.-backed opponent of the Sandinista regime would lend credibility to the process.

Some within the Reagan administration supported the candidacy of Arturo Cruz Sr., while others believed that the Sandinista candidate, Daniel Ortega Saavedra, could be defeated and democracy established in Nicaragua only by the use of force.

The Sandinistas won the election, receiving 67 percent of the vote and 61 percent of the ninety seats in the Nicaraguan legislature.

Victor Hugo Tinoco In 1984 there were two logics at work in the U.S. government regarding Nicaragua: the logic of war and the logic of elections. The Reagan administration rejected the logic of elections. It was not because of electoral conditions; in many countries elections are held in conditions much more difficult than the circumstances that then existed in Nicaragua. In Nicaragua the logic of war had taken over.

In 1984 we had the support of the people. The worst moment for us came after the elections. Because of the war, in 1985 and 1986 the situation began to deteriorate. Nicaragua became a test case in the East-West confrontation. Nicaragua was geographically close to the United States; it was easy for the U.S. to make Nicaragua a symbol of the larger struggle it faced.

Some have said that there were also psychological factors, that President Reagan was acting as someone obsessed with Nicaragua. But from a political view, they were testing their global view. And the place to test that was here, in Nicaragua.

Arturo Cruz Sr.   Once I was in Managua, I saw what was going on. I immediately realized that the Sandinistas were bluffing, that they wanted to tell the world, "We are having elections. We want the traditional political parties and labor unions to participate." But, in fact, they didn't.

It was a terrible mistake because we should have gone to the elections. I am to blame for all this — first, because I was not rich. They said to me, "You have to run." I said, "How can I leave my job? I have children still in school."

So the CIA, in the same way that it was helping everybody, decided to help me, and I accepted it. For a period of time I accepted from Mr. North an amount which was less than what I was giving up. Today I am receiving a fraction of the pension I should have earned because of all of the time I gave up, participating in the so-called revolution, and then in the so-called movement to liberate my country.

Miguel D'Escoto   We did have elections in Nicaragua. They were the most observed elections in history, and Daniel won, very handsomely. But the United States policy continued. To believe that U.S. policy had to do with elections is to believe that the United States cares about democracy.

They always supported Somoza, and there was never a good election here, ever. This is so phony; they don't give a hoot about democracy, or about the people. They only give a hoot about power, and increasing the power of the powerful.

Nicaragua Today

Arturo Cruz Sr.   I must admit that I made terrible errors as a Nicaraguan — first of all, with the Sandinistas, and second, in supporting the contras, although I resigned from the whole thing two and a half years before the end of the affair. I made an error because that war was unnecessary. I had tremendous empathy for Reagan's facing up to the Soviets, or outspending the Soviets, because that's how he defeated them.

As I look at it now, in hindsight, I anger people close to me, including my son, who gets furious with me when I say that that war was unnecessary because the United States was so powerful that on the one hand it was already defeating the Soviets in the cold war, but also that it was supporting the Salvadoran government and had made Honduras a fortress.

Why the guerrillas in Nicaragua? Just to establish a symmetry with Salvador? What I am trying to say is that it was overkill that is killing us now, because the consequence of that war was more poverty. It provides a fig leaf for the Sandinistas, who were corrupt and incompetent. When you tell them that, they say, "Oh no, we had the imperial United States on our backs; we were under aggression by the United States." So the war was unnecessary, inhuman, and unwise.

Miguel D'Escoto   Today Nicaragua is a veritable basket case, economically and socially. I don't think I can say to the people, "I am going to move on." I was part of their dream, and I think I should stay.

We were really Sandinistas, though there were a couple who would call themselves Marxists. Sandino — was he a Marxist? He would not accept communism. He said, "I do not have time to explore the success that these people have scored there. We are here."

We had a Communist party in Nicaragua. They always despised us: they were not with us in the struggle against Somoza; they were not with us in the years of revolution.

We knew about Marxism, but I myself never considered myself to be anything but a Nicaraguan who is a Christian and who wants to do well by what I know our Lord expects of us. I went to the seminary because I thought that would be the best way to bring about a just world.

Arturo Cruz Sr.   The most important financial source for the Sandinistas was not the Soviet Union; it was the United States. It was the political support they were given, and all the money that was raised in the United States. They raised so much more than what the contras were getting.

But to make a long story short, Mr. Reagan was right in his determination to face up to the challenge of the illegal war.

The worst moment for the Sandinistas was when they saw that the Wall in Berlin was coming down [and] there would be no more military or foreign aid from the Soviet Union; that Gorbachev, with his glasnost and perestroika, was coming to an understanding with the Americans.

That must have been a moment of despair for them. It's like, if I am a Roman Catholic and all of a sudden someone tells me there is no more pope. It must have been terrible for them. I would love to have listened to their conversations.

Some of them were Marxists. But as subsequent events proved, beyond a shadow of a doubt, they were just power drivers. The reason that they lost was that the cold war was won by the United States.

That is a cause for heated discussion with my friends, because my friends say, "No, it was because of the contras." I say, "No, it was because of one simple reason — that Mr. Reagan won the cold war."

They placed all their bets on one horse; these bets were that the Soviet Union was going to win the cold war. That is why they helped the rebellion in El Salvador and they became pawns of Cuba — which, in turn, was a pawn of the Soviet Union — in spite of the fact that Fidel Castro was fully aware that the superpowers at some point could understand each other and drop him like a hot potato.

Castro told me, in a visit that I made to Havana in 1980 as head of the Nicaraguan delegation to the celebration of the anniversary of the revolution, that he wanted to open Cuba up to the West. He said, "Don't you think I know that someday the two big ones might understand each other?"

The leadership of the Sandinistas who are now millionaires — most of them own businesses; they live lavishly — don't talk about Marxism anymore. They talk about democracy.

THE MIDDLE EAST

Reagan's Grasp of the Issues

Geoffrey Kemp   Ronald Reagan really had no strong background in the complexities of the Middle East. The senior people around him knew this. Indeed, their whole purpose in the first year was not to put foreign policy on the agenda, except in the sense of increasing the defense budget. The priority was to be the economy — domestic reform. Only then would foreign policy get a hearing.

But as everyone knows, the foreign policy agenda is not made in Washington. And in a matter of weeks it became clear that you couldn't ignore Cuba, Poland, and the Middle East. Therefore, Reagan had to get up to speed relatively quickly on these issues.

He was very good at understanding the big political picture; he was simply no good at mastering the details. So one of the powers of the NSC staff in the years I was there was that if you sent a memorandum to the president — and it's always the first one he reads — and attached to it memoranda from State and Defense, and made recommendations on it for him to tick off, he would invariably tick off what you asked him to. That meant that on a lot of these issues the NSC staff controlled a lot of events. There were exceptions.

Yehiel Kadishai   Our impression was that he is a man who knows a lot about everything, but when it comes to details, he doesn't know exactly what the administration wants of him. I noticed that he knew the facts of the Balfour Declaration and that the letter sent by Lord Balfour to Rothschild in 1917 included the fact that there is a connection between the Jewish people and Palestine. He also knew that Transjordan was included in the area to comprise the Jewish national home.

In the first days of his presidency, he expressed the view that three-quarters of the territory that was to be the Jewish home was taken away in the early 1920s by Great Britain and given to the Arabs. The State Department didn't like this view; it wasn't in line with the administration's policies. So we didn't hear him say this again.

The Iran-Iraq War

Geoffrey Kemp   The Iran-Iraq War started before the Reagan administration. During the first year of the Reagan term, the war was essentially a stalemate; it was basically a war of attrition in central Iran.

In the spring of 1982 the Iranians began to take the offensive and were pushing the Iraqis back. At that point the administration got very worried, because if the Iranians crossed the Shatt al Arab° and captured Basra, there was nothing to stop them from moving into the Arabian Gulf — to Kuwait and south. This was at the time when [Ayatollah Ruholla] Khomeini was talking openly about overturning all the regimes of the Middle East — culminating with the Israelis — and the Arabs were terrified.

Interestingly, the view in the administration was that now that the stalemate has been broken, we cannot allow Iran to win the war. That

---

° A body of water in southeastern Iraq formed by the confluence of the Tigris and Euphrates Rivers and flowing into the Persian Gulf.

was when the tilt toward Iraq began. The irony is that the Iranians by that point had won the war; they had repelled the Iraqi invader.

Had they stopped there, history might have been very different. But then Khomeini started his own crusade and launched the six-year war of attrition that ended with the defeat of Iran. Iran was defeated because, by the end of the war, Iraq was being supported by virtually everybody in the world — including ourselves.

President Reagan and Israel

Shimon Peres Israel was one of those issues about which he had a very clear opinion; he was unshakable — he was a staunch supporter. From that point of view, he belonged to the good people of this world.

Jerry Falwell I discussed Israel with him many times. Once, at the White House, I reminded him of the conversation we had had in New Orleans [in the summer of 1980] about Armageddon. I said, "Mr. President, I believe that God deals with nations in regard to how those nations deal with Israel; there is a lot of history to support that. There are a number of reasons why God has blessed this country, but one of them is that we blessed Abraham. So if there is any one thing that you as a president must never compromise, it is our commitment to Israel." And he didn't hesitate; he said, "I believe that."

Barry Schweid There is no way that I can measure — and there is no way that you would be able to if you talked to fifty people — how much it was Reagan's twentieth-century *Exodus*–Leon Uris depth of knowledge of Israel that caused him to be so pro-Israel.

I thought that Reagan-Shultz was Israel's best combination in Washington ever — the combination of Shultz's good manners and the underpinning from Reagan that he was going to treat Israel decently and fairly and look after their best interests.

Nimrod Novick He saw a compatibility in his perception of the American interest and his perception of what is good for Israel; he thought of these two things in concert.

Geoffrey Kemp The baptism for Reagan on the Middle East was in May and June of 1981, when we had the Israeli elections and, prior to that, the bombing of the Osirak reactor. Then a Jewish settler went berserk in Jerusalem and slaughtered some Arabs at prayer, with an AK-47, and

Reagan had to meet all the Islamic ambassadors in the White House, in a very emotional moment.

They were all in awe of Reagan because of his reputation. And in the Oval Office Reagan made some extremely homespun, low-keyed statements, saying that violence was terrible, [that] we wished there were more Anwar Sadats — which was not designed to endear him to everyone there.

From that point on, the realization was that Reagan was not going to pronounce policy in detail, particularly on complicated issues. We had to go out of our way to make sure that both Reagan and the senior White House staff, who were not familiar with some of these issues, did not put their foot in it by using buzz words irresponsibly.

Later on he did get much more involved and quite emotional, particularly over Lebanon. [He] became quite animated at one point in 1982 when the bombing of Beirut was reaching its peak.

Geoffrey Howe   America, as a whole, has always had a stronger pro-Israel lobby than Europe has, and stronger than Britain has. We almost all have reservations about the strength of the Zionist lobby in the United States.

Margaret Thatcher was less dismayed by that than some of the rest of us, for two reasons: one, because her own constituency in Finchley had a very substantial Jewish element; and two, because the Palestinians were identified with the PLO [Palestine Liberation Organization], which was a terrorist organization resorting to violence.

The Europeans were uneasy about the strength of the Zionist lobby in the United States, and the corresponding reluctance in the United States to acknowledge the legitimacy, and the importance, of the role King Hussein was playing. But the gap was never a wide one. When Europe did mobilize itself to urge the case of the Palestinians, it was useful and necessary.

The interesting thing is the extent to which the Zionist lobby remained as strong as it did in the United States. All the more reason for an independent European position. One of the important features of that European policy formation was that we were able to strike a different, and more hopeful, position — from the point of view of the Palestinians — than did America.

The Reagan administration's key Middle East interlocutors were the Likud Party leader Menachem Begin, prime minister of Israel from 1977 to 1983; his successor, Yitzhak Shamir, who held the posts of prime minister and foreign minister in rotation with the Labor Party leader Shimon Peres in the

Unity Government of 1984–88; and King Hussein of the Hashemite Kingdom of Jordan, a major Arab figure in dealing with the Israeli-Palestinian impasse.

Howard Teicher The president consistently displayed a great deal of warmth and admiration for Israel in general, and for Israeli leaders in particular. His relations with Mr. Begin were very correct, in part because Menachem Begin came from an old world school of European diplomacy: very correct, very proper, everything according to protocol, no outward display of affection or jocularity.

Yitzhak Shamir It is very easy for us to find common language with the Americans. Not so the Europeans. I have said many times to American friends, "You are the best goyim; among the goyim, you are the best." I believe this. I have many friends in Britain, in France; I have met many times with Mitterrand, with [Jacques] Chirac, with all of them. It's not the same. You can't trust them, but Reagan I could trust.

Howard Teicher Shamir was a former Mossad guy and was very good at concealing whatever was going on in his mind. It was a very correct relationship; I never heard Reagan utter an ill word about him. They developed much less of a relationship because when the president first met Shamir, it was in the context of the bombing of Beirut, right after a badly burned child's picture had appeared all over the newspapers. With Shamir, there was no real recovery from that; you could always sense this lingering bad vibe.

George P. Shultz He found Shamir difficult. That didn't mean he felt he was ineffective, but he was hard to work with. From the president's point of view, he was very intransigent in many ways.

But the president always had respect for the democratic process and [for] who the democratic process put into power. That's the person you're dealing with.

Alexander M. Haig Jr. I never found Shamir to be dishonest. Peres is a little more, although he is a dear friend and I respect him.

Howard Teicher In the case of Peres, the president was very happy to work with him, and Shultz was very high on Peres. There was a lot of hope that the initiatives we had taken on the peace process might have a better chance of bearing fruit.

In the end, the gridlock of the Government of National Unity proved to be more than we could do much about and not much happened. But there was more of a respectful relationship with Peres; he was more of a politician. Shamir was not much of a politician, and Begin was a quirky politician.

Eitan Haber, adviser to Defense Minister Yitzhak Rabin of Israel   Rabin was interested in America, whereas Peres was directed toward Europe. Rabin thought there were two superpowers in the world: Israel and America.

George P. Shultz   Peres is by nature an optimist — a dreamer in a way. Actually, the combination of Rabin and Peres was quite a good one, because Peres was willing to reach out and try things, and Rabin is tougher.

People in Israel have more confidence in Rabin — that he will drive a hard bargain and will be very concerned with security — and Peres might be a little more anxious to make an agreement than Rabin. And the tough, conservative guy needs to be pulled along, so the two of them together make a pretty good pair.

But Peres recognized, earlier than most Israeli leaders, that if Israel is going to make any progress toward peace, it has to be willing to give up some ground; it can't just stand there and say no to everything.

The president liked Peres a lot. In some ways Peres, in his conversations in the White House early on, gave him the feeling that it would be too easy. And I told him that. I said to the president, "It will be much harder to get anything accomplished than he led you to believe."

Eitan Haber   During the Unity Government, Shamir was very angry because Rabin had a direct line to the White House; Shultz consulted with Rabin at each step. In fact, almost all of the American officials became Rabin's friends.

Yitzhak Shamir   I was more or less aware of Peres's efforts during the period of the Unity Government vis-à-vis the United States. There were some people in the U.S. who sympathized with Peres and some who sympathized with us.

I always suspected Peres, but if I didn't know exactly what he did, I did know more or less. And therefore, I once sent [Moshe] Arens* to see

---

* A former ambassador to the United States, Arens also served as Israel's defense minister.

Shultz because Peres's plan was to bring us to a general conference with all the Arab countries and the permanent members of the United Nations Security Council.

I was against this because it was clear what the decision of such a forum would be: it would always be against us. I was interested that the United States' position was to oppose such a conference, and that was so for a long time; Shultz was against it. I asked him, "What is your interest in bringing the Soviets into this game?"

King Hussein   I will always treasure my first contact with President Reagan. I wish it had been possible for me to continue in the same way — when I was able to reach him directly and put a problem before him in black and white. When he focused on an issue, things moved in a different way. I respected him for that.

Vice President Bush and Israel

Yitzhak Shamir   Bush was always against us. He doesn't like Jews — not he, and not his wife. That we know. Bush believes that he lost the presidency because of his confrontation with Israel. I have no contact with him. I am friendly with Shultz and with Baker. He [Baker] said it was not he but Bush who was against us.

We had heard, when Bush was vice president, that he was against us in cabinet consultations, that his position was always against us, for example, in the bombing of the Iraqi reactor and about the Golan. We knew that he was always against us. But in the Reagan years his position was not so important for us because it was not decisive.

Secretary of State Shultz and Israel

On July 16, 1982, Shultz, an executive of the Bechtel Corporation who had served as a cabinet officer in the Nixon administration, succeeded Alexander M. Haig Jr. as secretary of state.

King Hussein   I had known Mr. Shultz before he became secretary of state, and I had a great deal of respect and admiration for him. But unfortunately, I think that we never saw eye to eye on a number of matters, starting with the Lebanese crisis, where I warned that there were dangers and suggested a different course.

But unfortunately, this was taken badly, not as advice from a friend.

Since then, this [relationship] deteriorated — like the attempt to focus on the Arab-Israeli issue, and the Palestinian problem as well.

But this is all in the past, and now we hope we are on the threshold not only of having achieved peace but of building peace in this region.

A high official of Israel, who declined to speak for attribution, informed us that at one time the Israelis thought it would be a good idea for Secretary of State Shultz to name Henry Kissinger as a special envoy to the Middle East so that the Israelis would have a good friend in Washington.

The Israelis asked a friendly intermediary in Washington to ask Shultz whether this could be done. According to our source, Shultz asked the intermediary, "Why don't you think that a non-Jewish person can be friendly to Israel? And secondly, do you really think that two serious people can deal together on one issue?"

Benjamin Ze'ev Begin, son of Israeli Prime Minister Menachem Begin
When Shultz was appointed, the feeling was that, because of his association with Bechtel, here was another Arabist. But it was a very nice surprise to see that Shultz was a man of high caliber and a square person.

Yitzhak Shamir In our first meeting he expressed to me, unofficially, that his relationship to Bechtel had nothing to do with his views on Israel, and that there was a necessity that the United States help Israel. So it was a good beginning.

Charles Hill The general feeling in the Middle East bureau was that Haig was pro-Israel and that Shultz would be pro-Arab. Haig was seen to be very definitively, overtly pro-Israel, more so than any other American leader in government at that time.

There was the feeling that any change would change this. It was assumed that as Shultz was from Bechtel — and since Bechtel was involved in a number of major projects in Saudi Arabia — Shultz would have a very different point of view, [and] that this would change the very nature of American foreign policy in its most severely tested area, the Arab-Israeli crisis.

Shultz was entirely fair and evenhanded. He walked into the middle of a war. There were those who simply wanted to stop the war, no matter what, and those who said we should find the right way to stop it, under the right terms.

Shultz wanted to do that. In that sense, he carried through what Haig had begun, although it got much more complicated and difficult than it had been during Haig's tenure.

Shimon Peres I had first met him when he was secretary of labor in the Nixon administration. He had paid a visit to Saudi Arabia and had come back through Israel. He called me — I was then, as I am now, in the opposition — and we sat together for two or three hours, and we started a friendship. And he was considered our friend throughout the Reagan years.

Yitzhak Shamir Shultz is a very decent man. He didn't play games with us; he told us what he thought, more or less. And we tried to be loyal to the United States. Of course, after the *Intifada* [Palestinian uprising] broke out [in 1987], Shultz hesitated because he feared that the Palestinians would glean something from this confrontation. But there was nothing to fear. My thought was, It will take time, but we will win. And it was so.

Barry Schweid I had covered Kissinger. He would never admit to any error, any fault of his. He would complain if you wrote that he had failed.

Now, Henry Kissinger had the AP and UPI wires somehow come to his plane. He always wanted to know how what he was doing was being reported, so on the plane, as he was going to the next stop, he would see the reporting on the previous stop. He'd come roaring back to the press section: "What do you mean, I failed? I never told you we were going to succeed."

Here I am on the plane with Shultz, and we come up front, and he's on the record, and I ask him, "Well, how did you make out?" And he says, "I failed. I got no place with them." And I'm looking at him. What? He was big enough, he had the character to say, "I failed." So I found him a remarkable person.

George P. Shultz When I came into office, there were two wars going on: there was the Iran-Iraq War — that we had no connection with — and there was the war in Lebanon, which was stopped fairly quickly.

Of course, we had our catastrophe there, but there were no more wars having to do with the Arab-Israeli conflict during the Reagan administration. There was a lot of effort and contact, and this was part of it. And we also had a very big part in getting the Iran-Iraq War to stop.

Geoffrey Kemp   [Shultz] became very supportive of the Likud position on a lot of issues. Only toward the end of the Reagan presidency did he become more hardheaded, when he helped to bring about the change in U.S. policy toward the PLO.

Barry Schweid   I was almost never surprised, but Shultz's action in opening a dialogue with the PLO stunned me. It was one of the most remarkable, unexpected developments since I had started as a reporter in Washington in 1956. I was stupefied by it.

I tried to ask a question at a news conference and actually choked, which surprised me. To look at Shultz, whom I had great respect for, and still do — those honest blue eyes — I knew that this was totally out of synch with the things he had tried in the Middle East. I was just amazed.

We kept going back to the Middle East; we must have gone twenty times. Once one of the correspondents asked Shultz, "Why do you keep bringing us back here?" And Shultz, who was not often emotional, said, "What else have I got to do with my time that is more important?"

But he really meant it. At that point, you realized that his settlement proposal was unlikely to go over, but his point was that this was important work.

Secretary of Defense Weinberger and Israel

Eitan Haber   Weinberger was the bad guy; Reagan was the good guy. Rabin had very warm relationships with American officials in general, but it was not the same with Weinberger. But we received everything we wanted from the Reagan administration, although the president was critical of our handling of the *Intifada*. He was likely influenced in this by the U.S. media.

Nimrod Novick   In the American Jewish community, Weinberger was dubbed an enemy from the outset. People in the American Jewish community perceived him as hostile to anything Israeli and Jewish, and they behaved accordingly, and sooner or later he started to react, which is only natural and regrettable.

But we didn't want to push him into a corner by attacking him. I was trying to judge him on the merits of what he was doing, and I didn't see anything hostile in his actions or in his statements or in his deeds. I saw a very capable man trying to the best of his abilities to fill the position of secretary of defense — and not everything he did in favor of the Saudis was, by definition, anti-Israel. But the truth of the matter is that eventually his was the less friendly voice in a very, very friendly administration.

Richard Secord I was with him on his first tour to Israel after he became secretary of defense, in early September 1982. I was the only senior official with him. People have accused him of being anti-Semitic. In my view, he is not anti-Jewish. But he was of a mind that the U.S. had to have more than one friend in the Middle East.

He believed that the Begin government was extreme in some regards and was not operating in the best interests of the United States. I think that he was basically correct, but he took a lot of heat over it.

Geoffrey Kemp I can't explain his particular anger toward Israel. But the Pentagon as an institution was extremely antagonistic about Israel in those days, to put it mildly.

The moment the oil crisis hit in 1973–74, the prevailing view in the Pentagon was: the Gulf is a critical, strategic region we have to be prepared to fight for. The fall of the Shah [of Iran] made it more important to have good relations with the Arabs. And then the Soviet invasion of Afghanistan [in December 1979] was the last straw. The Carter administration enunciated a truly dramatic doctrine — the Carter Doctrine — which said that we would fight for the defense of the Gulf. That required an extraordinary logistical and planning effort, particularly because the Russians were seen as part of the problem in those days.

The Arab Community and Israel

Adnan Khashoggi, Saudi Arabian financier In the heart of the Arabs, I have never seen people hating Jews. We mix with Jews in Paris, in New York; we go to parties with them; Jewish lawyers represent us. So how can this contradiction exist, you ask yourself? It doesn't.

If my neighbor starts making noises and poking holes in the door, of course I get angry. I go outside; I knock his face; I say, "Stop this!" And suddenly I find it has nothing to do with the Frenchman who is on the other side. It was not hatred, but a neighbors' clash between the Jews and the Arabs. The peace process proves this — outside of Hamas [Islamic Resistance Movement], who are serving other interests.

I have sat together with Peres many times. No one was as pro-peace as Peres. Even Rabin was not that hot. He had a military mind; he was still afraid. He was closer to the Likud [position] than Peres was.

I sat with Menachem Begin before Sadat's visit to Jerusalem [in November 1977]. I spent three hours with him. I talked for ten minutes, and he gave me a lecture on the Jewish Bible. He was really convinced that these territories — Jerusalem — were all his.

So I said to him, "What is the long-range thinking? You will go, and your children will remain. Do you think that the Arabs are not going to be sophisticated and well educated? They will have weapons. How long will it last when we start burning the oil fields? We can live on dates and camels, but the Americans can't. They will turn against you; there will come a time." So he looks at me and says, "That will be a long time."

The Iraqi Reactor Bombing:
An Early Point of Tension

On June 7, 1981, the Israeli Air Force attacked the Iraqi nuclear reactor then under construction at Osirak, near Baghdad.

Yehiel Kadishai   The issue was debated in the Israeli cabinet on quite a few occasions; there was a process of convincing some members of the cabinet, who opposed the raid. It took time — over a few months — until there was a majority in favor of executing this operation.

It was not so much that people were against the raid; they were hesitant. But when our experts said that when the center of the reactor will become hot — this was the expression they used — it will be impossible to do the operation without harming hundreds of thousands of innocent Iraqis, the cabinet was convinced of the importance of immediate action.

Begin knew that he would take heat. Peres said that it would hurt relations with Egypt, but Sadat, whom Begin had seen only a few days prior to the raid, said, "I am against what he did, but he was right not to tell me." The Labor Party in Israel said that Begin did it as a trick before the elections. This was a stupid claim, because, God forbid, if something would have happened to our pilots . . . It is not a calculated risk before an election.

The operation took place on the eve of Shavuot. The prime minister was at his home in Jerusalem. I was told to be at [his] residence in the afternoon. At about half past three, the prime minister came in, and then, one by one, the other ministers came in, and they didn't know what they were coming for.

They gathered in one room, and Begin told me to sit in his study.

There was a direct line to the chief of staff. Begin dictated a statement to me in Hebrew, and from the statement I understood that they were already on their way. And then came the call on the direct line, and Begin learned that the boys were about to land in Israel. He then went into the room and told the ministers what had happened and read to the cabinet members the statement he would make after the operation was publicized and it was clear that we had done it.

There was emotion in the room. The cabinet members shook hands, but they were worried. What is the world going to say? And it was exactly as they expected; the world condemned us in the sharpest terms. It is illegal, dangerous, a catastrophe.

Geoffrey Kemp It was a dramatic event. The consensus was that it was a political ploy by Begin to get reelected. The polls showed Peres ten points ahead; we were all hoping for a Peres victory.

The bombing was a clear violation of the norms of international relations. Iraq was a signatory to the NPT [non-proliferation treaty]; even Jeane Kirkpatrick supported anti-Israeli resolutions at the UN.

Yehiel Kadishai Begin had been sad for some months — his wife, Aliza, noticed this, but he couldn't tell her what made him so sad — when he saw the children walking in the streets, going to school. He would think, What's going to happen to them when this wild leader of Iraq, Saddam Hussein, will have this terrible instrument in his hands?

We had informed the Reagan administration that Iraq was in the process of developing the capability of producing nuclear weapons. As the planes were on their way back from the attack, we gave a report to the U.S. ambassador, [Samuel] Lewis. There was an outcry from all over the world, even from Mr. Reagan. We had anticipated this reaction. We had been warned by Peres in a letter a few months earlier. We would be, he said, "like a tree that grows lonely in the desert; no one will talk to us."

Then came the flood — the avalanche of condemnation from all over the world.

Benjamin Ze'ev Begin It was a very disappointing reaction, knowing that our action served not only Israel but democracy. We didn't expect that people in North America would give us an official blessing, but to condemn it was simply unfair. And then, only nine years later [during the Gulf War early in 1991], people scratched their heads and said, "Oh God, if they would have had the reactor, where would America be?"

Israel's 1981 Elections

Geoffrey Kemp One generalization you could make about the United States and Israel is that since 1973 — really since the first disengagement agreements that Kissinger negotiated — American strategic interests, and America's moral sense of the rights and wrongs of the Palestinian problem, have been very much in favor of a territorial compromise, as set down in UN resolutions 242 and 338. It was the cornerstone of the Carter administration; it became the cornerstone of the Reagan, Bush, and Clinton administrations.

Now, once you accept that principle of withdrawal for peace, you are inevitably at loggerheads with a political party in Israel [the Likud] that completely rejects that in its philosophy; that wishes to retain the West Bank; that argues that Israeli settlers have as much right to be in Judea and Samaria as anyone else and that we should create facts on the ground to make it impossible to withdraw.

The sense of every administration has been that the Likud policy was disastrous for America, for Israel, and for the Palestinians, and that it would foment endless conflict in a region of growing strategic importance, when it was important for us to have the Israelis and the Arabs on the same side.

So no matter how graceful and gentlemanly the Likud Party members were who came here, I cannot recall any official ever endorsing the principles they stood for. Therefore, the assumption was that if Peres became prime minister, the peace process would start up again.

The AWACS Sale

Very early in his administration, President Reagan had to decide whether to fulfill a commitment made to Saudi Arabia by President Carter to sell that country AWACS (airborne warning and control system) aircraft.

Despite strong opposition by Israel and its supporters in the United States, the administration went ahead with the sale after conducting a strenuous lobbying effort in the Congress.

Richard Secord The Reagan administration lived up, to the commitment made under Carter. They didn't want to; it was quite a big bite to have to take in the first days of that presidency. It was a courageous decision of Reagan's. I guess I'm the only one of the gang who has called him a coward in public, but I give him full credit for the AWACS.

If the Saudis hadn't gotten the AWACS, the Gulf War would have been quite different. So it was absolutely crucial.

The Carter administration recognized the importance of the sale. They were hardly flaming supporters of Saudi Arabia, but it was crucial then, and history has shown it to be a wise thing to do.

Geoffrey Kemp In retrospect, Desert Storm [the U.S. military operation in the Gulf War] couldn't have happened without all this prior Pentagon activity in Saudi Arabia. Weinberger and his personality — and his particular anger toward Begin and Sharon — is one thing; the Pentagon's position on Israel was quite another. The view was that, "Yes, Israel is a friend, but they should not have a veto over strategic decisions that affect America's most forward deployment of forces in a critical area. Goddamn it! They're the ones who are going to benefit from this!" That was not just Weinberger; it was everybody else in the Department of Defense.

Essential for our strategy was to have well-equipped Arab allies, from Jordan to Bahrain, with the Saudis being particularly important. The Pentagon always saw Saudi Arabia as an enormous potential strategic asset; the Israelis always saw Saudi Arabia as a potential threat.

Therein you have a fundamental difference of opinion. If your mandate is to defend the oil and fight the Russians as far forward as possible, you have to have Saudi Arabia, and they must have as much air surveillance as possible, particularly since they have the money to pay for it.

So this was not a simple issue of liking, or disliking, the Israelis. It was a question of strategic priorities. That was what the whole AWACS debate was about.

Opposition to the Sale

Richard Secord I was the head of the team that fought it through the Senate. It took most of 1981 and was excruciatingly difficult. There was a terribly close vote in the Senate, but we won by four votes. Two senators shifted at the very last minute, under great pressure from us.

The opposition of the Israeli government to the sale was very strong. I talked with Begin personally. Their air force commander was hardheadedly and dumbheadedly against it; I argued with him until I was blue in the face. Some have said that it was American supporters of Israel who opposed the sale, not for military or strategic reasons, but because it was an arms sale into the Arab world. This was something they always opposed.

Begin came to the United States on a state visit. It was agreed it wouldn't be on the agenda for public comment. Then he went to New

York and blasted it. So I said to my colleagues in the Pentagon, "That's it. We don't trust him, and we are not going to trust him." I didn't question Begin's sincerity.

We have a still-secret agreement with the Saudis.* I wrote the draft and negotiated it with Prince Bandar and briefed it to the crown prince, now King Fahd, and it is still the rules of the road. We could never have gotten it through the Senate otherwise. It was a considerable concession of sovereignty by the Saudis.

Getting the Sale Approved by the Senate

Richard Secord This was going to be a bare-knuckles fight. We were not going to build a consensus; we were going to drive it down their throats. That was what we had to do in the end. I was placed in charge. We went up the Hill in the military way.

Uri Simhoni Who cares about the AWACS? I cannot see how the AWACS sale influenced our security. It was business; millions of dollars were involved.

Benjamin Ze'ev Begin If there is a proclaimed policy that the United States should see to it that Israel retains its so-called edge — its technological and scientific edge — then one should understand that the net, ultimate result of such sales to Arab countries who do not have a peace treaty with us is inherently contradictory to the policy.

I would put it on the table bluntly, directly: the decision on the AWACS sale heralded a stream of top-line technology being sold to the Arabs that continues today.

The Lebanon War

On June 2, 1982, Arab terrorists shot and seriously wounded Shlomo Argov, Israel's ambassador to the United Kingdom, in London. Four days later Israel launched Operation Peace for the Galilee, a military incursion into Lebanon that would have far-reaching ramifications for U.S. policy in the Middle East.

Yehiel Kadishai The PLO in Lebanon was a state-within-a-state. They had their own army of almost one hundred thousand men; they had huge amounts of weapons and ammunition in bunkers; and they would de-

---

* The agreement is that the Saudis will use the AWACS only defensively.

velop into a more organized army. Their aim was to destroy Israel, to annihilate us. It's true that we were stronger, but if one day the PLO would succeed in having a certain territory — even smaller than Jericho — they would declare this territory an independent Palestinian state, which would be recognized the same day by many other countries and by the United Nations.

This state would then claim the implementation of the United Nations resolution of November 29, 1947: they would claim Lod [the site of Israel's international Ben Gurion Airport], Ramla, Jaffa, and an internationalized Jerusalem. And if you are a statesman and you worry about the next generations, you should anticipate such a development.

The danger was that such a Palestinian army, which called itself the PLO, wanted to "liberate Palestine." You have to do everything possible to prevent this enemy from fulfilling its aims.

Rafi Eitan, adviser to the Israeli prime minister on defense and security; member of the Defense Committee, Israeli Ministry of Defense We were under constant threat in the north from the growing terror organizations of the PLO. You must remember that in 1982 the PLO was an organization of about fourteen groups, and these groups had headquarters in Beirut. They occupied key areas in Lebanon, including Beirut, and the Lebanese government, which was a weak government because of the friction among the various parties [a friction that exists to this day among the Christians, Druze, Shia, and Sunni], helped them to do that.

Let's say that when they [the PLO] conquered half of the Shia area, the Shia at the time couldn't do anything. So we felt that sooner or later we would face a big problem in the north. So the decision was made to act — to push them out.

Yitzhak Shamir Shultz and Reagan thought we were putting too much pressure on the Lebanese. The Americans didn't understand the situation in Lebanon; they thought we were exaggerating. Their point was that the Lebanese have to be independent. I once had a conversation with McFarlane, and I told him he did not understand the situation. I said, "Lebanon is not a free country. If you think they have their own army, their own intelligence, you are wrong."

Benjamin Ze'ev Begin Haig was a true friend. It was very telling for me, coming from a friend, when Haig said that America would not understand an action by Israel in Lebanon unless there would be an unusual amount of bloodshed. This was unacceptable. I don't think that any foreign country should have the ability, or the moral responsibility, for judging how much bloodshed is reasonable.

If this comes from Haig, how can I expect others to behave? Or to feel? Or to act? How much bloodshed is reasonable? Two people killed? Five people killed? What's reasonable for the United States? How much bloodshed is a reasonable amount in order for the United States to act upon it?

Israel must be able to retain its strategic independence. That was my lesson: we must develop — and retain — an economic, strategic, military ability to be in a position to defend ourselves.

Geoffrey Kemp   Fairly soon after his meeting with Sadat, Reagan started to say, in salutations to letters, "Dear Anwar." So then it had to be "Dear Menachem." This was in 1981. Now comes 1982, and Begin is bombing Beirut, and Reagan is still writing, "Dear Menachem."

I had to go down and brief Jimmy Carter two or three days after the Lebanon War started, and that was one of the things he was furious about — I had taken him the correspondence. He says, "Goddamn it! Why does he keep calling him 'Menachem'? This is the time to say, 'Dear Mr. Prime Minister.' This will get his attention. I wrote to Begin in 1977 — when they invaded Lebanon the first time* — and I wrote, 'Dear Mr. Prime Minister, you will be out of Lebanon in seventy-two hours. Sincerely, Jimmy Carter.' And Begin said, 'Mr. President, what else could I do? You are the president of the United States.'" Carter's view was that Reagan was a softy who didn't know how to deal with these people.

Richard Murphy, ambassador to Saudi Arabia; assistant secretary of state for Near Eastern and South Asian affairs   The Saudis' position was very consistent: we want to see a peace settlement; those who must make peace are the front-line states — Egypt, Jordan, Lebanon, and the Palestinians. When they have agreements, you will find the rest of us ready to come to agreements ourselves.

We considered the Saudis to be definitely supportive of the peace process, but definitely not willing to be out in front. They were very upset by the Israeli invasion of Lebanon in 1982. I was in Jedda at that time. They received President Reagan's special envoy, Philip Habib. They expressed their great unhappiness about the Israeli invasion of Lebanon.

---

* An IDF (Israel Defense Forces) unit went into Lebanon, as far as the Litani River, in 1977, in order to respond to repeated terrorist attacks against Israel.

John Poindexter   Beirut was a terrible mistake from the beginning. Once the Israelis went into Beirut, we were in a very difficult position. We felt we would have to do something to stabilize the situation or we would have serious problems.

The Defense Department — to put it mildly — was not enthusiastic about going into Beirut. As a result, our troops were badly deployed and not used very effectively.

General Ariel Sharon and the Lebanon War

Ariel Sharon, Israel's minister of defense during the Lebanon War—and then, as now, one of the most controversial figures in Israel—played a major role in the formulation of the policy that would take Israeli troops beyond that nation's previously stated forty-kilometer objective.

One of the more intensely debated issues of the war was whether the Reagan administration had known in advance of Sharon's intention to move Israeli troops into Beirut. A source familiar with Secretary of State Haig's activities stated his view that Haig knew ahead of time that Israeli forces were going into Beirut—not that Haig encouraged them, but that he didn't inform the Israelis of how seriously their move would be taken by the administration, and that he did nothing to stop them from moving into the Lebanese capital.

Rafi Eitan   We were supported by the United States. At the time, General Haig was the secretary of state, and the first decision was to go up to forty kilometers [from the northern border of Israel]. Then, when we were there — by the way, forty kilometers is up to the suburbs of Beirut, if you take a direct line from the northern part of Israel directly toward Beirut — that development pushed the government to decide to go farther and to join with the Christians in Beirut.

Haig was for the war; at the beginning, everybody was for the war. Haig left office in the middle of the war. All the time that Haig was secretary of state I think that the United States fully supported the war, that they agreed to the whole intent of the war.

Eitan Haber   Rabin was sure that Haig had given Sharon a green light on Lebanon. But in many discussions Rabin had with him, Haig said this was not true.

Geoffrey Kemp   I don't believe for one minute that Haig gave the Israelis a green light; we can be absolutely certain that he did not give Sharon a green light. Sharon was the type of individual [to whom if] you said explicitly, and preferably in writing, "General, if you put your forces into this area, we will cut off military aid to Israel within twenty-four hours," that would have been a red light. Anything short of that to Sharon could have been worse — he interpreted the absence of a red light as a green light.

Uri Simhoni   If there was a green light, I am sure it was for what he [Sharon] presented as his plan, not for what the real plan was. He may have said, "I would like to do *a*, *b*, and *c*," and have gotten the green light, and then he went there and did *d* to *z*. That is Arik Sharon's way of getting the green light.

I was a paratrooper all my life. Arik Sharon was my battalion commander forty years ago. I believe that at that time he was a military genius as a field commander. But not in the 1980s and the 1990s.

In the war in Lebanon, purely militarily, he was not good. I was the deputy commander of the northern command during this war, so I was very close to him. Every day I saw the way he reacted, and I made a note to myself that he was no longer first-class. He was ready to listen only to people who thought the way he did. This was part of the closing of his mind; he became narrow-minded. I believe that he still lives in the 1960s.

Alexander M. Haig Jr.   In the spring of 1982 Sharon came and briefed a plan, one option of which was to go all the way up to Beirut. Not only was he told no in the open meeting, but he was then brought into my office, and I told him no again. And on top of that, there was a very strong message sent by me to Begin, telling him, "No way!"

So the "green light" stuff is just pure hogwash. It is absolutely untrue that I gave Sharon a green light.

Richard Murphy   He was a jump ahead of Begin. Sharon fell into a trap of assuming that an army could kill an idea. The PLO was an idea as much as it was an organization. As an organization, it was a shambles. As an idea, it was kept well alive; you couldn't shoot it. Sharon was going to eliminate the PLO by his moves in the Bekaa Valley and up the coast — and just shell it to death. It didn't work.

The Shelling in Beirut

During the war U.S. officials frequently expressed consternation over Israel's tactics. A vivid example involved American perceptions of Israel's bombing of Beirut on August 12, 1982.

We were present at a meeting that Prime Minister Begin held in the Knesset that day with a delegation of fifty-five American Christian clergymen. Addressing the group, the Israeli leader outlined his vision of a new Middle East in which Israel, Lebanon, and Egypt would be linked economically and culturally—a linkage that would be the first step toward a broad-based Middle East peace.

Uri Simhoni   The shelling in Beirut, which some people described as a holocaust, was very ineffective. It caused little damage and casualties, and it was highly exaggerated; most of the shelling was not in the populated area. We didn't want to cause heavy casualties in Beirut; we were mostly hitting empty areas.

I told General Eitan, the chief of staff, "Look, we are only hitting rats on the ground, not the PLO. Why not the PLO? Why don't we hit the headquarters?" It's a war. If you go to war, you should do what has to be done and [not] pay any attention to political factors. If not, then don't go to war. If you do go to war, there is no half a war, because if you do half a war, it will be a disaster militarily; the number of casualties will be high. War has to be short, powerful, and decisive. No matter how strong you are, never be involved in a long war, because it will destroy everything morally, economically, and militarily. There are no winners in long wars.

The August 12 Telephone Call

Richard Murphy   Reagan was deeply upset by the bombardment of Beirut. Pictures came in of a baby with an arm blown off in the streets of Beirut that really grabbed the president. He made it very plain that he wanted this to come to a stop when the human side was pushed in his face.

Geoffrey Kemp   Reagan had seen all these pictures of the bombing of Beirut. He had been watching television — he was an active video man; if you wanted to really impress him, you sent him videos — and he was furious.

He said, "I have to talk to Menachem." I monitored the call, and Reagan used the memorable phrase, "Menachem, this is a holocaust," to which Begin bristled — you could almost feel it on the telephone — "Mr. President, I know all about a holocaust."*

---

* Begin's parents and other family members who had lived in Brest Litovsk, Poland, were murdered during World War II in the Nazi genocide against European Jewry that came to be known as the Holocaust.

Then Reagan essentially said, "It's got to stop." And then it did stop. That is the only occasion I can remember of Reagan's truly choking with anger.

Rafi Eitan   As far as I know, Begin got a call from the president. Begin asked the government to gather; the meeting was held in the Knesset, not in the normal place. During this meeting there was a very tough discussion between Minister of Defense Sharon and Prime Minister Begin, and Begin ordered Sharon to stop the bombing. Sharon gave his reason for why he felt the bombing should go on. There were harsh words between the two. I was in the middle. And at the end Sharon gave in and the bombing was stopped.

Benjamin Ze'ev Begin   As far as I remember, when the president called it was already after the prime minister had ordered the army to discontinue the bombing.

The relevant detail on that issue was that the prime minister was surprised, not by Mr. Reagan, but by the action — by the bombing — something that he referred to later, in the government. He was asked, in the cabinet, whether he knew about the bombing, and he said, "I know everything, sometimes beforehand, and sometimes post facto."

Howard Teicher   Begin was shocked when Reagan basically read him a speech — that we had prepared — which seemed, finally, to get through to him, [saying] that as much as the president liked Israel and liked Begin, he was not happy with the way in which the U.S. believed Israel was treating America, in the context of the war and in the nature of the communications between the two leaders.

I don't think that the president was particularly comfortable doing that. He clearly had a great deal of affection and admiration for Israel, the underdog, the island of democracy in the sea of totalitarians; all the labels you can think of would apply.

It was unnatural for Reagan to be harsh; he was quite forgiving. During the war, when the people at State in particular were pushing for very harsh measures against Israel — as was Weinberger — Reagan said, "No. That's not how we treat an ally. They have a problem; we have to work with them."

That, of course, did not prevent Weinberger from doing whatever he could do unilaterally — which he consistently did [and] which the president never upbraided him for. There was a contradiction there.

Charles Hill   We now had the opportunity to bring it to a conclusion. I felt that something truly remarkable was happening: that very clearly the Israeli government had split; that the prime minister was being lied to by his defense minister; that he [General Sharon] was telling the prime minister, "We are not shelling," [and] at the same time he was saying, "Shell them some more"; and that this was preventing any conclusion to this war.

Alexander M. Haig Jr.   Reagan was tempted to react in the wrong way after the [Israeli bombing of the] Iraqi reactor. But foreign policy is not run on chemistry; it's got to be run on interests. And those interests were as strong then as they've ever been.

Begin was a hard man to love. There were a lot of reasons for that; he wasn't a Hollywood character. But I don't think Reagan had any problems with him until the Lebanon invasion.

When Lebanon occurred, the president decided that he was going to listen to the other side on this issue, and that was Weinberger and Bill Clark and Jim Baker. And that's a shame.

The Deployment of a Multinational Force

George P. Shultz   The Israelis were putting a lot of pressure on Beirut. We had started a process of negotiation designed to get the PLO fighters out of Beirut. It had just started, and the idea of a U.S., Italian, and French multinational force had been agreed to and was already in play. It was present when I became secretary of state, and I carried it forward.

Rafi Eitan   [Yassir] Arafat, as head of the PLO, was pushed out of Beirut at the time. I say to everybody who wants to listen that if Arafat had not been pushed out of Beirut, but had stayed in Beirut up to this very day, we wouldn't have been able to have the peace process, because the Syrians — Assad — wouldn't enable Arafat to go into negotiations with us. Not if Arafat were in Beirut to this day.

So indirectly the 1982 war caused Arafat to be weak, and the result was that he was ready to come and negotiate with Israel. In Beirut he was not able to do that.

King Hussein   When the troops landed, my view was that there should have been a clear position, insisting on the withdrawal of all foreign troops from Lebanon — meaning not only the Israeli forces but other forces that were there with the idea that they were protecting Lebanon against the Israelis. The attitude should be one of trying to recover Lebanon's sovereignty over its territories as a whole, and enabling the Lebanese to have a dialogue to resolve the problem.

I was therefore shocked to learn later that there was a question of a treaty with Israel. I realized that this treaty wasn't going to work. I said that it wouldn't work, and unfortunately I was proven right in terms of the terrible disaster in Beirut and everything that followed.

But instead of the views I articulated being taken at face value — as the views of a sincere friend — there was a lot of animosity and hostility from the architects of that policy. That was the beginning of the deterioration of our relations with America, which continued to slide until recently.

Giandomenico Picco The arrogance of Secretary Shultz in the Middle East was one of the reasons why the Reagan administration never did anything there. The Arabs are very nice people, but they don't like to be taken for granted.

When Secretary Shultz in 1982 got his agreement at the end of the year in Lebanon, and then, because he didn't consult the Syrians — which the embassy in Damascus had tried many times to convince him to do — the Syrians said, "Well, the secretary of state thinks he has an agreement with us. We will show him!" And the agreement folded in 1983, and he was then viscerally against the Middle East because he felt humiliated. He thought he could make an agreement in Lebanon without talking to Syria.

Abraham Tamir, director general, Israeli Prime Minister's Office; general officer, Israel Defense Forces (IDF); national security adviser to Prime Minister Shimon Peres; director general of the Israeli Foreign Ministry After we negotiated the peace treaty with Lebanon, I came with Shamir to Washington. We went to the White House; we were sitting on one side, and Reagan, Shultz, Weinberger, and their people were on the other side. Shultz said, "After signing this agreement with Lebanon, we have to continue with the peace process with Jordan and the Palestinians. Syria should be isolated from the peace process."

But we were left without the agreement,* the multinational force was evacuated, and we began to suffer casualties in Lebanon from Shiite terrorism.

---

* The agreement was abandoned after the assassination on September 14, 1982, of the Lebanese president-elect, Bashir Gemayel, in the bombing of his Beirut headquarters.

Rafi Eitan   Later on, when Bashir Gemayel was killed — murdered — the decision was made to occupy Beirut and to push the PLO out of the city altogether. No doubt, in the Israeli government at the time there was a discussion as to whether to go up to forty kilometers or to go further. But no doubt all steps were approved and decided by the government.

I was one of the few who took part in all meetings — all government meetings, all military headquarters meetings, and most of the meetings between the minister of defense and the commander in chief. And there was not one move that was done without the approval of the government.

It is true that most of the ministers at the time didn't realize that the war could go up to Beirut, though some of them had questions. In the first meeting — where there was a decision to go to war — there were questions: What would happen if the Syrians became involved? What would happen if we were not able to push the PLO groups outside range? What should we do? The reply was: We will go farther.

Sabra and Shatilla

On the evening of September 17, a unit of the Phalangist Lebanese Forces entered the Palestinian refugee camps known as Sabra and Shatilla. Once inside the camps, the militia, ostensibly searching for PLO weapons caches, carried out the massacre of somewhere between 250 and 700 civilians.

A commission of judicial inquiry was established by Prime Minister Begin to investigate the massacre. On February 8, 1983, the commission, headed by Israel's chief justice, Yitzhak Kahan, reported on its findings: Israeli officials had been remiss in failing to anticipate the possibility of a massacre by Phalangist forces entering the camps after the killing of their leader, President-elect Bashir Gemayel.

The Kahan Commission also sharply criticized Israeli officials for not immediately ordering the Phalangists from the camps once it was known that a massacre was taking place.

Rafi Eitan   The question of Sabra and Shatilla caused a big discussion in Israel. The issue was brought before the court, and the court decided that it should have been anticipated.

It's very difficult to say how you could anticipate it. No one really anticipated it in the military command, not even the people who discovered what was happening and warned the Ministry of Defense about it. Anyway, we didn't get any alarm call beforehand from the intelligence services.

Both camps were bases of the PLO; a lot of weapons were found there. But it does not help to analyze it today. I remember when the war was over, I was asked, "Do you know that Yassir Arafat said that although

he left Beirut, he left many guerrilla people with weapons in all these settlements and camps in Lebanon?"

I said, "Yes, he did." And for a few months this caused a lot of trouble. Again, that's warfare. In guerrilla warfare, people are killed; there is
a risk for civilians. Believe me, Prime Minister Peres did not intend that
anything like this would happen [referring to an incident that took place
in Lebanon in April 1996, during an Israeli military operation].

Could you ask today that he should anticipate that people would go as
refugees to a UN camp and that the camp's borders would be bombed?
It happened. In any war things like that happen. That has been my experience in about five or more Israeli wars.

Yehiel Kadishai One of the most terrible distortions of events that took
place was what emerged from the Kahan Commission; they came to conclusions that were harmful, that were false. I was sitting next to the prime
minister when he answered the commission's questions. He answered
every question without hesitation, [and] without any lawyer.

They did not accuse him. They said that, as prime minister, he had to
have known in advance that such things would happen — if the Phalangists would enter into the camps, terrible things would happen. The
prime minister was surprised by the commission's conclusions because
he knew the truth: that we did no wrong.

The Phalangists wanted to clear the two camps of the terrorists.
Everyone knew that there were many, many terrorists in Sabra and
Shatilla, and they got permission to enter and do the job. We had felt that
they hadn't done enough in our fight against the PLO. We had losses,
and then they had the fruits of getting the terrorists out of Lebanon.

So they did fight the terrorists, but they also massacred civilians in
revenge against the deeds of the Palestinians. So how did Begin say it?
"The goyim kill goyim, and the Jews are to blame; the Christians kill
Muslims, and the Jews are to blame."

This is what happened. No one of our people could imagine that they
would kill women and children. Unfortunately, these are some of the
characters we have to live with in the Middle East.

The Deployment of Another Multinational Force

Geoffrey Kemp I came to Washington two or three days after Sabra and
Shatilla happened. The most ominous political legacy was that the decision to send back the U.S. marine force that was then on ships off the
coast of Naples was based entirely on the emotional shock of Sabra and
Shatilla.

Whereas the first deployment of the multinational forces had been highly specific — with the goal of getting Arafat and the PLO out of Beirut; the moment it was successful Weinberger pulled them — the second mission was open-ended. There was no clear delineation of responsibilities; there was no time limit; everyone was writing their own mission statement as to what the force should be doing.

Howard Teicher   It was my view that the exercise of American diplomacy which was trying to stop the fighting among the Israelis, the Palestinians, and the Syrians — and the separate but related goal of the removal of the Palestinian fighters from Lebanon through diplomatic means — required some increase in American power in Lebanon.

To that end, U.S. diplomats, led by Philip Habib, cleverly negotiated an arrangement whereby a multinational force would be assembled to protect the Palestinians during the departure of their fighters [in August 1982 after their rout by Israeli forces]. The essence of the mission was not combat; it was confidence-building — leverage-building — in order to convince the Palestinians to leave Beirut and its environs. It was the goal also of the Israelis, U.S. diplomacy, and the Lebanese Christian community.

None of us had coordinated how we would achieve these goals. The Israelis were trying to do it militarily, as were the Christian Lebanese, and we sought to do it diplomatically. I don't think that the Palestinians would have agreed without the presence of American military power. They would have gone down fighting, and there would have been that much more bloodshed in Beirut.

John W. Vessey   I suppose that the assassination of Bashir Gemayel and Sabra and Shatilla would have taken place whether we had been there or not. The [Joint] Chiefs and Weinberger wanted the marines to leave. Then, of course, after the massacre we didn't want to go back in, but there wasn't any good argument for not going back in.

For us, it was: What are we to do? American military forces are reared in the doctrine that says that if you are going to use the forces, you need to give them a task to perform. What is it that you want them to do? Well, we never got a sufficiently defined task that either we or the forces on the ground really understood.

Perhaps the contributing factor to the fact that we lost the marines was the fact that there was this debate about whether or not we should stay or not stay. For me personally, it was the saddest day of my military career.

Weinberger's Opposition to the Deployment

Howard Teicher Weinberger did not want U.S. power to be perceived among the Arab community, in any way, shape, or form, as being associated with Israeli power. The fact is that everyone perceived U.S. power as being allied with Israeli power. But Weinberger wanted to delay its reality, and he did everything in his power to try to prevent the deployment and, once the deployments were made, to hamstring the ability of U.S. commanders or U.S. diplomats to do anything.

The manner in which Weinberger acted tended to weaken American diplomacy because the perception grew that the Americans were last in and first out, were not willing to take any active measures in Beirut, and were totally confused. That's the politest way in which I can describe how American marines, and American policy, were characterized.

Weinberger did his utmost to ignore the president's repeated, stated desire to see American power play a role in ending the conflict. He consistently disobeyed in his own way, which was basically a mix of stubbornness and wishful thinking.

John W. Vessey The issue is more that we saw the major danger to the United States. For those of us who oscillated between Vietnam and Europe, we watched a very capable force that was a good deterrent to the Soviet Union go downhill until it was a paper tiger. And we certainly didn't want to get involved in something that would detract from our ability to deter the Soviet Union again, in a major area of our interest.

We gave our best military advice, which was: Don't stick American troops between the Arabs and the Israelis. We didn't want to go to Lebanon primarily because sticking ourselves between the Arab countries and Israel didn't appear to be a good thing for us to do. That is why we didn't want to get ourselves pinned down in something that would detract from our overall ability, even though we understood the importance of keeping peace in the Middle East.

Caspar Weinberger I felt very strongly that we had done our part in the first multinational force and had lifted the PLO army out of Beirut and stopped a bloody house-to-house combat. I didn't see any particular necessity, or desirability, in our going in the second time, because there was nothing — no clear-cut mission — that was supposed to separate warring factions that had agreed to peace.

Sadly, the Syrians had never agreed to it, and the Israelis had only agreed to it with secret concessions and conditions, which made it actually impossible for a multinational force to do anything. The multinational force had no mission, no rules of engagement. They weren't even allowed to protect themselves.

It was, I thought, a very wrong enterprise, from start to finish, and I begged the president not to go ahead with it and to take our people out. But that tragedy, which was easily predictable, unfortunately happened before we decided to come out.

Moves Toward Peace

King Hussein After 1967 we tried to shoulder our responsibilities regarding the West Bank. We tried to seek the recovery of that territory, with the possibility of some minor adjustments regarding borders.

As far as Jerusalem was concerned, we put forth that it should never be a divided city again but should be the symbol and essence of peace. Over time this was obviously resisted more and more by the Palestinians, who wanted to have their say regarding their future on their national soil.

We were left in the difficult position of wanting to support and help and bring about a solution. The situation changed, and the PLO became the sole legitimate representative of the people of Palestine. Its leadership assumed that responsibility, and we agreed to that.

So there was a different set of circumstances in the region. There was that reality, but there was also the very special relationship between Jordan and Palestine. And the idea was put forward as to how this relationship could develop to enable the Palestinians to move and to enable us to help them make a breakthrough in the direction of establishing peace.

Finally, it became very obvious that it wasn't possible to get anywhere, and that was when we disengaged.

The Reagan Plan

In a nationally televised address on the evening of September 1, 1982 —the day of the final evacuation of the PLO from Lebanon—President Reagan announced a new Middle East peace initiative that came to be known as the Reagan Plan.

The plan called for a five-year period of full autonomy over their own affairs for the Palestinians of the West Bank and Gaza; an immediate freeze on Israeli settlements; and negotiations that would lead to the creation, in association with Jordan, of a Palestinian entity, which would be something less than an independent Palestinian state.

Yehiel Kadishai This was something! Begin was in Nahariya [in northern Israel], and he received a message that the president was going to announce his plan, which was not in line with Israeli policy. Begin didn't like it, and he asked Sam Lewis to ask the president not to declare the plan openly before we could discuss it.

That same day there was a reception for Caspar Weinberger, who was then visiting Israel, at the Tel Aviv Hilton. I went to the reception to find Lewis, to tell him that the prime minister would like to know the answer from Reagan. Lewis said, "The president is going to announce his plan."

Begin then declared that he was not going to accept this policy that the president was promoting. This resulted in a break in relations. Begin said that Israel was not a puppet state, a banana republic.

Geoffrey Kemp The Reagan Plan was the child of Lebanon and Beirut. It was an attempt to jump-start a peace process at a time when the two key protagonists, Syria and Israel, were on their backs.

The fight in the White House [over] how to handle Lebanon, from September 1982 through May 1983, was about strategy and tactics. Some of us felt that this was the time to assert American leadership and power and, essentially, to dictate to both Israel and Syria, "Times have changed, guys. Syria, you've lost a little war with Israel. Israel, you've blotted your copybook because of Sharon. Now you have to listen to Uncle Sam."

That, of course, would have required a more assertive policy than either the State Department or the Congress was prepared to go along with, so it got nowhere.

Alexander M. Haig Jr. It was in the wake of my departure that George Shultz was steamrollered into that peace initiative by the White House staff and Cap Weinberger.

George P. Shultz It was a time when there was an obvious need for something; there was a lot of turmoil. Sometimes, at least in my experience, turmoil is an opportunity if you can put something into place that clarifies matters. It always seemed to me that in the Middle East it is very important to have something constructive to be working on. If there is no program — no plan, nothing — it leads people to despair, and things tend to fall apart.

If there's something, even something that people criticize, at least there is a positive effort. So I tried to work up something, in coordination with the president. I think it actually turned out to be a very positive part of the picture. It never quite jelled, but nevertheless, it provided a lot of groundwork.

Abraham Tamir   After the Reagan Plan was published, Begin looked at Reagan like a traitor. Why are you coming with such a plan? It meant that the United States had given up Camp David.

In closed meetings, Begin criticized the Americans all the time. But he knew that without the Americans he could not move. That was his problem: to Begin, an agreement was a holy thing. You couldn't violate that agreement; it was holy forever. So he was very angry.

Benjamin Ze'ev Begin   The contents were one thing; the other thing was the surprise, which was very disconcerting. Usually the two governments pledge not to surprise each other. Of course, there are limits to this. But strategically you do not surprise allies. This was a surprise, and a bitter one. The idea of cooperation is that these conflicts should be on the table for the parties to consider.

Yitzhak Shamir   The Reagan Plan was not exactly his plan. But you can have differences among friends, and he and his secretaries of state were friends. It was a matter of conviction, and it was very useful to Israel.

Max Kampelman, head of the U.S. delegation, Madrid CSCE (Conference on Security and Cooperation in Europe) conference; chief U.S. arms negotiator, Geneva talks with the Soviet Union   The American Jewish community looked upon Reagan as a friend of Israel; there was no question about that. One leader, later on, said to me, "The difference between Reagan and Bush is that if Israel did something foolish — which it was likely to do at any time — Reagan's reaction would be, 'Let's not rush about anything.' Bush's reaction would be, 'Let's slam 'em.'" The community was familiar with, and sensitive to, that subtle difference.

What made Reagan such a friend? Superficially, one might say that he had been in Hollywood and must have had a lot of Jewish friends. But the more perceptive idea, or explanation, attributed it to the fact that during the war, when he was on that public relations board,* his job was

---

* During World War II, Reagan, denied a combat role owing to poor eyesight, was assigned to Army Air Force Intelligence, which was making training films for the air force as well as documentary films shot in war zones. During the closing days of the war, the California-based unit began to receive classified Signal Corps films showing the liberation of Hitler's death camps.

to look at the photographs of the concentration camps. Friends of his told me that those photographs had a tremendous impact on him and therefore remained with him throughout his lifetime.

King Hussein   I didn't have prior knowledge of it, except in a very short space of time. The plan was worthy of our support, and a positive step.

Adnan Khashoggi   The history of the United States is to try to have peace in that region; it is a valuable area for the U.S. economy. Reagan found that it is not easy to make peace between the Arabs and the Israelis. He found that the Arabs are a stubborn people. They are nationalistic; they are semi-organized; they have the Arab League; they have a hundred million people. Israel has five million people. So the U.S. recognizes that if one day they have to save Israel, they will have to be involved themselves against the Arabs. It is best to have peace, so the U.S. efforts were always around that point.

Now they were also looking at the Israelis, who are as stubborn as the Arabs, so they were never successful at breaking through on this point until the Gulf War.

Abraham Tamir   Begin and Shamir torpedoed the Reagan Plan because it would have allowed for another sovereignty on this [the West Bank] side of the Jordan River. Shamir would never accept a process that would result in Arab sovereignty on the west side of the Jordan, whether it would have been an independent Palestinian state or a state in confederation with Jordan.

Actually, if the Reagan Plan had been accepted, the PLO, as of now, would not be in the position of being the sole entity, along with Israel, on this side of the Jordan. There could have been a Jordanian-Palestinian state, or even an Israeli-Palestinian-Jordanian entity.

Adnan Khashoggi   I sent my proposal on the Reagan Plan to Reagan, and I also gave it to Mr. Peres — it was not a secret — and I also gave it to our king.

At the end of my plan, I said something was missing in the Reagan Plan: Where is the carrot so that people will sit around the table and talk? The Middle East, with all its wealth, is still an underdeveloped region. Israel is getting a lot of aid from the United States, but still they are underdeveloped, still involved in agriculture. They are not as sophisticated as the United States, so the reason for these people to sit together is to share the wealth of the area.

One of my proposals was to tax the oil and put the proceeds in a bank, a special IMF [International Monetary Fund] bank for the Middle East, and everybody would have a share. So people would be occupied with working rather than going into the streets and burning flags.

Richard Murphy The Saudis felt, as a general rule, that the Democrats were more friendly toward Israel than the Republicans. But certainly Reagan's comments on the settlements were duly registered. The September 1982 initiative was seen as an American effort. The Saudis didn't think very highly of it; it didn't promise any great transformation in American policy.

It came shortly after Shultz took over at State, in the wake of the Israeli invasion of Lebanon, when the Arab world was not only deeply upset by the invasion but potentially open to a new diplomatic initiative.

Adnan Khashoggi The Egyptian president arrived in Washington for talks. He was trying to find a solution: How to accept the Reagan Plan? I spoke to [Egyptian President Hosni] Mubarak when he was in Washington, and he told me he didn't know how to handle Washington on this problem because the Israelis were blocking all the opportunities for the Palestinian state.

I said, "You must come out with something, Mr. President, that will show the Americans that you made this effort, so that they will cooperate with you." He said, "Yes, but how?"

In the evening they invited me to a dinner that Reagan gave for Mubarak. I met Reagan, and I had the opportunity to tell him that President Mubarak was a bit disturbed that he could not come away from Washington with some kind of plan complementary to Reagan's own plan.

And at that moment I saw a leader before me. He was not afraid to talk. He said to me, "I want the same thing." So I said, "Well, what do you think if we create a committee, with the United States, Egypt, and Jordan, and the three of them can make a protocol acceptable to the Palestinians and the Israelis?" He said, "I like that."

So I went to President Mubarak and told him what had just happened and said, "You must push on this point." He said okay. He went to Reagan, and they agreed to this plan in principle. The next morning I was awakened at seven o'clock by President Mubarak. He said, "The State Department doesn't agree with Reagan because they are afraid the Israelis will not accept." So I said, "If they want the blessing of the Israelis, I will call Peres myself."

So I picked up the phone, and I called Peres. I said, "I am here with the president of Egypt. We discussed the situation yesterday with President Reagan, and he likes it, and we don't want the people in the State Department to convince you differently. Would you inform McFarlane that you approve?"

He said, "Give me a few minutes. I will call you back." So he called back and said, "Tell Mubarak that I will not do it because my principle is to negotiate directly. But I will do it only for President Mubarak, and I would like him to call me." I said, "Here is his number. He is waiting for your call. I just had him on the other line." Peres called him and said, "Adnan spoke to me," and this broke the ice between Peres and Mubarak after Sadat's death.

At that moment McFarlane got a call from Richard Murphy, who says, "Well, you did it." Murphy then calls me and says, "We have approved the plan, and we will announce it." So I said, "That's fine, that's beautiful."

So I called Mubarak and said, "Murphy just called me, and they are going to announce the committee." Before the meeting between Reagan and Mubarak, Murphy calls me. "Adnan, we are having a problem. The Jordanians won't accept." So I called Mubarak and asked, "Did you call King Hussein?" He said, "I forgot to."

But this showed that Reagan was a leader. He didn't even think of the State Department when I spoke to him. He made his own decisions. This is not a small man.

Begin's Resignation

Rafi Eitan Begin was a very sick man. During his prime ministership, he had a heart attack. He felt that unless he stepped down, he would die in service. Also, he felt that because of his sickness, he was not able to work efficiently. That's the reason why he stepped down. I have no doubt about it; that is the only reason.

Yehiel Kadishai In the late 1970s Begin spoke to three thousand boys and girls who were then graduating from high school. The meeting was held in the Mann Auditorium in Tel Aviv.

When he ended his lecture to this group of sparkling youth, there were questions. A boy from the gallery screamed, "Mr. Prime Minister, when are you going to step down from politics?" Begin smiled and said, "Don't worry, young man, when I'm seventy years old, I won't be in politics anymore. I'll sit down to write the four or five volumes of the generation from destruction to redemption."

In 1983 he became seventy and he resigned. But this was not the reason; he could have continued for another few years. [He gave as] one of the reasons he resigned: "I cannot continue." He had lost weight; he was tired. He told me, "Look, when I put my tie on, there is room for two fingers. I cannot do it anymore."

The reasons why he was so weak were the losses he suffered in Lebanon and the passing away of [his wife] Aliza. She was his raison d'être. He was coming home and he knew his Alla was there; he knew that he had somebody there at night, and in the early morning. And from November 1982, she was no more.

He continued for another eight months, until the end of August 1983. Those were hard days for him to come home and Aliza was not there. I know it well. He lost the taste for life. In addition, there were all these attacks on him.

And there is one thing, which I am telling for the first time. This is not the reason for his stepping down, but the timing of that day — not a week before and not a week later — was. Why on this day? The day after his resignation, Mr. Kohl came here on a visit. Begin had already met earlier with Mr. Genscher, the German foreign minister. He had explained on that occasion, "I am not meeting with him as Menachem Begin, but as the prime minister of Israel."

But for Begin to meet Kohl as prime minister, when he knows that he is going to resign very soon anyway — he may have noticed that they were putting up the German flags — he decided, "I am not going to see him. I won't have to shake hands with him."

Laying the Groundwork for Peace

George P. Shultz   The participants in the peace process since 1983 — the president, the secretary of state, Peres, and Rabin — all write to me and tell me that our work laid the groundwork for what is happening today.

You need to go back to the time of the early resolutions in the United Nations; it's been a gradual, evolving, building process. And everyone has built on what came before. This is one of the areas where the Clinton administration has done well. One of the reasons is the continuity: they didn't try to do something different; they tried to carry out what was there.

THE SOVIET UNION

Richard Perle, assistant secretary of defense for international security policy   It was tremendously exhilarating to have a president whose view of the U.S.-Soviet relationship was not in the direction of finding as many cooperative ways of dealing with them as possible, but one of someone who was able to resist the idea that the Soviet Union was a permanent fixture. He was revolutionary in that regard. It was a sharp break with all previous administrations, and certainly with the recent administrations of Carter, Ford, and Nixon. They all, to varying degrees, believed that the central task in the management of the U.S.-Soviet relationship was to find ways to get involved, to ameliorate differences, and to search for joint projects.

Reagan, who saw things quite differently, wasn't particularly interested in cooperating with what he regarded as an evil empire. He wanted to first rebuild American defenses so that we could deal with them from a position of strength. But if we were then going to deal with them, it was not going to be with the view of cooperating with them, so it was a very sharp change.

Alexander M. Haig Jr.   I believed that we had overlooked the real role of the Soviet Union in a host of trouble spots where U.S. interests were involved, to a larger or lesser extent, and where, for reasons associated with what some administrations would have liked things to be, we never called a spade a spade. I felt that was a terrible mistake, because it contributed to misjudgment and risk-taking on the part of the Soviet Union, which it otherwise should have recoiled from.

That was true all during Vietnam. It was also true in Latin America, where there was no spontaneous movement toward Marxist-Leninist ideology, but a stirred-up level of revolutionary activity supported by Soviet funds, direction, and leadership and implemented with some vigor and enthusiasm by Castro's Cuba.

Vietnam taught me that you cannot take these issues on locally without dealing with the bigger picture — the source of the problem — or you would end up doing what we did in Vietnam, which was to squander fifty thousand American lives for an unsuccessful outcome.

And the impact of that failure over a long period on the United States' psyche was very debilitating, so I thought we should get away from that. And the president agreed, and he took the issue on, head-on, in his rhetoric and in the policies we pursued.

Bernadette Casey Smith At an early meeting with Reagan and his top staff, Dad said, "If we want to win the cold war, we have to defeat the Soviet Union. What do we have that the Russians don't have?" That was money.

So every place they had a fire — Angola or Afghanistan or Poland — they would have pressure on each front and make them spend more money around the world. His idea was: If you follow the money, you know what's happening in the world. He had a business mind, and he treated everything as a business enterprise.

Geoffrey Kemp Casey was an enigma because he was extraordinarily smart but extraordinarily inarticulate. Some of us who didn't know him — and who were arrogant and were new on the job — thought he was a bit senile because he would mumble.

Later on we realized that he didn't want us to hear what he was saying; he didn't want us to know. His agenda, I think, was extremely simple. The number-one, -two, and -three threat to the United States is the Soviet Union, and anything we could do to make the Soviet Union uncomfortable, particularly in the Third World, we will encourage. My guess is that Casey's priorities were shared by Ronald Reagan.

Jerry Falwell Mr. Begin, Mr. Reagan, Margaret Thatcher, and the pope of Rome were the four people who, at a particular time in history, brought the Soviets down. And Ronald Reagan was far and away chief of staff of that quartet. He may have been sleeping over there when the pope was talking, but the pope wasn't sleeping when he was talking.

Frank Carlucci Howard Baker came to me one day and said, "Now, Frank, we're coming into a pretty heavy agenda with the Soviets, and we have to get the president better prepared. I've got an idea: Why don't we bring in people the president likes, and respects, for briefing sessions?"

He had a lady named Suzanne Massie.* She would talk to the president about Russia, the kinds of things that he loved. She was really the only one talking to him with any depth of background about the Soviet Union.

---

* The American-born daughter of a Swiss diplomat, an author and fellow at Harvard's Russian Research Center, Suzanne Massie traveled to the Soviet Union many times, starting in 1967. She is the author of books on Russian cultural history, including *Land of the Firebird* (1980), and collaborated with her former husband, Robert Massie, on *Nicholas and Alexandra* (1967).

Suzanne Massie, author, unofficial adviser to President Ronald Reagan on the Soviet Union Sometime in the spring of 1983, the administration had begun negotiations over resuming cultural exchanges, which had lapsed under Jimmy Carter. There were also plans to open a U.S. consulate in Kiev. On September 1, the Soviet Union shot down the Korean airliner [KAL 007].

I had been battling to get back my visa to the Soviet Union for a long time. I received it in the spring and made plans to go to the Soviet Union in late September. At that time, because of KAL, relations were in deep freeze.

When I arrived, I called the USA Institute* to thank them for helping me with my visa problems. To my surprise, they asked me to come right over. I found when I got there that they were desperate; they were backed into a corner, and they were very worried.

I had several conversations with high-ranking members of the institute and was very outspoken, as I always am. I told them: "You did a terrible thing [shooting down the airliner]. And you have handled it very badly." In one very troubling conversation with a deputy director of the institute, a man reputed to be very high in the KGB, the discussion grew very heated. At one point he pounded on the table, his eyes flashing, and exclaimed, "You don't know how close war is!"

There was terrible demonization going on in the U.S., cranking up for the [1984] election. Tempers were high. Most frightening, [U.S. and Soviet] bureaucratic relations had virtually stopped. I felt that we had to find a way to talk about something — anything. At the institute, after hearing a barrage of "nyets," I said, "There seem to be only two things we can agree upon: mothers and culture. If we can't talk about mothers and culture, we're finished." After a long pause, they said, "Well, there is some logic to what you say." So there was a crack.

I came home. My father, a Swiss diplomat, had raised me to believe that every citizen should — indeed has a responsibility to — act. I had a very strong feeling that I should try to see Reagan. I knew several senators, and so I went down to Washington and started with my good friend Bill Cohen [R-Maine]. I said that in my opinion the heated Soviet reaction was much more than the usual Soviet truculence, that they felt cornered, and that it was an extremely dangerous time. "We have to find a way to talk," I urged. After a long conversation, Bill said to me, "You ought to see Bud McFarlane."

---

* The major Soviet think tank on U.S. affairs, staffed by academics and political analysts.

I was given a twenty-minute appointment. I practiced beforehand to keep it to exactly twenty minutes. My pitch was very simple: I believe that there possibly is an opening to discuss the cultural agreement again. I realized that the situation was so inflamed that the discussion had to begin with something nonthreatening to both countries.

To my surprise, when the twenty minutes were up, Bud McFarlane didn't get up. He stayed, and he said, "What you have to say is very interesting. Could you come back and talk for two hours?" I said yes, and I did come down again, and I talked for two hours. I made a bold proposal: "Send me. I can talk to them." I had a lot of nerve, but I knew I could. I know Russians well, and I was sure that there was a way to discuss this with them.

McFarlane said, "Put it on paper," which I did. A few weeks later, at Christmas, I was called and told to go. At first I was told, "Go for three days." I said no, that I had to have more time. People have to be able to think over what you have to say. For the Russians, everything is long.

It was agreed that I would have ten days. But I insisted on one thing. I said, "You know, gentlemen, this is no disrespect to you, but the Russians are very personal people, and all of the president's men don't add up to the president. For his credibility, not mine, I must be able to say, honestly, that I have looked the president in the eye, and that it has come from him. It won't take very long; I only need to ask him one question. Five minutes will be enough." Shortly after, I was told, "Come to the Oval Office." That was on January 17, 1984, a few days before I was to leave for Moscow.

I was brought into the Oval Office by McFarlane, and to my surprise, a whole group, including Bush, Baker, Meese, and Deaver, were there, waiting, I don't know why. To my surprise, it didn't go, "Hello, goodbye." Instead, the president said to me, "Sit down, Mrs. Massie." So I did. And all of those men sat down, in pecking order.

It was an overwhelming moment for me. I had a moment of panic. I thought, I'm not prepared. I was ready for five minutes. I'm nervous, and they are going to say, Look at that dumb broad! The way we were sitting meant that if I tried to talk to both the president and the group, it would be like a Ping-Pong match. I made an instant decision: I decided to try to forget the others and look into the president's eyes, to talk to him as if we were alone, which is what I did. And he stayed for forty-five minutes.

When a person is terrified — which I was — you can feel the atmosphere more acutely. To my astonishment, I felt that the president was a bit nervous; I thought that maybe it was because someone had told him that I was an "expert." I wished that I could reach out and say to him,

"Mr. President, please don't feel that way. I know a bit about this one subject, but you know so many things I don't!"

The first question he asked was a very good and interesting one: "How much do they believe in communism?" I answered, "Mr. President, I can only tell you what the Russians say about their leaders. They call them 'the big bottoms,' and say, 'They love only their chairs.' "

In his speech, given the day before, the president had talked about small steps toward improving relations with the Soviet Union. My question to him was, "If you are reelected, will this policy of small steps be a continuing policy of your administration?" Reagan sometimes had an eagle's glance. Sternly, he said, "Yes. If they want peace, they can have it."

Later, in Moscow, during my negotiations with the Soviets, which were successful, there was a time when I said, "I am a writer. I have seen many powerful men. I have looked him [Reagan] in the eye. I believe he is genuine." Happily, there is the same proverb in Russian as in English, so I said, "Don't look a gift horse in the mouth. Think it over." And I left the room.

A few days later I was called back for some very serious, and substantive, discussions. And in the end they said yes, that they would start talking again.

Afterward, in the U.S., I never said anything about this mission. Finally, four years later, when I was invited to the White House dinner for Gorbachev, there was one particularly relentless White House reporter who kept at me, asking, "What is your relationship with the president?" My answer to the press up to that time had always been, "He likes my book [Land of the Firebird]." He did, actually. But this reporter kept pounding away, and I thought: This makes me sound like Reagan's Rasputin, and I'm not. So I called Bud McFarlane and said, "May I say that you sent me?" And he answered, "It's about time."

So that is actually how I met the president. It was not about my book; it was because I had said, "Send me," and they decided to do it. And it worked. It resulted in the cultural agreement two years later and the first Reagan-Gorbachev meeting in Geneva. That was the beginning.

Frank Carlucci   Suzanne Massie would go into the Oval Office alone; nobody knew what happened. So I went in to the president and said, "I'd like to put this into some kind of context." She didn't object. In fact, she and I developed a good relationship. It was a very interesting episode.

Suzanne Massie   In my conversations I did not presume to ask him, "What do you want?" I felt that I was at his service and that whatever he wanted to hear about, I should tell him. I had no axes to grind. I wanted things to be equalized, and for that you need a win-win situation; people can't lose face.

Despite the fact that he was very quiet in meetings, there was only one president. Usually the national security adviser was there, and myself, and that was it. And before Geneva, the vice president was there. There is no question that Reagan was the man. I never, ever felt, in any situation, that he was the puppet. Far from it.

I never expected to be seeing the president on any kind of a regular basis. I never thought about it, but then it kept going. He kept the relationship going. He called every so often, to my astonishment, and then it got so that I saw him before these meetings. I was not aware that I was having any influence on the president.

These meetings were a remarkable occurrence. If you were a writer, you were used to seeing a lot of remarkable people in a lot of remarkable situations. I heard later — I don't know if this is true — that one of the things he respected was the fact that I never asked for anything. But that seemed to me to be perfectly natural. You are a citizen; you do what you can.

Frank Carlucci There were all kinds of strange things going on: [Edward] Kennedy had some back-door channel through one of his staffers; the president liked [Zbigniew] Brzezinski [Carter's national security adviser]; he liked Richard Perle. He did not like Henry Kissinger, but we really hit a home run when we suggested Richard Nixon. We brought Nixon to the White House by helicopter. I was the first person to meet him there after he left the White House in disgrace. I took him to the Residence, to the study. There was just the president, Howard Baker, Nixon, and me. Nixon spent a good hour to an hour and a half with Reagan, talking about policy toward the Soviet Union. He was brilliant, and Reagan listened and absorbed. Those sessions were very useful.

Suzanne Massie At one point when he asked me to come down, I said, "It would mean a great deal to me if Mrs. Reagan could join our meeting." And she did. After that meeting the three of us had lunch together.

I was very impressed with Nancy Reagan. I think she got a very bad press. It was very clear to me that this woman had one thing in mind: her husband. She loved him, and she was totally loyal to him. He was lucky to have her.

It was very apparent that with her he relaxed, absolutely. I felt he was always on his guard with his aides, but with her he would relax and begin to talk. At another private lunch with them I screwed up my courage and said, "Mr. President, what is it that you want from the Russians?" Decisively he answered, "I want to get rid of those atomic weapons. Every one."

It was a big surprise to me that that would have been the one thing that he would have chosen to say. That was the closest I have ever heard from him to an expression of his intention.

The "Evil Empire"

On March 8, 1983, President Reagan, in an address to the annual convention of the National Association of Evangelicals in Orlando, Florida, described the Soviet Union as the "Evil Empire."

Oliver Wright   When he was first elected, people here were very worried at what we'd got, because this was a different person from any president who had gone before. We were in Germany at the time, and people there were worried about the "Evil Empire" concept.

Hans Dietrich Genscher   Reagan was interested in making his position clear. He couldn't argue with the "Evil Empire." He had a constituency in the U.S. But he was a man who was ready to talk substance. In the last phase of his presidency he was more flexible than his collaborators.

Nicholas Daniloff, Moscow correspondent, *U.S. News & World Report*   I attended a press conference in Moscow given by [the longtime Soviet foreign minister and Politburo member] Andrei Gromyko, and he really was very offended by that phrase. I remember it so well, because he said, "Never have the stars smiled more brightly on the Soviet Union than they do today. What's this 'Evil Empire' business?"

Sergei Tarasenko   At the Foreign Ministry, we were quite indifferent to this remark because we understood that it was normal. If you look at the relationship between the United States and the Soviet Union, it was normal for our leaders to exchange rather unflattering remarks about each other. We called you names; you called us names. It was part of the game. If you look at our propaganda, we used awful names — imperialist, capitalist, and the nest of all this evil — so for us, it was nothing. I barely noticed it.

Michael Reagan   The "Evil Empire" speech was one he always wanted to give. In a sense, he gave it in other ways, but it wasn't until he became president of the United States that he was able to use that form — and that bully pulpit — to say what he needed to say, and to have attention paid to it by the Soviet bloc.

The press was all over him. How can you say the "Evil Empire"? They interpreted the speech to say that he meant that the people of the Soviet Union were bad people. What he was saying was that the leadership was bad, and that their policies were terrible, and that their people were living in poverty because of those policies, and that the "empire" itself, the leadership, was very vile. He called it the way he saw it.

Suzanne Massie The reaction to the "Evil Empire" speech was different in the U.S. and in the Soviet Union. Here, there was nothing but criticism of the president, while in the Soviet Union many Russians approved. Several said to me, "Finally, someone has said it! Right on there, Ron!"

Stuart Spencer I had concern about the term "Evil Empire" because I thought it might be pushing the button too hard. But he liked it; he really believed it. And it was also a tactic: I give with the one hand, I take with the other. That's where they don't give him credit for his leadership.

Cal Thomas The "Evil Empire" speech was great, but I think his greatest speech was the one he gave in 1988 at Moscow State University. That was one of the most consummate communications I've ever heard of what America — the free market, free speech, and freedom — is all about.

It was glorious; it was a great speech. I still have it in my file, and I read it every now and then, just to encourage myself, especially when I see a Bob Dole interview. Dole said, "If you want me to be Reagan, I'll be Reagan." Man, he couldn't be Reagan any more than you could guard Michael Jordan.

Jack Matlock It amazed me that people got so upset. You could say, "This isn't tactful or diplomatic, but it's true. They did lie and cheat, and if you don't recognize that to start with, people are much more apt to think you don't understand them."

Actually, as it turned out, it was a brilliant stroke, because later, when he was asked about it, when they were changing, he could say, "Yes, they were, but that was another time, another place." It in effect legitimized the changes in the Soviet Union, so when Reagan finally turned up in Red Square, kissing babies and saying, "You're on the right track," it had an enormous impact.

It was also good that he used the expression only once — although the press constantly repeated it.

David Abshire   Reagan wasn't an intellectual, but his sensory capabilities were there on certain big issues. The outrageous remark he made on the "Evil Empire" that disturbed everybody rattled people because it was provocative. He did other provocative things: he went to Red Square and talked about human rights.

Max Kampelman   I was supported in the human rights area in every way by the president. At one point, in 1982, I concluded that the Russians were going to give us everything we had asked for before Madrid ended.* I told this to Shultz, and I told him that I was no longer satisfied with it. I said, "These are only words. I really feel that I can't defend any more words, to myself or to the Congress, unless I get some people out."

George said, "We have to talk to the president about this," and we went to see him. I told the president what I thought, and he turned to George and said, "This makes sense to me." He then asked me if I could do it. I said, "Yes, but we will have to be tough." I alerted him, "When Kohl finds out about this, he will call you; and George will get a call from Genscher; they will be very unhappy, but we have to stick with this."

The president agreed, but he said to me, "How are you going to decide which ones?" I said, "I don't know. I don't like to play God." Then he said, "You know, I would like you to get those Pentecostals out of our embassy in Moscow."† And he told me something I had not known; he said, "I wrote a letter to Brezhnev some months ago, in which I told him that it was very important to get these people out, and I haven't even had the courtesy of a response."

As we were ready to leave, he goes to his desk and opens a drawer, takes out a piece of paper, gives it to me, and says, "See what you can do about these people too" — it [bore] the names of some Jewish re-

---

* Ambassador Kampelman headed the U.S. delegation to the 1983 Conference on Human Rights, held in Madrid and sponsored by the Conference on Security and Cooperation in Europe.

† On June 27, 1978, five Russians, members of a Pentecostal family, had dashed past Soviet police stationed in front of the American embassy in Moscow, and were granted refuge in the building. Their plight was repeatedly raised with Soviet officials by both President Reagan and Secretary of State Shultz. On June 26, 1983, the five Pentecostals were allowed to leave the embassy and go to Israel with ten other family members.

fuseniks. So he couldn't have been briefed with this paper, and why he had it, I don't know. But it indicated what was on his mind.

Afterward, more than sixty Pentecostals — including the embassy group and their families — were let out. The president was very pleased.

Alexander M. Haig Jr.   On one of those few occasions when the president and I had a lengthy discussion, I pointed out that we had to have a balance between the vital interests of the American people under a real-politik rubric and traditional American values, such as human rights, and other democratic values — that to have a successful foreign policy, you had to have a balance between the two.

Suzanne Massie   Reagan did a very important thing in projecting will. Carter was a very fine man, but the Soviets had a very hard time understanding him; his style was often interpreted as weakness.

The Soviets had come to the conclusion that we had no will. Somehow Reagan convinced them that the United States had will; he came across to them very clearly, and they believed what he would do. That is very important: it can prevent you from making some very big mistakes. That was his strength.

The Soviets respected patriotism of the right kind: pride in your country. Reagan personified that. What I hoped was that nobody would try to mute that in him. I thought to myself, The Russians respect exactly the qualities he has.

Reagan and Nuclear Defense

James Abrahamson, lieutenant general, U.S. Air Force; associate administrator for space flight, NASA; chief of the Strategic Defense Initiative   President Reagan was a very interesting man. He certainly was not a technologist; however, he appreciated technology. He formulated the idea that we ought to be able to defend ourselves [from a nuclear attack] based on several things that had happened earlier in his lifetime, one of them being that he was the first governor of California to visit one of our key nuclear laboratories, the Lawrence Livermore Laboratory.

When he visited there, they dazzled him with their technology. There were several key people there who believed in defenses; one of them was Dr. Edward Teller, the father of the H-bomb. He was convinced that we could find ways to defend against ballistic missiles. He had in mind a nuclear approach, which, of course, has been very controversial. But, nonetheless, they talked to Mr. Reagan about their technologies. I believe that

that planted the idea in his mind that it might be possible — not that any one of the technologies they advocated was the right one.

Edward Teller, nuclear physicist; member of a presidential scientific advisory board on strategic missile defense   When he came to Livermore and heard about missile defense, it was very new to him. He didn't want to come out for or against it. After being president for two years, he came out very strongly for missile defense but wanted, if possible, that the system not utilize nuclear weapons.

So, on the subject of missile defense, Reagan took our advice but modified it; the modification was his, not ours. He asked questions and, for a long time, did not give the answers. He took fifteen years to make up his mind. And then he came out with not what had been put into him, but with something better than that.

Reagan did shoot from the hip, but his hip-shooting in the case of missile defense took him fifteen years. I have evidence that during this period of time he had thought about the subject again and again; he had talked to people, collected information, and then acted.

Colin L. Powell   He was very much against nuclear weapons. We used to have to constrain him from talking about his desire for a non-nuclear world, because we couldn't get there in the foreseeable future, as we saw it. We sort of had to protect him from the right wing.

Max Kampelman   He had an understanding of these complex arms control issues, in a simple way. Take the issue of a nuclear-free world. Nobody in the Reagan administration supported that program except one person, and that was Ronald Reagan.

I heard at least one or two arguments with him where everybody would point out why this was not a good policy from America's point of view. The argument against disarmament of nuclear weapons is that if we get rid of these weapons, the Soviets will have supremacy — because they have a massive conventional force — and that the deterrent is the existence of nuclear weapons, all of which is correct, valid, and persuasive.

But you couldn't dent him; he would come back, in a simple kind of way. His answer at one discussion involved Chernobyl, which was civilian power. What has happened as a result of Chernobyl? We can't get a nuclear power plant now in the United States, but the Soviets are going ahead with their nuclear power plants. Let's assume that Chernobyl was not civilian public power, but nuclear weapons. The result will be that we, in the United States, will have to stop nuclear weapons — all of Europe will have to stop nuclear weapons — and this doesn't mean that the Soviets will have to stop nuclear weapons. Aren't we better off to try to get an agreement to stop? There's a kind of common sense here.

Caspar Weinberger The president and I had talked many times — even when he was governor — about the basic philosophy of mutual assured destruction [MAD] and the ABM Treaty, which forbade us to deploy any defenses. Neither he nor I liked that. I talked — in two or three interviews during the transition and immediately after the confirmation hearings — about the importance of trying to acquire a defensive capability.

He supported the idea [that we should try] to acquire a defensive capability as the very best way of keeping the peace, and that without it, we were dangerously vulnerable. I think that events since then prove that that was entirely correct.

Edward Teller I was invited to dinner at the White House in March 1983. I did not know the reason. It was after I got there that I found out that Reagan would talk about nuclear defense.

To my mind, there were only three possibilities: wipe out the Soviet Union so that they can't retaliate; submit to their demands; or have a deterrent. In that situation, mutual assured destruction as a deterrent was a realistic and effective policy.

Reagan was unusual in that he did not simply see deterrence; he admitted that the policy of deterrence could easily lead to massive damage and human destruction.

Richard Perle MAD had been gospel, but it was controversial gospel. It had been criticized in particular by people who wound up in the Reagan administration. I was among the critics of it; there were others, in the White House and elsewhere.

We didn't like it for a lot of reasons. First of all, we didn't think it was credible to base the whole of your security on the threat to commit suicide. It seemed to me predictable that in exactly the crises you wanted deterrence to work, it was likely to collapse.

There was a tremendous disconnect between [the real world and] the world of military planners — where serious, intelligent people would sit in a room and discuss whether to add five hundred targets to a list of five thousand, each one of which was to be hit with a nuclear weapon, and if they were going to add five hundred, which five hundred? Which pulp factory in Kazakhstan should be added to the list?

I'm sure that the planners were deadly serious about this. But they were living in a dream world. I couldn't imagine a political leader who would ever give orders to strike thousands of targets. If we had been struck massively, like that, it would be completely pointless to launch thousands of nuclear weapons, a lot of which wouldn't be available if we had been hit first. Even the prospect of a handful of nuclear weapons was very sobering.

So there was a real question as to whether mutual assured destruction had any depth. And if it didn't, then to build a security strategy for [a situation in which], faced with imminent danger, people might suddenly decide, "Hey, that's crazy. But now what do we do? What do we have to put in its place?"

That was a real problem. So there was a strong desire to find alternatives. This happened to fit in very well with Reagan's own view: that vengeance was decidedly inferior to preventing a war in the first place.

Frank Carlucci   He had always been very much against nuclear weapons, even before he got into office. I guess that some of us didn't realize that. I can remember a session when I went over with Cap — we were discussing the MX missile — and the president said something to the effect of, "Wouldn't it be nice if we could have a weapon that would make all wars obsolete?"

He had always been searching for that weapon. He had wanted to get rid of nuclear weapons, and I had to tell him, "Mr. President, bear in mind that nuclear weapons have kept the peace since World War II." He would have gone faster than any of us in getting rid of nuclear weapons. He really loved the INF Treaty.

The Strategic Defense Initiative

James Abrahamson   The policy basis for SDI was fairly straightforward: if you can defend against ballistic missiles, and if you can demonstrate that that defense will eventually build up to be very, very effective, then the value of offensive ballistic missiles to the other side would go down. If the value goes down, they ought to be willing to trade them away, or to negotiate limits.

You must recall that we had never been able to negotiate a serious stop to the escalation of the nuclear threat; it had always increased. There was SALT I,* but what happened when they put limits on the

---

* An interim agreement reached between the United States and the Soviet Union during the early 1970s to limit strategic arms.

numbers of ballistic missiles was that they then put multiple warheads on ballistic missiles and kept it going.

So the policy basis was: find a defense that is more effective than their offense, and they will look somewhere else. That was the thesis.

The concept was a multiple layer system, so that when they fired their missiles in large volleys — and with all kinds of gear and techniques to hide the missile warheads and to cause confusion — you had to have layers of defense. And as the missiles or the warheads went to the first layer, you might get 50 percent of them. Then, as it went to the second layer, you might get 50 percent of what's left. And when it goes to the third and fourth layers, you get chunks of that.

So they would be faced with different techniques involved in each layer that they had to build countermeasures against, finding ways to penetrate all these multiple layers. The last layer, of course, was the old concept of "terminal defense," that is, around the key cities and target area you would have ground-based missiles that would fire up and get the few incoming ones remaining.

But the controversial part was: what could you put in space that would begin to get the missiles as they were fired first, or just as they left the atmosphere? And then, what layers could operate in space and continue to weed out the numbers of missiles?

John Poindexter The SDI has an interesting history. I guess it was in late '82, or early '83, that we were trying to get an agreement from Congress about replacing the MX missiles — the land-based missiles — and we had failed in our most recent attempt.

I wanted to pull together a group of people to look at strategic defense, so I brought together a half-dozen people to start looking at the issue. It turned out that, coincidentally, Bud had been talking to General Paul Gorman, who was assistant to the Joint Chiefs. He said that the Chiefs had just been discussing strategic defense. My group concluded that, though there were lots of problems, it was worth looking into as an initiative.

The president had a meeting scheduled with the Chiefs in February 1983. Bud put strategic defense on the agenda. Independent of all this, there was a group called High Frontier. Back in 1981 they had met with the president and had encouraged him to think in terms of strategic defense.

The president met with the Chiefs, and they agreed to look into the issue. The president was certainly in favor of it, so I had the staff start writing a speech for him. We knew that it was going to be a very controversial issue. The speech was prepared, and at the last minute it was sent to Secretaries Shultz and Weinberger for comment.

Then the ruckus began. The State Department, before the program was announced, wanted to do all this elaborate consultation with the allies. Bud got calls from Shultz and Weinberger, and from Richard Perle, who had sat in for Weinberger at the February meeting with the Chiefs, all urging that the president not make the speech.

At that point Bud began to waver and told Clark he didn't think the president should make the speech. Bill asked me what I thought, and I said that the president should go ahead with it, that we had known in the beginning that it was going to be controversial, but that it was something that needed to be done. Bill agreed with me. He told the president about the opposition, but the president said, "I'm going to make the speech."

William J. Crowe Jr.   The reason the president was so adamant on SDI was that Weinberger had told him all that stuff; Weinberger was a fanatic on SDI.

The Chiefs had a little bit different view on the matter. It's not that we were against SDI, but we thought, one, that it was a very, very challenging technical problem, and that we were a long way from solving any of that stuff; we were really in an experimental mode. But in order to satisfy Weinberger and the president, Abrahamson spent a lot of time talking as if the damn thing was in the parking lot. But it wasn't in the parking lot at all.

The Chiefs were suspicious of anything with so many uncertainties, with so many problems in developing. They spent an incredible amount of money on this. The Chiefs felt that we ought to go slow and see if the technical problems were amenable to solution.

Before I left, it was obvious that we could shoot down a missile, barring no other complications. Whether we could weaponize the SDI, and whether we could afford the SDI, was never obvious while I was chairman. And we thought that both of those questions should be explored in great depth before we went too damn far.

But there were a lot of people pushing hard for SDI — just push, push, push, spend, spend, spend, let's get it! They really thought we would really have a defense that would stop a missile. It was never clear to the Chiefs that we could build the kind of defense they were talking about.

It might have become clear when all these questions were answered, but it never was clear while I was the chairman. The Chiefs never felt that they had their hands around the throat of the thing; it was never under their control, in many respects.

But we were a great deal more suspicious than anyone else in the government. I was convinced that it looked like the expenses were going to be such that either we were going to have SDI or we were going to have a military. We couldn't have both.

James Abrahamson   When the president made his speech, in March 1983, there was very little warning in the Defense Department. I think it was only the day before that the president had called Cap Weinberger and said, "I'm going to add this little section to my speech on military preparedness. What do you think of it, Cap?" I think [Weinberger] was a little astounded — it was essentially a reversal of years of formal U.S. deterrent policy.

There were very few people who knew what the president was going to say. He wrote it, very personally; he didn't have speechwriters help him out for this one section. It was a paragraph at the end of his speech.

The key section of the SDI paragraph had three elements. He said, "Wouldn't it be better to save lives than avenge them?" To me, that clearly meant that there must be a better deterrent strategy. In the next line, he said, "Isn't it possible to find a technology to make nuclear missiles impotent and obsolete?" Of course, that was the foundation of the technology side of the program. Then, in the last element, he challenged the negotiators to get rid of the missiles themselves.

And, of course, he was right: we were never able to stop the growth of offensive nuclear missiles and/or nuclear bombs, and we certainly were never able to reverse that. But when Reagan challenged all the conventional theory, we were able to reduce whole classes of nuclear missiles. So he was dramatically right.

Was Reagan Premature in Announcing SDI?

Caspar Weinberger   It was not received as hoped for. We had hoped very much that people would appreciate that it was a system designed to destroy weapons, and not people, and that it was a system that had no offensive capability.

But the academic community and the defense specialists all leaped on it and poured scorn on it, on the idea that it upset all of the conventional wisdom. They shouldn't have been surprised, because the president upset conventional wisdom many times. He was generally convinced that conventional wisdom wasn't all that wise.

Max Kampelman   The Reagan administration screwed it up, and I have to blame Cap for this. We had a consensus in the Congress behind it at the beginning. [Georgia Senator] Sam Nunn [the ranking Democrat on the Armed Services Committee] was behind it because the logic of it is so clear. All we were doing was extensive research, and the idea of defense was sensible.

There is a secondary question that follows, which is: Do we deploy when we are ready? My view was always that since we're not ready, we don't have to make the decision about whether, and how, we deploy. Let's first know that the research is done and know what we want to do, know that it's economically feasible and technically feasible. And Congress was behind us on that approach; we had a clear majority in both the House and Senate.

But Cap felt the need to deploy . . . what, I don't know. I remember him saying to the president, at a meeting, "We'll be ready to deploy in six months, Mr. President." I knew that was nonsense, I had the technicians on my delegation, I had been to Los Alamos. I don't know what he was going to deploy in six months.

It certainly wouldn't have been effective. But they were trying to sell the president on this idea that we don't have time. And that was a fundamental mistake.

Abraham Sofaer   SDI became a convenient issue on which to hammer the administration — one in which Sam Nunn and the others exploited their majority control. There was only one Democrat who read the record and voted with us.

I don't believe that Sam Nunn read the record; there is no way he could have read even one-hundredth of the record in the hours that he logged in in the record room. The same thing is true of [Joseph] Biden [D-Del.] and [Carl] Levin [D-Mich.] — those were the three who attacked me the most vociferously — and I was amused. I was "Outstanding Graduate" of my class, I was editor in chief of the NYU *Law Review*, and I know what I'm doing when it comes to legal analysis. And this guy Biden — he allegedly crawled through a transom to pass an exam — he and others are very aggressive people who have gotten ahead with their wits, and they act as if I am an illegitimate person who manipulates words and the law, whereas they are honest and full of integrity and are going to uphold treaties. They refused to deal with the fact that many other distinguished people agreed with my work, including Nitze, Shultz, and Kampelman.

It was just a charade. The national security people, even a lot of Republicans, believed that it was not worth fighting this fight. It had no political support, so when it became a political issue and Nunn controlled the Congress on the question, he exploited it to the hilt.

James Abrahamson The Defense Department did not know what to do, so like all government agencies, they pulled together a study. They pulled it together under a former NASA administrator, Dr. [James] Fletcher; it was called the Fletcher Commission, and it was called the Fletcher Report. For about seven months his many teams studied the technology, really trying to convince themselves, and others, that it might be possible to build defenses.

During the same time there were a lot of policy implications, because this was a total reversal from the long-standing policy. So there was a second policy team, led by Dr. Fred Ikle, who was a high-level official in the Department of Defense.

During that time the administration looked for a civilian director for what they had already determined was going to be a new agency inside the Department of Defense, but at a level so that it reported directly to the secretary of defense and, through him, to the president.

I believe that they were right in wanting to look for a civilian of a very high technical stature. Everyone knew this was going to be a place everybody in the world was going to be shooting at, and they couldn't find anyone who would accept it.

They were beginning to wring their hands and say they could not find the right person. One of the senior officers said to the president, "You are going to have to give up on the idea of having a civilian director. I have the right guy. He is an air force three-star general, and you know him — and he thinks he is a civilian anyhow."

Reagan laughed at that, and Cap said it was a good idea, and they contacted me over at NASA. I was thrilled with the idea that this was going to be a program to reverse this concept of mutual terror, or at least to modify it. And I was thrilled that I had been asked.

The "Star Wars" Label

John Poindexter We tried to find a name for the idea. The media immediately started calling it "Star Wars." We wanted a catchy name but couldn't come up with one, so I finally said, "Let's call it SDI."

James Abrahamson The way the "Star Wars" label came about was that there was a little newspaper in Connecticut that said, in its headline, "The President Is Advocating Star Wars." And Teddy Kennedy picked that up and began to pound that theme, that this is ridiculous, it's fiction, it's like the movie *Star Wars*. That is how the name stuck.

Edward Teller   To my mind, the term "Star Wars" never made a particle of sense. It was invented by a person who was very good in influencing public opinion.

The Reaction

Sergei Tarasenko   In the Foreign Ministry, we were rather complacent about this initiative. It was a political thing. Among my colleagues, we did not think it was real stuff, a real menace, a real threat to the Soviet Union.

We saw that the main battle was in this rhetoric shield, that we had somehow to undermine the presidential initiative and put it against the ABM Treaty. For most of the time our efforts were concentrated on arguing with the American side that the SDI was not consistent with the ABM Treaty.

Our scientists did not believe it could be deployed. But from the propaganda view, we saw a good chance of accusing the United States of undermining the strategical parity of balance, or trying to get advantage over the Soviet Union militarily. Therefore, this whole issue moved into the areas of propaganda and public argument, not in the real research and military-related argument.

David Abshire   Reagan was right on some of the things that may have grated on the European allies. The so-called Star Wars grated because the European allies wanted to bury their heads in the nuclear deterrent theology that was totally appropriate before we reached parity and the Soviets gained superiority in certain areas.

Reagan, before he became president, became convinced — correctly so — that there was a real problem with this deterrent doctrine. This really rattled the Europeans, because it was like a Christian questioning the Trinity. Have faith; if you have faith and don't rock the boat, this doctrine will work.

And Reagan was correct in recognizing that if you got into real crisis management, you had problems. There were two ways out: one was a massive buildup of conventional forces, which the Europeans didn't want to do; the other was to seek to enhance oneself defensively. The search for the Strategic Defense Initiative was a way out of this, and it helped to win the cold war.

Donald T. Regan The SDI was to cost only several billion dollars to start and then gradually increase until sometime in the early 1990s. Then it would be much more. But once you spent that, you had it, and it was not going to be an ongoing expense, except for maintenance.

My point of view was that I firmly believed that we needed a shield of deterrence against intercontinental ballistic missiles, and I still believe in 1996 that we need it: we have no such protection today. I don't know how people can go to a movie like *Independence Day*° and not think about what protection we have against outsiders — I'm not saying extraterrestrial outsiders, but an errant missile being lobbed our way, out of some rogue country.

If the president wanted such a thing, I felt, all right, if we want it, we will have to cut back on other things. So if SDI is a priority, we will have to downsize something else.

My sense was that we couldn't have all these missile cruisers and aircraft carriers if the Pentagon was insistent on SDI. I also felt that there was a lot of waste, fraud, and abuse in the federal government. I still think so.

Caspar Weinberger Some people thought that it couldn't be done; secondly, that you shouldn't try to do it; thirdly, that it was too expensive; and fourthly, as President Reagan always used to say, "Why didn't I think of it?"

The scientific objections should have been long since set to rest, because we demonstrated, even with a fairly brief period of development and research, that we could do it, and could do it very well. The issue of expense is always raised; people who had no idea of what they were talking about used to talk in the trillions. It still engenders fierce emotions because of this feeling that if you defend yourself, you're being provocative and you're going to use it for offensive purposes, which I've always thought to be utter nonsense.

The theory seemed to be, If you were preparing an event, you were obviously thinking about an attack. Nobody paid any attention at all to the fact that the Soviets, from the day after they signed the ABM Treaty, had been trying to develop this capability.

Geoffrey Kemp We knew that the Soviets were working on all sorts of Star Wars technology. We know, from our own experience, that it is

---

° A 1996 film in which Earth is invaded by extraterrestrials intent on the annihilation of the human race.

frightfully expensive. This, combined with the endless studies that were coming before Gorbachev on the cost of Vietnam, of Cuba, of Syria, and of Angola, was an enormous drain on their treasury. These facts, together with the fact that Ronald Reagan was as hard-nosed as he was, were very salutary.

Oliver Wright   My view is that [SDI] is one of the major contributors to the downfall of communism. Up until SDI, the Soviet Union had managed to match the United States, weapons system for weapons system. But with SDI, whether or not it was going to be successful — the Russians felt that it might be successful — the Russians knew they couldn't do it, because there was nothing more by way of resources to squeeze from the civil economy.

So Ronald made them cry uncle. This was an idea that he had thought up himself — that there must be a better way of handling superpower relationships than mutual assured destruction. So he got his scientists together and asked, "Isn't there a better way?"

Nicholas Daniloff   As I understood Star Wars, it was a very ambitious system which was going to be able to shoot down incoming Soviet missiles by American missiles based in space — and possibly based on land — but it was a very fragile system and the Russians were going to work, I think, to play on those fragilities and make Star Wars ineffectual.

As time went along, there were a number of serious disputes. There was the issue of intermediate-range missiles to be placed in Europe; they were very concerned and upset when it looked like the United States had succeeded in convincing the Western allies to impose those missiles in Europe.

Horst Teltschik, national security adviser, Federal Republic of Germany; deputy chief of staff of the Chancellery   The question for us was, What does SDI really mean? We understood it as a huge program, subsidizing American research on basic scientific issues, things like lasers and computer technology. It was understood that the American government would spend billions of dollars for such programs.

Our scientists wanted to participate in these programs because they believed that the research involved would give the U.S. tremendous advantages.

Bernard Ingham   Mrs. Thatcher firmly believed that there had to be a balance of nuclear terror, that this was what had kept the peace for so long. She was very skeptical as to whether science could ever devise a 100 percent secure system. But she felt that even if it could be 80 percent, it was worth going along with.

Charles Powell Mrs. Thatcher was very supportive, from early on, of his Star Wars initiative — initially the research, but subsequently also the idea that it ought to be deployed. She saw SDI as a thing for the future; it was looking forward, to a future strategy.

Was SDI Feasible?

Richard Perle [The feasibility of the Strategic Defense Initiative] depends on what is meant by SDI. The president's concept — or what became known as the president's concept — of a hermetic shield was never technically feasible, and certainly wasn't affordable, even if you could imagine the technology that could put it together.

But it wasn't necessary to imagine the perfect defense in order to believe that SDI was exactly the right thing to do, for several reasons. First, if we didn't make a start on developing the technology, it was clear that we were never going to have it, and the Russians were working on it, and it was impossible to tell, without making the effort, what could or could not be done. Secondly, the mere prospect that we might be developing ballistic missile defense had such profound, and then troubling, consequences for the Kremlin that it would have been worth doing even if it evolved into a charade.

It wasn't a charade; there was real research and development behind it. So I think it was imaginable that we would develop a technology that would at least give us limited defense. It was important to embark on the program, even though the utopian vision was not in any foreseeable future.

James Abrahamson The scientific skepticism revolved around [the questions]: Would it be perfect, and what would the costs be? The problem was that we had some wild advocacy groups who would promise a perfect, leak-proof defense, and they would define it as a bubble over the United States that no nuclear missiles could get through.

That is nonsense! Nothing that man ever creates is perfect. Obviously, we were going to make it as good as we could, but it was clear the other side would look for countermeasures to get through that system, so we would always have to be upgrading it. That is no different from any other weapons system.

In my testimony to Congress, I would say, "This is a research program at this point. Our job is to do the research to get an extremely capable set of components to put in place, and to bring the cost down to a level that the nation can afford." I firmly believed that we could find something quite reasonable.

Colin L. Powell   We thought it had operational viability; that's what we were trying to find out. As Weinberger always testified, "We are not coming to you [the Congress] to put something up until we have something that will go up and actually work. So what we're asking your support for is to pursue the research, because we think we can do it."

The opponents of SDI did not want us to aggressively pursue the research because, Lord forbid, we might be able to do it, in which case all of their thinking about mutual assured destruction would be down the tubes.

Reagan, in my judgment, was in a slightly different world. He had his inherent belief in the power of American technology to do what it says it can do, almost a "We will go to the moon in ten years" kind of thing. But beyond that, he believed, with all his heart, that nuclear weapons were terrible, that nuclear war was unthinkable, and that we had locked and loaded for forty years to destroy each other with nuclear war in times of crisis.

He believed that we had to change that paradigm, and he believed with all his heart in the shield approach — that is, "Let's get rid of our big guns, because we both have shields to defend us." And what could be wrong with having a shield? Shields don't attack anybody; they defend from somebody.

Nicholas Daniloff   There were a lot of concerns — major concerns — about the Star Wars program, which they [the Soviets] saw very quickly as something that could bankrupt them if they were to do what they had done in the past, which was, basically, to try to mimic every weapons system that the United States created, plus to create a counter to that weapons system.

In the case of Star Wars, they decided that they couldn't match it, that it would, in effect, bring them into financial difficulties, and they knew that much better than we did at the time. They decided, if need be, that they would create a spoiling system to render Star Wars ineffectual. So from 1981 on, to the death of Chernenko, relations were extremely cold and tense and difficult.

David Abshire   It really didn't make a difference whether this thing would work exactly as Reagan envisioned it. It probably wouldn't, but it was the final blow in the cold war.

We know that the Soviets felt threatened by the strategic initiative, and also, on the tactical initiative, [that] they felt they would lose conventional superiority by the midnineties. And Gorbachev was smart enough to turn around. So Reagan — who was belittled in Europe because of the SDI and because he rattled the boat — rattled the boat that helped bring this thing to a conclusion.

George Bush   I felt SDI should be supported. I think that the Soviets were scared of SDI.

Craig Fuller   Bush saw it as strategically very useful. He had greater doubts about whether it was ultimately deployable or not. I don't think that he was as thoroughly motivated to deploy it at any cost as President Reagan was.

Nimrod Novick   Shimon Peres was fascinated with the concept of Star Wars. He studied the issue from scratch. He would say, "Gentlemen, this is the end of the Soviet Union." We would ask why, and he would reply, "America is divorcing the Earth and going into the heavens, and the Russians are not going to be able to compete. This is it: Reagan is going to destroy the Soviet Union."

None of us on the staff understood the trend that Peres saw evolving out of this. He admired Reagan for going for it.

Joseph Metcalf III   I thought that SDI was the way to go — and it worked. It was a fog job, in many ways a bluff, but we did convince the press that we were doing it.

Caspar Weinberger   It was a big factor in ending the cold war, because they [the Soviets] saw, correctly, that while they might not be able to do it, we almost certainly could, and that would render impotent a huge amount of their military capabilities.

We didn't want it for any military advantage; the president's willingness to share it with the Soviets proved that. What we wanted was to defend ourselves against any kind of attack, Soviet or otherwise, from these most horrible weapons.

Criticism of SDI

Gerald R. Ford When you talk about SDI, you mean the way-out program to shoot down missiles. I was not consulted on this, and I had the impression that not many other people were consulted.

Among my areas of expertise in the Congress, and in the White House, was our space program. I was there at the beginning, and I followed it closely because I had a personal interest in it. When I read what President Reagan had said — I didn't see the speech; it's my understanding that this language was almost entirely written by President Reagan himself — I couldn't believe they were making that kind of promise. People like Dick Perle will try to convince you that it was feasible and doable; Dick is a fine public servant. But very few people I knew who were experts ever said that we could develop that kind of a technical capacity in the foreseeable future. I'm not saying you couldn't way, way down the road.

Martin Anderson There is a simple way to explain criticism of SDI. There is an almost 99.6 percent correlation between one's opposition to, or support for, Star Wars and one's political registration. You can look at all the scientists who think this is a crazy idea, and right now they are all Democrats.

The big mistake we make is that we think that all intellectuals and academicians have integrity. That's the last place you'd want to look for integrity.

James Abrahamson I believe that it is important to focus on who the opposition was: the strongest opposition came from the Union of Concerned Scientists. They believed that this nuclear dilemma — they can destroy us, we can destroy them — was foolproof; that it would work; that the only thing wrong with it was that it kept escalating; and that somehow that was the fault of the militarists on both sides. And if we could only be reasonable about it, we could get back to about seven or eight ballistic missiles, and the cost would go down, and that money could be spent on peaceful purposes.

Caspar Weinberger SDI, in effect, repealed the education of all these specialists who had been talking for years about how if each side was capable of destroying the other, and there was no defense, there would be no attack. It was a very peculiar idea that you were only completely safe if you were totally vulnerable.

To have that idea challenged by the president of the United States infuriated some people. You have no idea of the emotions that this proposal brought forth. There were people who saw their whole educational careers, and their whole military specialties, being attacked, and they were furious about it.

It was perfect nonsense. The president did not want superiority; he even offered to share it with the Soviets after we developed it. But he and I felt that it was a very dangerous thing to go into an area of tremendous Soviet nuclear capability without any defense whatever.

James A. Baker III   The president succeeded in foreign policy in spite of the national security apparatus. When I say succeeded, [I mean] he won the cold war — he beat back communism — and he did it in a way that was controversial at first. Remember the "Evil Empire" speech? And SDI? The establishment said, "Tut, tut, there's a crazy cowboy off the reservation."

And the truth of the matter is that he was right on both of those things. I know, from talking to Gorbachev, that the SDI thing scared the Soviet Union to death; they couldn't compete.

Pavel Palezchenko, interpreter for the U.S.-Soviet arms talks; interpreter for Soviet General Secretary Mikhail Gorbachev and Soviet Foreign Minister Eduard Shevardnadze   The debate in the U.S. on SDI was followed very closely. What was important for Gorbachev was that he didn't want SDI to scuttle START [Strategic Arms Reduction Talks]. On the other hand, he could not ignore SDI, so he had to play a very cautious game. And therefore he was attentive to the U.S. debate.

He was also working very closely with the Soviet scientists and academics to try to see whether SDI could be skirted or circumvented in some way. When he came to the conclusion that it could be circumvented, he moved very aggressively on both INF and START.

It was a very difficult thing for Gorbachev — like squaring the circle. He knew, on the one hand, of Reagan's commitment to SDI, and on the other hand, he knew that some taking into account of SDI was necessary for any arms control agreement.

David Abshire   The cold war was a war of attrition: we built resource upon resource. [SDI] strained the Soviets and in part led to their collapse. They knew that they could not keep up with the technical revolution. So we broke loose from an attritionist strategy and went around their flank.

James Abrahamson   I don't think that anybody understood the real implication of what was going on in the economy and in the structure of the Soviet Union.

I believe that we had a marvelous, unintended consequence. And while SDI was not the only factor in that, it was a significant factor. A lot of Russian generals have told me that SDI was one of the major factors in the demise of adversarial communism in Russia.

George P. Shultz   As far as the ending of the cold war is concerned, it was over by the time we left office. What was left to do was to manage the endgame.

Jack Matlock   In fact, we couldn't have done SDI in anything like ten or fifteen years. It was probably oversold with the American public, but to get money for anything you have to oversell it. And besides, Reagan was a true believer.

Most of us didn't think it could work. But as a political bargaining chip and lever, it was extremely important — something the critics never gave us credit for.

If you look at the Soviet decision process, they will tell you that they could not have convinced their military to make these concessions if we had not been threatening SDI. Now, Reagan might have made a deal on it at that time. But if he had, it would have had the unfortunate effect of convincing Gorbachev that he could get the relaxation of tensions just with arms control.

We were still determined to make human rights and the opening up of their society important, as well as settling conflicts in the Third World. As long as they were fighting in Afghanistan and — through the Cubans — supporting the Sandinistas in Nicaragua, we had a problem. We did not want to delink all of this and let them have their arms control, which would let them reorient their economy without opening up their society. We considered that very important for long-term peace.

Robert C. McFarlane   The outcry against SDI came because it wasn't orthodox. For forty years the NATO strategy of offensive nuclear power deterrence had worked. Why tinker with something that works? If you go for defense and build the Astrodome over America, you will separate Europe from us, and this will invite Soviet intrusion. Then, the cost was very high.

Finally, with SDI we seemed to suggest that the United States wanted to have a first-strike capability. If you protect your own people and don't have to worry about getting hit, it is safe for you to attack them. If it looks that way in the Kremlin, won't they attack you before you get SDI built? So you are making the world a much less stable place.

We had to go through that calculus well before we ever made a speech, and say, "Those are fair points." It is true that the average American today — and then — really did like it. It was an appealing idea to be protected; the balance of terror had never been liked by Americans. The media didn't like it, but the people did. There was opposition in Congress and in Europe.

It wouldn't have worked unless we had an orthodox logic, which, frankly, Reagan didn't agree with. It was: if we spend money on what we do best, if we exploit our comparative advantage in economics, and if we spend one dollar and require them to spend two, then that is more effective than trying to match them tank for tank, plane for plane — where they would always win. The logic was: if we do that, and they begin to be stressed, their reaction will be to stop SDI. But how can they stop it? If we say, "The price for stopping it is for you to reduce your offensive ability to strike first," then they might do that, out of self-interest. Up until then they didn't have an incentive. If we give them a reason to worry economically, any Russian leader will say, "I can't deal with this. I can't afford it."

Reagan didn't quite agree. He said, "I am going to build this thing." I said, "Mr. President, that is going to be a hard sell on the Congress, and I don't think you will have to build it." He asked, "Why?" I replied, "If you can get the Russians to come your way — to come down gradually from six thousand warheads — they will reach a point where you don't need an SDI. When you get down to three thousand warheads, it will not be feasible for the Russians to strike first; they couldn't hit all our targets." He said, "You may be right, but I see that my moral obligation to the American people is to protect them. Until I see a very different Russia, I will not move away from my commitment to build this thing."

7

Operation Urgent Fury

A period of self-doubt is over. . . . History will record that one of
our turning points came on a small island in the Caribbean where
America went to take care of her own and to rescue a neighbor-
ing nation from a growing tyranny.

Ronald Reagan, October 25, 1984

*At 5:46 A.M. (Atlantic time) on Tuesday, October 25, 1983, a seventeen-
hundred-man force of U.S. Marines and Army Rangers invaded the small
Caribbean island of Grenada at the invitation of the Organization of Eastern
Caribbean States (OECS). Eugenia Charles, chairman of the OECS and
prime minister of the island of Dominica, had made an urgent, personal appeal to President Reagan to help contain the spread of Marxism that threatened the region in the wake of the overthrow of Grenada's leftist government
by an extremely radical faction.*

*Among the other reasons for the invasion, code-named Urgent Fury, the
most readily apparent was the possibility that approximately one thousand
American students enrolled at the island's medical school might be taken
hostage by the radical regime that had ousted and murdered the leftist prime
minister, Maurice Bishop, and some members of his New Jewel government.*

*There was perhaps another, more obscure reason for the U.S. military ac-
tion: President Reagan was delivering a message to the Sandinistas, to Fidel
Castro, and to the Soviet regime that his administration would not tolerate
their continued activities in the region.*

THE PRELUDE

**Hudson Austin, general; military leader of the government of Grenada
during the Bishop administration; military leader of the anti-Bishop**

coup   In his campaign for the presidency, Reagan made a promise that he would get rid of the revolution in Grenada. Soon after his election, he cut off diplomatic relations with Grenada by not assigning his diplomatic representative in Barbados to Grenada.

The U.S. had conducted maneuvers off Puerto Rico, which, we believed, were a prelude to an invasion of Grenada; they were called Amber and Amberines, which we saw as Grenada and the Grenadines. We were aware of this, and of the fact that, from the very beginning, the Reagan administration was hostile to the Grenadian revolution.

Kendrick Radix, attorney general of Grenada; minister of legal affairs; ambassador of the People's Revolution and government of Grenada to Washington and to the United Nations; minister of industrial development   There were, from the outset of the revolution, belligerent noises made by Ronald Reagan. I mean the "Evil Empire" speech and, by that, the projection into any area of the world where he perceived an evil empire.

We are a sovereign country. You have relations with Guatemala; we don't have any. You have relations with South Korea; we don't have any. You orchestrated [President Augusto] Pinochet's Chile; we wouldn't have. If Cuba is your problem, that is your business. You had relations with mainland China; we didn't, because we didn't like the behavior of the Chinese. The U.S. could have strengthened Bishop's hands with normal relations.

Oliver North   The actual events that led up to the rescue operation in Grenada — that's how I prefer to characterize it, because that's what it really began as and was — began in the summer, with the New Jewel Movement's collapse and the ascendancy of Cuban-supported radicals.

Maurice Bishop came to the U.S. to address the Organization of American States. There was a secret meeting arranged between Bishop and Bill Clark. We tried to make the effort to entice Bishop away from the Cubans. Bishop had been put in command by the Cubans; he realized he wasn't radical enough for what they wanted to do.

Eugenia Charles, prime minister of Dominica; chairman of the Organization of Eastern Caribbean States   Bishop came to the States in the spring [of 1983]. His visit was very downplayed. He met with people in the administration, but he didn't meet Reagan or the attorney general or people like that.

Robert C. McFarlane   The president's not having received Bishop was not on ideological grounds. There is a threshold of a country's importance, and because of limitations on the president's schedule, Grenada at the time didn't rise above the threshold. There were lots of presidents he never saw.

Kendrick Radix   I was ambassador in Washington for one year. While there, I was concerned by the very strident nature of some of the statements of the prime minister.

On my return here, I tried to temper some of the rhetoric and also to advocate a different approach in dealing with the government of the United States. By the time the prime minister had made his trip to the United States in 1983, there had been a turnaround, in terms of seeing the need not to antagonize the Americans. With the revolution, we had become the pariahs of the Caribbean.

So, despite the mistrust, we sought to send out a feeler to see what the possibilities were. They never really took it as a serious initiative, because they had no respect for us as a country, or as a government. A fellow in the State Department says, "You people are going to establish relations with Cuba. The government of the United States will view with great displeasure any establishment of relations with Cuba."

Keith Mitchell, professor of mathematics, Howard University; consultant to U.S. agencies; Grenadian minister of works and communications   While I was in Washington, we were in touch with a number of senators and congressmen, from both sides of the fence. I would naturally identify with the Democrats, but I found them lacking in understanding of what was happening outside the United States.

Maurice Bishop was seen as a popular Third World leader in the liberation of black people. It sounded nice, but I thought that the Democrats never understood what was happening in Grenada. I thought they saw it as a black versus white issue — Reagan, the white president, wanting to intervene in Grenada, a black country.

And they never understood the extent to which Maurice, while articulating beautifully the cause of black people in the international arena, was himself an oppressor of black people in his own country. That is where I found myself completely disillusioned with their own behavior: they seemed to be able to find justification for Maurice's wrongdoings in Grenada. I couldn't understand that.

They were not prepared to listen to people like me, because I seemed to them an American lackey.

Kendrick Radix I had known Maurice Bishop from when we were children. We were actually the first young people in the world to come into government as the product of the 1960s.

Why the New Jewel Movement? It must be understood that we had had about twenty-nine years of [Eric] Gairy.* He became corrupt — secret police, violation of human rights, autocratic behavior. So, to redefine our presence here, we took up the cudgels to get on a more acceptable road.

The New Jewel Movement believed in popular democracy; we sought to champion the cause of the poor and the dispossessed and to organize on behalf of the downtrodden. Ninety percent of the people were opposed to Gairy, and when they heard of the revolution, they came out, went to police stations, and took power in the country — people's power — and so we began the process of implementing our program of mass democracy.

Dr. Michael A. Radix,† physician at Richmond Hill Prison, Grenada At least 60 percent of the people — and over 90 percent of the youth — were genuinely pro-revolution, because what was put to them was this: These are the people who have been running the country for so many years, and they have ruined the whole thing. You should be part of the development, but you're not.

It was very appealing to young people, who were told that they should be a part of the future. And it also appealed to youngsters to run around with guns and ammunition. So they bought it. The actual overthrow of Gairy was a joke: a couple of dozen guys, including Austin, made the "Green Beasts" [Gairy's forces] run away. Hudson got an opportunity to be the big man. The whole nucleus of this revolution took place in Saint Paul's, where he lived, where I lived, where Bishop lived. We were all friends. He was then made a general.

---

* A Grenadian trade union leader who had won five out of seven general elections between 1951 and 1979.

† On the day of our interview, in an attempt to find Kendrick Radix, we by mistake went to the offices of Michael A. Radix, a prominent physician who had received his medical training in Ireland and then remained there for some years, until after the U.S. invasion of Grenada. While chatting with Dr. Radix, we learned not only that the physician was the younger brother of our intended interviewee, but that his political views were diametrically opposed to those of his sibling, and that he had a great deal to say about the Grenadian revolution and the U.S. invasion. We then arranged to interview Michael Radix as well.

Kendrick Radix When I was a young boy, my father used to talk to me about Africa. He also told me how he had to travel to Cuba at age fourteen to cut cane, and then go to Colombia, and to the United States, where he worked and sent himself through school and experienced racism in America.

When he returned to Grenada — we were the first indigenous, educated family of professionals in Grenada — we were not accepted by the ruling class. This took root in me more than in Michael, because we all have different chemistries.

Michael A. Radix I am a capitalist; this is the way I was brought up, and I never changed. I was scared of communism because, as far as I was concerned, communism robbed people of initiative; it pulled people down rather than elevated them.

Quite a lot of the early meetings of the New Jewel Movement, which was the nucleus of the People's Revolutionary Government, took place in my mother's dining room on Saturday afternoons. I visited my mother on Saturday afternoons, not to pry into the New Jewel's affairs, but it just so happened. So I often overheard quite a lot of things that were being discussed.

What I used to hear was that this was an organized Marxist program; there were no halfway measures. That was generally talked about because there are many capitalists here: nearly everybody here holds a little land, a cow, a few chickens. It was very different to introduce their system into a place where everybody has a bit of land, so it was generally talked about that they would have to do an easy squeeze, that it couldn't be a sudden sort of thing, and that they were out to sort of gradually change the system — but change the system they would.

Maurice Bishop

Desima Williams The moment made the man, and the man was right for the moment. Bishop was an extraordinary human being: he was educated, compassionate, and talented.

He was middle-class, yet he was committed to poor, working-class dispositions and sensibilities. Later on he would be very dismissive and arrogant toward those who objected to the revolution, particularly those in the upper class — rich people — who were very hostile; he was very hard on them.

Paul Scoon, governor general of Grenada   Bishop was charismatic, he was well-spoken — a very articulate young man — he was good looking. The girls liked him quite a lot, and he liked them too.

He obviously had been delving into these socialist things for a number of years, although I think that his deputy, Bernard Coard, was more deeply involved; he was more incisive when it came to communist ideology.

But Maurice had a crowd appeal, which, in my experience, no politician in this country had, except for Eric Gairy when he first came on the scene. People liked Bishop; they followed him. They weren't concerned in those early months about whether he was a Communist or not. In fact, we didn't know anything about communism. Bishop was the man; he was the leader.

There was a lot of talk that Bishop was supported by the Cubans, and that Coard — who wanted to move faster — was supported by the Russians. We know that Bishop simply adored Fidel Castro; I don't know if Castro adored him equally. What I would say is that the Coard faction — and Bernard Coard in particular — was more ruthless than was Bishop. And perhaps he wanted more ruthless things, more quickly. Bishop had a more human touch.

Michael A. Radix   There is a myth that Bishop was some kind of a moderate and that Coard and his people were radicals. All the programs Bishop had were 100 percent Marxist. There were all kinds of people here from the Communist-bloc countries — I used to play tennis with the Cuban ambassador — so when it is said that if Bishop hadn't died he would have made peace, no way. Bishop idolized Fidel Castro; whatever Castro said, that was it. It was heavy stuff.

The Bishop movement was a combination of the middle class and the upper class, who never liked Gairy because he was an upstart: he had the wrong color; he preached violence against the plantation owners.

The Bishop revolution had to do with youngsters, the middle class, the upper class, and the Catholic Church. I couldn't understand why the Catholic Church, which was supposed to be against Marxists, had a very strong part in the overthrow of Gairy. In fact, the rifles for Bishop's people were stored in the Catholic college.

The Airport

Donald Gregg The vice president had been concerned about Grenada for some time, particularly the airport. There was a real logistic problem for the Soviets to get things into that part of the Caribbean; they really didn't have a place to land, and this would give them a launching point.

Michael A. Radix This island was being prepared. There were people who had come from other islands: Trinidad, Saint Lucia, Jamaica, and Barbados. And after Cuba, we were the next stronghold, because we were the first people to have a revolution in the Caribbean.

There were a lot more planned, a lot more. They were all going to go: Dominica was going; Saint Vincent was going to go. This island was exporting terrorism. They were training people here to export terrorism.

Also, this large airport that could take a Concorde tells you something. Of course it was a jump-off point for Russia and Cuba.

Kendrick Radix The talk about the export of Marxism is a real joke. The real thing is that governments like ours — who take power through revolution, who are among the people, who seek the integration of one Caribbean — are considered dangerous, and therefore they have to be dealt with.

So they were involved not only in military preparation but in economic stranglehold, where Reagan tried to sabotage our number-one project, which was the airport. They started to intervene in the Caribbean Development Bank, giving express directions that Grenada could not get funds that were for infrastructure.

The airport was a civilian airport; there were no underground facilities. We realized that we needed an airport that could provide us with international connections to our country, both to bring people in and to send our exports out. We were going to exploit tourism because that was the only real future for the country; our agricultural products could not sustain a modern economy.

The idea that the airport was for other purposes was American propaganda; America saw everything in its own interests. Our people down here were dying for a ten-cent tablet, but the Americans didn't send any. Our people didn't have water in their houses; our roads were in terrible shape.

But as soon as you rise up to change some of these things, you are branded as anti-democratic, as being Communists. This was the mind-set of those rabid Reagan Republicans.

Joseph Metcalf III   I believe that our policy toward Grenada was bank-rupt. I visited Barbados when Carter was president, and I met with our ambassador and discussed Grenada. The decision had been made during the Ford administration not to help them with the airport; low-level bu-reaucrats had determined that the number of flights projected over a ten-year period did not justify the expense.

They forgot the objective: this guy, Bishop, is a Commie. And it's been demonstrated with despots like him that if they came to us first and we didn't help, he would go somewhere else — which is exactly what he did.

Kendrick Radix   I was present at the United Nations in 1979 when Mau-rice Bishop requested Fidel Castro to give assistance in the building of an international airport. It was not the other way around. I was there.

Joseph Metcalf III   In many ways the best part of our Caribbean policy was the military aspect, which at least made clear to people like Castro that we weren't going to put up with this fooling around.

The whole thing with Bishop was completely mismanaged; we should have built that airport for them. It was going to cost ninety million dollars — compared to nineteen killed and over half a billion dollars.

It was shortsighted; our policy in the Caribbean over the years had been shortsighted, I don't care what the administration was. It was the professionals in the State Department and the CIA.

Kendrick Radix   Here, the focus was on tiny Grenada's building of an international airport. One can recall Reagan's speech on national tele-vision, holding a satellite map in his hands, saying that these guys are building an airport with a nine- or ten-thousand-foot runway for Russian jets, and with underground fuel storage, and all this nonsense.

In fact, Reagan could have saved the Americans millions of dollars — as Maurice Bishop said — by just sending someone down there with a Kodak Instamatic camera and snapping that.

Sergei Tarasenko   I can confide that a couple of days before the inva-sion, the Grenadian government asked us for emergency aid — to the tune of five million dollars — because they were at the end of their wits. In Moscow we had no interest in this affair. We refused to give them that sum. Grenada would fall by itself.

THE ARREST AND KILLING OF BISHOP

On October 12, 1983, Maurice Bishop and several of his associates were seized by dissident members of his New Jewel Movement. He was held under house arrest for several days but was freed when thousands of his supporters marched to his home and then escorted him toward Fort Rupert.

En route, soldiers loyal to Coard separated Bishop from his supporters and marched the prime minister and his entourage to the fort, where they were executed the same day.

Kendrick Radix   The explanation for the coup against Bishop is purely the matter of domestic, personal, and individual ambition, married with the ultra-leftism of the so-called Communist elite in the Caribbean. Having attained a university education,* there developed in the Caribbean these elitist Marxists who were even higher in understanding Marxism-Leninism than was the Lenin school in Moscow, and who were ex cathedra Communists in the Caribbean.

Bernard Coard worked for a while in Jamaica, where he was a member of the Workers' Party. When he returned to Grenada, he started a movement. He had ambitions for personal leadership. I never liked him; he was mechanistic, Machiavellian, and devoid of warmth. He tried, in the 1970s, to clandestinely subvert Bishop's leadership. It was Bishop's task to keep him in check.

I worried about Bishop, but he would tell me that I failed to understand the balance of forces and realpolitik. He was right, in that sense, because there was no basis in the country for the advent of Coardism. I raised this a thousand times with Maurice; I even told him they were going to kill him. But life continued, as did the surreptitious penetration and destabilizing of Bishop's authority — the treachery of Coard, masquerading under the guise of joint leadership, and getting a plurality in the Central Committee by weeding out Bishop supporters. And Bishop, being the consummate democrat, fell for this ploy — that, in fact, here is democracy at work because of this artificial plurality.

Michael A. Radix   Toward the end Bishop felt much pressure; he lost a lot of weight. He knew that these people were plotting against him. While he claimed to have the public behind him, the hard core in the Central Committee were with Coard.

---

* Bernard Coard had been educated at Brandeis University.

Kendrick Radix When I heard that Bishop was under house arrest, I tendered my resignation from the government. I could not conceive how one could deescalate this crisis; that people would actually put their hands on Bishop, I could not understand.

At night I would go around the country, secretly readying the people for demonstrations in order to try to save Bishop's life. On Saturday, the fifteenth of October, I went to the market square in Saint George's and began speaking, informing the population that Bishop was under house arrest, that Bernard Coard was trying to seize power. I led a demonstration, calling for Bishop's immediate release. I developed the line, "No Bishop, no revolution!"

After that I was rounded up at my home, disarmed, and confined to Richmond Hill Prison as a counterrevolutionary.

During this whole crisis, Fidel Castro had sent a telegram to the existing Central Committee, asking them to treat Bishop with compassion and kindness and pointing out the fact that he was loved, by the Grenadian people and internationally.

Their response was that Fidel Castro had made himself into a god in Cuba, and that Maurice Bishop was not going to do that, so he was spurned.

Desima Williams Bishop and Coard were both pragmatic. Bernard had continuously focused on power, whereas Maurice was concerned about the people's welfare and his role in history: Did he do the right thing?

After the coup, the problem was what to do with Bishop. House arrest wouldn't solve the problem; sending him to Cuba wouldn't solve the problem.

Michael A. Radix The Central Committee of the New Jewel Movement met and decided that Bishop was a traitor, and that he should die. Bishop had a kangaroo court — a couple of hours, and up against the wall.

Keith Mitchell Bishop's own action led to his death. The minute you start instituting the military as an arm of decision, it must later engulf you yourself. It's just a natural process. These weapons were meant to control the population and to control power.

I believe that the killing of Bishop was due to personal rivalry. I am not one who would try to say that there was that big, fundamental difference between Bishop and Coard in terms of ideological position. Maybe there was in terms of the method of approach to instituting their own control. I would not want to say that one was much more extreme than the other.

Paul Scoon   I was at Government House when I learned that Bishop had been killed. I was shocked, and very sad, because although Bishop had his own ideology, he knew what I stood for and I knew what he stood for, so we could understand each other.

I knew that there was going to be a march up to his residence, which was located just behind where I was. And before the crowd arrived there, I had in my office one of his ministers, who got killed later, at the fort.

He came down to say to me, "All the people of Grenada are looking to you to try to solve this problem, so we really want you to do something about it." I simply smiled and said, "There is nothing I can do except if the prime minister advises me to. I want you to understand, I did not appoint these ministers."

He then left. I could see from my verandah the procession going into town. I didn't know whether Mr. Bishop was actually rescued. The next thing we heard was the shots from the fort, and we rushed to our front verandah and saw people jumping down the walls. I said, "We are going to have a lot of people dead, and a lot of people maimed for life."

The minister who had been in my home called me and said, "The prime minister has been rescued; everything is all right." Then the killings took place in the fort. They lined the chaps up against the wall and shot them. I heard the shots, but at first I didn't know what had happened.

The reports were not clear. At first I heard that Bishop was badly wounded. But I was really shocked when Mr. Austin — General Austin, as he called himself — came on the air in the evening to say what had happened. I was really shocked when he started to rattle off the names of the dead. In those circumstances, I thought I should adopt a wait-and-see attitude. I thought that there certainly should be some inquiry into the shooting.

Kendrick Radix   On the nineteenth, we could hear from our cells the automatic fire, but [did not know] exactly what it was. This was at about 1:00 P.M. Sometime later in the afternoon some of my other political colleagues, who were held in a special section of the prison, were taken out in an armored personnel carrier and taken to a dungeon up in Fort Frederick. And at about five or six o'clock, one could sense the tension in the air without knowing exactly what had happened.

Then we heard the soldiers talking — that Bishop was dead. We were never officially informed of that fact. We were kept in an underground place. They didn't give us food or water; we got a little water when rain fell. Of course, it was traumatic, because we realized that our very existence — from our days as students, from our days as activists, from our days of struggling to reorganize and to lead the people along a new path — had been dissipated and lost.

A flare went up at the fort after the executions. I inquired of the soldiers what it meant, and they told me it meant that the orders had been carried out.

When we were taken on the nineteenth of October from the prison up to Fort Frederick, Coard was up there with some of his colleagues, and one of the things that was said was that the proletarian revolution had arrived.

Paul Scoon The next morning Mr. Austin called on me because we were now being controlled by the Revolutionary Military Council [RMC], with Mr. Austin purportedly its head. I must say that when I heard him speak, I knew that was not of his composition; he is not a very capable man, from a literary point of view. I thought it was all Coard's doing, because I'd taught Coard for six years.

Austin looked distraught and tired. We chatted, and he said that the men had been killed because they were in the line of fire — that they were caught in some kind of crossfire. I didn't believe this, but I said, "This is a very sad thing for Grenada." I asked him how he intended to run the country. He replied that he was going to have some civilian people helping the military.

I said, "This looks reasonable, but what about the bodies of all these dead people? After all, we are still a Christian country. Perhaps what we can do is to have a quiet burial for these people." And he agreed. I also spoke to him about having an inquiry about the people who had been killed at the fort, and he agreed to that.

That afternoon I was shocked when Austin sent an emissary to me to say that the bodies could not be moved because it would result in pandemonium. I was told that the bodies were burnt and buried. This threw a different light on everything. I realized that I couldn't believe Mr. Austin anymore.

Kendrick Radix When Bishop was rescued from house arrest by the people, he went to Fort Frederick. His opponents sought a military solution because they thought he was arming himself, getting militarily ready. And the treachery had been exposed.

They either had to kill, or be killed, whereas Bishop was getting ready not for a military solution, but for a broadcast. Coard's analysis was: Bishop has come to get me because I challenged him for power; he escaped, and therefore I have to kill him.

Hudson Austin   At the point in time that Maurice was killed, he was very popular and the people were traumatized at his killing, so at that time they would support anybody who helped them.

The people were aware that Reagan was not a friend — that his administration was working against us. Not the people of the United States: we had many friends in the United States apart from the people in Washington; there were many Grenadians in the United States.

If the American administration had acted in a more friendly and diplomatic way after Maurice was killed, they would not have had the cause to invade the country, because I was willing to talk with them. I went to talk with the people at the medical school, which was the closest link we had with the Americans at the time; I pointed out the situation to them.

What was very disheartening to me was the attitude of the governor general, because I went to him and spoke to him about what we should do, even appointing an interim government. I would hold on to the army until the interim government decided to appoint somebody to take over the army. But behind my back, he invited the Americans to invade. It was treason.

THE DECISION TO INTERVENE

Robert C. McFarlane   We didn't have any great love for Bishop, but we hadn't been able to find any worthy successor. Indeed, the evidence, as it turned out, was that the more extreme radicals, even worse than Bishop, were the alternative. We didn't intervene out of pique that Bishop was gone — although the violence was a breach of law — but we just didn't have any better than what we had.

Our intelligence there was primitive. There was virtually none, really; we had no history of relationships with more viable candidates who might have been supported. Had we known about it two years ahead of time, we could have acted.

Oliver North   There is great evidence now, in what we call the Cuban Documents [seized by U.S. forces during the Grenada invasion], that in late 1982 and all the way through 1983, at the direction of the Soviets — with the help of the Soviets — they were building what we recognized as a backfire recovery base on the island of Grenada. They were storing up massive quantities of weapons; it was basically a weapons storehouse and an insurgency training center out in the Caribbean, for what Ronald Reagan would accurately describe as the last gasp of the Soviet empire.

All of that led us to conclude that we might be able to entice Bishop away from them and perhaps shore him up through what used to be called covert operations. That effort was unsuccessful, and Bishop went back and was placed under detention; eventually he was jailed.

At that point we intercepted a great deal of communications back and forth between Havana and the Cuban hierarchy and the people they had put in charge in Grenada. The bottom line was that the young students were potentially at great risk. The perception of that risk grew from August onward, so the contingency planning actually began well before the October operation.

I became the coordinator. We had a lot of meetings with the contingency planning group that I had kind of chaired at the White House, and with the interagency group at the State Department.

One of the unsung heroes of the whole thing is George Bush. In the structure we had at the time, I was kind of the executive secretary for the crisis preplanning group. I would send out the agendas and meeting minutes and basically draft the paperwork for the vice president, who chaired this group. If there was a decision coming from there requiring the president's authority to do something, I would draft the national security decision directive [NSDD], and it would be sent to the president.

As the crisis developed in Grenada, we had a series of meetings that started in mid-September or October. I can vividly remember the president saying — because there was a lot of concern, the situation was deteriorating rapidly — that there was some doubt that Bishop was still alive.

Kendrick Radix   What had prevented an invasion all along was the unity of Grenada's people: you can't invade a united people. Had they invaded under Bishop, grandfathers and their grandchildren would have resisted.

Even twenty to one hundred fatalities in Grenada would have been too many for Washington, and under Bishop, it certainly would have been a people's war. In the chaos of Bishop's murder, the Americans knew that if the leader of a government who was popular with 99 percent of the people could be murdered like that, then the people were terrorized and traumatized; that's how terrible it was. So in that moment the invasion was the way to crush them.

Keith Mitchell   The death of Bishop made U.S. intervention much easier — and much more acceptable — than it probably would have been under normal conditions. So the intervention in 1983 was a popular move, a popular event. Even people who normally would not have accepted the intervention of an American president in Grenada accepted it, because of the total chaos that existed at that particular time.

The OECS Chairman Asks for U.S. Intervention

Eugenia Charles   When they killed him, and there was no government in Grenada, then it became our affair. We figured that, at that time, we had a right to do something about it. Also, we got word from Paul Scoon, through the Venezuelan ambassador, that the OECS must do something; he didn't tell us what to do — he didn't even hint of what he was thinking of — he just said we must do something.

First of all, CARICOM [Caribbean Community and Common Market] called a meeting, and we in OECS decided that it was important for us to take a stand — that is, after Bishop was killed — so we arranged for all of those going to the CARICOM meeting to first stop in Barbados so we could have a meeting among ourselves and have an OECS point of view.

Everybody came with the idea that we had to go into Grenada, but we had less than two hundred men. There are little things that happen that later have importance. One of them is that both myself and [Prime Minister John] Compton [of Saint Lucia] had, the month before, attended U.S. military exercises in Puerto Rico. We were on the *Independence* and had seen what that vessel could do.

We learned that the top Cuban brass had arrived in Grenada. I had been arguing all the time with everybody else — even with the military in Barbados — that these Cubans who were in Grenada, building the airport, were soldiers, not masons and carpenters.

We had unemployment at home — why would you bring in Cubans to pour concrete? You would use your own people. So I was concerned about the Cubans who had just arrived in Grenada. I said to everyone, "Why has the top brass come? Are they going to pour concrete too?"

I was more and more determined that we needed the Americans to come with the *Independence*. I thought that one boat would be sufficient; I knew nothing about military matters.

Donald T. Regan   Eugenia Charles put in a very poignant plea to the president that moved him immensely, to the effect that, "If you don't stand up now, not only Grenada but my nation, and other nations in the Caribbean, will be lost to you forever. You will have another Cuba on your hands, where there will be a complete Communist takeover."

Eugenia Charles   On Monday morning I returned to Dominica, but I was worried. I knew that the Americans had sent a special representative to Barbados, and that the plane he came on would return to Washington later on Monday. So I phoned the U.S. embassy on Barbados and asked if I could get a ride on that plane to Washington — I had to get permission for the plane to land in Guadeloupe because it was too large to land in Dominica — and that afternoon I was picked up and flown to Washington.

We had to refuel in Miami, and before we took off again the U.S. representative told me, "We are going into Grenada at your request." I said, "Why didn't you tell me this in Guadeloupe? I would have returned home. The only reason I was coming up was to see that you would go in." He said, "Well, you didn't tell us why you wanted to come to Washington."

Oliver North   Her influence was critical; she was the Margaret Thatcher of the Caribbean. She was regarded across the Caribbean as a staunch believer in democracy; she was highly regarded by the Organization of Eastern Caribbean States, which she importuned to invite us to do all this. She was absolutely critical in convincing others. We joked, at the time, that Eugenia Charles was the best man in the Caribbean. She was tough — so solid.

John W. Vessey   I guess that Mrs. Charles and the other Caribbean leaders viewed this as far more dangerous than we did. The recognition by the president and his immediate advisers that he had some support by the people in the Caribbean certainly helped push the idea.

Craig Johnstone   That it was desired by her and the other leaders in the area is indisputable. They were pushing it harder and faster than we were prepared to respond to it.

Her own presence here in the immediate aftermath was a very major factor. Congressional attitudes were very dicey on this issue. The

Department of Defense thought this would be a public relations disaster of Vietnam proportions; they were reluctant to get involved in the operation at all.

Planning the Operation

Craig Johnstone   The operation was designed in the Department of State and was put to the president by Shultz.

George P. Shultz   President Reagan was willing to make a decision and anticipate what was happening, and to do something about it before it got out of hand. Don't wait until the students are hostages; act before they become hostages. So you prevent something that seemed to be very possible.

Joseph Metcalf III   He was the best commander in chief I ever served. He clearly supported the military. There is no doubt that the president made the decision to go into Grenada. Once he made it, that was it. The order to the military was: "Go out and do your thing."

John W. Vessey   North was a staffer at the NSC. Once the president decided to do the Grenada operation, it was ours: the conception, the planning, the execution — good, bad, or indifferent — was totally ours.

John Poindexter   I don't want to downplay Ollie's importance — Ollie did a lot of the liaison with the Joint Staff — but I wouldn't say he had a major operational role. Ollie was a fine staff officer: when given a task to do, he didn't say, "Well, how do I do this?" He would go and figure it out.

Robert C. McFarlane   North was the staff officer, the lead staffer, for the operation. That means that he attended the meetings with Defense, State, and the CIA, who came together to deal with contingency planning.
    The actual writing of the plans was military, and the briefing of allies was State Department. But reporting what was going on and making sure, from the White House perspective, that what needed to be done was being done was North's job. [It was] journeyman staff work, no operational responsibility.

Joseph Metcalf III   Certainly, North had nothing to do with the combat dispositions, and nothing to do with the timing. That was decided by myself and the commander in chief of the Atlantic fleet.

Fawn Hall   When Grenada started to happen, I had already seen that Ollie was very energetic; he threw himself into whatever he was working on, and he was very passionate about it.

From what I saw, there was a lot of military intelligence and papers being coordinated. And this would be the first time they could parade it about that they had overturned a Communist coup; it had never been done in history.

I was sort of scared, because I was the youngest person at the NSC. It was very heady. I was very naive at that age; I had never read the newspapers. When I was growing up, I was very proud of the fact that I knew nothing of what was going on. But at this point in my life, I started to be interested. I really didn't know where Grenada was.

They were doing a military exercise where they would play out a scenario. We were in the Crisis Management Center, utilizing it during a military exercise — a crisis management exercise — and Grenada started happening, so they switched gears.

I was really proud of Ollie. I remember, there was a stalemate about what to do, and obviously, Ollie was for going in and doing something.

I saw him do the pitch of why it was necessary to do this. He is very charismatic, very convincing — someone who can convince you of anything almost. He really made the turning point, because these guys were fighting back and forth; nothing was going anywhere. I don't know what decision had been made at this point, but I remember seeing him blend it all together and something came out. And I thought, that's a great asset — to have the ability to bring a bunch of different people together who don't agree. That is where my adulation, as you might say, began.

The Second Fleet Prepares

Langhorne Motley   We have had experience with Americans in trouble overseas. We went through the steps for fourteen days, and we were rebuffed at every step.

The first step is to go to the government and seek assurances that they understand their obligations, under the Geneva Convention, to protect U.S. students. But this was not a government. They had a shoot-on-sight curfew.

We tried to send in consular officers in a private plane from Barbados, but the plane was waved off. We leased three Pan American jets and had them ready at Miami. We said: "Okay, no hard feelings. Why don't you let us bring the airplanes in, and we will get our people out?" We were told they couldn't land. We got an agreement from one of those love boats in the Caribbean to pull up to the dock, but they wouldn't let it dock.

Remember that the taking of civilian hostages was the weapon of choice at that time, so we needed ironclad assurance that this would not happen in Grenada. But as we went through these steps, we did not get assurances.

[Then] at a critical juncture — when the president was at Augusta [Augusta National Golf Club in Augusta, Georgia] — the Lebanon re-supply had left Norfolk and the idea came up: Why don't we keep it going south before it turns and goes east?

Admiral [Arthur] Moreau [special assistant to the chairman of the Joint Chiefs of Staff], representing the chairman, was very firm in saying no. He said, "The chairman will not change the movement of the fleet unless he gets a direct order from the president." So the meeting broke up, and McFarlane and I chatted, and he got Ollie to draft the message. McFarlane took it to the president, who then ordered the change.

Joseph Metcalf III   As commander of the Second Fleet, I received or-ders to stand by for the rescue of U.S. citizens who were in peril. On about October 19 or 20, I was told to send a flotilla — which was on its way to Beirut as a normal rotation relief — south. And that got my atten-tion: What were we going down there for?

At the same time there were rumblings that we might have to inter-vene in Grenada. An operation order had been put together that nobody but a damn fool would, in my judgment, have thought militarily feasible. It mixed everybody up together, which is not the way to fight wars in peacetime, because you should fight wars with people who train together, and who shoot the enemy instead of themselves.

I went to the command center, where the basic plans were being made. The first question was: Do I have enough forces? I said to myself: I wonder why they are not letting the marines do this? Then I said to my-self: That is a dumb question; this is going to be a joint exercise, even if we have to make it one. That was pretty apparent.

John W. Vessey   It was annoying to have to turn the fleet, which was on the way to the Mediterranean to replace our force in Beirut. But with the forty-eight-plus hours we had in which to plan it and get it done, there wasn't much choice to do it any other way.

THE RUN-UP TO THE INVASION

Friday, October 21

Hudson Austin   On the Friday before we knew that the invasion was going to take place, there was a meeting in Trinidad about the situation on Grenada — all the Caribbean nations were there — and at the close of the meeting I had a call from a Guyanian official that some countries of the eastern Caribbean had asked the Americans to invade Grenada, but that the countries of the wider Caribbean — the Bahamas and Jamaica — were not in favor.

So we began to make preparations for an invasion, but we couldn't defend against bombs and battleships. I wanted to open discussions with the Americans. I contacted a friend of mine — a Grenadian who had contact with an official at the U.S. embassy in Trinidad who was with the American ambassador — and asked him to see if there was a possibility for discussion. He sent me a cable saying that Washington had said there were to be no discussions with the government of Grenada.

Donald T. Regan   The president had made the decision on the invasion of Grenada on Friday, before we flew to Augusta. In view of that, we felt that the trip to Augusta would divert the presidential mind and, at the same time, make sure that reporters and White House watchers would be reassured that there was nothing going on that they needed to pry into. If the president is going down to Augusta to play golf, sure as hell there isn't much happening.

To the dismay of the members of the club, the White House had set up quite an elaborate communications system on the grounds so that the president could stay in touch with everything. So, on Saturday, as we played golf, all was well, until the hostage-taking took place.

The assistant golf pro and one of the salespeople were taken hostage by this former textile worker who was out of a job, was about to be divorced from his wife, was distraught, and wanted to see the president. He crashed his truck through the gate, fired a couple of shots in the pro shop, and all hell broke loose.

Saturday–Sunday, October 22–23

Donald T. Regan   That Saturday night, because there had been so much excitement, the president of the club quietly suggested that we have dinner by ourselves. The next morning we were to play the par-three course and then get in an eighteen, come back, get cleaned up, have lunch on Air Force One, and arrive back in Washington by midafternoon.

That was the schedule. Well, sometime shortly after midnight I became aware of the fact that there were people talking downstairs. I wondered what it was all about, so I put my robe on and went downstairs to find the president with Shultz, both of them in their bathrobes, and Bud McFarlane, in slacks and a shirt, saying that somebody had just rammed a truck into the marine barracks in Beirut. We were under the impression that maybe five to ten marines had been killed.

Well. What to do? First of all, how do you find out who's responsible? We went through all of that. During this time nothing about Grenada is on the presidential mind; the presidential mind has turned. Grenada was not the subject of conversation at the Saturday night dinner; Grenada was not the subject of conversation while we played golf. The president checked with McFarlane after we left the first tee. And after we came back and were getting cleaned up, McFarlane briefed the president.

As the situation in Beirut turned worse during the night, I finally said to the president, "There is no way we can stay here and play golf." He said, "I know it, Don. We have got to get going." We decided we would be wheels up at 6 A.M., or shortly thereafter, so we told our wives what had happened and that we had to go back to Washington.

So a very mournful group proceeded out to the airport, and we landed in Washington at about seven-thirty. I stayed at the White House all of Sunday; I did not go home. We were all trying to find out what had happened, who was responsible, and what our reaction was going to be, so the Grenada situation sort of got shunted aside.

In the meantime, the military commanders had the green light, and they proceeded — like good military people — to disregard Beirut. That was somebody else's watch; their main thing was to get into Grenada and get out. And that's exactly what they did. It was a very successful operation.

Robert C. McFarlane   Reagan was a guy who did his duty. When you would wake him — as I did a dozen times — he understood that that was his job. He was always alert and thoughtful.

It happened twice down there. The first night it was the Grenada decision; the second, the explosion, the marine bombing in Beirut. He was very serious, but acute, in both the Grenada decision and the Beirut bombing — acute in that he understood right away that the issue here was the safety of Americans.

But, he said, "the real issue here is that we have four countries — the East Caribbean states — asking us to help. And if we get that request and say no, what signal does that send to NATO, to London, Bonn, Tokyo, and industrial countries who are relying on us? When somebody asks for help where there is such blatant provocation, we can't say no. We have to say: 'We have to do this.'"

At two o'clock in the morning, that's a fairly serious little thought. He wasn't precipitous; he thought about things. He spent an hour when he woke up that night, asking, "Is there anything else I ought to know that I haven't thought about?"

Oliver North   On that Saturday Bush came out with a recommendation to go on Tuesday. Bishop at that point was dead, and the students would be taken hostage.

The President Decides the Invasion Is a "Go"

Oliver North   The ultimate go decision was made on Sunday morning, when the president came back from Augusta. That decision would have been made even if Beirut hadn't happened.

George P. Shultz   It happened suddenly. President Reagan was concerned about our troops and their success. He was convinced — and it turned out rightly — that these so-called construction workers were also heavily armed military people. So it wasn't a little joke to go in there. Surprise would be important — and it was.

Colin L. Powell   One of the reasons why people say it was thrown together was that a fleet that was not supposed to be conducting an invasion was suddenly turned south and told to be prepared to conduct an invasion.

Paul Scoon   Sunday came. Everything was quiet. You just heard of more and more people being picked up, especially the Bishop supporters. There was a camp; some people described it like a Hitler camp during the war. A number of people had been killed, and since then a number of people had been taken out, and nobody knew where they were.

It was a very, very tense situation. People were denied going to church on Sunday; it was the first time in my life that I had ever heard of this. There was a curfew on, and although it was lifted on the Friday before — to allow people to go to shops — it was still very tense.

Monday–Tuesday, October 24–25

Paul Scoon On Monday morning, Mr. Austin — or the RMC — decided that people should go to work; the civil servants were asked to report for duty. I remember a gentleman who came into my office that morning whose greeting was, "Your Excellency, where are the Americans? Why don't they come in?" I told him to be patient. And the next morning it all happened.

Joseph Metcalf III I put together a meeting of all the commanders who were available on Monday morning. That's where I met [General Norman] Schwarzkopf [who would become well known during the 1991 Gulf War]. He was my deputy; he was assigned by the chief of staff of the army because I was a naval officer. And how was this thing going to be run by a naval officer with all those army guys? So he sent one of his best commanders, Schwarzkopf. And off we flew to the USS *Guam* — and Grenada. And the operation began right on time the next day.

Langhorne Motley When we were done with all the briefings and recommendations that Monday night in the Situation Room, he sat there for about fifteen seconds — although it felt like five minutes — and he didn't make a speech. He said, "Okay. Let's go." Once the decision was made, he would let it go; he would not micromanage.

Joseph Metcalf III At about seven-thirty in the evening a lieutenant commander comes up to me and says, "Do you mind if we don't have public affairs and the press in this operation?"

I wasn't particularly anxious to have press either, but if I thought about it — and I did afterwards — that was not the thing to do. We should have had the press.

John W. Vessey The exclusion of the media in the beginning was only to keep the thing a secret until we landed. We wanted as few casualties as possible among our own troops, among the Grenadians, and certainly we didn't want any of the American students hurt, and we didn't want to kill any Cubans as long as we didn't have to. We wanted it to be a total surprise.

We had expected to let the media in immediately. In fact, we wanted to let them in because if I could have had a couple of reporters with the Rangers and with the marines without tipping off the operation in the first place, I would happily have done that. It would have gotten us a lot of support, because those troops did their job very well. It would have been nice to have the American people see that.

But Joe Metcalf got hardheaded down there and kept them out for another whole day, and we got everybody in the media mad at us, which is a stupid thing to do — and got us a lot of terrible publicity. We should have found a way to put them in from the beginning.

James A. Baker III   This was the first time that the Reagan administration had used force. We got a lot of grief from the press about not informing Larry Speakes so that he could tell them about it, but my view was: The hell with it! American lives are at stake, and we are not going to tell anybody; that would risk American lives.

Because of that risk, we advised the president not to consult with anybody. There weren't any British soldiers involved. We didn't tell anybody, including [Speaker of the House] Tip O'Neill [D-Mass.]. We called him up to the Residence a few hours before the operation, and Tip, after listening to the presentation by the generals, said, "This is not a consultation; this is notification. Good luck, Mr. President." And walked out.

Paul Scoon   The RMC were told that the Americans were going to come in. I was told by the RMC that the Americans seemed to be invading us. Preparations were visible in other parts of the Caribbean; they had some fairly sophisticated instruments, and they could see the ships out of the harbor.

They made certain preparations; they went into one of the grocery shops in Grand Anse [an area close to the coast of Grenada] and almost emptied it out. There were also radio announcements, calling on Grenadians to come out and face the enemy. They didn't realize how powerful air power would be; they thought people would just come ashore and fight face to face.

The Call to Noriega

The U.S. government, which continued to have a relationship with General Noriega during the Reagan years, used the Panamanian leader to contact Fidel Castro and urge him to keep his troops in Grenada from firing on the U.S. invasion force.

Those of our interviewees who were involved in the incident differ on who made the initial call to Noriega, as well as on who else may have been on the line, either speaking or listening.

Oliver North There was a contingency plan to have us use bases in Panama. By agreement, we had to confer with the powers-that-be there — and Noriega was the power at that time. That was all done simply as a precaution: if we had to put a large force on the ground, Noriega was going to pick up the phone and call his friend Fidel and tell him what was going on.

Earlier on Noriega communicated [with the Cubans], and we sent the same message through the Yugoslavs, here in town, where there was a Cuban interests section. We communicated that this was to be a limited operation; that they were not to interfere; and if they did, there would be terrible consequences for them. That message was also sent to the Russians. My recollection is that that was basically the message Noriega was to send Monday night to Fidel.

Craig Johnstone I was involved in the debate as to whether we should tell the Cubans, prior to the invasion, that they should back off. The Department of Defense clung to the view that any kind of advance warning would compromise people's lives.

I had qualms about that position, because I didn't think the Cubans would mount a defense if they thought they were going to get into a fight with us. Indeed, the Cubans went into an enormous state of shock after Grenada because of the potential risk to them — as they indeed did in Managua too. In both cases, people saw this as sort of a precursor to an American invasion of their country.

We had an ambivalent relationship with Noriega. I don't think that State ever had a good relationship with him; the CIA had a much closer relationship with him. He played all sides off against the middle.

Langhorne Motley People who were in a position to know told me it didn't happen. I doubt if Bush talked to him. I have lesser doubts about Casey; you never knew what Casey was up to. One of his people had communication with Noriega; it may have been Clarridge.

Noriega had met with the vice president in Panama much earlier than that; I was with the vice president on that trip. We had lengthy discussions as to how valuable Noriega was as a conduit to Fidel, and he was discounted more than a junk bond.

Duane Clarridge Bush and Casey didn't make the call; I made the call, through my station chief [in Panama]. I got the request from the vice president, through Donald Gregg. First of all, it wasn't a request to go to Noriega first. It was, how can we get a message to Castro to tell him,

"Let's stop this nonsense of fighting to the last man." This was probably Tuesday evening. The invasion had started that morning.

Manuel Antonio Noriega   I didn't know about the invasion, but I was not surprised by the call. With the United States, you are not surprised.

This call came at the moment of the invasion because when they were advancing in the invasion, they knew that they had a problem with this area of the localization of the students and the population. They did not want these Cuban soldiers in Grenada to respond to the United States' fire.

They called me. Mr. Casey said, "Mr. Bush is on the line." Mr. Casey and Bush were on the line, and on the other line the interpreter and me. They observed that in making the invasion the United States had a problem because the American students, and other students, are behind the targets of the fire. The United States didn't want the students to die in this moment.

They sent a message to Mr. Castro: No confrontation with the Cubans; not to respond to the fire, so that it would not produce the death of the students, or the population.

The invasion was incorrect — totally. I was concerned about the liberty and the dignity of the other country, and the violation of its sovereignty and its rights. What was the right of the United States to intervene? But at the moment of the telephone call, I was only a transmitter of the message, and my concept was to help.

I communicated by telephone with Fidel. He said to me, "Noriega, the United States wants this now. But in this moment, they are firing. Your call is very late, because they are firing. But the Cuban troops are not responding to the fire." After I spoke to Fidel, I communicated immediately to Mr. Casey.

John W. Vessey   The night we went in, we had a meeting in the White House — upstairs in the residential area, because we wanted to keep it a secret. The president had Tip O'Neill and Senator [Robert] Byrd [D-W.Va.], and other leaders. Cap and I took our maps, and I briefed them on the operation. The president asked me some questions. By that time we had airplanes on the taxiways, and I told him that if we were going to do it the next morning, he had to give the order by a certain time. I explained the time-frame in some detail to him. And Bud McFarlane said, "Mr. President, we have the White House Situation Room open all night long. We'll be ready to brief you anytime you want to be briefed."

The president said to me, "What are you going to do?" I said, "Mr. President, I'm going home to bed. The Chiefs have gone over the plan; we think it's a good plan. We have well-trained troops to execute it, and unless you call it off, there's nothing I can do between now and the time they land in the morning. I'm going to wait until they've been on the ground for a couple of hours, and then I'll have someone come in and tell me what's going on." The president said, "I'll go to bed too."

The Invasion Plans

Langhorne Motley   The details were put together by the interagency group, and particularly by me, Moreau, and Clarridge. From there, it went right to the president's level — that is, Weinberger, Shultz, and McFarlane.

Joseph Metcalf III   The rules of engagement for the operation were strictly written by a politician — not even North could have dreamed this one up — because they said, in effect: there are to be minimum casualties on both sides; nothing is to be destroyed, or minimum destruction.

We were supposed to establish a legitimate government. It was very straightforward; there wasn't any doubt about what I was supposed to do, which was, essentially, to take the island, restore the government, and protect the people who were there.

It was very, very difficult to execute. You take an armed force in there, and you're not supposed to hurt anybody? This is absolutely against the principles in which you are trained, particularly in those days; we were trained to beat things up.

This was the first operation I'd ever been in where this business of lives was very prominent in the operation order. So based on that, we did our thing. But I had no doubt about what I was supposed to do: although Scoon wasn't mentioned, I was supposed to put him in. As things went on, I got very little direction, which was fine with me. Once the operation began, I sent a message every half-hour, saying what the status of things was.

Credibility was important to me. I had been involved in the evacuation of Saigon, where credibility was very low because people had been misleading and lying to the press for years and nobody trusted anybody. In Grenada I decided to tell everything that was going on — and some of the things I told were wrong, which is the fog of war.

Tuesday, October 25: Mrs. Charles's
Meeting with the President

Eugenia Charles At seven o'clock on Tuesday morning, I went to the White House. I met with Reagan, Weinberger, and Shultz. I had heard people say that President Reagan was not "with it" — that he didn't always know what was happening around him. That was completely untrue. I found him very much clued in on what was happening. He may have been briefed the night before, but he knew what he was talking about; he understood why we were worried. And he was the one who said, "You must go and talk to the OAS [Organization of American States] about this while you are here."

Oliver North I went into the Oval Office totally exhausted. I had gone into my office at three o'clock Sunday morning, after getting a phone call about the Beirut bombing.

By then I was deputy to the director of political-military affairs, which really meant that I was the coordinator for these kinds of crises, and particularly with terrorism — which, of course, the event in Beirut was.

Tuesday morning we were bringing the various prime ministers in. We would bring in one and take out another; it was public diplomacy. The two I remember most vividly were Eugenia Charles and Prime Minister Compton, who brought his wife with him; she was his young, second wife — very attractive. When the meeting with Compton was over, the president stood up and said, "Thank you very much, Mr. Prime Minister, for your support for this operation." And Mrs. Compton said, "Mr. President, there is one other message my husband did not give you from our people. Our people have enormous regard for you because, Mr. President" — and she gestured — "you have big balls." And the president went, "Well, I'll tell Nancy you said so."

Eugenia Charles Reagan was going to brief his cabinet, and he said to [Undersecretary of State] Kenneth Dam, "Mrs. Charles has been here since seven o'clock. Why don't you get her some breakfast?" Kenneth Dam said, "Yes, and while she is eating, I will brief her." Reagan said, "You won't. She will brief you."

Then the president asked me to brief the cabinet, and I was worried that he didn't have consensus. Shultz gave me his chair — I didn't know that every cabinet member had a little silver nameplate on the back of his chair — and then the president asked me to go to the press conference with him.

I was given the draft of his speech, and I changed some things that were not correct: the draft did not specifically mention that we were concerned with our own safety, that we felt that if what was happening on Grenada succeeded, they would come and pick us off, one at a time.

Kendrick Radix Having Prime Minister Charles come to Washington was merely public relations; it looked good having her come to Washington and appear on television, standing by President Reagan. She was supposed to get an airport for that. Instead, she got about four miles of road.

THE INVASION

On the first day of Urgent Fury, in one of the bombing raids designed to destroy specific military targets, a 180-bed mental hospital was mistaken for a military base when Grenadian troops were observed entering the building, and it was attacked by a 500-pound bomb dropped from an A-7 Corsair light aircraft.

According to an official U.S. estimate, at least twenty-one patients were killed in the bombing raid. The United States officially acknowledged the error six days later, on October 31, reportedly after a Canadian journalist visited the site and made the incident public.

Paul Scoon The PRA [People's Revolutionary Army] set up their headquarters in the building next to the mental hospital. There is a little bridge connecting the two buildings, and we were told by people who worked there that the RMC chaps went over and gave guns to some of the inmates. These are mad people, you know.

I think that it was a genuine mistake by the Americans. Not only guns, but a flag was planted there; this was deliberately done by the PRA to give the impression that the camp extended there. When you see that kind of a situation, what do you do?

Hudson Austin It was a miscalculation on their part. They thought the whole structure belonged to the army. The building had that barracks shape; it had been a military barracks before it was turned over by the British to become a mental hospital. This was in 1856, after the cholera epidemic in Grenada.

Desima Williams I had traveled to Nicaragua two days before the invasion. I was traumatized very deeply between the assassination of Bishop on the nineteenth and the invasion on the twenty-fifth.

It was very early in the morning on the twenty-fifth when I heard the news on the BBC broadcast. On the twenty-second, the day before I left the United States, I had spoken with a U.S. official, a diplomat. I was then receiving reports of impending action; he flatly denied it. He was either outright lying to me, or he was lied to by his government.

When the invasion occurred on the twenty-fifth, I was angry at this person; I was angry at myself; I was angry at the action. Anger, frustration, and rage swept over me. I was in shock. My two bosses were dead — the prime minister and the foreign minister.

I thought that one of the most important things to do would be to rally Latin American support for our country, so I commenced going to Nicaragua, Mexico, and Cuba. There was a Latin American response of solidarity; they did everything in terms of communication. The Cuban government had offered to do a number of things prior to the invasion and, immediately afterward, withdraw their citizens and cease belligerence. The Nicaraguans were very forthcoming.

I immediately tried to address the Organization of American States, to put forth a position there that this was an unprovoked act and that it should be condemned.

Oliver Wright We had got wind that the operation was happening. I was in almost hourly communication with Larry Eagleburger at the State Department, trying to find out what the United States' intentions were. I was doing my perfectly legitimate task of warning my government what was going to happen, and Larry was carrying out his perfectly legitimate task of not telling me.

We were good pals, but we had to go through this ritual dance. When the invasion came, it didn't prevent my prime minister from blowing her top. And what are ambassadors for, but to transmit the blowing of the top to the receiving government?

We disagreed with the United States. The U.S. did it by force; we would prefer to do it by political and economic measures. It would, obviously, have taken us very much longer to do so. Actually, I think that the U.S. was right and we were wrong.

John Poindexter We were very anxious that the whole thing happen relatively fast. We were also very much concerned that it be a total surprise.

Later on I was heavily criticized for what was said to be misleading the press, but we considered operational security to be very important for the success of the mission, to minimize the loss of life on both sides.

Craig Johnstone When you plan an operation, you look at what might go wrong. And the potential for things going wrong in Grenada seemed to be very high. One specific negative that was cited was that we didn't know whether runways had been built yet, or whether they were still soft. The prospect of planes trying to land and the wheels going right through the runway horrified people.

We didn't have a strong intelligence base as to what was there. It was clear that time was of the essence; we didn't want to be in a three-week preparatory stage, where the Cubans would find out about it and reinforce their troops. That really would have been a mess.

Joseph Metcalf III We operated for the first few days on Esso° maps; we didn't have a map of the place. Where do the roads go? I had a chart prepared by the Brits in 1898, for the depth of the water; the Esso map kind of said where things were.

There was great complacency in our intelligence — that we were going to overwhelm them, and that this was going to be a nonproblem. The whole thing was, Gee, just land and walk off, and no problem. That complacency was reflected back in the way the army — the Rangers — were going to jump out of their airplanes. They were going to make administrative jumps.

People jump out of airplanes for stupid reasons, so I said, "No, we're not going to do that. We're going in here in combat; we are going to be ready to fight. I don't care what the intelligence is."

Of course, the first thing that happened was that we started getting shot at. And fortunately, they did a combat jump, because if it hadn't been a combat jump, there would have been more casualties, because whoever had a gun was aiming at our guys.

John W. Vessey The thing has been hashed and rehashed, and criticized, but the fact of the matter is that we had a very short time in which to do it. If we were going to accomplish the objectives, we didn't have time to rehearse or do the sorts of things that one usually does in preparing for that type of thing.

For that reason, some things didn't go as well as they might have, and we lost a few people that we shouldn't have lost.

° The former name of Exxon; "S.O." stood for Standard Oil.

On the other hand, I would suggest that nobody in the world would have done it in the period of time that we did it in and as well as we did it.

Eugenia Charles I was shocked at the U.S. media reaction. I think that Americans don't like to go to war. Reagan was quite brave to stand up to it, because it was not in his benefit as a politician. But if he hadn't done it, I believe that all of the islands would have gone the way of Grenada. We must remember that the Communists already had cells in each island. All of us were going to go; it wasn't only Grenada.

Kendrick Radix Under the cover of the invasion, we — having made previous preparations — brought in some big stones and broke down the [prison] bars and escaped.

We were supposed to have been shot. The soldiers were agonizing about carrying out the order. In the decaying security situation — many soldiers were not seeing real leadership — they just changed their clothes and faded away.

After I escaped from prison, I stayed in a couple of people's homes, and eventually I decided to seek refuge in the Cuban embassy. During the invasion the 82nd Airborne Division surrounded the embassy and ordered them to put everybody on display. This was not permissible under the Geneva Convention, but they did it. [As a result,] my presence became known.

I remained there until the proconsul of the United States of America, through his minion, the governor general Paul Scoon, said it was all right for me to go home. As I was going home, some of those mentally subnormal military people took great offense at my presence; the soldiers had listened to interviews I had given from the embassy that were critical of the invasion, so they were uptight about it. They threw me down and tried to shoot me. It was a really nasty experience.

I went to my parents' house, only to be visited by the U.S. security officials, who pulled me in, and I was debriefed by Barbados police looking into the murder of Bishop. I also told American security about this.

Paul Scoon It is not true that I only learned of the invasion when I saw U.S. troops in my garden; to say that is a big joke. In fact, when the planes came in, I got a call from my ADC [aide-de-camp] — I was still in my bedroom — and these were his words: "The action has begun."

I knew exactly what he meant. In fact, I thought the troops had come in on Monday morning, rather than on Tuesday. I knew the boats were gathering offshore. I felt that the longer they stayed away, the more chaotic things would become in Grenada.

Desima Williams When the invasion occurred, the then–governor general, Paul Scoon, issued an edict that all the representatives abroad resign and return home immediately. This was around the thirty-first of October, events having occurred starting with the invasion on the twenty-fifth.

I refused to resign. I challenged Scoon's authority. I suspected — without any evidence in hand — that he was acting on behalf of the Reagan administration, and I was not going to cooperate. That was my way of not cooperating with the invasion.

Rescuing the Governor General

Joseph Metcalf III He was surrounded in his house for a couple of days. We did an amphibious landing and got him out for breakfast.

Paul Scoon That morning there were shots all over the place. I told my staff to get into the basement, and we all did. Soon after, a helicopter hovered over the front lawn. It couldn't land because of an incline, so some chaps came down. A second helicopter came a few minutes later and landed on the tennis court. It was shot at, and one of the crew was wounded; he later came back to Grenada and visited me.

In no time at all we could hear the troops in the house. They were shouting my name, so I decided to go out, much to the consternation of my wife. She thought the soldiers might have been the Cubans, or the Russians. The soldiers had my photograph. We were all taken into the dining room; that was about the safest place.

There was shelling in the area. I spent the entire day lying on the floor in that dining room. As darkness came on, the shelling became more intense. The Barbados radio was informing people as to what was going to happen afterwards, namely that the governor general would take over and carry on until new elections.

Joseph Metcalf III He wanted to talk to the queen — he was a representative of the queen — and our public affairs people wanted him to get on the radio and broadcast to the people of Grenada all this blather: Give up.

He wouldn't have any part of it. He was a cautious fellow; he was playing this thing close to the vest. He was cooperating with us within the frame of reference he thought his position was. It was clear that we were going to use him to set up a legitimate government — he was key to that — but he wasn't playing the game the way we wanted him to.

Paul Scoon   The shelling really became intense, and one came very close. The Seals were hoping that they could take us away in the night. I thought this was very dangerous, so we spent the night in the house. And in the morning, at about nine o'clock, reinforcements arrived — army people, who had landed, and we were taken to Queen's Park. We walked there, guarded by the soldiers. We were shot at, and I was very heartened when I got to River Road, a very densely populated area, and the people cheered me and encouraged me.

From there we took a helicopter to the *Guam.* After that, I was taken to Point Salines, where we spent three days before going back to Government House.

Hudson Austin   I was picked up by the Americans and taken aboard the ship *Guam.* I was questioned and fingerprinted; they put an iron chain on my leg.

They weren't obeying the Geneva Convention. You don't take a prisoner of war out of his country and put him on a ship on the sea; you treat him as you would your own soldiers. We were not treated as prisoners of war at all.

Kendrick Radix   They took me to a prisoner-of-war camp they had at the airport. They reconstructed the tiger cages of Vietnam, in that they had this wire tunnel and you had to get down on your hands and knees, like an Eskimo, to get into this area, which was guarded by a large marine with a big rifle, to create a psychological disorientation. I was there for three or four days. So, I have been jailed by Gairy, by Coard, and by the Americans.

Joseph Metcalf III   Austin and the Coards were hard-core Marxists; we saw that in the brig of the ship. They were fortunate that they were found by the marines and not by the people.

They ran the military part of the operation, which explains why, when the communications went out, the whole thing fell apart.

Kendrick Radix   We had a highly centralized party. It acted upon political orders; nothing happened without the party's dictate.

You must look at the personality of Hudson Austin. He really was a mere fig leaf, a figurehead. Even though he was a general, he took direct orders from Coard as to what to do and when. He was scripted because he enjoyed the good life of dolce vita — he enjoyed that, driving around in his car and entertaining women and that sort of thing. Coard did not discipline him for these deviant tendencies that he developed.

Michael A. Radix   Anyone who says that the trial of the conspirators was a kangaroo court must be joking. They had the best attorneys — the best — from Guyana, Jamaica, and England. Don't forget that the Communist, left-wing movement was behind them. People even brought students from various parts of the world — from the U.S. — to attend the trial; it was something like the O. J. Simpson trial. The Grenadian government is still paying off the bill for the trial.

Eugenia Charles   They should have hanged them; I don't think they should have been forgiven. I suppose that public opinion said that there were too many people to hang — that they didn't feel they could pick out the Coards and not hang the others.

WHAT THE INVASION FORCES FOUND

The Arms Cache and the Cubans

John W. Vessey   When we got in there, we found things that we hadn't known. I went down there a couple of days later and went through those warehouses loaded with propaganda leaflets and arms. Clearly, they weren't for defending Grenada.

Hudson Austin   As one American journalist put it, the arms we had could be found anywhere in the world. We had some British weapons, like the Sten gun; these were the weapons used by the militia. And what would we use to attack another island? If we wanted to go to another island, we had to rent a barge.

There were very few Russians on Grenada. They had an embassy here, but we did not have any Russian military advisers here. We did send some of our officers to the Soviet Union for military training, but we never had any Russian military instructors; we had Cuban military advisers. The Russians we had were teachers.

Paul Scoon   When Mr. Reagan took his pictures and said, months before, that it was not a commercial airport they were building, the man knew what he was saying, because if you looked at that airport — and looked, for instance, at the enormous area they had for a restaurant — they obviously had a place where troops could get their meals and stay over.

What I didn't know was that when you leave the airport, and coming into Saint George's — you see the American embassy on one side — that route was not there at all; I knew nothing about it. And the Russians had offices there, and the Cubans were on the other side.

I remember going down to that area one Sunday on a drive, and there was a whole set of Cubans coming in. There was no road there. The point I'm making is that there was no road there; this became the airport road afterward. And I said, "Where are all those people coming from?" In my ignorance, I thought they were living in a little house, but they had all these buildings, and Grenadians didn't know what was happening. I don't think the British were fully informed.

Joseph Metcalf III   The intelligence had told me that four guys had arrived from Cuba the day before. Sometimes you have a feel for what is going to happen. I said, "Those guys have come here to take charge of this defense." And they did; they placed some guns around and sharpened up the whole defensive scheme. So my feelings were right; we did get opposition.

It was a Soviet-style command and control system. I wanted to take the center out with an airplane; it would have been very hard to take out with a gun because the gun doesn't shoot straight and we might go over, or under, the target, and I was worried about collateral damage.

The Cuban troops were effective until about noon, when we knocked out their communications. After that they fell apart.

Hudson Austin   At the time there were about six hundred Cubans on the island. There could have been more; it was hard to tell because they frequently changed their people.

Some of the Cubans would have been soldiers. We had military instructors who were living in that area; our military involved the police, the militia, and the army. We had about 2,400 people, but the majority were workers from the Cuban construction company.

Fidel Castro gave the Cubans on Grenada direct instructions not to fight; any fighting that was done was carried out by Grenadians. They only tried to defend themselves; a number of them were killed.

Keith Mitchell I was not surprised at the warehouses filled with weapons, because the country had become a military base; people had guns all over the place. That is what led to the demise of the revolution.

Langhorne Motley They had tried a coup against Mrs. Charles. They were feared in the eastern Caribbean as troublemakers. We found all those weapons — one hundred thousand grenades, one for every man, woman, and child on the island.

Michael Ledeen I was asked to look at the documents that were brought back from Grenada. I went through them with a team of government people, which I headed.

Joseph Metcalf III I saw documents with Soviet signatures, including Gromyko's. The East Germans had built the main building. It was clearly a military building, with reinforced walls, and the landing strip was ten thousand feet long and well constructed.

I was ticked off when we found the arms: two bullets for every man, woman, and child in the Caribbean. We didn't even know it was there. That, to me, is an outrage; the CIA had no idea!

John W. Vessey I went down there and talked to some of the Cubans two or three days after the landing, to see how they were being treated. The Cubans were what we would call construction engineers — military construction engineers. By and large, they looked like a rear area engineer construction battalion in the United States Army; they were more mechanics than soldiers.

They were organized into squads and platoons; they had their weapons, their machine guns. They were clearly military people, with military ranks. How well they were trained, I can't tell. But they put up a fight. A handful of Rangers defeated them in a short period of time, but they were the best troops we had in the United States Army.

Paul Scoon If you speak to any of the Cubans, they will tell you that they were soldiers first. They had military training, and not only them; the Cuban doctors here had military training. From my personal knowledge, there were Cuban instructors for the police force and for the militia; it's hard to make the distinction.

We are not a warlike people. I can't understand why we had to have all these weapons. It's either that Mr. Bishop was always preparing for an invasion — possibly by the Americans — or that they were going to be exported to other islands, Grenada being the headquarters, so that if, and when, an invasion took place in Saint Vincent, or Saint Lucia, they could always get arms from here.

Michael A. Radix If the invasion had not taken place, the Coard coup would have quickly collapsed. For sure, there would have been an uprising. Then they would have used more violence, and that would have inflamed the people.

THE ROLE OF THE STUDENTS' SAFETY IN
THE DECISION TO INTERVENE

Craig Johnstone The issue of taking military intervention in Grenada came up before the students were on the radar screen; the first impetus to do the operation was not directly related to the students.

On the other hand, it was discovered that we were facing a problem because of the students, and everyone said: "What the hell are students doing there?" So we started looking into the situation, and we discovered the existence of the two campuses and the students, and we said, "Oh brother!"

The initial reaction was, "This is the end; we can't do anything because of the students being there." Then we began to get indications that the students were being eyed as potential hostages, and it became a melding of, Do we have to do something because of the students? and, Do we want to do something because of this overall geopolitical argument?

They came together; combined, they were clearly sufficient cause, from the administration's perspective. I believe that the students would possibly have been sufficient cause, once that problem became clear. The attractiveness of doing something geopolitically would probably not have been sufficient cause.

Paul Scoon All of Grenada was in danger; certainly the students were. Because the American troops were coming in, it was very easy for the local people to take some revenge on the medical students; they were the group in the country that was most vulnerable.

Having said this, I must admit that all during the revolution nobody really interfered with the American students, or American citizens, except for one or two who were asked to leave the country.

The rescue of the students was not the priority, but once the confrontation began it was the best thing to get the students away. After all, they were asking non-Grenadians — whether they were Americans or British — to get away.

Hudson Austin   The assertion that the students were in danger is the lie of the twentieth century — you can tell the world that I say so — because I personally went down to the medical school to speak to the vice chancellor: there was no such thing as a threatened medical student. The vice chancellor even told me that they called to the United States to tell the parents that they were not under any threat. Not at all.

It was really Ronald Reagan and the White House, trying to justify the invasion on the grounds that the medical students were in danger. We had no plans to take the students hostage. Where would we put them if we took them hostage? What would we do with them?

John Poindexter   If one had to go back and identify what first got the president's attention on Grenada, it would be the students. In the perspective of what had happened in Beirut during the Carter administration, the president did not want to get into a position where those students could be taken hostage.

Langhorne Motley   It was about two years since the 444 days of Tehran. What drove it, no doubt, was the 600 Americans. There was no doubt in my mind that Ronald Reagan would not sit still for 444 days. So when this thing started to unfold, we went through the normal drill.

George P. Shultz   Had it not been for the students, first, and then the real concerns of the leaders of the little island states — the democratic states near Grenada — about what was happening on that island, we wouldn't have gone in. Those were the two big factors. You had small island democracies that were terrified about the emergence, in their midst, of a relatively large, Cuban-dominated, Soviet-dominated, aggressive state.

And, of course, we tried to get the students out. We tried to get a large ship in there to take them off; that was refused. We tried to get permission for an aircraft to land and take them off; that was refused. So they were trapped on that island, and the place was experiencing a very bloody, somewhat chaotic situation, so they were in peril.

Donald T. Regan   American lives were at stake. That was the icing on the cake.

WAS THERE A MESSAGE
IN THE INVASION FOR
THE SOVIETS, THE CUBANS,
OR THE SANDINISTAS?

James A. Baker III There was some legitimate concern about the students; it wasn't just manufactured. But it was important to knock down this little tyrant who had appeared there; it was of the same ilk as the Sandinistas and the Cubans. We made it clear that this was not something we were going to permit.

John W. Vessey We did it in a fashion to make sure that it was a message to the Soviet Union, and to Nicaragua, and to Cuba; that is the way we structured it. But nobody said, "Let's send a message to the Soviet Union, Nicaragua, and Cuba by doing this." The reasons for doing it were the trouble in Grenada and the fact that we had a bunch of American students down there, and the president told us to get them out.

Victor Hugo Tinoco We were aware that there was a real possibility that, as the U.S. had invaded Grenada, they could invade us. In many respects, we had taken into account that possibility; so many decisions in economic and political terms were made because this was a real possibility.

I believe that they were unable to create internal conditions in the U.S. to invade Nicaragua — this was less than a decade after Vietnam — and before invading a small country like Nicaragua, the government has to create the political condition. The U.S. government never had the possibility to create that atmosphere inside the U.S.

Of course, also, Nicaragua was a well-organized society, and it wouldn't have been as it was in Grenada, where the U.S. lost maybe fifty soldiers. In Nicaragua, the U.S. troops would have had to stay five, six, or ten years after an invasion.

Langhorne Motley Two days after we went in, our ambassador in El Salvador was called in by Nicaraguan Defense Minister Umberto Ortega, who said, "Look, if you ever want to get your citizens out of here, call me. Here is my private number." People in the press in Europe — and to some degree in the U.S. — who had painted Reagan as a paper tiger now saw him differently.

Robert C. McFarlane The operation's effect on the Ortegas was discussed; Reagan was very conscious of that. Also, he thought it would probably send some shivers up Castro's spine about whether or not they might be next. He said, "That's fine. They might be."

George P. Shultz It was a big message to the Soviets. In fact, it was noticed all over the world — kind of like Reagan taking on the air controllers. It showed that this was a person who was willing to take action — and was willing to take action with lots of people opposed — if he thought it was the right thing to do. And he used force. It raised the credibility of the U.S.

WAS THERE A CONNECTION BETWEEN THE GRENADA INVASION AND THE MARINE BARRACKS BOMBING?

Kendrick Radix The invasion was caused, to a large extent, by the blowing up of 256 marines in Lebanon, to have a palliative for that most brutal event. They sought to immediately draw away public opinion from that tragedy, into the invasion of a tiny country, which didn't have a submarine, which didn't have a navy, an air force. We didn't even have a tank.

They used planes that flew over Grenada in less than one second: they couldn't even drop a flaming bomb because by the time they let it go, the plane was on the other side of the country.

It was most racist and most arrogant — the display of the military. They played some classical music while the helicopters gallivanted through the skies. It was most distasteful, like in an Oliver Stone movie.

Caspar Weinberger It had nothing to do with the marine barracks. First of all, it couldn't have been planned that quickly. And it wasn't; it was planned, and decided upon, before that attack in Beirut. They happened to fall on the day after each other, but that had nothing to do with it; the decision to go into Grenada had been made at least two or three days before.

When the marine barracks were attacked, we simply proceeded with the Grenada activity and the rescue operation on the Monday and the Tuesday of the next week.

Langhorne Motley   The unfortunate incident at the marine barracks had one positive note: it gave us cover to meet at the White House that Sunday. Without this, we could not have gotten away undetected.

Oliver North   The people who try to make a linkage between Beirut and Grenada both overestimate our ability to respond instantly and have ignored all the prior contingency planning, both militarily and diplomatically, that had gone on for many, many weeks before that. It turned out successfully everywhere, except in a place called 10 Downing Street. That was the one place where there was absolutely total shock that we had done this.

THE JOINT CHIEFS' OPPOSITION
TO THE INVASION

Craig Johnstone   The initial reaction from the Joint Chiefs when it was broached to them was, "Are you guys out of your minds?" They were focused on domestic public reaction, and they misread it substantially.

John Poindexter   I don't think that Cap and General Vessey were ever in favor of using military forces. We used to say that General Vessey was a charter member of the Vietnam Never Again Syndrome.

Colin L. Powell   There is a tendency, when people examine the military's reluctance to do this, to sound-bite it by saying we're suffering from "Vietnam Syndrome." But I think it is more than that. There is a natural reluctance among military leaders — a useful one which has served the American people quite well — not to get ourselves into wars because somebody gets mad one day, but to make sure that we understand the consequences of going to war; that we know what it is we're trying to do; and that we put the force to that objective with full knowledge of what we're getting into.

William J. Crowe Jr.   Anytime anyone has proposed the use of military force, Vietnam was right there, in the middle of the table. A lot of questions were asked: Why are we doing this? What are the objectives? And most important of all, will the American people support this in a sustained fashion?

Politicians don't like questions like that. It's hard to get a politician to tell you why he is committing a military force; they usually don't know. Colin Powell had the same problem in Desert Storm. The politicians mumble generalities; then they say the military is cautious. A lot of people believe that the military is eager to go out and shoot somebody, or that it should be; that's what they expect from the military. The modern military is not like that at all. In my experience, the civilians in the government were always more eager to go shoot somebody than were the military.

I heard George Bush say, after Desert Storm, "The shadow of Vietnam is behind us." Number one, that's not true, and number two, it shouldn't be true. We learned too much in Vietnam. Why do we want the shadow of Vietnam to go away? Most of my approach to life today in government is conditioned by things I learned in Vietnam.

Charles Hill   The Pentagon — with Weinberger as spokesman and leader — did not want to use the military for anything. Not for anything. Zero. I suppose that if the Russians had actually had an amphibious landing in South Carolina, they [the Pentagon] would be willing to do something. But in this case, they did not want to do anything.

Caspar Weinberger   It is just not true that the military and the DOD were against the Grenada operation. I don't know of anybody who opposed it within the Joint Chiefs; certainly, at the time, no one presented any reasons why it shouldn't be done. The military, first of all, does what they are told to do, and does it very well.

There wasn't any question about whether we should, or should not, do it. It was a question of how it should be done, given the fact that we had to act very quickly, given our worries about having another set of American hostages held for years — comparable to the Iranian situation — and given the fact that there was total anarchy down there, with a bunch of cold-blooded murderers running around shooting everybody.

These were conditions we could not tolerate, and neither could our neighbors; we were begged to come in by the other Caribbean states. At the end, there wasn't the slightest argument from anybody, because it was a matter of saving approximately one thousand American students who were there in a completely anarchic situation.

John W. Vessey   I hope you don't make Grenada a bigger issue than it really was. Grenada was not central to either the presidency or foreign policy or national security. It was a passing incident, the sort of thing that one will see quite frequently, I think, in the world of the future — the Grenadas of the world, where there is trouble, disruption of civil authority. So we either need to rescue Americans or do something quickly and get out.

MRS. THATCHER OPPOSES THE U.S. ACTION

There was consternation in the administration when Margaret Thatcher, widely regarded as President Reagan's staunchest ally in the West, voiced strong opposition to the invasion.

Langhorne Motley It was an enigma to us at first. There was only one ally with whom we could consult; that was Mrs. Thatcher. The president spoke to her twice; neither conversation was satisfactory. He was disappointed and dismayed at her vehemence. What came across from him — although he did not articulate it in this way — was: We did everything for her on the Falklands issue, yet here our citizens were at stake. He wondered why she reacted this way.

Charles Powell I don't think she's ever quite forgiven the fact that she was not properly consulted and only told at the last minute, in a telephone call. My recollection is that President Reagan said that he got pretty much of an ear-battering from her when he rang up to tell her about it.

  She felt at the time that the American intervention in Grenada without us being informed in advance was a slur on our sovereignty. We had a governor general there — the queen's governor general — yet we knew nothing of it. Indeed, very shortly beforehand, we had been given the impression that no invasion was planned. She felt that that was not the way in which one close ally should behave to the other.

Alexander M. Haig Jr. That was poor staff work; that was mismanagement. I don't blame it on the president. You don't surprise your best ally in an area of very special interest to Great Britain by telling her, after the fact, that you are invading.

George P. Shultz Margaret Thatcher and Geoffrey Howe made statements in the Commons saying that nothing was going to happen in Grenada. They were asked. They went way out on a limb. There's no reason why they should have done that. They had no information from us that we weren't going to do anything; they just assumed we wouldn't do anything unless we got their okay. And therefore they were embarrassed and jeered when they went back to the Commons. It's the woman scorned, I guess.

Robert C. McFarlane   She was embarrassed; it was the embarrassment of having it exposed that the relationship [between Thatcher and Reagan] wasn't as strong as it ought to have been. I don't think she would have opposed it if we had not already told her we didn't intend to land.

Geoffrey Howe   We felt that there was no intrinsic justification for the operation, and that the way we were treated in terms of consultation was entirely cursory.

We couldn't understand how the government of the United States could be so preoccupied with such a trifling thing. Above all — as Mrs. Thatcher said later in the week — if the United States is entitled to walk into a country because it doesn't like what's going on there, how can we complain about Russia's walking into Afghanistan? However sharp this disagreement between Reagan and Thatcher was, it didn't color their relationship at all.

Eugenia Charles   We had been sending faxes to the Foreign Office in England, and they had changed their fax number, and the faxes were going to a plastics factory in Ipswich.

The people in the factory kept calling London, saying, "We have some faxes for you; they seem important," and they were told to put them in the mail.

We never blamed Mrs. Thatcher, because our approach was to the Americans. We knew the capability of the *Independence*, and [we knew] that it was going to be in our waters.

If it hadn't been for that, we probably would have gone the usual route. In fact, we tried that route, but they weren't getting our messages; the factory in Ipswich was.

James A. Baker III   It was the only time we got crossed with Margaret Thatcher. She didn't like it a damn bit, and yet it was her style of action.

Later she would tell Bush he should just go in and kick Iraq out of Kuwait — just the United States and the U.K., and to heck with an international coalition. Let's go in and do it the way I did the Falklands, and the way Reagan did Grenada!

THE AFTERMATH

Hudson Austin   Had the Americans not launched the invasion, there would have been an inquiry into the prime minister's death, and the people responsible for it would have been punished.

But the Americans came in and picked up everybody, lock, stock, and barrel. They picked up everybody — party, army, government — threw them all in jail, got charges made up against them, and tried to get everybody convicted. What they did was in their own interests, not in the interests of justice. My trial was not really a trial as such.

We were not hostile to Washington, but there were some people in the Reagan administration who were very hostile toward us. From the beginning of the Reagan administration no American official came to meet with us on Grenada; Casey was very hostile to us. But I don't think the problem was with Reagan but with his handlers.

Langhorne Motley   We spent a great deal of time trying to figure out how to make their economy work. It was very difficult: their economy is based on sugar. They have to import their foodstuffs; they don't have the infrastructure for light industry. Their best bet is tourism.

George P. Shultz   There was a lot of skepticism in the Reagan administration about what you accomplish by pouring a lot of money into a place. And properly so; it doesn't always do that much good.

We helped them get the airport concluded; we helped them to get on their feet. It wasn't as though we had gone there at their request with some promise of aid; we went there to preserve their freedom — which we did — and the freedom of surrounding countries. That's the greatest gift you can give.

Desima Williams   We've gotten roads, and we've gotten road mirrors, so I can drive from my home to Saint George's with less fear and a little less temerity than I would have had before. You have multi-party politics, and other good things have come.

Some of them have come because of the natural maturity of the society. But some of them have come because of the postinvasion years. For example, young Grenadians are going back and building houses in the country; they feel that the Communists will not take their houses, so they are returning.

But there is a deeper level for me: I believe that we really lost the opportunity to turn around at the end of the twentieth century. Our socioeconomic program and model of participatory economics and politics has been lost. And that, for me, is an irreplaceable victim.

Paul Scoon   It is absolute nonsense to say that the people are worse off since the invasion. This kind of talk has been generated by the chaps at the universities. They had an adult education program, which, in itself, was a good thing; there were a few adults who used it to good effect. But when you look at the material used, it was a way of indoctrinating the people. And that, to me, was a minus.

If the invasion had not taken place, there would have been horrors and more horrors. There would have been killings, because you had a situation where people might have taken the law into their own hands. People would have lost a lot of their prosperity and businesses. If the events of October had not taken place, they would have declared Grenada a socialist republic.

Kendrick Radix   The Coard government would not have lasted, for the simple reason that this is an island. The Caribbean governments had cut air links; without air links, you can't get in and out. Our money supply was eastern Caribbean currency. What would the new government have done? Would they have gone to IOUs? They had no support internationally. Who would have come to their aid? I don't know who. The only place that I really think would have come to their aid was Albania.

You have to understand that when Bishop was killed, the people were traumatized, so if people had come from outer space to save them, they would have been appreciative. That is the context in which the invasion should be seen.

There was also a political dimension, in which a lot of people — in their simple and naive understanding of the real world — thought that the Americans would just open Fort Knox, and that the Grenadian blacks would be better off than the indigenous American blacks.

That has not happened, and there is a lot of bitterness and frustration about the abandonment of Grenada and the "special relationship" that was supposed to have been engendered by permitting the Monroe Doctrine to apply to the English-speaking Caribbean.

With the invasion has come the advent of crack cocaine into our society, which came on the tails of the military troops — it wasn't there in the revolution — and also the increase in crime, serious and increasing crime, as a result of the invasion.

Michael A. Radix   I am extremely grateful to the Americans for coming here. This is where my brother and I disagree. It is very hard to dissect two people; it is very funny to understand how two children, born in the same house, into the same family, with the same Catholic upbringing, the same school, can be just the opposite.

To him, it was terrible that the U.S. came in here. I was so grateful for the U.S. action that I wrote Reagan a letter from Ireland, thanking him that I could now come home.

PART THREE

THE SECOND TERM

8

The 1984 Campaign and Administration Changes

THE 1984 CAMPAIGN

William P. Clark I had hoped there would not be a second term. I told the president that I hoped he would consider the fact that we had accomplished what we had set out to do, both on the domestic front and internationally, and that I hoped he would consider handing the reins instead to the vice president, who well understood — and was in agreement with — our policy. I had proposed it half in jest: Have we not done our job? Can we go home now? I'd rather not go into his reaction.

There was a certain sense of fatigue among the key players. I wanted to get back to California, and I tendered my resignation. I know that the president gave great consideration to my suggestion. I don't think he came close to that alternative.

In the 1984 presidential race, the Reagan-Bush team was opposed by former Vice President Walter F. Mondale and Congresswoman Geraldine Ferraro of New York.

President Reagan's campaign rhetoric was suffused with the optimistic concept of a "mythic America."

In a major campaign commercial, the administration's first-term achievements were highlighted and it was proclaimed that "It's Morning Again in America." The commercial concluded with the question "Why would we ever want to return to where we were less than four short years ago?"

Cal Thomas Reagan was able to do something no other president in my lifetime has been able to do: he was able to restore the American people's confidence about their nation, their institutions, and about themselves. That is nothing short of miraculous.

It was more than "feel good," because "feel good" is superficial. He made us realize that something we had inherited from our parents and our grandparents — going way back to the founders — could be made new again in our time. That's what "Morning Again in America" was in 1984.

The Decline of the Moral Majority

Cal Thomas   Two things happened. First of all, the energy that had been brought about began to dissipate very quickly. Politics abhors a vacuum, and if one group isn't there, the other group is going to be there. Reagan pretty much won a second term without a vision that he had had in the first term.

The Moral Majority, and other groups who came along, began to treat this as mostly a fund-raising machine and did not adequately create a political system that would last beyond Reagan. When the leader left, there was nobody else; there was no support — no foundation — because it was all built on personality, and on an individual.

The Debates

Within a two-week period in October, President Reagan debated his opponent, first in Louisville, Kentucky, and then in Kansas City, Missouri. During the first debate President Reagan appeared nervous and confused at times, stumbling badly before a television audience of millions and raising questions about whether he was too old to carry out a second term.

Realizing that he had performed badly in this high-stakes campaign appearance—he attributed his poor performance to overpreparation—the president took a more relaxed stance in preparation for the Kansas City encounter.

Displaying the Reagan charm, when queried as to whether his age would be an impediment in a second term, the president replied, "I am not going to exploit for political purposes my opponent's youth and inexperience."

Joan Quigley   I did pick the times of the debates. The one glaring mistake I made for them — this sounds awful, but it was almost amazing that everything worked out as well as it did — was that I thought that Mondale had such a drippy personality that I'd make his personality shine out and he'd show what a drip he was.

The terrible thing was that Mondale came to life and did the best he'd ever done in his whole life. But it really turned out better in the long run, because in the second debate all eyes were focused on it because it was so unusual for Reagan to give a lackluster performance and Mondale to give a good one.

James A. Baker III   Laxalt and the first lady and some other people wanted to fire Dick Darman* after the first debate in the 1984 election. They said that the president, who had performed badly, had been brutalized in the preparation. They were finding a convenient scapegoat.

They came to me and said, "You have to fire Darman." I said, "Good luck. When I hear that from the president, then we'll fire Darman." I knew that the president would never tell me to fire Darman, and he didn't.

Stuart Spencer   I hear all those stories about Louisville. The bottom line is that Ronald Reagan didn't do his homework; he got lazy. Before Louisville, he was given his briefing books. He took them up to Camp David, and they sat over there, and he was watching old movies.

And he knew that he blew it. When we got back to the room, I said, "You didn't sound so bad." He said, "I was terrible." And he got ready for the next one. He did his homework the second time.

On November 4, 1984, Ronald Reagan was reelected, carrying 49 states, winning 59 percent of the popular vote, and receiving 525 electoral votes. The president's only failures were in the District of Columbia and in Minnesota, where native son Walter Mondale carried the day, winning 10 electoral votes.

And despite the fact that Mondale had selected a female running mate, 54 percent of women voters cast their ballots for the Republican Party candidate, up from 47 percent in 1980.

STAFFING CHANGES

Craig Fuller   I would have to conclude that there was a better combination of people for Ronald Reagan in the first term. The second term had some very good people for him — including Don Regan, a man who had achieved a lot in his life and was very successful — but that combination of people didn't serve the president as effectively as did the combination in the first term. There is no one person to pin it on except, ultimately,

---

* A key White House aide and Baker ally, Darman left that post to serve under Baker in the Department of the Treasury in Reagan's second term.

the president. He gets the credit for thinking through, and assembling, the team.

Because Reagan delegated so much, he didn't really fully appreciate the value of the people who worked for him. He appreciated them but didn't necessarily know how much people were doing, and how important those relationships were within the group. So when he set up the group in the second term, the fact that they didn't work as effectively was a bit of a surprise to him.

William P. Clark   In the gubernatorial days, Mr. Reagan didn't want anyone to make government a way of life; he felt that the transitioning of personnel was very important. I did too. I spent two very good years as chief of staff in Sacramento.

If you look at the turnover in posts like the chief of staff and national security adviser since World War II, I think the country has been best served by moving new people in, not only at the top but at midlevels as well. It was my feeling that things had gone very well during the first term. You reach a certain plateau of success, and it is very helpful to hand over the reins. I think that the American people feel the same way.

A crucially important staffing change followed James Baker's decision that he no longer wished to be chief of staff; a job switch with Secretary of the Treasury Regan was proposed.

Michael Deaver   Jim Baker wanted out; he had tried a couple of other times to get out. And I wanted out. I had been in the hospital in January 1985 with this renal infection. I decided then, because I was so sick, that I was going to have to get out of there.

James A. Baker III   It was a tough job [White House chief of staff], and at the end of a couple of years I was ready to move on to other things and seriously considered the offer of the baseball owners to be baseball commissioner.

Ultimately, I decided against that, in favor of staying and running the 1984 reelection campaign. But I really wanted out and didn't know how I was going to get out after four years, until Regan had this idea. It was his idea.

I didn't think he was serious at first. But he wanted power, and that's where the power is. I don't think that he understood that it comes with a heavy dose of politics and that even though you're powerful, you're still staff. And the chief of staff who doesn't understand that never does a good job.

Donald T. Regan   The job [secretary of the Treasury] was becoming old hat to me. You go through that stuff for four years, battling with Congress over taxes. And each year you have to prepare the revenue side of the budget and come up with tax ideas. And then you have to go before two or three different subcommittees of the Ways and Means Committee, and then the full committee. You have to do the same with the Senate Finance Committee. You have to go to the House and Senate Banking Committees and God only knows how many other committees.

You do this fifteen or twenty times a year, and you get an idea of what it is to prepare for congressional grilling; a Republican cabinet secretary going before a committee with a Democratic majority is red meat to the lions. I was frustrated because everything I wanted to do in the way of tax reform was being blocked. I couldn't see eight years of being secretary of the Treasury.

Michael Deaver   I came home from the hospital, and Jimmy came over to see me and told me that while I had been sick he had talked to Don, and that Don would like to switch, but that Don wanted to talk to me about it. So Don came out to the house, and he said, "Jimmy and I have talked about this. If you want to be chief of staff, I won't stand in the way. If you want it, it's yours to have." That was the last thing I ever wanted. I wanted out. So I said, "I'll be happy to support this."

Don asked me if I would propose the idea to the Reagans, which I did. The president's response, when I raised it to him, was kind of curious. It wasn't, "Well, that's an interesting idea." I remember that he didn't commit on our first conversation. I didn't know whether he had someone else in mind or whether he thought he could talk Jimmy out of it again.

Donald T. Regan   We used Deaver as our go-between because we knew that this would provoke quite a bit of surprise in Washington circles and would provoke some surprise in the East Wing of the White House, and we wanted to make sure before we did anything that everybody had been alerted, so Deaver was the logical one.

I didn't realize until later the major role Deaver would have to play in getting the first lady's agreement to this swap; if she were to nix it before the president's agreement, the thing would not go. Deaver apparently was successful, because he said, "I think you guys ought to at least put the idea in front of the president and see what he has to say." So Deaver, as keeper of the schedule, put us on for a certain day, and the three of us went in together.

Now, whether or not Baker, as chief of staff, had mentioned to the president, "Don and I are thinking of swapping jobs; he's coming in to talk to you about it," I don't know. I never asked Jim Baker about it. All I know is that when I first told the president about it, the two of them stood silent. They said, "Okay, Don. It's your idea; you tell the president." I felt that was a hell of a note. Here these two guys are his chief lieu-tenants, and they are leaving it up to me to explain something to the man. But anyway, I did.

He said, "Are you all in agreement?" We said yes. He said, "Well, let me think that one over." He didn't say no, or yes, or that much about it. So after a very few minutes of conversation — not much more than fif-teen or twenty minutes — we agreed that we'd keep it quiet, he would muse over it, and then we would get a decision as to whether he would permit it or not.

Stuart Spencer   Two things were happening at that point in time: Jimmy Baker and Mike Deaver had total burnout. Normally, they would call me and ask for my reaction. They knew me well enough to know that on this one they should tell me after the fact. They never knew how far I would go, whether I would try to call the president and try to submarine it. I knew that Don Regan would not make a good chief of staff. He wasn't the chief-of-staff type; to me he was a CEO. On this one I was called and told about it half an hour after it was announced in the White House press room.

Michael Deaver   I look back on this and think of all the "what ifs." I probably would have thought it was a lousy idea if I had not been sick myself and desperate to get out. I had spent five years there. I was the guy who'd had to hold them together, and I was just sick of it. I was not look-ing at it rationally; I wasn't looking at it in a responsible way. If I had been, I would have done a lot of things differently.

Edwin Meese III   I thought it was a great idea. Jim had been there for four years. It gave Don a new lease on life; he had been at the Treasury for four years and had done an excellent job.

But you never know about people until they are in their job. Jim did the Treasury thing reasonably well. But Don really had trouble adjusting to being a staff member after he had been a chief executive in private life and then had run his own department for four years. I was glad I had done it the other way around.

James A. Baker III   It's probably not a good idea to have someone who has been a principal in their own right being chief of staff, because even though you are really powerful, you weren't elected, and the press and the American people don't want to see a whole lot of a chief of staff, exercising that power. Everything in that job is derivative of the president, and you constantly need to keep that in mind.

Regan Is Accused of Aggrandizing Power

Stuart Spencer   He was a premier, a prime minister to the president. Look at any picture during that time in the White House, and Don Regan is in the picture.

He had a big ego. He had been secretary of the Treasury and head of Merrill Lynch. That's not the role; he didn't fit the role, any more than Baker fit the role of chief of staff when he came back for Bush. I knew there would be problems for Don. He didn't understand the Reagans, their relationship as a team.

Craig Fuller   Baker understood Washington and its various component parts: the Congress, the executive branch, and the media. Don Regan, as successful as he was — his success came in the private sector — didn't have that same feel.

Regan felt he was going to be chief operating officer and make lots of decisions. The nature of a staff position — even a chief of staff — is that you support the person who makes the decision. If you have the ability to exert influence, you'd better do it in a way that gives people the feeling — whether in fact it is true or not — that the decision was made with the full support of the president.

Don didn't always do that. And he paid a price for it.

Donald T. Regan   Sure I have an ego. Who doesn't? Most people who have any success have egos, so I plead guilty to having an ego. But on the other hand, enlarging my power? No. I used the system I had been brought up on, as far as how I thought a chief of staff should operate.

There are probably a thousand people who have one reason or another to contact the president of the United States at a given minute, and I'm not talking about some ordinary taxpayer who has a gripe. I'm talking about people in the government — be it a cabinet member or one of the

435 members of the House or one of the 100 senators or heads of agencies or heads of foreign governments — all of these people, at one time or another, have reason to contact the president. Somebody has to screen that process and prevent the wasting of the president's time. Somebody has to set priorities.

The president says what he wants done, and somebody has to try to organize and carry that out. Somebody has to act as doorkeeper, to keep the president from being overworked. President Reagan was an older man, not a young guy like Clinton, and not nearly as active and itchy and anxious to get around and look into things as George Bush and Jimmy Carter. Reagan wanted to come in at nine and leave at four.

I had to replace three guys — Baker, Deaver, and Meese. The net result was that I naturally came to the attention of the press more than any previous chief of staff because the three of them would share views with the press. I was doing it all on my own, so therefore it looked like I was playing up my own role.

I tried to get a deputy who would be stronger, but Mrs. Reagan didn't want it that way, and neither did the president. They said no, they didn't want a strong deputy. The president got accustomed to bouncing problems off me, so if he asked for something, I had to have an answer. So therefore I was poking my nose into a lot of things. Was that a grab for power? I don't know. All I know is that I hate for anyone to ask me a question and not have the answer.

Edwin Meese III Don was starting from scratch and had to adapt to the rhythm of the White House. When there were three of us — Jim, Mike, and myself — we had divided up the responsibilities. Don pretty much took it all on his own shoulders. He was a good guy; it was kind of like a Greek tragedy to see what happened to him.

McFarlane Resigns

On November 30, 1985, Robert McFarlane resigned as national security adviser and was replaced on December 4 by his deputy, Vice Admiral Poindexter.

Oliver North I don't know what motivated McFarlane to leave as precipitously as he did. I do know that, as a consequence, there was no small degree of chaos at the top end of the administration.

There were a lot of people out there who saw opportunity in this. As a consequence of this, I don't have a particularly high regard for George

Shultz, particularly for what he did, or tried to do, to John Poindexter. With the exception of people like John Poindexter, there are not a lot of people in this town with backbone.

Michael Ledeen   In the summer and fall of 1985, McFarlane had a nervous breakdown — or what in the old days you would have called a nervous breakdown. He just collapsed, in part because of frustration. He felt he wasn't getting through to Reagan; he felt that he, personally, was the wrong sort of person to deal with Reagan.

All the other people there had a great rapport with Reagan. They went back a long way with him; they were all self-made men — wealthy people, business people, people of the world. McFarlane was a military guy — a marine colonel, with a certain political dimension — but he felt that he wasn't getting through.

Then people started spreading rumors about him — that he was having an affair with [NBC Television White House correspondent] Andrea Mitchell. That upset him tremendously; he is a very proper person.

Charles Powell   Mrs. Thatcher was intrigued by the changes in the national security adviser. She liked Bud McFarlane. I remember him coming down to stay one weekend at Chequers.* I think she found him a bit opaque. Of course, we were not really in the picture in what was going on in Iran. He wasn't telling us, and I think that subsequently colored her view of him.

Mrs. Thatcher thought of Admiral Poindexter as a bit too much of the straight-up-and-down military man — not really having the breadth of experience to advise the president. She certainly didn't dislike him; she thought he was a very honorable man. But she didn't relate to him very much.

In early 1987, Admiral Poindexter was forced to resign as national security adviser owing to his involvement in the Iran-contra affair. He was succeeded by Frank Carlucci, deputy secretary of defense in the early part of Reagan's first term.

In December 1987, when Carlucci succeeded Caspar Weinberger as secretary of defense, Lieutenant General Colin Powell, the highest-ranking African American officer in the U.S. military and Carlucci's deputy at the NSC, succeeded Carlucci as national security adviser.

---

* The official country residence of the British prime minister.

Charles Powell [Thatcher] saw Frank Carlucci as a much more substantial person — a man who really got things done, who was really getting a grip on the operation of the national security adviser's office.

And she was very attached to Colin Powell, although she has been critical of him subsequently, about the Gulf War.

Frank Carlucci When I was asked to be national security adviser, I met with President Reagan. One would normally have expected the president to say, "I want you for this job because you have a certain amount of ability" or "a certain amount of experience," or, "I like you." Instead, he said, "I want you for this job because you're the only person that Cap and George can agree on."

George was unhappy with me at the outset. He wanted the national security adviser to be a glorified executive secretary. But we eventually worked things out.

Colin L. Powell President Reagan had a tendency to follow the path of least resistance on personnel matters. You had McFarlane sitting there, readily available; you had powerful forces in Shultz and Weinberger, who did not want to see an equal of theirs as national security adviser, i.e., a Jim Baker.

When Bud finally got tired and realized that since he was not equal to Weinberger and Shultz, he couldn't really survive, and the only way to reconcile the difference between these two guys was to start doing things on your own — which lit the fuse on Iran-contra — he gave up, and they turned it over to John Poindexter, who also was not a coequal of these guys. But it was the path of least resistance.

And then it all exploded. In comes Carlucci, who is a match for Weinberger and Shultz, and guess what they do when Carlucci leaves to become secretary of defense? They go the path of least resistance. Colin Powell, whom Ronald Reagan knows, is sitting there. I saw my role not as a shadow secretary of state, but as making sure that the secretary of state and the secretary of defense carried out the policies determined by the president.

9

The Issues

BITBURG

At 2:45 P.M. on May 5, 1985, President Reagan arrived at Kolmeshohe, a small cemetery located in Bitburg, West Germany. The president's visit to Bitburg was one of the most controversial issues of his entire presidency.

While the president had hoped that his visit to the cemetery would promote the cause of post–World War II reconciliation, press reports in advance of his trip revealed that members of the Second Waffen SS Panzer Division, a unit that had massacred 642 French civilians at Oradour-sur-Glane in June 1944, were buried in the cemetery.

Donald T. Regan He went because of one name and one name only: Kohl. Kohl was faced with an election, and he wanted the president there, and Reagan gave his word to Kohl early on that he would go back to Kohl's constituency in Bavaria and be seen with him.

Having given his commitment to another world leader — and an ally and a good friend — Reagan was not about to back off. He felt that as a leader of the free world, if he had given his word to an ally, he had to carry it out. You can't let Kohl down, because next time you want him to do something, he might let you down.

You have to remember that at the time of Bitburg we were still facing the Soviet Union as a very strong and very active enemy, and we wanted the Germans on our side. And Kohl was a strong ally against the Soviets.

Edwin Meese III When Bitburg was planned, the presence there of SS soldiers was not known. Then, of course, the press played it up. I don't know whether there was any way it could have been changed.

Horst Teltschik Once we knew about the SS dead at Bitburg — and knowing that these SS people were seventeen to eighteen years of age, and knowing that some Germans were forced to become members of the

SS, having no alternative — the question was, Should this be a reason to cancel?

Later on, when the Jewish community in the United States raised concerns and there were a lot of threats on both sides, in Germany and the United States, we said at the very end, "Let's alter it." But then there was the famous telephone conversation between Reagan and Kohl, and Reagan repeated, three times: "I'll do what we agreed on. Let's do it."

Elliott Abrams   A very large part of it had to have been the very close relationship with Kohl and Kohl's appeals to Reagan on a political basis — if you cancel, it will really hurt. Also, the president had some advisers who were pushing him [to go] — Don Regan, for example.

Don Regan is a very good and decent man, but his understanding of this was completely flawed. I am about 95 percent sure that when Elie Wiesel made his appeal to Reagan, Regan made some comment to the effect that he was just trying to sell books.*

He was completely tone-deaf on the issue. To whom was the president listening at this point? It was Don Regan, the chief of staff. The president was getting bad advice from everybody, except Shultz.

The president just dug in his heels. It was a mistake. One can say it didn't do all that much damage to Reagan's historical reputation. Whether it would have damaged Kohl had Reagan canceled, I don't know. This is one of those rare cases where Reagan's own inner radar totally failed him and he came out on the wrong side of an issue.

Horst Teltschik   The main advantage Helmut Kohl had was that he had met with Reagan when Reagan came to Bonn while governor of California. And Reagan never forgot that Kohl had received him. This was the beginning of a good friendship. And when Kohl came into office in 1982, Reagan remembered the earlier meeting. From the beginning, the most important factor in their relationship was that they could rely on each other. When Kohl promised something, you could rely on it; the same was true with Reagan.

Robert C. McFarlane   Once Reagan learned that Kohl would really be badly damaged by a withdrawal, he said, "We can't do that; I owe him."

Deaver, who was quite concerned, said, "We have got to find a way to

---

* Wiesel has written extensively on his experiences as a teenager incarcerated in a concentration camp during the Holocaust, and of the Soviet Jewry movement, including a seminal work, *The Jews of Silence*. He is also a playwright.

do this, Mr. President. Do you mind if we make one more try to measure Kohl's level of vulnerability? I know Horst Teltschik. We can at least get a candid view from him and, in the process, let him know that it is a pretty big downside here."

Shultz said I should write to Teltschik. So I drafted the letter, Shultz approved it, and I sent it out from the White House.

Horst Teltschik   A cancellation would have hurt Kohl personally, but he would have survived. He was ready to say, "Okay, I can't take the risk that something might happen to Reagan" — or to him — "so let's cancel." This was made clear to the Americans.

Sure, if the chancellor had been ready to cancel earlier, Reagan might have agreed. In the last call — eight or ten days before the visit — the chancellor, for the first time, said, "Ron, if you decide that it is better to cancel, you have to know, I am ready to do it."

Lyn Nofziger   [Reagan] was willing to take the heat from the Jewish community in the U.S. — and some of his very close supporters were Jewish — but he was also willing to take the heat from some of those around him, including his wife.

Robert C. McFarlane   It was one of the times when the president and the first lady disagreed. On those occasions, Nancy would come around a bit. She'd come to me — and to Mike — and the two of them would come to me, as they did. I said, "We are trying one more time."

Joan Quigley   I was shocked when I heard the president say on television that they wouldn't visit a concentration camp because it was time to put those things behind us. It was later decided that he would go to Bergen-Belsen.

The problem was timing. Nancy put me on the phone with Mike Deaver. I said, "What are you planning?" He replied that they were planning Bergen-Belsen for the morning. I said, "Oh no, it's wrong. Afternoon, because at around noontime is the most prominent time." I wanted to pick the longest, and most prominent, time for Bergen-Belsen. I also said, "I want the Bitburg time to be as short as possible."

We needed Bitburg; we needed to get the missiles in Europe. If Kohl's government had fallen — which it would have done if Reagan hadn't made that visit — we couldn't have gotten the missiles in Germany. The missiles, along with SDI, would be Reagan's lever with Gorbachev. He had to have that.

But for moral reasons, we had to accent Bergen-Belsen. I said to Mike, "Get through Bitburg in ten minutes — fifteen at the outside — just enough time for him to lay the wreath." It happened, the trouble died down immediately, and we went on to deal with Gorbachev.

Michael Deaver   Reagan took the long view of almost everything, which is one of the reasons he will be recorded by the historians as a great president. Nancy and I took the short view. In Bitburg, when we had three weeks of constant barrage in the media, Nancy and I would say, "We have to get this behind us." Ronald Reagan would say, "Three weeks of the media? What do I care about that?"

I recall that two days before they were to leave for Germany, I was heading out to Andrews Air Force Base for my third trip there. I was really exhausted. Nancy had already told me I had ruined her husband; it was my fault. In the car, I get a call from the White House, telling me to turn around; the president wants to see me.

So I go back, and the president meets me upstairs, at the elevator, and takes me into the den, and shuts the doors, so Nancy can't hear the conversation. The president says, "I'm sorry to have to call you back. I know you and Nancy don't want me to go through with this, but I don't want you to change anything when you get over there, because history is going to prove I'm right. If we can't reconcile after forty years, we are never going to be able to do it." In principle, he thought it was right. He was saying that reconciliation was important; he was not bowing to pressure.

That was one of the few times he ever gave me a direct order. So I get back into the car, and I go out to Andrews, and I fly to Bonn, and I put it together. It was a horrible, horrible two days.

There was not an anti-Semitic bone in his body; he was one of the best presidents the state of Israel ever had. I don't think there was even a hint in his mind that he was doing something that was anti-Semitic. I remember being in the East Room of the White House about a week before we were going to leave, and Elie Wiesel made that plea to him on national television, "Mr. President, don't go!" But he believed it was the right thing to do.

CENTRAL AMERICA

Panama

Manuel Antonio Noriega   When I changed — when I expressed my honest opinion and the opinion of my country about the United States' political system in its relationship with Central America — the United States did not see me as a friend, because I was a critic. I was very critical of this political system of the United States to Central America, and Nicaragua especially.

Donald Gregg Bush had a very strong sense of what was right and what was wrong. And my speculation is that if somebody had done something wrong — particularly related to drugs, because he was very concerned about drugs and terrorism — he felt that he ought to be held accountable.

Elliott Abrams My first exposure to Panama was the removal of [Nicolas Ardito] Barletta [president of Panama, 1984–85] by Noriega. We had accepted Barletta's election even though the opposition actually won. Noriega put him in, in part, because it was more troublesome not to, and nobody wanted to take that issue on. And Barletta was a good guy; he was — and is — a distinguished, honest, intelligent man.

We were unhappy with his removal. I recall talking to him on the day before, or the day of his removal, urging him to hang on: "Don't let Noriega push you out." That was the beginning of what turned out to be four years of trouble with Noriega.

There was, in a sense, a progression from Noriega's removal of Barletta to Noriega's being jailed. Removing Barletta was misbehaving; increasing corruption was misbehaving. Normal, old-fashioned corruption — theft at customs — and then drugs, which was a new form of corruption, were in the end what brought Noriega down.

In an attempt to ease the Panamanian president out of office without the intervention of the U.S. military, the Reagan administration began negotiations with Noriega during the spring of 1988.

Elliott Abrams One of the first ways we reacted was to have Casey deliver a message to him — he was actually invited to Langley to be given this message — and Casey didn't give it to him. So we decided to do something else. We would send a messenger down to meet with him, and yell at him, and that messenger would not be from the CIA because we didn't trust them.

It was decided to send Poindexter. I went with him. The purpose was to deliver the message: "You are misbehaving, and you'd better knock it off." Later he got messages from others, including the Department of Defense, to which he paid no attention.

We met Noriega at the officers' club at Howard Air Force Base; it was just Poindexter, our ambassador, Briggs, and me. What I remember most about Noriega was that he was an amazingly ugly man — one of the few people I've met that the first thing you say to yourself is, What an unattractive fellow.

But I will say this for him: he gave a very good answer at that meeting. Poindexter delivered the message: "You have to turn it around." Noriega's reply was: "Your embassy people go to all the cocktail parties in Panama City; you know every millionaire in Panama. But you get out there where the Panamanians live, and they support the PDF [Panamanian Defense Forces], and they support me. Of course, the upper class hates me. You put them in power. That is not the way it is, and that's not the way it is going to be. You ought to get out there into Panama, and see what's going on."

The truth is, he was right. Not about the corruption, but about the support; he could have won an election. Later, as the corruption and the oppression became greater, he lost that support. But at that moment, he gave a terrific answer.

Duane Clarridge They didn't send the right people. You don't send Poindexter to talk to Noriega; you send [Department of Defense official] Nestor Sanchez, or you send me — somebody he knows. You have to conclude that they didn't really want him to go.

On February 4, 1988, Noriega was indicted in a U.S. federal court on charges of drug trafficking and racketeering. In the following months an intense debate took place within the Reagan administration over whether Noriega should be allowed to seek asylum in a third country, in which case the United States would not seek the Panamanian leader's extradition but would maintain the indictment as leverage against any attempt by him to return to Panama.

The main opposition to this proposal came from Vice President Bush, who was concerned that a deal with Noriega would impede efforts to curb the flow of drugs into the United States and hurt his chances in the 1988 presidential campaign.

Noriega rejected the proposal, leading Bush, on December 20, 1989, as president, to launch Operation Just Cause. The military operation led to Noriega's surrender on January 3, 1990, to U.S. forces.

Subsequently tried and convicted on eight counts of cocaine trafficking, racketeering, and money laundering, Noriega is currently serving a forty-year sentence at a federal facility in South Florida.

When asked by us why he turned down the Reagan administration's proposal that would have allowed him to leave Panama and not be prosecuted by the U.S. government, Noriega, who moments earlier had been smiling and loquacious, turned in his chair, shrugged, looked up at the ceiling, and threw up his arms.

Manuel Antonio Noriega I believed Reagan when he said that if I left Panama, the indictment would be dropped. This was signed in draft by the attorney general, Meese, and by Shultz; I saw the letter. There were two options: the political and legal. The legal was, kill the indictment. The indictment disappears — I would be out of the PDF, and the government would be out of Panama for some years, because the United States wanted to have more interference in the Panamanian government.

Reagan wanted to be able to say he had resolved the Panamanian problem before he met with Gorbachev in Moscow, so Shultz delayed his trip to Moscow for one day. Shultz continued waiting for my decision, and all the papers were ready for the United States.

The plan was under the direction and control of President Reagan. Shultz waited because he thought I was going to sign. It was a political moment for me; I would have to compromise with my soldiers, my government, my citizens, and with my party. I would have to politically compromise, and I thought more about the political compromise than about my personal situation.

I was an idealist in this moment. I thought, if I sign, all the people will say, "Look, he lost."

The reality was that in one moment, I did not think about my own person. Today I would look at it differently. The time has changed.

Craig Fuller We were out on the campaign trail in June of 1988. We were in California, doing law enforcement events prior to the California primary, and there were negotiations going on with Noriega. President Reagan was being persuaded by Secretary Shultz that an agreement with Noriega was desirable.

The vice president felt that the terms of the agreement — as they were being communicated to him in California — were totally unacceptable. Bush saw Noriega for what he was, and was very troubled that we not make a bad deal that would only perpetuate his influence over his country. He was very frustrated because he wasn't there, so he had me talking to Ken Duberstein and Colin Powell, who was trying to get the president on board. But it wasn't working. And the vice president — in what was extremely rare in the middle of an issue — sent a memo to the president, and ultimately called him, with his concerns. And Shultz wasn't very happy with it, nor was Powell.

It was particularly difficult because the negotiation with Noriega was being reported on, and people wanted to know where Bush was on this issue. He was to speak to the Los Angeles Police Academy, and I said to him, "I don't see how you can go out and give a tough speech on crime. I know that you believe that Noriega is someone with whom we should not negotiate."

So I put that in the speech. The *New York Times* missed it entirely. The *Washington Post* knew that something was going on. Howard Baker went out and commented on CNN that day that this was, in fact, a concern that Bush had.

And that led to the ultimate derailment of the negotiations, so people realized that Bush was willing, prior to the Republican convention, to take a slightly different view from Ronald Reagan's.

Manuel Antonio Noriega   In his campaign for the presidency in 1988, Bush opposed the draft agreement between me and the U.S. only for political reasons. He did not want to give the Democrats political help, because the Democrats had questioned the relationship between him and me.

The personality of Bush is hypocritical. All the time he was head of the CIA, he had one appearance to the public, but really, in his life and in his decision-making, he was very focused. When he has power behind him, he expresses hardness, but in his own personality he is weak.

But he is also a devil; this is the pattern of the conduct of his life. In the Second World War, when he was flying and the Japanese were surrendered, he killed Japanese; he shot at them from his plane. This is him: when he has the power, he is the devil.

Abraham Sofaer   I thought that we had negotiated a pretty good deal with Noriega. There was a time when he could have been taken to Spain, but he basically pulled out of the deal at the last minute.

He made a big mistake; he couldn't believe that we'd actually go in and get him. But we did. I was convinced that we would. I knew that Bush was not going to allow him to humiliate us repeatedly.

Manuel Antonio Noriega   The plan for the invasion of Panama existed before Bush; Reagan knew the plan. It was presented to him; he heard all the opinions. But he did not accept the plan. He never accepted it because Reagan was more honest; he realized that the invasion of Panama was unnecessary.

And Bush, in his personality — in his pattern of conduct — wanted to kill, to give the international appearance of being a strong man.

George Bush I did not want to see Noriega pardoned — or see anything done that would keep him from being brought to justice.

Duane Clarridge I suppose that Noriega was not a very nice man. I never saw any involvement in drugs; I met him several times and never saw any evidence of his using drugs. The DEA found him useful. Were they taken in? I don't know.

THE MIDDLE EAST

The Shultz Interlock

In January 1988, Secretary of State Shultz began one last attempt to achieve peace between Israel and the Palestinians. He and his associates were determined to attempt a new initiative: trying to bring the parties to engage in final status negotiations whether or not transition arrangements had been agreed upon or put into effect.

Shultz's mission was complicated by several factors: the Unity government in Israel, where Prime Minister Shamir and Foreign Minister Peres wanted to implement competing programs; the ongoing Intifada, or Arab uprising, in the West Bank and Gaza; the intransigence of PLO Chairman Yassir Arafat; and the hesitation of Jordan's King Hussein to agree to the U.S.-brokered terms.

Shimon Peres I flew to London to see King Hussein secretly; I told [only] Shamir. The idea was that if we should reach an understanding with the king, it would not appear as an understanding between the king and us — this would be inconvenient for the king and impossible for us — that this would emerge as an American proposal.

When I flew to London, I didn't have a plan in my pocket. I met with the king for eight hours, and I saw that we were in agreement, so I suggested that we should put it in writing, and he agreed. We then worked over the points and agreed that we would hand it over to the United States, and that the United States would adopt the agreement and say, "This is an American proposal for the two sides." And then the two sides would reply to the proposal.

I came back and met with Shamir and read the agreement to him and told him that this should be an American paper. One of the issues was the international conference, and Shamir said, "Leave the paper with me." I said, "No sir. I can't leave it with you because it will leak from your office. It will never become an American paper."

King Hussein The international conference concept provided the beginning of the real dialogue, when all of us here decided it was time to move into negotiations. This didn't happen during the Reagan administration, perhaps because the cold war still existed and the world was still divided.

Richard Murphy He [King Hussein] counted noses and saw that he had very little support on the West Bank. Earlier he had had some bitter experiences with Arafat. In 1985 Hussein brought a plan to Washington: I would have a meeting with non-Palestinians. The PLO would see the holding of that meeting as a signal.

The participants were not members of the PLO, and certainly not of their executive committee, but they were men of substance. They would move to accept [UN resolutions] 242 and 338. Then we would have met with the PLO. And then everyone would have gone, hand in hand, to an international conference. And there would have been direct negotiations from there on.

If we had moved ahead and had the meetings, it would have at least tested the PLO's capacity and capability to do what Arafat finally did, three and a half years later. We could have — and should have — done more in 1985. But I'm not saying that it would have brought the kind of transformation on the political scene that caused the collapse in Moscow — the disappearance of the Soviet Union — or the situation caused by the defeat of Iraq [in the Gulf War] that increased the misery of the Palestinians.

George P. Shultz The president really didn't trust Arafat at all; he didn't want to have anything to do with him as a person. We finally did deal with him when he met our conditions.

Richard Murphy The Israelis had tried to kill Arafat. They bombed an apartment building in Beirut, killing many people, because they understood that he was holding a meeting in that building. Arafat was considered to be the devil incarnate. It is amazing how attitudes have shifted in the past decade.

The Saudis went through ups and downs with Mr. Arafat because they felt they were dealing with a man who had promised to make certain moves — which he didn't make.

Arafat was a mixed blessing. They never tried to deal with anybody else, but they felt quite embarrassed that he had pledged to do something that he did not deliver on in terms of moving the talks ahead in the areas of opposing terrorism and recognizing Israel's right to exist.

Abraham Tamir   Peres completed an agreement with Hussein in London, without consulting Shamir, only consulting with Rabin, because Rabin was all the time changing from one position to another position. He never went on one straight position in his life. I know this: I was his chief of operations for many years.

When Peres finished the London agreement, he asked Shultz to present it as his paper. There was a problem with the PLO. I met with the PLO, through the mediation of the Egyptians. It was a secret; we met in an East African country.

Shimon Peres   Shamir was unhappy — even mad. I sent my assistant, Yossi Bellin, with the agreement to Finland, where Shultz was staying on his way to Moscow [in May 1988 for a U.S.-Soviet summit]. Bellin saw Charles Hill, Shultz's assistant, and showed him the paper. We were sure this would be published.

Then, I don't know exactly what happened, but I know that Shamir sent Mr. [Moshe] Arens to Washington to see Shultz. I don't know exactly what Arens told Shultz. But apparently he said that this was an intervention in the domestic affairs of Israel, so I was left dry.

I thought of resigning, but I couldn't give the reason why I would, since the matter was very secret. The king was very disappointed.

But I never asked Shultz to be an intermediary between Shamir and myself; I myself informed Shamir of the whole story.

Abraham Tamir   Hussein was ready to go for a solution under Jordan — a Jordanian-Palestinian solution — only after the United States, or someone, maybe Israel, would do the job with the PLO for him. He said he couldn't do it with Arafat on his back.

To me, if you want peace, you have to give it all back, including East Jerusalem. So after the Lebanon War — which was the Yom Kippur War for the PLO because all their infrastructure was destroyed — an Egyptian-American initiative started, on the basis of the Reagan Plan, to renew the peace process. Arafat, who was then weak, agreed to this initiative.

Hussein welcomed this initiative because it was a Jordanian-Palestinian solution, which meant a Jordanian role also in the West Bank and in

Gaza. That is why he signed the agreement with Peres. Then, after the *Intifada* started, he went part of the way out, but not completely. He said, "First reach an interim agreement on autonomy with the PLO. Then, when you come to the final status, don't forget Jordan."

King Hussein   The idea was that it wouldn't be a Jordanian-Israeli suggestion. Peres said that within forty-eight hours he would reach the secretary of state, but that it would come as an American suggestion, which would be accepted by both Jordan and Israel.

Two weeks passed and nothing happened. Then later, we understood that that particular agreement was sent to Prime Minister Shamir as an agreement between myself and Peres, for his comments.

As far as I could tell, that destroyed any chance of its getting anywhere. That was the situation as I saw it: Prime Minister Shamir had the view that the territories occupied by Israel were Israeli territories. And obviously this was something that was impossible for us to accept. So we didn't make much progress during that period.

Yitzhak Shamir   Shultz had proposed a peace conference under the auspices of the two superpowers, the U.S. and the Soviet Union. He asked if I would accept the idea, and — to his great surprise — I said, "Yes, I accept."

But then he had to get the consent of King Hussein and the Soviets. He went to London to see Hussein, but the king did not accept the proposal. Hussein knew that the other Arab countries would not accept the proposal, and he did not want to stand alone.

I was in a very good position. I had accepted this American proposal; it was not against our interests. And it did not become a reality because of the refusal of the Arabs.

Eitan Haber   Rabin was having lunch with Shultz at a Jerusalem hotel. He told Shultz that the "interlock" was not going to work.

Nimrod Novick   There was the administration's inability to pursue opportunities presented to it on the Arab-Israeli peace process. It did not do what it could and should have done, from our parochial perspective. There were great, great opportunities to push the process forward, and they fumbled the ball for reasons that were not valid.

If the United States perceives a historical opportunity to serve American interests, most secretaries of state will go for it — or they will at least try. But this was not the position of George Shultz. I think

Kissinger, and later Baker, would have said, "Sorry, Mr. Foreign Minister, my president is sending me, so I am going. If the prime minister doesn't want to see me, that's his prerogative, but I have to do what the president says."

Shultz should have created a situation where either Shamir goes for it or is forced to expose his true position, which is hostile to it. What Shultz allowed Shamir to do was to block it without presenting the Israeli public with the truth of his position, so that he could portray himself as a champion of peace while blocking peace.

An American secretary of state cannot shield himself by noninterference. Whatever he decides to say, or not to say, he is interfering in Israeli domestic affairs. If you say that the Middle East is ready for peace and there is only one son of a bitch who is blocking it, you're interfering; if you don't say it, you're interfering because you are allowing this same son of a bitch to claim to his own people that he has the backing for his policy of the United States of America.

So it's a mixed bag. It's real appreciation, forever, for the friendship and support, and regret that they missed historical moments for which we eventually paid the price.

Abraham Tamir   When Shultz came to Israel, he saw that the country was split on the plan. He worried that this might result in early elections, whose outcome could not be predicted, so he gave up on the plan.

Yitzhak Shamir   Hussein is very smart, but he is weak. He doesn't present a strong factor in our area. He is very positive, but at the same time he can isolate himself from the rest of the Arab world.

He believes it is important to maintain good relations with us, because he is sure we would befriend him in an emergency, so he trusts us. He trusts me. He once told me, "I trust you more than all the other people in the Middle East."

The same was true during the Gulf War. I had an agreement with him that he will do nothing against us, under any conditions. This was important to us at that time.

George P. Shultz   In order to do anything in the Middle East, you have to recognize that your dealings with the leaders of the Middle East are the tip of the iceberg. You have to be dealing with the American Jewish community, and with the Congress, every step of the way. You just don't go out and have some initiative without consulting people — letting them know that something is coming. The president recognized this. We all did.

Yitzhak Shamir   After the *Intifada* started, I came to Washington and the U.S. ambassador to Israel, [Thomas] Pickering, accompanied me all the time. Why? Because he wanted to see how I was accepted by the Jewish community. And it was beautiful; he saw that everywhere I went I was received with great support by all of the American people.

And this was reported to Shultz and Reagan, and it was clear to them that I represented the policy that was welcomed by the Jewish community in the United States. This was important: the U.S. did not change its policy toward us in Reagan's time. But afterward, with Bush, it was different.

King Hussein   I believe that the concept others may have, that the United States can deliver Israel, or any Arab state, is a wrong approach. U.S. help is welcomed, but in the final analysis the people who are going to be neighbors and who are going to resolve their problems must do it themselves.

Why Was Peace Not Achieved During the Reagan Years?

George P. Shultz   The Soviet situation was gradually turning around. I think it is fair to say that the cold war really ended in the Reagan years, though we hadn't been able to reap the harvest of that everywhere, including in the Middle East. [Syrian President Hafez al-]Assad is something of a spoiler.

Adnan Khashoggi   To be honest, the Israelis had difficulty in accepting that the West Bank should have a status. They were not convinced; they have some fears — and some grounds for them. At the same time the Palestinians want a state; they are going back to the 1947 United Nations decision to partition the land. It is difficult to partition where people have lived and occupied. So not only the Arabs but the Israelis were not in a hurry to make it work. Mind you, the Likud ruled during this period. They are the stubborn side of the Israelis. Peres and Rabin saw the benefit of sharing the wealth.

Giandomenico Picco   Baker was much more subtle; he learned that the arrogance of the Reagan years could not deliver anything in the Middle East. The Bush people were more knowledgeable; Baker had learned from Shultz.

King Hussein   The history is one of many, many lost opportunities. It might not have worked during the Reagan years. I believe that the

United States can play a very major role — can help in a very constructive way — and obviously has a voice that can be heard by both sides. But
when it comes to the bottom line, we and the Israelis were able to put
our peace treaty together because we worked it out ourselves.

THE TWO GERMANYS AND
THE SOVIET UNION

*On June 12, 1987, President Reagan, addressing tens of thousands of Berlin
residents gathered at the Brandenburg Gate, then the dividing line between
the city's eastern and western sections, invited Soviet General Secretary
Mikhail S. Gorbachev to come to the site and "open this gate, Mr. Gorbachev! Tear down this wall!"*

Horst Teltschik   Reagan was a man with fundamental principles. One
was, to tear down the Wall. Two years later the Wall came down.

When Reagan was planning to come to Berlin, there were discussions
as to whether he should speak in front of the Wall. Most Germans were
against this, but I was in favor of it. I said, "It will show that the main
world power is ready to support our main interest. What could be better
than such a speech at the Wall?"

Hans Dietrich Genscher   Schmidt was in the hospital, so I was head of
the German delegation to the [G-7] meeting in Cancún [Mexico] in the
fall of 1981. I was sitting next to Reagan; to his right was the president of
Venezuela, to his left the Saudi ambassador. There were no interpreters.

Many problems were discussed. There was a question about European
borders. I said, "Mr. President, you are a country of continental size, with
only two neighbors, neither of them hostile. Look at Germany. We have
three neighbors; we are the country with the most borders. We are sixty
million people, with no more than three hours to be at the next border.
Can you imagine what that means?"

SOUTHEASTERN ASIA

Marcos Is Ousted in the Philippines

*In February 1986, Ferdinand Marcos, the pro-American president of the
Philippines since 1965 whose administration was marked by corruption and
dictatorial excess, was defeated in his bid for reelection by Corazón Aquino.*

Marcos refused at first to accept the election result. But later he was per-suaded by the Reagan administration to leave office, and Corazón Aquino succeeded him in a peaceful transition.

Nicholas Platt   It was presented to us as a fait accompli. We knew that Marcos was corrupt and that he had lost the support of his people — and of the economy as well — so we welcomed his removal. We felt that his time had come and that it was in America's interest to have new leadership and a restoration of democracy.

I believe that President Reagan had very mixed feelings about this. But I think that he also understood the realities of the situation — that Marcos could no longer legitimately rule, and that for the United States to continue to back him would be costly, over time, to our interests.

THE SOVIET UNION

Gorbachev Comes to Power

Stuart Spencer   He had a plan, to build our defense up so that we would be so tough that they would have to come to their knees. It didn't work with Brezhnev because he was an old man; it didn't work with Andropov because he was sick. But Reagan was lucky — he was always a lucky politician. Along came Gorbachev.

Bernard Ingham   We got down to a short list of two, as to who was likely to become the new leader of the Soviet Union. One was Gregori Romanov, and the other was Gorbachev.

Afterward, Mrs. Thatcher asked, "How does this system throw up that kind of a maverick?" He was such an untypical Russian leader. He didn't read from papers; he argued, he discussed. He could give and take hard knocks.

Mrs. Thatcher had an important role to play in helping Gorbachev make an impressive entry upon the world stage. She was very pleasantly surprised at the Chequers meeting, which led to my saying to the world that night, after I had discussed it with her, "Mrs. Thatcher thinks that Mr. Gorbachev is a man she can do business with," which was one of the more famous sound bites, and quite prophetic.

Charles Powell   It was really rather extraordinary. We were in this big, oak-paneled room, with a fire blazing away, and either Mrs. Thatcher or

I occasionally got up to toss a log on it. Gorbachev and Mrs. Thatcher sat side by side, in armchairs.

Gorbachev had no enormous brief, no speaking notes — all the things one had associated for fifty years with Russian leaders. He had some notes, in green ink, that he pulled out of a small briefcase; he occasionally referred to them.

They settled down for an entirely uninhibited discussion. She really knew she was on to something quite different. After dealing for years with the Brezhnevs and the Andropovs — who read out these absolutely meaningless notes — here was someone you could argue with like a Western politician, who had the confidence, the articulateness to develop an argument.

Mrs. Thatcher thought, starting with our discussion with Gorbachev over lunch and continuing in the afternoon, that he realized there were fundamental weaknesses in the Soviet system and that unless those weaknesses were dealt with, it would go into the next century as a Third World country.

Therefore, he was open to persuasion about certain things — in the crudest terms, that communism didn't work in the form in which it was being implemented in the Soviet Union. He was open-minded enough to accept that possibility. He could be told that some things were simply counterproductive and that what they were doing in Africa and in the Middle East was highly dangerous and counter to Russia's real interests.

So she believed he could be changed and, through him, the Soviet Union could be changed. This was in the early days; this was even before he became party secretary.

The postluncheon meeting had been scheduled to be forty-five minutes to an hour. As it was, we went on for about three and a half hours. The poor Soviet ambassador was twitting away outside — postponing engagements one after another — as Gorbachev showed no inclination to stop talking.

Nor did Mrs. Thatcher. At the end, she felt very elated: this really was something new. But we didn't know when he came that he was going to be such a revolution to us.

Geoffrey Howe The meeting far exceeded our expectations. He was clearly speaking from his own analysis. The note that impressed us most was when he quoted Palmerston, that Britain has no permanent friends, no permanent enemies, but only permanent interests. He said, "We have interests that we need to identify with yours. And we need to work on those to see if we can get on together." The whole tone was set by that.

His style made such an impression that it led her to say, "He is a man with whom I can do business." The fact that Gorbachev made that impression on Margaret Thatcher then was wholly unforeseen, and very important. The fact that she was then able to impress Reagan, and myself, and Shultz — with the picture we'd had of this man — has made an inestimable contribution to East-West relations; she sold Gorbachev to Reagan. I don't think that Reagan would have taken him without that testimonial.

Horst Teltschik Sometimes you need the luck of history. The luck was that when Reagan was ready to move, Gorbachev came into office. And the liberalization process had already started in Poland, and later on in Hungary, and then, under Gorbachev, in the Soviet Union. All this came together to change Europe.

On July 2, 1985, Soviet General Secretary Mikhail Gorbachev appointed Eduard Shevardnadze, first secretary of the Communist Party of the Republic of Georgia, to be the foreign minister, replacing the veteran diplomat Andrei Gromyko, who was given the ceremonial post of chairman of the Presidium of the Supreme Soviet of the USSR.

Although Shevardnadze did not have a foreign affairs background, he soon entered into a close working relationship with Secretary of State Shultz and went on to play a major role in U.S.-Soviet relations.

Arthur Hartman, ambassador to France; ambassador to the Soviet Union When Shevardnadze was picked by Gorbachev, it was clear that Gorbachev was going back to a very early relationship. They had both been Komsomol* leaders in the old days.

We knew Shevardnadze by reputation. What we had heard was not too good. He had been the interior minister in Georgia and had put down demonstrations there in a very harsh kind of way.

Gorbachev must have had reason to believe that Shevardnadze also favored making changes in the system, and changes in the way the party worked — not as [Boris] Yeltsin later did, in getting rid of the party.

Nicholas Platt Shultz greeted Shevardnadze's arrival in office as an opportunity for a new relationship, and with the feeling that Shevardnadze was a breath of fresh air.

When we were preparing the papers for his first meeting with She-

---

* The Young Communist League, the traditional road to power for the party leadership.

vardnadze, Shultz looked at the usual talking points and said, "This is just the same old stuff. Shouldn't we change our approach? Can't I say to Shevardnadze, 'Look, this isn't about emigration from Russia; that's part of it. This is about your survival as a nation, competing in the world. Any nation that cannot abide the free exchange of ideas and information cannot compete. There is a direct relationship between survival and freedom.' Shouldn't we say that?" And he did. And Shevardnadze and Gorbachev responded.

David Abshire   When I got involved with very important people in Washington, one of the things that struck me was that there are certain areas about which they don't know much. [They] didn't begin to have the leadership ability with which to see one, two, or three important things correctly. Reagan saw that we had to break out of where we were on the old concept of deterrence — to begin to look in a different direction. He was ahead of his advisers in seeing that Gorbachev was headed for a U-turn. That bothered his advisers.

He sensed certain things. I remember that at one NATO meeting, George Shultz, who had great admiration for Reagan, made a statement, "Reagan has got his finger on the pulse of youth; he senses things."

Gennadi Gerasimov, editor in chief of the *Moscow News;* chief of the Soviet Foreign Ministry Information Department; spokesman for Secretary General Mikhail Gorbachev   In our society, there was always a contradiction between ideology and the practical outworking of foreign policy. Ideology said that the world was going to be Communist, that communism was the wave of the future. But diplomacy was different; we had to find accommodation with our neighbors, especially in the nuclear age. Today, with ideology out, there is no contradiction.

Andropov said that we didn't know the country we lived in; that there was no feedback between the rulers and the country; that the KGB reported to the leaders what they wanted to hear, not what really happened.

Gorbachev understood this. You cannot solve the problem if you don't know the problem, so he needed feedback; this was the reason for glasnost. He invited us to discuss our problems, but when we opened our closets, we found lots of skeletons — too many for Gorbachev.

In this sense, he released the forces which, in the end, he could not contain. But his main achievement was that he ended the cold war. He was aided in this endeavor by Reagan — and by Bush, in Malta, where Gorbachev and Bush buried the cold war in the bottom of the Mediterranean.

Pavel Palezchenko The key person in the relationship with the Soviets was Shultz; we called him "Prime Minister." We knew that he did a lot of the background work for Reagan. The relationship that Shultz developed with Shevardnadze was very important.

Sergei Tarasenko There were some thirty to forty meetings between Shultz and Shevardnadze. Without George Shultz, we would not have reached that kind of understanding and approach to the president, because the U.S. secretary of state and our foreign minister had the most difficult task, of crossing this water of distrust.

The chemistry between them worked right. When Shevardnadze told Shultz that we would get out of Afghanistan, nobody in the U.S. administration believed him. But Shultz bet ten bucks against one of his colleagues who said that this was just nonsense, and Shultz won the bet.

I believe that Shultz would agree that the most important thing during this period was that he and Shevardnadze had mutual trust. They had a lot of disagreements, a lot of problems, but whenever they reached some understanding, they would keep it. Theirs was a slowly built confidence — that we would deliver to the Americans what we said, and they would deliver what they said. This was very important.

Nicholas Daniloff Shevardnadze came out of nowhere. I think that everybody was surprised and shocked when he was named to replace Gromyko as foreign minister. Shevardnadze and Gorbachev were very close friends. They were similar thinkers in the Politburo; they felt that socialism hadn't produced the benefits that had been expected of it, that it was an inefficient system, that Russia was being left behind by the rest of the world, and that something had to be done.

Jack Matlock Psychologically, they were very much alike — very personable and open — and if given confidence, would return it. In the fall of 1988, while President Reagan was still in office, Shultz and Shevardnadze began to have discussions about the possibility of the breakup of the Soviet Union. We had reached that degree of confidentiality.

Up until then, when we made our usual pitch on human rights, the Soviets would say, "It's our business." This time, he said, "Thank you. We are going to look into it. If mistakes have been made, I can assure you we will do everything possible to set it right."

He said, "Look, George, I want you to understand, I am not doing this because you asked me to. I am doing this because my country needs it. We can't have a modern society if we don't take care of these things."

George stood up immediately — they were sitting across from each other — and pounded his hand and said, "Eduard, that's the only reason you should ever do anything like that."

Human Rights

Elliott Abrams At the level of ideology and policy, Reagan internalized human rights and then made it the theme of his second term. There was an interesting change here, and I take credit for being part of that change.

In the early days of the administration, there was a tendency to throw human rights in with the rest of the failed Carter foreign policy that the Republicans didn't like, to view it as a form of American weakness, as part of the policy that Jeane Kirkpatrick had talked about with great eloquence, of beating up American allies and giving American enemies a free ride, the examples being Iran and Nicaragua.

I didn't have that view, and there were others who also felt this way; they were the "neo-cons." It was not an accident that I sought the human rights job [head of the State Department's Bureau of Human Rights and Humanitarian Affairs, December 1981–85]. I had worked for Scoop Jackson. I was part of that group of Jackson Democrats that included Jeane Kirkpatrick, [Washington-based author and commentator] Ben Wattenberg, and Admiral [Elmo] Zumwalt [chief of naval operations, 1970–74], who were very disaffected about what had been happening in the Democratic Party from 1972 on. Once it became clear what the race was going to be — Carter against Reagan — it was clear to me that I wanted Reagan to win, and once he did win, I wanted to serve in his administration, in a foreign policy job.

Reagan had said relatively little about this except to denounce what we all viewed as the mistakes of the Carter administration. We came up with a Republican theory of human rights that said that human rights was the center of our foreign policy, but that, given that we were in the middle of the cold war, the center of any human rights policy was going to be anticommunism, because the greatest threat to human rights was the Soviet Union.

Now you were talking in a language that the president not only understood but had himself employed, as had every conservative Republican. The service that the neo-con intellectuals performed was to provide the magic key to the scriptures.

It was a useful service. The president instantly recognized that, from both a principled and political point of view, this was a very good thing. And it really was significant for American foreign policy.

Nicholas Daniloff   There were a lot of [Soviet] dissidents at that time. The question was, did they represent only themselves, or did they represent certain worldwide trends that were more important than just themselves individually?

In the early 1980s the general attitude of the Soviet leadership was that they were a bunch of troublemakers — that they were not very important. As that period evolved, the intellectual community in Russia — either openly or secretly — sympathized with many of the goals of the dissidents: freedom of speech and of activity, an easing of the restrictions that were placed on Russian citizens.

I've always felt that one could overestimate the importance of the Helsinki Agreement. It is often said that the agreement helped to open Russia up, that it gave the Russians the recognition of postwar borders that they were looking for — but at a price. And the price was more communication between East and West.

I think that the opening up of the Soviet Union did not really come with the Helsinki Agreement; rather, the agreement ratified a process that was going on, a process that started with Khrushchev's purchase of U.S. wheat in the winter of 1963.

What happened from then until 1975, when the agreement was signed, was that this was a period when the Russians were experiencing deficits in many areas, forcing them to trade actively with the West. This trade required Russian and Western businessmen to go back and forth more easily, so this is the opening up that preceded Helsinki.

Rozanne Ridgway   You have to give Max Kampelman [head of the U.S. delegation to the Madrid Conference on Human Rights of the Conference on Security and Cooperation in Europe (CSCE)] a lot of credit on this issue. The first time Shultz met Gorbachev and raised human rights, Gorbachev went nuts: "This is our internal affair. Who do you think you are? You don't treat people any better than we do!" It was god-awful.

But meanwhile, Max had elaborated — and continued to do so — the legal notion that by signing the Helsinki Accords the Soviet Union had taken upon itself an obligation to police its own human rights record. Having signed the document, they had done it to themselves. Max was trying to get them to understand this argument. This was not the U.S. pushing them around; it was the Soviet Union living up to its own obligations.

Nicholas Platt   Both Reagan and Shultz were very assiduous about human rights issues; they presented them in all the meetings, as was required. Their hearts were in it; it wasn't just a perfunctory exercise.

But Shultz had a different slant on it. He was looking at it from the point of view of the impact of technology on human rights. For Gorbachev and Shevardnadze, it was a chance to do something different.

George P. Shultz   There was a lot of toughness. When, as a human rights buff, I look at the way Clinton handled human rights in China and contrast it to the way we handled the subject with the Soviet Union, it makes me gag at the setbacks in China.

Reagan was so much more quiet about it; he accomplished a lot more. Take, for example, the Pentecostals. Nobody even knew how that happened because Reagan was interested in helping people, not in getting the credit for it.

Richard Schifter   The Pentecostals were mostly Russians. The way they handled it was to let them emigrate as Jews. They had to get an invitation from Israel in order to obtain a visa, and the KGB told them what number to call in Rome.

Rozanne Ridgway   Reagan used the emigration argument, but the thrust of it really was that modern societies looking to the next century were going to have to use every intellectual resource at their command, and you could not exclude large portions of your population from the creative requirements of the next century. And by having this kind of human rights regime, [by] doing this to creative minds and creative people and producing a population of four hundred thousand people who wanted to leave, you were punishing your own future. You were taking away an enormous capacity to be a modern state. It took a while, but it began to seep in.

Whatever you thought of the president, he was a fully integrated mind — a fully integrated person, including the contradictions — who really believed that a country that had all those different people in it was very much like the United States, and that the success of the United States had been in capturing the talents of all of those people.

He very often said to Gorbachev that he was the president of a country of immigrants, so naturally he wanted to talk to Gorbachev about how our people here, with their basic ethnic backgrounds, were interested in what was happening in East and Central Europe. Polish Americans were worried about Poles, Czech Americans were worried about Czechs, and American Jews worried about Soviet Jews.

East-West Relations

Horst Teltschik   Kohl was the first visitor to the White House after the 1984 election. We signed a communiqué that was very important to us. We got Reagan to agree that the Western alliance would try hard to reestablish arms control and reduction negotiations between East and West, to start again with summit diplomacy between the two world powers.

Fortunately, with the coming to power of Gorbachev, the negotiations were able to start again. It was a basic concern for us that if we could get the two powers to meet, we could achieve our goals vis-à-vis the German Democratic Republic, Poland, and Hungary.

Rozanne Ridgway   There had to be a channel, and it wasn't going to be [Soviet Ambassador to the U.S. Anatoly] Dobrynin; I was pleased about this. Shultz was determined to control the dialogue on the U.S. side, and he knew he needed somebody on the Soviet side. Shultz has a particular capacity for measuring people, and he believed that Shevardnadze was a different kind of person. And from what we could see, that seemed to be the case.

His relationship with Shevardnadze was very carefully constructed. At Helsinki in 1985 — at the tenth anniversary of the CSCE — it was Shultz who walked up all of those steps to shake hands with Shevardnadze, who was arriving for the first time and, we learned, arriving with a Mrs. Shevardnadze. That had never happened before.

It was then that the Shultzes decided that Mrs. Shultz would extend her friendship to Mrs. Shevardnadze, and they toured downtown Helsinki together. When Shevardnadze came to Washington on the eve of UN meetings, Shultz decided to invite him to his home. It was an extraordinary evening, a mix of cultures. There was George Shultz, who had a kind of entertaining uniform — gray slacks, white shirt, and bow tie, and a burgundy-colored sports jacket — turning steaks in his fireplace. The Russians were in their blue suits.

From this evening, there developed a personal respect; you don't abandon principle when you add personal warmth. Properly done, it makes it more likely that you will deliver your message in [such] a manner that it will be understood. That's what Shultz had in mind.

And that's what Shevardnadze reciprocated. Four years later, at the final party in Washington, the Shevardnadzes arrived with letters from their grandchildren to the Shultz grandchildren.

THE SUMMITS

George P. Shultz   Gorbachev and Shevardnadze were more knowledgeable than their predecessors about what was really going on in the Soviet Union. They were aware that it was a bad scene. And I thought that they were quite different people from their predecessors. After all, I had dealt with some of the same leaders back in the 1970s, under President Nixon.

Gorbachev and Shevardnadze were different. We saw in that an opportunity. Many people in Washington said, "There is nothing different, these are just personalities. Nothing can be changed." That was the CIA view; that was Cap's view; that was the view of all the hard-liners. They were very critical of Reagan, and more so of me, because they felt I was leading him into dealing with Gorbachev. They were terribly wrong. Gorbachev was an important figure.

Suzanne Massie   The president mentioned to me that he was struck by how much Gorbachev talked about God. He had mentioned God in his first U.S. interview. Our journalists did back flips to explain that, while he measured every word, this was one he didn't.

It was interesting to me, as a writer. It interested Reagan as well.

Cal Thomas   I don't think that the Religious Right was frustrated when Reagan sat down with Gorbachev, because they trusted Reagan; they didn't think he'd give away the store. They said, "Yes, he is smart enough to do this and not have his pocket picked." They had enormous faith in Reagan, and still do to this day.

Frank Carlucci   The president was certainly enthusiastic about the prospects of negotiating with the Soviets. He never lost his faith that if they just understood us, they would change.

The Geneva Summit

On November 19, 1985, a new era in U.S.-Soviet relations began when President Reagan met with General Secretary Gorbachev at Geneva, Switzerland. During this summit—the first of several such meetings between the two leaders—Reagan and Gorbachev established a rapport that facilitated their discussion of arms control, human rights, and other major issues.

George P. Shultz   The chemistry between Reagan and Gorbachev was good. He admired Reagan because he saw what Reagan accomplished; he saw the strength of the man; he saw that he could carry out what he agreed to.

It was peculiar, because Reagan had kind of a paternal attitude. Gorbachev was much better informed on all kinds of things than Reagan was, but Gorbachev had enough intelligence not to try to take advantage of the fact, although sometimes it frustrated him.

Pavel Palezchenko   The relationship had its difficulties in that Gorbachev likes to improvise and Reagan liked to work from the cards. But they both believed that political leaders make a difference; they both believed that they were the people who could make decisions. Gorbachev always said to us that we should work with the available partners, that we should not set conditions so far as style, philosophy, or ideology were concerned.

Nicholas Daniloff   When Gorbachev came to power, things began to shift, and to change. The Russians began taking major initiatives that we hadn't seen before. We had more or less assumed that it wasn't in their character to take initiatives; it was more in their character to respond.

With the appearance of Gorbachev, you had a breakthrough, you had a different partner who really put public relations on a different basis; in the process, he destroyed the Soviet Union.

Then, of course, there was the Geneva summit, which I attended. At the Geneva summit, Gorbachev and his crew surprised the West by their openness and by their willingness to put forward influential Soviet managers and leaders and to open them up to the press. Essentially, the American administration and the American journalists felt that the Russians had beaten the Americans at their own game.

Pavel Palezchenko   It was a get-acquainted meeting, and the result was a good one. They were able to agree on an important declaration, which included the statement that nuclear war cannot be won and must not be fought. This was a breakthrough.

George P. Shultz   Whenever we got together with the Soviets in the Reagan-Gorbachev meetings, SDI was always on Gorbachev's mind. He seemed almost ready to concede anything if he could only manage to deep-six that program.

There was a very dramatic moment in the Geneva summit in which Gorbachev attacked SDI. And when he got through, Reagan gave a very personal, impassioned statement about why it was important. And it was very powerful.

Reagan's words were being simultaneously translated, and when he stopped, there was this absolute, dead silence in the room that seemed to go on forever. And then Gorbachev said, "Mr. President, I don't agree with you, but I can see that you really mean it."

Suzanne Massie   Reagan had a triumph at Geneva; it was an image that went around the world. Up until Geneva, the Russian people had seen no pictures of Reagan other than caricatures. On our side, Reagan was being described as old — a person who sleeps — while our press reacted to Gorbachev as though he were the new football hero; he couldn't do anything wrong.

And then Gorbachev arrives for the first session, and he gets out of the car and looks up the stairs, and there is Reagan, bounding down, without a coat. The Russians' reaction was electric. What kind of a country is the U.S.? The man is seventy years old, and coatless; our guy was bundled up. This was never forgotten by them.

The Post-Geneva Release of Anatoly Sharansky

On March 15, 1977, Anatoly "Natan" Sharansky, a computer specialist who became an activist in the Soviet Jewry movement and a spokesman for Soviet dissidents and who sought to live in Israel, was arrested by the KGB on trumped-up charges of treason, a capital crime in the Soviet Union.

Convicted, sentenced to hard labor, and incarcerated in several harsh regime prisons, Sharansky continued to play a heroic role in the human rights struggle as a prisoner of conscience—the designation for those who were imprisoned for leading Jewish lives, including speaking, and in some cases teaching, Hebrew, and wishing to emigrate, mainly to Israel.

Sharansky's plight became a major cause in the West owing to advocacy on his behalf by Soviet Jewry organizations, leaders of the free world, and his wife, Avital. Avital Sharansky, who married her husband in Moscow shortly before he was seized by the KGB, was told at that time that if she did not leave immediately for Israel, she would never be allowed to do so, and so she left, believing that she would be better able to advocate from the Jewish state for her husband's release.

On February 11, 1986, Sharansky was expelled from the Soviet Union in a prisoner exchange and emigrated immediately to Israel, where he was re-united with his wife. He soon became a spokesman for Soviet Jews living in

*Israel, as well as a major political figure. He is currently a member of the Is-
raeli government.*

Max Kampelman   I made that deal in Madrid. What the Soviets wanted
was a letter from Sharansky. I drafted a one-sentence letter — it was addressed to Gorbachev: "I hereby request a release from prison" — which
the KGB man I dealt with accepted. He sent it to Moscow, and it was
accepted.

What I was trying to keep away from was anything that might indicate
acquiescence in guilt, or that Sharansky's past behavior had been improper. I said to my Russian colleague, "Okay, we have now got a letter,
and we expect him to send it. I have to check it, but you haven't given me
a pencil, and you haven't given him a pencil."

He thought I was crazy. He said, "What are you talking about, Max?" I
said, "Who is going to explain all of this to him? Will you do it? Do you
think he will believe you? Will the warden [at Chistopol, a harsh regime
labor camp] explain it? Will he believe the warden? Will Gorbachev go and
explain it? Are you going to let his mother [Ida Milgrom, who then lived in
Moscow] explain it to him? You haven't let her in there for more than a
year. You have to let his mother in there; she has to explain it to him."

She did visit him and recommended the letter. I had first talked with
Mrs. Sharansky, and she accepted it. She went back to Israel — she was
working with a very deeply religious, Orthodox Hasidic group — and
they persuaded her that this was not the thing to do. But I don't think
that Sharansky was influenced that much by her. I think he decided not
to do it; it was his own strength that decided this.

The Prelude to Reykjavík: The Arrest of an American Journalist in Moscow

*The arrest on August 23, 1986, by the FBI of Gennadi F. Zakharov — a sci-
entific attaché with the secretariat of the Soviet Mission to the United Nations in New York City — as he passed money to a young man in exchange
for classified documents provided for that purpose by the FBI, set in motion
a series of events that would at one point call into question whether the second U.S.-Soviet summit of the Reagan administration would take place as
scheduled.*

*One week later, on August 30, the Soviets, in retaliation, seized Nicholas
Daniloff, who was then in his tenth year as the Moscow correspondent for
U.S. News & World Report, only seconds after he accepted from a Soviet na-
tional a package containing materials marked "Top Secret."*

Daniloff was taken to Lefortovo Prison and charged with espionage, a capital offense in the Soviet Union. President Reagan reacted viscerally, suggesting to Gorbachev via the U.S.-Soviet "hot line" that if Daniloff were not released, he would be considered a "hostage" and that "serious and far-reaching consequences" would ensue.

A debate then occurred in the administration as to whether or not Daniloff's freedom should be obtained by exchanging him with the Soviet attaché. The situation was complicated when it was discovered that five years earlier Daniloff, although not paid for his activity, had delivered a package to the U.S. embassy in Moscow that had found its way into the hands of the CIA.

After intense diplomatic negotiations and the conclusion of an arrangement whereby Zakharov would be tried in a closed session in New York and released to Soviet custody on the freeing of the American journalist by the Soviets, Daniloff was released from Lefortovo Prison on September 12.

Nicholas Daniloff   The FBI, for good and sufficient reason, arrested Gennadi Zakharov. They were not acting as a rogue intelligence agency; they had the goods on him. Furthermore, before they made the arrest, they went around to all the departments in Washington that would be affected, including the State Department, and everybody gave their approval.

I have asked American officials, "Why an arrest at that time, when Reagan and Gorbachev were doing the minuet about whether they would set up the Iceland summit? Why not let the summit go ahead, and then arrest him?" The answer I got was that the case on him had been built, and the FBI was anxious to close the case.

And what is slightly appalling is that little thought was given to what the retaliatory consequences might be.

Abraham Sofaer   When I talked to Reagan about Daniloff, he had a view about the Soviets. He told me that they had set this guy up, that he was innocent, that this was an outrage. And then he started to tell stories about Commies, what they were like. He was teaching Abe Sofaer how to understand Ronald Reagan. And they were funny stories, good stories.

I was trying to make a point that related to America's interests — and to our responsibility to Daniloff as a human being — that superseded the ideological point he was making. He was uneasy throughout; you could see that something I'd said had an effect on him.

What I said to the president in the Oval Office was that, based on the evidence that I knew the Russians had about Daniloff, they had enough so that if we had had that evidence against a Russian in the United States, we could have convicted him of espionage in a federal court. I put it that way so that he would understand what was going to happen down the road.

The president was shocked; he didn't know the facts. No one had really briefed him on what the Russians had on Daniloff. They had planted stuff on him; the CIA guy in Moscow had spoken on an open line things that were highly prejudicial to him; some of the documents that he had been given — and kept — were very artfully done, so that they had "classified" markings on them. All in all, Daniloff clearly wanted to have classified information. He got set up; it got him into trouble.

The president obviously understood the implications of this. It was quite clear to me that he was very upset.

Shultz was convinced that we had struck out. I said, "No, he understood what I said, and he's going to change his mind." And Shultz said, "Maybe."

I was as firmly against the Soviet Union as Reagan was, and I thought that once he understood the situation, he would look on it differently, because there was really no sense in allowing a public trial of Daniloff in Moscow, where it would show everybody that there was evidence against him. It might have been trumped-up evidence, just as we trump up evidence against people — and, in fact, we set Zakharov up.

At first he didn't believe me, and when it sank in, and I insisted that he understand what I was saying, Reagan was shaken. Thereafter, they asked for this to be confirmed by the Department of Justice. So I called the chief of the Criminal Division, and I sent the materials over to him.

He examined them and reached the same conclusion, and this was confirmed to Shultz and the White House. And that created a new environment for the Daniloff case to be considered [in], which was very important from Nick's point of view. I just felt it would have been a terrible, terrible thing to make him suffer because of the need to seem tough. We could be tough, but we didn't have to be tough at his expense.

Nicholas Daniloff   When Zakharov was arrested, I was in my last week in Moscow, and I was packing my bags. My replacement had arrived. I had no particular reason to suspect that I might be the target. The CIA was sloppy; there was no need for them to have mentioned my name. It came up in a couple of ways. Where I first became aware of the CIA's having incriminated me, as it were, was in the interrogations in Lefortovo Prison, where my interrogator brought forward these various statements — that I was an agent of the CIA, according to him. He accused me of collecting information on the instructions of the CIA and taking it to the CIA station in the U.S. embassy.

This was fatuous. I had never had any contact with the CIA people in Moscow. I did not seek them out; they did not seek me out. I received no instructions from anybody to gather anything, except instructions from *U.S. News & World Report*, which was interested in a variety of things, and I tried to fulfill their wishes.

There was one point where the interrogator showed me a letter, which was presumably written by an American CIA person to a dissident rocket scientist, or to his contact man. He accused me of having lent my typewriter for this letter to be printed on. My typewriter was a totally different type. I told him so. This was a ridiculous accusation. "This letter — this is not my typewriter."

That was where I learned that there had been some kind of incrimination of me by the CIA. My reaction was, this is serious business. What they are doing is phonying up documents, and they are going to claim that these are true documents. I didn't believe that they were true documents; I thought that they were phony documents.

Abraham Sofaer The CIA made a mistake by making a call to Daniloff. I think that they genuinely believed there was a certain person who wanted to reestablish contact and provide very useful information, as he had in the past. This was a very exciting thing for them, and they called him to ask him to come back and discuss the thing with them.

And that got Daniloff into trouble, because the Soviets were waiting for that call. They were waiting for this kind of thing to happen, having given him some phony stuff to start with, and having sent him a phony letter from this person.

At some point in the middle of this, I went up to see Cy Vance, who was counsel for *U.S. News & World Report* and who had Daniloff's interests very much at heart. He was, I thought, appropriately concerned that Nick not pay the price for face-saving. I don't know how you put it. When you have a reputation for being against the Soviet Union and you want to preserve that reputation, there is always a danger that you won't do the right thing.

Not with Shultz. The thing about Shultz is that if he thinks something is not right, he won't do it. And the same with Reagan. The question was just getting through to him. Once we got through, and he realized it, that decision was made: this case is going to be handled in a different way.

Then my job became to negotiate with the Department of Justice and the court system the whole end-scenario for the turnover of Zakharov. I came up with the idea of the nolo contendere [no contest] plea, and all the other mechanisms, even his going into the courthouse through the basement. I knew the eastern district had a basement; you could drive into it and avoid the press. All these things were worked out, down to the last detail, with the U.S. attorney, who was a very good friend of mine.

There was one problem after another. The Soviets were totally unused to this kind of cooperation from us; it was a new way of dealing with them. In a very real sense, the Daniloff case was a turning point. All of a sudden, we are trusting each other, to the point where we are allowing a process to go forward. We are turning someone over; they are turning someone over without knowing for sure that everything has been done. These two guys, Shevardnadze and Shultz, are trusting each other and instructing their staffs that they are going to be trusting each other.

From the U.S. point of view, it was just a fabulous deal, and it allayed the Soviets' fears about what we were doing, what we were really up to. Were we going to renege? Was Zakharov going to be kept? Was he going to be asked questions?

Gennadi Gerasimov   He was arrested because the Americans arrested Zakharov. Shevardnadze had a very high regard for Zakharov; the impression was that he was innocent. In our view, it was a very silly arrest — the game that intelligence services play. From the very beginning it was clear that it was just a game of reciprocity.

Nicholas Daniloff   It was a frightening and extremely unpleasant experience. They started by treating me like an ordinary prisoner, and I lost a lot of weight very quickly, and then they began feeding me better. The Russians would tell you that I was given preferential treatment, but I wouldn't say that it was very wonderful.

The worst thing about it was that I knew too much about all these things. I knew that people had been horribly tortured in the Lefortovo Prison. It's right next to a construction bureau that makes aircraft engines, and sometimes these engines would be tested, and the noise would be very loud, and that's when they would torture people. I knew this, and that made my imagination work overtime.

And the worst thing really was not knowing what was going to happen from one minute to the next. I was in that prison for two weeks, but two weeks that went by minute to minute. If you measure your day minute by minute, it goes for a long time.

Gennadi Gerasimov   Daniloff simply behaved very naively. He received a package containing secret things; he said it was a provocation. I don't know.

This was an unfortunate episode — maybe the last episode — of the cold war. But it started in New York, not Moscow.

Nicholas Daniloff The CIA station must have been under pressure to make contact with anybody they had a reasonable judgment could be helpful to the United States, in terms of technology, so they were reaching out.

The letter I found in my mailbox — and that I gave to the embassy — was apparently one of those cases. Now, I was always, from the beginning, suspicious of the contents of that letter. It was a big problem for me to decide what I should do with that letter. There were a number of choices. I could take that letter to the embassy, which is what I did, or — and I contemplated this — I could have taken it to the Soviet Foreign Ministry and said, "What the hell is this letter that's appeared in my mailbox?"

They would have given me a blank stare. But it would have been an action that would have told them, "Don't try to involve me in your lousy espionage operations."

I didn't do it for one reason, which was that, maybe, this was a bona fide spy; maybe this wasn't just a trap. Do I want on my conscience that I betrayed a Soviet who was an American agent, and he was now going to get arrested and be executed?

So I took the letter to the American embassy, and we opened the letter, and it was apparently a letter from a dissident rocket scientist. So I told them, "Take this and do what you want, but keep me out of it." Of course, the CIA paid no attention to that.

My experience suggests that the CIA didn't give a damn. This was, possibly, a windfall for them, and they wanted to pursue it because Casey was putting on that pressure. Well, fine for them. But to say, over an open, monitored telephone, that Nicholas Daniloff passed this on to us, and our friend Nicholas did this and that, is baloney. I never met the operating officer in that.

But once I get into the interrogation chamber at Lefortovo Prison, my interrogator is telling me that I am [Moscow CIA station chief Paul] Stambaugh's friend, and that he is my control officer. I said, "This is ludicrous. I've never met him."

In prison I put forth a proposal. I said, at a meeting with my wife, in the presence of the interrogator, "This is a bad thing that everybody is doing. It's not good for you to be holding me in prison and for this to become a great international incident. And what you need to do next is to release me to the custody of the American ambassador, and Zakharov to the custody of the Russian ambassador. And then you have to get the diplomats on both sides to negotiate a sensible compromise." And that indeed did happen.

The interrogator was bowled over when I said this. His immediate reaction was, "Who told you that?" I said, "Nobody told me that. I figured that out from past history." Believe it or not, I was not just interested in getting out of prison. I was interested in seeing that the two superpowers had a more honest, and a better, relationship. That was always my posture during the whole thing — that this is an evil action that has been taken by a security service in order to resolve their problem with their guy, who is being held in New York. Get rid of that problem, and let's get back to the major issue of our time, which is how to produce a better relationship between the United States and Russia.

The Role of Armand Hammer in Daniloff's Release

Armand Hammer, the chairman of Occidental Petroleum, who had longtime connections to the Soviet Union, was instrumental in securing Daniloff's release.

The industrialist also played a role in the release of Dr. David Goldfarb, a noted Jewish scientist and hero of the World War II battle of Stalingrad; he lost a leg in that conflict.

Dr. Goldfarb, whose son Aleksandr was an activist in the Soviet Jewry movement and a close associate of prisoner of conscience Natan Sharansky, was brought to the United States in an aircraft belonging to Hammer. It was discovered shortly after Dr. Goldfarb's arrival in the United States that he was suffering from lung cancer. He died several years later.

Nicholas Daniloff I was always fascinated by Hammer. I had interviewed him in the 1980s, and I was aware of his career. He was an unusual guy.

He played a useful role in this crisis. Hammer flew to Moscow, and his role, as I understand it, was, with the blessing of people in the U.S. government, to try to convince the Russians that Zakharov should change his plea from guilty to nolo. The Russians didn't understand that because nolo was not a plea they were familiar with.

He liked to claim that he was the originator of this device, which was a key device in unlocking the situation. If you look into it, you will find that he was not the only one who had this idea. But the benefit Hammer brought to the situation was that he was trusted by the Soviet side; he was one more confirmation that this was okay.

While the American public may have felt that what Reagan did was to swap a non-spy journalist for a spy, the resolution was much more complex than that, and much more interesting.

It's always been my view that the Americans got the better part of the deal. I think that Shultz was very intelligent in the way he negotiated the resolution. What happened in the resolution, as I know it, was that Orlov* was released from Siberia and allowed to come to New York with his wife. The Russians paid the premium of letting Orlov out, but I believe that they also agreed that they would quietly allow ten or twelve other Russians to leave to get medical treatment in the West. My particular friend, Dr. David Goldfarb, was allowed out, and I believe that was part of that very quiet agreement.

I was given back my passport. While the charges were not immediately dropped, I left the country with a passport and a valid reentry visa into Russia. Subsequently, the case was closed, and the charges were dropped.

I've now been back to Russia any number of times. Zakharov changed his plea to nolo, was given a five-year suspended sentence, and was expelled. While none of this is necessarily perfect, it is a pretty good package. The Americans got the better part of the deal.

Arthur Hartman People tend to make up broad theories about narrow events. We made a mistake. We had gotten a piece of paper that indicated that somebody wanted to communicate. The only way we had of getting back to this source was if Daniloff handled it.

It was my fault, because I should have known that this put a newspaperman in a very, very bad situation. I should have refused to let that happen when they came to me and told me what they wanted to do, because it gave those on the Russian side — who were looking for a way of getting an incident that they could then use to slow the process down — the opportunity.

When people say that the Russians were testing us, no way. First of all, there wasn't one view in Russia. There were people on the security side who didn't like the idea that some of these talks were progressing. They didn't like Gorbachev very much; they were looking for an incident, and this was made for them. We handed this one to them.

Daniloff was not a spy. He didn't even know what this was. He had just been handed something, and we said, "Look, hand it back to the same person. And then get out of it. We don't want to use you." It was wrong. We shouldn't have done that at all.

---

* Yuri Orlov, a major figure in the Helsinki Watch group (established by Soviet dissidents to monitor compliance with the 1975 Helsinki Accords), and his wife were released from Siberia in the fall of 1986 and arrived in New York on October 5.

Nicholas Daniloff When I was released from prison, I was taken to the American embassy, and I had a confidential conversation in the bubble[*] with Richard Coombs, the deputy chief of mission.

My wife[†] was also with me in the bubble, and she exploded in rage. She said, "I will not permit this conversation to go on any further. Nick, don't say a word! These bastards have blackened you for no good purpose. Let us get out of here."

Throughout the whole thing she was immensely angry; I was always very restrained and controlled. I didn't think that spewing large amounts of emotion was going to help anything very much. I think that she was right and I was wrong. In the end I was negotiated out and the Iceland summit took place.

The Reykjavík Summit

In the period following the Geneva summit, U.S. and Soviet negotiators sought progress on arms control prior to the convening of a summit in Washington. The failure to achieve such a breakthrough led Gorbachev to suggest a preparatory meeting between the leaders.

On the weekend of October 11–12, 1986, Reagan and Gorbachev met in Reykjavík, Iceland. This summit, characterized in some quarters as a failure, marked a turning point in U.S.-Soviet relations.

For Gorbachev, the summit's key issue was arms control, while Reagan wanted to add human rights and regional and bilateral issues to the discussion. During the two days of intensive conversations, Reagan accepted Gorbachev's proposal for the eventual elimination of nuclear weapons, but he refused to agree to limit SDI testing to a laboratory setting.

The meeting, which appeared to result in a stalemate, nonetheless led to important progress on arms control, paving the way for the INF (intermediate-range nuclear forces) Treaty, which eliminated the whole classification of intermediate-range nuclear missiles.

Joan Quigley My mother died on September 18, 1986. The next morning Nancy called and said, "I want to talk to you." I said, "Nancy, my mother died yesterday, and I just don't feel like talking." She said, "But, Joan, this is important. Ronnie and I are the only people who know — you will be the

---

[*] A special device enabling conversations to go undetected by any listening devices planted by the Soviets in the embassy.
[†] Ruth Daniloff was very involved in helping to secure her husband's release from Soviet custody.

third: Gorbachev has just invited Ronnie to a secret meeting in Reykjavík, Iceland. Should he go? And should the meeting be kept secret?"

I said, "Give me an hour." I worked for an hour, and Nancy called back, and I said, "He not only should go, but he will go, and it will never be kept a secret. The whole world will know."

I picked the time for them to leave for Iceland. I said they should negotiate as long as they possibly could, that they should stay until the very last minute.

Lyn Nofziger   Reagan was kind of conned into it. Gorbachev made people think things were easing up over there. A lot of us were afraid that at Iceland Reagan would be conned into giving away the store.

I called over to the White House and said I would like to speak to the president. And when I go over, it is just me and Ronald Reagan.

I said, "Mr. President, a lot of us are fearful of what is going to go on in Iceland. We think there is talk about making a deal, and I want you to know that there are a lot of people out there who support you because of your strong stand against the USSR."

He said, "Lynwood, I don't want you to ever worry. I still have the scars on my back from the fights with the Communists in Hollywood. I am not going to give away anything." So we sat around and told jokes for twenty minutes, and I went away.

Reagan's weakness is that he thinks that if people like him, they are also going to like his views. He could not conceive that a man as outwardly congenial as Gorbachev could really have ulterior motives. Reagan doesn't believe in ulterior motives; he never had an ulterior motive in his life.

Sergei Tarasenko   We saw in President Reagan a human being — not a politician, but a human being, dedicated, and believing strongly in certain ideas. You could not argue with him; you could not productively argue with him on his so-called pet projects. If he believed in these things, he really believed them, and you felt it.

Gennadi Gerasimov   Reagan was looked at as a big danger because he was talking tough. Then, when we started negotiations, everything changed. For this, Gorbachev respected Reagan, although he had some misgivings about Reagan's intellectual capacities.

Arthur Hartman   Gorbachev had infinite confidence in his own abilities, to the point where he would never listen when people tried to tell him his facts were wrong, when he determined that he was going to do something in a certain way, no matter what kind of advice — even good advice — he got.

It came to the point where his principal adviser at the time, Aleksandr Yakovlev, quit several years later, because he felt he wasn't listening. He wasn't listening to anybody; he was doing his own thing. And we saw the first evidence of that in this episode at Reykjavík.

Human Rights Discussions at Reykjavík

George P. Shultz   We got the subject officially on the agenda. That was a breakthrough in Reykjavík; people don't realize how important Reykjavík was. Shevardnadze said, "We only do things if they are of benefit to us. We don't do things just to please you." Shevardnadze would talk to us about the subject of human rights.

I felt that all of this trade-related work on human rights — and the whole notion of linkage — was wrong. And we changed that. That was a big part of changing U.S.-Soviet relations — to get rid of this doctrine of linkage that kept everything bound up. So I developed an approach. I thought about it very carefully, and I wrote it out, about the impact of the information age on society, that this was where the future was.

I said to him, "This is the way the world is going. Any society that wants to be part of the future has got to be involved in this. And an information knowledge society has got to be an open society. So your conception of the relationship between the individual and the state has got to change, for your own benefit. And that has human rights implications."

I wrote all that out, and unlike many of my presentations to Shevardnadze, I asked for some time on this, which he gave me. Dobrynin came, and I read it out. Their note-takers took it all down. I made similar comments to Gorbachev.

I've asked Shevardnadze since, and I've asked Gorbachev since he left office, "Do you recall that meeting?" and he said, "Yes. I reported that." Gorbachev liked the subject of how the world was changing.

The Soviet Jewry Issue

Rozanne Ridgway   On the human rights side — which Shultz always talks about — we were continuing to do a work list on human rights; we handed over God knows how many names.*

---

* The National Conference on Soviet Jewry provided Secretary of State Shultz with a list, compiled by the Anti-Defamation League, that contained the names of eleven thousand Jewish refuseniks and prisoners of conscience. Secretary Shultz, in turn, gave the list to the Soviets.

We had agreed to a human rights statement; it never got published. That would have been a breakthrough. But Reykjavík was the turning point on human rights.

Elliott Abrams The Reagan administration kept beating the Soviet Union over the issue of the Soviet Jews and kept telling them, "You have to deal with this question. You will not be able to establish the kind of relationship you want with us unless you have dealt with this question — the question of emigration and the question of what you are doing internally."

At a certain point Gorbachev came to the realization that the way they were running the country was failing. I think that Reagan and Shultz had something to do with that realization. But the notion that Gorbachev came to power and the following day decided to open up the Soviet Union to democracy is very foolish. Historians can debate what role Reagan policy played in forcing, or bringing, the Soviets to these changes. But the record will not sustain the view that there was a steady trajectory of change within the Soviet Union — including change toward democracy, openness, and human rights — that was unchanged, and unaffected, by pressure from the United States. We had endless discussions with the Soviets on human rights. It was really at the top of Shultz's agenda with the Soviets. This was a period — as the 1970s had been — of phenomenal human rights abuses.

Yitzhak Shamir Reagan's interest in Soviet Jewry was immense; it was close to the first issue on the American agenda and was part of the confrontation between the two superpowers. And Reagan and Shultz were excellent in this confrontation. I have no doubt that they brought about the defeat of the Soviet Union.

The Soviet leaders told me that every time they met with Shultz, he raised the issue of Soviet Jewry, and they would ask him, "Why do you do this?" Shultz answered that this was very important.

Gennadi Gerasimov I have notes on their human rights discussions at Reykjavík. Reagan said, "Jews want to practice their religion, so they want to leave the country." Gorbachev dismissed this idea about religion, but he accepted the idea that they wanted to leave.

Gorbachev was the one who defused the issue of human rights — at that time mainly the right to travel, to leave the country. Gorbachev lectured Reagan on our understanding of human rights as involving social and economic issues, such as job security and medical care. The dialogue on this issue was very polite.

Gorbachev thought that the human rights issue was one of the cold war weapons. For instance, we don't have any lines today at food stores in Moscow, but there are long, long lines at the American embassy, and the embassy is refusing many requests for visas. The American position is, yes, everybody has the right to leave the country, but not every country has an obligation to accept everybody.

Arms Control Discussions at Reykjavík

Caspar Weinberger Reagan did not put any offer on the table. Gorbachev had four major aims: to decouple us from Europe, to get us out of NATO, to have us stop work on Stealth, and to stop work on the strategic defense. He coupled and linked everything to that. And the president had no intention of giving up strategic defense; quite properly, he rejected Gorbachev's proposals.

Jack Matlock He didn't sign on to anything of a technical nature without consulting his advisers. They worked on the technical details almost all night — Akhromeyev* on the Soviet side and [U.S. arms negotiator Paul] Nitze heading our team, with several arms control experts.

The only commitment the president made which would not have been approved by the others — but one he felt sincerely about — was the agreement that we should try to phase out our nuclear weapons by the year 2000. More and more people are now coming over to that view, although not necessarily fixing a date. Reagan was before his time on that issue. It was another case of his following his instincts.

Richard Perle The notion that it was all kind of careening out of control was based on the idea that he offered to give up all nuclear weapons. What in fact happened was that we had laid down a quota to eliminate ballistic missiles. This was a self-serving proposal, to be sure, because the big Soviet advantage was in ballistic missiles.

Jack Matlock His proposal to eliminate ballistic missiles was very well thought out by a narrow group of people, including experts. Now, the 630 other people who worked on the issue in the U.S. government — and thought they weren't consulted — could say that he didn't know what he was doing.

---

* Sergei Akhromeyev, marshal of the Soviet Army and chief of the Soviet General Staff, later served as an adviser to Gorbachev and was involved in the abortive August 1991 coup attempt against Gorbachev, following which he died, most likely by suicide.

That's nonsense. That proposal came out of the Defense Department. We didn't consult every expert in the government who thought he should have a piece of the action. But a lot more thought went into this than the president was given credit for.

Richard Perle   The important thing about our proposal to scrap ballistic missiles was that it forced Gorbachev to answer the question: If we are going to eliminate ballistic missiles, then what's the problem with the defense against ballistic missiles? It becomes irrelevant; it is a kind of insurance against cheating and has no significant impact upon the strategic equation.

In the course of discussing that, Gorbachev, in his frustration, said, "Why not give them all up?" Reagan said, "That sounds good to me." An exchange of that kind is interesting, and it can have some pretty far-reaching consequences. But it is not in the same category as a proposal in writing, handed to the other side, that they study before they reply to you. It's more in the form of the surrounding debate, or dialogue, than the negotiating process itself. And it was a rather offhand, breezy suggestion — an expression of his frustration.

William J. Crowe Jr.   The newspapers suggested that Reagan had been very close to making a deal with Gorbachev on doing away with nuclear ballistic missiles — that the president was very close to making a dramatic decision on nuclear weapons. The newspapers went on to say that he had not consulted with the Joint Chiefs of Staff, and they asked, how could he do that?

Of course, the commander in chief can do any damn thing he wants to do. There is nothing wrong with the president making a decision without consulting the Joint Chiefs of Staff. Now, it may not be the prudent thing to do; it may not be wise.

He felt that he had an opening, and he wanted to take advantage of it.

Arthur Hartman   I blame Gorbachev for trying to take advantage of the president. The president had been saying that we ought to get rid of all nuclear weapons. The Russians knew what he meant — that it was a long-term goal, that many things had to happen first.

Paul Nitze and [Soviet Deputy Foreign Minister] Aleksandr Bessmertnykh had held preparatory discussions prior to Reykjavík and had made some progress on the various issues. When we got to Iceland, it was as if those discussions had never taken place. Gorbachev started right in; he focused entirely on "Let's have an agreement on nuclear weapons." It drove everybody up the wall because, in a sense, the president always said that was his objective. But he was kind of caught when that became the principal objective and all the preparations just sort of went down the tube. I think that the president felt, Where am I?

He had been briefed on a variety of things — in the embassy we said, "This is what we discussed with them" — so I think that the president felt double-crossed by Gorbachev. He also probably felt that we hadn't prepared this thing very well. This was such a surprise, and it was impossible to get the conversation back to these other points we had discussed.

Then the question was, how to play this publicly? And here, I think, George [Shultz] overreacted; he set the tone by saying what a disappointment this was. We could have been more straightforward, saying, "This wasn't the script we were playing with. We don't know what they have in mind, but we hope they will come back to the table."

William J. Crowe Jr.   The whole time I was chairman, arms control was a huge issue. The Chiefs were generally satisfied with the Republican approach to the issue until, all of a sudden, Reagan decided that he wanted to move out. Reykjavík was the watershed of my chairmanship; he essentially did some things at Reykjavík without consulting with anybody.

The preparations for the summit were really quite superficial, in that nobody thought anything important was going to happen there. It was to be a presummit meeting for a subsequent summit meeting, so the preparations were really not very detailed.

The president went to Iceland with a whole entourage of advisers, but neither Weinberger nor I was there. Curiously enough, Akhromeyev was there. Shultz came back from there and told me what a wonderful man he was. He said, "You two should get together." That's when I first heard about Akhromeyev.

Richard Perle   In Akhromeyev we saw a different personality — an apparently much more relaxed person, more voluble, with a sense of humor, more authoritative, not just looking over his shoulder, apparently more flexible, because he was in the position to make decisions.

But some people got carried away and went beyond that, thinking that he was something other than a tough-minded Soviet general who had the best interests of the Soviet Union, and not the United States, at heart.

I didn't share that rosy view of him. I thought he was a tough adversary — a much more agreeable personality, but a tough adversary nonetheless.

Reagan's Offer to Share SDI Technology

John Poindexter I didn't have a problem with Reagan's offer to share the technology. I think he was very sincere about it. I think he was probably naive — I don't mean that in a derogatory way. It was such a unique proposal that there wasn't any way the Soviets could believe that we would really do that.

Horst Teltschik Reagan's offer in Iceland to share SDI with the Soviets was a real surprise for all Europeans — something like a shock wave — because we hadn't been consulted beforehand.

Most Europeans were worried, because we were not sure of Reagan's intentions. Gorbachev was such a warm and sympathetic person that I could understand how Reagan could be overwhelmed by his personality, so there was a fear whether there could be such an arrangement between the Americans and the Soviets without integrating the European alliance.

The main impact of SDI was not whether the Americans would have been able to establish the system; the most important impact was that the Soviets were convinced that if the Americans want to do it, they can do it, and they will do it. The Soviets knew that they could not do it because of their lack of financial resources; their system was already bankrupt.

Colin L. Powell He had undying, Reaganesque American faith in the ability of American industries and laboratories to provide him with such a shield, so he went out and acted on those beliefs and shocked the Russians; they could not believe that the guy really felt this.

And Reagan could say to them, "Look, not only do I believe this, I'll give it to you." Now, that used to drive us nuts, because he actually meant it. We would have been shocked to ever have given such sophisticated technology to the Soviets, not knowing how they would ultimately have used it.

But Reagan meant it with all his heart, because he wanted them to have as strong a shield as we had, because only then would they be comfortable about getting rid of those horrible missiles. So that was it. He believed in the concept: he wanted to defend not only America, he wanted to defend the Soviet Union for America.

It was really quite noble and far-reaching conceptually, and it scared the hell out of a lot of people — both on our side and on the Russian side — who couldn't believe that this guy meant it. He was giving them his marker: he would give them the technology to defend themselves against us and therefore we could both then disarm. Gorbachev couldn't believe it.

Summit's End: Breakthrough or Disaster?

Nicholas Daniloff   At the Iceland summit, Gorbachev presented a whole series of concessions, which were largely aimed at getting the Americans to come off of Star Wars, and Reagan refused to come off of Star Wars. But he was sorely under pressure to do so.

Again, the Americans were taken by surprise at Iceland, by the imaginative and wide-ranging nature of the Russian proposals.

Max Kampelman   Both the president and George Shultz thought at the end of the day Saturday that, by Sunday noon, when it was supposed to end, we would have it. And it was Sunday morning when Gorbachev came in with his push on SDI. Much to Gorbachev's surprise, he found Reagan immovable on this.

The rest of us caught the enthusiasm of Saturday night, because after the Saturday session we had a meeting among ourselves and then we were put to work. Akhromeyev was in charge of the Soviet group, which we viewed as positive since he — unlike the Foreign Ministry people — was a decision-maker.

So when it broke up the next day there was disappointment, and Shultz showed this disappointment. He was exhausted; we had awoken him at three o'clock on Sunday morning.

Shevardnadze came in to our U.S. meeting at about lunchtime on Sunday. He saw that the thing was coming to a dead end. He apparently knew what Gorbachev was planning, and he saw the stubbornness on Reagan's part. He was desperate, so he pleaded with us. I remember, he turned to me and said, "You have a reputation for being creative. Can't you come up with something that will bridge the gap?"

It was at that point that we floated an idea we had been floating among ourselves for weeks, the idea of the elimination of all ballistic missiles.

We mentioned it to Shevardnadze, and he said, "This is worth exploring, but I do not know what Gorbachev or Akhromeyev will think of it." We then said, "We don't know how Reagan will react, because we haven't talked to him about this." Reagan came back to Hofdi House between one-thirty and two o'clock, and we put this to him. And he asked us, "What do you think?" Just at that point, without any politeness — he didn't knock — Gorbachev opens the door and barges in, so we couldn't keep talking. If somebody had said, "Gorbachev is waiting for you in the meeting room," we would have rushed our conversation, and maybe Reagan would have had something to say. But as it turned out, Gorbachev rushed in, so we all left without having a position.

I do know that Reagan was eager to get back; he was angry at Gorbachev, so he just went back. Remember, the Iceland meeting wasn't supposed to be a summit; it was supposed to be a preparation for a summit. But Gorbachev came in with a whole agenda.

Jack Matlock The president's position on SDI at Reykjavík was a turning point. I think that if we had stayed until the next morning, we probably could have worked out some formula on SDI. But the fact is, without the threat of SDI up until the Iceland summit, Gorbachev could not have convinced his own military on the 50 percent cuts in heavy missiles — which was one of our prime objectives.

Rozanne Ridgway Shultz is sorry to this day that, tired as he was, he went out and did that [post-summit press] briefing. He looked tired; he looked disappointed. And the press said, "Tired and disappointed — it must be a failure." But the nuclear dialogue changed at Reykjavík.

Charles Hill It was an amazing turnabout. Reagan had completely convinced Gorbachev that SDI would work, and that we were going full steam ahead. Reagan was willing to cut Gorbachev in on this because he believed it; he had convinced Gorbachev that this was the way the world was going to go for the next generation.

The great strength of the Reagan presidency was that he knew exactly what his position was on the key points, and in the nicest way possible, he would never move, so people didn't try to get him to move. You couldn't change his mind. So when he looked at Gorbachev and said, "No, we can't do that," Gorbachev was just drained. It was over at that point; there was nothing more.

The most remarkable thing of the 1980s was that on a certain day, at a certain hour, Soviet behavior — individual, personal behavior — totally changed. Before that time, you could not have a conversation with any Soviet official. It was impossible. For decades they simply wouldn't talk to you. You'd say, "Good morning," and they would give you a diatribe back about ideology.

Charles Powell The trouble is that President Reagan wanted to eliminate nuclear weapons before there was anything to put out in their place. At Reykjavík, he seemed to be on the brink of negotiating that with

Gorbachev. And luckily for us, Gorbachev insisted that the Star Wars program be stopped.

Mrs. Thatcher said that she really felt the ground moving under her feet when she heard the president's position. We raced over to Washington a week or two later, and she got him to issue a joint statement with her, reaffirming his commitment to nuclear deterrence and modernization of the British nuclear deterrent, which was a vital part of her whole political position.

If that had been undermined by the president's statement, she would have suffered severe political damage here, because the Labor Party at that time was against nuclear weapons and would have said, "We're on the same side as President Reagan. It's you, Mrs. Thatcher, who are the odd one out."

The president's sense of Reykjavík, as he explained it to the prime minister in their Washington meeting, was that he had got very close to his objective, but that Gorbachev had been totally unreasonable on the subject of Star Wars, and therefore it had been impossible to reach a full agreement.

Richard Perle   Reykjavík ended in a tremendous victory for the United States and the West: Gorbachev did not get what he wanted. He wanted to kill SDI; he was prepared to pay quite a lot to do that, so it was already a vindication of the president's decision to proceed with SDI.

The speech announcing SDI was made in March 1983, and Reykjavík was in October 1986, so in a little over three years, for an investment at that point of five or six billion dollars — for that modest investment — he had produced a situation in which the leader of the Soviet Union was prepared to cut their strategic forces in half, and all they asked for in return was that we wouldn't proceed with SDI.

Rozanne Ridgway   The extreme views of Reykjavík represent the ideological battle. Those who think it was a failure — and want it to have been a failure — were those who were reluctant to negotiate with the Soviet Union and who really did not want to reduce nuclear weapons.

In the campaign, Reagan had said that he hated nuclear weapons; he hated mutually assured destruction. I guess that his colleagues on the right didn't believe him. They never believed that he really meant that. But it turns out that he did mean that.

When we went to Reykjavík, it was with the notion that we would be following up on Geneva. These two men were on the record that we were going to get rid of nuclear weapons.

A lot of things happened at Reykjavík. Not only INF was on the agenda; it became strategic weapons as well. But Reagan and Gorbachev got caught up in a game — which many people see as a poker game — that got out of control. Maybe it did, but it wasn't as if people didn't know what cards were in the deck.

What did happen was that folks started talking reductions. At the end of the day, it looked as if Gorbachev was prepared to say: "I'll take this down to zero, provided you give up SDI." And for Reagan, who was a very integrated person, it couldn't work without SDI. He wasn't prepared to strip away offensive ballistic missiles and stand naked before the Soviet Union with nothing, so he required a ballistic missile defense in its place. One would come down as the other went up.

There was a moment in the middle of it when the people for whom it really mattered thought they were within reach of a conceptual deal — of less offense but more defense — on a phased basis. And when Reagan pushed back from the table and said, "No, not without SDI," people who thought they had seen this thing were disappointed. Shultz was one of them.

There were people in the delegation who were nearly dead of fright that something was going to come out of this. For Gorbachev, it was one last roll of the dice to play Europe against the United States on INF and on SDI, in which he had failed at Geneva. He left Reykjavík and went immediately out on a big campaign. And while the Europeans were horrified that so much respecting their future had been discussed at Reykjavík without their presence, they also understood that they could not side with Gorbachev on this one, so it was only a few months later that we got the signal from the Russians to start again, and then we got right through and INF was gone within a year.

Reykjavík, in nuclear history, must be seen as the two days in which the world stopped building up nuclear weapons. If that was the mountain we were climbing, at Reykjavík we got to the top and started down. To this day that is not well appreciated.

Gennadi Gerasimov   SDI was the reason that Reykjavík was originally considered a failure. This was unfortunate, because SDI was nothing but a bluff. The Soviet delegation had a meeting before we started the negotiations, and like some others, I was given two or three minutes to talk. I said, "The Americans are bluffing; they don't have the technical possibility to have a nuclear shield, so don't worry about this." But Marshal Akhromeyev dismissed my views as those of an amateur.

My feeling was that Akhromeyev viewed SDI as a real danger — that the Strategic Defense Initiative was going to work — which meant that it was going to ruin the strategic stability. Akhromeyev bought this bluff, and Gorbachev accepted his view.

John Poindexter   The Russian chessmaster, [Gary] Kasparov, described SDI in a speech as "the straw that broke the camel's back." It wasn't the only thing that brought about the demise of the Soviet Union, but it was sort of the last nail in the coffin.

The Soviets were very, very concerned about it. They held our technology in very high regard and felt that if we set our minds to it, we could do it.

William J. Crowe Jr.   Many people think that SDI was the crucial item. It certainly played a part: SDI scared them. It scared me too; I thought it was going to put us both out of business.

I believe that the crucial factor in the downfall of the Soviet Union was the worms in their own system. All of a sudden, you have a man like Gorbachev, who was smart enough to see that they were just going down the wrong road.

Jack Matlock   In a sense, the failure at Reykjavík gave the Soviets another push to start to open up their society and to deal with human rights issues, and to start talking turkey about how to get out of the Third World conflicts.

As they later said, they realized that the arms control agenda was not enough for us to deal with them. The fact is, the issues are interrelated. They had to realize that if they invade another country, Congress will not ratify even the best arms control agreement; if they are depriving their people of the right to emigrate, we are not going to be able to build up trade. Our political life forces this upon us. Therefore, let's be realistic.

Finally — it was 1987, the year after Reykjavík — he began to seriously make these changes. So Reykjavík was the hinge summit; it was a breakthrough — probably the most important summit we had. What was decided there — with one or two exceptions of detail — eventually became the treaties. So to look at it as a failure is to look at it in a very superficial way.

Charles Z. Wick   I remember flying back from the Reykjavík summit with all the dejected guys from the National Security Council, who thought that Ronnie had blown it. And I said to Ronnie, "You've really

come through; you just won the cold war. You called Gorbachev's bluff."
And he said, "I had no alternative."

The Release of Andrei Sakharov

*The release of the dissident physicist Andrei Sakharov, a leading monitor of
compliance with the Helsinki Accords, and his wife, Dr. Elena Bonner, from
internal exile in the then-closed city of Gorki in December 1986 would be a
turning point in Gorbachev's approach to human rights. On December 16 —
just over two months after the Reykjavík summit—General Secretary Gorbachev telephoned Dr. Sakharov in Gorki, and he and Dr. Bonner were soon
allowed to return to Moscow.*

*Sakharov, whose wife was Jewish, was a staunch supporter of the cause
of freedom for Soviet Jewry.*

Richard Schifter I recognize that the people who were there in Geneva
made a great deal of the fact that the Soviets were now willing to discuss
human rights. But they didn't do a thing about it for another year; the basic decisions on this issue were made in the fall of 1986. The first evidence was in December 1986 — the return of Sakharov from Gorki, that
really made the difference.

Arthur Hartman As much as I'd like to think that the Americans had a
great deal to do with changing the Soviet policy toward human rights,
Gorbachev decided for his own reasons, because of the kind of change
he wanted to make.

He was a trained lawyer. He kept saying, "We have to have a society
that is ruled by law." He wanted to illustrate the break with previous practice. He's a harsh guy. He would have thrown people in jail — I'm sure he
did in his earlier years — but he decided to make an example, and the example he chose was Sakharov. It wasn't because we insisted that he had to
be released or we wouldn't talk to them. It was for Gorbachev's own reasons that he decided to release Sakharov, get him back to Moscow, and
get him involved in politics, because he knew he was a patriot.

He wanted to move the country in the direction of a more normal
kind of political dialogue, and to break with past policies. Getting
Sakharov back was the way to do this. I talked to Sakharov after he got
back to Moscow, and I think he believed this.

Richard Schifter Beginning in 1987, there was a whole set of new developments. We made clear to them that just listening was not enough;

doing something about it was what counted. And that message got across to them.

This was one of George Shultz's great contributions: to begin to intertwine human rights concerns with the rest of the agenda, which, as far as they were concerned, was principally an agenda dealing with arms reduction.

The Washington Summit

The major achievement of the Washington summit, which began on December 7, 1987, was the signing of the INF Treaty.

On Sunday, December 6, 1987, designated as Freedom Sunday for Soviet Jewry, more than 250,000 Americans, most of them Jews, rallied in Washington, D.C., to express their support for the U.S. administration and to call attention to the cause of human rights for Jews still remaining in the Soviet Union, including the right to emigrate. The rally was coordinated by the National Conference on Soviet Jewry, the organized American Jewish community's mandated agency for advocacy on behalf of the Jewish community of the then–Soviet Union. (In the wake of the dissolution of the Soviet Union, the National Conference continues to act on behalf of the individual Jewish communities of the fifteen nations of the former Soviet Union.)

Among the speakers were Vice President Bush, Senator Al Gore, and a number of former refuseniks and/or prisoners of conscience, including the recently released Natan Sharansky and Ida Nudel.

Gennadi Gerasimov   Gorbachev didn't comment on the rally. When he didn't like something — when he was in a difficult position — he tried to ignore it. When we were in China, there were many students demonstrating in Beijing. He tried to ignore this, so as not to embarrass his hosts. The same, I guess, for this Jewish thing.

The rally was not mentioned at the summit. I can read some of my notes on the subject, from the Reagan-Gorbachev discussion in Washington:

> REAGAN: There are divided families. Of course, we understand that you can have difficulties if a lot of the people go out of the country simultaneously. But we know that the Jews have their own country;° they want to practice their religion.

° Central to the Soviet Jewry movement was the concept of Israel as the national homeland of the Jewish people. Thus, Soviet Jewry regarded emigration to Israel as repatriation to the Jewish national homeland.

GORBACHEV: Oh yes, maybe you are right, to a certain extent. We do have some things that must be done in this sphere of national traditions.

REAGAN: Approximately every eighth American is an immigrant from Russia [I don't think Reagan was telling us the exact figure] and about one half million Jews want to go because they can't practice their religion.

GORBACHEV: No [he disagreed with Reagan because he did not believe that the majority of Soviet Jews wanted to practice their religion].

REAGAN: By our Constitution, everybody can go anywhere and choose any God he wishes.

GORBACHEV: We interpret human rights much wider. We have freedom of religion, and you limit immigration.

REAGAN: But we cannot accept everybody.

GORBACHEV: Then other countries also can talk about the regulation of emigration, if you talk about the regulation of immigration.

REAGAN: We want to build a fence in Mexico.

GORBACHEV: But for our people to leave the country, they must enter some other country.

Richard Schifter   What the American Jewish community did was to put the Soviet Jewry issue on the U.S. government's human rights agenda. And the U.S. government, in turn, put it on the Soviet agenda.

The rally in Washington took place on a Sunday. The following Tuesday, Gorbachev met with Reagan, and the person who was the note-taker at the meeting told me that Reagan started out by saying to Gorbachev, "You know, there was this rally on the Mall the other day." And Gorbachev said, "Yes. I heard about it. Why don't you go on and talk about arms control?"

And for five minutes, Reagan kept on talking about the rally and the importance of the Jewish emigration issue to the United States, when Gorbachev wanted to talk about something else.

Frank Carlucci   There was one episode at the December 1987 Washington summit, where Reagan asked to meet alone with Gorbachev, with only the interpreter present. We were all abuzz: What does he have in mind? The staff never wants to leave the president alone.

The interpreter later told us that what the president wanted to do was to take Gorbachev to task about the lack of freedom of religion in the Soviet Union. And Gorbachev lashed right back. According to the interpreter, it was not a particularly happy session.

Robert C. McFarlane   He liked the man and believed he was open to change. He had seen that Gorbachev was a fast study. Reagan felt that if someone was open to persuasion, he could persuade them. He believed he could change history — that he could forestall Armageddon.

The Moscow Summit

On May 29, 1988, Reagan and Gorbachev met in Moscow two days after the Senate had ratified the INF Treaty. There was no further significant progress during the summit on arms control, as SDI remained a major stumbling block.

President Reagan, who was making his first visit to the "Evil Empire," placed human rights at the top of his summit agenda.

Rozanne Ridgway   There will be many who will say that Reagan really didn't know what was going on. He certainly knew enough to run the Soviet relationship. And on his final trip — the one to Helsinki, Moscow, and then to London — he was able to articulate for the United States a vision of what this was all about, and what it represented. And what more do you want of a president?

10

The Pollard Affair

On November 21, 1985, Jonathan J. Pollard, a civilian employee of the U.S. Office of Naval Intelligence, was arrested outside the gate of Israel's embassy in Washington, D.C., and charged with spying for that nation.

Pollard, who had first handed over classified materials to the Israelis on July 19, 1984, would eventually plead guilty to espionage and receive the surprisingly harsh sentence of life in prison without possibility of parole from U.S. District Court Judge Aubrey Robinson, whose decision was based in part on a memorandum submitted to him by Secretary of Defense Caspar Weinberger.

Among the many unanswered questions concerning the Pollard affair are: What echelon of Israeli officialdom authorized the running of an American citizen as an agent in Washington? Was Pollard recruited as part of a rogue operation? And did Pollard have an accomplice—whether known or unknown to him—within the U.S. government who identified specific documents and areas of information that Pollard's Israeli handlers instructed him to obtain?

In speaking with both American and Israeli officials involved in the Pollard affair, our interest was also piqued about a possible connection between Pollard's activities on behalf of Israel and Israel's interest in helping the United States to effect an opening to Iran in order to facilitate the release of the American hostages being held in Lebanon.

Our rationale stems from the fact that the Israeli leadership, believing that the material supplied to Israel by Pollard was essential for Israel's security and never contemplating that Pollard's espionage would be discovered, felt obligated to return Pollard's favor by acting on behalf of U.S. interests with the Iranians. Indeed, in the very month that Pollard was arrested, Israel shipped U.S.-manufactured HAWK (Homing All-the-Way Killer) missiles to Iran.

Geoffrey Kemp Pollard was my student. He came to me when I was teaching at the [Tufts University] Fletcher School of War and Diplomacy. He was assigned to me as an advisee.

He was absolutely fascinated by the Middle East. After the first three or four weeks, I really had to put a huge crimp in his style, because he would be outside my door every day with ideas and enthusiasm, but there were other students to see.

After one term I went on leave. When the story broke, much later, I wasn't the slightest bit surprised. This was a guy who had an almost super-romantic view of Israel — a belief that the Holocaust could happen again, and that we were systematically cutting the Israelis out of a lot of the intelligence that he felt was highly relevant to their security — so I understand where he was coming from. The fact that he was a spy is neither here nor there.

Roy Furmark, U.S. businessman; associate of Adnan Khashoggi   How do we know that Pollard wasn't a rogue spy? He wanted to be a hero for Israel and deliver this secret stuff. I cannot believe that the Israeli government knew, and sponsored Pollard to do what he did; I cannot believe that the Israeli government would sanction a Pollard; I cannot believe there was the slightest chance that the Israeli government was officially involved — even unofficially involved. The fact that he was being paid made him something else, completely.

In Israel you have a lot of rogues; they all have different ideas about their Israel. But the established government, the established intelligence — I cannot believe it. There is so much at stake: public opinion in America against Israel.

What prime minister was going to sanction this? To get what from this guy Pollard? What are you going to get out of it? Nothing. And to lose three billion in aid and lose the support and respect of the U.S. and the world. They have the atomic bomb already, so what are they going to get?

THE REASONS FOR POLLARD'S ESPIONAGE

Howard Teicher   As I understand what occurred, Sharon, [when he had served] as minister of defense, had set up his own little covert intelligence operation outside the mainstream of the Israeli intelligence establishment. I think that Sharon did this in response to Weinberger's repeated denials of his requests for strategic intelligence that he, Sharon, considered to be very important.

It was both the type of intelligence and the process. Sharon asked for a satellite downlink so that U.S. satellite imagery could be provided in its raw form to Israel, so that Israel could interpret photographs themselves. The nature of the relationship was such that the U.S. would provide what we call narrative interpretation of what our photo interpreters saw — the time/date stamp that on this date we saw geographic coordinates x, y, and z. The only country that I am aware of that got photos in real time was the United Kingdom. That was really what a "special relationship" meant. There was nothing you wouldn't share with the prime minister of England, or their intelligence establishment.

Israel was not in that category. So the fact that Sharon played the U.S. card anyway — his diplomatic leverage was to show Israelis that he was tough enough to stand up to America; he gained popularity in the street by being this tough guy — all fit in with his politics.

My guess is that he called in his guy, Rafi Eitan, and said, "Rafi, how can we find out if Weinberger is deceiving us or not?" In this context, Eitan goes out and finds this idiot Pollard, who has got Walter Mitty fantasies and tells everyone he's a Mossad agent.

I had never met him or heard of him. He was about as off-the-scope, low-level an analyst as you could find in Naval Intelligence. But in that capacity, he could get his hands on all the things Sharon wanted and wasn't getting. Sharon was mad, and Weinberger was denying him intelligence information. I'm not saying that the U.S. should, or should not, have provided it. But putting that aside, there was such hostility between them that Sharon wanted to find out if he could prove, somehow, that the U.S. was not telling him everything.

Maybe that's not too logical, but it makes sense to me, having been in meetings with these guys and seeing the nasty electricity — two negative fields of highly charged ions coming together.

Geoffrey Kemp My assumption was that the reason the Israelis were so interested in Pollard was not that he was going to tell them something about the Syrians that they didn't know. In my view, the most important concern to Israeli intelligence at that time — and for that matter today — is what we know about what the Israelis are up to, particularly their nuclear, chemical, and biological programs.

Now, Pollard was in a position to get access to American intelligence reports about Israel, as well as about the Arabs. It could well be that in the documents Pollard turned over there were some unbelievably sensitive items that have compromised American agents in Israel — and we don't know how many American agents in Russia were compromised.

Caspar Weinberger   The Israelis were probably trying to get as much information as they could, and certainly some of that information that Pollard gave them went to other countries, which was the reason why it was so heavily classified.

WHICH ISRAELI LEADERS
KNEW ABOUT POLLARD?

Shimon Peres   I wasn't aware of all of it. You must understand that the intelligence services do not have to inform us of all their agents. I didn't have any idea that there was spying going on in the United States. In the middle of the night, Shultz called me and told me the story; he was very excited and very angry. I told him I would do everything I could to cooperate.

Abraham Sofaer   Certainly, Peres was very sorry; he was very remorseful. I believe that a very serious mistake was made over there. Peres could not bring the people involved in the negotiation with me to be straightforward and honest in their dealings.

I believe that they antagonized the Department of Justice lawyers tremendously by lying to us several times; we had to go back and show them that they had lied to us. And then they would tell us a new story. And that really soured these prosecutors, not that they needed much souring — they are a pretty sour bunch. They were very hostile toward Pollard and Israel, but they were certainly justified in feeling that they were misled and lied to, and that the government of the United States was terribly mistreated in this.

What the Israelis did made no sense at all. If you are going to cooperate, you want to do it in a manner that will not get you into more trouble than you were in before you cooperated.

Yitzhak Shamir   The Pollard affair was a rogue operation; I personally didn't know that it existed. It was idiocy. It did not cause any great rupture in our relationship with the United States. It could have, but it didn't. I think that Shultz trusted us — that the government had had no part in it.

Howard Teicher   Sharon, meanwhile, loses his job as minister of defense, but the operation keeps going because they have got a gold mine here. Whatever the Mossad may be doing, the minister of defense is telling the prime minister. And that's why they want him back, because at the end of the day the government benefited, regrettably, from Pollard.

Shimon Peres It was partly necessary, partly not. We got the material — not in the original form — but the content was important because it showed the deployment of forces in the Arab countries; that was its importance.

Uri Simhoni What happened was unnecessary — totally unnecessary — and in many aspects irresponsible in terms of relations between Israel and the United States; irresponsible in terms of relations between Israel and the American Jewish community; [and] totally unnecessary as far as the quality of the information needed. We could have survived without it.

Information is just information; believe me, it's not that important. When you look at the test of secret information historically, you find that its price cannot justify it. People are ready to pay too much — economically and physically dangerously — to get information that is related to curiosity but is basically of very little help.

AMERICA'S SENSE OF BETRAYAL

Uri Simhoni I believe that the administration viewed Pollard as an insult, as something that shouldn't have happened. A day or two after Pollard was arrested, I felt I had to go to see my friends in the Pentagon to say something. It had happened, and I just could not leave it without speaking about it. So I met with Richard Armitage and told him that I was as surprised as he was. I had no idea that this had been going on.

Then I met with Secretary of the Navy [John] Lehman, who was a very good friend of Israel. I was ready to be thrown out of his office, but he said, "Uri, why did you do this?" I said, "I don't know." He said, "Do you know what kind of information he passed to Israel?" I said I didn't know. He said, "Why didn't you ask me for this information? I would have given it to you officially." I said, "I don't know." He said, "Look, Uri, did it ever happen that you asked for something and we refused?" I said, "No."

Everything we wanted from the navy, we got. Everything. His door was always open, and he felt personally hurt.

Duane Clarridge You have to understand that the two institutions in the United States with the hardest feelings about the Pollard case are the National Security Agency [NSA] and the navy.

There is history there. The United States Navy will never forget the *Liberty*;* number two is that the Israeli Navy as an institution is a non-event. Therefore, unlike with our army and our air force, there has never been any close interaction. So that kind of relationship — which is so important among military services — was never built up.

Now you come to the NSA, which in many ways is the father of the Israeli Signal Service — the Israelis are in many ways dependent on their signal service, not on their spy service — so the NSA had reason to feel enormously betrayed as well, not to say that there aren't other institutions in the United States that don't feel strongly too.

You also have to remember that there was an agreement of long standing — probably not in writing — between Israel and the United States, that we wouldn't spy on one another. James Jesus Angleton [longtime director of CIA counterintelligence] was probably its author. It was scrupulously carried out by the U.S., so in that sense the betrayal goes beyond the navy and the NSA.

ISRAEL'S RESPONSE TO POLLARD'S ARREST

Uri Simhoni   Israel could have reacted totally differently. The intelligence organization, as an intelligence organization, should have behaved differently. We should have cleaned the table immediately. We didn't do that. We started to hide information. Instead of telling the truth, accepting responsibility, and apologizing, we did everything wrong. We added insult to the blame.

Abraham Sofaer   What Israel should have done was to accept responsibility for this. They should have said, not just that they were sorry, they should have said, "We encouraged Pollard to be a spy on our behalf. We took advantage of his sympathetic — maybe even neurotically sympathetic — feelings toward our country. It was wrong for us to exploit his feelings in that way, and we feel that you should put the blame on us more than on him and reduce his sentence. And we, in response, recognize that we should do something for the United States at some point, to show our appreciation for that."

---

* The *Liberty*, a U.S. Navy vessel on patrol in the eastern Mediterranean in June 1967 during the Six-Day War, was shelled and sunk by Israeli forces when it failed to identify itself properly. The Israeli government has apologized for the incident and paid compensation to the families of the victims.

If that had happened, there would at least have been a chance that Pollard would have been treated sympathetically. I don't believe that Israel has been properly guided in this regard, and I believe that the pro-Israeli lawyers here have been very politically oriented; they try to attack all the time.

Movement people — people who have a purpose beyond helping a person — can frequently damage that person. To help Pollard would have been to keep his mouth shut — to keep him from criticizing the United States the way he foolishly and wrongly did — and to get Israel to step up to its responsibility.

WEINBERGER'S SEVERITY

Caspar Weinberger I have a basic feeling against spies and traitors, and I thought that he had abused a position of trust in a way that caused enormous injury — as well as enormous potential injury — to the United States.

I said all of this in a classified affidavit to the judge; it was submitted at the judge's request. I don't talk about it because it is classified, but the damage was there and was stated in a factual way to the court.

Abraham Sofaer Weinberger wrote a memorandum to the sentencing judge. I've read it; I don't know of any false statements in that memorandum. He said that the information Pollard gave the government of Israel had done grievous damage — very severe damage — to our relations with friendly Arab states and compromised our intelligence-gathering system. I know that is true from personal experience — having seen the documents involved — and from having talked to the countries involved.

Uri Simhoni Weinberger's reaction was emotional; he felt he deserved better treatment from us. I believe that behind this was that he is half Jewish: Why did you do this to me? I basically opened my system for you. You wanted the satellite information; I gave it to you. You wanted $a, b, c,$ and d; you got it. Why spy? If you know the door is open, why come in through the window?

Colin L. Powell I have no insight into Weinberger's views on Pollard. I can't believe that you are speaking of Weinberger's being soft on Russian spies. I found him to be down on anybody who would spy against the United States.

THE SENTENCING OF POLLARD

Abraham Sofaer   I led the negotiation to convince Israel to cooperate with us on Pollard. I don't think that Pollard was given a raw deal. I didn't have anything to do with his sentencing — they certainly were enthusiastic to get him — but the reason Pollard suffered so much was not the Department of Justice. Nothing they could have said or done — or [that] Weinberger [could have said or done] — would have hurt as much as did his interviews with the press, and Wolf Blitzer's interview with him.*

Pollard had agreed with the district judge not to talk to the press. He had admitted his wrongdoing — which was really very serious wrongdoing; it cost the government of the United States a staggering amount of money to undo what he had done — and he came before a wonderfully honest and balanced judge for sentencing, Aubrey Robinson, an old-time liberal. I had clerked for Judge Skelley Wright, and he and I and Judge Robinson frequently had lunch together; he was one of Skelley's favorites. He was warm, generous, and balanced, not at all anti-Semitic. On the contrary, he was very warm to me, and to everybody.

And suddenly, you go before this district judge, you tell him you did this terrible thing to your country, that you never should have done it, and you promise not to speak to the press while he considers what your sentence should be. And on the day of sentencing you have already spoken to the press, and you've told the press that you lied to the district judge — that you really feel that you didn't do anything wrong and that you did absolutely the right thing. It's crazy to think that you would have anything but the maximum penalty imposed on you in that situation.

Was Weinberger very upset about Pollard? Clearly he was. He was very vigorously in favor of the maximum sentence. I don't believe that even that memorandum would have had the effect of getting Pollard a life sentence if it weren't for what Pollard did at the sentencing.

Nimrod Novick   There were legitimate reasons for wanting to see Pollard put away for a long, long time. There were no legitimate reasons for wanting to see him put away forever — and never yielding, and never softening, and never accepting repentance.

---

* While Pollard was in custody, awaiting sentencing, he was interviewed twice by Wolf Blitzer, the Washington correspondent for the *Jerusalem Post*. Blitzer's articles based on these interviews appeared in the *Washington Post* as well as the *Jerusalem Post*.

There is no doubt that there is something in Weinberger's position. Compared with other cases of espionage, he was overdoing it, and there was a perception here — perhaps not justified — that there was more than just doing justice, that there was also a certain vendetta, that he was acting not just on the merits of the case, that there was more than that. I don't presume to know exactly what it was, where the hostility originated.

But again, it was not just Weinberger; it was others in the Pentagon, relevant to the story, and there were people there who were not happy, for professional reasons, with the intimate relationship between the two countries.

WAS THERE AN ACCOMPLICE?

Uri Simhoni   I do not believe there was somebody with Pollard. At that time in Washington so many names were dropped. Some were very good friends of mine. I know that they knew nothing; they were not involved. But when the environment became suspicious, a lot of damage was done. Some people got harmed, and I don't know if the damage has been corrected.

Howard Teicher   I have a hard time believing someone else was involved. They have enough professionals of their own who could figure out, based on their own relationships, what to ask for without needing another mole.

Michael Ledeen   After Pollard, it was clear that a lot of people in government started to look at Jews differently. Every high-ranking Jew in the government was subjected to very intense scrutiny by the security people, and lots of people were called in and asked all kinds of questions. Not me, but a lot of my friends were. That was particularly true in the Pentagon, and there's always been a lot of anti-Semitism in the CIA.

Duane Clarridge   I do know that in the aftermath of the Pollard case — it is still going on today — there are some thirteen to seventeen cases that may still be open on people who are suspect, in various forms, of spying for the Israelis.

WAS A THIRD COUNTRY INVOLVED?

Rafi Eitan At the time Weinberger was sure that Pollard was the reason for the capture of a few agents of the United States in Russia, so he wrote this to the judge, and that decided the fate of Pollard.

Now we all know that Ames* was responsible for the capture of these agents. So it is a question for me as to why Pollard is still in jail.

Robert C. McFarlane For Cap to have been so severe implies that the nature of the breach [of security] and the information must have involved our most sensitive sources and methods, that it got to the Russians. But if that was true, you would have thought it would have come out by now. At the end of the cold war we are having seminars on everything from the Cuban [Missile] Crisis to SDI, and so somebody would have said something.

Uri Simhoni The Americans still believe there was a third party, and this may be part of the reason they are still not ready to close this story.

SYMPATHY FOR POLLARD?

Abraham Sofaer It was very unfortunate what Pollard did. Since then, there has been a big push to get his sentence reduced.† Unfortunately, I believe that people have approached the issue in the wrong way, by arguing things like, it's okay to spy for a friendly nation, and that what he did really didn't harm the United States. This is total craziness, and it didn't help Pollard at all.

Yitzhak Shamir It's a pity that a man like Pollard is suffering so much; he is suffering more than all the other spies who have been arrested by the Americans. I don't see any justification for it. After all, he did nothing against American interests.

---

* Aldrich Ames, a CIA official, was apprehended in 1995, tried, convicted, and sentenced to life in prison for espionage conducted on behalf of the Soviet Union.
† Pollard's immediate family and his new wife, Esther, to whom he was recently married, as well as Jewish organizations and individuals, have repeatedly petitioned President Clinton to pardon Pollard, to no avail.

Michael Ledeen   I was in favor of executing Pollard. I am in favor of executing traitors, so whatever they did to Pollard was fine with me. I am not moved at all by the argument that, after all, he was helping Israel. If you were the KGB and were trying to recruit a Pollard, you certainly would not go to him and say, "Hi! I'm your friendly KGB. Please work for me." You'd go to him and say, "Hi! I'm your friendly Mossad. Please help us." It doesn't justify what he did at all.

Eitan Haber   On his last day here in the Defense Ministry, the day before he was assassinated, two minutes before he left for home, we discussed the idea that Rabin, as the prime minister, would write to Mr. Weinberger, asking him to ask the president* to try and ease the punishment. We decided that he would think about it in the next week.

---

* In July 1996, President Bill Clinton denied a pardon to Pollard. The announcement was made in the White House by Clinton's press secretary as the president met in another room with a leadership delegation of the Conference of Presidents of Major American Jewish Organizations.

11

Taking a Stand Against Terrorism: Libya and the *Achille Lauro*

THE *ACHILLE LAURO*

On October 7, 1985, the Achille Lauro, *an Italian cruise ship that had begun its voyage four days earlier in Genoa, Italy, and was scheduled to dock at Ashdod, Israel, later that week, was hijacked off the Egyptian coast by four Palestinian terrorists who had boarded the ship with false passports. They were commanded by the PLO executive committee member Abu Abbas, a close aide to PLO Chairman Yassir Arafat.*

Abbas, who directed the operation from Egypt, would later escape capture when an aircraft carrying him and the hijackers was intercepted and forced to land at an airbase in Sicily.

Owing to lax security measures, the terrorists had been able to bring aboard heavy weapons. Their original intention, however, was not to hijack the ship but rather to stage an attack on land when the Achille Lauro *docked at Ashdod.*

Their mission changed when a ship's steward, entering one of the cabins occupied by the terrorists, discovered them cleaning their weapons, which included guns and hand grenades. The terrorists panicked, rushing into the ship's dining salon and rounding up many of the passengers, including Leon Klinghoffer, an American who was confined to a wheelchair.

The following day, October 8, the terrorists, pressing their demand for the release of Palestinian terrorists in Israeli prisons, murdered Klinghoffer, threw his body and his wheelchair into the sea, and threatened to kill other passengers unless their demand was met.

On the day of the hijacking, the CIA heard that an Italian cruise ship had been hijacked "somewhere in the Med"; one of the agency's terrorism specialists, Charles Allen, identified the ship to the NSC as the Achille Lauro.

The United States Responds

Howard Teicher [Navy Captain] Jim Stark shared office space with Ollie; there was a political-military office suite with North, Stark, Dick Childress, and one other person. Jim told me that he had the idea that we should just do what we did to the Japanese,° so he told Ollie.

Jim was a policy person; he was not involved in any operational activities. North, by contrast, had insinuated himself into all of these counterterrorism activities and channels. He had three different computer systems and three different secure phone links — at least it appeared that he did. He could call things up and communicate with people.

He immediately went to work on trying to make the intercept happen. I walked in because I had some ideas; anyone who had an idea concerning an issue that wasn't in their action had to go to see the action officer. It was North's responsibility in [that he was] the staff officer with any lead on this.

We began to brainstorm as to how we could find the airplane if they [the Egyptians] were to fly them [the hijackers] out. I said, "Let's use our Israeli friends." Whatever I did was minor. I tracked down the attaché, General Simhoni, who was at home, in the shower; it was quite amusing.

Uri Simhoni The official task of the military attaché is to work with the Pentagon on purely military subjects, such as technological and intelligence exchange. The official task is not always what you are doing.

It was a very intensive period of unofficial relations that really flourished between us — and because of the many things that happened, such as the *Achille Lauro.* It is something that is unbelievable even now: the cooperation between two administrations to carry out together a mission on a third party's land.

John Poindexter We were preparing to take the ship over before it got to Port Said, in Egypt. We had special forces in the Mediterranean. Doing something like that is obviously very complicated: it had to be carefully planned, or else there was the danger of loss of a lot of lives. We were moving with deliberate speed, but the ship arrived in Port Said before the opportunity presented itself.

When the ship went to Egypt, we had pretty good intelligence, both

---

° During World War II, U.S. warplanes, acting on intelligence information, shot down an aircraft carrying Admiral Isoroku Yamamoto, the officer who had led the Japanese attack on Pearl Harbor on December 7, 1941.

technical and human. Our first attempt was to try to convince President Mubarak to turn over the hijackers to the United States. He obviously did not want to do that; he told us that the hijackers had left Egypt.

But we found that to be false. The National Security Council had developed a very good working relationship with the Israeli embassy in Washington. Ollie, because of his work on the hostages in Beirut, had developed a good, informal working relationship with the Israeli military attaché, General Simhoni. Through Ollie's connections, we not only found out that the hijackers were going to leave that day, we found that we could learn the flight number before they left Egypt.

The president had a short trip planned for that day out to the Midwest; the president and Bud McFarlane had gone on the trip. I called over to the office of the chairman of the Joint Chiefs, and I spoke to Admiral Art Moreau, who was a friend of mine. I said, "It looks like they are going to be leaving today. What do you think about discussing in the Pentagon the possibility of intercepting this airplane?"

At about that time Ollie came into my office, and he had information from Simhoni that confirmed our own information. Then I reached Bud on Air Force One and briefed him on my conversation with Moreau, and asked him to talk to the president and get his view on the possibility of an intercept. Bud called back and said, "The president says, 'Go ahead with the planning and keep me advised' " — which is what we did.

Howard Teicher He [Simhoni] came in, and they went to work for us and found the airplane.° North didn't have anything to do with that. He did something for McFarlane, probably a short paper, enabling McFarlane to go to the president and say, "We have an option."

This one was really the president's call. If anyone really made it happen, it was the president — and McFarlane, because McFarlane prevented Weinberger, who was desperate to stop it, from reaching him on the phone to tell him it was disastrous and not to do it.

North played the key role operationally. There were a lot of other people involved, but Ollie took all the credit. In the grand scheme of things, I don't think it really matters, because this was one where a presidential decision was required.

° The hijackers were placed on board EgyptAir flight number 2843 — a chartered 737 — bound for Tunis, then the PLO's headquarters. The flight, which took off at approximately 11:15 P.M., Cairo time, was forced by F-14 Tomcat fighter aircraft launched from the USS *Saratoga* to land at the Sigonella Italian/NATO base in Sicily.

We thought about this: Should we bring the plane down in Israel? We knew there would be no trouble there. Here, the striped-pants cookie pushers said, "We can't do what will be the biggest slap in the face to the Egyptians. What we have done is bad enough." We understood that we couldn't bring the plane down in Egypt, or in Tunisia. We thought Italy would be best.

Uri Simhoni   I was in my office at the embassy in Washington in the afternoon, and I got a call from Oliver North. Oliver was a very good friend; we used to meet almost daily. He opened the door of the National Security Council for me; he used to take me in every day.

So this particular day he tells me that some terrorists have taken a ship. I was told that after Mr. Klinghoffer was killed, the president made a decision to intercept the plane that would carry the terrorists from Egypt to Tunisia.

North told me that they would like to do this but they didn't have enough information — how to identify the flight, how to know what time the flight would take off. Sometimes Oliver moved faster than others. I said to him, "Are you sure that is what you are going to do? Because if we try to make phone calls, we will alert all the system. Just confirm to me that you are not acting on your own."

He told me, "The president is in Chicago, visiting the Sara Lee facility." When it was confirmed to me, I called General [Ehud] Barak, the chief of intelligence, from Oliver's office. I said that they needed information. He said, "Where are you now?" I replied, "I am sitting now in the basement of the White House; I heard Oliver checking it with the president's people." Barak said, "All right. We will start to work on it."

Within an hour Barak called back and said, "The tail number is — ; they are going to take off from runway number — ; the airplane is a Boeing 737, and here is the time of takeoff." I gave this information to Oliver, who almost fainted. He said, "Are you sure of this?" After all, no one wants to down a civilian aircraft; that would be a disaster.

The information was verified three times and was passed to a carrier in the Mediterranean. Four American jets took off from one of the carriers, identified the Boeing, and signaled with their wings for the Egyptian plane to follow them. Then the problem was where to land, because the Italian government didn't want to give landing permission to a hijacked aircraft.

I was back in my office, and Oliver asked me if the plane could land in Tel Aviv, so I called Barak and said, "They are flying near Malta. Can they land at Ben Gurion Airport?" Ehud told me to hold the line while he called Rabin. Rabin asked Ehud to ask me if the president was aware of this request.

This was something very unusual. I called Oliver and said, "Look, Rabin asked Ehud to ask me to ask you if the president is aware of this request. Is this a presidential request, or an Oliver request?" Oliver said, "Hold on, please." A few minutes later he said, "This is an official presidential request to land in Tel Aviv."

At the same time they continued to work for landing permission in Italy. Oliver called Mike Ledeen, who happened to be a good friend of the Italian prime minister [Bettino Craxi]. Craxi was not there, but Ledeen said, "I know the number of his mistress." It was after midnight; he found Craxi, and he approved the landing at the U.S. base at Sigonella, Italy. This operation could only have happened as a result of the good personal and trustful relationship between Oliver and myself.

Michael Ledeen   I was not involved in the planning; that was done by North, Stark, McFarlane, and the others. I was at home at about seven o'clock that evening when North called me and said that they were having trouble getting permission for the plane to land at Sigonella, and would I please call Craxi.

So I called Craxi in his hotel in Rome, the Raphael Hotel. I had first met him in the mid-1960s, when I was working on my dissertation. We were both interested in girls, and this forged a good friendship. I saw him a lot; I think I was his only American friend.

The embassy could not reach him that night; they would call, and his protector would say, "I don't know where he is." So I called and said, "This is Michael. I really must talk to Craxi." His protector said, "He's not here." I replied, "This is a real crisis; people may die tonight if I don't talk to him. If people die because you have said Craxi's not here when he's carrying on with the usual woman in the room next to you, you are going to have your picture on the front page of every newspaper."

So he said, "Just a minute," and Craxi came on the phone. I explained the situation. He said, "Why here?" And I said — it's my best line in government — "Because no other place on earth can offer the perfect weather, the fabulous cuisine, and the cultural tradition that Sicily can provide." And he cracked up and said, "I'll get right on it."

Duane Clarridge   Once the intercept was decided on, it all went into motion with the military; the NSC wasn't involved.

I was at the Pentagon, and I heard Art Moreau give the rules of engagement to EUCOM, which in turn gave them to the Sixth Fleet. Once the idea was launched and accepted, the NSC had virtually nothing to do with it anymore. If the truth be known, the military cut the communications between the NSC and the forces, in order to keep them out.

John Poindexter We had a battle group in the eastern Mediterranean. We gave them the tail number of the aircraft that we had gotten from the Israelis, and the time it took off. It was the forces on the scene who came up with the plan of how to intercept the plane.

And Moreau got back to me and said, "If the president authorizes it, I think we can do it." I passed that to Bud, and the word came back: Proceed ahead with the planning as if we will do it, and when the president gets back to Washington, he will conduct a conference call.

In that call the president made it clear that we could fire live ammunition in front of the plane, but we could not shoot it down. Weinberger was out of the country. We later found out that he was not anxious for this to be happening; he had tried to reach the president from his airplane, but there were communications difficulties.

Robert C. McFarlane Cap was against bringing the plane down; he thought it would have the impact of damaging our relations with the Arab states. We were in the airplane coming back from Chicago — where the president had given a speech and met with the families of the hostages — and Cap called, and I said, "You ought to tell the president that," and I put him through. And he said, "I don't think we should do this."

The president, to his credit, said, "Cap, it is pretty cut and dried. This is a guilty party; we cannot let them go." And the president approved the Pentagon's going ahead. We were disappointed when the Italians misbehaved and let them go.

John Poindexter The intercept was made, and the plane landed at Sigonella, in Sicily, where there were problems with the Italian police.

Oliver North I have a great deal of difficulty today, in 1996, in looking at this great peacemaker, Yassir Arafat. Abu Abbas was the chief terrorist for Arafat; he was in command and control of the attack on the ship. The target was eventually to be Israel.

Abbas was allowed by the Italian government to escape, and they not only allowed him, they assisted his escape, just as Hosni Mubarak assisted the terrorists in getting out of Egypt. He lied to the president on the phone; I was listening to the conversation. It's hard to figure out who were the worst actors in this event, the Italians or the Egyptians. There was moral weakness.

Michael Ledeen   Abbas was smuggled out. Mubarak was afraid that if Abu Abbas ended up in an Italian jail, he might be shot, or there might be terrorism in Egypt. He was very upset.

The Reaction

Howard Teicher   This was a dramatic initiative. It turned out well in the domestic arena, but badly overseas, particularly in Italy, because we failed to get Craxi to cooperate with us the way we should have before we did this. That is the price of unilateralism; it is the risk you run.

Sometimes people will think they have to cooperate. Craxi's political calculus was: If I give in to the Americans on this, I'm a dead man in Italy politically. Had he been asked in advance, maybe he would have agreed. But on the other hand, when we bombed Libya, Mitterrand had agreed beforehand to let us overfly, and then he refused to cooperate. So even when you ask people, they don't necessarily cooperate.

John C. Whitehead   Shultz was away, and I got word of a situation with Prime Minister Craxi of Italy, regarding the *Achille Lauro* incident. The White House had criticized Craxi for having allowed Leon Klinghoffer's killer, Abbas, to escape. Craxi saw it differently: he thought he was the savior of the 399 other Americans on the ship. He was very offended when President Reagan had said how angry he was that this terrorist had been allowed to leave. Craxi felt that, in a free government, you cannot arrest and hold a man when there is no evidence against him.

Craxi was so angry that he said he would not come to the summit that was to take place in a week or two in Washington. So Reagan sent me over to Italy to talk to him. I met with Craxi and allowed him to fully express his view, which he did, from many pages of notes on a yellow pad. After more than an hour of this, he was like a balloon that had lost its air; all the venom was gone. I said, "I will report this to the president." Craxi then said, "Then the president will understand what really happened" — some of which was not what happened — "and I will be glad to come to Washington." I had hardly said a word, but I learned that you sometimes get more from listening.

THE U.S. BOMBING OF LIBYA

In another, more controversial, stand against terrorism emanating from the Middle East, on the evening of April 14, 1986, U.S. forces bombed sites in Tripoli and Benghazi, Libya, in retaliation for the bombing a few weeks earlier of a West Berlin discotheque frequented by U.S. military personnel. One American had been killed in that attack and many others injured.

At least two of the bombs fell on Splendid Gate, the barracks headquarters of the Libyan dictator, Mu'ammar Muhammad al-Gadhafi, killing his adopted infant daughter, injuring two of his sons, and inflicting casualties on many other Libyan citizens.

While the U.S. action was largely condemned by European and Third World nations, many Americans welcomed the bombing as proof that President Reagan was willing to pursue terrorists on their own turf.

Craig Fuller   Prior to the attack on Libya, we were on a trip to the Gulf States. While we were there, planning was under way for this assault. I called back a few times and said, "Don't forget where we are." In the course of the discussion, Bush was very carefully, and subtly, giving the rationale for having to do something with Libya.

That was a factor in tempering the Arab response to what we did. And I am certain that it served Bush well when he then had to get a coalition together to deal with the invasion of Kuwait.

John C. Whitehead   Shultz was in Moscow at that time. We had earlier discussed what we should do about Libya. It was a place where terrorists were trained and funded; we had very good evidence of this.

I was told that there would be a meeting of congressional leaders at the White House at eight o'clock on a Sunday night. There was a military plan to bomb targets in Libya. My task was to describe the diplomatic situation. I listed evidence of terrorist training and information on canceled checks of Libyan payments to terrorist groups, which we had tracked through the banking system.

The president, after the Defense Department outlined the military plan, said that because France would not allow our aircraft from Britain to overfly France, the planes had to take a long, circuitous route and were now in the air. He said, "They will be refueled five times in the air before they arrive over Tripoli, so at the conclusion of this meeting, I could call off the operation. I am not presenting you with a fait accompli. We will decide in this meeting whether to proceed."

He then asked each of the congressional leaders to give their view. All of them were concerned about possible civilian casualties and the possibility of our planes being lost. The president said, "I would like to ask if any of you believe we should cancel the operation, which I can now do by placing a call from this telephone. Please raise your hands if you believe we should cancel." No hands were raised. The president then thanked the leaders and cautioned them about the privacy of the meeting.

Edwin Meese III   The president had maps all over the floor of the Oval Office, looking at the targets that had been designated. I remember his going through the targeting and determining of which targets we should or shouldn't hit, as a matter of policy. He crossed out some because they were too close to civilian installations and approved the targeting of the military installations.

Oliver North   I wrote the NSDD [national security decision directive] on that. The target was the terrorist infrastructure — the support bases, the communications infrastructure that allowed Gadhafi to carry out these kinds of attacks.

In point of fact, it worked; there was a serious diminution of terrorism in its immediate aftermath. Its purpose was not to assassinate Gadhafi. The president wrote — and had me put into the directive he signed authorizing it — that it was not to be construed as such.

Duane Clarridge   I was there when the targeting was decided on. The president ruled out the intelligence headquarters because we might hit the French embassy — and we hit them anyway.

There was certainly no discussion — or anyone making any smart or ad-lib remarks about hitting Gadhafi's command center — that we might get him. Did we think that was a possibility? I'm sure that we all did.

But there wasn't. The command center was something to take out. Nobody knew that he had his tent and his children around; we knew that he lived around the area. Was it seen as a way of getting rid of him? I don't think so.

Afterward, I was talking to Casey. I felt the hypocrisy of the whole damn thing: we weren't allowed to take out a contract on Gadhafi — have somebody put a bullet through his head — yet we can drop a two-thousand-pound bomb on him, intentionally or not.

There is a certain amount of hypocrisy in that. I thought we had come up with better ways in our counterterrorism center, with my technical guys — that there were better ways of sending a message to a leader short of sending in the U.S. Air Force and the Navy.

The Reaction

Charles Powell There was no enthusiasm at all from Geoffrey Howe for the bombing of Libya. When Mrs. Thatcher consulted the members of her cabinet, they were all pretty well unanimously opposed to our giving support to the United States by providing the airfields.

She simply overruled them and said, "This is what allies are for." The Foreign Office said, "If we support the United States on this, all our embassies in the Middle East will be burned up, and commercial interests will suffer." And indeed we did suffer: two of our hostages in Lebanon° were killed following the bombing of Libya. But she was absolutely determined to do it, against the advice of the bureaucracy — the Foreign Office and the institutions.

Her thinking had evolved from the time of Grenada on the justification for intervention. But it was absolutely clear in her mind that Libya was supporting terrorism — and was caught virtually red-handed in support for terrorism — and that the way to deal with that sort of thing was a preemptive strike.

I think she would have been happy to participate directly, if we had had the military capability to do so. As it was, the contribution President Reagan sought from us was the use of the airfields and the use of Cyprus as an emergency landing base for any aircraft that couldn't get there, or get back.

Geoffrey Howe The original purpose that was put to us disconcerted Margaret Thatcher and myself almost equally because, again, it was a demonstration of the recurrent failure of American presidential foreign policy, with its willingness to talk in terms of retaliation. Americans, for whatever reason, so often talk about: "We must have a response to this." On the other hand, self-defense is legitimate; it was possible to make a case for the bombing of Libya on the grounds of self-defense.

We had thought it through for a day or two and concluded that the operation could be justified on the grounds of self-defense. We per-

---

° Leigh Douglas and Philip Padfield. An American hostage, Peter Kilburn, the former librarian at the American University in Beirut, was also killed in retaliation for the raid.

suaded the Americans to present it substantially along those lines. We were therefore prepared to give it our backing. It's an interesting illustration of the thought process.

The fact that we were the only European country willing to give it our backing was, of course, of enormous importance. It created a huge clamor from many of our European partners and many people in this country, not the least because it was thought that we were agreeing to the use of American bases in response to American authority, rather than consultation, which was a bad portent in relation to the use of nuclear weapons.

We had no doubt that it was right to do it on the grounds of self-defense, to deter Gadhafi from doing it again. And we were warmly applauded by the U.S. government and Congress for having given that support, which did make it much easier for us to persuade Congress to ratify the extradition treaty that came not far afterward.

Bernard Ingham   Mrs. Thatcher felt that it was justifiable in international law; we looked at that very carefully indeed. She had no illusions about Gadhafi, as he was a terrorist; he was supplying the IRA with weaponry.

Once she believed that it was justified under international law, Mrs. Thatcher felt that it was her duty in supporting Reagan's strike against a terrorist state. Gadhafi has not been the same since.

Donald Gregg   I had an incredible reaction from an Arab diplomat who is a friend of mine. He said that when Gadhafi was seen carrying the body of his dead child out of the wreckage, he lost all stature because it was shown that he couldn't protect his family.

PART FOUR

IRAN-CONTRA

12

Trading Arms for Hostages

By late January 1985, six Americans were being held hostage in Lebanon by the radical Shiite group Hezbollah (Party of God), a branch of the terrorist organization Islamic Jihad (Holy War). These Shiites were loyal to Iran's fundamentalist Islamic leader, Ayatollah Ruholla Khomeini, and were opposed to the government of the United States, which they blamed for, among much else, the Israeli invasion of Lebanon. In addition to the kidnappings, the Islamic Jihad claimed responsibility for four attacks on U.S. diplomatic and military installations in the Middle East during 1983-84 — including the marine barracks and the U.S. embassy annex in Beirut—that killed some 315 people.

At this same time Manucher Ghorbanifar, an Iranian national and independent arms dealer, was soliciting covert Western military aid to his country, which was then at war with Iraq. He initiated a series of meetings with Al Schwimmer, a founder of Israel Aircraft Industries, and Yaacov Nimrodi, a businessman who had spent a considerable amount of time in Iran during the era of the shah. Both of these Israeli citizens had ties to the arms industry and to the government of Prime Minister Peres. Ghorbanifar proposed himself to Schwimmer and Nimrodi — and by extension to the state of Israel— as the broker of an agreement for a Western sale of arms to Iran. His position was given legitimacy in the eyes of the Israelis by the backing of Adnan Khashoggi, a Saudi financier well known to Schwimmer.

Ghorbanifar, a sometime informant for the CIA since 1980, was considered by the American intelligence community to be an unreliable source. Indeed, in July 1984 the CIA had issued an internal memo advising all personnel to regard him as "an intelligence fabricator and a nuisance." This is probably why the CIA disregarded information that Ghorbanifar had given to a former Agency official, Theodore G. Shackley, during one-on-one meetings in Hamburg in late November 1984. Ghorbanifar told Shackley that the Iranians might be willing to release the American hostages in return for cash, and that the Iranians were in desperate need of U.S.-made antitank (TOW) missiles.

At the urging of the Israeli government, Ghorbanifar was now given a fresh hearing by the U.S. State Department. He was flown to Washington for a series of interviews that led, in August 1985, to the initial sale of American arms to Iran: ninety-six TOW missiles, to be shipped from the Israeli arsenal and then replaced by the United States.

For many in the Reagan administration, Iran was an outlaw state, a major supporter of world terrorism to be shunned by the United States. After the overthrow of the shah in 1979 and the subsequent occupation of the U.S. embassy in Tehran, America broke off all diplomatic and trade relations with the new Khomeini government. Throughout Iran's war with Iraq, the United States refused to support either side with arms. After the Hezbollah-sponsored murder of Malcolm Kerr, president of the American University in Beirut, on January 18, 1984, President Reagan publicly denounced the Iranian government. The State Department initiated Operation Staunch, a campaign to discourage other nations from selling arms to Iran.

But for others in the administration, especially those who recalled America's strong ties to Iran during the era of the shah, Iran was a former ally to be won back to the fold or lost forever to Islamic fundamentalism and growing Soviet influence in the region. These persons also shared the president's concern for the hostages, a concern that was heightened when Hezbollah released a video depicting the torture of one of the hostages, William Buckley, the CIA station chief in Beirut.

It should be noted that CIA Director William Casey was troubled by the possibility that Buckley might, under torture, reveal secret information that would jeopardize U.S. operations and operatives in the region. At the prompting of National Security Adviser Robert McFarlane, Casey commissioned a paper recommending a new national security decision directive (NSDD), which, had it been approved, would have allowed U.S. allies to strengthen ties with Iran and perhaps even support it through arms trade. The directive was opposed by Secretaries Shultz and Weinberger.

Israel also had complex motivations for its involvement with Iran. Unofficially, Schwimmer, Nimrodi, and their friends in the government viewed the arms sales as a lucrative opportunity and the first stage in Israel's renewed economic activity with Iran. On an official level, the government had a genuine interest in aiding the United States in dealing with the hostage crisis.

During the first week in May 1985, Michael Ledeen, a consultant to the National Security Council on terrorism and Middle East issues, met privately in Israel with Prime Minister Peres to discuss Israeli intelligence on Iran and the possible sharing of this information with the United States.

One month later, David Kimche, the director general of Israel's Foreign Ministry and a former high official of the Mossad, went to Washington to meet with Robert McFarlane. He told McFarlane that certain Iranians—namely Ghorbanifar—had contacted his government with an offer to intervene in an effort to free the hostages. A good-faith U.S. response, said Kimche, should include the possibility of offering weapons for sale to the Iranians.

Inherent in the Israeli analysis of the offer—as well as in American expectations—was the idea that Ghorbanifar was the hitherto unexpressed voice of moderation in Iran, and that he and his fellow "moderates" would be able to temper Khomeini's extremism if they were to obtain weapons from the West to be used against Iraq. Upon the death of the ayatollah, who was then already quite elderly, these "moderates" would be expected to lead their nation into a more positive relationship with the West.

American officials also assumed that an Iran indebted to the United States would use its influence in Lebanon to help free the hostages.

In early August 1985, Kimche returned to Washington, this time seeking assurance that the Reagan administration favored the arms sale initiative. President Reagan, who had discussed the issue with McFarlane during his recuperation from colon cancer surgery, convened a high-level White House meeting on August 6 at which he, the vice president, Secretaries Shultz and Weinberger, Chief of Staff Regan, and McFarlane discussed Israel's request to sell to Iran one hundred U.S.-made TOW missiles, which would then be replenished by the United States. Shultz and Weinberger strenuously objected to the proposal.

Several days later the president, in a telephone call to McFarlane, approved the sale, and on August 19, Israel—working through Nimrodi and Schwimmer, and with bridge funding from Khashoggi—shipped 96 TOW missiles to Iran. That shipment, however, did not result in the release of any hostages, perhaps because the TOWs were seized by members of an extreme faction, the Revolutionary Guards. It was only on September 15, the day an additional 408 TOWs arrived in Iran from Israel, that a first hostage, the Reverend Benjamin Weir, was freed.

THE HOSTAGES

A total of fourteen American hostages were held in Lebanon during the two terms of the Reagan presidency.

William Buckley, kidnapped on March 14, 1984, was the first of the hostages. He died at the hands of his captors on or about June 3, 1985, of natural causes after having been brutally tortured during his captivity.

Jeremy Levin, CNN's bureau chief in Beirut, was kidnapped on March 7, 1984, and was released, or escaped, on February 13, 1985.

The Reverend Benjamin Weir, a Presbyterian missionary, was kidnapped on May 8, 1984, and was released on September 15, 1985.

Peter Kilburn, the librarian at the American University in Beirut, was kidnapped on December 3, 1984, and was murdered on or about April 14, 1986, following the U.S. bombing of Libya.

The Reverend Lawrence Jenco, a Roman Catholic priest and director of Catholic Relief Services in Beirut, was kidnapped on January 8, 1985, and released on July 26, 1986.

Terry Anderson, the Middle East bureau chief of the Associated Press, was kidnapped on March 16, 1985, and released on December 4, 1991.

David Jacobsen, director of the American University Hospital, was kidnapped on May 28, 1985, and released on November 2, 1986.

Thomas Sutherland, dean of agriculture at the American University, was kidnapped on June 9, 1985, and released on November 18, 1991.

Frank Reed, director of the Lebanese International School in West Beirut, was kidnapped on September 9, 1986, and released on April 30, 1990.

Joseph Cicippio was kidnapped on September 12, 1986, and released on December 2, 1991.

Edward Tracy, an American writer, was kidnapped on October 21, 1986, and released on August 11, 1991.

Alann Steen, Jesse Turner, and Robert Polhill, teachers at Beirut University College, were kidnapped on the college campus by armed terrorists disguised as Lebanese police officers on January 24, 1987. Steen was released on December 3, 1991, Turner on October 22, 1991, and Polhill on April 22, 1991.

In addition to the Americans, French, British, and German nationals were also taken hostage. The most noteworthy of them was Terry Waite, a lay leader in the Anglican Church who, after spending several years shuttling between London and Beirut in an attempt to free the hostages, was himself taken prisoner on January 20, 1987. He was released in November 1991.

President Reagan and the Hostages

Frank Carlucci   When I came in every morning, he'd ask about the hostages, and he'd talk about terrorism. It was part of the man's character. That was why he worried about the Pentecostalists in the Soviet Union, and about individual human rights.

John Poindexter   It's an exaggeration to say that the hostages were the president's first and last thoughts every day. But that is not to say that there wasn't concern. He made a distinction between individuals and groups of people; if individuals were in adversity, the president would be very concerned. It was similar to the Nick Daniloff situation.

The hostage issue was important to him also because of its potential for U.S. citizens in foreign countries. He wanted to make the point that the U.S. would not tolerate this activity. That's why he readily agreed to the *Achille Lauro* plan.

Edwin Meese III The hostages had an important impact upon the president; he was concerned about them. But it wasn't just the hostages; the whole Iranian initiative was presented as a much broader picture. The Israelis were very interested in this too.

The president, having seen Carter with his hostage experience — where we had obliterated any relationship with Iran — and knowing at the time that the Soviets were very much interested in what was going on in Iran, had a lot of good reasons for us to be on a path toward regaining communications with a post-Khomeini government there. If he had not had these other ramifications, I don't think he would have gone for the initiative.

Lawrence Walsh, independent counsel, Iran-contra affair To me, it has always seemed that his prime motivation was the recovery of the hostages and that the so-called Iran initiative was a cover for that, although I believe that there was a sincere hope for some achievement in that regard. But the professionals in the State Department and the Defense Department had no respect for that objective; they believed we were deluding ourselves.

Duane Clarridge First of all, let's give everybody their due. Let's say that uppermost in everybody's mind was an opening to Iran, which was a reasonable thing to undertake. There was no way that the president could have undertaken an opening to Iran without dealing with the hostage issue.

Therefore, he was caught right away in that issue, plus the fact that he's got all this pressure on him to do something on the hostages. You have no idea what was going on. There was a major U.S. effort; people's time was being spent on this business far beyond what it was probably worth. These things take on a life of their own. So all of that pressure came in on the president. I can see where he had no choice.

John Poindexter The thing that frustrated me in the aftermath was the disbelief that we really did want a strategic opening to Iran.

Iran was — and is — very important to the United States. It is a very strategic nation, and it is not in the interest of the United States to have an antagonistic relationship with Iran. It was probably more important then: the Soviets very much wanted an opening into the Indian Ocean.

We thought that there was an opportunity for a strategic opening. And contrary to popular opinion, it was not simply just a cover for arms for hostages; from my standpoint — and from the president's — the real motivation was to work toward more normal relations with Iran.

Colin L. Powell I would disagree; I think it was more the hostages. Reagan always had this desire for reconciliation, almost a Hollywoodesque fading scene — everyone walking, hand in hand, into the sunset.

In this case, I think he was motivated, from a human standpoint, by his desire to see the hostages released and also to get rid of this lingering black mark on American power and prestige, by having American citizens under the control of a bunch of kidnappers.

Early Efforts on Behalf of the Hostages

Terry Anderson, Beirut bureau chief of the Associated Press In general, I have no complaint about what President Reagan did. I am in no doubt of his personal commitment to the hostages, and to the hostage families; I know for a fact that he was deeply affected by our situation. And in fact, his personal commitment was what led to the mistakes he made: I am referring to the arms-for-hostages episode. Several of his advisers advised him very strongly against it.

But it never died, because if the president wants something, it gets done — particularly when the executive in charge happens to be a marine. They are very well known for allowing nothing to stand in their way. I place the biggest burden for those mistakes on Ollie North — again, not doubting the personal commitment to us.

Oliver North I spent more sleepless nights flying back and forth to Europe than I care to count. I would leave my job at the White House at four o'clock in the afternoon, jump into a White House car, race to Dulles Airport, take Pan Am flight 60 or 61 — whatever it was — to London, get off at six in the morning, meet at Heathrow Airport for three or four hours, jump on the Concorde, get off in New York, and fly in the shuttle back to Washington so I could be at the 4 P.M. staff meeting so no one would know I had been gone.

I did that countless times, trying in one form or another, working with a foreign intelligence service, or some other organization or entity, to try to get those Americans freed. I did it to the point where the White House Travel Office was saying, "How the hell are we going to pay this guy's travel bills?" It was that bad.

Donald Gregg   There was a sense that North was really on the cutting edge and was as close as anybody to being able to get these people out. I think that was one way he built his reputation.

The key relationship he had was with Bill Casey. I think that Casey, North, and President Reagan all had deep similarities and that some of the things North wanted to do really played extremely well with President Reagan and Bill Casey, because this was going after the bad guys.

Fawn Hall   I remember the hostage situation. Ollie had real concern. He got very, very close to Peggy Say.* He made himself available to her, where for a lot of people it was just a job. You know, it's ten o'clock at night, and the wife is at home, and the kids want you there — "Well, sorry, Mrs. Say. It's time to go home." That wasn't Ollie; he would extend himself, and I really admired that.

The President and the Hostage Families

Terry Anderson   McFarlane told me that he very strongly advised against allowing the president to meet with any of the families. He knew what was going to happen — that Reagan would be affected very personally.

Fawn Hall   I don't know if Ollie originated the thought that the president should not meet with the families of the hostages. But after a few of these meetings, the president would be consumed by grief; he needed to be kept objective. So after a few times they said, "We have to stop these meetings."

Oliver North   I remember writing a paper before a meeting; I think it was in Chicago. Don Regan was chief of staff at the time. He called and said, "I need a piece of paper quickly on a meeting with the president and the hostage families." I thought: Oh, my God. Why would we do that? If we are concerned about the direction of the policy now, wait

---

* The sister of the hostage Terry Anderson, Peggy Say waged a constant campaign — with the administration and in the media — for her brother's release.

until he meets with these families. Because I had had to do it on a regular basis — it is the most gut-wrenching ordeal.

I wrote, "You can forget anything else after this because the floodgates are going to open. This is a bad idea; there's never going to be a time after this that Reagan won't pull out all stops to get the hostages out." Poindexter backed me up, and Regan overruled him because the PR guys got to him and said, "You have to have this meeting."

William Buckley

Oliver North   The terrible mistake was having Ronald Reagan meet with the hostage families. It [also] broke his heart to know that he had met with, and been briefed by, a guy [William Buckley] who was being tortured to death. You can say to yourself, a president shouldn't have that kind of compassion for people.

Howard Teicher   What Casey cared most about — and what mattered to Reagan — was to try to free Bill Buckley, and this was justified. The government has an obligation to try to rescue government officials who are held captive by enemies. You have policy justification and human justification.

There is no doubt in my mind that, without Buckley, North would have continued to receive frequent appeals from the families of the hostages, but I don't think he would have gotten the support of the intelligence community to do what was eventually done to rescue some clergymen, educators, and journalists — all of whom had been warned not to go to Beirut.

Bill Buckley, on the other hand, was a patriotic American who had given his life to government service. We knew he was being tortured and was possibly dead. It was worth it to try to save him, or at least to recover his remains. I think that was what Casey was most interested in; he was going the extra mile for his covert people.

Martin Anderson   Casey showed Reagan the videotape of Buckley, who had been tortured. I can see Reagan taking it very personally.

Casey should never have brought the video in. The White House chief of staff shouldn't have allowed it. Reagan never should have watched it.

George P. Shultz   The White House staff people didn't appreciate and try to understand their man. When you are working for somebody in government, you realize that every person is a bundle of strengths and weaknesses, and your object, as a staff person, is to build on the strengths and compensate for the weaknesses, so that they don't have a chance to express themselves.

That's why I thought it was such a terrible thing that people played on the president's clear concern for the hostages.

Terry Anderson Buckley died early in my captivity. I believe that Casey knew Buckley was dead considerably before he acknowledged that he was dead. Yet, as far as I know, this information was not given to anyone else in decision-making circles for a long period of time.

Casey was personally concerned only with Buckley, for good reasons: Buckley was an experienced, senior CIA operative. As far as I can determine, Buckley never gave up any information destructive of American interests.

David Jacobsen, director of the American University Hospital in Beirut
After Father Jenco was released, at their instruction I had made a videotape. They didn't give me a script. I said, "Look, the situation is bad. I hope you will do something — negotiate for us, get us home."

They had a general idea of what I was going to say. I ad-libbed, and I expressed my condolences for the widow and the children of Bill Buckley, because I honestly believed that he was married and had kids. I wanted Buckley's family to know that he was dead so that they could get on with the grieving process, and get on with their lives.

One night they came into the room where we were held with a VCR and said, "Mister, you are going to enjoy seeing this." They put in the tape I had made, with the volume off. But I had made the tape, so I knew what I was saying. In the lower left-hand corner of the picture was a box, containing a picture of Buckley, that was captioned "CIA." In the upper right-hand corner was Tom Brokaw, who was talking. There were the words "Coded Message" under the picture of Buckley, which had been recaptioned "bachelor."

I knew what was going to happen, and two days later it did: they beat the hell out of me. I then had to make another videotape, at which time I had to look into a camera that was being held by a man who did not have a mask on. It was Mehdi Najat.°

° An Iranian who was a major negotiator with the Americans and characterized himself as a Revolutionary Guard. He was also the brother-in-law of one of the Da'wa prisoners, whose release had been sought in the TWA hijacking and whose freedom the negotiators continued to demand throughout the hostages' ordeal in Lebanon.

Military Plans to Free the Hostages

Oliver North We tried over a dozen different initiatives, some of them military; some of them intelligence-related; some of them diplomatic, through the Algerians, the Moroccans, the Japanese. You name it, we tried it.

And nothing worked to get Buckley — to get them all — back, and to stop it. And good people died in the process: Americans were killed in various parts of the Middle East, trying to get them back and to prevent more of it.

Donald Gregg It was frustrating to us. We were building up this Delta Force; I went down with Bush to a demonstration. They were impressive people. Here was this capability, and a kind of fantasy about the bright and shiny good guys going in and rescuing the hostages from these disreputable terrorists. North got very close a couple of times. So there was a sense that here we had this capability. There was frustration; terrorism is frustrating.

Duane Clarridge We were working on going in with a Delta Force, but it was a very complex problem. It is no simple matter to find out where the hostages are, and to know where they are all the time, and to bring a force in there and extract them.

This very difficult operational problem was being worked on night and day; a lot of things were actually done. But the chances of pulling it off were minuscule.

Richard Secord They would have launched an operation in a heartbeat if they could have pinned down the locations, which is what I kept telling McFarlane we ought to be doing. We could have done this with money; with money, you can buy all of Lebanon.

The CIA was so crippled in the clandestine service at this time; Stansfield Turner's tour of duty just about wiped them out. The truth of the matter is that the deputy director for operations, John McMahon — who later became deputy director under Casey — had never had an overseas assignment, had never been chief of station. He was an administrator, but he was head of the clandestine service; he wouldn't know a spy from a man on horseback. You can't create these people overnight.

They were relying on the military to mount the raids [in Lebanon], but we didn't have the critical intelligence for the military to act. What we should have done was to take a bunch of suitcases full of money and set up camp in Beirut and start paying for intelligence.

Benjamin Weir, Presbyterian minister working in Beirut I do remember well that in that conversation with North — and afterward — [I was] opposed to the idea of a military rescue. I was convinced that the place where the men were held was so heavily guarded, and so loaded with explosives, that if anyone tried to break in I was sure they would all die.

In fact, at the time I was held I was quite convinced that if anyone had tried even to approach the building, that would probably have been the end.

David Jacobsen Having lived in Lebanon for thirty years, Ben probably knew where we were located. We were held in that penthouse apartment for thirty-two days after Ben's release, and every day I prayed for a Delta Force to come through the window with a concussion grenade. One concussion grenade would have immobilized our guards. We weren't wired with bombs; we could have been rescued safely in a couple of minutes.

Giandomenico Picco The kidnappers did fear a U.S. raid to free the hostages. Their perception is that the U.S. knows everything — that there is a big computer at Langley, and that the computer knows the life and death of every single human being, that you even know what they will think tomorrow, not only today. So they are absolutely terrified.

People believe that the Americans are absolutely a super-race, so it was strange to me that a president like Reagan was so far from understanding that the world actually believed that America was much stronger than it actually was. After all, that was Reagan's myth — his objective to make America the strongest possible whatever.

He didn't have to go very far, because the perception of the strength of America was already much higher than he ever imagined. But if he had no one to explain this to him because the people he worked with had never done anything except selling oil from Texas or California, what do you expect? They can't explain to you how the world looks at you.

THE PRELUDE TO THE ARMS SALES

U.S. Relations with Iran

Robert C. McFarlane   In Iran we were totally in the dark — by choice. In 1978 the Carter administration, at the urging of Admiral [Stansfield] Turner of the CIA, decided, at the president's direction, that we should rely less on human collections and spies than on overhead collection — electronic photo imagery, infrared, listening, communications intelligence. That certainly has its place, but there are certain kinds of threats that those means are ineffective for, and that could only be dealt with by human beings.

We severed our relations with six hundred assets — spies, people who were on the payroll. This left us vulnerable to using third parties. It also made anybody whom we asked five years later to help us very leery of doing it, because anytime a spy risks his life penetrating a government and is cut off, he is not going to go back to that country again for a long time.

So we had very, very poor intelligence. We relied on the British, Israelis, anybody we could find — all of whom had different interests from ours. We ended up being quite ignorant.

Giandomenico Picco   When the Iranians realized that Reagan had won the 1980 election, they thought perhaps they could deal with him. These are people — despite the description we read about them — who are very pragmatic. They go for their own advantage, and they don't really worry too much about it.

The fact that Carter was a Democrat and Reagan was a Republican was a subtlety of no consequence; that is why the embassy hostages were released on the day of Reagan's inauguration. They thought: There is a new president coming in; let's see if we can tempt him to be a little bit different.

Howard Teicher   The issue of U.S. policy toward Iran was complex. From the first day at the NSC in March 1982, I was assigned the project of conducting an interagency review of U.S. policy toward Southwest Asia; within that, the real issue was Iran policy. It was conducted completely aboveboard over a period of two years, with multiple subcommittees. The scope of bureaucratic involvement was probably seventy to one hundred participants; it was as correct an enterprise as possible.

On the issue of Iran, we basically ran into what I call "the Shultz problem," which was actually more significant than Weinberger's on this: the notion that we could not deal with Iran as long as they supported international terrorism. We could not talk to them, let alone have normal relations.

The notion that they were important was not disputed — that they had all this oil, all these people, that they were potentially a destabilizing influence. You had this huge column of reasons to deal with them, and then it was vetoed. It was like the Security Council: Shultz just vetoed doing anything, and Weinberger basically agreed with this.

Giandomenico Picco We tend to forget that [the nations of] the West — and the United States in particular — were for over eight years military, political, and economic allies of Saddam Hussein. By June 1988, the Iraqi side was winning [the war with Iran] militarily.

It took them until the day — August 8, 1988 — the armistice agreement between Iran and Iraq was actually concluded to accept that that war would come to an end. So we are talking about an inability to understand what was going on. I can tell you that the Reagan administration did not want the end of the Iran-Iraq War. I say this out of direct experience, because I was personally involved.

Donald T. Regan We were assured by McFarlane, and by Casey also, that there were forces there — [Speaker of the Iranian Parliament Ali Akbar Hashemi] Rafsanjani was the one who was usually mentioned — who would be more forthcoming in dealing with the United States after Khomeini passed. That if we irritated them now, they would be intractable enemies, just as much as Khomeini was. So the president made contact in order to gain insight into Rafsanjani, and others.

Eitan Haber Rabin thought that Iran would be our biggest danger in the future, and he was right. He tried to find ways to the Iranians. That's the reason why he thought what we now call Irangate was the right step. He read the intelligence reports and thought we could find moderate Iranians. He thought, if we assist Iran secretly now, they will pay in their policy in the future. In any case, he said that we must try.

Ghorbanifar Meets the Israelis

Adnan Khashoggi It started with me. I met Ghorbanifar, and he was telling me how people in Iran are dissatisfied with Khomeini. Of course, as a Saudi man who knows the policy of our government, we were not very happy with Khomeini either. He was trying to export his revolution to all the Islamic countries, and in a very radical way. We are all true Muslims; we love our faith. But our faith doesn't say what these people are saying we should do.

So I listened carefully to Ghorbanifar, and I went to His Majesty [King Fahd] and explained the intelligence I had received. He said he didn't want to be involved.

So I said, "Do you give me the freedom to discuss it with the Americans? With the Egyptians? With others?" He said, "I give you nothing; I know nothing. You are a free man." So I went to Egypt and talked to Hosni Mubarak and informed him as to what was happening in Iran.

He wanted to check out this guy, Ghorbanifar, so they brought him to Egypt. They talked to him — Egyptian intelligence — and after a while the Egyptians said, "Listen, this is something higher than we have the ability to handle. There are different groups in Iran; they could be interchanging their intelligence. It could be a problem to Egypt." So the Egyptians withdrew.

So I thought: the Israelis had a great presence in Iran during the period of the shah, and they know the Iranians better, so why don't I talk to Mr. Peres? I asked him if he could send someone to me to discuss something important, so they said they will send me Schwimmer and Nimrodi. I knew them because, for years, they were always around Peres.

I met Schwimmer. I said to Schwimmer, "This is what is happening." He said, "Nimrodi is the one who is an expert on Iran." So he brought Nimrodi in. He had lived in Iran during the period of the shah. They liked the situation. They saw it as an opening — that there were people in the regime to recognize Israel's role. And maybe it could influence peace.

So I said, "Fine, talk to him." They also took him to Israel and put him under proper intelligence, and they were convinced this guy was for real — that he was representing this group of people who want to moderate Iran.

Roy Furmark   I had introduced Khashoggi to Ghorbanifar. Adnan said, "I don't know if this guy is for real. The only way to find out is for him to talk to the Israelis. They know the Middle East like the palm of their hand, and they will determine whether this guy has any truth in him."

Then Adnan arranged for Ghorbanifar to meet the Israelis. I went with Ghorbanifar to Israel. We met with Nimrodi, his partner Al Schwimmer, and with David Kimche. They were skeptical, but they met with him, had sessions with him with Israeli intelligence. And apparently they felt he had a lot of good intelligence; he passed the test.

David Kimche, director general of the Israeli Foreign Ministry; ambassador-at-large   The government didn't know Ghorbanifar. Shlomo Gazit, who used to be the head of military intelligence, had met him; the Mossad had met him; of course, Nimrodi and Al Schwimmer had met him; and later I was introduced to him.

There wasn't a view of Ghorbanifar; there was a person who claimed certain things. The question was, were those things correct? Could they be used? Could it be exploited, if you like, to the good of that particular subject? Don't forget, not every person who helps an intelligence operation is necessarily the son of a rabbi; it doesn't work that way. Whether he was a man with tremendous integrity or not wasn't the question.

The question was, could he be used in any way to help in forwarding a very important subject — the subject of preventing Iran from sliding more into the camp of the Soviet Union, and also of further extremism?

Roy Furmark   Ghorbanifar came up with this plan. There were the moderates — the chance to change Iran's direction, to bring them closer to the West, and to get the hostages released. I said to Khashoggi, "It sounds good. Is this guy for real?" He said, "Call the Israelis."

In the end, the Israelis said: "This is something we will do only if we have approval from Washington." So the next step was to bring Washington in. He had to pass tests with the Israelis and in Washington before this thing proceeded.

Adnan Khashoggi   They realized they could not do anything without checking with the United States, so they went to America and they talked to McFarlane.

Roy Furmark   He was invited to Washington, and I went down to see him. That was where I met Ledeen. I said, "Manucher, how do you satisfy the U.S. government on your credibility?" He said, "I'll tell you. In two days the Iranian Navy will board an American freighter in the Gulf, and they will go through the ship and then leave the ship alone. That will be the signal to the U.S. government that it was prearranged and therefore that Mr. Ghorbanifar is bona fide in his discussion."

Lo and behold! A couple of days later the Iranian government boards an American freighter in the Gulf. This helped to create his bona fides with the U.S. government: he said it was going to happen, and it did. So, if you were Ollie North, or the CIA, or whoever he went to see while he was in Washington — boom! What he said was going to happen did happen, so it must have been preplanned.

ISRAEL, AMERICA, AND ARMS FOR HOSTAGES

Albert Hakim, international businessman   The Iran project started through the Israelis. In the past I had had very, very close ties with the Israeli government, and I knew most of the players then, such as Yaacov Nimrodi. And the whole operation — I really want to be as modest as I can — was something I introduced: that you cannot negotiate with the Iranians just for the release of hostages. And that is why Israel was not successful.

I never worked for the government, and I don't know what the chain of events was. What came from the president and how it was later interpreted by Ollie — that I cannot comment on. Maybe, from day one, they wanted some fundamental relationship with Iran beyond the release of the hostages; that I cannot comment on. I can comment on what was presented to me, and that definitely, at the beginning, was a focus on the release of the hostages.

Adnan Khashoggi   There was no mention of the hostages at the beginning. But later, since [Reagan] was probably obsessed, he thought: If these guys [the Iranians] are going to open up, get me the hostages. A normal request. But not to trade hostages against weapons.

It could be that the Israelis sold the concept on the hostages, knowing the weakness of the president. But they didn't have an okay on the hostages to start with. This is very important historically — that Kimche did not have any okay on the hostages.

Abraham Tamir   The traders came forth with the idea to push weapons and to do business, to release the American hostages. This was a wrong approach, a wrong policy. I was against it because I don't think that Israel, with all its problems, should interfere in the internal problems of other countries.

Howard Teicher   There was a Khashoggi memo, which I staffed for McFarlane, which talked about this Persian — who turned out to be Ghorbanifar — who thought he could help bring about freedom for the hostages. Then McFarlane said, "Let's do this again," and [Donald]

Fortier and I did a draft national security decision directive based on all the work that had been done. McFarlane circulated it on a very limited basis. Casey came back and said, "It sounds great to me." Shultz and Weinberger came back and said, "Over our dead bodies."

So we were told to forget about it.

Caspar Weinberger   His very human concern for the safety of the hostages led him to agree with the very bad advice he was getting — that there were some moderate factions in Iran that we could work with, which, of course, was totally untrue.

He got advice — from people like McFarlane and North — that it was possible to have an agreement with the moderate elements in Iran. I kept telling him that the moderates had all been murdered and were in the cemeteries, that there weren't any moderates in any effective positions, and that none of these people who were making the promises were to be believed.

I wish he had followed my advice, but he wanted very much to do anything that would help get the hostages out. And there were constant presentations by people who had daily access, such as McFarlane. Eventually he was led to believe it could have results. Obviously, it couldn't; the president acknowledged it himself. He said, "George Shultz and Cap Weinberger were right, and I was wrong."

Craig Fuller   The president always insisted that he believed he was being asked to reach out to a moderate faction that had influence over the hostage holders — therefore, in his mind, separating the notion that if I build a relationship with you by giving you something you value, and it affects your actions, then I'm not trading arms with you to get the hostages released. It was a hard argument to sell but was very much what President Reagan has always had in his mind.

Duane Clarridge   Reagan, as a human being, was terribly tried by all of this. He had that constant barrage of pressure on him. Every once in a while he would have to see these hostage families.

Someone should have told him that he was going against his own policy. That's where I blame Shultz and Weinberger. They had more access than anybody; they let it happen.

I suspect that they knew exactly how he felt. And he might have turned to them and said, "If you don't want me to do this, what are we going to do?" And nobody had any good ideas. They may just not have wanted to take the president on.

Robert C. McFarlane   The president believed passionately in the potential of the individual himself as the heroic figure, as the person who can make a difference. The leader who takes risks — as long as his heart is pure, we win.

In this instance, he became so absorbed in getting the hostages back. Since nothing else had worked, this might work. The risk element for him — appearing to deal with terrorists, or at least thugs — made him vulnerable. He clung too easily to the notion, "I'm trying to get back human lives. And as they are portrayed to us as [being] against terrorism, I'm willing to defend [my action] in public." I say "too easily" because, whenever human lives were at risk, he was more willing to take risks — even against the interests of the country, certainly his own interests politically.

The real blame, however, is my own, because I knew that Reagan was a humanitarian, and vulnerable. The anguish of the loss of a single life was more important to him than anything else. And knowing that, when I saw it going wrong, I should not have let the administration go on, because there was nobody he trusted more than me. Never did Ronald Reagan do something that I said, "Don't do [it]."

Giandomenico Picco   The Reagan administration [had a] simplistic way of looking at the world. I don't think that they were intellectually equipped to deal with Iran.

God knows, we told the administration not to pay gangsters, because gangsters will always come back against you.

MICHAEL LEDEEN GOES TO ISRAEL

Nimrod Novick   I got a call from a friend at the National Security Council telling me, "Michael Ledeen is coming to Israel, and he wants to see the prime minister." I sent the prime minister a little note saying, "He says he is not coming on behalf of the president, or McFarlane, but with their knowledge."

At the time I didn't attach any importance to the request; I didn't recommend one way or the other. I thought that Peres had known Ledeen; I didn't know for sure.

Peres agreed to see Ledeen privately. We did not know what the issue was going to be. There were people in Israel telling Peres there might be an opportunity in Iran, that maybe we should explore it.

But he was not ready to do that. Peres handled it outside of the Israeli administration. He listened to Ledeen; he did not react, and he wanted to find out whether he was really speaking on behalf of the administration. That is why he sent Dave Kimche to find out what was going on.

And Dave came back and reported that everybody was in line — from Reagan to Shultz — which was what he heard from McFarlane. It was a written report. Dave didn't know that the close staff of Peres was not involved.

Michael Ledeen   My instructions were to arrange a meeting with Peres outside of government channels. That I was to go there and have no contact with the embassy in Tel Aviv, and talk to Peres and come back and report to McFarlane. Period.

Basically, the White House thought that everything that happened at the State Department leaked, and that most everything that happened at the CIA also leaked. Bud always told me, "Don't tell Casey; don't tell anybody at CIA."

So I did what I was told. In fact, I told Peres, "One of the conditions of sharing information on this is that the CIA is not to be informed." My brief was to ask him how he felt their intelligence was about Iran, because there was a possibility that we might want to take a fresh look at Iran — people had told us that Israeli intelligence on Iran was very good — and if he was happy with his intelligence, would he be willing to share it with us?

That was the entire discussion; I did not bring up the hostages. I had been sent by McFarlane, and we had not as yet had contact with Ghorbanifar. There was nothing on the table, as far as I knew, about the hostages. It wasn't until after I talked to Peres that Schwimmer came to Washington and told me for the first time about Ghorbanifar.

John Poindexter   Mike is a complicated character, as we all are. Bud had a close relationship with Mike. I never developed a close relationship with Mike. He has wanted to have lunch with me for a long time, and I just put him off.

Ollie was uneasy about Ledeen. He was uncertain about Ledeen's relationship with the Israelis, and exactly what connections he had. I have no question about Ledeen's loyalty.

Roy Furmark   After I met Ledeen in Washington, I knew he had gone to Israel. He had just come back. I knew that he was going back and forth and that he wanted to play a role. Ledeen is a play-maker; he is right in the center of power in Washington. He may not be the power, but he knows everybody, and many people take his opinion very highly.

He believed that Israel was important to the U.S. and that the U.S. was important to Israel, and he wanted to do everything he could to maintain and see that relationship grow. I don't know whether he had any special agendas. I can remember him saying that the Iranian hostage crisis was affecting the whole region.

Michael Ledeen   My contact with Peres came from the work I did for Haig. One of the things I did for Haig was the Socialist International. I have a lot of friends there: Craxi was a close friend; I knew Mitterrand's people very well, from my days at the *New Republic*. Peres at that time was head of the Labor Party, and the Labor Party was part of the Socialist International. My task was to go around to its leaders for Haig and explain our policy, so I went to see Peres in Israel several times. It didn't have to do with Israel; it had to do with socialism.

Howard Teicher   We had paid for him as a consultant at the beginning and sort of started the whole thing. I had been leery of the fact that Ledeen had gone to Israel. Apparently he believed that McFarlane had said it was okay for him to talk to Kimche about what we were going to do about Iran, which led Kimche to then go to see McFarlane and tell him that we have this link — and for Khashoggi to do his thing. One thing led to another.

Roy Furmark   The Israelis had two agendas: one was the Middle East regional agenda — Iran is a big export market — and the second was that the Israelis wanted to show the Americans that they were loyal.

Everyone was trying to take credit for saving the hostages. Without the hostages, the pressure on Iran by the West wouldn't have been so extreme; possibly there could have been a thawing out much earlier between the U.S. and Iran. But the fact that the hostages were there — and all the evidence proved that [Iran was] directing, supporting, and paying the hostage takers — made [Iran] become ostracized.

If you hadn't had the hostages, I don't believe that would have happened. You might have had somebody trying to buy arms in Iran, but it never would have been on this basis; it would have been a standard way of buying some arms from the Israelis, or from other sellers. Because there were Americans involved, it became a mega-situation. Whatever happens in the world, if Americans are involved, it is front-page.

Yaacov Nimrodi, Israeli business executive   In Israel we thought it was tremendously important to help the Americans. Reagan asked Shimon for a favor: he wanted only the hostages. Shimon is a doer. He called Schwimmer; he called me and told us the story.

At the same time we came in with Ghorbanifar's story; it became parallel. This was before Michael Ledeen.

Nimrod Novick   To this day Shimon says that his main motive was not the opportunity to penetrate Iran — he was a bit skeptical about that — but that it was Reagan's request for help on the hostages. He felt: Reagan is a real friend, national and personal; this man is pursuing policies that are very, very helpful for Israel; he helped me; he helped us on many occasions. When he asks for my help, I am going to do it.

David Kimche   Ledeen went to the prime minister and said, "We have a problem as far as Iran is concerned. How can you help us?" The prime minister said to me, "Look, if we can help the United States on this subject, we are duty-bound to help them. They have helped us in many things, such as the Russian immigration and the Falashas° from Ethiopia."

He stressed that very strongly to me when he briefed me. He said, "We have to help them if we can, and if we have this possibility, through Ghorbanifar, we have to do it for them." He saw it mainly as aid for the United States, not as something for Israel.

Shimon Peres   The first information I had as prime minister was that the United States was very interested in bringing home the hostages who were in the hands of the Iranians.

We wanted to help the United States. I understood that they wanted to do this, rightly or wrongly, outside of official channels. I didn't have the slightest idea that there was a division of views within the administration, because we were approached by the president — an envoy of the president, Michael Ledeen. He was the first one to come over. He had shown a general interest in what was going on in Iran in reference to the

---

° Ethiopian Jews brought to Israel.

hostages. He said, "Look, it's to the advantage of all of us not to do it through official channels."

KIMCHE SEES McFARLANE, JULY 3, 1985

Yaacov Nimrodi The government — Yitzhak Rabin — decided to send David Kimche to speak directly not with Reagan but with McFarlane. Kimche met Michael Ledeen, of course; he was involved. They brought the subject to President Reagan. Nobody believed that he would agree, but he did.

David Kimche We never spoke to the president of the United States; our partner was Bud McFarlane. The operation was geopolitical, and the subject matter was certainly geopolitical. It was practically theoretical — and humane, if you like.

Oliver North It was Kimche; Ghorbanifar was brought in as a consequence of Kimche's overture. This thing started way before I got involved. My first involvement was simply to set up the apparatus to monitor those guys.

David Kimche The prime minister called me and said, "I understand you are going to the United States on Foreign Ministry business." I went to the States purely on Foreign Ministry business at that time, and I was briefed before I went by the prime minister and other people here about this whole business of Ghorbanifar. The prime minister asked me if I knew Bud McFarlane well, and I said, "Yes, we're good friends." He said, "I had a visit from a guy by the name of Mike Ledeen," whom I also knew very well, and he told me the story and asked me to go and speak to Bud McFarlane.

It had to do with a strategic opening; it had nothing to do with the hostages. When I spoke to McFarlane, the subject of the hostages hardly came up. It was purely a question of what's going to happen in Iran — the dangers of Iran — especially if Khomeini will be succeeded by one of the fanatics, or someone close to the Soviet Union; it was purely strategic.

This coincided with Israel's interest, which was not to see Iran continue as a fanatic country. We were also worried about what was going to happen after Khomeini, and if there would be any way to prevent this continuous move toward more and more fanaticism and extremism. There was a complete identity of interests between us and the United States on this issue.

Michael Ledeen When Kimche came to see McFarlane, we didn't know anything about Iran. Nothing. We were very bad on Iran all along; we were bad on Iran in 1979. That was a general intelligence failure.

Kimche had a personal relationship with McFarlane that dated to the time when McFarlane was special representative for the Middle East. When McFarlane would go to Israel, the person he would talk to was Kimche, who was running the Foreign Ministry. Kimche and McFarlane were made for each other; a lot of it had to do with personalities.

Robert C. McFarlane You have to meet David and know him to really get a good answer as to why one would trust him. He is a man of enormous intellect, but that is not enough. At the time there were sixty thousand Jews in Iran, and through them, Israel had the best intelligence — far better than ours. Their interests are different from ours, and they could easily have been drawing us into something that would have, from their point of view, worsened our relations with Muslim countries.

You have to go beyond that, and I did ask David, "Why do you believe these people?" He presented some pretty good evidence. He said, "These are people who live there and therefore are vulnerable. They have put themselves at risk to us by being photographed with Jews — with Israelis. And with me. They seemed genuinely willing to take risks for their purpose here. We said, 'We have checked out what they have told us. They have given us a fairly detailed order of battle — of where people stand in the lineup for and against Khomeini. Their information checks out with our own people. So we tend, by association, to think these people are legitimate.'" That was not true. It was an erring judgment on David's part — and on mine.

Richard Murphy He is a very able person. He also benefits from the assumption that Israeli intelligence is unmatchable — which is not necessarily true.

The general assumption in Washington at that time was that an Israel under threat is an Israel whose antennae are unusually sensitive; they are making damned sure that their facts are straight, so their words carried extra weight. And Kimche was a very personable and persuasive man, with an enormous amount of experience.

Adnan Khashoggi McFarlane for some reason liked it — it's an opening to Iran, it's not bad to have a dialogue. But he was nervous. He's not a weak man — how would I call it? He's a careful man — like if I sit with McFarlane for three hours, I have to speak for three hours and he speaks for one minute.

THE "MODERATES" IN IRAN

David Kimche It was no secret that we had been collecting intelligence on Iran; it's a target country, obviously. So we were in contact with a lot of Iranians. But Ghorbanifar was a man who said he had access to the very top, and he happened to come along at the time when Michael Ledeen made his approach to Peres.

Ghorbanifar was a charmer, a slippery charmer, slippery like an eel — you could never pin him down. But he certainly knew the subject matter of Iran. Our brief was to try and help the United States on this matter; every snippet of intelligence we got from him was immediately passed on to the United States.

I remember very vividly asking Bud McFarlane, "Look, we have passed you this information. You must have checked it and double-checked it. Please tell me, is it right?" He said, "Yes, and we find it extremely valuable and very important. Please continue to get as much as you can in this area of intelligence."

As far as I was concerned, that was vindication that we were doing something positive, because I had my means of knowing whether what he was saying was correct or not; my means of knowing that was what Bud McFarlane told me. He was very enthusiastic about the information; he thought it was extremely valuable, so we continued.

Oliver North There were very thoughtful people writing papers on the absolute urgency of reestablishing some kind of activity with the new leadership. And at the same time Casey was saying, "Somewhere in Iran, there are people who are going to replace this regime at some point, and we need to be in touch with them now." At that point there was still an Evil Empire, and nobody knew that it was going to collapse in 1990.

Robert C. McFarlane It was portrayed originally by David Kimche — and throughout 1985 — that those with whom he had dealt wanted to form a new government to overthrow the ayatollah. They were anti-terrorist — people who had awakened to the vulnerability of Iran, both in the war with Iraq and [as they looked] at the Soviet invasion of Afghanistan, as perhaps presaging a Russian move into their territory, and therefore [they wanted] to turn away from this theocratic crusade in Iran. That's how it was portrayed to me, and how I portrayed it to the president. And for the three months between July and October, it looked to me like it wasn't achieving what we had hoped it would: connecting us to genuine anti-Khomeini elements.

Michael Ledeen   One could see then that the revolution was starting to generate internal opposition and that there were important Iranians who at least said they were prepared to deal with us to try to mitigate the more extreme forms of what was going on there.

All the Iranians really want, on the one hand, is to be embraced by America. On the other hand, they also hate America, because America threatens them [and] everything they believe in. They are complicated.

The issue was of pro-Americans and anti-Americans, pro-Western and anti-Western. There were no moderates in Iran. I never believed there were; Kimche never believed in moderates. It had nothing to do with moderates; they were all Islamic fanatics — Shiite fundamentalists. Among them were lots of people who believed that Khomeini was going to incur America's wrath, which Iran could not survive, and who believed that for Iran to survive, they must have a decent relationship with the United States. That was the cutting edge; that was already enough, from American interests.

My view of Iran was, and is, that we must play there. Iran is a very important country, and we must have contacts, people, however you want to do it. If you want to declare war, fight them; if you want to cozy up to them, cozy up to them; if you want to appease them, appease them. But you have to be there; you have to talk to them, have channels to them. To avoid Iran is just madness.

Roy Furmark   Everybody was trying to resolve the hostage crisis; every Iranian in Europe was working on it. But all of these other Iranians did not have the access, and didn't meet with a lot of important Iranian officials in other countries, like Ghorbanifar did.

Ghorbanifar is a businessman, but he was also hoping to bring Iran back into the Western world to a certain extent. And you have to start someplace. The Iranians were being blamed that they controlled the hostages, that they controlled the hostage takers. So Ghorbanifar's idea was that this would be a way to improve Iran's relationship with the rest of the world. And in addition, the Iranians felt, if we do this, what do we get out of it? They are not in the charity business; they don't have a big charitable foundation system like we have in America. Everything they do has a bazaar mentality; it was a simple bazaar mentality in the Middle East.

It began as a confidence booster. Of course, the Israelis were happy to sell; for them, it was business. Who knows what they sold them, and if it worked. Was it secondhand equipment? Rejects?

Giandomenico Picco   In any situation it is very handy to project the image of the good cop and the bad cop. If you have to negotiate, or you have to play a game, it's a very handy way of proceeding. So the Iranian government had no difficulties in projecting the image, true or false, that there were better people and worse people.

Among the people who worked in the Tehran government over the years were people who were all educated in California. To this day they are called "the California boys." Were they very powerful? At times, yes; at times, no. The war against Iraq ended because of them. They were the ones who sacrificed personally; some of them were purged.

There were also others who took advantage of the confusion and decided to set up their own money, their own network, and their operations, in Lebanon and wherever. The question of creating two sides to a story gave them tremendous flexibility.

If you do this, you want to have two cards — the more cards the better. Who is the great negotiator? He who invents cards that do not exist and transforms them into something that exists. It has often been said that it is not difficult to be an American negotiator, because you have atomic weapons, money, everything. But when you don't have these things, you have to invent things — and make them real. That is virtual reality.

Roy Furmark   I had been to Tehran in the good old days. Before Khomeini, it was the good life, especially for the upper echelon and the government people. Those were the good times, and I'm sure that a lot of people there remembered those times. How could you all of a sudden become so dogmatic as to how the Iranian people were going to live?

I'm sure that today there are still a lot of moderates, but they are afraid to come out. In those days there was so much pressure on them because of the hostages; they wanted to get that burden off their shoulders. I am convinced that the moderates Ghorbanifar was talking about were there — and still are today.

THE GREEN LIGHT

In mid-July, as President Reagan recuperated in the hospital from colon can-cer surgery, he was visited by McFarlane, who outlined a plan for a strategic opening to Iran. McFarlane later stated that the president, who during that visit authorized McFarlane to make contact with Iran, was "all for letting the Israelis do anything they wanted" regarding dealings with Iran.

John Hutton The president handled this as if it had been a minor op-eration. I remember the day Bud McFarlane came out. I think he came out with the vice president; I remember Mr. Bush calling and asking me if they could come out. I said, "Sure, there is no problem at all."

Adnan Khashoggi McFarlane went to Reagan. And the truth has to be told — that Reagan was informed from day one by McFarlane. And he got the green light from the president to go ahead, and to keep it con-fined to the White House.

Why? I think it was stupid; they should have involved the National Security as a whole. This is one of the weaknesses of the system. And McFarlane then depended on what I call "a little boy named North" in something bigger than him, because they don't see the dimension.

North was involved in Nicaragua; he was involved in a specific target. Now you involve him in another secret mission which is more compli-cated politically than Nicaragua. We didn't know North; he was not a player to us. We played on the level we should play on: to bring the in-formation to the White House.

When it reached the president's level and he okayed it, the Israelis were happy. I know that there is a document that was executed between the two governments, but it disappeared. It will appear someday, but it doesn't exist somewhere now, because nobody has referred to it. But Schwimmer and Kimche would know more if it is for real, or if just word of mouth was enough. But the Israelis were more careful than just to ac-cept word of mouth.

The basic deal was not the hostages; the basic deal was that he could accomplish peace. Reagan was frustrated to make this peace. He couldn't, because of the Arabs and the Israelis.

Let's put ourselves back into that time. Why did he authorize it? He had four advantages: one, the peace with Iraq; two, to contain the radi-cals in Iran; [three,] to get this crazy man out of the picture; and [four,] the Israeli involvement in the peace process that would put them back into the process — and there was good reason at that time, because Peres was the prime minister.

So he was playing his game for peace. Reagan understood that more than all of the people around him. Look at what he did in Nicaragua: he didn't care about legality. He wanted accomplishment; this is a man of accomplishment.

Maybe he never read things himself. Maybe he never had the right advisers around him, because they were all like McFarlane, who is an honest man, but he's not a Scowcroft — a cunning little man. McFarlane wasn't like that. The only man sitting there with a complex mind was Reagan himself.

Donald T. Regan   To the extent that there were twenty or twenty-one captives in the Middle East (some of them having been captives for several years), and that we, as a strong nation, were unable to extricate our own people — the president took that very seriously.

To get Iran to somehow intercede with these Middle East fanatics, to get them to give up their hostages, he was willing to try to get into the good graces of certain forces within Iran, in order to see if they would intercede.

This was the proposition put to us by the Israelis. They knew that the Iranians needed spare parts for the HAWK missiles they had purchased from us during the days of the shah, and they wanted those HAWKs in top shape. If the Israelis were allowed to sell HAWK parts from their supplies to the Iranians, and we replenished the Israelis, then we weren't literally trading with the enemy. At least, that was the rationale Reagan developed for himself.

That is what we agreed to: Israel was the interceding party, whereas we were letting them sell the arms to Iran for us, and we replenished the Israeli supplies.

Yaacov Nimrodi   The most important day for me concerning the Reagan presidency was the day the government of Israel asked permission to find a way to supply arms to release the hostages.

We agreed that we would supply the five hundred TOWs immediately, from our stock. Even then, Rabin sent Dave Kimche to get permission. I don't know if he got it, but something happened. McFarlane went to see Reagan in the hospital and came back and said to Dave, "It's okay." I was impressed that Reagan made the decision alone — not with Weinberger, and not with Shultz.

THE RELEASE OF REVEREND WEIR

Benjamin Weir   At the end of fourteen months in isolation, when I was kept with four other men, we began to get a sense, after some weeks, that TWA 847* was under negotiation, and we realized we had been brought together at about that time. So we began to wonder if, possibly, our release was related to that negotiation.

My captors never specifically discussed the question of who had the power to free me. But sometime in the first week, I remember seeing through a doorway in the hall a picture of the Ayatollah Khomeini. Also, at another time, someone walked through a hallway in a lightweight, long white robe that was characteristic of Iranians, but not of Lebanese. These were only suppositions on my part.

Still later — perhaps a month after I was held — I was able to look through a crack in a shutter and saw soldiers in uniform. Still later I saw men in uniforms that were not Lebanese uniforms. I began to get a sense that there was some Iranian connection. But it became clearer later on, on Tuesday nights, when the guards would gather and chant religious chants for a long period of time; one of those chants was in reverence and honor of the Ayatollah Khomeini.

Putting these things together, I began to get the idea that there was some Iranian inspiration in what was happening, but it was never said explicitly to me that Iran was behind this movement — Islamic Jihad. But it did become clear that someone was providing a small monthly wage to the Lebanese men; they looked for that wage every month. And one of them had said to me that he had received training outside of Lebanon. He never said Iran but suggested it had been the Soviet Union — or somewhere else.

Giandomenico Picco   The hostage-taking was part of a strategy — at least by some people in Lebanon — and [it was] definitely supported in the early and middle 1980s by Iran. You could say that hostage-taking

---

* On June 14, 1985, TWA 847, carrying 153 passengers and crew — most of them Americans — was hijacked by Shiite terrorists while en route from Athens to Rome. The aircraft was flown to Beirut at the behest of the hijackers. There they murdered one of the American passengers, navy diver Robert Stethem, and threw his body onto the tarmac. Almost two weeks later the hostages were released, but only after Israel began a phased release of seven hundred Shiites who had been detained in Israel.

once or twice was a coincidence, but the holding of tens of kidnapped people would support the theory that this was thought out.

The premise that, if we can deal with these Iranians they can have influence in Lebanon, is accurate. I have lived that connection; there is no question that there was a profound connection.

When these people took hostages, no matter what the connection was — as everybody now knows — each hostage, or each two or three of them, were the physical responsibility of a small cell, which usually was a real family. Yes, the Iranians have tremendous influence, but the physical well-being, until the last second they are released, is the responsibility of that particular family.

What does it mean to say that Iran is responsible for 90 percent? If the guy is dead or alive, 10 percent or 1 percent is the same thing. The percentage of responsibility — or of control — is theoretical thinking, part of a political science book; it has no significance in practice. If the individuals who are physically responsible for the day-to-day life of the hostages can also kill them, the fact that somebody is responsible 99 percent, politically, is fine. But they can kill them in one second. I think even Oliver North would understand this.

David Jacobsen We knew who our captors were: we knew that we were being held by Shiites; we knew that they were Hezbollah. There were seven or eight group names used, but basically there was only one group, using seven different names, to confuse everybody. But we did not know at the time whom they represented. It took a period of time and exposure to these people — and then to come out and to be able to research as a free man — to identify who was pulling the strings on them.

When the TWA plane was hijacked, we knew that talks were going on. We knew that there were a certain number of passengers on the flight and that the number they were negotiating about increased by seven — that would be the total number of hostages on the ground — not associated with the plane. Those talks continued for several days, and from the radio we knew that we were excluded; the number dropped back to just the number of passengers.

From time to time we would get old magazines. One of the Syrian ministers would say he was doing everything to get us free. We knew that there were some actions, but we didn't know what our government's role was — if they were trying to do anything.

REVEREND WEIR'S HOMECOMING

Benjamin Weir   I never met President Reagan in person. My family did not ask; I never asked for, nor did I anticipate, a meeting with Reagan. In fact, plans had been made initially that I would be released in or near Switzerland and that I would have a time of rest there, so I did not go to Wiesbaden but was flown directly to Norfolk, Virginia.

Oliver North met me in the middle of the night when the plane landed at the Norfolk Naval Air Station. A few days after my release, I was present at a meeting with Vice President George Bush and some members of the National Security Council, and Oliver North was there.

The meeting with Bush and North had been planned with hostage families prior to my release and included some members of the Jenco family, my own family, and, I think, Peggy Say. It was intended as a briefing.

I stepped off the C-130 cargo plane and at the bottom of the steps was met by a person in civilian clothes who said he was there to welcome me back and to discuss what the next steps ought to be. He led me into the lounge. I saw that there were other people there. He said that there was a nurse and some other people from the government.

We sat and talked a bit. He said that he recommended that since there were still hostages being held, and since there was still some hope that the hostages might be released, he wanted to be sure that the matter would be kept quiet, for at least a time.

I said, "How long?" And he said, "A matter of days." And he suggested that I, and my family, go to a secure location; as I recall, it would be on the Naval Air Station base. I said, "I haven't talked to my wife. What does she have to say?" I understood him to say that she was in agreement. I said, "Well, I really don't want to make that kind of a decision until I have had an opportunity to talk with her."

Colonel North seemed friendly; he seemed supportive, encouraging. He seemed to have a clear idea of what he wanted. When I made it clear that I really didn't want to make any decision until I talked with my wife — I insisted on it more than once — he seemed to accept that, and to be concerned about my health and welfare.

Finally he said, "We'll take you to the hotel where she is staying." There was a psychiatrist who rode in the car with me; there were several cars, and men who, I understood, were from the FBI. We arrived at the hotel. It was then after midnight; I think it was probably nearly two o'clock in the morning. We waited for a moment in the car. Then they said it was all right to go in.

It wasn't the main entrance; there were no people around, no strong lights. I went with the psychiatrist, who took me upstairs, and pointed, and said, "Your wife is there, at that doorway," and left me. And Carol came to the door. She couldn't believe I was there. That was my return to my family.

Yaacov Nimrodi   I remember when later, Rabin, this bastard — I am sorry to say that — called me and said, "Yaacov, are you sure that they released the hostage because of the TOWs?" Rabin didn't believe us. He didn't like me; he didn't like Schwimmer, who is a good friend of Peres.

Reverend Weir's State of Mind on His Arrival in the United States

Benjamin Weir   I was not angry; I was relieved, and elated to be back in the United States and to anticipate seeing my wife and family. I had no idea where my children were.

I remember so well, after I was flown to the Sigonella base, in Sicily, and on board the C-130, as we approached the North American continent. It was a clear night. We flew down along the coast, and I was delighted with the view of the lighted cities, seeing them one by one as we flew south, toward Norfolk.

It was really with a deep sense of thankfulness that I was back home. I did not feel a spirit of blaming anyone. I must say that I had then — I had previously — a sense that I wanted to be my own person and did not want to become manipulated in whatever might take place.

I didn't know that would happen, and I should say that a dominant thought in my mind — before and afterward — was that from the moment I was told I would be released, my concern was for the other four men with whom I had spent nearly two months. I remember asking Colonel North if there had been any more releases, and if there was a prospect of those men being freed. I was very concerned for their release and appalled that I probably would carry the burden of trying to do something for them, and believing I could do very little, if anything at all.

Was Reverend Weir Uncooperative
with His Debriefers?

Benjamin Weir   It is true that for many years prior to my capture, I had been very much concerned about U.S. policy in the Middle East, especially with relation to the Palestinian people, and feeling that the U.S. was a very uncertain peace broker. I opposed the U.S.'s almost unlimited support to Israel; that is still true today.

But it is not true that I sympathized with my captors; I was always suspicious of my captors. I never allowed myself to think that I wasn't in imminent danger. On the one hand, I had lived in a Shiite Muslim community in Lebanon, so I had many friends among them; I had sympathy for them. But I also knew that most people in that community would be not only opposed to but dismayed at this small, radical group's taking of hostages.

I thought their proposition of bringing about an Islamic revolution in Lebanon was preposterous; I certainly did not sympathize with their goals. But I certainly had some sympathy for what I supposed would be the pressures on some of the young men to join the group and to have at least some kind of livelihood. But I certainly didn't justify in my own mind what they were doing.

Perhaps there were two points where I was considered uncooperative. One was when I was asked repeatedly to describe my captors: I had to honestly say that I never saw them. I was always blindfolded in their presence; I certainly could not identify them.

Secondly, the first or second day after I returned to Norfolk, I was asked if I could look at some photos and perhaps identify people. I had said in that initial interview, "Here I am, ready to respond to your questions as best I can. But I don't want this process to go on and on, and as far as I am concerned, this is the opportunity I'll have for debriefing." I didn't see that I could provide anything beyond what I had told them.

Later, within a day or two, people came back, from the FBI and perhaps Naval Intelligence, asking if I would be ready to identify some pictures, and I said, "No. I told you previously that I was not ready to continue this."

It came up again in telephone calls — maybe once or twice — and that was my reply each time, so perhaps that's what Colonel North saw as my lack of cooperation.

13

The Ante Is Raised: From the HAWK Sale to a Visit to Tehran

The release of Reverend Weir raised the hope that additional arms sales would lead to the release of the remaining hostages.

On October 27, 1985, Ghorbanifar—whose credibility had been enhanced by Reverend Weir's release—met with Ledeen, Nimrodi, and Schwimmer to discuss such additional sales. At that time the Iranians upped the ante by mentioning their interest in acquiring HAWK anti-aircraft missiles.

Then, on November 5, Israeli Defense Minister Yitzhak Rabin met with Robert McFarlane to alert him to an impending HAWK shipment to Iran and to determine whether President Reagan was in support of the shipment. McFarlane, in order to ensure the replenishment of Israel's stock of HAWK missiles, asked Oliver North to deal with the issue.

That shipment would be complicated by logistical problems and errors. From November 18, when the president was informed of the imminent shipment of the HAWKs, until November 25, when only eighteen of the intended eighty missiles arrived in Iran, a series of blunders occurred: there was difficulty securing a replacement delivery aircraft to make the landing in Europe; the CIA's involvement in the episode was unplanned; the Iranians were disappointed on discovering that the missiles they received were not capable of shooting down high-flying aircraft, and they were chagrined that some of the missiles bore Israeli markings.

These blunders led to the undermining of the Israeli middlemen's credibility; as a result, the decision was made to remove them from the operation and to opt for direct U.S. involvement in future arms sales to Iran.

The removal of the middlemen also caused the government of Israel to become more directly involved in the operation. Amiram Nir, the prime min-

ister's adviser on counterterrorism, a former journalist, and the son-in-law of one of the prime minister's most influential supporters, became Israel's liaison to the initiative.

The ill-fated HAWK shipment led also to Oliver North's deepening involvement in the initiative, as did McFarlane's resignation, on December 4, as national security adviser and replacement by his deputy, Admiral John Poindexter. In this reorganization of the NSC, North was given McFarlane's arms sales–related responsibilities, although McFarlane continued to be in touch with the operation through an NSC computer hookup to his home.

North was now at the center of the two major operations being run out of the White House and the NSC: the resupply of the Nicaraguan contras and the Iran initiative—whether defined as an effort to free the hostages or as a means by which to develop a strategic opening to Iran.

On December 5, North suggested that an additional fifty HAWKs, as well as thirty-three hundred TOW missiles, be sent to Iran, in five installments, with one or more hostages to be released following each shipment.

On that day President Reagan, at the CIA's insistence, signed a finding retroactively covering the Agency's participation in the November HAWK shipment—a document that Poindexter would destroy in late 1986. A signed copy of the document, which specifically mentions hostage rescue rather than the larger issue of a strategic opening to Iran, would be found later by investigators.

On the following day, December 6, according to the official chronology prepared by the government of Israel, North told Israeli officials of his intention to divert profits from the arms sales to the contras. North would later say that the idea of the diversion was first broached to him on January 22, 1986, by Ghorbanifar, during a break in a London meeting.

On December 7, the president met with his key advisers to discuss whether the Iranian initiative should continue; over the objections of Secretaries Shultz and Weinberger, but with the assent of CIA Director Casey, it was agreed to continue the initiative. This meeting would be recalled during the subsequent investigations of the initiative, when notes taken on the session by Weinberger would confirm that the president had been aware of the November HAWK shipment.

Two days later, on December 9, North, in a memorandum to Poindexter and McFarlane, suggested that Major General Richard Secord, who had retired and was involved with his partner, Albert Hakim, in supplying aid to the contras, be used to control both Ghorbanifar and the weapons delivery operations. With Secord in place, the president, on January 17, 1986, signed a finding authorizing direct U.S. involvement in the transfer of weapons to Iran.

In February one thousand TOW missiles were transferred by Israel to Iran. However, this shipment, along with the supply to Iran of intelligence information on Iraq coordinated by the CIA, failed to produce the release of another hostage.

On April 4, North drafted what would become known as the "Diversion Memo." In it he stated that profits from the arms sales would be used to purchase critically needed supplies for the contras.

Then in May a major attempt was made to free the remaining hostages: McFarlane and a small entourage flew to Tehran with one pallet of spare parts for HAWK missiles, in a good-faith gesture to the Iranians. A larger parts shipment remained in Israel, to be shipped if McFarlane were to indicate that his negotiations were producing results.

McFarlane, however, did not authorize the shipment because he was disappointed with both what he perceived to be the low level of Iranian participation in the talks and the lack of progress in securing the release of the hostages. After three days of fruitless negotiations, McFarlane and his entourage left Iran, with the disposition of the unshipped HAWK parts unresolved.

The issue of these spare parts prompted North, Cave, Nir, and Ghorbanifar to meet on July 21 in London, where they discussed the need for a further hostage release prior to the parts shipment. Five days later, Reverend Lawrence Jenco was freed. Jenco's release, however, failed to satisfy Poindexter's order that the parts not be shipped until all of the remaining hostages were released.

Some weeks earlier, on June 29 —the day Vice President Bush met with Nir in Jerusalem to be briefed on the issue—the president had approved a plan, generated by North, to apply a carrot-and-stick approach to the hostage situation and allow for the transfer to Iran of the remaining HAWK parts, which arrived in Iran from Israel, contained in twelve pallets, on August 13.

THE HAWK SNAFU

Adnan Khashoggi   The Iranian side wanted to be sure that we were dealing with the Americans, and not just the Israelis. They wanted evidence that this was so, so they asked for spare parts for the HAWK missiles for a million dollars.

Now they have the problem: Who has a million dollars to spare? I could not believe that the whole American intelligence could not supply a million dollars; it didn't make sense to me. But later it made a lot of sense when I knew that only McFarlane was sitting there with his disinformation. Then I realized, he doesn't have even a penny in his pocket. So I said, "I'll give you the million dollars; you'll give it to me when you receive the funds." The Iranians, through Ghorbanifar, accepted that I bridge the financing.

The goods were shipped; they arrived; everything went smoothly. The Americans were convinced that they were dealing within the structure. What surprised me was that the Iranians lied to Khomeini that they had the Americans' support; I don't know what kinds of lies they told Khomeini. But he also supported the opening with the Americans. It was not something he did not know; they opened the door with America with his knowledge, and then they became stronger in the country than he was.

This was games-within-games. Now, the parallel becomes so amusing: in America, which is more sophisticated, the same thing happens. McFarlane whispers in the president's ear, he gets the okay, and nobody else gets involved, not even the legal counsel.

If Iran does these things, it's acceptable, but not in America. But it happened in both countries that this secrecy developed, with a lot of mystery and games-within-games. And suddenly, for a stupid reason — I don't know who injected this idea in their minds — they want to show that the Iranians are really sincere, that they will release the hostages.

Ghorbanifar came to me and said, "They want us to show some evidence of the release of the hostages." I introduced the idea that I gave a million dollars. And then Ghorbanifar said, "They will do it, but they want more evidence that America is also sincere. They want ten million dollars more, in spare parts."

In the war between Iran and Iraq, one million or ten million dollars is nothing; it's one minute in the whole operation. I said to Ghorbanifar, "You have to be careful. This is going to be an opening for you guys, and if you start pushing the Americans too far, you will create a problem for the whole area, and you will lose in what you are trying to accomplish."

He says, "Well, we will not release all the hostages to them. One hostage." I said, "If you admit that you have hostages and you are going to release one, you have put yourself in more serious trouble, because until now, as a state, you don't know about these hostages — who took them. But now you tell me you can release them one by one, like popcorn. I think this is crazy."

He left my place. They took him to America; he met with North; they put a lie detector on him. Some of the people were convinced that he was sincere; some of them said he was a double agent. You have to accept that he was a double agent for his country and for the purpose he wanted to use the Americans.

Now, because the Americans did not go the way they should go, they played into his hands; they started dealing, and suddenly I was isolated. There was one big deal, for eighteen million dollars, that Nimrodi and Schwimmer got involved in. And in the end they fell into this same situation — that they had no bridging for financing. They thought the Iranians would put up the money.

The Iranians would not trust them with a dollar, so they came running to me. I said, "I don't know whether I can be involved in something like that. It is too complicated for me." Then Nimrodi said, "You go ahead. We will protect you." So I gave them five million dollars.

I didn't want them to ship everything at once. They said they would give me a profit on it. It became like a business deal: they paid me 15 percent above the five million dollars, in about thirty days. It was a good return on the money. Later they wanted another ten million dollars. That was given, and that's the end of the story, because then the story was out, and the ten million dollars are to this day frozen in Geneva. So really, from a business point of view, we lost money.

Yaacov Nimrodi I have said what the real story was one hundred times, but nobody wants to listen to me. Before Nir came in, they had decided to release the rest of the hostages; I was the contact with Iran. They asked for one hundred HAWK missiles. They gave us proof that the moment the missiles will arrive, they will release the hostages.

We tried to find an airplane. I signed a contract: for twenty-four million dollars, we were giving them eighty HAWKs, the new model.

David Kimche We had no idea these HAWKs were defective in any manner or form. No one had the brilliant idea to send them defective HAWKs.

What probably happened was that someone in the air force that had to supply these HAWKs thought: Why give them good ones if we can give less good ones? We certainly had no intention of making a double-cross — we, meaning the ones who were leading and handling this operation.

Yaacov Nimrodi A week before the shipment, I got the money from the Iranians, but someone in the Ministry of Defense decided to send the old, old kind of missiles. My assistant, Yehuda, was at Mr. Schwimmer's house when representatives of the IDF and the Defense Ministry were talking about how to send the missiles.

Mr. Schwimmer speaks only English, and the officials were speaking in Hebrew. They discussed sending the old missiles: "Because they are Persians, they will not understand that."

Richard Secord McFarlane was in Switzerland with the president, and he called Ollie and had Ollie call me, because, unbeknownst to me, they already had under way a transfer of improved HAWK anti-aircraft missiles to Iran in a secret deal coming out of Israel.

They were really screwed up; it was laughable. We talked with Bud on the secure phone. Bud asked me if I thought we could arrange for a black [secret] flight through Portugal; we had been dealing in Portugal in support of the contras. I said, "Given time, I am pretty sure we can. But the government is changing there right now."

So he said, "Go out there and see if you can." He asked me to go to Israel and talk to Al Schwimmer. I knew Schwimmer when he was the head of Israel Aircraft Industries. McFarlane also wanted me to see David Kimche and Mendy Miron, who was the director general of the Ministry of Defense and was a friend of mine.

They wanted me to track through all of this and how it got so badly screwed up. So I met with each of these people and finally got the story on this incredibly snarled snafu — a perfect example of how when you get a bunch of slicksters together to try to do a deal, they don't know anything about the technology; they keep the experts frozen out because they don't want any help.

This little plan for HAWK transfers to Iran had been hatched by Yaacov Nimrodi and Al Schwimmer and Ghorbanifar and one other Iranian — we were never sure who it was. It was one of the ayatollahs. They hatched this plan in a meeting in Europe. None of those fools knew that the Iranians already had the largest HAWK deployment in the world, including the U.S. Army.

The Iranians wanted a high-altitude surface-to-air missile, and the HAWK is optimized for low-altitude, low fliers. They wanted to shoot the high fliers and fast movers coming out of Iraq. The U.S. doesn't have any such weapon; the Russians do. That's why the Iranians were so furious. Their people said, "We already have seven hundred of these HAWKs. What? Are you crazy?" Then they were demanding that the HAWKs be removed, which we did. I got sucked into that thing like it was a whirlpool.

Yaacov Nimrodi   I was in Geneva — in a hotel with Ghorbanifar, the head of Shabak [Shin Bet], and three Hezbollah guards — waiting for the missiles. The telephone rings. Who is speaking? The [Iranian] prime minister. They opened one box — only one box. First, they saw the Star of David, then Israeli numbers, and that the missiles are not new ones but a very, very old series. The prime minister spoke with Ghorbanifar. He told him, "You are a liar; your friends are liars. If tomorrow you do not bring the money, we will kill [some of] the hostages."

After the prime minister spoke to Ghorbanifar and warned him, I took the telephone and spoke to him in Farsi. I explained that this was a mistake. I said, "Tomorrow morning I will pay the twenty-four million dollars back." I assured him that everything would be okay, but that I would check on it. I called Schwimmer and asked him to check with the Ministry of Defense in the morning.

They told Ghorbanifar, "All your family is here; we will kill them." Ghorbanifar started to cry. So Schwimmer spoke with Haim at the Ministry of Defense, and Haim told him, "The missiles are new. They have to look in the head of the missile; we did some changing."

In twenty-four hours I got the money back from the ministry. I went to the bank with four Hezbollah and with Ghorbanifar. Then they released the airplane and the pilots [who had flown to Tehran], without the missiles. So now what to do? It was a mess.

Oliver North   I never met Peres in all of this. My initial introduction as an active participant, not simply as someone who was tracking on it, was when I got a call. I believe it was November 17, from Geneva, Switzerland, where Bud McFarlane was meeting with the president. He said, "You are going to get a call from Yitzhak Rabin." Well, I'm not used to getting calls from defense ministers of foreign countries. And Rabin called me in my office, on an unlisted number.

I said, "Bud, he's already called me." So Bud said, "Get up to New York right away. Take the shuttle and go meet with him. Here is his room number in the Waldorf-Astoria. See if you can carry out what they want to do."

David Kimche   I have never heard of any New York meeting in December 1985. The person in charge on the political side in December was myself; on the operational side, it was Yaacov Nimrodi and Schwimmer. Nir wasn't in the picture at the time, so it could only have been one of the three of us.

Why should Rabin have had to meet with North when we had an

open line to Bud McFarlane? It's not logical. I was present in that London meeting in December, and there was no meeting with Oliver North beforehand. Definitely not.

Oliver North That was my first act of operational involvement in this endeavor. Up until then, my job was, if we knew that Mike Ledeen had a meeting with somebody like Ghorbanifar, to make sure — it is a matter of public law that when you wish to have wiretaps or surveillance in this country it is conducted by the FBI — that the surveillance warrants and court orders were properly handled.

I would prepare the documents in my office and take them to the director of the FBI and head of the CIA. Of course, the first person to sign off is the national security adviser. The attorney general takes it to the court, and then the FBI guys call me back and say, "Where do we need this stuff?" That was my job until November 17.

I came back to Washington after meeting Rabin, prepared the paperwork, and said, "Here's what he wants to do." And Bud said, "Go do it." Notwithstanding his alternative recollections today, there are documents. There are two things that, if I was at all smart, saved me. One was that I documented everything; number two was that I never had a meeting with any of these people that was not recorded. I insisted on it, Casey supported me on it, and they went into extremis sometimes to provide that kind of surveillance.

I did not want anybody — days, weeks, or months later — to say that North was off on his own, doing things that other people didn't know about. I was not ashamed of what I was doing, but I sure didn't want anybody to misunderstand, to think that in what I was doing I was exceeding my mandate, or doing things that other people weren't aware of.

Ultimately there was salvation. None of us ever expected the thing to turn into what it did. We all knew that it was a serious political liability, but no one ever thought he would be accused of criminal behavior.

McFarlane Breaks Down

Michael Ledeen I called Kimche and said, "Bud is having a crisis. You're the only person I can think of who might be able to do something about it. Please come."

And he came. He saw McFarlane and North, and I had lunch with him right after that conversation. Kimche said, "Look, it's hopeless; he's gone. Strong people, when they stand against the wind, some of them bend and ride it out; others try to stand against it and break. And he's broken. My experience is that you can't put him back together again. Forget it; he's not going to do this."

And that is when North got out of control, because McFarlane could control him and nobody else could. Poindexter might have, but he had another tragedy: he had asked [Donald] Fortier to monitor North, and Don got cancer. Poindexter, who is a terrifically honorable person, had been told by the doctors that if he replaced Fortier, it would be a psychological blow; his chances of recovery would be diminished if he saw that his job had been filled by somebody else. So John didn't fill that slot.

NIMRODI AND SCHWIMMER ARE
REMOVED FROM THE OPERATION

Uri Simhoni   Nir wanted them out; he pushed them aside. There was a lot of money on the table, and he wanted to do the money himself. I believe that this was the motive. Nimrodi still believes that Nir made millions; this was supposed to be Nimrodi's money and was taken by Nir. It could be true or not true.

Yaacov Nimrodi   Nir arranged that the first person to be removed from the operation was Ledeen. They pushed him out; they put him outside like a dog.

He was a good man, but without *betzim* [balls]. Some say that Ledeen got money from the first TOW sale, but I don't believe it.

Michael Ledeen   I don't know why I was cut out. My suspicion — and what seems to check out — is that North wanted me out of there because he wanted to take over the whole operation so he could get his hands on some of the money for the contras, and he certainly knew I wouldn't have gone for that, because I didn't think we ought to be doing anything for the hostages. So North planted the story that Nir had said I was getting money for it — which cost me two years of Judge Walsh [the independent counsel in the Iran-contra investigation].

Roy Furmark   Once the private sector had been eliminated, the Israeli government wanted to know what was going on, so they moved Nir right in so that they could keep their hand in. If anything happened, they wanted to get credit for it.

With Schwimmer and Nimrodi out — and it's all taking place via Washington — they wanted to know what was going on. They didn't want to be left out of their "baby," which they had originated, because Ghorbanifar was their baby, and they brought him to Washington.

Eitan Haber   We did it secretly, here in this office [Israel's Ministry of Defense in Tel Aviv]. There were, let's say, four or five people involved in this story. We thought we were doing our best. Nobody knew. A huge part of the story has not yet been published. One day I'll write the real story of Irangate, because it looks to me as if I'll be the only one to survive.[*]

When Irangate came to this office, it was after Nimrodi and Schwimmer were out of it. Rabin wanted the government involved, not the arms dealers. He said, "This is a story of a government, not of arms dealers." He hated arms dealers.

Uri Simhoni   There was nothing behind it from the very beginning. Ghorbanifar and the others were all middlemen. I will never understand Rabin's involvement: you have the power and you go around your own power, the same as in the Pollard affair. I cannot understand how someone who is responsible — who gets the proposals, who sees the papers — won't know that it's bullshit. People are mistake-prone; given the opportunity to make mistakes, they grab it. There is something in our brain that is preplanned genetically to make any possible mistake.

ENTER AMIRAM NIR

Rafi Eitan   Prime Minister Peres came to power in 1984, and one of the first things he did in the first week was that he called me and said, "Look, I'm going to replace you with Amiram Nir." I said, "Okay. Give me a few months." What could I do?

Richard Secord   When they put Amiram Nir into the mix, he was very persuasive and influential. Nir had the ear of the prime minister; there is no question that he was the prime minister's guy.

Craig Fuller   Nir did appear at some briefings we had. He sat in the back of the room; he never said anything. I saw him as somebody who

---

[*] We interviewed Haber on March 25, 1996, less than five months after the assassination, on November 4, 1995, of Yitzhak Rabin, who had become prime minister of Israel for a second time. Haber was deeply traumatized by the assassination of Rabin, with whom he had had a long and close relationship.

was basically an intelligence officer, as a very buttoned-down operative who was running a covert program for the Israelis.

Howard Teicher The truth is that once again, as in the case of Rafi Eitan, we were not dealing, unbeknownst to us, with a professional. Indeed, when Nir took this affair over from Kimche and the Mossad people, it basically became a Keystone Kops operation.

Amiram Nir — no disrespect to the profession — was an Israeli television correspondent who fancied himself a counterterrorism expert. He made Oliver North — who at least had some years working on this — actually appear to be a true counterterrorism expert. Ollie really wasn't a counterterrorism expert. We were all bureaucrats assigned to issues. It became Ollie's issue.

Nir was Walter Mitty again — tough guy and hard-nosed Walter Mitty — and really political. He was in this job because his father-in-law had basically put Peres in office, and his father-in-law was owed, big time. And Peres took care of him; he gave Nir this job.

Rafi Eitan It's completely right to say that Nir didn't have the background for the position. But it is the privilege of the Israeli prime minister to change his advisers and to choose whom he wants — with experience or without experience. I felt awkward about it, but I knew that this was the privilege of the prime minister.

Richard Secord I liked Amiram Nir; he was really a good guy. He was a reserve officer of some standing, like a lot of men in Israel. He had only one eye; the other one was knocked out in an accident, not in war. I met his wife a couple of times; she was the daughter of a powerful family in the news media business.

Judy Nir Shalom, widow of Amiram Nir Amiram was Peres's campaign manager in the 1984 election. Before that, Amiram had been a military journalist for television, and in the military he was a tank battalion commander. And he did his doctorate at Tel Aviv University.

Amiram was a Zionist — an idealist. He could do anything. After he left the army, they asked him to come back for a year. He loved the army. We had our honeymoon in Lebanon.

Nimrod Novick Nir and North appreciated each other, felt very comfortable with each other. That was a very important instrument in Nir's taking the operation away from Nimrodi and Schwimmer: he managed to produce evidence from the White House that it was their preference. And the one who produced the evidence for him was his friend Oliver North.

Adnan Khashoggi There were two American channels dealing in Iran: the Ghorbanifar track, and the CIA, through Secord and Hakim, with Rafsanjani. And the White House is sitting there, dealing on one track, and the CIA on another.

Now, Rafsanjani was also considered a moderate, and here is Khomeini, and both of them [the two American channels] are showing them [Rafsanjani and Khomeini] options to the Americans. And being a cunning old man, he [Khomeini] okays both channels. At the end these two channels conflicted with each other; this is where the mistrust came of Ghorbanifar and Rafsanjani. If they had opened up with the CIA and with each other, this thing would not have happened; they could always have double-checked what was going on.

When the CIA discovered there were two channels, they wanted to coordinate, using North; the CIA had been involved with him in Nicaragua and all these other places. So suddenly North became very strong, because he had two roads to work on: the Ghorbanifar road and the Secord road.

One of our interviewees, who was close to the operation and declined to be quoted for attribution, told us that Nir was able to convince Prime Minister Peres to remove Nimrodi and Schwimmer from the arms-for-hostages operation because they could ostensibly cause trouble for Peres, and that Peres would never have removed Nimrodi and Schwimmer on his own.

Our source stated further that from that time on Nimrodi tried to destroy Amiram Nir, and that his animosity toward Nir may have explained why he purchased the newspaper Ma'ariv.

Yaacov Nimrodi After Irangate was revealed, I went to *Yediot Ahronot* with a small article explaining what had happened — Amiram Nir married into the *Yediot* family; Judy Moses, Nir's wife, is a *Yediot* heiress. The article went from *Yediot* to *Ma'ariv*, and the editor said, "This won't be published."

So I said to the editor, "There was collusion. I will buy *Ma'ariv*, and on the first day I will fire you and your dog." And I bought the newspaper for fourteen and a half million dollars, and today it is worth one hundred and fifty million dollars.

Of course, Nir removed me, Mr. Schwimmer, and Dave Kimche, all in one shot. I put the blame for all this on Rabin, not on Peres. Because of the quarreling between Rabin and Peres, Rabin brought in Amiram Nir against Shimon.

Oliver North   I did not trust these people [Schwimmer and Nimrodi]. It seemed to me right from the beginning that this was an endeavor fraught with enormous political consequences. If it goes awry, there has to be someone — not the president — who is going to take the spear in his chest. It was very clear to Poindexter that there were going to be one or two people to do that: one is named Poindexter; the other is named North.

Under these conditions, you would at least like to have a little more control over the outcome. I am not a control freak, but at that point you basically put the fate of a presidency, your own personal situation, and probably the future promotion of a man who, in my opinion, was capable of being chairman of the Joint Chiefs of Staff in the hands of people you have absolutely no control over whatsoever. So let's get them out of it and let's take control of this operation. And John supported that.

Yaacov Nimrodi   I put most of the blame on him [Rabin] because he adopted Amiram Nir. Poindexter wrote a letter — from Reagan to Israel, and Nir and all the group removed us, Schwimmer and me, from the story.

John Poindexter   It was not North's suggestion to remove the Israelis. It was actually Ed Meese who expressed the opinion that if the president were going to proceed with it, we should do it directly, and not through Israel. His reasoning had something to do with the Foreign Assistance Act.

David Kimche   Nir went to the United States. He came back saying that the new people in the game, Poindexter, wanted a new team — wanted him — and for that reason Peres said, "Okay, you take over." But there wasn't a conscious decision to remove Nimrodi or Schwimmer — definitely not. Schwimmer is one of the closest people in Israel to Peres; he has complete and absolute faith in him. He never would consciously remove him. Never.

Nir was a manipulator, and he manipulated himself into this operation. He lied a few times to us about what he was going to do; he went to the States and convinced them that he had to be the man working opposite North. That's more or less how the change took place.

Fawn Hall Nir was kind of quiet; I don't think of him as much of a personality. He was hard-working, very serious and dedicated. He came into the office a lot. I would call him at midnight, at his wife's house: "Ollie's calling." He did not have Ollie's charm.

Yaacov Nimrodi After the incident with the HAWKs, we said we would supply the Iranians with three thousand TOW missiles. And here Amiram Nir entered into the picture. He said he could do it better than us. He came to the government here and said, "Let the Americans do it. We have to take the missiles from them. We will give them a base here, in Eilat; the missiles will come from the United States to Eilat, and then from Eilat to Tehran. They will use us as a transmission point."

So they said, "Okay. This is a very good idea." They didn't tell me, nor Al, nor David, that we are out at all. We continued: we were dealing with the Iranians; the Americans were dealing with Nir; he is dealing with the Iranians — with the same Iranians, with the same Ghorbanifar!

The Americans did it in their way, which was not the right way. Nir, who was the fuse in all of this — and was more clever than they were — taught them, but he never worked with the Iranians, with the intelligence. He was *mishooga* [crazy]; there was something in his head, exactly like Colonel North. They were the same. They did it alone.

We had decided to do it as private people. I bought the missiles from the Israeli ministry; I paid for them and showed the Americans that I had handled it with the Iranians, merchant to merchant. They [the Nir-North combination] came after the HAWK missiles, and it became official. That was a disaster.

Nimrod Novick Nir's most hostile partner was Rabin. Rabin didn't like him; he didn't like the appointment. Rabin was very happy when everyone was blocking Nir out.

But during his operation he gained Rabin's confidence by representing the Defense Ministry's perception and interest in the story — which was secondary and marginal — on the question of: Do we or don't we supply, off the shelf, and what happens to our stock at that time? [These were] parochial concerns of the minister of defense.

Nir came up with very creative solutions. He knew how to sell his merchandise; he knew the buyers very, very well. It was more his initiative and talent in obtaining the green light than the eagerness on the part of his superiors.

The turning point was a note Rabin wrote to Shimon during a cabinet session, saying something like: "I am increasingly appreciative of Amiram.

He proves to be creative." And Rabin became more supportive of Nir's involvement than Peres.

Albert Hakim   Money was keeping them together. When the second channel was introduced, that stopped. The whole purpose of that union was profiteering. This was an area where they could profit. A businessman works on a profit. You must differentiate between that group and myself.

Of course, Nimrodi wanted to help his country. The Israelis probably did. But they used an agent of theirs, Ghorbanifar, whom they knew would make deals with the mullahs and create a profit-sharing momentum.

They knew they could also benefit from this profiteering momentum created by the Iranians. Probably Ghorbanifar, brainwashing his connections in Iran, said, "What the hell, let's just make some money out of this thing. None of you can be assured that you can stay on." So the profiteering, in my opinion, was: buy into Ghorbanifar. And the Israelis had a free ride not only for making money but also for pursuing their political objectives.

THE RULES OF ENGAGEMENT

Oliver North   They were brought in by the Israelis and/or Ghorbanifar as the "financiers" behind the thing; everybody had to pay for things in advance. The rules of engagement that I had, which had been set up before I ever got into this thing, were that nothing will move from the United States of America, or from U.S.-controlled assets — meaning weapons that had been shipped to Israel that were essentially theirs but were restricted by U.S. sanction as to what they could do with them.

The rules of engagement, which were reaffirmed to me on a very regular basis, were that nothing will move until it's paid for, so somebody had to come up with the money. It turns out that the Iranians weren't putting up the money. We learned this in the aftermath — that it was coming out of Khashoggi, Schwimmer, the whole crowd, this bridge-financing operation that would, once we had the money transferred to a U.S.-controlled account, meaning the CIA, then be transferred to the Pentagon. And then the missiles would be picked up at Redstone [Arsenal in Huntsville, Alabama] and flown to wherever they were going to be distributed.

Roy Furmark   Nobody could trust anybody, but Khashoggi said, "I'll bridge it — I'll trust the Israelis, and I'll trust the Iranians," because the supplier wanted to be paid before the goods left his warehouse and the Iranians wouldn't pay for it until it landed. So you needed a bridge, because the supplier didn't know once the goods got on a ship whether he would be paid. And if the Iranians prepaid for the material, they didn't know whether it would ever reach port, so Khashoggi was taking a risk.

MOTIVES OF THE PLAYERS

Michael Ledeen   It was clear to me — at the level I was talking to Kimche, Schwimmer, and Nimrodi — that they all felt that if the Iranian initiative was a success, it would help alleviate the damage done by Pollard. So, certainly, from the Israeli side, there was a motive.

Yaacov Nimrodi   We were three people: I was the businessman; Mr. Schwimmer knew about missiles, about aircraft; and Dave Kimche was the politician. We started without the Americans; with the first five hundred missiles, they were not in the picture. We took five hundred missiles from here, brought an airplane from South America, loaded the missiles, got the five million dollars, and sent them. And after three weeks, they released the first hostage.

Amiram Nir then thought: If they can do it, I can do it. He had been appointed the prime minister's adviser on antiterror warfare, without any experience. Peres took him in; he had nothing to do except to write articles about antiterror warfare. He brought North into the story.

Michael Ledeen   For Israel, that is absolutely standard. That's the way they operate; it gives them deniability. If a Schwimmer is out to dinner with a Khashoggi, so what? Two businessmen are talking to each other. The fact that Khashoggi is reporting back to the king of Saudi Arabia, and Schwimmer is reporting back to the prime minister of Israel? Well, all right, the prime minister and the king can always say, "I don't know what he is doing."

Oliver North   Most of the financiers were in it for the money. I never talked to Khashoggi about it; I never met Furmark; and I never met the rest of these clowns. I did meet Ghorbanifar, and there is absolutely no doubt in my mind what his motivation was. I don't think he's got a drop of human kindness in him. He could put on the best act in the world, but I don't detect any great empathy for the hostages.

Michael Ledeen   I like Khashoggi. He's fun to be with; he's intellectually fascinating; he has one of those constantly febrile minds that's looking at all sides of everything, trying to understand things, trying to see how to get a profit out of it.

And he really wanted to advance peace in the Middle East; there is no doubt about that. He was intrigued by Ghorbanifar for these reasons: a fun personality; a source of money; a channel into Iran at the highest level; a way to advance political goals in the region. It was Khashoggi, as I understand it, who really brought Ghorbanifar to the Israelis.

He always had Israeli friends. My understanding is that the Schwimmer-Khashoggi friendship goes way, way back, and that it was one of the basic channels through which contacts were passed between Israel and Saudi Arabia.

Roy Furmark   He [Khashoggi] did it for a lot of reasons. He is a visionary; he saw that if this worked out and the hostages were released, Iran would come closer to the West, and there would be development in Iran, and he could participate as a businessman.

And looking at it as a Saudi, if Iran started to prosper, they would no longer be a potential threat in the area; they would be happy — working, prospering, and enjoying life. So these are the reasons Khashoggi got involved.

He had the blessing of the Israeli government and the American government, so he said to himself: Where's the risk? He wouldn't have done it if the Israelis hadn't gotten the green light and the Americans hadn't proceeded. This was not an off-the-wall thing.

Craig Fuller   Our national security people had a pretty good idea of what motivated the Israelis, but you never know. And, again, there is no doubt in my mind that the constant reporting on the hostages had an emotional impact upon people. If we were just talking about a strategy to establish relationships, or contacts, with moderate factions for the purpose of having a relationship, then it never would have gone to some of these lengths. It was because of the feeling that they could help us with the hostage issue.

Nimrod Novick   Every important thing Peres has done he has done outside the establishment — and more often than not, against the establishment. When this operation happened, his natural inclination was not to give it to the Mossad, which is what should have been done; they are the ones responsible for special operations and countries we have no diplomatic relations with.

But he said, "I am going to test it first, with these two guys, one of whom [Schwimmer] I trust very much; he's been my outside, right-hand man for over thirty years. The other one [Nimrodi] knows the country, and I know that he is a shrewd operator. Let these two guys find out for me what this is all about."

That is classic Peres. Had he brought it up for discussion in the government, had he brought it up to the internal cabinet for security, I don't think it would have been accepted as the way to proceed.

SECORD AND HAKIM

As the arms sales to Iran and the contra resupply program developed, Richard Secord and Albert Hakim, who had entered into a business partnership in 1983, became involved in North's activities under the rubric of the organization that was indentified as "the Enterprise" during the Iran-contra investigation.

Albert Hakim   In 1983 General Secord and I became partners in Stanford Technology Trading Group. We started one or two projects that were not successful. And then, in 1984, this project was offered to me. However, both of these projects were ongoing.

They were not successful because they did not have the businessman's ingredient: they did not have a financial institution that could give them what they were trying to get. In my opinion, what they wanted to get — when I say they, I mean the Reagan administration — was to make sure that the objectives were achieved without the financial involvement of the United States government. It takes a businessman to have the creativity and the financial, legal, operational network to achieve that. They tried it without that institution, and it was not going well.

It was only then that they contacted me and asked if I would be willing to participate and to use my total business structure and network, including what I had had in Geneva since 1971 or 1972. So that institution was not created for the purposes of Iran-contra at all; it was an existing entity.

Richard Secord   I first met him [Hakim] in Iran in the midseventies, when I was the U.S. Air Force commander. Our mission in Iran — the

Military Assistance Group [MAG] — was the largest one at the time. Hakim was a contractor there, and he came to see me to protest about something a person on my staff had done, about advising the Iranians on a communications program; he was just raising hell. He came to see me again, in the Pentagon, in 1980 or 1981.

Albert Hakim It became necessary for me to contact him for a project that I was trying to implement for the Iranian Air Force. He was the chief adviser to them; that's how we became acquainted.

Actually, our relationship started with a clash; that is what brought us closer together. The nature of my business — it has never been arms, it has always been governmental, I have never dealt with a nongovernmental organization — has been in the area of high technology.

Richard Secord When I retired in 1983, I went to work as a consultant for the corporation that trained the Saudi National Guard. And Hakim called me one day and made me a business proposition to start a company called Stanford Technology Trading Group International [STTGI]; he offered to put up the necessary capital, which he did. That is how we got together.

Albert Hakim The word *partnership* has deep meaning; there was no such partnership. We were working on one project, and we had certain arrangements for that project. To be a partner means that you have many activities, that you share the losses and the profits. That was not the case.

There were actually two projects: the Nicaraguan project and the Iranian project. General Secord and I had a partnership, Stanford Technology Trading Group International, which was basically designed to handle systems projects for the Middle East — where both could use our connections.

Then I had a separate company, Stanford Technology Corporation, that was established in 1974, for manufacturing and, later on, only for systems integration. General Secord was not a partner in that. Basically, Stanford Technology Trading Group International turned out to be the company giving service to the so-called Enterprise; there was no such institution established as the Enterprise. We adopted this name during the course of the investigations. That was the only time it became necessary to call it in a nondescriptive way for the purpose of the hearings.

And Stanford Technology Corporation was a company that had the capabilities of implementing the work that STTGI would generate. STTGI was, effectively, a marketing company focusing on specific projects, whereas Stanford Technology Corporation was a traditional company, manufacturing systems integration implementation and primarily focused on high-tech areas. That's where my background is.

The STTGI died with the conclusion of the two projects, i.e., the Nicaraguan project and the Iranian project. That company was dissolved; so was our partnership.

Richard Secord I was aching to get back at Iran. In 1980, after the Desert One fiasco,° the Carter administration called on me to form a new task force, and I did. I put together a quite powerful secret task force. Desert One had eight helicopters; my force had ninety-five choppers and five thousand troops.

Howard Teicher When he showed up in the Tehran operation, Ollie said, "Secord is handling all the logistics." I had no idea what Secord had been doing. He thought of himself as an Iran expert. North once said, "Secord really wanted to be involved in this." There was never any sense that there was anything unpatriotic about what he was doing.

North said that all this had been approved. When you have an NSC-supplied dedicated satellite up there to support you, and you see that everybody is working with it, you figure that this is an approved operation; we are not here doing something on our own.

And Secord knew how to get all the covert stuff — how to get an airplane, and take a tail number from another airplane. That was the nature of his activities, along with logistics.

John Poindexter Although Ollie is given credit for involving Dick Secord, it was Bill Casey's decision to use Secord as the agent. The finding made the director of Central Intelligence responsible for the overall program; it was his responsibility to decide how it was going to be implemented, and he decided to do it through a third party — Secord.

THE ARMS SALES AND THE ADMINISTRATION

Vice President Bush

Robert C. McFarlane At the outset, in July and August of 1985, when the request came and I briefed the president, together with Shultz, Weinberger, and Casey — in four or five meetings in the Residence [the

---

° A failed attempt by the U.S. military to rescue Americans being held hostage at the U.S. embassy in Tehran.

family quarters of the White House] after Reagan got back from the hospital — in that window of three weeks, Bush was party to those briefings.

He heard the arguments; he heard Shultz say, "Don't do this," [and] Weinberger say, "Don't do this." And then the president made the decision, and I notified the vice president, so he's witting about it.

If you spend very much time in this town, you find that part of the political culture is that we become expert at obfuscation — portraying events to the self-interest, to be self-serving. I say that because I don't think George Bush lied about this; he did what a politician does. He said, "I wasn't in the loop." What does that mean? To you and me, it means he didn't know anything about it. But to him, it doesn't mean that; it means that he didn't make the decision — and that's Washington-speak. A court of law probably wouldn't have said it was perjury. But he was there; he knew about it.

Nir Briefs Bush in Jerusalem

Craig Fuller I learned about Iran-contra through what became a fairly well known meeting that George Bush had with Amiram Nir in Jerusalem. As I heard this story, told by the Israeli operative — North's counterpart — I was surprised at what I was hearing. Vice President Bush had told me that we couldn't necessarily rely on this person to tell us the truth, but I was supposed to record what he was telling us. I was told, "Don't talk to anybody about this. Seal the document. Give it to North."

Donald Gregg I went to Israel with Bush in 1986. There was a meeting that North arranged. I was cut out of it; I expected to go to it. Craig Fuller said, "No, I'm sorry, Don, you are not included in this meeting." I was taken aback, because that was one of the few times that that had ever happened. Bush was very open and inclusive when he could be.

I think that North was very careful to keep me out because he knew me quite well, and I think he knew what my reactions would have been to some of the things he was involved in.

I was not briefed about the meeting with Nir [on June 29, 1986]. The first time I ever heard about it was when I read Fuller's memo.

Craig Fuller It was presented to me by Ollie North that this was important to the prime minister — that it was important to the effort that was under way.

Peres never said anything in my presence to confirm that. He did acknowledge that he understood that we had the meeting, and that he appreciated that. I don't believe that he and the vice president ever discussed it privately.

Shimon Peres Nir told me this was a request that came from Washington — that he was asked by his counterpart in America to brief the vice president. It wasn't my initiative. I said okay.

Oliver North It wasn't important to me that Nir brief the vice president in Jerusalem; it was important to Nir. He was very close to the Likud bloc at the time when you had a Labor government; he wanted to make sure he wasn't going to be aced out. At the same time he was looking for a little bit of reassurance from us that he had our backing.

Craig Fuller We were told that it was important to Peres that we have this meeting. I was never sure that he knew exactly what the meeting was about. But North indicated that having this meeting was important to keep the program on track. That is what he told me, which is what I told Vice President Bush. The vice president said, "Did he tell you what the program was?" I said, "No."

The meeting lasted about twenty minutes. If I had known what the subject was, I probably would not have taken such good notes; they are practically verbatim, written in very quick fashion, as Nir was talking, and he spoke slowly.

George Bush said almost nothing. When we were through, I spent some time literally rewriting the notes. When I came back, I typed up the report and gave it to Oliver North. What made the notes unique was that they were one of the only accounts that anybody ever took of any conversation, or any meeting, in which we had an Israeli telling us what, exactly, had transpired.

I knew when George Bush was hearing all this that he knew more than I did, but not a whole lot more. He wasn't entirely familiar with the details that were being relayed to him. Of course, it was all on the effort to deal with the factions in Iran; it had nothing to do with the contras.

The vice president felt he did not want to have the meeting alone — which could have proved to be a mistake in some ways. He told Poindexter that he would have the meeting but wanted me there to take notes, so he got a sort of dispensation for me to know only what was revealed in that meeting.

We never discussed it. The only time it ever came up was around November 1986, when I remember him saying, "We have some reason to believe we may see another hostage come out." We were in Houston at the time, on election day, and he said, "Touch base with the National Security folks, and let them know where you are, because we may have something on the hostages." So that was the only indication that I had that this thing was continuing to go forward.

I have asked myself a few times since then: Should I have had a different reaction? Because I had basically been given the details of what had been going on for several months. I think that all of us looked at it as an effort to deal with this horrible situation concerning the hostages, and wanted to believe the Iran part of the Iran-contra deal was legitimate — that we were trying to find factions with whom we could deal.

Lawrence Walsh   Secord believed that the meeting made the vice president an advocate for a continuation of the arms sales. The meeting came at a critical time, when the Iranians were refusing to pay for the HAWK parts that Ghorbanifar had bought from the United States, through Secord. A small planeload had been delivered, but the major planeload was still in Israel.

Poindexter and McFarlane shut down the deal. Nir was urging its reopening, because Ghorbanifar was in a very difficult position — he had prepaid for the arms and could not pay his bankers for the amount he had borrowed to make the prepayment. He was actually fearing assassination at that point.

It was not just concern for Ghorbanifar, but a concern for his talking that, I think, motivated the Israelis, through Nir, to try to persuade the president and the vice president to let this go on. I think that two days after this meeting, President Reagan authorized the full delivery of the HAWK missile parts, and then, about two weeks after that, a hostage was released.

Bush has always claimed that it was a general discussion; Nir claimed that he was explaining to Bush the need for the serialization of the hostage release, rather than releasing them all at once, in advance. And that became the basis for the continued arms sale, so there were circumstances that suggested that the meeting may have had more significance than Bush claimed.

Shultz and Weinberger

Adnan Khashoggi I didn't know that Shultz was not informed; it was a shock to me. The least you do is inform inside your house. Until now it is a mystery in my mind: Why weren't they informed?

Now, they say that Bush didn't know. It is possible that he didn't know, because if we see that Shultz, the most important man after the president, was not involved, then it is just as well that the vice president would not be involved. After the fact, I think that when it got hot, everybody was involved, but it was too late.

Now, whose mistake is this? Is it McFarlane's to keep it limited? Does he see political benefit in working with the Israelis — with the president to give him all the credit — without the others involved? All kinds of stupid reasoning can come out of it, but none of the reasons making sense.

Robert C. McFarlane The evidence is contained in the cable that George [Shultz] wrote when I laid out a full explanation for what Kimche had said, and what I thought the risks were — the answer that George sent back that said, "Well, there are risks, but we could not let an opportunity like this go by, and I think you ought to take the next step; you ought to take the next step — not me."

But to his credit, when the ante was up on the arms side, he did come out and say, "No, I think the risks are too high." And he maintained that position all along. That said that he was quite witting of everything, and for him to have said he wasn't is just false. The evidence of that is in his own notes — Charlie Hill's notes.

The reason those notes were taken was because at meetings of what was called the "Family Group" — which George originated [and which consisted of] himself, Weinberger, Casey, and me; we would have lunch in the family dining room of the Residence as often as we were all in town, once a week was the target — there were no note-takers and no subordinates there.

I briefed them: "Here's what has happened on the Iranian front." And he'd go back and one-on-one with Charlie Hill; that's where the notes came from. To deny it is tawdry; it's not only dishonest, but it's disloyal. When the story broke — because I was responsible, it was my bad judgment — I had to say, "That's a time when people ought to stand up and be counted, from the president on down, to say: 'This is what I thought; this is what I did; I'm sorry it didn't work.'"

I think that if they had, it would not have gotten to be a scandal. But George said, "I never knew. They never told me." That's outrageous. Of course he knew. It's clear now — in the report of the independent counsel — in black and white.

George P. Shultz McFarlane fell into the Iran-contra trap, although when he left at the end of 1985 it was, for the moment, over; the episode had run its course. We had a meeting with the president, and Cap and I spoke out strongly, and things basically came to an end. But not for very long — the Israelis kept stimulating it.

Michael Ledeen Shultz was very tricky about this whole subject. He knew too much to be innocent and too little to be secretary of state.

I briefed Weinberger on what had happened in the summer of 1986. He was fascinated; he hadn't known anything about these political contacts and about the possibility for some kind of working relationship with what were called the dissident mullahs. He said, "Shultz really needs to know that. Would you brief Shultz?"

I said, "Sure. Set it up." He sort of laughed and said, "You will have better luck getting to him yourself." So I called Charles Hill and said that I had briefed Weinberger, and here's what it's about, and that if Shultz wanted to hear about it, I'd be happy to do it.

Some days later he called me back and said that Shultz was not interested. I think that Shultz wanted to put himself in a position that, if the thing succeeded, he would be able to say: "Well, I had my doubts, but I was a good soldier." And if it failed, he would be able to say: "I was against it from the beginning."

Alexander M. Haig Jr. By the time I left, I was convinced that Irangate would happen. It was an inevitable consequence of the procedures being pursued in the Reagan White House that there would be a screwup in the area of covert action.

I admire and respect Bill Casey; I don't blame any of this on him. There was a lack of systematic control of that area of our foreign policy apparatus that was at fault.

From my experience in prior administrations, I knew that the worst thing you could have is an administration that leads the president to believe that he can do tough things covertly and not share knowledge of what he is doing with the American people.

The men around the president, especially Bill Casey, believed they could achieve policy goals with covert action. I'm not against covert action, but it has to be done in peripheral areas, not in critical policy areas.

Giandomenico Picco   Every government has a stated policy and then they do twenty-five other things which are against that policy. Once I said to a very senior American diplomat, "I don't think this is consistent with what you told me three months ago." He said to me, "Johnny, are we talking about consistency or politics?"

The fact that any American government has many voices is taken for granted all the time, every day of the year, by the rest of the world. Every foreigner knows there are various decision-making centers in the United States — and that you have a struggle between four or five basic players.

The December 1985 White House Meeting

George P. Shultz   At the December 1985 meeting in the family quarters of the White House, I felt that Cap and I had won the day. And as it turned out, the next contact was the one that ended things.

Then, when McFarlane left, it started again. One of the Israelis visited Poindexter, and he went back to the president. Then we had a meeting in January, where I sounded off and Cap agreed with me. But I could see that around the room everybody else, including the vice president, was on a different side.

David Kimche   We made a choice to do everything we could on this operation. We would have done completely different things with a man like Ghorbanifar if there hadn't been the American angle. So, first and foremost, we wanted to say to the United States of America that we were an appreciative ally.

I was not aware of the dissension in the Reagan cabinet. How could I be? I assumed that if we are talking to the adviser to the president of the United States on national security — who sees the president every day — we are talking to the American administration. That's like talking to the president himself. None of us had any inkling that this was something that was not considered to be the right thing to do. We assumed that this was the United States of America that was asking us to do these things. We had no reason to question the internal machinations of the American administration — none at all.

Uri Simhoni   Oliver was a very good man. I am very sorry he tried to do too much without understanding the name of the game. The whole idea was stupid; the chance to do it was nil from the very beginning. There was nothing behind it; there were just stories. Oliver told me, "Your people said this . . ."

I said, "Oliver, what is the Israeli side? How come I don't know it?" He told me, "Amiram Nir."

Amiram came from nowhere. He was a journalist — not bad, but not a very good one; let's say a medium journalist. I believe that many facts in his personal history are not true. For example, he told me that he had been injured during a war, and later on I learned that it had happened in a car accident. Small things like that make the red lamp in your head start to blink about the man.

Through family relations — through the *Yediot Ahronot* family that was close to Peres — he became close to Peres during the election period, and Peres committed himself to making Nir something in the system. Nir wanted to be head of the Mossad, a job for which he had zero qualifications. So they made him the head of a small organization, one that had been promised to a brigadier general who had qualifications for the post. The general, who was twenty years older than Nir, was to be his deputy. The general said, "A month ago he couldn't even talk to me, and now he will be my boss? How come? How can you justify it?"

But Shimon Peres needed a channel between him and the Moses family, with all its powerful positions in Israel. Nir now had the job, but nothing to do; he could have spent two years looking at the ceiling. That was what people wanted him to do. But Amiram was a very creative man; he was very smart and adventurous, but with zero background and zero know-how.

And he started to make all the noises. For example, in a new book by the Israeli journalist Ron Adelist, it says that Nir used to meet regularly with Casey, that he reported to Peres that he met with Casey. I swear to you that he never met with Casey. If you understand the system, Casey cannot meet with Amiram Nir without reporting it to the head of the Mossad, just as the head of the Mossad cannot see an American official in Israel without reporting it to Casey.

I believe that what really happened was that Nir used to meet with Oliver North. North met with Casey. North would come back and say: "I told Casey . . ." Nir, who was much more sophisticated than Oliver, and more manipulative, used North.

I said, "Oliver, Nir talked with you on selling missiles to Iran? He is not supposed to do that; this is not his job. Why don't you call the Mossad? They can tell you if this is real or not. Nir can play with you and act like a big shot. But there is nothing behind him — no people, no organization, no logistical support. He has only one secretary, one small car, and one room, and that's it."

He said, "Uri, Rabin and Peres called me and told me to do it, to do it with Amiram, and now you tell me to do it with the Mossad. What am I supposed to do?" I said, "You know what you are supposed to do; you are supposed to listen to them and do the opposite. Listen to me: it will never happen; it will explode in your face. Only somebody who is totally unfamiliar with the whole structure of relations with Iran could ever dream of this. Believe me, this is crooks speaking to crooks, speaking to crooks. No one can really influence the thing."

President Reagan

In his desire to obtain the freedom of the American hostages being held in Lebanon, President Reagan developed a rationale for trading arms for hostages. His first reaction upon being presented by McFarlane with a plan for Israel to supply missiles to Iran in exchange for the release of the hostages was negative; the president insisted that the United States would not do business with nations that sponsored terrorism.

But by December 7, 1985 —Pearl Harbor Day—during a meeting in which Secretaries Shultz and Weinberger voiced their opposition to trading arms for hostages, the president had changed his mind, expressing his rationale this way: "It's the same thing as if one of my children was kidnapped and there was a demand for ransom. Sure, I don't believe in ransom, because it leads to more kidnapping. But if I find out that there's somebody who has access to the kidnapper and can get my child back without doing anything for the kidnapper, I'd sure do that."*

Ten years after Reagan rationalized his approval of trading arms for hostages, his supporters argue for having engaged the Iranians, while his critics continue to regard the episode as a black mark for the administration.

Nimrod Novick It may be surprising for someone who is not involved in politics. In politics you run into moments of conflicting interests, and then you have to decide which one you are pursuing at the moment — which one you compromise on, and to what extent. So you may be anti-Iranian, antiterrorist, through and through, but then you have an opportunity to save a few lives and you compromise. We've been there.

---

* As quoted by Reagan in his memoir *An American Life* (New York: Simon & Schuster, 1990), 512.

Oliver North   Their motivation was to keep us from getting cold feet. Nir knew from earlier meetings with him that I had grave reservations about this whole thing. I'm certainly not the author of the phrase, but "dealing with terrorists is not my way of dealing with terrorists." I like to deal with them the way we did with the airplane at Sigonella and with the raid on Gadhafi — that's my way of dealing with terrorists.

Terry Anderson   The day I came home my kidnappers told me that it [the taking of hostages] had not been a useful tactic. They have not engaged in those kinds of tactics since; they have had almost no kidnappings for political goals since that episode.

Had the arms-for-hostages thing gone through, and had we been released in that manner, it would have put Americans in serious danger. There would have been a great many more kidnappings. These are people without ethics or morals; they are only interested in the success of their strategies.

In that sense, you make mistakes. Those mistakes quite possibly cost us a lot of time in prison, but they didn't matter in the long run.

Benjamin Weir   Once I arrived home, I did not have confidence that the government would be able to secure the release of the four others [in my cell]. I regarded it as a very complicated situation. I understood, from the meeting with George Bush, that there would be no negotiation — which I understood to really mean, no communication with the captors.

On the other hand, at the time I was in the American embassy in Beirut I was told that people there were hoping that there would be another release. I was told that the U.S. government had in some way had a hand in my release, but I was not given any details about it.

David Jacobsen   I was the one hostage who came out who publicly supported President Reagan and Ollie North and Admiral Poindexter and Dick Secord.

President Reagan believed that it was in our interest not to let Iran lose the war — even though he disliked them for what they were — but to give them the defensive missiles so they could sit there and shoot back and forth with the Iraqis and continue the stalemate. Thus, our two worst players in the region would not have the time or money to go out and bother other people.

If we hadn't done that, the Soviets — who already had troops in Syria, twenty-five thousand in a military cadre in Iraq, and perhaps half a million troops in Afghanistan — would not have had a problem in moving troops into Iran. So if Iraq had won that war, perhaps the old Soviet Union wouldn't have broken up as early as it did.

David Abshire The president saw it as dealing with a faction in Lebanon that was dealing with a faction in Iran; it wasn't state to state. I showed him a poll that said that about 90 percent of the American people didn't believe that, and he looked at me and said, "Dave, I might be the only person in America who believes this wasn't arms for hostages, but that's what I believe."

He has a photographic memory. He takes a picture, and once he does, you don't change him. He felt that arms for hostages was immoral.

George P. Shultz Why is it that the United Nations last year traded arms for hostages in Bosnia? That's what they did, and the newspapers didn't even make anything out of it. The answer is that people who feel desperate about something will overlook the implications of what they're doing.

And I think that the staff people in the White House saw a weakness in President Reagan, that it just bothered him — "bothered" isn't the word — it just drove him nuts that there were these American hostages being mistreated. And he felt it was his responsibility to do something about it.

And there didn't seem to be anything to do, and here comes somebody who says: "I've got a deal for you, Mr. President. We have this problem with Iran. We'd like to turn our relations with Iran around, and we need to put forward a little good faith in the form of arms sales — and incidentally, Mr. President, we're going to get our hostages back in the process. How about it?"

He buys into it because he has such a wish about the hostages. And then people create this rationale, and then they distort the intelligence, and you're off to the races. That is the way I think it happened. But who knows? I'm tired of the subject.

Shimon Peres Usually meetings with the president were never under four eyes. This time, after a meeting, the president called me and said he would like to speak with me tête-à-tête. He said, "I want to thank you very much for all you are doing."

Benjamin Weir At the time I returned to the United States, I had a very brief conversation with President Ronald Reagan, who assured me that he was glad I had returned and that there had been no payment of money for my release. Later I received a telegram from him, reiterating that there had been no payment, and no trade of any kind, for my release.

It was quite a long time afterward — I think it was through the report of the Tower Commission — that I began to get a sense that there had been some shipment of arms to Iran. And much later, through the testimony, of arms shipments to Iran. But I understood that it had really begun prior to my having been taken hostage and had been provided by Israel, without the explicit consent of the American government.

Shimon Peres North became active with one of our people; the man who kept in touch with North was Amiram Nir. The president sent Amiram a thank-you note, which is most unusual.

At one point during our interview with Judy Nir Shalom on July 31, 1996, at her home in Ramat Gan, Israel, she showed us President Reagan's thank-you letter to Prime Minister Peres, written on October 3, 1986, one month before the Al-Shiraa disclosure, in which the U.S. commander in chief demonstrated knowledge not only of Israel's role in trading arms for hostages but specifically of Amiram Nir's activities on behalf of the endeavor. Reagan wrote:

> Dear Mr. Prime Minister,
>
> I want you to know of my personal gratitude and that of the people of the United States for the extraordinary efforts being undertaken on our mutual behalf by Mr. Amiram Nir. As you are aware he is participating in an endeavor of great importance for both our nations and peoples.
>
> Throughout, Mr. Nir has demonstrated exceptional discretion, perseverance and personal courage. He is a rare man who well serves both our countries in a common cause. I share your hope that this initiative will arrive at a swift and successful conclusion.
>
> Sincerely,
> Ronald Reagan

While a staff member could, conceivably, have drafted the letter, signed it using a mechanical pen, and sent it to Prime Minister Peres without President Reagan's knowledge, it is unlikely that anyone on the president's staff would have risked such an action, given that the letter's recipient, a prime minister, might then have mentioned the letter to Mr. Reagan.

THE TEHRAN MISSION

At 7:30 A.M. on May 25, 1986, after a flight from Tel Aviv in an unmarked Israeli Boeing 707, McFarlane—accompanied by North, former CIA official George Cave, NSC staff member Howard Teicher, an unidentified CIA communications specialist, and Amiram Nir, whose participation was potentially dangerous—arrived at the Tehran International Airport.

The mission originated from a suggestion made by Ghorbanifar in April, during a visit to Washington—that a high-level U.S. delegation travel to Tehran to meet with top Iranian officials. McFarlane, who had the president's approval, viewed the mission as both an intensification of efforts to free the hostages and an attempt to establish a dialogue with Iran. Following the mission's failure, McFarlane and his group left Tehran for Tel Aviv at 8:55 A.M. on May 28.

Shimon Peres   Amiram Nir had the idea that we had to create a group to deal with the Shiites and the fundamentalists, for good and for bad. He convinced his American counterpart [North] to proceed with research. It was Amiram who prepared the whole story with the cake and the Bible. We were also interested in recovering the bodies of fallen IDF troops.

Barry Schweid   I'm the idiot who called McFarlane's office once and the secretary said, "He's not in." And I said, "Will he be back?" And she said, "No, he's traveling in the Persian Gulf region." And I'm thinking: What's he doing there? Later we learned that he was there with a cake and a Bible.

Albert Hakim   Who were they? They came with a copy of the Koran and what? A chocolate cake? Do you think that the Middle Easterners are that naive? McFarlane had been national security adviser; the Iranians have seen a lot of retired people. They are not stupid in analysis. Believe me, they know it from experience that unless they get to the heart of the structure, everybody else doesn't count.

I told them, "Don't go. That is not the way you should do things; it won't work." Nir was there; Secord was there; Ollie was there. I told them, "Don't waste your time, because the broker is not reliable; the Iranians do not accept the broker, Ghorbanifar. If they don't accept the broker, they are not going to work with you. They are going to look at you at the same level that they look at the broker." None of them wanted to realize that the meeting didn't have any foundation, regardless of who went there.

Michael Ledeen What is the Iranian reality? The Iranian reality is that they didn't trust Ghorbanifar. They talked to him; he was one of them. He had an incredible access; he could pick up the phone and talk to the president of the country and to the deputy prime minister, but they didn't believe him.

I am sure that when McFarlane landed in Tehran, the Iranians were flabbergasted; they never expected he would go to Tehran, even though they had been told he was coming. You have to understand a bit about Iran. The Americans cut out the only people who were culturally equipped to deal with this: Nimrodi, who knows Iran as do very few living people — he is a fascinating person, and all kinds of terrible slanders have been written about him; he is really an excellent person — and Kimche, who is intellectually far and away the smartest of all of those guys.

Roy Furmark The Israelis were impressed with Ghorbanifar and his ability to deliver. He arranged the Tehran meeting. How do you do that if you can't deliver? How many other people could arrange to have this important group fly into Tehran?

The fact that the meeting didn't work out is really a question of what actually happened. If you have nonbelievers going on this trip, and they go reluctantly, what happens is that if things don't immediately work out, they go home.

If you're dealing in Iran, or Saudi Arabia, it takes a long time to get things done. For them to think that the Iranians operate like the Swiss National Railway is beyond being rational; it just doesn't get done overnight. Even with patience, it's difficult.

Oliver North There absolutely was a sense that there could be a breakthrough. Not from Ghorbanifar. He would simply tell you, "Here is what it looks like is going to happen." Then we would start to monitor certain activities, and it would be basically confirmed that something was about to take place.

We had a very good sense at the time, based on the travels of certain Iranian officials and based on certain communications. You put it all together and said, "This makes sense."

There was a great deal of risk for the people involved in the mission — and a great deal of risk for the country if we didn't come back.

Robert C. McFarlane North almost was insubordinate. When I arrived in Tehran, I hadn't been part of it for six months. I felt that North was really the only one with a corporate memory. He was the only one who met with Ghorbanifar on the White House side of things; he knew more than I. Therefore, as long as he had somebody — that is, Bill Casey — to protect him back in Washington, it was okay for him to freelance.

But as a practical matter, the delegation had no integrity. What I was saying in the formal sessions was being undermined by Nir and North. I didn't know that at the time, but it's pretty clear from North's testimony.

Yaacov Nimrodi I heard about the visit to Tehran only two or three days after they came back. I was told by President Herzog, who was a good friend. When I heard about it, I went to Shimon Peres and shouted at him. I had been in the dark for three or four months, and Nir is going and telling stories. Peres was very busy, Rabin was very busy, and Nir was doing what he wanted to do.

Howard Teicher The primary reason it failed was that both sides had been lied to by the middleman, and so expectations were totally misplaced. Ghorbanifar was a typical business broker. In trying to bring people together to make a deal, a broker sometimes has to convince people to do things they don't want to do.

He figured that once we were there, he could make it happen, so he wrote this letter that said what the Iranians would do in exchange for our doing x, y, and z. And at a certain point in the meeting, we brought this out, and the Iranians said, "We don't know what you are talking about; we never said any of this." They seemed genuinely surprised. When you saw the sweat pouring off Ghorbanifar's face, you had to conclude that he got caught lying.

All we could do was tell him we would kill him if we could. They would kill him if they could. He had been good to them: he had delivered some TOW missiles, so he had credibility. He delivered us; we showed up. He told them that we would show up with all these spare parts; they became concerned when we didn't have anything with us.

What North told Ghorbanifar, and what Ghorbanifar told the Iranians, I don't exactly know, but it was clearly not what they had expected. It's very clear that in this context McFarlane, right or wrong, decided that we were too far apart — that they would not do what needed to be done. McFarlane understood, correctly, that both sides had been duped, and that the people we were dealing with were not at a level where they could deliver anything.

Adnan Khashoggi I know McFarlane was going to Tehran; I did not know that Nir was going. If I had known, I would have warned him. It was silly; why take these risks? Nir could have whatever happened in the meeting in his pocket the next morning, so he didn't have to really be in the meeting.

Judy Nir Shalom I didn't know exactly what he was doing. But I met Ghorbanifar in Europe. He was very charming. He sent me very nice presents when my son was born; he knew the good life — the good restaurants. I also met Secord and North — under the name of Mr. Goode. Ollie was very nice to me.

One day my husband told me he was going someplace and he had to disguise himself. He went to a fancy hairdresser. They put him behind a curtain, and he had his hair colored. He was very anxious. He also put on a mustache.

Howard Teicher We are really dealing here with that most interesting and amorphous level of foreign affairs known as the human factor. Just as everybody in Washington knows that the important thing is to be in the meeting, so Nir understood that in order for him to get what he wanted, he had to be there himself. So in terms of Tehran, this was the party, and Nir did not want to miss the party.

I don't think the Iranians knew he was an Israeli. He had an accent, but lots of people have accents. The Iranians were certainly willing to buy arms from the Israelis if the Israelis would sell them to them. And from their point of view, that's what this was about; this was the Middle East, wheeling and dealing behind the scenes. The only danger to Nir, personally, was if the word leaked to the bad guys that there was an Israeli in the penthouse.

Albert Hakim Nir definitely had the interests of his country at heart, and he did not want to give up the power with the first channel. So in order to be able to maintain that, he went there. Nir was daydreaming that he was going to go there and continue to do some good for his country. The whole thing was without a foundation. There was nothing to build on. Everybody was daydreaming, McFarlane included.

Nimrod Novick Nir was blocked out by the intelligence community. They criticized Peres for having appointed him to this type of critical position. They didn't like the fact that he was appointed to the job; they didn't think that a journalist should be involved in this kind of business.

Nir was a very dynamic operator. He was looking for a niche, a way to express himself. He felt he could and wanted to do things, and he asked me to help him on some occasions because of our common background of the Center for Strategic Studies at Tel Aviv University; we were there together.

I was the only friend he had in the Peres entourage, and our friendship was limited. This was his big thing: for the first time he felt he could make a breakthrough and have the appreciation of the intelligence community and maybe build a more substantial agenda and power base.

Richard Secord Nir knew that I opposed his going to Tehran. I argued it almost to the point of scuttling the mission. I thought it was the dumbest thing he could do. The trip was dumb to start with. I facilitated it, but even Ollie would not tell you that I drummed that trip up. I was present when we made the ground rules, but I urged that it be called off when they changed the ground rules.

Every now and then I put my old policy hat back on. I thought that a meeting on an island in the [Persian] Gulf was viable; we could protect our people there with our special ops forces. At the last minute, when the Iranians said, "We have to do it in Tehran," I said, "These people are Persians. You must be nuts; you are going into the heart of darkness." I lived there for four and a half years. I know how far away Tehran is. We can't come and get you; Ronald Reagan can't come and get you.

Everybody who went on that mission was crazy. Ollie was nuts for going on it; McFarlane was nuttier — he was the boss. I thought Howard Teicher, who had worked for me in the Pentagon, had better sense. I've seen a lot of brave things in my time, but this was bravery to the point of craziness.

Robert C. McFarlane Our group was fragmented. The Israeli participant should not have been there; Amiram Nir clearly had no loyalty to me, whom he had never met. But more importantly, he had no loyalty to the United States; he was there on behalf of his own government, with his own instructions and mandate. Although I told him, "You will not deal with these people," he just ignored this.

Yaacov Nimrodi When Nir came back to Israel from Tehran, he reported that he had met there with Rafsanjani. It was a lie. When I met with our president a week after he came back — I had gone to see the president on another matter — he told me, "Listen. Amiram Nir met with Rafsanjani; he met with all these people." I said, "You know it is a lie."

McFarlane Decides to Leave

Howard Teicher   Ghorbanifar's henchman, [Mohsen] Kangarlou, was an educated, nasty man who did not deliver on his principles. Once we realized that they had no ability to get anything done, McFarlane decided we had had enough.

The dynamics were that the imam — the man who held the hostages in Beirut — had a personal stake in all this, and he was not controlled by the Iranians. He would undoubtedly have let two hostages go and, as quickly as he could, taken two more. For all we knew, they couldn't find him while we were in Tehran. As far as we could tell, they weren't even in touch with the key guy in Beirut, the Shia Islamic Amal terrorist whose brother-in-law, or first cousin, who was very close to his wife, was one of the Da'wa bombers in Kuwait. What he really wanted was to get his relative out of the Kuwaiti jail; that's what this was all about, and all these other things got built up on top of it.

Once we and the Iranians saw in Tehran that we had both been duped, it suddenly became apparent that it would be very unlikely that we would achieve our goal.

Albert Hakim   I met McFarlane only once, when he came to Geneva to change planes, so I have no ties with him whatsoever. He definitely is a good soldier, and he was used, most probably, by Ollie. So when he realized there was no foundation, he left. If the proper analysis had been given to him, he would not have gone on this trip.

Oliver North   I don't recall the conversations as having been as acrimonious as they are portrayed. I do remember conversations with Howard Teicher, and Bud McFarlane, and George Cave, in which I was an advocate for waiting another twenty-four hours to see if they would actually fulfill what they said they would do.

Bud was adamant: "No. We are going home." I don't want this to turn into an "Ollie Versus Bud McFarlane" debate, but I'd seen Bud act that way once before, when he was very tired, down in Honduras. He had stormed out of a meeting and said, "That's it. We're going home. I'm the national security adviser to the president of the United States, and I'm not going to be pushed around by some tinhorn dictator." That very abruptly ended a meeting with Walter Alvarez, who was subsequently murdered and who at the time was the head of state in Honduras.

In retrospect, Bud was not the kind of person who, once he had made up his mind, was going to change it. It affected all of his policy. Bud clearly decided in early 1985— well before I was engaged in it — that this was what we were going to do. And in my writing a paper saying that this was a bad idea, I wasn't going to dissuade him from this course of action in leaving Tehran.

Would we have gotten two out that day? I don't know. According to David Jacobsen, they were preparing to move him.

Richard Secord I think it was desperation that caused them to go; they saw the operation failing. I urged them to dump it. I honestly thought they would be held there. It's a miracle that they weren't — probably because the Iranian regime was tottering at the time. We knew that, and we had hooked our wagon to the right star. History has proven that.

David Kimche After I left the operation in December 1985, I had no further involvement or information on it. As far as the McFarlane visit to Tehran is concerned, if I had handled such an operation, I would have worked out the minutest detail before I went. I would never have gone on such a visit on the off-chance promise of meeting someone, and then working out negotiations.

In such a visit, you have to say, "We want *a, b,* and *c,* and we want an agreement, beforehand, of what we are going to get." Without that, they shouldn't have gone.

Michael Ledeen McFarlane felt he had been lied to by Ghorbanifar; the meetings he had been expecting to hold had not taken place. They really expected to see Rafsanjani. I told them not to go. I thought it was a mistake, because whatever came of it, it would strengthen the regime — and our interest in Iran was to weaken the regime.

I think that if they'd stayed longer, put in another few days, it might have worked, for all that I was against it. They might have been able to get a couple of people out and get some kind of dialogue going with the Iranian regime.

Judy Nir Shalom I remember that they came back tired and dirty; he was full of dirt. We all went out to eat. The mood was very good, but it was very frustrating for them to speak, because I was there. He was on the telephone all night, calling people in Washington. He told me that I would find out what he was doing in twenty years and that I would be proud of him.

14

Opening the Second Channel

The release of Reverend Jenco, while gratifying to the Reagan administration, did not alter the fact that after eleven months of arms sales to Iran, most of the American hostages remained in captivity in Lebanon.

Thus, in late August 1986, Secord, in an attempt to open a "second channel" to the Iranians and to remove Ghorbanifar from the operation, met with Ali Hashemi Bahramani, the nephew of Ali Akbar Hashemi Rafsanjani, the speaker of the Iranian Parliament. Subsequently dubbed "the Relative" and "the Nephew," Bahramani became the central individual in this latest effort to secure the freedom of the hostages.

From September 19 to September 21 —only days after two more Americans, Frank Reed, director of the Lebanese International School in Beirut, and Joseph Cicippio, the deputy comptroller of the American University of Beirut, were taken hostage—the Relative visited Washington, where he met with North and others involved in the effort, and was taken on a late-evening tour of the White House by North that included a brief stop in the Oval Office.

While the continued kidnapping of Americans appeared to confirm the fears voiced by Secretary Shultz and other administration officials that the arms sales would only lead to the development of a cycle of hostage-taking, arms sales, releases, and then additional abductions, Secord and Hakim may have regarded this progression in a positive light: additional arms sales and the resulting profits would both augment their own financial resources and provide North with ongoing funds for the contras.

North later described the ensuing discussions as having gone extremely well. They covered the weapons sales and hostages, and the status of the Da'wa prisoners then being held in Kuwait, as well as the future of Saddam Hussein, the Iraqi leader.

Then North, Secord, Hakim, and Cave met with the Relative from October 6 to October 8 in Frankfurt, where they presented him with a Bible signed by President Reagan.

North rushed back to Washington from Frankfurt after learning that a Fairchild C-123 aircraft belonging to Secord and Hakim's Enterprise operation had been shot down over southern Nicaragua during a supply mission. The two pilots had been killed, but an American cargo handler from Wisconsin named Eugene Hasenfus had survived and been taken prisoner by the Sandinistas.

At around that time, Secord left for Brussels, leaving Hakim and Cave behind to deal with the Iranians. In one of the more bizarre twists in the arms sales affair, Hakim, a private citizen, negotiated a nine-point plan that North soon told him was signed off on by the president. The plan became known as the Hakim Accords.

On October 7, as Hakim was negotiating with the Iranians in Frankfurt, CIA Director Casey informed two senior Agency officials of a telephone call he had received that day from Roy Furmark, an old friend of his who was a business associate of Adnan Khashoggi. Furmark told him that the two Canadian businessmen who had loaned Khashoggi the money with which to bridge the arms sales were threatening to expose the operation unless they were repaid, with interest.

Furmark and the CIA officials then met several times to determine ways in which to lessen the impact of the now-likely exposure of the arms sales initiative. North would later testify that Casey called to warn him that the diversion could be exposed.

Three days later, on October 10, Israel, in accordance with the U.S.-Iranian agreement, shipped an additional five hundred TOW missiles to Iran. Although even after the revelations of both the arms sales and the diversion of funds to the contras the White House attempted to keep the initiative alive—Iran received a total of 2,004 TOWs, 18 HAWKs, 17 of which were returned, and 240 spare parts for the HAWKs—the October 10 shipment would prove to be the final such distribution to the Iranians.

On October 29, North, Secord, Cave, and Hakim met again with the Relative, this time in Mainz in the Federal Republic of Germany, where the Relative informed the Americans that a student faction in Iran, as well as members of Hezbollah, had publicized within Iran the story of the U.S.-Iranian arms-for-hostages negotiations; he explicitly suggested that this information could have wider circulation. The Relative also stated that representatives of both the first and second channels planned to serve on an Iranian government commission established to determine whether the initiative should be continued.

The Relative's warning of the possible wider exposure of the arms sales initiative would be borne out within days, following the release of hostage David Jacobsen, with the publication by a weekly Lebanese newspaper of an

*account of McFarlane's visit to Tehran—a leak some U.S. analysts attributed
to Ghorbanifar, who was angry, they believed, at being removed from the
initiative.*

Roy Furmark   The second channel was to cut Ghorbanifar out because
they couldn't control Ghorbanifar. They wanted to get somebody who
was in their pocket; Ghorbanifar wasn't in their pocket.

He created the deal — it was his white paper. He did everything, and
it was working: the ground had been broken because all the hard work
had been done by Ghorbanifar. Now Secord and Hakim want to get rid
of him, to have a puppet of theirs to be involved.

You don't break a channel that is working. But they got greedy: if they
could get rid of Ghorbanifar, nobody would know what was going on.
The Israelis wouldn't know; Khashoggi would not know if Ghorbanifar
was gone. They would have their own puppet.

GHORBANIFAR'S CREDIBILITY

Craig Fuller   There was probably an initial misreading of Ghorbanifar;
he was initially presented as a credible person. But I know that Bud
McFarlane saw through this — that Bud McFarlane, after spending
more time on it and getting personally involved, recommended that this
whole effort be stopped, that Ghorbanifar could not be trusted.

I have never fully understood on what basis it started again; that is a
mystery to me. I don't know what went through people's minds to cause
Poindexter to get it going again, and for McFarlane to conclude that the
president was behind it.

Oliver North   He was totally unreliable. Mike Ledeen will swear, to this
day, that Ghorbanifar is the most honest man on the planet, and that the
lie detector test was cooked, and that Ghorbanifar can be trusted with his
darling daughters. He probably knows Ghorbanifar better than I do, but
I wouldn't trust the guy farther than I could throw him.

Duane Clarridge   Let's face it, the polygraph had been developed by
Westerners, for Westerners. It works very well on Americans, who have
been brought up with a sense of what's right and what's wrong — guilt
and that sort of thing.

To a Shiite, who is absolved by God about lying, the fact that he is a
Shiite under pressure puts a whole different view in his mind on right

and wrong — and lying. It makes Arabs — and Persians in particular — very difficult to test.

Ghorbanifar was a scumbag, but he seemed to have the right connections. And they did get Weir out.

Michael Ledeen   He's a whole volume. I thought that the whole Iran initiative was dead; I thought that the CIA should use him on terrorism, which was my brief. In December [1985], I went to the CIA — with North's approval — and talked to Dewey Clarridge and Charlie Allen. I told them about Ghorbanifar, and of the information Ghorbanifar had given us about terrorism, which was terrific and which we had not known. He predicted, with an amazing degree of specificity, an impending Iranian-sponsored terrorist attack in Saudi Arabia. He told us the targets that were going to be attacked, and it happened exactly like that.

Plus, in a general way, the picture Ghorbanifar gave us about Iran checked out: the internal political divisions; who the radicals were; who the relatively pro-Western people were. We hadn't known any of that.

No one believed his general claim that it was Iran that was running Islamic Jihad; we all thought it was Syria. Certainly he said things that weren't true. So what?

Albert Hakim   Ghorbanifar is the slickest liar that you can put your hands on; the guy is extremely talented in fabricating information. As a matter of fact, in a meeting in Germany — where I had disguised myself — he started fabricating information right there and then. He did not know who I was. I was introduced to him as a special interpreter for the president and with a fake name; he thought that I was American-born and that I would not understand his zigzags. So right there and then, he played Ghorbanifar: he lied through his teeth. That's his style. He doesn't know how to talk about the truth.

WAS GHORBANIFAR AN ISRAELI AGENT?

Fawn Hall   Michael Ledeen is very close to him; I just never understood that. If Ghorbanifar was an Israeli agent, that's why Michael would like him.

Roy Furmark   I don't believe for a minute that Ghorbanifar was an Israeli agent.

Richard Secord   He was obviously an Israeli agent because that is how we came to him: he had made a number of trips to Israel under their control before I met him. I also thought he was a French agent — and very successful — after our time, too, in Lebanon.

I always said he was his own agent. He has the Persian bazaar mentality: he is absolutely corrupt and shameless, to the point that he has a certain amount of charm. He is cosmopolitan: he has been with big money lots of times, he has lots of money. He is the kind of guy the fighter pilots say is okay — as long as you keep him at twelve o'clock and don't let him slip around to ten, much less six o'clock.

Judy Nir Shalom   Bullshit! He was always promising things and changing his mind; he would say things and not deliver the goods. He was only for himself. It used to drive Amiram crazy.

Shimon Peres   He was not an Israeli agent; he was an Iranian who was in touch with us. He claimed he represented a group. We thought that, through him, we had an opening, because he was well placed and had shown an operational capacity. He wasn't an agent.

Duane Clarridge   He had been an Israeli agent, but you have to be careful about the word *agent*; in my business, an agent is somebody who is under control, who is usually being paid. Let's say that Ghorbanifar was an asset of the Israelis — what piece of their apparatus, I don't know. Nimrodi had known Ghorbanifar for a long time.

Oliver North   To this day I still believe that Ghorbanifar was the agent of the Israeli government.

Ghorbanifar had worked for these guys; he had been an agent of several Israeli companies over there, and he had represented their commercial interests. I still maintain that Ghorbanifar was working for them.

OPENING THE SECOND CHANNEL

Richard Secord   Rafsanjani was not in control at that time. And remember, his nephew was our guy; I was the one who discovered him. I told Hakim and Ollie, when the Ghorbanifar thing really screwed up, that we had to have a second channel or get out of business. So we put the word out and, through Hakim's contacts, screened through a few groups.

I knew most of the ex-generals; Hakim knew them better than I did. This one group seemed to be quite interesting: they allegedly came from the right place, so we worked up a little session. Hakim met with them first, and called me and said, "It's real." I replied, "I sure hope so."

So I went to Belgium and met with them for several days. That was the first of several steps. There was a kind of Agency trade-craft — step by step vetting to the best of your ability. But sometimes you have to take the plunge, because you can't submit them to all the tests you'd like to do.

We got them to take some secure communications equipment back into their headquarters, the Rev[olutionary] Guard, the devils themselves; we were dealing with devils. Over a period of several months, I grew more confident about those guys. I wrote some reports on them, and finally we developed a second channel, which proved to be real.

Now, you could argue about how valuable they were. We certainly got one hostage out as a direct result of their actions, and we would probably have gotten some more. My preference, as I told these guys, was: Just give us their locations. Ollie worried that I would scare them away, but he didn't know them that well. They would ask, "What will you do?" I said, "You don't want to know, but we'll do something." They never would do that [supply the locations], but they thought about it a lot.

SECORD AND NORTH MEET WITH RAFSANJANI'S NEPHEW

Richard Secord   We brought the Nephew to Washington to impress him — to show him that they were dealing with people at the top. They had been concerned that they weren't.

I didn't know that they had brought him into the Oval Office until after it happened. I had been over in the OEOB [Old Executive Office Building] on the first day, and then I had gone home.

The Nephew, whose name I have — and whose name we protected even during the hearings because he was in great jeopardy — was pretty stable. And even though he was young, he thought politically. And even though he was a young guy, he had a lot of experience; he had been in a lot of battles. I questioned him very thoroughly about these battles, and he had all the right answers, so he had a lot of credibility with me. We thought that he was as close as you could get to Rafsanjani; he had grown up in his household.

Albert Hakim That was just a beginning. He was a young boy. His mission was short-lived. The Engine* took over. The Engine had more understanding of political issues at an implementation level, so he helped me and drastically went out of his way to make the Iranians understand what I was talking about; he was promoting what I had started.

And what I started was — the Iranians bought into it — that we will have a relationship, and we will say where this relationship will take us in the future, with no preaccepted conditions.

They had told him many times, directly, that I was representing the American government. And he trusted me; he still does.

He went into this the Iranian way, the Middle Eastern way: "I trust Albert, who would not lie to me. So if he says this has been authorized by the U.S. government, he is authorized by the U.S. government." There was also the fact that North had been with him in many meetings; they became buddies.

Richard Secord While the Monster proved useful from time to time, he could not be trusted. He was a real SOB; he was a Rev Guard, through and through. He had spent a lot of his life in jail under the shah's regime. He is older than Rafsanjani's nephew, and much more volatile. He would get real furious. You could see it in his face; he was a real killer.

He actually broke down and cried one time in Geneva. I was on him so fiercely because of the way things were turning, and he started crying. I had never seen such a pathetic wreck.

WHAT WAS THE IRANIANS' BOTTOM LINE?

Richard Secord We asked ourselves all the time: What is the Iranians' bottom line? I think they were in the stage where they wanted at least a partial rapprochement with the United States, because they saw enemies everywhere, especially in the Soviet Union; they had been at war with the Iraqis for years. And their economy was ruinous. They were afraid politically — the revolutionaries are the ones who always get killed, and then the business guys take over. And Rafsanjani had not yet ascended to the top spot.

---

* An Iranian Revolutionary Guard intelligence official also known as the Monster. This officer was called the Engine by Hakim because Hakim viewed him as the key to an agreement. The others on the U.S. side viewed the Iranian as the Monster because he consistently took negative positions, insisting on concessions to Iran.

Albert Hakim I was totally convinced — and I am today — that regardless of the messenger, everything that I negotiated and discussed with them got as high as Rafsanjani. As to whether he took it beyond that, Rafsanjani, in a speech, said: "If you get the arms dealers" — referring to us — "back to deal with us, we will have no problem dealing with them." So he knew. I was talking to the people who could get the message to Rafsanjani.

HAKIM'S NINE POINTS

With North, Secord, and Cave having departed from Frankfurt, Hakim felt under tremendous pressure to negotiate an agreement that would allow North, by the time he reached Washington, to report that the meeting had been successful.

For Hakim—and Secord—the stakes were very high, since failure to reach an agreement would probably mean the closing of the second channel.

This pressure led Hakim to make a number of concessions, including the release of the Da'wa prisoners; the delivery of five hundred TOWs before any hostages would be released; the release of fewer hostages than had been insisted on by North; the promise to supply an additional one thousand TOWs; updated intelligence information; and technical support for the HAWKs.

Albert Hakim It's not that they left; it's that: "We have had it. There is nothing that we can do." I said, "You are wrong. We must talk, and talk, and talk some more." They said, "Fine. We give you" — I forget now. Twenty-four hours? Forty-eight hours? A short time. "You stay on. You think you can do it? You stay on; we have had it." That's when we worked almost twenty-four hours a day to get the nine points done.

What I was presenting was a harmless relationship; it did not have any political involvement. And the Iranians liked that. But the three others [North, Secord, and Cave], who were raised as government employees, could not see anything beyond their immediate mission: they wanted to see how quickly and how many hostages they can release today — a one-night stand.

The Iranians said, "No. Our revolution is not about the hostages. We have the hostages because we have no other way of fighting the West. So we want to force you to sit down with us, and talk to us, and understand us." I had the patience; I understood what they said; I stayed on. The others didn't have the patience, and they wanted just the hostages.

The Da'wa Prisoners

Seventeen members of Al Da'wa al-Islamiya, a dissident Shiite political
group headquartered in Tehran, had been imprisoned in Kuwait following
the bombing in December 1983 of the U.S. and French embassies there.

The brother-in-law of one of the Da'wa prisoners was Imad Mushniyah,
the leader of Islamic Jihad, the main group involved in the taking of the
hostages in Lebanon.

Albert Hakim I had my own connection with the Kuwaiti government. I
relied on my capabilities in negotiating the release of the Da'wa prisoners. I had talked to some of the Kuwaitis, and the issue was very clear: I
will try to do it, based on my own personal contact and understanding
that in the Middle East everything is negotiable. You have to sit down
and negotiate, and you have to have patience — and you have to drink
tea, and drink tea, until it's done.

There is nothing in the Middle East, even today, that cannot be negotiated; that is the culture. In all the problems that exist today and they are
trying to resolve, what do you think they are doing? They are negotiating;
that is the structure.

David Jacobsen The big smokescreen that was put out at the time
Anderson and I and the others were being held was over the Da'wa prisoners in Kuwait — the smokescreen that we were kidnapped to be used
as leverage in negotiations for the release of those people.

One of those seventeen prisoners was the brother-in-law of the man
who was the number-one agent acting for Iran in Lebanon, so he obviously wanted his brother-in-law to be out. The brother-in-law was handicapped. He could not be a street fighter but had received special
training: he was the individual who assembled the bomb that killed our
241 marines; he may have been the person who helped to blow up the hijacked airplanes that were held in West Beirut in the mid-1980s. So this
was a wonderful smokescreen that they wanted us to use in exchange for
the Da'wa prisoners.

The real reason for our kidnapping was that it was to be used to get
the return of the Iranian assets that were frozen by President Carter in
1979. At the time of the negotiations for the release of the embassy
hostages in Tehran — which were successfully concluded with their release on the day President Reagan was inaugurated — these negotiations
were finalized in what was known as the Algerian Accords.

One provision was that Iran and the United States would litigate in a special tribunal in the World Court in The Hague for the return of the frozen assets. The estimate was that the U.S. government and corporations held approximately ten billion dollars in Iranian assets. The shah had been required to pay cash in advance for many of the orders; the Iranians had had to put up one billion dollars in an escrow account — they always had to keep five hundred million dollars in that account — so that American firms that were litigating against Iran for confiscating their property could get restitution out of that one-billion-dollar fund.

Whenever we returned a large sum of money, something good happened: somebody came home. When we did not return funds — or we returned a small amount of money — something bad happened: somebody was killed, or more people were kidnapped. When the final sum was returned, Terry Anderson, Tom Sutherland, Terry Waite, and Joe Cicippio were released within days.

I, along with other people who have studied this terrorism problem with the Iranians, am absolutely convinced that the attacks against American citizens and property were primarily based on their demands to get return of the frozen assets and the interest that accrued on those funds. The World Trade Center bombing — which is known to have been Iranian-instigated — was probably over a struggle, or a conflict, with our State Department on the interest that had accrued on the original ten billion dollars. That was the message: we want our money.

In the Algerian Accords, our State Department had waived the rights of Americans who had been held in the embassy to sue Iran for damages as a result of their incarceration. At the time the Foreign Sovereigns Immunity Act prevented American citizens harmed by other countries from suing for restitution. But it could well be that those hostages in Tehran had a right to sue based upon the concept of commercial terrorism, which would not be covered by the Foreign Sovereigns Immunity Act.

The Fate of Iraqi Dictator Saddam Hussein

Albert Hakim As a matter of fact, when I put that in the nine points and sent the information to Ollie — he had started with five points, and I had eleven, and ended up with nine — I was definitely left with the impression that we [the United States] would assist in neutralizing Saddam. That was their understanding; we were very specific about that. I think that Iraq was neutralized without killing him, or having to destabilize their nation.

We are not a nation, the United States, that can tolerate negotiation. Even day-to-day businessmen want a quick fix; that is the American way.

In these countries they don't look at it this way. You must bargain and negotiate, and bargain on all the issues.

We agreed, regardless of what is written in that paper, that I had the approval of the U.S. government, by phone, to sign it on their behalf.

There was the understanding that it could lead to the two nations' working with each other without necessarily having to interfere in each other's way of doing business. That was basically the Iranians' fear. The United States is well known in any country they move into, to hammer in their own objectives and not that much of the host country's. So that was an issue that I had to resolve. And that resolution took place.

The CIA agent who participated in some of these discussions told me, walking down the stairs in Geneva at the Intercontinental, "Albert, this would not have been accomplished without you." He spoke Farsi, and he was listening to my debate and argument; the debate and argument was definitely beyond the issue of hostages.

The other issue was how the two countries can work together in areas that would not cause interference by the United States in Iranian affairs. That covered many areas — anything that the two nations could find necessary for their relationship. That includes trade, intelligence-sharing, and other areas. The component that I set forth in establishing that relationship was trade: you first establish a trading relationship with Iran — and that I can help you to achieve — and that could also give you the possibility of releasing the hostages. But don't come into this with the idea that you want to release the hostages, to hell with the Iranians.

As a matter of fact, the Iranians were ready to invest fifty million dollars in this relationship, in the so-called Enterprise. And that is the basis of my counterclaim in the Virginia court — that this was the money the Iranians were prepared to put in to expand on this trade relationship between the two countries.

It is a platform that I introduced then in a very general form, and all the court documents refer to the fact that I expected to have many larger projects after the two nations had the relationship — and the benefit from it. So since the beginning — the very beginning of the investigations and the hearings — when STTGI was dissolved, I immediately established another company, pursuing the same trade platform.

Richard Secord   Hakim didn't write the nine points; Dick Secord wrote the nine points. North and McFarlane, blessed by Poindexter, actually had seven points. This gets confusing. They really got it bollixed up on the Hill; politicians don't like complex stories because they don't play well in sound bites. So if there is a complex story, they will usually truncate it.

But this one was clear. I remember it very, very well. There were seven points. But the Iranians wouldn't buy them; we spent hours and hours trying, for two days. Ollie left; he had to go back because of the Hasenfus situation.

Albert Hakim I stayed on; I am a very dogmatic, persistent person. As a matter of fact, the release of Jacobsen reflects that. In the letter he wrote to the judge, he said, "All the Americans gave up and left, except Albert, who stayed on to finish the work."

We made a commitment. We promised, and then when the political issues got hot in the United States, we didn't care about our honor and our agreement; we just backed off. To the Iranians, that's double-crossing.

Richard Secord I stayed,* and I said, "Ollie, I am going to give it one more whack." And I went straight back to the Steygenburger Hotel, near the airport in Frankfurt am Main, and went at it again. It was nighttime by the time we really got cooking. We went back and forth, and I finally said, "How about this?" I fashioned a compromise; Albert had to translate it word for word. They'd argue over the words, and this went on and on. And finally we came up with the nine points.

Albert Hakim I presented a draft of the agreement to Secord. We sat down in a hotel room and through the equipment that he had transmitted it to North. North took it to Poindexter. Where it went from there on, I have no idea.

And they came back. After an analysis, they said that this was even better than the original mission given to me, and they approved it. Knowing the government structure, I don't think Poindexter would *not* have mentioned this to other cabinet members; they were all sitting and waiting to see what was happening, so he had to say something to them. Not because he wanted to report to them. He had to say, "Okay, there is some hope." The cabinet members wanted to know what to tell the president, and when there would be hostages released. So he had to tell them, "Albert is having some success."

---

* Secord, who had left for Brussels on a business trip, returned to Frankfurt, from where he eventually transmitted the nine points to Washington.

Richard Secord   I sent them back by KL-43 [special communications equipment], and it took quite a few transmissions because there were too many characters for the KL-43.

The transmission was there shortly after Ollie got back to Washington. He took it to Poindexter, and they blessed the nine points. They became known in the testimony as Hakim's points. Albert Hakim is not a diplomat; he couldn't have written those points if his life had depended on it. And by the way, he wasn't interested in them either, not at all. What he was interested in was in getting a deal closed.

I'm the one who wrote the language about the Da'wa prisoners; I know the history of the Da'wa mess very well. I wrote it very carefully because I knew what could be done. I'll stand up today for this point, which we took a lot of gas on. It was a well-written, diplomatic, workmanlike piece of professional international negotiation. It didn't say that the United States would pressure the Kuwaitis — not at all — or promise them anything. It said that they — at the foreign ministry level — had to establish contact with their counterpart, i.e., the foreign minister of Kuwait, and work out arrangements that would satisfy the Kuwaitis.

There is nothing wrong with that. The bottom line was that it was approved in the White House by Poindexter, and he admitted it. You can say all you want about retired generals dabbling in diplomacy, but it really doesn't make any difference who wrote that language. My signature on it would have no meaning. That's a red herring; there were a lot of them in this.

On November 2, 1986, Al-Shiraa, a Lebanese newspaper, published a story that would not only expose the arms-for-hostages sales but lead to a further disclosure—one that would threaten the future of the Reagan presidency and cast a shadow over the Reagan legacy.

15

Disclosure of Arms for Hostages
and the Diversion of Funds
to the Contras

The Al-Shiraa *disclosure on November 2, 1986, of the McFarlane mission to Tehran and the information that the United States had been selling arms to Iran—claims that were confirmed the following day by a senior Iranian official—came the day after the release of U.S. hostage David Jacobsen.*

That disclosure caused great concern within the White House. Between November 4 and November 20, the administration scrambled to find an explanation for the arms sales.

During this period the president denied that McFarlane had visited Iran, insisting that the United States did not deal with terrorists but was considering its long-term relationship with Iran.

WHY THE *AL-SHIRAA* LEAK?

Oliver North   The timing for the *Al-Shiraa* disclosure was the [1986 U.S. congressional] elections. I am absolutely convinced that this was either KGB- or GRU[East German intelligence]-inspired. That newspaper was not started by fundamentalists with Islamic money; it was started by the KGB as a mouthpiece, an organ.

The Soviet intelligence service knew what was going on well before the American people did. Many of the leaks, or disclosures, that occurred came about as the consequence of their effort to undo Ronald Reagan. I suppose they succeeded, to a certain extent.

Adnan Khashoggi   It was deliberate. When McFarlane visited Iran, promises were made, and I think the Iranians gave up because of the two channels. In Iran, both channels were lying to Khomeini, so when they got exposed, they had to cover themselves. Both of them suddenly went undercover and united under Khomeini and said, "The Devil was trying to work with us."

Of course, Khomeini wanted to put the United States into trouble with the Arab world and to confuse the Iraqi issue. It was another weapon in their hands.

David Jacobsen They released the news through their Syrian allies, using a small newspaper in Lebanon. That newspaper hit the streets of Lebanon at about nine o'clock in the morning on Sunday, November 2, 1986 — two hours after I was released.

The release of Weir, Jenco, and me was really one of the nice side benefits of the sale of the missiles that would keep Iran from falling to Iraq. The Soviet Union was very aware of the missiles that were sold to Iran — whether they came out of Israeli inventories or from other sources. They knew that if this information became public, there would be a political feeding frenzy in this country.

The Soviet Union wanted to protect two of their allies: first, the Iraqis, because they had twenty-five thousand troops there; and the Sandinistas, because they knew of the diversion of funds to the contras and they wanted to protect the Sandinistas because they knew they were losing the war.

Terry Anderson and I — held in the same building, on the same floor, but in separate cells — were to have been released the same day. Terry Waite was serving as the cover for that release, by humanitarian efforts that would mask whatever was being done as far as the arms sales went.

I came out at seven in the morning, the paper came out at nine, and Anderson's release was canceled; he was supposed to come out that evening. I don't know their logic. I sat all day in the American ambassador's residence in East Beirut. They asked me if I would wait, because they expected one more American, in the evening. So we waited. And the next morning there was no release. We knew that because of the story in *Al-Shiraa*, Anderson's release had been canceled.

JACOBSEN'S WELCOME AT
THE WHITE HOUSE

During the White House Rose Garden ceremony in which he was welcomed back to the United States, Jacobsen and President Reagan were asked repeat-

edly by White House correspondents whether efforts were being made to free the remaining hostages held in Lebanon.

David Jacobsen I was not aware at that time of any ongoing efforts to bring the remaining hostages out. But I was aware of the fact that the kidnappers watch our television; the number-one leader of Hezbollah in North America lives in Dearborn, Michigan, and the videotape of that broadcast was probably made in Dearborn and sent to Lebanon.

I was aware that there are plenty of Hezbollah — Iranian and mullah supporters — in this country, and I was deeply concerned and troubled by the nature of the questions that were being asked, [concerned] that they would be misinterpreted by the kidnappers and that harm could come to my friends who were still hostages in Lebanon. My experience with the kidnappers was that they would believe the media but that they would not believe an American president, or anybody associated with the government.

I was still angry that an American anchorman had claimed that I had sent out a coded message when I had not. I had told the kidnappers that, but they didn't believe me; they believed the media. So the question that was asked in the Rose Garden — it was a grossly irresponsible, speculative question — made me believe that whatever the president's answer, the damage had already been done. There was the chance that Anderson and Sutherland and the others would have holy hell beaten out of them — like what happened to me.

Jacobsen was also questioned about the role of the British Anglican Church official Terry Waite in helping to secure his release, to which Jacobsen responded that Waite had been acting on humanitarian grounds, without any connection to any government.

David Jacobsen When I said that about Terry Waite, I honestly believed that he was a humanitarian and a church leader working independently to bring us out. Our government has never told me to say anything. On occasion after I came out, I would contact the men I had met on my release and in the debriefing, people who were with the State Department, the Justice Department, and the CIA. I would call and say, "What should I do? I don't want to screw it up if something is going on."

They always said to me, "Dave, you are a private, free citizen. You say what you want to say. We are not going to advise you on how you ought to react." I was never told what to say or what not to say. Anybody who says anything to the contrary is a goddamn liar.

Following Al-Shiraa's disclosure, President Reagan, in a televised address to the nation on November 13, acknowledged that the United States had indeed shipped arms to Iran. The president, however, in an attempt to soften the impact of this statement, denied that the arms shipment had been part of an attempt to secure the return of the hostages.

On November 19, President Reagan told a news conference that the United States had had no role in the November 1985 HAWK deal, and that the United States had had nothing to do with other countries, including Israel, and their shipments of arms to Iran.

Twenty minutes after the news conference ended, the White House issued a statement saying that a third country had been involved in the secret U.S. initiative to Iran.

Two days later, on November 21, the administration launched a fact-finding investigation into the matter, headed by the attorney general, Edwin Meese, following comments from State Department counselor Abraham Sofaer that Secretary Shultz objected to an NSC chronology that reported the 1985 HAWK sale to have been solely an Israeli operation.

During the weekend of November 21–22, North, after learning that Meese's aides intended to examine NSC files, shredded or altered documents. While a considerable amount of material was destroyed, North and Fawn Hall were not able to complete their work, and Meese's aides discovered North's April 4, 1986, diversion memorandum.

The discovery of the diversion memo led to North's firing and Poindexter's forced resignation. At a meeting of the National Security Planning Group on November 24, Meese, who would later be criticized for the manner in which he was conducting his investigation, told the NSPG that the president had been unaware of the November 1985 HAWK shipment. Those present knew this information to be inaccurate but did not contradict the attorney general.

The following day Reagan and Meese held a noontime press conference at which they revealed the diversion of funds from the arms sales to the contras. One hour after the briefing's conclusion, North—who was at that moment meeting with Secord in a Virginia hotel—took a call from the president in which he was told that he was an American hero.

During that conversation the president also said, "I just didn't know," an assertion North believed related to whether the president had known of the diversion prior to its revelation.

On that day Shimon Peres telephoned Meese, informing the attorney general that Israel planned to deny assertions made during the press conference concerning Israel's culpability in the affair.

In an atmosphere of growing skepticism, the president appointed a spe-

cial review board. The mandate of the Tower Commission—named for its head, John Tower, a Republican senator from Texas—was to examine the Iran-contra affair and to evaluate the NSC system.

Then, on December 16–17, the House of Representatives and the Senate established a special joint committee to investigate Iran-contra. Also on December 17, a three-judge panel of the U.S. Court of Appeals appointed a former federal judge, Lawrence Walsh, to the post of independent counsel.

While Attorney General Meese had wanted the independent counsel's inquiry to be limited to an investigation of the arms sales and the diversion, the court gave Judge Walsh the authority to investigate the broader issue of support for the contras.

As the various investigatory bodies were being formed, events in the Middle East continued to unfold in a familiar pattern. On January 20, 1987, Anglican Church representative Terry Waite was taken captive in Beirut, and four days later, on January 24, three more Americans—Alann Steen, Robert Polhill, and Jesse Turner—were abducted.

On the following day, Speaker of the Iranian Parliament Rafsanjani displayed in public both the Bible signed by President Reagan and the bogus Irish passport used by McFarlane on his then-secret visit to Tehran the previous year.

In the United States, CIA Director William Casey resigned on February 2, after he collapsed and was diagnosed as suffering from a brain tumor. And one week later McFarlane—in an apparent suicide attempt—took an overdose of Valium.

Casey died on May 6, 1987, shortly after allegedly being visited in his hospital room by the Washington Post *correspondent Bob Woodward, who, in his book* Veil, *claimed that Casey had admitted to him his culpability in the Iran-contra affair.*

On February 26, the Tower Commission—the first of the investigative bodies to present any conclusions on the Iran-contra affair—issued its report, placing blame on the president for failing to ensure the proper functioning of the NSC. The commission was particularly critical of White House Chief of Staff Donald Regan and former National Security Adviser John Poindexter.

On November 17, the joint congressional committee—following twelve weeks of televised hearings and interviews with more than five hundred individuals—issued a 690-page report that, with a dissenting view from the Republican minority, criticized North, McFarlane, and Poindexter on the operational level, and Casey for approving the operation, and concluded that the ultimate responsibility in the affair rested with the president.

While the Tower Commission and the joint committee made headlines, the potentially most important investigation was conducted by the office of the independent counsel. Lawrence Walsh—who would later be accused of using lower-echelon officials to attempt to gain indictments at the cabinet and even the vice-presidential and presidential levels—achieved considerable initial success, with convictions and/or guilty pleas obtained involving North, Poindexter, McFarlane, Secord, Hakim, and other officials and participants in the Iran-contra affair.

Judge Walsh lost ground later, however, when North's and Poindexter's convictions were overturned and other convictions—and Weinberger's indictment—were nullified by President George Bush's pardon of these individuals on December 24, 1992.

THE FIRST REVELATION:
ARMS FOR HOSTAGES

King Hussein I was surprised and shocked to learn about the arms sales to Iran. I communicated my views to the Reagan administration within the context of friends talking to each other to express our surprise.

We were led to believe exactly the opposite by our friends in Washington. Just a few days before the revelations of Irangate, I had a visit from representatives from the Pentagon and the armed forces, who categorically denied that anything of this nature could be possible.

Adolfo Calero I remember talking to Ollie North about his trips to the Middle East. He didn't say anything that would reveal deals; he never mentioned that they were going to ship weapons to Iran. I knew absolutely nothing about that. He said that there were agents doing some efforts for this rescue, but he never mentioned that they were going to ship weapons. I only knew about that when it burst.

Michael Ledeen When the story broke, I was very upset because I didn't think that we were doing a proper job of presenting what had happened. What I was saying to both North and McFarlane at the time was, "Look, what is all this nonsense about Israel?" It wasn't an Israeli initiative, it was an Iranian initiative. They came to us — Ghorbanifar came, and it's clear that he came with a blessing from Iran. Inside that, he had a second agenda. He said from the beginning, "I know mullahs in Tehran who want to change things and can help strengthen their position. We can work with them."

So I said to both McFarlane and North, "I don't know all this late stuff

I am now seeing on television, so anything they ask me about this, I can't do any damage. Let me talk to the press and explain how it started." They did not want that; Congress did not want that. I demanded to testify.

THE ATTORNEY GENERAL'S INVESTIGATION

Meese would later testify before a congressional committee that he had uncovered what would on its disclosure become a bombshell—evidence of the diversion of funds to the contras—but that he had failed to act on this information, enabling North to destroy key evidence of the diversion.

Edwin Meese III We did talk about whether it would be proper to use the FBI, and the answer was that it was not.

My purpose was not to conduct an investigation. We had no inkling on Friday and Saturday that there was anything wrong, no inkling that there would be any attempt by North, or anyone else, to shred any papers.

Even when we found the diversion memo again, there was no knowledge that anything illegal had happened; the fact that it might be illegal wasn't developed until Monday or Tuesday. And as a matter of fact, nobody has ever found anything illegal in the diversion of funds.

Our whole idea was to find out what happened, because different people had different parts in this, so they would be sure that any testimony they gave would be true, accurate, and consistent with each other's.

Bernadette Casey Smith I was at the house the morning Ed Meese came and told about finding out what Ollie North was doing. He came to Dad's house at six o'clock on the morning of November 24 to tell him what was happening. And I don't think Dad knew the extent of what Ollie North was doing. He knew that Ollie North was helping the contras; he knew that Ollie North was raising money to send down to the contras. That he knew, but the diversion of funds and all that business? I think that was an Ollie North original.

Fawn Hall I don't think Ollie ever thought it was going to happen. When I came into the office the morning before he was fired, I asked, "How was your weekend?" He said, "I was in here all weekend with the Justice Department." It wasn't a criminal investigation, it was questioning by the attorney general.

I was panicked; I was just on overload. We had done the shredding. I found out that he had been fired. I went up to Bob Earl and said, "I found these e-mails about the TOW missiles." I didn't know what they were looking for. I just felt they were after us.

I didn't have detailed memories of Watergate. My feeling was that the administration had wanted these things done and that Ollie was doing them, with every good intention. And as far as I knew, everything was on the up-and-up. These things were leaking, and things weren't good politically, and therefore we had to get rid of everybody.

Bernadette Casey Smith   North, when he made his confession to Meese, never mentioned that Bill Casey was the mastermind behind all of this. I wrote a column against Ollie North. If Dad was doing all these things that Ollie said he was doing, why did he wait until Bill Casey died before he mentioned it?

My husband, who is a lawyer, said, "You can't quote Ed Meese without showing it to Ed." So I faxed it to him. He agreed with me that Ollie North never used Bill Casey's name when he saw him that first time, or said, before Dad died, that Bill Casey was involved in the diversion of funds. I said, "Do you mind if I print it?" He said, "Go right ahead."

John Poindexter   One of the mistakes I made was the failure to develop a plan if it began to leak out; we were not prepared when that happened. Because the program was so sensitive — and we knew it to be controversial — there was a very minimum amount of paper actually ever created. That was also true on the support of the contras.

One of the problems we were faced with in November 1986 was reconstructing everything that had happened. But I do think Bud made a mistake in 1985: the Iranian program should have been defined in a finding much earlier than January 1986.

In December 1985, after the CIA had helped the Israelis with the one HAWK shipment, they wanted to cover their backsides. They sent over this very brief finding that only addressed the arms issue. This was in the first days after I had taken over as national security adviser.

[Deputy CIA Director] John McMahon was pestering me to get it signed. Unfortunately, I reacted to his pressure and got the president to sign it. I told McMahon that it was signed, but I didn't release it because it was not adequate from my standpoint. It only addressed one small part of the issue.

In the middle of December 1985, I asked Ollie to pull together a more elaborate finding, based in part on work that Don Fortier had done earlier and that addressed the strategic import of Iran. Ollie did this, and it was eventually signed. But that should have been done in 1985, when Bud first brought the issue up. But Bud liked to keep things very close to his vest, even more so than I did.

Fawn Hall Is Called by the U.S. Attorney

Fawn Hall [U.S. Attorney] Jay Stephens called me. I don't like that man at all; he was personally very abrupt with me. He asked if I had shredded. I said, "Yes, we shred every day." Of course, we shredded more than usual. I did not offer that information; I didn't know who the enemy was anymore. We had been working for these people, and now they were ready to scalp us.

I made a lot of mistakes due to the fact that I didn't know what was going on. In many ways, I blame myself for making it look like I was taking the documents out. If I hadn't taken what I took out, the whole thing about the cover-up wouldn't have been so intense. What I took out was nothing; it was a bunch of e-mails. They were in the computer.

The FBI Interview

Fawn Hall Bob Earl was going in to be interviewed by the FBI and I was next. Bob had told me he wasn't going to get a lawyer; there was no reason to do so. I felt the same way. I really didn't think, at the time, that I had done anything criminal. It wasn't as if I were trying to save Ollie from something I knew he had done wrong.

It was more about protecting the operation. I felt that the administration was going to dump all those secrets out there that we had been protecting. And they weren't necessarily political secrets. They were things that were going to harm people out there; they were going to affect the hostages.

I just panicked. I got really, really scared. I needed someone to help me. I didn't want to hurt those who were already being attacked, so I called Brendan [Sullivan] and said, "I need to talk to you." I went to see him and said, "I shredded documents. You asked me about this stuff a month or so ago, and I told you nothing."

It was funny; this was Ollie's lawyer, and he was saying, "Tell me everything." This was the guy who was going to be helping Ollie. I was scared to tell him; my protectiveness was something I had learned from working for a long time in government. It was a mistake; it did a lot of damage that didn't need to be.

At that point I hired a lawyer. I didn't want immunity. I questioned my lawyer: "Why do I need immunity? I didn't do anything wrong. It is going to make me look guilty." I was willing to go to jail. My lawyer said, "Trust me," and I thought: This is the guy Ollie's lawyer told me to go to. I was just not trusting anybody.

THE DIVERSION BECOMES
PUBLIC KNOWLEDGE

Craig Johnstone   I was called in Algeria by the *Washington Post* before any of Iran-contra broke. I was asked: "Can you tell us anything about the relationship between Ollie North, Khomeini, and the contras?"

I said, "What? How could you possibly construct a relationship between them? This is so far off the radar screen — such an absurdity."

I couldn't understand what would motivate such a question. All kinds of screwy ideas come up all the time; they are a dime a dozen. They are seen as such fairly early in the process and get slapped down. Every once in a while one slips through. But not this nutty.

Howard Teicher   When I asked North, "Where's the money coming from? Where's it going?" he said, "Howard, you don't have a need to know, and you don't want to know, and I am not going to tell you." So I didn't find out about the diversion until everyone else did — when it was made public.

Adnan Khashoggi   I only knew about the diversion afterwards. It was a big shock for me because it was silly. Silly things cannot be played in these games of big nations.

Judy Nir Shalom   Unfortunately, it came on my son's birthday. Because of that, the last thing that interested him [Amiram] was his new baby. I understood that this opportunity to work for the [release of the] hostages was important to the U.S. and to Israel. I was proud of him, of course.

Benjamin Weir   I learned of it through what was reported by the Tower Commission. I was dismayed, not only because I thought that to divert funds to the contra action was decidedly interfering in another country's activity. And frankly, I saw it as support of oppression rather than of freedom for the people of Nicaragua. It was an illegitimate activity to sell arms to Iran, contrary to the understanding with Congress.

On the other hand, when I became aware that there had been arms provided to Iran and that it was presumed — though not quite by me — that it might have had something to do with my release, I was in a dilemma. On the one hand, yes, I very much wanted to be free; but no, I didn't think that that was a justifiable way to go about it. I saw it as being very contrary to what I understood to be legal and ethical.

David Jacobsen   I thought it was a hell of a brilliant idea because we were selling missiles at an exaggerated price to our enemies and taking the proceeds and using them to support our contra allies in Nicaragua.

There is nothing illegal about selling arms to terrorists, or nations that sponsor terrorism. The argument against Reagan was that he had said he would never, never deal with these terrorist nations.

Nimrod Novick   There were two elements to the reaction. One was: Oh boy! — the administration working against the law, against Congress, that is very strange. The second was that we didn't consider it a major trauma from our perspective, because the whole issue of the contras was so remote and irrelevant to us.

Not that we didn't appreciate the domestic consequences. But we didn't think it was such a major international disaster. From our perspective, Iran-contra was a juicy scandal that was totally irrelevant to the real things — the kind of friendship and support we got throughout the Reagan years.

Rafi Eitan   You have to divide it into two categories: one professional and the other political. We know now that politically it was wrong; professionally it was the right thing to do.

Donald T. Regan   I knew about the Iran phase. I went along with that. I see nothing wrong with that; it's statecraft. It's for the president to decide how he wants foreign policy handled; he can do as he pleases.

I definitely supported the contras, and I still think that O'Neill and Boland and the rest of them were wrong in tying the president's hands as he tried to suppress communism in the Western Hemisphere. But I never would have — and still would not, and have so testified publicly — condoned any misuse of government funds.

The only illegal thing done was that money from the sale of those weapons was to have gone directly to the Treasury; it should not have been diverted to a Swiss bank account and then further diverted to the contras for their use. That was what was wrong. But there was nothing wrong with the Iran policy, and nothing wrong with the contra policy. It was the diversion of the funds that was the federal offense.

Edwin Meese III   I was deeply shocked when I learned about the diversion. It took two controversial issues and put them together — like putting a match and a stick of dynamite together.

David Kimche   We heard it from the press when it blew up. We never knew anything about the contras. The word *contras* never came up, not in my time, not even as a whisper, not even a hint. We were surprised; at least I was surprised. Very surprised.

Poindexter Resigns and North Is Fired

In the wake of the revelation of the diversion of funds, President Reagan accepted Admiral Poindexter's resignation and fired Colonel North.

George P. Shultz   He was one of the stars of the navy; they picked an able man when they picked him. But Poindexter was not able to deal with the political level. I felt he was a good, intelligent guy to work with on many matters, but he was way off the beam on this one.

Fawn Hall   I never dreamed he would be fired; I was completely shocked. I don't think that others around me were shocked. I remember someone saying to me a couple of days before it happened, "This is going to explode!" I was so busy that my sense of an explosion wasn't as imminent.

I believe that the president distanced himself from Ollie purely for political reasons. I believe that Ollie was prepared to step down and be the scapegoat, but I don't think he really believed that he was doing something illegal.

I know that they tried very hard to walk the line — to do everything legally — and they took advantage of loopholes. People do that, especially when you are talking about getting hostages home.

And you're talking about Central America, something they felt very strongly about; it was one of the president's top agendas.

Cal Thomas   Ollie had a few successes, and people said, "We're on a roll; just don't tell us." And as long as it was working, they were happy to take credit.

Of course, when things went wrong, they started looking for a boogeyman. If North had been successful, nobody would have said a word. When he was interdicting the hijacked airliner, it was great stuff, and everybody else wanted the credit. But when something went sour — "Not us, we didn't have anything to do with this. It's the guy in the basement."

HOW DID THE DIVERSION COME ABOUT?

Roy Furmark   The Americans said, "We have to come in and bail these people out. They are a bunch of stumblebums. We'll do it." Then, as they were doing it, they dreamed up this scheme of the pricing and leaving the profits in the [Enterprise] account.

Only the people on the inside in the U.S. government knew what the CIA transfer price was, as opposed to the market price. I don't know what it was, I'm sure Ghorbanifar didn't know what it was, and I'm sure Nimrodi didn't know what it was. The Americans knew. So that is key as to how this diversion began. Somebody who knew the transfer price as compared to the market price, which they were charging the Iranians. That was where the profit was.

Elliott Abrams   In the case of Central America, the failure to fill the vacuum — the vacuum that was created when Congress cut off military aid to the contras — was a form of drift. How do you fill it? The president filled it, in a sense, with rhetoric — in speech after speech, saying that this was an incredibly serious national security issue — but with no action. There was a very clear gap between the issue as he defined it and the action the administration took.

Into this vacuum, which nobody wanted to fill, stepped North. And when he stepped in to fill it, the feeling around the White House was relief. That meant that the president didn't have to do anything else differently.

James Baker III   The truth of the matter is — and I know that this is not the general wisdom — that Iran-contra was basically a policy dispute between the Congress and the executive branch. Because of the Boland Amendment, people in the executive branch were doing some things they shouldn't have done.

John Poindexter   It's fair to say that I was upset with Congress over the Boland Amendments. As to that being the only reason I signed off, no. We had a situation where we did not want to undercut the Israelis and indicate to the Iranians that they were paying the Israelis more than they should have, so we kept the price the same.

That meant that we ended up with extra money; there was more profit than Secord and Hakim needed. We had the other problem of finding money for the support of the contras, and it just seemed like a good idea — although admittedly controversial.

Albert Hakim   It came from the United States of America, from the Democrats. There was no diversion; that's why I am staying on and fighting it. What diversion? Of what funds? My money? The Enterprise's money? These are not U.S. moneys. And I am about to win that case.

I came up with that strategy first. After we established our relationship, I said, "In the same way, we are making a profit by buying the arms that General Secord was buying through Portugal." We were marking it up and designating it for our own benefit, and we wanted to donate, like other Americans who wanted to donate for the cause. We donated for that.

It is wrong to tie these things together, the two projects. I made the profit for the Enterprise, and I decided to buy arms with that because the Nicaraguans were fighting. I paid the United States government in full, plus 10 percent profit. That was the end of the deal; any other markups were my profit.

And what I want to do with my profit is my business. That's why I have taken ten years to stick to this, and that is why the lawsuit is going on. And finally, I think, I have cornered them and they are talking about settlement. And it's not going to get settled unless it's settled in the right way. The case is being settled in three jurisdictions: Geneva; in federal court in Virginia; and now in district court in San Jose [California].

That's what I have managed to bring it to. They have to come up with actual proof that the money is there — a contract, or witnesses. That they don't have, because the witnesses that they have heard have testified throughout that the profit was Enterprise's.

Roy Furmark   All of the money Hakim and Secord are trying to obtain is Khashoggi's money. He wasn't paid ten million dollars; the U.S. government got the Swiss government to freeze the account. And without a doubt, the money — this is money that Khashoggi lost — belongs to Khashoggi.

Hakim and Secord think that this is their retirement profit. They didn't lose any money; they didn't put any money up. When Secord established the Enterprise and went into business, that's what Khashoggi risked his money for; that's why he did the bridging, in the hope that out of this whole thing would come a business relationship in Iran. The Enterprise put no money up whatsoever. It was financed with Khashoggi's money. The Enterprise was financed with the profits — the profits that didn't go to Nicaragua.

Fawn Hall   As a result of the Boland Amendment, Congress was supposed to be informed in a "timely" manner about covert operations, and everybody was saying, "You didn't tell us." And I thought to myself: Look up the word in the dictionary. "Timely" means, by an appropriate time. The intentions were good. There was no self-motivation; they weren't pocketing money.

John Poindexter   One of the mistakes the administration made early on, going back to the very first Boland Amendment and the lack of a line-item veto, was reluctantly accepting these Boland Amendments.

I had argued earlier that we should not accept them and that the president should veto the entire bill. I could never get any support for that until I became national security adviser. In 1986 I convinced the president that we should not compromise with the Congress and that we should insist on legislation without any restrictions. And eventually, in 1986, we got it.

I was convinced, from the very beginning, that the reason we won was that the Democrats did not want to be held responsible for losing Central America to the Communists.

Richard Secord   *Diversion* is a bad word; it has legal connotations. There was no diversion, and even the special prosecutor never alleged such. I made conscious decisions to spend money in a way that my Enterprise was legally entitled to spend it. These were my funds; I could have spent that money any way I wanted to — with Hakim's concurrence, of course. Hakim was the CFO; I was the CEO, so I was over him in that relationship.

The Enterprise was chartered outside of STTGI. Hakim wasn't even involved, and didn't know anything about it, until sometime in 1985, when I saw the Iranian side start to creep in and brought him into it. The terms under which we would split the profits if there ever were such — I told Albert there might never be — were fifty-fifty. But there was no question ever about the command relationship, nor could there be. He was on foreign ground. He didn't know anything about this sort of thing; Albert wouldn't know a light machine gun from a hand grenade.

He was good with the Iranians, though. I brought him into the policy side because we couldn't get a Farsi speaker — a good one — from the CIA. George Cave was the only one we had. They tried to give us a woman at one point. I said, "Are you crazy? Look whom we're talking to." You could make a good cartoon out of that.

Oliver North Ghorbanifar was the guy who suggested it to me overtly. It was almost immediately seconded by Nir, which kind of confirms my initial suspicion that Ghorbanifar was working for the Israeli government. If you put those two things together, there must have been some degree of collusion there that we were not totally aware of.

Ghorbanifar mentioned it, and Nir seconded it. I wrote a document to John Poindexter and said, "Here's what has been suggested. And if we are going to continue to do this thing, we might as well get something for it." That was my whole motivation for endorsing the proposal.

Edwin Meese III There is a system of checks and balances which, in this case, was breached, not by the president and not by the chief of staff.

Ollie was a very zealous guy. He was a very patriotic, very loyal person; he wanted to accomplish the president's objectives. He took it upon himself to do a lot of these things. Poindexter should have had a shorter leash on him — staff people should never be given operational authority — but he was overworked himself and didn't understand the political ramifications.

Charles Hill They exercised influence by the communications revolution. I could see it happening — going back to my notes of a couple of months in 1983. Before 1983 the State Department controlled communication; the United States dealt with the world officially through State Department diplomatic communication, which was coded and very carefully controlled. It was a monopoly. You had good secretaries of state then. This couldn't have happened.

At the time I was chief of staff and in charge of communications, and I could see that the guys in the White House were building their own communications system — their own State Department — in the basement of the Executive Office Building. They could do so because the State Department was thwarting what they wanted to do.

I had my personal encounter with this when North, on some other issue, called me in the middle of the night, saying, "We would like you to send a cable saying x," and I said, "We are not authorized to say x." He was very mad, and said, "I'll get back to you." This happened again; he called again at four in the morning and said, "Well, now I have authorization that you are to send this cable," and I replied, "I need that in writing or I can't do it." He became furious, and I later learned that he had sent his own communication out, which appeared to be as authoritative as any could be. Essentially that broke the monopoly; the White House could send its own communications — and North and Poindexter and McFarlane grabbed that and ran their own foreign policy.

Adnan Khashoggi   Thus developed the Nicaragua funding. If the Iranians want the equipment, let's give them what they want, but let's hike the prices so that we can get the difference and buy weapons for Nicaragua.

Suddenly North became a businessman — the clearinghouse for equipment and collecting commissions, and using the Secord company in Geneva to act as a clearinghouse for this money. It was nothing personal; they didn't benefit. They just wanted the money to buy equipment to go to Nicaragua.

Now, most of the Iranians are not stupid. They are trained in the United States; they have lists of prices. So when they saw that suddenly the prices are five or six times what they're buying, they got upset. And this is when North's plan with Secord fell apart, because it became unacceptable business.

And this is the pettiness of the Iranians. They should have let them make the profit and have benefited from the channel. They could have gotten more equipment; they could have had more input. But you are dealing with technocrats — an officer sitting there with the prices: "Oh! They're cheating us!"

And this is what exposed them: the hungry desire to get money because they couldn't legally get money from the U.S. government for Nicaragua. So they went to Iran to get the money, which is very stupid. But it happened.

Roy Furmark   I don't think they were bothered by the markup in prices — the fact that it went to Nicaragua. What bothered them was that they did not get what they paid for; it was overpriced, even on the market price. If the market was ten, they were charged thirteen. Anybody would be a little upset about that.

Motives

Michael Ledeen   North had a motive to keep it going. He was driven to have money for the contras, to keep them alive, so he was constantly wanting to do more and more things with the Iranians, because that generated funding — the tail wagging the dog, if your major concern is Iran.

Oliver North   This assertion is outrageously wrong. The end result of the revelation was, of course, that more hostages were taken. And one can argue — as I did at the very beginning of this endeavor, and at several points during it — that this could indeed result in prolonging the activity.

One of the most difficult things in my life — having seen people die in my arms — was to say that the price of an American citizen was five hundred TOW missiles; that was just a very difficult thing for me to accept. Why not ten thousand at that rate, or ten million?

There is certainly nobody that I know of in the administration who wanted this thing to go on any longer than it did; certainly I didn't. Having not wanted to start it in the beginning, that is a very solid position.

Howard Teicher   I suspect that Reagan and Casey got many a good laugh over the fact that the ayatollah was supporting the contras against the Sandinistas. But I am not so cynical as to think that North, at his level, or the president, at his level, wanted to keep this going as a way to pump money into the contras.

Michael Ledeen   Ghorbanifar had a motive: he was trying to get something to happen. Various people were perhaps making money out of this. At the end of the day, I think that Khashoggi and Ghorbanifar lost money.

Nir was undoubtedly driven by a lot of things that [also] drove North: personal success and all the Israeli motives, which were to do something great for the Americans.

Adnan Khashoggi   Nir was suspicious of North — and he was right. I don't think the Israelis knew too much of what North was cooking, using the price differentiation for Nicaragua. Nir was supposed to have been in an intelligence unit; he knew a bit of these games. And Peres chose him. Because Schwimmer and Nimrodi wanted to make money, he had to get someone independent from those guys.

WHAT WAS THE HIGHEST LEVEL OF
KNOWLEDGE OF THE DIVERSION?

Duane Clarridge I suspect that the president didn't know about the diversion. I'm not even so sure that Casey knew about it.

Adnan Khashoggi Casey was involved with the Rafsanjani connection. This is a fact. I sent Roy Furmark to tell him, "You have to honor the commitment to pay the money." Casey did not like what Furmark was telling him; this Casey considered as a threat. At that time Casey got wind of what was happening.

Roy Furmark knew Casey from the time of Nixon, so he had a personal relationship with Casey and could talk frankly to him. But the thing we did not realize was that Casey did not know, which we couldn't believe. I mean, here is the CIA, and they would not know what was going on between Israel and the United States?

Suddenly Casey knew something from us that he had not known, and he started pushing his own people — Secord and all these guys — and then he realized they must work as a team.

Oliver North Bill Casey and John Poindexter knew absolutely everything I was doing, and Bill Casey is probably the only one who knew all the dimensions of it. I took a lot of advice from Casey.

Bill Casey was a part of everything I did for the Nicaraguan assistance. He was a part of everything I did for the hostage operation. He gave me a ledger to keep track of the finances on this thing so that no one could ever accuse me of mismanaging someone else's money.

Casey was very actively engaged in every aspect of it, including giving me not just an Irish passport. I had a blue U.S. passport that had my picture in it, but it didn't have my name in it. I had a pocketful of cards — what they call "pocket litter" in the trade — that said "William P. Goode, National Security Company" so that if I should ever blurt out "NSC," it would make sense.

I had equipment I used to carry back and forth through customs all over the world that would explain what the NSC Company did — "security work for your company and your government." By the way, here's a phone number in Rosslyn, Virginia, where you can call and confirm my employment.

George Cave once watched the British — who by then knew what was going on — take me apart at customs in a big show, because I had all this [encryption] equipment that I got from Bill Casey.

The joke among the Caseyphiles was a meeting where Dewey Clarridge was present and I took out this now-famous notebook and started to make notes, and Casey looked up and said, "What are you doing?" And I said, "I am taking notes on what you just said." And he replied, "If you need to take notes, you don't belong in this business."

Well, I knew I didn't belong in this business. From the very first days as a marine officer, the very first thing a commanding officer says to his subordinates when he's giving out orders is, "Take notes." And I did, because I don't have the facility to remember everything and get it all right.

Bernadette Casey Smith   Now, he knew about helping the contras; he knew about raising money to send down there. I don't think he knew about selling the arms and giving the money down there. That is the only portion of it that I can see as having been shady. I think helping the contras was a great thing to do.

Everything he did was pointed at outfoxing the Russians; that's why he was so keen on the contras. But I am convinced that he didn't know about the diversion, mainly because it was such an ill-thought-out intelligence plan. Dad would never do something that had the same people operating all of the different systems.

Harry Shlaudeman   Certainly Casey had to have signed off on it in some way. They all must have had some kind of general idea that these things were going on. I can't believe that they didn't.

But I think that they didn't know about the actual manipulation of the money; this is one of Ollie's crazinesses.

Roy Furmark   Once they had set this up, Washington never had to know what was going on with [Willard I.] Zucker [who had a fiduciary agreement with Hakim and Secord] in Geneva, because Zucker took his instructions from Secord.

On the day-to-day supervision that some people say existed between Casey and North, once the funds were flowing into Geneva and Zucker's account, they spent it the way they wanted it spent. Secord and North would say, "Send x, y, and z, or do this or that," and it was done.

I don't know who managed the account, but it was controlled in Geneva by Zucker and, I presume, Secord. So when people talk about supervising North day by day, who was supervising Secord? Who was controlling that account? Was it Casey? Of course not. Was it North? If it had been higher than North, somebody would have gotten a legal opinion. These are not stupid people. In government, whatever you do, you get an opinion, so I don't believe that everybody knew about it.

Alexander M. Haig Jr.   I think Bill Casey knew everything, the good and the bad. He was a peripheral villain, if he was one at all. He was not one of the real villains.

I did my best to get my arms around Bill Casey. I had lunch with him once a week. I think he was as open with me as I was with him.

He always lived on the edge. I did respect and admire him; he did a lot of things to help the CIA. On the other hand, in the long run he did a lot of things to harm it.

Lawrence Walsh   Casey was unavailable by the time I was appointed; he died shortly thereafter. So without ever having an opportunity for him to explain his own position, we were always reluctant to build a case against him, although we did what we had to do to understand his activities.

Poindexter is quite firm in his belief that North saw Casey every Saturday morning when they were both in Washington. He kept him informed and then, in a sense, told Poindexter afterward about what he and Casey had discussed. So Casey had an important role in it, and his death deprived us of a source of information that could have been valuable.

Michael Ledeen   Poindexter kept inviting Shultz to go to these meetings so he could brief him, and Shultz did not go; he did not want to know. If he had taken his responsibilities seriously, he would have found out what was going on.

Bernadette Casey Smith   He was a little bit mad at Shultz on the contra thing. Not too long before the Iran-contra revelation, Dad told Reagan that he was upset with what Shultz was doing. Shultz said he didn't know about it, but Dad told my husband that he was sending a letter to Shultz, telling him exactly what he had told Reagan.

Lawrence Walsh   There is a limit as to how much you can do as a cabinet officer — how many fights you can fight and how much you can do to deter a willful president.

I would be hesitant to say that Shultz and Weinberger could have done more than they did to try and discourage this activity. On the other hand, after it was exposed, Weinberger attempted to conceal it. Shultz less so; he advocated full exposure.

Michael Ledeen   Weinberger thought it was dead; he thought he had killed it. As far as I can tell, he behaved quite properly. He argued against it; he didn't want anything to do with Iran, ever. "Not one screwdriver," he once said. Nothing.

Barry Schweid   I'm a great fan of George Shultz; Shultz was very good at taking care of himself. Weinberger did not know how to take care of himself. Shultz and Weinberger are fine on objecting to Iran-contra. There are some who might say that Shultz is a rather smooth operator, that he knows how to keep his distance from something that's unseemly, unpleasant. But I see him as a man of incredible character.

President Bush responded to our request for an in-person interview, and then to our request to speak with him by telephone, by electing instead to respond, on July 18, 1996, by faxed letter, to a list of questions we had prepared.

He declined, however, to comment on a variety of questions we posed to him having to do with the Iran-contra issue. We had asked the vice president:

"What is your view on the genesis of the arms sales to Iran? Did you know in advance of either the arms-for-hostages decision or the later diversion of funds? What was your view of Director Casey's knowledge of the diversion? How did the unfolding of the Iran-contra episode affect the president? Did the president come close to impeachment?"

Bush responded, "No comment," to all of the above questions. And to our query concerning his own knowledge of the arms sales and/or the diversion of funds, he added the notation, "Refer to previous public statements."

We find Bush's silence notable in light of the candor of our other interviewees concerning their roles in the Iran-contra affair.

Michael Ledeen   As far as I know, Bush did not attend these high-level meetings. I never briefed Bush; I never heard his name mentioned. And furthermore, if you look at the briefing Bush got from Nir, that is a soup-to-nuts briefing — the kind of briefing you give a person who does not know the background. He gave him a full briefing, from the beginning.

Elliott Abrams   I don't think he was very much involved. I suppose that Donald Gregg had some kind of information flow because he had formerly been in the Agency. So I assumed he was tapping into information — exactly how much information, we'll never know.

How much did [Gregg] pass on to Bush? The answer has got to be less than 100 percent of it. I say that in the sense that I did not pass on 100 percent of my information to Shultz, partly because he had other things to do than Central America.

I think you need to separate the two questions: what information Bush had, and what actions he took. He had some information; pinning it down will now be impossible. In a certain sense, the hearings failed to do this, and Walsh failed to do this. Walsh failed even to pin down precisely what information Don Gregg had. What did the vice president do? What involvement did he have?

Miguel D'Escoto   I believe also that Bush knew. What would have been the reason for not telling this? I think that Reagan was an adventurer, who wouldn't care. And besides, when you have this concept of so much power, so many people fear you.

When they were prevented, or impeded, from using funds, they would look elsewhere — and, of course, the drug traffic. Bush knew quite a lot about that.

There is no doubt that in its efforts to finance, not the contras — the contras is only a little thing — the United States, from all the conservative and responsible estimates, put the level of American expenditure in this overall effort to get rid of the Sandinistas at more than ten billion dollars, and drugs were used in connection with that. I think it is quite clear that Bush knows about that.

Oliver North   One of the things I have found most offensive is the suggestion that North would do business with drug dealers; that is absolutely unconscionable. I had working with me on detail from the attorney general two DEA agents.

That story — that the contras are being supported by drugs, and therefore by the North connection — starts in Mexico in early 1985. It is a plant by a Mexican newspaper that is run by the Cuban DGI [Cuban intelligence service], which funded it with KGB money. They knew that the congressional cutoff had occurred; they knew that the contras should be withering on the vine and yet they were growing dramatically, and that the training continued and airplanes were dropping supplies. So their explanation was that they were doing it with drug money.

Well, in point of fact, anybody who knew of anything to do with drugs immediately got shut down or was turned over to the DEA.

Adolfo Calero   There were accusations that planes would leave this air-field near Homestead Air Force Base, bring arms to us, and go back loaded with cocaine. That's the most ridiculous thing you can imagine!

There was also the story about the airport in Arkansas — that we used to run drugs in and out of there, run arms out and drugs in. We never had anything to do with drug dealers; they never helped us in any way. Those are ridiculous accusations; it made no sense.

I am speaking for the FDN; I don't know if people in Panama — Noriega — helped Pastora. That might have been drug money.

Craig Fuller   The piece of it that I don't believe was ever reviewed with the president, or the vice president, was the contra piece. I know it wasn't; I was with George Bush when he learned about what had happened and how this money had gone to support the contras. He was absolutely shocked; it was like somebody had hit him in the ribs and knocked the air out of him. He came back to the office and just sank into his chair and said, "You're just not going to believe what's happened."

Oliver North   If the vice president knew, I didn't tell him. I had many, many meetings with the vice president. To my recollection, this issue was never addressed.

I don't think John Poindexter was deceiving me. I would prepare memos to the president of the United States. On most, my name appears in the lower left- or lower right-hand corner: "a memo for the president from John M. Poindexter, assistant to the president for national security affairs."

I prepared several of those documents, laying out exactly the trans-action that was going forward. And they came back with an initial — approved by the president. As I said in my testimony before the [congressional] committee, as I said in my trial, and as I said at the trials of others, "I would not have done any of this if I had thought for a minute that the president of the United States had not approved it."

That's not my wont. I was trained for thirty years — not just twenty-two years of active service in the marines, but as a prior-enlisted re-servist in the marines, and at the Naval Academy for five years. I wasn't about to buck the chain of command. I was a good officer — I wouldn't have gotten into the NSC if I hadn't been a good officer —

and you don't get to be a good officer by simply ignoring the wishes of your superiors.

You sometimes have to take the initiative. I certainly did that in combat, in training, and in a lot of other places. But you don't take the initiative in directions that your commanding officer doesn't want you to go.

And so, in my testimony — and what they focused on in *Time* magazine — was that I believed then, and I believe today, that the president knew exactly what was going on. And I think John Poindexter is one of the bravest people I have ever met.

Robert C. McFarlane I find John Poindexter's explanation plausible in saying that he didn't tell the president, because John, knowing it was wrong — and knowing it was already done when North told him ex post — would say, "The only way I can protect my commander in chief is for him not to know."

But I can also well imagine that John, in the dozens of encounters in which the president was surely frustrated at the congressional cutoff, would have said, "We are getting things to them, and Ollie found a way." It seems very likely to me that that would happen, and it's equally likely that Ronald Reagan would have said, "Good, great" — and the next morning would never have remembered it.

Director Casey probably would have told Reagan, because he would have been proud of it. He was a guy who believed what he was telling North: "The president would want you to do this." He thought he knew Reagan better than anybody.

Bill got so frustrated with the Congress and the restraints imposed by it, and with the White House staff, with me, with Meese, Baker, and Deaver — they were not doing the president's bidding.

I don't have a factual basis for this, but Bill really was driven to do what he believed his president wanted him to do — and the law be damned. His own agency had told him: "We're not going to do what the Congress won't let us do." So he had no in-house means.

Richard Secord I would think that Casey would have told the president. He was a cabinet officer; he had frequent, personal meetings with the president; he had the kind of access Weinberger had.

George P. Shultz There isn't any doubt that the president signed on as far as the arms sales were concerned. I don't think that anyone knew —

as far as I can find out — about the diversion of funds. The president didn't know; I don't believe the vice president knew. This was all done within the circle of Poindexter and Casey and North.

David Jacobsen Ollie took the rap to take the political pressure off the presidency; he didn't do anything illegal. He was not a loose cannon; his superiors knew exactly what was going on. It was nice for others to say, "We knew nothing about it. It was just that colonel." Of course, I am biased about him. He saved my life; he freed me; he is one of my best friends.

Miguel D'Escoto I have no doubt that Reagan knew. This is what really makes one wonder about the sanity of the president. He gave more time and attention and creative energy to his efforts to destroy the Sandinista revolution than to any other political situation elsewhere in the world.

Maybe Shultz did not know. He was foreign minister but, from my perception, not really in the inner circle. I was the foreign minister of this country for eleven years; I am the godfather to all of Daniel Ortega's children; we are very, very close. I think it would have been most difficult to be in the Foreign Office and not be very close and have access like thirty hours a day.

Manuel Antonio Noriega When North was speaking, it was Reagan and Bush. He insisted, "Mr. Casey is not my chief; the CIA is not my organization. I depend on, and I respond only to, Reagan and Bush."

Because I sometimes wondered about North, I checked with Mr. Casey. I said to Mr. Casey, "North said that . . . ," and he said, "Okay, I will check." And he checked. I knew that Mr. Casey was a man who said what was right; he was honest. He said to me, "Yes, the president is in charge."

The responsibility for this operation was with Bush and Reagan. I would not have spoken to North if he had been speaking for himself. He had to be speaking for the government.

Albert Hakim I don't think that he even cared, or that the others reported to him. Because we were working at a level that was unreportable, how would he know?

Michael Reagan I think that people around Ronald Reagan knew what was going on, but I don't think that Ronald Reagan did. Had Nancy not been shut down by Donald Regan, Dad would have gotten more information, because there were people out there who knew but just couldn't get through to him.

Lawrence Walsh The Weinberger trial would have exposed the activities of the senior foreign policy advisers to cover up President Reagan's personal participation in the shipment of arms to Iran through the Israelis in 1985.

The president, the vice president, Weinberger, Shultz, Poindexter, and Casey — all listening to Meese — fed them a false history they knew to be false, to conceal the president's participation in a HAWK shipment in November 1985 which was particularly embarrassing, because the CIA had been drawn into it without appropriate authorization and because it was very offensive to the Iranians — it was a botched-up job by the Israeli arms merchants.

It is less likely that some of these same people were aware of the diversion, although through his intelligence sources, Weinberger knew of the controversy about the payments the Iranians claimed they were being overcharged.

WHO ORDERED THE DIVERSION:
THE SCENARIOS

Judy Nir Shalom In the beginning, Mr. Meese said it was my husband's idea. That wasn't the case; the congressional committee found that out. It was a very difficult time for him, to be blamed by the Americans.

He was willing to take the blame to help Israel. He asked Prime Minister Shamir* if he should, and Shamir said no. So did Rabin. Rabin talked to him every day during this time, to show that he was not alone; he knew it was not true.

Duane Clarridge I know for a fact that it was Nir's idea to up the prices to provide funds for the contras.

Roy Furmark I met Nir after the CIA had issued a statement based on my interview that suggested that there had been a payoff to Nir.

Khashoggi called me and said, "Come to Paris," and there was Nir. There was this accusation that Nir had taken a 15 percent payoff [from

---

* Shamir would succeed Peres as prime minister in 1987, under the terms of Israel's Unity government.

Ghorbanifar], so I wrote an affidavit, which he took back to his government, explaining what I had said to the CIA: there was no payoff; this was never mentioned.

Nir was really upset because he felt that they were out to get him, through me. He was upset because he had been called in to the prime minister's office and asked, "What the hell are you doing? Look at what the U.S. government says."

So I flew to Paris and spent two days with him — he flew on a government plane to meet me — and prepared an affidavit, which he took back to his government; he flew right back with this affidavit. It was critical, because he was being accused of being paid off by Ghorbanifar.

I had the feeling that Nir was a key person because he was in the network: he wasn't on the periphery, he was right in the middle. That feeling was based on my spending two days with him in Paris, talking with him.

William Casey

It has been suggested by Martin Anderson and others that at the time the decision was made to divert funds to the contras, Casey was already suffering from the effects of his brain tumor, and therefore, if he was involved in the decision, he may have been confused about what he was doing.

Sophia Casey   I never heard of that before. Martin Anderson is very much against Bill Casey. He never knew him before. In that group, there were two or three people who didn't like Casey.

Bernadette Casey Smith   Dad would push the White House people out of the office and speak to Reagan alone. I'm sure Dad talked about domestic things, and people thought he shouldn't do that.

We were mad when Martin Anderson said that. I don't think so. The doctors told him that it was a very fast-growing tumor. I talked to other people who had tumors like that, and they were fuzzy on unimportant things, but on their work they were fine until very much the end.

What Martin Anderson is saying is that Dad masterminded Ollie North; I don't think that Dad knew what Ollie North was doing. Months before I had asked Dad, "Who is this guy Ollie North?" And he said, "Oh, he's in the National Security Council." That's all he said.

I'm sure he knew Dad, but he was a small-time player, and I think he just ran with the ball. But Martin Anderson is saying that Bill Casey did mastermind it, and that's why he's saying he got fuzzy.

Roy Furmark   I would see Casey half a dozen times a year while he was in government. He always looked vibrant. I never noticed anything. Casey looked the same; his voice was the same. I'm a voice person; I can usually tell if someone is upset, by the slightest change in their voice.

It may have been his speech; he would always talk fast, and therefore it was like he was mumbling. His diction wasn't clear like a debater's, but his mind was so fast, and so brilliant.

When these things come on, they move quickly. With Casey, right up until my last conversation with him, which was during the hearings, I never noticed anything. In fact, in October 1986, when I flew to New York with him, he was going to go play golf.

Albert Hakim   I know very little about Casey. I have a lot of respect for him, God rest his soul. I personally think he was the designer of the whole thing. I never met him, but I really respect him. He and Secord got along fine because, basically, they come from the same way of thinking.

I believe Casey designed both the Iranian project and the Nicaraguan project — that he was really overseeing this thing very closely. I know that from the regular meetings that took place between Secord and Casey, and Ollie and Casey.

Casey didn't get to the level of the Enterprise. He saw two parts. How are we going to fund it as long as we don't use U.S. government money? He didn't care; it was our neck. If he did anything illegal, our neck would go with it. If he didn't, God bless him.

When you design a system and give it to someone to implement, the architect and the mason are two different people. I can look at the same drawing and build it differently.

Roy Furmark   Casey is not here, so whatever went wrong, it's Casey. He was so busy, traveling all over the place, that for North to say that they took showers together going over this project . . . you have to look at Casey's travel schedule: he was always on the road.

Edwin Meese III   I know that Casey was not encouraging North in the diversion of funds because I talked with Bill. Maybe North, in his own mind, thought this was something Casey would approve of. And, of course, he testified that Casey was involved.

By that time Casey was incapable of testifying, and I always felt that Ollie gave Casey more credit than was probably due for his involvement.

Bill Casey was smart — so smart that he would know the political downside of this, the dangers involved.

Abraham Sofaer   I believe that the person who managed this whole affair was Casey; I don't have any doubt about it. I knew Casey from before. I admired and liked him, and when I blew the whistle on the whole thing, it was Casey who, I felt, regarded what I had done as treason. Shultz thought it was great. Reagan thought it was fine, that if that was the truth, let it come out; he didn't want to be impeached. But Casey and Ollie really, really resented what I did.

My sense of it was that Casey and Ollie and — to the extent that they knew what was going on — the other national security people and a lot of the State Department staff knew a lot of this stuff. It had seeped back, all this arms-dealing and stuff.

Michael Ledeen   I loved Casey. I thought he was something wonderful — everybody's favorite uncle. The Woodward allegation is a proven lie.

Oliver North   I've never read Mr. Woodward's books. Quite frankly, I've never had a particularly high regard for Mr. Woodward. I find it hard to believe, knowing the security arrangements Mr. Casey had, that he ever had such a conversation — at least as I have seen it reported.

Sophia Casey   Bob Woodward never got near my husband. There were about five people watching the room, besides us.

Constantine Menges   I have no idea whether Woodward got to see Casey. I went to the hospital several times, and I was not able to get into the room because he was sleeping, or resting, or it wasn't the right time. And I was known to the security detail.

I don't know how anybody could take whatever Casey said after the operation [to be] probative; I don't believe that whatever response there may have been had any significance. If you ask someone something this complicated when a person is in enormous physical and emotional stress, sometimes people understand it and sometimes they don't. It's really hard to know what is understood when there is a partial impairment of the brain. So I don't think that Woodward's scene tells us anything.

What to me is significant is that no member of this huge investigation — with a million documents — [could find any] documentary evidence whatsoever of Casey having this role that North alleged, and as the report said, only North's allegations tie Casey into the initial activities.

The evidence is very clear that Casey was determined to keep the CIA out of it and to abide by the letter of the Boland Amendment.

Bernadette Casey Smith   The people I knew in intelligence said that Bill Casey wouldn't have organized it because it wasn't thought out; it was badly done and didn't have his earmarks. He was too smart an intelligence officer to have the same people handling the Middle East and Central America.

An Oliver North wouldn't have known everything that was happening; it wouldn't have gone through one person. I don't know North, but I am very dubious because North never mentioned Dad's name as being involved in the diversion. Oliver North never mentioned Dad's name until after Dad died.

And he thought — and everybody thought — that until Dad died, he could speak and could correct the information. After the operation there were four months in which he really couldn't communicate. We didn't let that out. Ollie North didn't know that Dad couldn't talk. Bob Woodward didn't know that. And they both got caught.

Abraham Sofaer   I doubt that Woodward had the discussion with Casey in the hospital. However, I don't doubt that Casey had made a deal with Woodward to tell the whole story, that he had told Woodward the whole story in exchange for Woodward's not printing it until Casey died. I read Woodward's book, and there's true and accurate stuff in there that had to have come from Casey, so I infer that Woodward and Casey had made a deal.

So his fib about the hospital encounter was not a real lie, because the information he got was reliable — and he got it from Casey himself. We still don't know the whole story. I'd like to hear the Iranian side of it.

Bernadette Casey Smith   All we knew was that Bob Woodward was writing a book. He told Dad that he was writing a forty-year retrospective on the CIA; he didn't tell Dad that he was writing a book on him, so Dad talked to him. I don't care how many times Dad talked to him; there were only a dozen times on record at the CIA. But he absolutely, positively, never got into the hospital room.

If you read Woodward's book, it's a scenario: the sun is coming in the room . . . but where the room was, the sun couldn't come in that way. It was all done for a screenplay, for which he was supposed to get a half-million dollars; I think it was pulled. He had no ending; he didn't know how to end his book.

I never heard Dad say, "I believe. I believe." His quotes throughout were unlike Bill Casey's speech patterns. In the back of Persico's book on Casey, he has the verbatim interview with Bob Woodward, where he says, "Ah, ah." That is not the persona Woodward would want to present, or does present.

John Hutton   Woodward writes about his going in and seeing and talking to Casey. It's nonsense: the left side of Casey's brain had been removed to get this lymphomatous tumor out. Everybody I've talked to — I talked to his neurosurgeon twice a day so I could keep the president informed, and I would talk to the CIA physician, who was a friend of mine — said that he had gotten a total expressive aphasia. In other words, the part of his mind that controls speech was, for the most part, obliterated.

Also, Woodward never got through to see him. He tried to push his way through, but it was a shoving match and he got pushed down on the ground. And even if Woodward could have gotten in there, Casey couldn't have said anything.

Bernadette Casey Smith   It was a Saturday. The *New York Post* had written "Deathbed Confession." We were coming home from somewhere; we saw it as we were going through the tunnel. We bought the newspaper, and Mom sat very quietly in the backseat and said, "I don't know what I am going to do."

The next day Woodward was supposed to be on *60 Minutes* to talk about it. That afternoon Mom called *60 Minutes*; she wanted to be on with Bob Woodward. They said no, that it was already canned.

We watched the show, and Woodward was asked about something Mom had said that afternoon on a broadcast. She did go on *Nightline*, on the morning shows, and on *Larry King*, so they could have done it if they'd wanted to. The next day Mom got a call from *Sixty Minutes*; it was Mike Wallace, asking her to be on the next week. He said that they had had an agreement with Bob Woodward that they would have no one else on the show who would contradict him. No expert. No one. That is telling in itself.

Roy Furmark   The first thing Casey said after I told him about the Canadians* was, "I want you to brief one of our people on this," and he called Charlie Allen, and Charlie Allen came down, and I went through it.

---

* The financiers of Khashoggi's bridge funding. This conversation took place during a meeting between Casey and Furmark on October 8, 1986.

Casey said, "This is not our operation; it is probably an Israeli operation. I want you to tell every single thing that you know; don't forget one single thing." I didn't finish with him because Casey said, "I'm going back to New York; my wife and I are going back. If you want, I'll drop you off at La Guardia." So I flew back with him.

Then Charlie called me, and he came up to New York. Then I went down to see him in Washington. I recall that there had just been a cabinet meeting and something that Casey had proposed was approved, and they were all elated — it had to do with Russia.

Then, the last time, when I read about the prices in the paper, I called Bill, and I said, "Bill, these figures are all wrong; I know they're wrong." He said, "Come down and see me," and I flew down that night. It was that night that I told him that Ghorbanifar had mentioned that this profit was going to Nicaragua — to the contras. I had never mentioned it before. It was only when I read that there was a big difference between what I know Khashoggi had funded and paid for and what they said was the price in the newspaper that I said to Casey, "These figures are really wrong, Bill. I don't know what happened to the rest of the money."

He then tried to reach someone by telephone. The person wasn't there, and Casey left a message. That's when this whole thing exploded. I was bringing Casey new information. When I had said to Casey that the Canadians were putting a lot of pressure on Khashoggi, he said, "File something."

I said, "You're the government, Bill. All you have to do is have one more shipment so that Khashoggi can try to get his money out of this. Why should he be out ten million dollars? He put the money together, through the Canadians."

Bernadette Casey Smith Dad loved the contras; he thought it was wonderful that people down there wanted to fight their own fight and that our men weren't down there.

He didn't see anything legally wrong with helping people with intelligence, helping to raise money for arms. And his was one of the best legal minds; he was too good a lawyer, besides being a good intelligence officer. He wouldn't have done it if he had thought it was illegal.

Jeane J. Kirkpatrick Casey has had a terrible rap. He was a man of great intelligence, education, and integrity — a really good man. He was very devoted to serving Ronald Reagan.

He cared about the law; [he] had written books about the law. Nobody ever made the case that there was no violation of the law in Iran-contra;

that was the case that Casey was working on when he had his stroke. He is almost treated as if it were a matter of fact that he violated the law, and knowingly violated the law.

I had a very interesting personal conversation with him about this; it has never been published. I was in Europe at the time that the Iran-contra charges began to surface, and when I came back, I called Bill and said, "Hey, you guys have really messed up." He said, "What do you mean?" I said, "You guys are getting the president in trouble; it looks to me like you've broken the law."

He said, "Now calm down. Nobody has broken the law. What law do you think we've broken?" I said, "It looks to me like you have violated one of the provisions of the Boland Amendment." He said, "How long has it been since you've read the Boland Amendment?" I said, "It's been a while." "Well," he said, "nobody's violated the law. You go back and read the Boland Amendment, and you'll see for yourself. There was a specific exemption made — negotiated on the formulation of the amendment understood by the committee — and nobody's violated the law."

I had lunch with Bill and Sophia on a Friday, a few days before his stroke, and he reiterated this position and said it would be made clear. After lunch we went to his office. He asked me something about the trip I had recently made.

He was sitting at his desk — he had been working since about seven o'clock that morning on his testimony — and he said to me that he felt depressed, as if what he did didn't really matter. But, he said, his testimony was going to make a difference.

He never gave that testimony, but I don't doubt that Bill Casey was himself convinced that there had been no violation of the law. He's gotten a very bum rap. This has caused me great pain, as I know it has caused Sophia and Bernadette great pain.

Oliver North

Edwin Meese III   In the two situations that gave rise to the name "Iran-contra," the first one, the Iranian initiative, was so secret, so compartmentalized, that the CIA had a certain function and the Department of Defense had a certain function. Because it was so compartmentalized, and because it was so tightly held, the only place to have somebody coordinate was in the White House.

And that's when Ollie, as head of the political-military bureau, took this thing over. It was in that guise when he telephones and says, "This is the White House calling." People on the outside assume that it is the president, and that he, North, is operating with the proper authority. He overextended that authority beyond what the president had approved when he diverted the funds from the Iran initiative to the contras.

In the contra situation, the Congress had passed different appropriations measures — a different one every year. Some years you could give military aid; some years you could use DOD [Department of Defense] or CIA; other years you couldn't use them, but you could use private funds.

In 1985 and 1986 — the years of the two initiatives — there was nobody in the departments who could do that, because of the congressional legislation, so the only person who could do it was somebody in the president's own office, and that's how Ollie got involved. In other words, in those two instances, which were different from the normal pattern of governmental activity, he had both the opportunity and a very major mission.

If he had stuck with the freedom fighters and done what they were supposed to be doing — which was all proper — or if he had stuck with the Iranian initiative and what was going on there — which was all proper . . . But it was when you took the funds from one and used them for the other that you brought two volatile operations together and put the president into that position of vulnerability.

Adolfo Calero In my dealings with North, I had the impression that what he was doing came from the top down. The first time I met with Reagan — this was in 1985 — North went into the meeting. It was in McFarlane's office; I don't remember McFarlane being there.

The president was very warm toward North; I think he called him Ollie. North venerated Reagan: he was like a god to him. Ollie was a real loyal subject.

Roy Furmark Secord being a general, and North being a lieutenant colonel . . . in the military you always look up to your leader. I've thought it was North listening to Secord, because it ended up that Secord controlled everything, through Switzerland. The decision was made to do it, and now it had to be implemented. And who controlled every single thing? The bank accounts were controlled by Secord and Hakim. At least that is what I have read in the papers.

William P. Clark It all happened with McFarlane. Poindexter, of course, inherited the Iran-contra situation from McFarlane. Whether North had the relationship, and the green light, from the deceased Bill Casey, or not, will always be a question, I suppose.

Robert C. McFarlane I don't think he [North] trusted me after I left the White House; he knew that I'd turned it off. He was sitting there when I came back from London and told the president in the Oval Office, "This is not working."

If he did something else, he wouldn't have told me anyway. Even if he had done something really stupid, it was not something that would threaten the republic; North's not that smart.

Craig Fuller There is no doubt in my mind that North was aided and abetted by Bill Casey, who, again, wanting to do what he thought was right, was looking for ways to get things achieved. But Ollie was someone on whom people could rely to make things happen; he somehow worked in the system without people having a clear idea of how he was going about what he was doing.

He was also in a unique position, because the portfolios he had could meld together, in a way that people didn't fully appreciate at the time, with, I think, Bill Casey's help.

Bernadette Casey Smith North gives conservatives a bad name. We had Dad's wake at home. North called up and asked to come. Of course he wrote in his book that Mrs. Casey had invited him. It was all right; the house was open to anyone who wanted to come, but he invited himself. That was before he said that Bill Casey had done everything. My family was very pro-contra, and they thought he was a hero.

Jeane J. Kirkpatrick I personally doubt whether Ollie North was ever as close, personally, to Bill Casey as North implied after Bill's death — just as I don't believe that Bob Woodward ever had that interview. I have been doubtful about both these things because they were not consistent with my own knowledge about Bill's views and his habits of association.

There were lots of times that Bill Casey would bring together five or six people who were particularly interested in Central America, as he was. As Sophia said, "No matter how many people were in a room, we would end up together, in a corner of the room, talking about the importance of Central America to American national security."

This group never included North; he was never, ever, in one of these meetings. There were various people at them, but never Ollie North. That is one of the things that made me a little bit dubious about him.

Constantine Menges I think that North did it on his own, that he did not do it under orders; he did it in spite of orders, and in spite of his knowledge that it was improper.

I believe that there is very strong documentary evidence — in his own, contemporaneous notes — that contradicts his sworn testimony, that contradicts everything he's written since, that contradicts his whole allegation of his relationship with Casey, which, of course, he used only after Casey's death. And he dropped that allegation when alleging that Reagan knew everything would sell his book better.

The evidence for all of us who know the people, who know the story, and who know the institutions, is overwhelming that this man acted on his own, for his own purposes, and, in fact, for all the tens of millions of dollars that he controlled.

If Casey had not had his stroke and operation, and incapacity, and died, then North never would have made those kinds of allegations, and the political nature of the thing would have had an entirely different resonance.

Stuart Spencer The president had one conversation with me about North. It involved a pardon; there was pressure to have him pardoned. But he didn't pardon him. Maybe that tells it all.

John Poindexter

Richard Secord John was in the navy. It's a pristine service; that's why they wear white. I'm a graduate of the Naval War College; the navy culture is different. John was somewhat ill served by that culture.

I suspect them all, including the president, and the vice president as well. They are, first and foremost, politicians; they didn't get there by being good guys by and large — or maybe even ever.

Craig Fuller I'm sure that Poindexter and North and Casey were involved in the contra piece of Iran-contra, but I don't know how much was shared between North and Poindexter. I think that John Poindexter became very frustrated, because a president who wanted to achieve certain things was constantly having to deal with people on his staff, or his secretaries of state and defense, who were at odds with each other.

Poindexter fell prey to wanting to do something, and make something happen, when, again, the only person who really could make the decision to overrule people like the secretaries of defense and state was the president. And the staff ought not to go about subverting that relationship,

even if it meant that you were up against very tough decisions. And ultimately the president paid a huge price for this.

John Poindexter   The highest level of sign-off on the diversion was me.
It was Ollie's recommendation to me, and I decided not to tell the president, or the vice president, or Bill Casey — and I don't think Ollie did
either.

I didn't tell my superiors because I knew that if it ever leaked out it
was going to be very controversial. I wanted the president to have some
deniability, which he had. Although I would much have preferred that it
had not leaked out, it worked out just the way I had intended it to, if it
did leak out.

James A. Baker III   After all this broke, I saw Poindexter in a White
House hall and he said, "I'm really sorry that we cut you out of these
meetings." I said, "Are you kidding, John? You did me the greatest favor
by not inviting me to those meetings."

Lawrence Walsh   Poindexter claimed that he kept President Reagan informed on almost a daily basis — and Bush also — about the progress of
the so-called Iranian initiative. Poindexter denied that he told the president specifically about the diversion, but you have these very sophisticated people knowing that we are shipping arms to Iran and getting no
results, and keeping it up. Why? The obvious explanation seems to be
that there was an advantage coming to this country in other ways, which
would be support of the contras at a time when Congress had cut off that
support.

The fact is that Poindexter continued to deny that he had supplied
that information. North claimed that he understood that the president
knew about it — until after the exposure, when Poindexter told him he
had not told the president. But everyone is almost on equal ground in
speculating why it was continued when it was so humiliating.

I think we know what we need to know. We know that the president
was willful, whether he said to divert the money or not. He said, "Go
ahead and do two things. Keep the contras in the field, body and soul,
and get the hostages back. And keep the activities going in both directions, in spite of Congress."

Now, whether he said to divert the money from this bank account to
another bank account is secondary. He knew that the process was going
on, and in his own heart he must have known it could not have gone on
legally.

President Ronald Reagan

Lawrence Walsh It's difficult to understand how President Reagan could have continued the arms shipments for months without the release of a single hostage, unless he saw some other advantage coming from it. That's as far as I've tried to go on that.

Manuel Antonio Noriega North had this power in violation of the whole system. But this was a special operation, by direction of President Reagan and Bush. They needed one close person, of any grade — it could be a sergeant — but they needed the person in whom they have confidence.

Craig Fuller Ollie North was somebody who got the job done. I've always thought that if he had been supervised more thoroughly, some of this wouldn't have happened. He came to believe that Ronald Reagan wanted certain things done that, I am convinced, Ronald Reagan never told him to do.

He would hear the president say, "I wish we could do this; I wish there was a way we could help the contras." Mind you, it was a very complicated period, with Congress having this on-again-off-again policy toward the contras. You begin to get these appeals for help, and any compassionate person is going to say, "I wish there was something we could do."

Well, the people who knew the law said, "It's a shame; let's try to change the law." Ollie said, "If this is want he wants to do, let's find a way to do it."

Robert C. McFarlane The Congress kept beating up on him, so Bill [Casey] became operationally a lame duck. He had to come out of that status and find somebody to work with — and he found North. And yet Bill was not a rogue. He believed that Reagan would approve. And for all I know, in private talks with him, Reagan did approve. My guess is that Bill — because he knew and because he didn't have any sense at all that Reagan didn't agree with him — probably told him about it.

Yaacov Nimrodi We in Israel were 100 percent convinced that it was Reagan's decision to go ahead. It was the right decision, but the problem was this rubbish in America. They didn't know how to work; everyone only thought about himself; they were stupid. Secord is a *gonif* [thief]; all he could think of was the money. I think that the money is now in his account — almost thirteen million dollars is missing.

Michael Ledeen   I don't see any reason to doubt Poindexter on the president and the diversion. I've been through Poindexter's depositions, line by line, and I can't find anything that I know to be wrong. It tracks exactly with the way they treated the president: there was a tacit assumption that there were certain things the president should not be told.

Everybody has complicated this beyond recognition. The president drove the policy — both policies. The president wanted the hostages out and said to everybody, "Do what is necessary to get them out." He wanted the contras preserved and said to everybody, "Do what is necessary to keep the contras alive."

The details were not something that you would ever take to a president like Reagan. He was a "big picture" president: he made policy decisions and then left their implementation up to his staff. So they staffed it. I have no doubt that, at some point, North and Poindexter said to each other, "Okay, this is going on, and we are just not going to tell the old man about it. It is something he doesn't need to know."

Edwin Meese III   The president would not have signed off on the diversion, and he would have had a lot of people, including myself, recommending that he not sign off on it. It was a very close decision on just the Iranian initiative. But something like this? No.

Stuart Spencer   Casey mumbled, and Reagan had a hearing problem. I can believe that Casey walked into the room and mumbled, and Reagan said okay.

Terry Anderson   I don't believe that the diversion was done without his knowledge; I believe he was fully informed, as was Vice President Bush. Reagan encouraged Ollie North to do what he was doing.

Presidents have a very strong tendency of deliberately not knowing. He indicated what he wanted done. He continued to indicate what he wanted done even when he was formally agreeing that it shouldn't be done.

And it was done, and he got caught. He successfully evaded responsibility. That doesn't make him any less responsible.

HOW DID NORTH AGGRANDIZE
SUCH POWER?

Charles Hill North was a not untypical officer, a service academy graduate of that era: North, McFarlane, Poindexter, and many others. I could
only surmise that they had been taught at West Point and Annapolis that
the country has taken a wrong turn. "We are the only people who uphold
the nation's good; therefore, when the time comes, you will have to make
some decisions that may appear to be illegal or untruthful, but you will
have to do that because only we can be trusted to uphold the nation's
interest."

I saw that again and again. Primarily, that produces liars — people
who will lie under pressure. North was not that unusual; I saw lots of
people like North.

Duane Clarridge I don't care what rank he is; he represents the White
House. What North was unique at — remember Haig was a lieutenant
colonel too — was filling vacuums. That's where you get the North phe-
nomenon, because North marched for the president. North was an activist, and because vacuums — or areas of need — developed, North was
always there to fill them.

He was very articulate on paper, as well as in speech. He worked all
hours of the day and was very bright, and he just picked up all these portfolios in a much more active and different role from the norm.

John Poindexter He was a very can-do kind of officer. When the Boland
Amendments put restrictions on the CIA and the Defense Department
from taking part in activities for the contras, it became important to figure out some other way to do that.

At that point Ollie had demonstrated the capacity to perform jobs
like that, and to do them very well. Contrary to what Bud has said since,
I think Bud relied on him a lot. When I took over in 1986, I was aware, in
general, of what Ollie was doing, and what his capabilities and — to some
extent — his limitations were. He continued to have my confidence.

William J. Crowe Jr. Anything connected with the White House has a
mystique about it. I worked in the White House when I was a lieutenant — I didn't have as grand a job as North had — and I could call
the navy and say, "Look, we have to get somebody over here. I need a
hammer." And I'd get a box, lined with velvet, with a very nice hammer

sitting in it, with a little plaque saying "For the White House." That's the way we were treated.

So, if the national security adviser supports them and lets them run free, they can do all kinds of things. That's exactly what happened in North's case. He was dealing with a subject that was very highly classified. He's very energetic, and very taken with his subject. He used the White House name freely. And nobody over there seemed to know or to rein him in.

It is very easy for that to happen if the staff is run shoddily and poorly, and if the action officer is unconscionable, you can do all kinds of things in the name of the White House. The reason he got away with it for so long was that everything was so highly classified — what they were doing in Nicaragua and in El Salvador.

You really get mixed up in your own ideology in these kinds of things. You had a group of people who felt that, no matter what, it was good for those people down there to prevail, whether it was legal or illegal, that it was in our best interests. And you had a whole bunch of people in the United States who didn't agree with that, and most of these people carried the Congress with them.

It's not some military officer's function to save the country from itself — and particularly one as dishonest as North. He was a pathological liar; he still is, I think. He said that I had said to him, "You had better straighten out, or I'll take care of you." I never spoke to North in my life. I had heard the name North; I knew he was over there in that organization somewhere.

Richard Secord   I didn't deal with North exclusively, or even all the time. I dealt first with Bud McFarlane. I frequently dealt directly, face to face, with John Poindexter, so it wasn't a matter of my being led around by a lieutenant colonel.

I seldom talk to North anymore, but he has matured some, I am sure, in going through all this mess over the past years. But North was a pretty sharp article even then. I likened him to the army mule. In warfare you would load the mule until you broke his back, and then you would eat him. That is exactly what the Reagan administration did.

He was a can-do kind of guy. They gave him special jobs; he accomplished a lot of them. You have to give him credit; he is an exceptional guy.

If you know anything about the National Security Council staff, they usually don't have too many exceptional people there. It is not a place where most diplomats or military people would like to go; they are seldom seen and are heard from even less. So I wasn't surprised at all at the disparity between his rank and the level at which he was operating. There are lots of less qualified marines than Ollie North who are wearing stars today.

A source told us that, as national security adviser, Judge William Clark had kept North on "a very short leash," believing that North was effective only for certain assignments.

Michael Ledeen I know that there were various efforts to get North a military posting, and he always balked; he did not want to leave. He was very effective in mobilizing these campaigns to keep him there. I do know that when Poindexter became national security adviser, he wanted North to move out. He had been advised that North was a terrible problem, and he set out to get North out of there. He had actually arranged for North to be a military attaché in London; it was set.

And North mounted a big campaign in Congress, in the bureaucracy, and in the press. There were articles saying how indispensable he was — he engineered that whole campaign — and Poindexter finally relented.

The good side of North is, when you are looking for someone to do difficult things, he is what you are looking for. The bad side is that, as a colleague, you can't trust him. The most terrible thing about North, in my opinion, is not what he did then, but what he did after: he abandoned everybody.

I was very happy working with North. He was terrifically effective. That was one of the few places in government where you could really get things done, and we did a lot.

I was fooled, as well as most other people. I thought he was a terrific colleague. He has a dazzling personality, and for an intellectual, an alliance with a man of action is always very exciting.

William P. Clark Ollie was on the staff when I arrived; Richard Allen had brought him in. I gave him the role of liaison and housekeeper for the Kirkpatrick-Kissinger Commission on Central America, studying longer-term social and humanitarian issues down there.

Kissinger and others liked Ollie because Ollie's favorite answer was a marine answer; you gave Ollie an assignment, and his answer would be, "Done." The first time or two, I asked, "You mean you've already accomplished it?" "No," he said, "but it's done." He was a man who could be counted on to see that people got to airports and were picked up; he handled all the logistics for that commission.

He was never in a role of big substance while I was there. Intelligence gathering, yes. And making recommendations, yes. But not in an operational or policy role. He was more of a military attaché, as Poindexter had been to Richard Allen.

Roy Furmark   Even though there is a chain of command and all that in the White House, everybody is busy, working eighteen hours a day just on their own thing, without worrying about what others are doing. It's not like the regimentation you have in the military or in the Pentagon.

There are many meetings each day in the White House; at the morning meeting they may go through an agenda of twenty-five items. And the president has his own schedule to fulfill, with all of its pressures. So they are not sitting down with North and asking him, "Whom did you see today? What did you do?"

Albert Hakim   Governments are not efficient in management. When you don't manage a lieutenant colonel, he can end up doing anything in his office.

What was he reporting to Poindexter? How he was reporting to him, I can only guess. He is very, very talented in the presentation of anything that doesn't eliminate his own twist. So how much twist he was putting into this, and how much twist Poindexter was putting in, and how much McFarlane was used by Ollie and others — I cannot say.

In my heart of hearts, I believe the power that Ollie had was something he arranged to have. It was not something that was given to him.

Michael Ledeen   One thing that people forget about North is that he was a consummate bureaucrat. He always made sure that he wrote the last memo; if he had to stay there till three in the morning, he would stay; and if it meant going two days without sleep, he would go without the sleep.

In government access is power. Anyone who gets the ear of the top guy is powerful; it doesn't matter what his title is. Kissinger once advised me, "When there is a crisis, just show up. Go into the room and sit down, as if you belong there. You won't find people with titles much more important than yours. Just sit there and work. In a crisis they want people who are willing to work."

And North was always willing to work. Don't forget that North's secretary, Fawn Hall, was the daughter of Wilma Hall, McFarlane's secretary, so whenever we wanted to see McFarlane, Fawn called Wilma, and we were there. So Ollie had instant access. And that's power; it doesn't matter what your title is.

David Abshire   He gained power because the hostage issue — and their wives — got such political attention that that created a political force in itself, and North was at the head of that.

I know some of the people who were at those meetings and thought he was next to God; this guy was going to save the hostages. Shakespeare or Eliot would have done such a good job on him because you had certain noble motives, but he wasn't in the Western tradition — that you've got to tell the truth. He never learned that at Annapolis.

But he's a politician, he's charismatic. Then, of course, you've got Bill Casey, so you had the culture operating there that increased North's leverage.

Michael Deaver   He was given a lot of authority by people: McFarlane, Clark, Poindexter, Casey. I guess I'm cynical, or suspicious, but he was exactly the kind of guy I wouldn't want around. He was kind of bright-eyed and bushy-tailed, and "Yes, sir," and "No, sir," and wore the flag on his heart.

Reagan was very impressed with him because he was exactly that kind of all-American kid. In many ways Reagan could see everything; in other ways he could be a fool.

Constantine Menges   He never had a political sense. He was a very good person to be the military liaison to the contras. He and his staff were not supposed to be the geopolitical strategists for the region; they were supposed to have a defined technical function. And North aggrandized that through his courtship of McFarlane and Poindexter.

I had breakfast with North every day for two years, after our seven-thirty meetings. And North was unctuous and crisp and courting of McFarlane and Poindexter at all times to their faces — and vicious and brutal in criticizing them behind their backs.

At a certain point I went to various senior people, saying that I was concerned about North — that I was concerned about having him in such a sensitive position, that I believed that he lied too much, that he lied to us, and that he lied about important things.

When Elliott Abrams became assistant secretary of state, I said to him, "North has many good qualities, but he lies and manipulates and will try to control things. Don't do anything in the real world based on what he tells you. You can't trust him; we have all learned this. We all regret it. He's charming and nice and personable. He means well, seems to be on the right wavelength in terms of issues, but this is something you have to watch, because he'll try to control you. If he says that there's a sudden incursion across the border and we need military assets put into Honduras — North always liked to move assets around — don't make a move until you check with CIA."

One of our interviewees who was close to the situation and who declined to be quoted for attribution, believes that Casey should have performed the function of éminence grise regarding North, rather than romanticizing North's activities—as if Casey were back in the OSS.

Robert C. McFarlane   Casey went back thirty years with Reagan. So North, whether he believed it or not, could salve his soul and say, "Well, I am obeying my chain of command. My president, through Bill Casey, would approve what I am doing." One could say North's conduct with regard to Central America had to do with Vietnam, that the burden of guilt that so many of us had in betraying our allies in Vietnam led us, North included, to say, "We will never do this again."

Maybe that holds water in Nicaragua; it certainly didn't in Iran, because there weren't any allies involved. Yes, there were hostages, but anyone who couldn't see that the people we were dealing with were not people of integrity . . . Our mission, originally, was to overthrow the government, but you couldn't do that; we had no business doing that. So North's justification was: "My commander in chief" — through Casey — "says so. Therefore, I am obeying my chain of command." And there was this arrogance, this hubris: I can make it happen.

Yaacov Nimrodi   North is a liar, a crook, a bastard. We dealt with him because the Americans appointed him to be our colleague.

Terry Anderson   Ollie North is a wonderful combat commander. He is a marine. I was a marine; I admire him for that. But marines don't belong in political positions. What in God's name gave anybody the idea that Ollie North, a straightforward marine, could engage in sensitive political maneuverings with a bunch of Iranian radicals and succeed? How did they think he could outsmart these people?

David Jacobsen   Ollie North did two things for me, as did President Reagan, and I will be forever in their debt. They kept me alive when there was an offer out for seven and a half million dollars to kill me, and they did get me released.

At the time we bombed Libya, Gadhafi offered two million dollars each for the killing of three hostages in Lebanon: Peter Kilburn, an American, and two British professors. Six million dollars was paid by Libya to the Hezbollah to kill these three hostages.

Later Gadhafi offered ten million dollars to kill four of us: Sutherland, Anderson, Jenco, and me. One day Said, one of my guards, came in and said, "Mr. David, how much do you think you are worth to your government?" I said, "Maybe two dollars." He said, "No, be serious." So I said, "Well, as a ransom, perhaps half a million dollars." He said, "No, you're wrong. You are worth seven and a half million dollars to the U.S. government." I asked how he knew this, and he said, "I know."

After my release, I was talking with Ollie, and he told me that he had heard on the street of an offer by Libya for ten million dollars to kill the four hostages. He took this information to the president and said, "Our intelligence tells us that there is an offer of ten million dollars to kill four of the hostages. What should we do?"

The president said, "Well, there is only one thing to do, and that's to outbid them." So Ollie said, "How much?" And Reagan allegedly said, "Thirty million dollars seems like a good amount. Thirty million dollars divided by four is seven and a half million dollars." So Ollie said, "Where do we get the thirty million?" And Reagan apparently took a three-by-five card out of his pocket and wrote down three names and said, "Call these people."

Ollie told me he called the three people, and in thirty minutes he had pledges for thirty million dollars. The offer was to be made by a third party, in Africa. I personally think that an offer was made by the sultan of Brunei.

Then the Hezbollah and the Iranians had a problem. Do we kill these guys for ten million bucks and lose twenty million dollars on the deal? And a decision was made not to kill us for the ten million, but also not to accept the thirty million, because they wanted more money — the billions held in frozen assets.

Uri Simhoni It's in the psychology of someone like North to go beyond the limits, to do more than people expect of him. Sometimes you are in a position to implement your dreams. Oliver and Amiram Nir were in a position where they felt, "Yes, we can go ahead and do things. We have the power."

You must get into the psychology of people who want to leave something behind, to do something that will be written about by historians — to be somebody.

I used to meet with Oliver almost daily. My job was to make sure the American decision-makers were familiar with our point of view. For me, Oliver was a reliable channel to transfer the information higher. As a result, Oliver was much better informed than others. He used this position: he knew how to speak; he was enthusiastic; people started to listen to him.

In most administrations people do not like to take responsibility. But he wanted to be involved, to express his ideas. He became a key player with no relation to his military rank; he was a lieutenant colonel, but he was much more than that because of where he sat. He was well informed, and suddenly he became important.

Now, there are talkers and there are doers. He was a doer; he was ready to go to Nicaragua, not to go fishing or take vacations. If not for Iran-contra, he could have made his way up, up, up.

Adnan Khashoggi Let's say that I'm a married man, and I have a good servant, and whenever my girlfriends come, he takes them around the corner; suddenly he becomes a very powerful man. North was given a job of secrecy that was illegal, unacceptable; suddenly he felt his muscles.

He was a brave soldier; he took the lead in initiating new mechanisms, getting money from different channels — from the Bahamas, for example — to buy arms for Nicaragua. If you start digging about how much money was spent in Nicaragua illegally, the Iranian money was nothing. It was just the tip of the iceberg, another creation of North to get more arms.

George P. Shultz His influence was very narrow. He had no impact on U.S.-Soviet affairs; he had no impact on our Asia-Pacific operations. He was focused on the Central America area, and I think that one puts their finger on it when they say that Casey was the driving force there.

It wasn't as though North accumulated power. Casey did. And the White House national security apparatus did. The basic problem — in addition to too much of a policy orientation on Casey's part — was the yen of people in the White House to be operational.

That seems to happen a lot in the White House. Look at Henry Kissinger, who, great as he is from a procedural view, basically shunted the departments totally aside. And Bill Rogers, who was secretary of state, didn't even know they were making an initiative toward China, let alone what they were negotiating on Vietnam. That was all being done in the White House.

Did North Have a Relationship
with President Reagan?

Uri Simhoni   When Rabin was in meetings with McFarlane, North was in the room. He might have been a lieutenant colonel, but he was in the room with a defense minister. If he was not important, why did McFarlane call him in? Or Poindexter? He was there all the time. I believe that he was a key player, with good access to the president.

James A. Baker III   North exaggerates his contacts with the president. I don't remember but one meeting with Ollie North in my office during the first term. But there is a lot of power in the national security adviser and with the director of the CIA. They don't have to get the president to sign off on every little thing they do, and I don't think they got him to sign off on a lot of what Ollie was doing.

Michael Deaver   I did my best to keep North out of the Oval Office. There is nothing to North's claim of a relationship with the president. North used to come into the Oval Office on Monday morning, having spent the weekend in Beirut, and with Bud sitting right there, tell Reagan he was winning in Beirut. It was ridiculous.

Fawn Hall   To my knowledge, there were no private meetings, no private phone calls. Ollie was obviously in a lot of meetings attended by the president.

The president knew who Ollie was. Ollie is not shy; he is very humorous and affable, and I am sure that he engaged the president.

Ollie definitely knew the vice president better than he knew Reagan because of the terrorism — the marine barracks and all that. The vice president headed a task force on terrorism, and Ollie, as the NSC representative, was in charge of coordination. Terrorism was clearly a crisis. The administration needed a policy to deter it. Ollie also sat in on cabinet meetings. The vice president was only a floor away from our office.

Constantine Menges   North had many good qualities, but he had an enormous problem of misstating facts and reality — and of self-promotion and self-aggrandizement — and he's giving speeches and saying he meets with the president twice a week. This is simply not true.

He told me he saw Nancy Reagan. One time he was telling me about how he had just had a talk with Nancy Reagan, which was, of course, absurd. I said, "Come on, Ollie, you're not talking to the Methodist

Women's Club. You didn't have a conversation with Nancy Reagan." He said, "Well, . . ." and kind of shrugged. My publisher took out the word *delusional*, [but] that was the view some people had of North.

The inaccurate statements became progressively worse, and I said to him, "Ollie, you have to stop doing this; you have to tell us the truth." And his answer would be, "You're right, Constantine. I don't know why I do that."

Oliver North   I have never said, or claimed, that I met with the president one on one. How that story got started, I don't know. There is more folklore about Ollie North than there is about Rip Van Winkle.

Geoffrey Kemp   Sometime in 1984 North was told by McFarlane, "Ollie, take it from me. If you are to have a career in the marines, you have to go back. The marines hate this White House. You've been here two and a half years; you are already overstaying your welcome. Go back into the field and get on with your career."

And Ollie packed his bags and was to go to Okinawa, or something like that. The reason that I know this is that my secretary was promoted to go to work for George Bush and Fawn Hall was assigned to me as her replacement. Then, at the last minute, there was another terrorist incident, and Ollie was brought back in.

Now, by that time he had shown extraordinary dedication and, secondarily, through bureaucratic smarts, parlayed his job as coordinator of the NSPG into being the point man on terrorism for the NSC. When you have a mandate that includes terrorism, you can do what very few others in the bureaucracy can do: you can legitimately get involved in everyone's business. So he could come into my office and say, "Why don't we have a chat about Abu Nidal and the PLO?"

Thirdly, you learn very quickly that if you truly want to get anything done, you have to have a good Rolodex of who your opposite numbers are in the key agencies: State, Defense, and CIA. These people are invariably career — this is the point at which you get to be nominated to be an ambassador or [for] another job requiring Senate confirmation — and you are very aware that what stands between you and that embassy, or that promotion, is the White House.

So all you have to do is call up and say, "This is Ollie North, from the White House, calling." The fact that he is a major* is irrelevant, because if you screw this guy up, he can make life very unpleasant for you. So you

---

* North was promoted while in the White House.

are able to parlay the name of the White House into extraordinary clout in the bureaucracy. And, of course, North did this.

Then, when you stay in there longer than anyone else, the new opposite-number people are going to be even more intimidated. And if your boss thinks you are doing a great job, and is preoccupied with other things, you bring things forward to the National Security Council, and you end up with Weinberger and Shultz shouting at each other, and nothing will be done. This is how it happens.

Robert C. McFarlane   North had no personal relationship with the president; he was never alone with the president, ever, in my time in the White House.

I had been asked by North to help him get a command and avoid being sent off to a staff job. I had done it once, and the second time — I think it was 1985 — he said he was about to get orders to a staff job, and would I help. I called [Marine Commandant] P. X. Kelley and asked if this was a problem, and he said, "Why don't you come over?"

I went over, and we had lunch in his private dining room, one on one, and he said, "There are some things you ought to know about North." He told me about this episode back in '74,* and he said, "Apart from that, what would have kept him from being a general is that so many people don't like him; his grandstanding and arrogance offend a lot of people."

I was surprised. A lot of very courageous marines are brash and flamboyant. And because North had been nominated to come over here by the marines and the secretary of the navy, I assumed that North was the genuine article.

But what Kelley was telling me was that North was unlikely to be promoted. He said, "We can give North a command, but I didn't want you to be misguided. I felt that there were some things you should know about."

Fawn Hall   I have heard the story that Ollie wanted reassignment from the White House; I have heard it from Ollie, and from others. Whether or not it's true, I don't know. I know that at one point they were packing to move to Camp Lejeune.

I think that Ollie wanted out. The part of him that wanted to follow

---

* In December 1974, North was hospitalized for eleven days at the Bethesda Naval Hospital, where he received psychiatric treatment for depression induced by stress related to both his military service in Vietnam and marital problems, which were resolved.

orders, that said, "Ollie, it's time to go," was willing. There was a part of Ollie that felt that something would fall apart if he wasn't there.

I think he was disappointed when they kept him on. Then later, as time wore on, at nearly the breaking point of this whole thing, I heard that Poindexter was quite concerned that Ollie was pushing too hard, and Poindexter felt Ollie needed to back off, or we needed to let Ollie go or take some of the responsibility from him — that maybe he was getting to the cracking point.

I never saw Ollie overwrought; he functioned very well. It's amazing. He would go on these trips; I would be dead tired, but he had the capacity to do it. At that point I heard that Poindexter was going to turn over Ollie's terrorism responsibilities to Vince Cannistrano, who worked right next to us.

It was the only time I ever saw Ollie . . . I was disappointed. We all have our disappointments in people, but it was quite profound for me. He didn't want that to happen, and he was pissed; he was clearly upset. I think he felt that it was his baby. And I can understand that.

He could have absolutely been a general. To me, Ollie was a combat field marine. That's where he was happiest; he was not a suit person. He came in there and got into it because he is a person who gets into things.

Joseph Metcalf North was a wild man. The basis for wanting him out was that he was unqualified for the job. At least three times that I know of, they — the military, the members of the Joint staff — tried to get him out of there. They were told no. Now, whether President Reagan or Donald Regan ever made an explicit decision, I don't know.

Oliver North I was slated for a field command; my monitor had slated me for command of a battalion. I tried to get out of the White House three different times; the commandant of the Marine Corps testified about it at my trial.

I had been on a career track to be a general officer before I went to the White House. If you look at my fitness reports — there are dozens of them, in some cases written by general officers, some actually say "commandant" — they say, "This man ought to be a general officer someday."

One of the reasons I did not want to go to the White House was that the U.S. Marine Corps is not the U.S. Army. You can find no record, in all of the different outside service assignments, where marines prosper [outside the corps]. I knew that. One thing I knew well was the U.S. Marines. Once you go out of service, you're gone.

I went over to see General Kelley, and I said, "I need to get back to the U.S. Marine Corps." He said, "Ollie, I am being told by the president of the United States to keep you there. I'm not moving you."

I knew that after three years in the White House my career was finished. At that point you start to think: What else can I do? I communicated that to Bud McFarlane on a number of occasions. That's when he started to talk about, "Well, maybe you can come over to CSIS."[*] He actually wrote me notes to that effect.

David Abshire   North's lawyer came in; they tried hard to get a pardon. I wouldn't meet alone with the lawyer; I had one of my people in the meeting. Of course, it went nowhere.

As a matter of fact, there was a meeting North attended with the Iranians in Frankfurt. I guess the NSA [National Security Agency] taped it; maybe North didn't know that. He told the Iranians that we really didn't have an evenhanded policy, that we were for Iran to win the [Iran-Iraq] War, that he had been with the president, and that the president had told him that personally.

We got that tape and took it in to the president. Don Regan was with me. This was the day after Bud McFarlane tried to take his life [on February 9, 1987, with an overdose of Valium]. It was the only time I have seen Reagan furious — he should have been furious twenty times — and he let out an exclamation and said, "The wrong man tried to take his life." That's how mad he was at North when he heard that prevarication.

The North-Nir Symmetry

Nimrod Novick   There is a parallelism between Nir and North. The two gentlemen have many common characteristics. In some ways they are almost mirrors of each other: patriotism, inclination for military security, clandestine activities, very dynamic and creative.

They part company where Oliver parts with the truth and with reality. Nir was very realistic and was not an obsessive liar; he would color the truth as a marketing instrument, but I don't think he was a liar. He would not knowingly mislead the prime minister or the minister of defense.

The relationship between Nir and North is a fascinating one. They got to know each other when Ollie was at the State Department, in charge of counterterrorism. That was Nir's only mandate at the time,

---

[*] The Center for Strategic and International Studies, a Washington think tank with which McFarlane became affiliated after his resignation as national security adviser in December 1985.

which was not a very satisfying mandate because at that time the position had no teeth, and no instrument of implementation.

When North moved into the White House, it was one of the greatest days of Nir's life. All of a sudden, he has a partner in an important circle, who sees things the way he does, which means: the two of us can get things done. This was the turning point in his career as adviser on counterterrorism.

Judy Nir Shalom   You could say they were two brilliant men. My husband could read when he was two, and Ollie was also smart. They knew that they were smart and that they could make the difference. Amiram wouldn't have minded taking the blame to help Ollie.

Michael Ledeen   He was just like North: super-ambitious, endless energy, very handsome, charming, charismatic. He was the Israeli equivalent of North.

THE INVESTIGATIONS

Michael Ledeen   Casey obviously didn't trust North. Everybody misses this. If you look at Casey's behavior toward North from the minute Casey found out that the Iranian thing was going on, he attached a line person from the CIA to North. From that moment on, there was always a CIA person with North. Every meeting North had with an Iranian, there was a CIA person there.

That is the opposite of what North testified to. His testimony said the operation was self-contained, off-the-shelf, independent covert action. Nonsense! It was before North took it over; once North took it over — and Casey found out about it — Casey said, "No, I want my people there." He wasn't going to let North do this by himself. No way.

All these people were saying that terrible crimes had been committed. That never happened; there was nothing criminal about Iran-contra except a couple of people cheating on their income tax.

It was a blunder, a stupidity. And like most stupidities, it was generated by the usual things that make people act stupidly: personal ambition, misguided loyalties, a vision of things that aren't possible, and lack of culture. I mean North — and I have plenty of good things to say about him. He was like the little girl with the little curl in the middle of her forehead: when he was good, he was spectacular; when he was bad, he was horrific.

House and Senate Committees
Hold Their First Public Hearings

On May 5, 1987, the House and Senate committees investigating the Iran-contra affair held the first of a series of public hearings in which testimony was heard from the major players in both the arms-for-hostages operation and the diversion of funds to the contras.

The public hearings would continue until August 3. On August 12, President Reagan acknowledged, in a television appearance, that he had been "stubborn in pursuit of a policy that went astray."

Lawrence Walsh   The joint committee moved very rapidly and tried to throw a broad net, but it destroyed its effectiveness in many ways by setting an arbitrary time limit on its work. It is just impossible to do a thorough job on activities of this complexity in the time it allowed itself.

Its controlling effort was to get everything over with before the presidential election year. In doing that, it not only failed to do justice to its own investigation but, by granting immunity to North and Poindexter as a shortcut, it hurt mine.

John C. Whitehead   They asked the secretary [of state] to be the first witness at the hearings, but he was away. Mike Armacost, the number-three man at State, was supposed to testify in Shultz's place. But at our regular morning meeting on the day of the hearing, Armacost said, "It looks like more of a political thing than a foreign service expert issue, and I wonder, George, if I should be the one to testify."

They both looked toward me: "What are you doing this afternoon, Whitehead?" So I was assigned to give the State Department testimony. This was the first time there had been any official statement about this Iran business. I testified for three hours — with lots of questions. We didn't know much about this transaction, so I said, "I don't know the answer to that question."

I thought I had handled it quite well. I drove back to the office from the Hill and turned on the television. To my horror, I found that my testimony was leading off the news on every channel. In the midst of three hours of testimony, I had occasionally made an unfortunate statement that was not entirely loyal to the White House position. Congressman [Robert] Toricelli [D-N.J.] said, "The president has remarked that he has seen a diminution of terrorism in Iran in the last few months as a result of improved relations [of Iran] with the United States."

I answered — not terribly wisely — "I hate to disagree with my president, but the information we have shows there has been no change in the degree of terrorism sponsored by Iran in the last months." So the headline was: "I Hate to Disagree with My President, But . . ."

It looked bad for the president on the evening news, as if I had undercut him. So I wrote the president a note, saying, "My testimony is playing very badly. I thought I had defended your position and your sympathy toward the hostages." He was always extremely sympathetic toward them; he used to say they were in his prayers every night, and he thought of them every day when he first woke up. You could tell that it [the hostage issue] constantly preyed on his mind. We all knew of this concern, and I am sure that things that were done by his staff were done out of a feeling that he would have wanted them to do what they were doing.

I didn't get an answer to my note that evening. The next day the newspaper headline was: "I Hate to Disagree with My President, But . . ."

Finally, late that afternoon, there was a message asking me to come over to see the president. I said to my staff, "Well, it's been fun." I'd been there almost a year; I thought I was going to be fired.

I met with the president alone, and he said, "You have been taking a lot of flack today. I want you to know that I understand how that can happen. You have been doing a terrific job, and I want to reassure you that something like this is inevitable, and I understand that you are doing your best." He couldn't have been nicer, and I was so relieved.

"But, John," he said, "I have to tell you how I heard about it. I had a very busy day yesterday. I got back to the White House at seven o'clock, went upstairs, took off my shoes and put on my slippers and lounging robe, and sat down to watch the seven o'clock news.

"You know how, when you turn on the television, the sound goes on but there are a few seconds' delay before the picture comes on? The sound said, 'I hate to disagree with my president, but . . .' I said to myself: Now, who in the hell can that be? And then, John, your picture came on — you of all people. I was so surprised."

So in that wonderful, warm way in which he made everybody feel good about their work, he let me know that I had hurt him. I was relieved that I didn't get fired.

Fawn Hall During the time that Congress was writing these letters, and asking about things, we pulled documents. In fact, Ollie went through them. There was a piece of paper that Bud had written on; there were serial numbers, identifying numbers for documents that were taped to his desk for years.

I had never changed documents before. I kind of took a deep breath. I thought to myself: But he must have instructions. When the whole thing blew up, some of the documents matched up. My feeling was that Bud had told Ollie at some point to take care of this. I don't know what the instructions were.

It bothered me, but I didn't think of it as being something so cynical, or really very bad. I wouldn't do things that were wrong. I felt that it was innocent, but I don't know.

Michael Ledeen   I was supposed to testify before North.* The Monday before the Thursday I was supposed to testify, we had a final deposition with Liman, so we ran through a lot of things. At the end of it my lawyer, Jim Woolsey — who went on to be CIA director — said to Liman, "How certain is it that Michael is going to testify?"

Liman said he didn't know. Then he looked at me and, with a tone of sympathy, asked, "Why are you so eager to testify?" I said, "Everyone is having so much fun telling my story that I thought I'd have a crack at it myself." He said, "There are a lot of people on the committee who don't like you." I said, "I know. Not to worry."

And then I made my big mistake. I said, "First of all, there is no question that can embarrass me. I didn't do anything wrong; I have nothing to be ashamed of. And moreover, when they are finished asking me their questions, I have a few of my own for them. You just make sure that [William] Cohen [R-Me.] and [James] McClure [R-Idaho] are there." And this look came over his face, and I said to myself: You idiot. And I never testified.

And one night [Daniel K.] Inouye [D-Hawaii]† called me at home. It was unbelievable. He said, "We just had a meeting, and we voted 16–0 that you shouldn't testify." There is a thing in bridge called a practical finesse on a hand that is not necessary. The gag everybody says here is, "He took a finesse to show everybody that he knew how to finesse." It was an out-and-out lie; he had no reason for it. He called because he figured it was time for him to lie to me. Lee Hamilton [D-Ind.], who was his counterpart in the House, just gave me the back of his hand; he never responded to anything. Even [Senator Joseph] McCarthy let people testify.

* North began his testimony on July 7, 1987.
† Senator Inouye was chairman of the Senate Select Committee on Secret Military Assistance to Iran and the Nicaraguan Opposition.

Fawn Hall   In the hearings they said to Ollie, "You told Secord you have a private relationship with the president, but we know that is not true." And Ollie answered, "I would have told Secord anything to get it done." And that is Ollie; he would exaggerate.

In reading his book [*Under Fire: An American Story*, with William Novak (HarperCollins/Zondervan, 1991)], I almost wanted to throw up, about his whining about not having a White House badge. I was a little bit ashamed; I was disappointed. There were some exaggerations that were Ollie. He does that; he's a storyteller. It crosses into being detrimental, into clearly lying. I think he's capable of lying.

When I defended him in my testimony, I was devastated by the onslaught of attack; I couldn't believe we were being attacked like that. I was very young and naive. Also, I couldn't see any discrepancies at that time; I had never seen him boldly lie.

Adolfo Calero   The congressional investigation was a lot of theater. The only thing they didn't do before I went on television was to put makeup on me.

One thing that I am proud of is that while Ollie and Secord claimed the Fifth Amendment, I never did. My lawyer told me that that was what I should do. But I said, "No. I have nothing to hide. I have nothing to be afraid of." He said, "Well, my duty as a lawyer is to tell you to do that." I said, "If I did that, I wouldn't need a lawyer, so all I want of you is to guide me legally. I did nothing wrong. I did not know about these things. I did not participate in making it up. We used the money correctly."

They investigated not only Iran-contra; they investigated all our funds — where they had come from, what they were destined for. I gave North unsigned traveler's checks; that was something this bank did for us in Miami so we could get around.

I felt that he was totally trustworthy. I told the independent counsel that I would trust North with my life.

Lawrence Walsh   North's activities today are an outgrowth of the joint committee hearings — the fact that they were in such a hurry to get their work done that they did not have time to litigate with Oliver North, to make him agree to giving private testimony before he gave public testimony. They made a deal which no lawyer would make, except under some extreme urgency of time — to permit him to go on cold as a witness, and take over the hearing, and make a hero of himself.

Everything he is doing today is still an aftermath of that one glaring error, which he and his lawyer ably capitalized on to raise funds for his legal defense, to sell his book, and to make him a very popular lecturer — twenty-five thousand dollars a shot during the period I was in office.

Then, even more pointedly, when he ran for the Senate, he not only made a nearly successful run in an important state, but he was getting homage from Republican presidential contenders at the time — with Dick Cheney, Jim Baker, and Dole all sending funds to him.

He achieved attention and power beyond the state of Virginia — and beyond even the Republican Party. All of this comes less from his activities in connection with the contras and the recovery of the hostages than in his turning the tables on the committee, which was an extraordinary, dramatic achievement.

The jury convicted him as a felon, but the Congress had laid the groundwork to destroy the conviction. The conflict with the Congress could not have been more dramatic. And it was not only the conflicting needs for his testimony, which we thought we had surmounted — and which Judge [Patricia M.] Wald, who dissented from the reversal,* also thought we had surmounted. Congress could have a witness and we could still convict him if sufficient precautions were taken. But that was stricken down by what I thought was an extreme opinion by the Republican majority of the panel that reviewed the case.

Judge Silberman was obviously the author of the more extreme part of it, and it had the ring of partisanship. And it is a shame, because there has to be a way to accommodate Congress and the courts in a legitimate performance of the duties of each. I think that Congress greatly exacerbated the problem by calling North without proper preparation and letting him make himself into a hero, and run free, and give an erroneous impression of his activities to the country.

Roy Furmark   Casey called me and said, "Roy, I just came out of an intelligence hearing. I'm sure that they are going to call you."

A few days later — I had left my apartment about six o'clock, I was getting a flight to Chicago — at about seven-fifteen in the morning, the doorbell rings, and there are two policemen and a guy from the Senate

---

* On July 20, 1990, a three-judge panel of the U.S. Court of Appeals, in Washington, D.C., suspended the three felony convictions: deceiving Congress about secret Reagan administration arms sales to Iran; receiving an illegal gratuity; and destroying government documents. The court set aside the convictions for the first two felonies and overturned the third conviction. The panel, which split two to one, consisted of Judges Laurence H. Silberman and David B. Sentelle and Chief Judge Patricia M. Wald.

Intelligence Committee. He flew in, the police met him at La Guardia Airport, and they drove, sirens blaring, to my house in Brooklyn Heights.

The doorman said that I had left already. They insisted on going upstairs. They rang the bell, and my wife's nurse opens the door. We have an Irish girl taking care of my wife because my wife is a quadriplegic [due to an illness-related spinal cord injury]. She thought they were after her, and she says, "Mr. Furmark is not here." They say, "He's here. Where is he?" And they insist on going in to see my wife, so they go down the hall, see my wife in bed — she is in bed, she can't talk — and he drops a subpoena on her.

Then I came home, and there was the subpoena. I talked to my lawyer, and he said, "You've got to take the Fifth." I said, "For what?" He says, "Who knows what they are going to do to you?" I said, "No, I'm not taking the Fifth. I'll tell what I know, and that's it."

So I went down to the hearing, and I complained, with all the senators there, about the tactics of the subpoena guy, almost breaking into my house, going in and dropping the subpoena on my wife, who is a quadriplegic and can't talk, and they said, "He wasn't served properly." I said, "I'm here; I accept your service; let's go on." And I told my story.

They were stretching. [Senator Thomas] Eagleton [D-Mo.] went after me inside the Senate Intelligence Committee; he wore the black hat as though I had secrets to everything. Who else can go and see the DCI? Who else can do all this? I said, "You know, Mr. Casey is a regular guy. He doesn't turn his back on old friends because he is now important."

Albert Hakim   My opening statement when I testified was that I had three objectives. And I am the only one who came clean and clear and said that: "I want to help my country, the United States; my native land, Iran; and make money." One of the senators, at the end of the hearing, said, "You are not a profiteer; you are a good businessman, and you definitely have helped the country." So there is a difference between being a businessman and doing this work for a profit, or a businessman who would create agitation between the two ends of the business to increase their income.

Lawrence Walsh   Hakim promised, at the time we permitted him to plead guilty to a misdemeanor, to assist us in obtaining the return of the money for the government, except for, I believe, $1.6 million that he claimed he needed for commitments that he'd already made.

Then, as soon as he had received the sentence, when we came a few months afterward to collect the money, he welshed on his agreement and would not cooperate. So we turned it over to the Department of Justice to pursue. But I believe that the money [$7.8 million, plus interest] is all there.

The Tower Commission

Lawrence Walsh   The White House at the time the Tower Commission was appointed was hoping to divert attention from the president and focus it on the National Security Council. The Tower Commission's area of responsibility was simply to review the activities of the NSC and criticize its overstepping.

It was part of an effort by the White House to publicly suggest a runaway conspiracy growing out of the National Security Council and, thereby, to divert attention from the president's own shortcomings. Actually, the Tower Commission went somewhat further than its assignment; it developed other testimony.

Roy Furmark was asked by the Tower Commission to produce both Ghorbanifar and Khashoggi; he did so, setting up meetings with them in Paris.

Roy Furmark   When I tried to convince Khashoggi to meet with the Tower Commission, I said, "Adnan, tell them what you did. You put up the bridge money; you introduced Ghorbanifar to the Israelis; and that was it. You didn't deal with the Americans; you didn't deal with the Iranians. You had faith in this thing. You put up the bridge money, and in the end, you're the only one who lost money. The Americans made money; the Israelis made money; the Iranians got what they wanted; Secord and company made money; the contras got money. And you lost your money." Khashoggi brought all his bank records to show them.

Adnan Khashoggi   Reagan tried to stop the Iran-Iraq War; this was a noble thing to do. Secondly, he wanted to neutralize this radical force that was developing in the area.

The Tower Commission came to Paris to interview me. One of the questions they asked was: "Why did you want to be involved in the situation?" I answered: "It was obvious that Mr. Reagan wanted to create peace on both fronts in that territory — the Iraqi peace with Iran, and containment of these radical Iranian Muslims into part of the whole tranquillity of the Middle East. And also [to have] Israeli involvement, so they are with us in this whole process."

Reagan was clever. I think he understood how stupid his people were

[so] he took this on his own. If I want to be an independent historical analyst of this man [Reagan], and Reagan said [to McFarlane], "Go," then he is not stupid, because he knew that it was an opening; he knew the advantage of it. It takes a complicated man to accept this whole plan.

The Independent Counsel

On December 2, the president requested that an independent counsel be established to investigate further what became known as "Iran-contra." The findings of the independent counsel, combined with evidence elicited in the congressional hearings, would result in legal actions against fourteen individuals and in the president being severely taken to task for his failure to stop what the counsel defined as illegal activities.

Elliott Abrams   Why not appoint a special counsel rather than an independent counsel? It worked in Watergate. It would have said to the Democrats and the press, "Something went quite wrong here, and we're going to have this investigated. But we are not going to do it your way."

What that would have said was, "You're not winning this; we are not collapsing; we are going to fight. We are going to have a real war here, guys." And the administration did not give that impression; it gave the impression of utter collapse.

Adolfo Calero   Walsh was a very dignified, very amiable man. For what they found out, the millions of dollars that they spent was, for me, something that created jobs for unemployed lawyers.

James A. Baker III   Walsh went too far; I think most people feel that way. He spent all that money. I don't know whether or not he was imbued with his own importance.

Lawrence Walsh   There is no way to conduct an investigation of this complexity cheaply, especially if you have to create a mini-agency in order to do it. We weren't given a room in any government building; we had to go out and rent space through the General Services Administration. They were the ones who selected the office in which we worked — and which had a high rental — because the intelligence agencies would not permit us to store their records in a less secure building. Twenty percent of our expenses were due to the classified nature of the material.

We had to build an office for each defendant, with the same security as our own. Our office, to settle the problem of redacting every document that came into it, had to have the same degree of security that the CIA itself has. Then you add to that the complexity of the investigation, and the withholding of documents consistently by the agencies of government, which prolonged the investigation at a very high cost of over ten thousand dollars for every day we were delayed. So you get some sense of where the money went, and why it was expensive.

The Investigation Process

Lawrence Walsh   If you think of ideal circumstances for a criminal investigation and prosecution, you would like to have complete secrecy about your own activities — complete secrecy as to the testimony you are developing — so that the witnesses are unsure of how much you know and therefore are [motivated to act] in their own self-interest, to tell the truth, because they don't know if you are in a position to contradict them or not.

That advantage was largely [denied] us — first, because the Tower Commission publicized a lot of the testimony and information very early in connection with its report, before we had really gotten fully under way. Then we had a problem with immunity — Congress giving immunity to our most certain targets, and ultimately our most valuable sources of information — [a problem with whether] they could be convicted and confronted with a prison sentence. That happened also in Watergate.

The Israelis would not let us interview their people, nor would they give us the bank accounts there, so we were deprived of that aspect of information.

We had a somewhat expanded form of the Israeli chronology [mentioned in the joint congressional committee report]; that was part of the settlement after we subpoenaed Kimche. The chronology was helpful, but it was not the same as questioning a witness. We always treated the document as classified.

Roy Furmark   I met with Walsh. They were looking for something. I was asked several hundred questions; they were trying to lead me into things that I didn't know about, or that weren't true. I said, "It's all there. You have my testimony between the Senate and the House. That's all I know; there is nothing more that I can tell you."

Abraham Sofaer   Walsh was definitely out to get Reagan and, later, Bush. I believe that Walsh was convinced that the president knew more than he had said.

Elliott Abrams   I'm not sure that they were after Reagan or Bush. I think it was a cabinet member. And the question was: Shultz or Weinberger? It was worth getting me, in the hope of getting someone else.

The Walsh operation was abusive from the first day to the last. In many ways it violated the law — for example, in the way it spent money. It was clearly in violation of various legal and ethical standards, and nobody cared about that.

More fundamentally, this was basically an anticonservative outfit, with strong policy and personal views of its own, [and], more amazingly, [it] proceeded to indulge those biases for five years rather than carefully screening them out.

Lawrence Walsh   We were not trying to "get" anybody; we were trying to unravel the facts and to deal with whatever crimes were exposed. We had no preconception of who our ultimate target would be.

When we started off, it looked as though it were a runaway conspiracy by North and, perhaps, Poindexter. There was more involvement at the cabinet level and in the White House than I had originally recognized.

Lyn Nofziger   The independent counsel thing is an outrage; it's a violation of a lot of things. You give a guy a chance to get the president and therefore go down in history. It's a corruption of the process.

Edwin Meese III   When the independent counsel comes in, he usually hires a bunch of young, avid trial lawyers. I think that Walsh got carried away personally, as well, with the idea that he was going to bring down a sitting president. It was going to be a replay of Watergate.

Lawrence Walsh   I hired the staff the same as I would have staffed a private case, with recognition of the nature of the case, but not the political background of it. The staff was picked solely for its abilities in certain fields. None of them were interviewed as to their political leanings, and there was no effort to obtain a political viewpoint of one sort or another.

Edwin Meese III   They were trying to find some way to get to Ronald Reagan. They made an offer to Cap Weinberger — whom they indicted — that if he would give them information that would implicate Ronald Reagan, he would go scot-free.

Richard Secord   Walsh is a snake. I assailed him; it is in volume 3 of his report. He is a tax evader [and] a liar many times over. He will do anything to try to salvage a ruined reputation.

He was always a bridesmaid, never a bride — this arrogant, patrician kind of guy. He never set foot in a courtroom; he hasn't tried a case since the days of Tom Dewey. He told me — with two FBI agents, an assistant of his, and my attorney sitting there — that he had seen my testimony on television and was very impressed. One of the guys choked on that. Later we confronted him on that, and he denied ever having said it. He is an absolute liar of the first magnitude.

Lawrence Walsh   Everything is relative. I thought he [Secord] handled himself well as a witness in his own interest. That is different from saying that I am favorably impressed by an individual, but I did think that he handled himself very well.

I could only hear those parts that did not relate to the financial side of his activities, because I had to turn the TV off and not listen to anything that could have been derived from Hakim's private testimony to the committee, or records that he supplied, so I did not hear all of it.

Richard Secord   He tried to get everything but ended up getting nothing; it was a Keystone Kops act if you ever saw one. The great tragedy was that it went on for so many years and ruined so many lives. And a totally unfettered kind of instrument has been spawned. I have to laugh a bit now that the shoe is on the other foot: the Democrats, who invented this instrument of justice, are starting to find out what it means.°

David Jacobsen   Of all the people in Iran-contra, I believe Dick Secord was the most honorable person. He was doing what he thought was in the best interests of his country; he was a patriot; he understood the frustration of dealing with the bureaucracy; in Vietnam he rescued American POWs; he was a do-it-now, seize-the-moment kind of guy.

He was charged with felonies that he did not commit; he was innocent. I was surprised when he took a plea bargain and pled guilty to providing the security fence to Ollie North. But at the time his immediate

---

° A reference to the Whitewater investigation, involving President Bill Clinton and his wife Hillary, by a special prosecutor, Kenneth Starr.

family was being crushed, so like a good soldier, he stood up and said, "I'll take your beating and let my family be free."

Abraham Sofaer   Coming close to indicting Shultz was the height of lunacy. I don't have the slightest bit of doubt that Reagan was innocent and that Shultz was innocent.

Walsh, the first time around, should have been more careful in looking at notes and getting the full story. It was not my job to look at Charlie Hill's notes; I never looked at his notes, except the portions he showed me. But I told Charlie to preserve his notes. And then, when they asked for his notes, I said to them that they could have them. And I told Shultz that they had to be provided, and I told Charlie he had to give them up. And he did.

Donald Gregg   I'm sure the Democrats feel about Mr. Starr the way we came to feel about Mr. Walsh. It seemed to come in waves: I thought I was completely clear of it, and then they came back at me again, after Weinberger had been pardoned.

They felt that if they could get me, they could somehow squeeze me the way they'd squeezed Weinberger, and have me say something about Bush — which, of course, wouldn't have happened, because there wasn't anything that I knew. A correspondent who had covered the issue for seven years told me that I had been totally screwed.

Lawrence Walsh   The drawing of President Bush into the pardon gave the public another demonstration of the high level of the cover-up; it was an atrocious thing. It was the first pardon issued by a president to block a trial and hide from the public the facts that would have been exposed in the trial — that would have been exposed dramatically — and a pardon by a president who might have been called as a witness himself.

Elliott Abrams   There was a lot of talk about a pardon. I knew that Judge Clark, among others, was pushing very hard to get Weinberger a pardon. It was also very clear that if there were to be a pardon, it would be between election day and inauguration day.

The only thing I did was to ask friends in the administration to put forward the argument that if there was going to be a pardon, it should include more people than simply Weinberger.

I believe that Reagan made a big mistake; it's obvious when you look at the feeble Reagan of the deposition. I don't know anybody now who does not share the view that Reagan could have gotten away with it without hurting his historical reputation. And he would have helped himself.

The answer to why he didn't is in no small part Nancy. There was a move to do this — Reagan was essentially amenable — and apparently Nancy was violently opposed to it and stopped it. As I heard the story, she later said to friends that she recognized that she had made a mistake.

I suppose there were other advisers as well who in good faith said, "This is a mistake, because it will hurt your reputation as it hurt Ford's."[*] I have another view of this, which is obviously somewhat personal — that the failure to do this really harmed Reagan's reputation among the people who care about that reputation most, not the *Washington Post* but the conservatives.

Reagan had a moral obligation to people; he did not meet that moral obligation. First, he did not meet it when the scandal erupted, because what he basically did was to say to everybody, "You're on your own, buddy." The best small example of what that meant was when administration officials were refused the advice of agency counsel in dealing with Walsh, simply because Walsh said, "I don't want to do that." The administration should have said, "Drop dead." But this was part of the pattern of abandoning everybody.

Reagan had a chance afterward to meet the moral responsibility, and he failed to do it. Somebody should have been able to say to him, "What you are doing is very bad. This is a real moral challenge."

Michael Ledeen He [Walsh] was trying to get important people. Reagan would have been wonderful, but he was happy to settle for Weinberger, McFarlane — and look what he did to Elliott Abrams. It was one of the most outrageous things I have ever seen.

It's not just Walsh; it's an occupational hazard with these special prosecutors. The whole institution is un-American. You give a guy unlimited money, staff, and time, and one target. It's hard to survive.

I was lucky, I survived. Thanks to North's intervention, they made me the subject of a criminal investigation. Otherwise, I would have been wiped out like so many other people. I was not because the Ethics in Government Act says if you become the subject of a criminal investigation by the special prosecutor and he does not indict you, the government pays your fees. So I survived.

I don't know why North invented these things about me. He hasn't spoken to me since.

---

[*] President Ford was criticized in some circles when, on September 8, 1974, he pardoned Richard Nixon, who had recently resigned from the presidency and was then an unindicted co-conspirator for his part in the Watergate cover-up.

Robert C. McFarlane   We haven't figured out how to translate theory to practice. The theory of having an independent counsel is eminently defensible; the idea of the Justice Department investigating itself is wrong. The practice is unjust because the motivation of the prosecutors is not the national interest; it is ambition. When you bring a battalion of young lawyers to town, they are going to prosecute. I sound like a cynic. I didn't think that before I went into this experience, but coming away from it, I certainly do.

Judge Walsh was as disconnected from it as the man in the moon. When Judge Walsh began, they told me and my lawyers, "For the first nine months of the investigation, we are not going after you; you are not even a target." Then the young lawyers took over and said, "We have to get a scalp here; we are going to nail him." Okay, I can see reasons why they could prosecute me. Information had been withheld from Congress, although nobody had been prosecuted for that ever before in two hundred years. But after that — and this is my point — they came back and said, "If you will nail Ronald Reagan, we won't charge you." That is not justice; it is abuse of the public trust.

Abraham Sofaer   It really was a terrible failure, because it didn't achieve the prosecutions that it should have achieved.

I believe that Judge Walsh set out to change the American system of government. His initial indictment in the Iran-contra affair — which was a draft that never saw the light of day — really alleged that the way government is conducted in Washington violates the Constitution and violates the rights of Congress; that Congress cannot be misled — never mind lied to — by the executive branch; that if you are telling the Congress to do something and you have another motive, the failure to tell Congress of your other motive might be a crime.

His concept of what the Congress should be told about was totally alien to everything that happened in American history. I know this; this is my field. If there is anything I know about, it is how the Congress and the president related to each other.

This got him way down the road on lots of things he didn't have to get involved in. If he had stuck to garden-variety crimes — straight-out lying, not telling Congress the truth, or misappropriating the assets of the United States, taking missiles that belonged to the Department of Defense and giving them to Israel so Israel could sell them to Iran — he might have been able to get to trial quickly on some limited charges.

In fairness to him, the other reason he didn't succeed was because it was more important for the country to have a hearing about what had happened than it was for Mr. Walsh to conduct a proceeding, and they undermined his capacity to do that by granting immunity to people.

Martin Anderson   The problem with the Walsh investigation was their basic error in strategy. Instead of trying to find out what had happened — instead of looking for the truth — they tried to see if they could stick it to Reagan, track it back to him. And it all fizzled out, and they went home.

Lawrence Walsh   At the close of the congressional investigation — at the close of the Tower Commission investigation — the public was told that this was a runaway conspiracy of North and Poindexter. That was wrong. The runaway conspiracy was a diversion by the White House, in a sense a diversion of public attention. The activities with respect to the contras and the activities with respect to the arms sales were known in the White House — not in detail as to the diversion.

For example, I can't prove that as to the president, but he certainly knew what was going on, and the secretaries of state and defense knew in general terms what was going on. They didn't know the details; they didn't have to.

The activities of North were fully supported by the CIA and by Abrams and the State Department. They knew what they had to know in order to give him the support he needed. So it was not North going off on his own, or Poindexter going off on his own. It was an administration activity. So that is what we accomplished.

FURTHER DAMAGE CONTROL:
ABSHIRE IS CALLED IN

On Christmas Eve, December 24, 1986, President Reagan, convinced that he increasingly lacked credibility with the American people and aware of the possibility that his presidency was in jeopardy, invited David Abshire, his ambassador to NATO and a highly respected scholar, to return from his post in Brussels to become special adviser to the president on the Iran-contra affair.

Ambassador Abshire accepted the president's invitation, and he was officially appointed on December 26 to head a special group to coordinate the administration's responses and strategies on the Iran-contra issue.

David Abshire   If the head of a corporation gets two decisions wrong in a year, he's in trouble. A president can make one or two wrong decisions — Nixon, for example, in getting into the Watergate cover-up.

Reagan phoned me at NATO and said, "Dave, I want you to come back. I want to get to the bottom of this and get everything out." Had Nixon phoned somebody the week after Watergate and said that, he would have ended up as one of the most successful presidents of this century.

I was called back to serve as an individual who had not been in the White House, or in government, during this period; we had no contact with the Iran-contra issue at NATO.

At first my brief was misunderstood; even Nancy Reagan misunderstood it. Some people thought my brief was to get the facts and give them out. Where did the money go? That was not it at all; that would have been a disastrous mission — one that would have led to a perception of cover-up, because nobody knew the facts.

My brief was to serve the Tower board, to serve the committees on the Hill and the needs of the independent counsel. In the three months I was in the White House, we had good relations with all three. I knew all the key Democrats on the Hill. They were asking me, "What is it going to mean if we have another president go down?" That's what they thought about.

Stuart Spencer Deaver and those guys would call me. Reagan would call me when decisions were to be made and they wanted my input. When Reagan was going to speak on Iran-contra, I felt he needed more points of view, more information.

I brought Tower in, very quietly, upstairs to see him. The Tower Commission was going to make its report. I said, "John, tell him what the hell is going on. He just can't go out there and give a speech and get blown out of the water by the report from the Tower Commission."

Geoffrey Kemp Iran-contra was a potential disaster that could have led to impeachment. It was a blunder of quite staggering proportions that could have been stopped had the two main opponents behaved like statesmen rather than spoiled schoolboys; Weinberger and Shultz could have stopped it.

It was so outrageous what was being done. Weinberger knew this; Shultz knew this. If they had buried their own animosity for a period of time and gone to Ronald Reagan and said, "This has got to stop, otherwise we are resigning," it would have stopped.

Edwin Meese III I didn't think the president could ever be impeached for what he had done. There was no basis for it; he had done nothing wrong.

I was concerned that if anything looked like a cover-up — it was a difficult position that Ollie and John had put the president in — if we didn't get it out as quickly as possible so that there was no attempt by anybody to think there was a cover-up, that would put him in a vulnerable position that some of his opponents, who were very bitter about Nicaragua, would try to use, and even threaten impeachment.

Donald Gregg   Impeachment for what? I remember Boydon Gray [the White House personnel director] coming in to me and saying, "Don, I want a chronology of your involvement in everything that you have had to do with North and with Iran-contra." We put that chronology out in December 1986, and it's never been modified because it was the truth. The mantra there was absolute disclosure.

Joan Quigley   I became involved in Iran-contra after his second operation for cancer, in January 1987, when Reagan and other people who were advising him openly wanted him to go around the country, defending his policy with the contras.

It seemed like poor timing after his operation. I felt — both from that standpoint and from an astrological point of view, and because I could never find any good times for press conferences during the period — that if he went out to defend his policies, he would not be well received, either by the public or the media.

So my advice to them was to do as little as possible — to be as invisible as it is possible for a president to be, and not to give press conferences, and not to go around explaining his ideas, because they wouldn't have been well received.

Looking back on it, I think my advice — which was based on astrology — was excellent, because they came out of it very well. I sent him a letter in August 1987, and Nancy put him on the phone to me, and he thanked me for all I'd done.

Frank Carlucci   When I became national security adviser, I found a very distracted president. It was hard for him to focus; he didn't seem to understand what was happening. I was the last person to see him before he went to the Venice economic summit. I said, "Mr. President, you are going to be at an economic summit with world statesmen. You are going to meet the press corps. The first question is going to be on Iran-contra. Don't answer it. Just say, 'We are at a summit; we are here to discuss economics. Take those questions back to Washington.'"

Well, of course, the first question was on Iran-contra, and he gave a long answer. He just couldn't seem to get away from it; it was almost like fly paper. It was very distracting. Gradually we got all that behind us, but it was a tough period.

Elliott Abrams My feeling was — and it's part of a broader criticism of the president's handling of this — that I am, first of all, critical of the administration for failing to bridge that gap between its rhetoric and its actions on Central America and, in a sense, leaving it to Oliver North.

Either the president should have stopped giving speeches or he should have done something. Then, when the scandal erupted in the fall of 1986, it seems to me what really happened was that the president — and the administration — collapsed under the pressure. The — if you will — Jim Baker view of this took over, which was, first of all, "Let's see how many people we can throw over the side. And we don't care about the morality of that. We'll just get rid of them if it helps us. And we'll say anything we need to say to get out from under the pressure."

What would have happened if the president had said, in essence, "This is not nearly as big a deal as the press is trying to make it. Mistakes were made, but they are not very large mistakes. I wish I had known about them sooner; I would have stopped them."

The administration increased the atmosphere and the sense of horror, scandal, and collapse of the administration by its sense of panic. There were two ingredients: one of them was panic, and the other was this kind of Jim Baker–Howard Baker attitude toward all of that, which was a kind of: "Put us in charge, and we'll fix all of this." The greatest nightmare was that somebody like Howard Baker should be his chief of staff.

Sorting Out All the Details

David Abshire I did not know what the president had been exposed to; I did not know what Poindexter was going to testify to. The North stuff . . . he never met alone with the president, but Poindexter was in there close; Bud McFarlane had been in there close. So we did not know what would come out.

As we got more deeply into the issue, my concern was whether Admiral Poindexter, in briefing the president, might have gone in there and maybe stuck this [the diversion of funds] in the middle. Since I could meet with Reagan privately, I went in and confronted him with this. I asked, "Is there any chance that John Poindexter came in and mentioned the transfer of funds, sort of in the middle of something?" Reagan would sometimes be clear as a bell, and he said, "Absolutely not."

Was the President Credible?

David Abshire   In the Nixon administration, Haig called me to come into the White House, and I told him, "I can't do it." I had just come back to the Center [for Strategic and International Studies]. I wasn't sure Nixon was telling the truth; I thought he was brilliant, but I rendered a correct judgment on a flaw in his character.

I did not know Reagan nearly as well as I knew Dick Nixon. I had met with him when he was governor and, of course, was with him when he visited NATO. I judged that he was incapable of conspiracy — that this degree of naïveté, which gave him political strength with the American people, was also a quality that made him incapable of plotting a conspiracy.

I believe that is absolutely correct. I believe that he had no knowledge of the transfer of funds. I was alone with him over a dozen times; I was able to talk with him in depth about things. He was able to box off problems to give him optimism.

It is true that it can be claimed that he drove the attempt to trade arms for hostages — even though he didn't perceive it that way — because he had tremendous compassion for those hostages.

But when you get to the thing that had the real degree of criminality, which is the transfer of funds, he would, in my judgment, have remembered that; he was, in my judgment, incapable of lying about such things. His mind doesn't work that way. Somebody could say he was forgetful; I think it would have stuck. Poindexter testified that the president didn't know.

Barry Schweid   There is a school of thought that says that Reagan was a real cunning guy — that he dumped it all on North, and on others, and that he knew what was going on; he was no dummy.

But the Reagan I saw makes me doubt that he was all that cunning, and that he could work out some clever scheme of covering his tracks. For God's sake! Nixon was ten times cleverer than Reagan and couldn't cover his tracks!

When I covered him on his trips, I saw Reagan following his script. I found it hard not to like Reagan. It was easy for me to believe the things about Nixon that turned out to be so; it would be very difficult for me to think that Reagan had the guile — or really even the misunderstanding of what kind of country this is — to be personally involved.

But I wouldn't have trouble believing that it was kind of said in front of him, and around him, and that he heard it, but didn't hear it.

Michael Deaver   If you go way back with Ronald Reagan and look at some of the polling that General Electric did when he was their spokesperson, his credibility was in the eighties. And after about eight years as governor of California we did polling and his credibility was in the eighties, because people said, "Whether I agree with him or not, he does what he says he is going to do."

That personal credibility — his personal credibility, what the media called the Teflon President — was what I fought to keep for him, regardless of whatever else happened.

Richard Secord   It would have been easy for Reagan to dodge this bullet had he gotten up and taken credit for it — sort of like the U-2 or the Bay of Pigs.° The Bay of Pigs was a horrible mess — so many people killed. Iran-contra was just an old ladies' tea party compared to that, yet Kennedy was smart enough to immediately take the blame.

George P. Shultz   The period after the Iran-contra hearings to the end of the administration was one of the most productive periods of any presidency as we reaped the gains of all the earlier work that had been done. That was the period when we made all the deals with the Soviets; lots of good things happened during that period.

But the revelations weighed on him, and I think the thing that bothered Ronald Reagan more than anything else was that before, he had always felt that if he believed something was in the U.S. interest, he could go to the American people and explain it, and they would support him. He tried to do that in this case, and it was obvious that they didn't support him.

Abshire's Advice to the President

David Abshire   I was telling the president, "Those committees on the Hill are responsible; they are concerned; they do not want to bring down a president; they are not the enemy. Cooperation is essential." I didn't want people telling him otherwise.

° A reference to President Dwight D. Eisenhower's acknowledgment that a U-2 aircraft piloted by Gary Francis Powers and shot down by the Soviets in Soviet airspace had been conducting a spying mission; and to President John F. Kennedy's admission that a force of two thousand exiled Cubans had received U.S. support and military training for what proved to be an unsuccessful attempt to invade Cuba and overthrow Fidel Castro.

When I met with Senator Inouye for the first time, he said, "Now, David, if at any time you think we are doing something that is out of line, I want you to speak up." I would tell Reagan this.

The period Reagan was in danger was in the three months I was in the White House. What I was doing in part when I went in to see him was talking about bipartisan support we were getting on the Hill — the process we were going through.

The president said to me, "I caused all this trouble. I should have said in the beginning, 'I can't remember.' If I had simply recorded in my diary that discussion in the hospital with McFarlane, I would have no problem."

I said, "Mr. President, if I on April 5, 1985, at NATO, went in to see Lord Carrington and somebody said, 'Abshire, come clean; what did you talk about?' I would say, 'I have no idea what we talked about. And what's more, I didn't think that as the ambassador I had to keep a diary. I thought I had other people who were supposed to keep the record. I thought you national security advisers were supposed to keep the record.'"

I couldn't resist saying this because Reagan was made to look dumb. This old man can't remember a discussion on August 5, 1985 — or is he not coming clean? Now, he was very precise in keeping his diary. I don't know how in the world he got the discipline to write in it.

Michael Deaver   Reagan did the best he could, given the information and advice he had been given. I went back on two occasions and talked to him. One of the problems was that, at the time, there weren't any people in the White House who could say what Baker and I could say to him.

DID BAKER'S JOB SWITCH WITH REGAN HAVE A NEGATIVE EFFECT?

Geoffrey Kemp   My read on the Reagan years is that you cannot understand Iran-contra and all that happened in the second term unless you take into account the dramatic effect that the departure of Baker had on the management of the White House staff. Baker was exceptionally smart at working with Reagan's strengths and weaknesses; he and Deaver and Meese were a great team.

Don Regan was exactly the opposite. He was ignorant about foreign affairs; he thought that by telling jokes to the president, he could handle him. And he wanted Reagan to be Reagan — and that's the last possible thing anyone wanted. They wanted Reagan to be charming and excellent on television, but to essentially sign off on the documents where he was told to. I don't think that Iran-contra would have happened if Baker had still been there.

David Abshire Don's critics say he was trying to have himself made prime minister. And he was the controller, so it's a mystery that all of this business could go on and he couldn't get in command of it.

When we talked, he said that governance at the White House is a difficult problem. I said, "Don, get out now, while you are on top of things, and write about this." He felt very strongly, once this broke, that he hadn't had authority in the national security field.

McFarlane didn't have much prestige. He had a complex because you had these multimillionaires in there; he wasn't of that school. He was a lieutenant colonel, and Don could remind him that it took him twenty-three years to make that rank and that Don had made it in three, during the war. So it is a mystery.

Poindexter didn't come in there with any kind of independent base. Judge Clark was there with a little bit of an independent base. When the Howard Baker people came in, the White House was not, as has been written, in disarray. Don was still running his staff meetings; he was the efficiency expert. As a person in command, Don was very strong, very well organized personally.

Michael Deaver I say this with as much humility as I've got: I don't think it would have happened if Jimmy Baker and I had been there. Baker had his pulse on so many things. He would have sent me in there; we would have gotten to the bottom of it. It would have been an enormous, ugly, uncomfortable time within the White House, but it wouldn't have happened the way it did.

Lyn Nofziger If Baker had known about Iran-contra, it wouldn't have happened, because those guys were protecting their backsides. It was so far-fetched that it doesn't even make good fiction.

Stuart Spencer If Baker had been there, I don't think it ever would have happened. We had these things going on with Casey. Other people seemed to have agendas that weren't the president's — or weren't in his best interest.

The chief of staff has to sort all that stuff out — to bring people in, to make other arguments. Some people had an agenda and moved it forward, and there was nobody there to say, "Wait a minute, let's talk about this." Cappy and Shultz should have been in the loop on a question like that. Baker would have tracked it a lot closer.

Craig Fuller The contra part of it — the diversion of funds — was really not known to people until the investigation was made public, so I fully believe that the people who kept this from George Bush, and Don Regan and others, would have kept it from Jim Baker, because Baker would not have stood for it. I don't know whether in these meetings, with only a few people present, Jim Baker would have come down, much like Shultz and Weinberger say they did, against it.

Some of the most damaging decisions made in the White House while I was there were usually made with only a few people involved, persuading themselves that they were acting properly. The Iran-contra program was held so closely that there just wasn't the opportunity for any kind of internal debate. Therefore, I think it's probably not fair to Don Regan to say, "If somebody else had been there . . ."

Michael Reagan My dad, if he could, would tell you that the worst mistake he ever made in his life was when he changed his chief of staff and treasury secretary. It was a terrible decision, because Jim Baker, although he came from the moderate side of the party, was much better as a chief of staff and had a better pulse than did Donald Regan.

What Donald Regan did that Jim Baker had not been able to do was to shut Nancy out. Had Regan not shut Nancy down, Iran-contra might never have happened.

James A. Baker III I don't think it would have happened if I had been there by myself, or if Ed had been there by himself, or if just Meese and Deaver had been there, because I don't think we would have let it happen. We never would have let Bill Casey go in alone, without getting a read-out from the president or Clark.

Regan Is Faulted for the Iran-Contra Affair

Frank Carlucci The Great Communicator wasn't always the greatest communicator in the private sessions; you didn't always get clear and crisp decisions. You assumed a lot in your decisions; you had to. And people who assumed wrong got into trouble, and they got the administration into trouble.

I don't think Don Regan had much control over what was going on.

The Tower Commission faulted him, to some extent. But there was a bit of inconsistency there, because they faulted Don Regan, but then they said that there ought to be a strong and independent national security adviser, with direct access to the president. But you can't have it both ways: you can't say that the chief of staff ought to supervise the national security adviser, and that the national security adviser ought to be independent of the chief of staff. I obviously opted for the latter.

Regan and the First Lady

While Mrs. Reagan offered opinions on policy and on staff appointments, when asked, she did not in most cases play a role comparable to those of two notably involved first ladies, Mrs. Carter and Mrs. Clinton.

An exception on personnel matters was Mrs. Reagan's crusade to achieve the resignation or dismissal of Chief of Staff Donald Regan. She went outside the White House to enlist the help of William Rogers and Robert Strauss in order to convince the president that Regan had to leave.

Donald T. Regan   I remember a crack I made: "I don't mind falling on my sword for the president, but it was the knife in the back that got me."

You have to have a fall guy. Somebody is responsible; somebody is going to take the blame for this or that. And who is going to get the blame? The culprits — McFarlane and North and Poindexter — seemed to be not that well known, particularly to the public. There had to be some higher-up who had to know what was going on.

This was aided and abetted by Mrs. Reagan's feeling that somebody should put a stop to this. Or, if you can't put a stop to this, you ought to get out of the way and get somebody in there who can put a stop to it. How do you put a stop to a congressional investigation? Only by telling the truth and getting on with other things.

She didn't want it that way, so, therefore, I became the guy. I should have, in their opinion, submitted my resignation immediately. It happened on my watch and therefore I'm responsible, not realizing that although it happened on my watch, it didn't happen under me. The diversion of funds was nothing that I could have known about or could have been responsible for.

Therefore, I wasn't about to be the fall guy and forever have my career under a cloud for having done something wrong, or evil, to the presidency. So I decided to stick it out. I said, "After the report is made, I will resign." I said, "Once the Tower Commission makes its report, I know I will be exonerated by the commission" — as I was, although they said I was responsible for what happened afterward. But after a crime has been committed, how do you stop it?

But they didn't want it that way. They wanted to push me out because I was being so damned stubborn.

There was a meeting with Paul Laxalt and a few other people in which it was suggested that I might have to resign for this, and I said, "I have already put in my resignation to the president." As soon as the Tower Commission reported this, I knew exactly what was going on. I didn't know of the meeting with Robert Strauss and Bill Rogers until much later on.

They knew that Bill Rogers was a close friend of mine, and they were trying to get Bill to plead with me to resign and get the hell out of the way. Strauss went along with it, obviously, as a Democrat. It would have made great headlines: "Chief of Staff Fired in White House."

Time heals all wounds. I am a big boy. In every speech I have given, I have always praised President Reagan and the presidency. My experience has never clouded my judgment. I have never, in any way, damned this president.

16

Looking Back

Terry Anderson   I have this recurring joke about getting into a New York taxicab and having the driver turn around and say, "Hello, Mr. Terry. How are you?" I might recognize some of my captors if I ran into them in New York. There was one who was involved for six years. I know his voice very well, and the way he carries himself. I might recognize his face, and I might not; it's been a long time.

I am not angry, I am not bitter. I take seriously the injunction that I, as a Christian, am given: to forgive. I am not sure exactly how far that goes, or where it leads me.

I have interviewed Ollie twice. He is a nice man. I disagree profoundly with him politically; I would hate to have him in the U.S. Senate. I have come, during his Senate campaign, to have serious doubts about his ethics. He is a long way from the simple, honest marine officer that he once was. He attempted to seriously mislead people about his role and his activities; he lied during his Senate campaign — quite drastically.

He probably cost me two years. There's no way to know that; it's a guess. The problem was President Reagan's saying, publicly and repeatedly, "We do not deal with terrorists." Ollie North, under his aegis, was dealing with terrorists. The terrorists knew that; it was not a secret to them.

Then, when it became public knowledge, Reagan — and then Bush — said, "We do not deal with terrorists, and we mean it." Well, it's difficult to convince the terrorists of that. It's hard to convince somebody that you're a virgin when you've been sleeping with them. It took a long time to understand the reality that they were not going to achieve anything this way.

David Jacobsen   You have to understand that forgiveness is not permitting the criminals to get away with it and go free; forgiveness is a cleansing of your internal emotions of hatred against a whole general class of people. But you do not abdicate an obligation, or a responsibility, to do justice.

I do not hate all the Arabs, and all the Lebanese, and all the Shiites, and the Druse, and the Iranians, so, in a way, I have forgiven all the Muslims. But I never, ever abdicated my desire to help in arresting the people that did it to us, and to be a witness at their trial, and to dance on their graves when they are executed, because they are evil men. And if we have this religious feeling of forgiveness, then let's open up the doors of every prison in this country and let everybody out.

Once Marty Jenco had said he hoped to meet his kidnappers in heaven. I called him and said, "Marty, if I get to heaven and I find you there, talking with our kidnappers, I'm going to leave and go to the other place, because I want to be with a better class of people."

IF I HAD IT TO DO OVER AGAIN . . .

Adnan Khashoggi At the time I thought it could stop this unnecessary war between Iraq and Iran. Honestly speaking, it was a lesson in life. If I had it to do over, I wouldn't be involved. I would not now trust any government to act in good faith and govern within their own structure, because you can't deal with individuals in a government. A government is a government; that's why it's called a government.

Fawn Hall Today, if I had it to do over, I wouldn't have taken immunity — and I wouldn't have taken the documents out, yet I don't think there was anything that important in the files. Everything was retrievable. I didn't file any secret notebooks with names and numbers; the documents were in my computer.

Elliott Abrams Looking back on it now, I would have pressed North and the CIA harder. I certainly would have asked for more information, although I would have to say, looking back on the situation I was in, I should have pressed everybody harder.

It would have saved me a lot of trouble on the Hill later if I had known that the Saudis were kicking in two million dollars a month. I think I would have pressed the entire system harder, but North in particular, to find out exactly what he was doing. I believe I would have been the only person who was doing so.

Oliver North If I had gone up before that committee, or even before then, if I had done what Ross Perot advocated that I do, and said, "I'm a victim of all this, I was just a poor kid carrying out my orders, and I just totally screwed things up, and I'm a victim of these crazies who are running the White House, and I'm just a poor little marine lieutenant colonel, and I'm a victim" — he used the word *victim* about ten times — I would still be a national hero for the *Washington Post* and the *New York Times*, because that is what we do today: your vindication is victimization. If you want to avoid being described as a scum-sucking, belly-crawling, low-life, right-wing goon, the way to do it is to go up there and basically whine and claim victim status.

That's never been my wont. I was a boxer at Annapolis. I was damn-near killed in a terrible automobile accident. My daddy taught me from the earliest days, when you get knocked down, you get back up. I have spent fifty-two years on this planet, and I still do the same thing.

One of the things you realize about government — no matter who the administration is — is that there are not a lot of heroes around Washington. I didn't set out to be one; I didn't try to be one; I didn't want to be there to begin with; I certainly didn't relish the end of it. But I am not ashamed of what I did while I was there.

Did I make mistakes? You bet, I made them every day. The easy calls are the ones you make between right and wrong; the tougher calls are between good and better. The worst calls you will ever have to make in life — and you hope you won't ever have to make many of them — are the ones you have to make between bad and worse.

I had to do that in combat; I had to do it in the White House. And you're always going to be second-guessed by somebody who survives the experience — that you should have made the other decision. Is my judgment flawed? Probably. Will I make mistakes again? Sure. My kids keep lists.

Fawn Hall   I think he's become a political animal, which I had never seen in him before. I had a dream, when he was running for the Senate and I was in the rehab place. He was walking down the street — it happened in my neighborhood — and my first reaction was: "Oh, my God!" It was like the old way I would respond to him: "Hi!" And as he came closer, I saw that he had on a wig and Margaret Thatcher–like putty on his face. And I reacted in horror. That to me is very symbolic of what he is today.

I never saw a motivation like, "I want Admiral Poindexter's job one day," or some kind of recognition; he never sought publicity. But it turned into something else. We all have seeds in us that if watered enough are going to sprout. I don't think he had the right people around him.

In 1993 Young Republicans for Freedom had asked me to come

down and speak. I really was resistant to those kinds of things, but I said, "Okay, I will make an appearance for you." I didn't know how radical they were, because I am not that way. They said, "We are trying to get Ollie, but he wants forty-five thousand dollars, and we can't raise that kind of money."

I said, "If you change your mind, and you get him, let me know. If you do get him, make sure that he knows that I am going to be there." Well, a few days later there is a phone call, a few days before the event. It's from the group, saying that Ollie's lawyers have instructed them to call me and tell me not to be there, that they had raised the money and I wasn't to come. And I thought: How humiliating! How many times do you have to be told that this guy wants nothing to do with you?

THE STATUS OF THE
NORTH-HALL RELATIONSHIP

Fawn Hall Betsy [North's wife] and Ollie didn't have an answering machine. In March, for Betsy's birthday, we got them one. Betsy called to thank us. I said, "Can I talk to him?" By this time I had been on the front page and all these offers were coming in, from *Playboy* and others, and Ollie said something to me that really disappointed me. He said, "Fawn, I just wanted to thank you for not doing that *Playboy* thing." And I thought to myself: What? It just devastated me. I thought that this man knew who I was; I would never do that. That was the last time I remember speaking to him.

I stayed on at the NSC office after Ollie was fired. In January they came in and said, "You are out of here at three o'clock. Pack your bags."

They tried to get me a job at AID [Agency for International Development], and this person wrote to the executive secretary of the NSC and said that Fawn said that AID was a pinko organization. I was so naive that I had never heard the word *pinko*.

I went back to the Pentagon. I worked in an office called "The Secretary of the Navy's Paper Reduction Task Force," and I thought: My God! This is like shredding paper! I got shoved from job to job. I became a political bombshell; people had presumptions about me.

I had four different jobs in four months. I was incredibly shy, and it was very hard for me. Tourists would walk by my office and look in. My sister, who worked for the air force, would walk with me through the Pentagon.

All these offers were coming in. I met with Norman Brokaw of the

William Morris office [a talent agency]. I wanted to do something positive with my life, but there were things I could not do. I was offered
Revlon for twenty-five thousand dollars and turned it down. They said,
"Okay, be our 'Woman of the Year,'" and I said no. Trump offered me
something like ten thousand dollars to shake hands for two hours, and I
said no. Part of me wanted it, but the other part of me felt that there was
blood all over the offers — the blood of the people I had worked for.

I was so angry about the things that were being said about me. I was
pleased with a lot of it too; I was proud when they would say "his loyal
secretary" — in the sense that I had always thought that I was very
dumb. I didn't have a lot of self-esteem. Ollie and I do not speak today.
The way I felt about him in that situation remains the same; the way I
feel about him today is totally different. I don't want to mix that up.

I came to work for him at a time when there was no direction in my
life; I was ripe to get passionate about something. He was the perfect
teacher. As the years went by — I don't think he ever really knew this —
he became like a mentor to me. I never really understood what a mentor
could be, nor was I seeking one; it just happened. So, for that reason, I
am greatly indebted to him in many ways.

I did see his foibles and his weaknesses at the time I was working for
him, and I was highly disappointed. When he was fired, he went into the
hospital, and they wouldn't let me go to see him. I needed to take care of
him. I couldn't believe that this person I admired — this whole thing we
had been doing — just stopped, like that.

My mom said to me one day — I was sorting his mail, like he was still
there, and wanting to go up to the law firm, and drop it off just to see
him. And I really want to be very clear about this, because it has been so
misconstrued: I am not in love with Oliver North. I loved him in a way; I
admired him a great deal. My mom said, "Cut the umbilical cord." I said,
"You still talk to General Scowcroft. Don't you understand what it's
like?" She did, but she is also a reality check for me.

And then the legal stuff happened and just cut it off. I believe there
was justification in saying, "You can't talk." But it was hard on me. Then,
as time went on, I realized that the justification was becoming an excuse,
and it was very, very painful for me.

I don't know what I did that he doesn't speak to me. As close as we
were — working for nearly four years, twelve to fourteen hours a day,
five to six days a week, and in such drama, and then to go through the
tragedy that we went through — normally there would be a bond. There
are people I have a bond with that if we don't speak for ten years, we can

pick up where we left off. I have that with everyone except for the man I worked for, and I don't understand that.

I moved to California; I was just trying to do something with my life. I met the man who would become my husband. The last person I ever dreamed I would be with was a heroin addict. I was very reclusive; I didn't trust people, and I went down that road with him after two and a half years of being with him, because I couldn't get him to stop and I just joined him. It was that I tried to save him. It's a trait of mine, whether with my husband or Ollie. As a result, I ended up in a lot of treatment centers.

I have to say that this thing with Ollie has hurt me deeply. As much as Iran-contra and his being fired, it broke my faith in the system as it was. It caused me a great deal of grief; I just couldn't get out of it. I tried to let it go — the process of grief, the anger, the denial.

A therapist said to me, "You have just got to resolve it on your own." People die and we don't resolve it. And you know, it still hurts. It will always hurt, like a death always hurts. But it doesn't concern my life, and for the most part I don't really know why I don't care anymore. I do, but I don't.

I didn't seek after him. He is older than I am; it's up to him to come to me. I have done nothing that I can see that's wrong. He knows that I am in pain, because everybody else around us talks. I talk to Dewey Clarridge; he talks to Dewey Clarridge. I talk to Bob Earl; he talks to Bob Earl. The only people who aren't talking are Fawn and Ollie.

There is no reason to think that this thing is driven by Betsy, because she and I were close. I think that it's politics. Someone else suggested that maybe he knew he had hurt me and didn't have the courage to deal with it. Obviously he meant more to me than I meant to him.

PROTECTING OLIVER NORTH

Oliver North   By 1987, when Gadhafi was able to send a message from Tripoli to McLean, Virginia, to carry out an attack on a U.S. government official and murder him and his family, they tried to carry it out. If we hadn't known of the communications method, I wouldn't be sitting here, because in February 1987, he dispatched the order from Tripoli, and a team was sent from McLean, Virginia, to kill me and my family. That is why we ended up with thirty-five federal agents living with us for the next ten or eleven months — and that is a lot of coffee.

The "Belly Button" Account

One of the ongoing questions concerning North's relationship to Secord and Hakim is whether the three men entered into a financial agreement.

This question took on added relevance when it was revealed that Hakim had earmarked a specific amount of money contained in a so-called belly button account.

Martin Anderson My feeling is that we don't know the whole story, that there is a lot more to be known. People have covered this thing up. There are enormous sums of money missing. Hakim and Secord are looking at potential business, with hundreds of millions of dollars of profits. A lot is at stake here. And the way things are set up, this young guy in the White House, Ollie North, has the switch and he can decide who gets the business.

He takes the business away from [General John K.] Singlaub* and gives it to Hakim and Secord, who are charging more, which, to me, means that he is violating the policy of the president — who wants to help the contras — and he is making weapons, food, and ammunition more expensive by dealing with Hakim and Secord.

Within months after Hakim and Secord set up this arrangement, Hakim says to Secord, "I am beginning to love Ollie like a son. We should do something nice for him. How about giving him five hundred thousand dollars?"

They decide that that is too much, and fix on two hundred thousand. And they plot how to bribe him while he is a sitting White House staff member with this kind of authority. They bring this lawyer from Switzerland to meet with Mrs. North in Philadelphia. Shortly thereafter, two hundred thousand dollars appears in their bank account.

They ask Ollie about it. He is shocked. If you read the testimony, nobody followed up. The reason was that the Democrats had no interest. They didn't want this little fish; they were trying to nail Reagan. The Republicans were embarrassed.

Then Hakim and Secord set up an insurance policy for two million dollars. If they died, North was the beneficiary while he was sitting in the White House.

There was also the question of the disappearance of the ten million

---

* A retired major general in the U.S. Army and chairman of the World Anti-Communist League, Singlaub was involved in raising funds for the contras.

dollars. The money was being wired. The entire foreign policy of the president of the United States was at stake. That's an eight-digit number; there are some numbers you don't get wrong.

We now find out that the money went into one bank account; this person took it out and put it into another bank in Switzerland and invested it in CDs. To this day we don't know who that guy was.

Fawn Hall   I had no idea about what was called the belly button account. I did not approve of that. But I do not question the motives of what they were doing. I can understand the security fence — he clearly had threats against his life — so I think the fence was valid. I think it was also illegal; he accepted a gratuity over a certain amount and apparently tried to cover it up. But I don't understand putting away money so his kids can go to college.

Lawrence Walsh   Circumstantially, there was reason to believe that North did know about the account. There was the fact that he had his wife go to Philadelphia — she says at his request — to give information to Zucker,° and her giving information as to her children and their educational needs, so that Zucker could set aside a fund which, with interest, would supply that need. And also, there was a telephone call from Secord on or about the same day. There was also a message of some sort from Secord to him, regarding a two-hundred-thousand-dollar insurance fund, which is ambiguous, but it fitted in, in the time zone.

Mrs. North's visit to Philadelphia was confirmed by her sister, who acted as a baby-sitter for the children that day and knew where she'd gone. Zucker's telephone calls from his hotel in Philadelphia to the North home are confirmed by records, and Zucker testified to his discussions with Mrs. North. It was never in terms of a payment, or a quid pro quo of any sort; it was getting the needs of the children [met], and the expectation that he would be able to do something about it.

It's hard for me to believe that Mrs. North didn't know what he was doing. But using Mrs. North's testimony against her husband would probably have been impossible because of spousal privilege.

° Zucker, a U.S. citizen and former lawyer with the IRS who owned a Swiss fiduciary company, maintained the Enterprise's records. Citing Swiss law, Zucker refused to talk to the congressional committees that investigated the Iran-contra affair. We spoke with him by telephone, but since our conversation was inconclusive, we did not include Zucker's name on our roster of interviewees.

THE FINANCIERS AND THE ARMS DEALERS

What Has Happened to the Money?

Richard Secord With the interest, there should be twelve million dollars in Switzerland — if Zucker hasn't stolen it. He's the only one who has access to it. Neither I nor the U.S. government has any way of knowing; they are so interested in it that they have never sought to get an accounting.

Lawrence Walsh The Swiss would not let us investigate the recipient of that money [the ten million dollars]; we could never get that account. All we could learn from the Swiss was that it was nobody related to the people we were otherwise interested in. As I remember it now, we don't know to whom that ten million was paid.

Richard Secord I am the one who was sued, as an agent of the U.S. government at all times. Hakim is the second guy in that case, as a subagent of mine. That is exactly the way the suit is filed. The complaint is an interesting piece of mythology. What it boils down to is the government's claim, in a suit filed against me and Hakim for millions of dollars — those moneys and millions of dollars of damages — [that] we violated our agency relationship.

I countersued; Hakim did not. My lawyer could not get down to the court fast enough. He was afraid they'd pull it because it gave us a vehicle; we hadn't had one before. It was almost like a gift, but they have managed to keep it tied up, and we are now going on three years. We appealed it, and the Fourth Circuit ducked because they claimed they didn't have jurisdiction because there wasn't yet a final judgment. But they also said that whatever happened, they had been assured by the government that there would be no negative res judicata effect as to Secord's interests. We maintain that that means that they can't dismiss it, although the government has filed dismissal papers.

They sued us as agents of the U.S. government, in a fiduciary sense, based on the operation of the Enterprise. There is not one witness to prove this; the Enterprise was private. They characterized it themselves, in the Clair George trial.° I was a witness, and they went to great lengths

---

° On December 9, 1992, the former CIA deputy director Clair George was convicted on two counts of lying to Congress concerning his knowledge of resupply operations to the contras. He was acquitted on five counts of perjury and obstruction. George was pardoned on December 24 of that year by President Bush.

to characterize me — they had big posters — as the commercial cutout, the private operator; they coached me on it.

So their case against me is preposterous; there is no way they can win that point, and they know it. That's why they want to dismiss it. We don't; we want to retry it. It should have come up several months ago, but the judge has been sitting on it. He must know we are right, but he doesn't want to rule for us. This case is going to the Supreme Court, for sure.

THE DEATH OF AMIRAM NIR:
WAS IT MURDER?

In 1988 Amiram Nir, who was no longer in government service, died in the crash of a small plane in a rural area of Mexico. The circumstances of the crash have led some individuals to suggest that there may have been foul play.

Yaacov Nimrodi   After Nir died, there was an investigation, and they said that I stole two million dollars. After three years of investigation, I went on television one night and told all of them — Shamir, Shimon, and Rabin — "You are liars; you are bastards. Nobody can trust you. When you wanted me, you called me, and I did what I had to do. When an accident happened, nobody came to help me."

Nimrodi then played a video for us of that broadcast on Israel Television. The narration, in English translation, says: "A general in Israel was nominated to investigate the case of Iranian money that was missing. Nimrodi sued the state of Israel, asking them to declare that he didn't owe any money to the government. It was announced this week that the file was closed. Therefore, Nimrodi canceled his claim against the state."

Judy Nir Shalom   My husband felt that Mr. Peres didn't give him backing on Iran. Amiram was very surprised by that. Only Mr. Rabin and Mr. Shamir supported him. It was politics. He didn't return Amiram's calls when Amiram was in a deep depression. I found a very sad letter from Amiram to him. It's sad when your mentor doesn't talk to you.

Until now, I didn't speak to Peres; I met him at parties and just ignored him. He tried to speak to me, but I didn't speak to him. Then, only three weeks ago, at a bar mitzvah, I came over to him and shook his hand. I excused him after all these years.

Yaacov Nimrodi When they wanted me, I came. I operated all my contacts, in Israel and outside. I realized all of my mission: my friends and I released Weir. It was a big success until a mishap occurred that did not happen because of me. All the leaders, and all those who put me on the mission, evaporated.

Just imagine if the person hadn't been Yaacov Nimrodi — like someone who had no means with which to clear his name from these evil people, jealous people, liars. I don't know what somebody else would have done. Maybe he would have died.

Eitan Haber I was the first one in Israel to get the news that he had died. The minute that I got the call, my first thought was that somebody had killed him. But then I heard a lot of information, and it looked to me as though it was an accident. But I don't know.

Richard Secord I grieved when he was killed. I thought he was a patriot. We handled a lot of money, and I never saw him being sticky-fingered at all.

Robert C. McFarlane The murder of Nir — the death of Nir — puzzles me a bit. I can't figure out a motive. There are a lot of potential motives, but I wasn't that close to Nir's involvement. I met him one time on that trip [to Tehran], and never before or after. This thing is a little too coincidental to me.

One of our sources speculated—not for attribution—that Vice President Bush, a former CIA director, may have involved the Agency in an attempt to harm Amiram Nir.

Adnan Khashoggi I think it was an accident, for the simple reason that nobody would benefit from his death. All the information Nir had, I give to you. This happened before the U.S. election and the question was raised on the involvement of Bush in Iran-contra.

The CIA, or any of the forces, will not dirty their hands to kill a man like this. There is no national security involved; there is nothing.

Uri Simhoni Don't believe all those stories; it was an accident. He was killed by accident in a small, remote field in Mexico. If you want to kill someone, you don't do it together with a pilot, somewhere in Mexico. How does the killer know where to wait? Things like that are so well planned.

He was already out of the system; he was not protected at all. If the CIA wanted to kill Amiram, a gunman would have knocked on his door and, with a silencer, put a bullet in his head. It would have been done in a very professional way.

Judy Nir Shalom Many weird things were happening when he was killed. There were four people in the airplane; two survived and two were killed. One of the survivors was a woman; she was a journalist. What was she doing on the farm? For a long time the woman didn't speak to journalists. I'm told she had plastic surgery. She lives in Canada. There was no autopsy. I didn't think about it then. Now I am sorry I didn't.

Yaacov Nimrodi I think that someone killed him. I asked: Why has the government or the family not sent anyone to investigate? As for who killed him, it had to be the Americans, or Ghorbanifar. Why Ghorbanifar? They had an account of eight hundred thousand dollars; Ghorbanifar would kill anyone for one hundred dollars. I think he got the money, took the account; nobody has found it. I had an account with Ghorbanifar, and he took what he wanted from it.

Judy Nir Shalom About six months after Amiram's death, there was a break-in at my house. Materials were taken relating to one of the people involved in Iran-contra. Also, Amiram's gun was stolen.

Oliver North I am not a grand conspiracy theorist; it was just a tragic accident. I do think he's actually dead, although the joke is that both he and Bill Casey are alive and well, and both living in Rio.

PART FIVE

THE POST-PRESIDENCY YEARS

17

The Reagan Legacy

REAGAN THE MAN

Harry Shlaudeman One thing I miss about the Reagan administration is Reagan. He was an extremely nice person to have at the middle of our consciousness in this country, because he was essentially such a decent guy.

Benjamin Ze'ev Begin He had a kind of human warmth you don't see in many politicians. I recall my father telling me how impressed he was when, at a function, Reagan went out of his way to shake the hand of a crippled person who was seated in a chair.

Michael Reagan When people would tell me how great my father was, it used to bother me; it was like I had lost my identity. When I found out who I was, I was then able to deal with who my father is. On his eightieth birthday, I gave him a toast and thanked him for having a heart big enough for the country, but also a heart warm enough to adopt a child. He brought me into his family, and loved me and cared for me.

When he was president, the media always referred to me as his "adopted son." I went to him one time, and I said, "Would you please have them stop referring to me as 'the adopted son of the president of the United States.' I'm your son."

He didn't understand the dynamics of this until he read my book. Then he came to me and said, "If you ever do a paperback, can I do the foreword?"

Suzanne Massie One of the things I grew to respect very much about him was his modesty and his great sense of humor about himself, as well as about everyone else. Look around at how little sense of humor we actually see in our political leaders; how unusual it is to be comfortable enough inside yourself; how few powerful people have their ego firmly, and quietly, in place.

As I met with him, I said to myself: he knows he is not brilliant; he accepts himself as he is; he understands what he has and doesn't have. And that's the beginning of wisdom.

I also thought he had an extraordinary instinct for people; he sensed them right away, without much speaking. After a few months I began to have great respect for him.

It's hard not to be fond of him — and his courage. A psychologist once told me that he had watched in slow motion when Reagan was shot. And I had said to my friend that I had occasionally seen in Reagan's eyes a flash of steel, and my friend said, "Yes. Most people when they are shot move back, or to the side; his first reaction was to go forward. This is an instinct that you cannot fake."

Abraham Sofaer   He wanted to be liked. He had very strong ideological beliefs; he couldn't bring himself to compromise them to be liked. He softened them; he would say them in ways that would maybe hold on to more people rather than alienating them.

Ultimately, he was the movie actor, six-gun-shooting type, who would fight if you wanted to fight. But basically, his attitude toward people was very positive; he engaged people.

Larry Kramer   I am fascinated by the Reagans. Did they have any sense of their destiny? Did she sense that he had something in him? Did he sense that she could help him realize it? She, obviously, was strong and pushing and ambitious and had a knowledge of the world.

I hate the man; I hate his wife. And yet, this is the man who brought us détente, or whatever you call it. I guess it's a good thing.

Nicholas Daniloff   Some aspects of his policies I really don't agree with, essentially in the domestic area. He was a credit-card president, leaving my son — and my eventual grandchildren — a debt to pay off which largely developed in the Reagan administration.

On the other hand, Ronald Reagan got deeply involved in the case I was entrapped in, and he did something that I think is very unusual.

It's an extraordinary thing for an American president to get so deeply involved in the case of one man. I have to say that he treated me and my family with enormous interest, and I am deeply grateful. Why did Reagan get involved like this? There are probably several answers. One might very well be the Sofaer argument, that, indeed, the Russians could make a case out of this, and if it had been reversed — an American situation —

there would be a trial, with serious consequences, so there would be a humanitarian issue.

There might also have been the fact that Reagan was very clear in his mind when it came to an individual, or small numbers of individuals, and my case was very black and white. Here was a journalist who was working hard, aggressively, but who was not an agent of the CIA, not an agent of any American intelligence service, who's going to get it in the neck. Therefore, I've got to do something about it — the same mentality that was applied to the hostages in Lebanon. Unfortunately, in that case, things got very bollixed up.

But could Reagan put that kind of emotion and imagination and energy into the problems of the United States? I wonder. Reagan was the sort of guy who could well understand the difficulties of one, or several, individuals. But could he understand the problems of twenty million?

THE GREAT COMMUNICATOR

Ronald Godwin　As an articulator of conservative ideals, Reagan was without peer. As a user of the presidency as a bully pulpit for traditional morals and values, he's without peer. As a unifier of the country, he's the last president we've had with that ability. As a steward of the national economy, we would have to give him much lower grades. Nevertheless, as a motivator and inspirer, Reagan is to me without peer in my lifetime.

Oliver Wright　He was instinctively in touch with his fellow Americans. That is why they loved him so much; that is why he was called the Teflon President, because all of your intellectual snobs and left-of-center commentators flung mud at him, but it didn't stick.

Intelligence is, of course, important. But what one wants in a president, or a prime minister, is wisdom — judgment in times of crisis. That Ronald Reagan had.

Bernard Ingham　Once, when we were at Camp David, the president said to Mrs. Thatcher, "It's a quarter to twelve. I've got to make my weekly radio broadcast to the nation. Would you like to come along?" So we strolled over to one of the cabins.

He had these two sheets of quite closely typed paper in front of him, and he sat there, waiting for twelve o'clock to come. And after sitting there for five minutes, Mrs. Thatcher's patience broke, and she said,

"Why are you not looking at your script?" At twelve o'clock, he read absolutely immaculately through these two pages, and absolutely on time. And he said, "Well, shall we go and have a drink now?"

If it had been her, she would have been in trauma before, and she would have taken a long time to wind down. He was an absolutely consummate communicator — if he had a script.

Gerald R. Ford His ability to communicate was his greatest political asset, going back to when he represented General Electric. Those five- or ten-minute things he used to do laid the groundwork for his reputation as the Great Communicator. He was a first-class communicator; he somehow defused a lot of criticism by his mannerisms, his way of speaking.

Adnan Khashoggi The man has an ability to speak; it is not easy to stand up before hundreds of millions of people and express ideas eloquently and win their hearts. There have been presidents since Eisenhower who have difficulties in doing what Reagan has done. Even Bush doesn't convince you; he has doubt in his voice. But Reagan was so sure of what he was saying that people were convinced. Maybe he was bullshitting them, but he did it. Bravo.

Rozanne Ridgway He's the only man I know who can wear brown suits to a ceremonial occasion and look good.

PRESIDENT REAGAN'S PLACE ON TODAY'S POLITICAL SCENE

George P. Shultz I think the view on Reagan has already changed. People are watching the current presidency and saying, "My God! — for Ronald Reagan to stand tall and represent us." I listened to a panel — mostly of reporters — talking about presidential politics right now, and there was unspoken recognition that the standard they were comparing people with was Reagan.

The things they talked about were steadiness, purpose, consistency, willingness to fight something through, not flip-flopping — these are the big things people realize you need in a presidency.

He was successful in all his leadership roles. When he left the governorship of California, it was universally acknowledged that the state was in better shape than when he arrived. And he was very popular. The same thing happened when he was president, not only on a national scale but on the international scale.

Lyn Nofziger It's as if there were no George Bush. It's because Reagan made this country feel good again. He is the eternal optimist; he instilled a feeling of optimism in this country, a feeling that this is a good country.

The best thing that ever happened to Reagan was losing to Ford in 1976, so we got Jimmy Carter. Carter talked about a national malaise, saying, "Maybe our problems are so big that we can't solve them."

This was made to order for Reagan, who knew he could be president with one hand tied behind his back, who had no doubts that the American people could do anything they had to do, and who didn't for one minute doubt that we could solve our problems. Look at Star Wars: we can do this. You couldn't convince Reagan that it couldn't be done.

People tend, in their own minds, to say those were good years. They don't want Reagan back because of the things he accomplished; they want him back because of the attitude he transmitted out to the country.

Geoffrey Kemp Look what came before! A highly intelligent nuclear engineer, Jimmy Carter. He understood the workings of cruise missiles, he wrote endless position papers on the B-2 bomber, and he was a bust.

And here you had Reagan, a guy who conveyed what people wanted to hear: the charming one-liners, the sense of humor, the certain grace under fire. He really endeared himself with those one-liners after he had been shot. Anyone who met Reagan came away liking him.

What is important is for people to go back to his 1964 Republican convention speech. It is one of the most powerful bits of oratory in American history — and does not have the later scriptedness of his presidential speeches, where he was clearly reading every line. In 1964 this guy was fantastic in getting ideas across. And look at those ideas! They were all six years ahead of their time!

The irony of Reagan is that by the time he became president, he was too old to implement his strong, articulate views on a lot of policy issues. But he could still articulate them.

When you voted for Reagan, you voted for a highly patriotic American, with a John Wayne aura, against the backdrop of the Carter and Vietnam years.

Michael Deaver His achievements were enormous. Not only was he able to get the Soviets to the table, but he was able to wipe the slate clean as far as Watergate and some of those horrible things we had gone through were concerned.

We began feeling good about ourselves as a country. Much of it was due to the force of his personality. He had about three things he wanted to do, and he wasn't bothered with anything else. It seems to me that that worked for him.

PRESIDENT REAGAN'S INTERNATIONAL LEGACY

Alexander M. Haig Jr. With every passing day, people are looking back with nostalgia about Reagan; I see it all over America. He's never going to be tarred with whatever his shortcomings were. He's going to be remembered for his contributions — not the least of which is the good fortune of having been president when the Evil Empire began to unravel, even though that process began the day Marxism was installed in the Soviet Union.

For us to consider that standing tall in Grenada, or building Star Wars, brought the Russians to their knees is a distortion of historic reality. The internal contradictions of Marxism brought it to its knees. I said in the early 1970s at NATO, "All we have to do is stay together, and stay strong, and they will collapse in our lifetime."

Frank Carlucci There is no question that he made America feel good about the strength of our country; it was an extraordinary period of cooperative relationships around the world. History will judge him kindly there. You can argue over the economic issues.

Jerry Falwell Mr. Reagan saved America. We would still be dealing with the Soviet Union today, in a much fiercer mode, if not for Reagan. He made patriotism a good word again.

International respect for America goes back to Reagan. He has been, without question, the greatest president of this century. There is no Ronald Reagan on the scene today, and I think the reason is that none is needed. God always has a man for the hour. Had he not come on the scene, America could have disappeared as the nation we know it is today.

Martin Anderson One hundred years in the future, when all the political dust has settled, I believe that they will say three things about Reagan. First of all, they will say that there was an extraordinary burst of economic activity. Secondly — and much more important — they will say that the cold war was won without firing a single shot; the Soviet empire disintegrated. But most importantly, they will see an extraordinary intellectual change, where an entire philosophical view of the world was declared bankrupt; the philosophy of communism was gone. This wasn't just Reagan, but it happened on his watch.

Historians will look back and say, "This thing had been going on for seventy years, and this battle between ideologies is now bankrupt. The well from which it sprang is gone." Even here, on the Stanford campus, no one proposes this as a serious idea any longer.

Colin L. Powell   When you look at the years after Reagan — what he bequested to Bush and then to Clinton — you had the ending of the Soviet Union, the unification of Germany, the Middle East peace process got under way, and every nation in Latin America — with the exception of Cuba — is now under democratic leadership.

Reagan's standing fast in El Salvador and in Nicaragua caused all of these nations, ultimately, to tumble into the column of democracy-loving nations. Cuba is just waiting for it to happen, when we find a way to give Castro early retirement.

DID REAGAN END THE COLD WAR?

Howard Teicher   If he is evaluated in terms of the East-West struggle, it will have to be said that he won the cold war. He did; the rest of it is details.

Robert C. McFarlane   The Russians will tell you that SDI brought them down. Nixon didn't do it, nor did Kennedy, Johnson, Carter, or the Eastern Establishment that has the reputation of great intellect. Kissinger didn't have the guts to try that. Ronald Reagan did it.

Gerald R. Ford   I feel very strongly that our country's policies, starting with Harry Truman and those who followed him — Democratic and Republican presidents and Democratic and Republican Congresses — brought about the collapse of the Soviet Union. Truman initiated the Marshall Plan, which brought peace and prosperity. Eisenhower was responsible for NATO and its concept of thwarting Soviet aggression. I signed the Helsinki Accords, which helped to stimulate striving for individual freedom and economic reform within the Soviet Union.

These presidents achieved their goals with bipartisan support in Congress. No president, Democrat or Republican, can claim credit for the collapse of communism. It is the American people who deserve the credit: for forty-some years they supported Democratic presidents and Republican presidents, Democratic Congresses and Republican Congresses.

The American people deserve the credit, not some politician living in the White House. So when some people say a president deserves all the credit, my answer is: hogwash! The American people deserve the credit.

Gennadi Gerasimov I am convinced that Reagan had nothing to do with the collapse of the Soviet Union. In general, the system was not working.

Gorbachev knew this and wanted to bring about change, perestroika. For this strategic aim, Gorbachev had to have peace with America, so the idea to end the cold war had nothing to do with Reagan. The idea was: we don't need it; nuclear weapons are too dangerous. We must have good relations with everybody.

Colin L. Powell It all came apart for a variety of reasons: Western solidarity, Reagan's strength in painting them as the Evil Empire, and then starting to cooperate with the Evil Empire.

The arrival of Gorbachev on the scene was the catalytic event. The man was a lawyer, in addition to being a Communist and an apparatchik; he could see things in analytical terms. The Red Army had become very large and proficient and, in doing so, had bankrupted the country, for no particular gain. [About] Soviet adventurism around the world, as Shevardnadze said to us and to his own people in 1988: "Comrades, look what we have done around the world; look at what causes we have supported. They end up with a strong, powerful alliance, doing well economically, and we end up with Angola, North Korea, North Vietnam, and a bunch of other basket cases. We have lost billions of rubles doing this. Comrades, we will never do this again." All of this was icing on the basic issue, which was that communism didn't work; the system they had been trying to get to work for seventy years was failing. With each year it was failing more rapidly and more obviously. They were living in a system that could not work.

All of these things contributed to bringing it down. It's too much to say that one thing contributed to it.

Adnan Khashoggi One of the things he did was to disturb the Soviet Union to the maximum when he started thinking of Star Wars. He didn't even worry about the cost. Maybe he wasn't serious about deploying this program, but he shook them up — and in examining themselves, they found themselves broke. Gorbachev had, in a sense, to surrender, and he did. So Reagan will be remembered in history as a man who played his role as president very well.

Jack Matlock   Although some people brag that the Soviets were on their last legs, that's not true. We did know that they were in trouble, and we also knew we could run circles around them if they really wanted an arms race. With 6.5 percent of our GNP, we could force them into 25 to 30 percent of their GNP, which was less than half of ours, for a country that had a lot more people.

As Gorbachev looked at the situation, he had sense enough to ask: What countries are successful economically? Well, Japan, which has had almost no defense burden, and Germany, which has had considerably less defense burden, whereas the Soviet Union had tied its whole future into the arms race. So he had to end the arms race, and — in the final analysis — on our terms.

Charles Powell   His role in the downfall of the Soviet empire was absolutely crucial. He came to office with this very clear vision that communism was evil and should be brought down. By greatly enhancing America's military strength to make it absolutely clear — which his predecessors, lamentably, failed to do — that the United States was not going to give up any ground at all, he confronted them with the stark realization that nothing they could do was going to win, and that they were far better [off] to try to reach an accommodation.

Eventually the by-product of this was to put the Soviet Union under unbearable pressure. And he had support in this from Mrs. Thatcher.

James A. Baker III   Not enough credit is given for breaking the back of communism. He teed it up in such a way that when the Bush administration came into office, communism was in the throes of collapse. It all happened in the Bush administration, but it wouldn't have happened without President Reagan.

Michael Reagan   I would like my father to be remembered as an Eagle Scout: he had to do something for his community to earn the designation, and he earned it by ending the cold war. He is not only my father, he is my hero.

My father's legacy is always going to be that piece of the Berlin Wall that is sitting out at his library. That is the way he would want it.

I've often said that when people are at the library, they look at the colorful side of the Wall. But that is not the story. What is important is to walk around and look at the other side, what the people had to look at all those years, the pock marks and the ugliness, because that's what communism was.

WILL IRAN-CONTRA BE A PERMANENT BLOT ON THE REAGAN PRESIDENCY?

Jeane J. Kirkpatrick I don't think that anyone even knows today what Iran-contra was. What was it? It wasn't anything. The only law that people were prosecuted on was perjury. There has never been a demonstration that there was a law broken.

Robert C. McFarlane I am not very objective on this question. I cannot imagine that it will be portrayed as very significant. In my life and yours, we have lived through a lot of crises in government, where ethical standards have been breached. In 1964, when I was on a ship off Vietnam, the Gulf of Tonkin episode occurred. It was portrayed by a president [Lyndon Baines Johnson] as one set of things that later turned out not to be true, but it was the proximate provocation that led us to escalate and, ultimately, go to war. Fifty-five thousand people died. That was a scandal. Four years later Nixon and Kissinger approved the invasion of Cambodia and countenanced the falsification of the bombing records, and people died — lots of them. That was a scandal.

In Iran-contra, nobody died; nobody gained any personal wealth. I suppose you could say the security fence [was personal gain], but that is not on a scale of real scandal, of willful abuse that leads to loss of life or serious threat of sustained violation of the law.

I don't think it's possible today to violate the law for very long in government. The press is very good; investigation is quite good; congressional oversight is quite good; and there are honest people all around you.

Iran-contra has certainly gotten far broader treatment than the Gulf of Tonkin or the Cambodian bombing. But at the end of the day, historians will write that in the big scheme of things, this was pretty small potatoes.

Abraham Sofaer I believe that historians will be puzzled by the importance that was given to Iran-contra at the time. To me, Iran-contra was important because it represented an inconsistency in Reagan's behavior that was very serious. He should have but didn't see it as inconsistent.

Iran-contra will be forgotten because it was a catastrophe that was averted. The big catastrophe would have been the cover-up, but it was not permitted. If someone had blown the whistle on the cover-up sooner, Nixon could have been saved.

David Abshire Iran-contra is a tragedy because it enabled people to ridicule Reagan, to suggest that the guy didn't know what was going on.

He was getting older, but the point is that he had done a lot of things right. The biggest thing he did wrong was the deficit situation, but he won the cold war.

But Iran-contra enabled all of those people to bring in that ridicule. This is too bad, because had it not been for that, Reagan would have had a clean sweep.

Gerald R. Ford I saw the Iran-contra situation develop, the Nicaraguan problem come to the forefront, and the Ollie North disaster. I was very upset because I thought it adversely reflected upon Governor Reagan's management of the NSC. The NSC under Reagan, inadvertently or otherwise, became an operational organization, totally different from what the law says.

Instead of having a think-tank concept, as the law stated, it became an operational unit for eager beavers; the people President Reagan put in charge weren't acting responsibly. The best example is Ollie North's running all over hell's half-acre, without anybody controlling him.

That was one of the most serious deficiencies in the Reagan administration. I don't think the president understood what was going on. That's tragic.

George P. Shultz I should think that practically no weight will be given to Iran-contra by thoughtful historians; it was a little blip on the screen. The big things in the Reagan foreign policy were this gigantic, seismic event of turning around the U.S.-Soviet relationship and basically ending the cold war and, at the same time, the start of a real Americas policy with the U.S.-Canada Trade Pact, which was designed by Reagan.

Iran-contra, of course, got a huge amount of attention — I think overattention. It wasn't like Watergate; Watergate had a rancid element. The things people did — even the things Casey and company did — they did for what they thought were the best interests of the United States. They were trying to fight the Communists in Central America, and they went about it in the wrong way, in a way that was not in accord with our Constitution, so it was wrong.

And Reagan's motives were, in a sense, good motives. He was worried about those Americans and wanted to get them back. The method was not a good method, but the intentions were honorable.

Elliott Abrams   It seems to me that the significance of the size of a scandal is not an objective fact; it depends in large part on who is in control of Congress and who is in control of the press. It is inconceivable that Iran-contra would have been what it was had there been a Republican majority in either house.

Its seriousness was much less than Watergate's because in Watergate you were basically talking about what the president had done. In Iran-contra, you were not; you were talking about what other people had done.

In retrospect, there is one bad thing about Iran-contra that was lost at the hearings, and that is the business of arms for hostages. That was really bad and should have been the focus. Instead, the focus was essentially political.

Lawrence Walsh   Iran-contra will always be a qualifying factor. People are going to see the good and the bad in any president's record, and Reagan invited more attention than most presidents will, and Iran-contra will be one of the bad factors that went with it.

It will show one of his weaknesses — sort of a flaw in the very important interlocking of government activities and procedure. In other words, it was both substantively bad, a bad judgment — it's always going to be a bad judgment call against President Reagan, particularly on the Iran side; he was emotional and willful about the hostages — and it also shows a popular president's administration's belief that it could bypass Congress on an international activity. It pushed to an extreme the president's control over foreign affairs — so-called control, because the president has never been given exclusive control over foreign affairs.

And it showed an outright defiance of the Arms Export Control Act and the National Security Act — not as though the president thought out these issues and disposed of them, but that his attorney general and his other cabinet officers went along with it. Whether they went along happily or unhappily, they went along. And some of them tried to cover it up, to the very end. When you have activities of that kind on a matter of such importance, I think it has to leave a scar on the administration.

Watergate had a sordid quality to it that makes it perhaps more dramatic in the public mind, but in constitutional terms, it did not touch Iran-contra in importance.

Colin L. Powell   In early 1987 there was enormous concern that Iran-contra had almost brought the administration to a dead stop, so clearly there was concern that it might turn out to be the dominating part of the last two years of his presidency.

It turned out to be a significant part of his presidency, but his presidency ended with 68 percent of the American people rating him positively, and with an over 80 percent approval rating for foreign policy conduct in our relations with our greatest adversary, the Soviet Union.

Iran-contra was a terrible screwup that shouldn't have happened. I believe that it will fade somewhat over time, when people step back ten or fifteen years from now, and they look at what happened between 1986 and 1989. We had the beginning of the end of the cold war; you had the first treaty signed that actually eliminated nuclear weapons; and you had the beginnings of other treaties that put an end to the nuclear arms race.

That is what is going to be looked back upon, not the scandal — which was terrible and a breach of a lot of things. In the future the achievements will stand out, and not Iran-contra.

Lyn Nofziger   Iran-contra will be there, but in about the tenth paragraph of his obituary. The American people have overlooked that; they have overlooked all the things that went wrong in the Reagan administration. They are not looking at what happened; they are looking at Ronald Reagan, the man. That's the guy they want back; they want Ronald Reagan, the leader.

HOW WILL REAGAN BE REMEMBERED?

Elliott Abrams   The main things people will say about the Reagan administration are about the end of the cold war and, to a lesser degree, the change in the view of government from a government of solution to a government of problem.

This didn't start with Reagan, but it took on a great deal of speed. If you want to look at the turning point at which Americans came to view government as the problem, it was election day 1980.

Caspar Weinberger   Reagan is denigrated today primarily because he was not supposed to succeed. He was sneered at by the intellectuals and by the media: he was "just an actor"; he had totally different ideas than did the conventional wisdom; it was impossible that he should succeed.

He cut taxes; he tried to cut popular spending programs; he pursued a very strong military; he was not conciliatory with anybody who opposed him; he wanted peace; he got a lot more results in the only treaty that actually reduced arms, the Intermediate-range Nuclear Forces Treaty.

All of these were great successes, but he was not supposed to succeed. The media and the intellectuals simply cannot forgive him for having been such a successful president.

Ultimately, history will assign him his true role, of having accomplished an enormous amount of change for the better, for both the United States and the world.

Oliver North   It will probably take one hundred years for Reagan to be regarded as one of the greatest presidents this country has ever had because of what he accomplished. He set out to reduce the size and cost of government in our lives, and to free up the entrepreneurial spirit of this country, and to bring down the Evil Empire. And he darn well did it.

He may not have seen it all happen during his tenure, but he made this world a far better place for my children than it had ever been before. We are old enough to remember having been taught in public school to get under our desks in case of nuclear attack: hide your faces, and cover your ears, and don't look up, because the blinding flash will get you.

Our children and grandchildren will never have to do that again. Why? Because of Ronald Reagan. That remarkable change is the direct consequence of Ronald Reagan's having been president of the United States. He certainly was the greatest president of my lifetime.

Stuart Spencer   He was one president who didn't have to spend a dime's worth of time working on his image and trying to protect it. When he was in power, he really reflected the thoughts of the American people — this great ability he had of reading the public.

And he was in the right place at the right time in history: the overriding thing, way down the line, will be his accomplishments with Russia. That didn't happen overnight. It started with Nixon, but Reagan brought it to a head; it happened on his watch. The credit he will get for that will be overwhelming in the long run.

Sergei Tarasenko   He was a great, great president. In a simple way, he projected American values — human rights, living standards, the technological achievements of America — toward a Soviet audience. That was important, because we looked at all the other American presidents as enemies. Maybe, for the first time, we saw a human being in President Reagan — not a politician, not an enemy, but a human being.

His greatest achievement was to translate political goals — political goals and ideals — into the personal sphere, so people at large could see this easily. It was much easier for people in the Soviet Union to understand what it was all about.

Benjamin Ze'ev Begin   It would be very presumptuous of me to say how anyone will be remembered in history. I don't even know how Menachem Begin will be remembered in history. In order to know that, we have to predict what kind of society will be there in one hundred years — what its values will be, what it will cherish in history. In one hundred years, there could be a society that would cherish Stalin. I'm not sure that even today people appreciate Reagan's role in the collapse of the Soviet Union. And this is only ten years.

Craig Fuller   I don't think the nation has seen a leader quite like him since, and I don't see one out there in the future. Clinton has communications skills like Reagan's, but I don't think that people feel there is sincerity behind it. People sensed that Reagan believed what he said.

I still think that people like to look up to their leaders and believe that they can put them on a pedestal and that they can stand the test. So, as people look back, they will see Reagan as a unique leader in this last half of the twentieth century.

18

"My Fellow Americans . . ."

With the following words, handwritten on November 5, 1994, and addressed to the American people, Ronald Reagan disclosed that he was suffering from Alzheimer's disease:

My Fellow Americans,

I have recently been told that I am one of the millions of Americans who will be afflicted with Alzheimer's disease.

Upon learning this news, Nancy and I had to decide whether as private citizens we would keep this a private matter or whether we would make this news known in a public way.

In the past Nancy suffered from breast cancer and I had my cancer surgeries. We found through our open disclosures we were able to raise public awareness. We were happy that as a result many more people underwent testing.

They were treated in early stages and able to return to normal, healthy lives.

So now, we feel it is important to share it with you. In opening our hearts, we hope this might promote greater awareness of this condition. Perhaps it will encourage a clearer understanding of the individuals and families who are affected by it.

At the moment I feel just fine. I intend to live the remainder of the years God gives me on this earth doing the things I have always done. I will continue to share life's journey with my beloved Nancy and my family. I plan to enjoy the great outdoors and stay in touch with my friends and supporters.

Unfortunately, as Alzheimer's disease progresses, the family often bears a heavy burden. I only wish there was some way I could spare Nancy from this painful experience. When the time comes, I am confident that with your help she will face it with faith and courage.

In closing let me thank you, the American people, for giving me *the great honor of allowing me to serve as your president. When the Lord calls me home, whenever that may be, I will leave with the greatest love for this country of ours and eternal optimism for its future.*

I now begin the journey that will lead me into the sunset of my life. I know that for America there will always be a bright dawn ahead.

Thank you, my friends. May God always bless you.

Sincerely,
Ronald Reagan

THE FIRST SIGNS OF ALZHEIMER'S DISEASE

Michael Reagan   When he wrote the letter, he knew what was to come, from the experience with his mother, who also had Alzheimer's.

At the time I would have said: he's getting a little slow. But after all, he was eighty years old. But if you go back, they started to do a diagnosis after he fell from the horse in Mexico; he took quite a fall.

The first public situation where it became evident was the birthday party for Margaret Thatcher, held at the [Ronald Reagan Museum and] Library [in Simi Valley, California, opened on November 4, 1991]. It was Dad's job to introduce Mrs. Thatcher. He had his little three-by-five cards, and he started by introducing her, and everyone applauded.

But then, he could not move the card, and he went back and redid the introduction. You know, everybody there clapped a second time, like it never happened the first time. It was apparent that there was a problem.

Were There Signs of the Disease During the Reagan Presidency?

C. Everett Koop   I never saw any evidence of the president's Alzheimer's. I've thought of all the instances when it might have been possible to diagnose it and can't come up with any.

If you go back and look at Ronald Reagan in his old movies, and you look at him as governor, or president, he always had a very winsome, hesitant way of speaking; he wasn't a person who went out and banged the lectern and said things in a bombastic way.

One of the reasons why he was such a good communicator was that he lowered his voice and said things in such a way that you thought he was talking to you. If you take somebody who talks like that, and say,

"Look, this is incipient Alzheimer's disease," somebody could buy that. But I don't believe it for one moment.

Miguel D'Escoto   I used to think that he was mentally off, because of this obsession [with Nicaragua] being so big; this is not the sign of a healthy psychological state of being.

I feel very sorry about his Alzheimer's because he is a human being. He did more damage to my country than any human being could ever do; he is actually responsible for the death and murder of so many people.

But on the other hand, when I heard of his sickness, I just prayed to God to make it easy on him. God only knows why we act the way we act. He thought he was doing the right thing. I cannot judge; only God can do that. He did us terrible harm, and I don't want to criticize him. All of us need God's pardon.

LAST CONVERSATIONS WITH PRESIDENT REAGAN

Eitan Haber   After Reagan left the White House, I traveled with Rabin to meet him in Los Angeles to interview Reagan for the Israeli newspaper *Yediot Ahronot*.* I am not sure, at the beginning of the meeting, that Reagan knew who Rabin was. There was a misunderstanding in the preparations for the meeting. When we arrived, Rabin started to ask questions, and after about ten minutes, Reagan signaled that the meeting was over.

Rabin was very surprised. He said, "I came from Tel Aviv to interview you." Reagan replied, "Nobody told me that; they said you wanted to stay for a few minutes." Then we stayed for another half-hour, and he gave us the interview.

Oliver North   I have not talked to Ronald Reagan since the night I left the White House, when he called me in my hotel room and said how sorry he was. It was a very emotional discussion. It was very brief. I will never forget it. I think it sums up the sentiment of the man accurately. There is a nobility to Ronald Reagan that many ascribe to his experience as a movie actor. I always believed it was genuine.

---

* Published September 8, 1991. Haber had been a journalist prior to becoming Rabin's adviser.

Lyn Nofziger   The last time I saw him was about two years ago; that was before they said he had Alzheimer's. He greeted me very warmly, but we had nothing to talk about. He showed me around the office, showed me all the mementos I've known about all these years. It was a very disheartening experience. I said to myself: I don't need to go back, I'd rather remember him in other ways. Now I feel I have to go see him again.

There was a very touching story. The Reagans had gone out to dinner with some old friends, and as they got up to go, everybody in the restaurant got up to clap. And Reagan turned around and gave them a salute. And most of the people began to cry.

Gerald R. Ford   I was in Los Angeles about six months ago [in October 1995] and called his office and said I'd like to drop by and pay my respects. They said fine, so I went to his office.

I walked in, and for the first five minutes I'm not sure he recognized me. But I kept prompting him about our relationship, and then, yes, for the next twenty-five minutes we had a good conversation.

Joan Quigley   I think that our relationship is over, well and truly. I don't think that the president would have fallen off that horse when he did; I don't think he would have been on that horse if I'd been advising them.

Jerry Falwell   Just weeks ago [in the fall of 1995], I was in Washington, speaking to an international group. Jeane Kirkpatrick preceded me. We wound up in the holding room between speeches. She asked everyone else to leave the room; she wanted to talk to me privately.

She had just come back from California. She dearly loves Mr. Reagan and always has. She told me, among other things that were very confidential, that he said to her — she could see the signs of Alzheimer's but for the most part he was very clear in the conversation — "Jeane, for all the years that I was in the White House, when I had that awesome power, I had one prayer that I prayed every morning. I started each day saying, 'Lord, not my will, but thine be done.'"

She said, "I've never seen him so somber or sincere." I know that had been his approach to the presidency — that he was God's servant, there by divine appointment.

Stuart Spencer   I used to have a lot of contact with the Reagans, but in the last year I haven't. We played golf about a year ago. I talk to Nancy on the phone, but I haven't seen him in a year. It's selfish; I can't handle it.

I hear he has good days and bad days. Of all the people I have ever known, he will handle this as well as anybody; he is that kind of person. Of course, it's tough on Nancy and the family. It has brought the family together in a lot of ways; it wasn't like that before.

PRESIDENT REAGAN TODAY

Michael Reagan   I think that my father is more comfortable at the office than he is at home. I think that is the nature of the beast: the office people say, "Yes, sir . . . no, sir . . . what can we do for you?"

You know that Dad is fine; Nancy is the one who needs the prayers; she is the caretaker. You have to know that there has got to be some anger. We've lived this life; we've been governor; we've been president; now we can finally retire and do all those things we never had time to do — and she can't.

John Hutton   I was with the president as he watched Nancy speak at the 1996 Republican convention. It would have been uncomfortable for him to have been present at the convention. It wouldn't have been terribly meaningful: as he watched the television, he was confused; he couldn't understand why Nancy wasn't with him. Yet he enjoyed seeing her.

His condition is drifting downward, but not at an accelerating speed. And some of his wit still comes through.

Michael Reagan   I feel an inner peace about him. I thought, back in 1989, that so often we blame our parents because they don't say, "I love you." It's easy to become a victim and say, "My parents don't hug me, or tell me they love me." So I thought to myself: When was the last time I hugged my dad and told him I loved him?

So I decided: every time I see him from now on I'm going to hug him hello, I'm going to hug him good-bye and tell him I love him. I remember, the first time I hugged him, I got one of these looks: What's going on here?

I'm perfectly at ease because, before this really started taking over, those hugs were worth more than all the other things we had ever done. Those hugs today are really what have bonded us as father and son and given me a comfort, so that I'm not looking finally for my father to say, "Gee, Mike, you are the greatest human being on the face of the earth. I'm proud of you." I don't need that anymore because I have been at peace with my dad from the period after January 20, 1989.

I do that to this day, and now, with the Alzheimer's, he may not be able to say my name, but he knows my face, and he knows there is a hug, so when I leave the house, I say: I'd better hug him, because I have started out of the house sometimes and realized that I forgot to hug him. And he will be standing there, with his arms open like there's something coming, and I'll hug him.

APPENDIX A:

THE INTERVIEWEES:

WHERE ARE THEY TODAY?

———

APPENDIX B:

SCHEDULE OF INTERVIEWS

———

BIBLIOGRAPHICAL NOTE

———

INDEX

APPENDIX A

The Interviewees:
Where Are They Today?

James Abrahamson left the SDI program in 1989 and established the transportation sector at the Hughes Aircraft Company, now known as the Hughes Electronic Company. General Abrahamson then served as co-chairman of the Oracle Corporation, where he became interested in air traffic control problems. He is now an investment banker, "putting together groups of companies, which I then help operate, aimed at improving the safety and efficiency of air traffic management."

Elliott Abrams has been a fellow at the Hudson Institute "for almost the entire period since the Reagan presidency." In addition, he is a consultant on investment in Latin America by American companies and the author of a recently published book on the future of the American Jewish community.

David Abshire has served since 1988 as president of the Center for Strategic and International Studies at Georgetown University. He was also a member of the President's Task Force on International Broadcasting.

Martin Anderson is a senior fellow at the Hoover Institution at Stanford University. He has written books on national policy, urban renewal, welfare reform, the military draft, and the Reagan presidency.

Terry Anderson, following his return to the United States in 1991 from his captivity in Lebanon, became chairman of a small information services company on the East Coast. He serves as a director of the Committee to Protect Journalists and is involved with the Vietnamese Memorial Association, which is building elementary schools in Vietnam. He has written a book on his experiences as a hostage, and in the summer of 1996 he returned to Lebanon to make a film about his captivity.

Hudson Austin continues to deny that he had any role in the murder of Prime Minister Maurice Bishop and those shot with him. Following the commutation of the death sentences imposed on him and thirteen others on December 4, 1984, General Austin remains in Grenada's prison, located atop a hill overlooking the Saint George's Botanical Gardens.

James A. Baker III went on to serve as secretary of state in the Bush administration. He then returned to Baker & Botts, the Washington, D.C., law firm founded in Houston in 1860 by his great-grandfather. He serves as an honorary chairman of the James A. Baker III Institute for Public Policy at Rice University in Houston; as a senior counselor to the Carlyle Group, a merchant banking firm in Washington; and on the boards of a number of nonprofit corporations, including those of Rice University, Princeton University, and the Howard Hughes Medical Institute.

Benjamin Ze'ev Begin served as a Likud Party member of the Knesset. In 1996, following the election of Benjamin Netanyahu as prime minister, he became Israel's minister of science, but later resigned that post.

George Bush succeeded Ronald Reagan as president of the United States. Following his 1992 defeat by Bill Clinton, he retired from politics and moved with his wife, Barbara, to Houston, where he is writing two books and is in demand as a speaker.

Adolfo Calero in 1990 returned to Nicaragua, where he went into the lumber business. "I got my house back, but not other things," he says. "It's incredible that we had to go through a war to get back to almost where we started from. Everything could have been done better. Of course, Monday morning quarterbacking is easy."

Frank Carlucci in 1989 became vice chairman of the Carlyle Group, a merchant bank in Washington, D.C., and since 1993 has served as chairman. He also serves on the boards of sixteen corporations and has received numerous governmental awards and academic honors.

Sophia Casey lives on the North Shore of Long Island, where she and her family spent many years prior to her late husband's service to the Reagan presidency.

Eugenia Charles remained prime minister of Dominica until May 1996, when she retired. A frequent visitor to Washington, she continues to be interested in political affairs.

William P. Clark, after leaving Washington, was asked by President Reagan to chair the Nuclear Weapons Review Group, as well as to continue his work on the settlement of Hopi-Navaho tribal differences. He was also asked by the president to become involved in the discussion of pardons for those implicated in the Iran-contra affair. Judge Clark lives on a ranch in California with his wife and five children. He practices international law, engaging in much pro bono work.

Duane Clarridge left the CIA in 1988. Since then, he has worked for the Electronics Division of General Dynamics. In addition, he says, "I have been doing international marketing for the last eight years. And I am writing a book."

William J. Crowe Jr. was a professor of geopolitics at the University of Oklahoma from 1989 until 1994, as well as chairman of the Foreign Intelligence Advisory Board from 1993 to 1994. In 1993 President Clinton appointed Admiral Crowe ambassador to the Court of Saint James.

Arturo Cruz Sr. has retired and returned to Nicaragua. He is building a house in the hills above Managua.

Nicholas Daniloff had a fellowship at Harvard University's Kennedy School of Government from 1987 to 1989. In the latter year, he joined the faculty at Northeastern University in Boston, where he is now a department chairman.

Michael Deaver, following his resignation, had major legal problems stemming from his years in the White House. He is an executive with Edelman and Company, an international public relations concern.

Miguel D'Escoto was the national head of Nicaragua's Communal Movement for one year. Father D'Escoto then resurrected the foundation he established twenty-three years ago, which feeds poor children, and brought it to Managua to work with the grass roots in order to develop strong neighborhood associations, in his belief that "this is how you build democracy, from the bottom up."

Rafi Eitan served as an adviser to Shimon Peres for a few months after Peres became Israel's prime minister in 1984, then retired. He is now the head of Israel's chemical industry.

Jerry Falwell disbanded the Moral Majority in the late 1980s. He continues as pastor of the Thomas Road Baptist Church in Lynchburg, Virginia, and serves as chancellor of Liberty University.

Gerald R. Ford serves on corporate boards, has lectured at more than 175 colleges and universities, and continues to be active in Republican politics. The former president has been associated with the Betty Ford Center and is "enormously proud of Mrs. Ford" for her courageous work in the field of addiction counseling. He is also involved with the Gerald R. Ford Foundation, the Gerald R. Ford Library in Ann Arbor, Michigan, and the Gerald R. Ford Museum in Grand Rapids, Michigan.

Craig Fuller served as co-chair of President-elect George Bush's transition team. During the Bush presidency he served as a member of the advisory committee for the economic summit held in Houston and as chairman of the 1992 Republican National Convention. After the election he became president of Hill and Knowlton USA, then a senior vice president for corporate affairs at Philip Morris Companies, Inc. until Governor Pete Wilson of California selected him to be chairman of his presidential campaign. In 1995 he became worldwide vice chairman of Burson-Marsteller, a Washington, D.C., public relations concern.

Roy Furmark and his wife now live atop a mountain in New England. While he is technically retired, he maintains extensive business contacts in South America, Africa, and Southeast Asia.

Hans Dietrich Genscher served as federal minister for foreign affairs and as deputy chancellor of the Federal Republic of Germany until 1992. He has also served as an honorary professor at the Free University of Berlin.

Gennadi Gerasimov served in the Soviet Foreign Ministry until 1990. Following the dissolution of the Soviet Union, President Boris Yeltsin appointed the former Soviet envoy as the Russian Federation's ambassador to Portugal.

Ronald Godwin has served as a senior vice president of the *Washington Times* and remains associated with that newspaper. He is also involved in international business activities.

Donald Gregg served as ambassador to Korea for three and a half years during the Bush presidency, starting in September 1989. During his tenure there, his efforts were directed toward transforming the Korean-American relationship from a military alliance into an economic and political partnership. In March 1993, he retired from his forty-three-year career and became chairman of the board of the Korea Society, located in New York City.

Eitan Haber will be remembered by those who attended Prime Minister Rabin's state funeral in Jerusalem — or who watched the rites on television — for his emotionally charged recitation, read from a piece of paper soaked with the slain prime minister's blood, of the "Song of Peace," which Rabin had sung at a peace rally just moments before he was shot. Following Rabin's death, Haber resigned from his position in the prime minister's office and is now an international business consultant.

Alexander M. Haig Jr. was a potential Republican presidential candidate in 1988. The author of three books, General Haig is an international business consultant based in Washington, D.C.

Albert Hakim lives in northern California and has continued his career as an international business consultant. He is involved in litigation regarding his claim that he remains under contract to the U.S. government.

Fawn Hall left Washington in the aftermath of the Iran-contra affair. She is now married and lives and works in southern California.

Arthur Hartman retired from government service following his tour of duty in Moscow. He has since become a consultant, serves on four corporate boards, and is president of Harvard University's Board of Overseers. He also heads an investment fund that has raised two hundred million dollars, privately, for investment in the Russian Federation.

Charles Hill was a senior research fellow at the Hoover Institution from 1989 to 1992. Since 1992 he has worked at the United Nations as a special assistant to the secretary general. He is also a lecturer at Yale University.

Geoffrey Howe, following his service to the government of Prime Minister Margaret Thatcher, was a visiting fellow at Harvard University's John F. Kennedy School of Government and a visiting professor at Stanford University. Lord Howe is the author of *Conflict of Loyalty*, published in 1994. He serves as special adviser on international affairs at Jones, Day, Revis, and Pogue in London.

Max Hugel resigned from his CIA post following allegations — for which he was never indicted and which were never proved — that he had been involved in unsavory business dealings. Involved in various business enterprises in Washington, D.C., he owns Rockingham Park, a racetrack in Salem, New Hampshire, and breeds thoroughbred horses in Florida.

King Hussein continues to reign in Jordan. Following the conclusion in early 1995 of a peace treaty between Jordan and Israel, Israeli tourists began to visit Jordan, and regularly scheduled air service now exists between the two nations.

John Hutton commanded an army hospital at Fort Lewis in Washington State. He was promoted to the rank of brigadier general, and after a thirty-nine-year military career, he recently retired. He is now a professor of surgery and chief of the Division of General Surgery at the Uniformed Services University of Health Sciences in Bethesda, Maryland.

Bernard Ingham left government service in 1990. He then wrote a book and returned to journalism. Sir Bernard is a director of various companies, serves as the chairman of B.I. Communications, writes columns for *PR Weekly* and the *Daily Express,* and does consulting in the public affairs field.

David Jacobsen, following his return to the United States, moved to California, where he resumed his career as a hospital administrator. He has written three books, including *My Nightmare in Beirut* (with Gerald Astor).

Craig Johnstone returned to private life as the international vice president of the Cabot Corporation and as the president of Cabot Plastics International. During the Clinton administration he returned to government service as the director of Resources, Plans, and Policies at the State Department.

Yehiel Kadishai served as the chief of bureau for Prime Minister Yitzhak Shamir, has worked on Menachem Begin's archives, and is an executive at the Jabotinsky Institute in Tel Aviv.

Max Kampelman in 1991 served as head of the U.S. delegation to the Conference on Security and Cooperation in Europe's Copenhagen and Moscow meetings on the Human Dimension. He is honorary vice chairman of the Anti-Defamation League, honorary chairman of the Jerusalem Foundation, and chairman of the National Advisory Board of the American Jewish Committee.

Geoffrey Kemp became a senior associate at the Carnegie Endowment for International Peace, where he was director of the Middle East Arms Control Project. The author of numerous books and articles on the Middle East and related subjects, he now serves as the director for Regional Strategic Programs at the Nixon Center for Peace and Freedom in Washington, D.C.

Adnan Khashoggi continues to be an influential international financier and retains a strong interest in the geopolitics of the Middle East.

David Kimche has left government service and now lives north of Tel Aviv. He is involved in consulting work.

Jeane J. Kirkpatrick is a senior fellow at the American Enterprise Institute in Washington, D.C., a post she has held since 1977. She is also a syndicated columnist and a professor at Georgetown University. In 1996 she was co-chairman of Robert Dole's presidential campaign.

C. Everett Koop is a senior scholar at the C. Everett Koop Institute at Dartmouth College. He also serves as chairman of the board and medical director of a new company, Time-Life Medical, and runs the Safe Kids Campaign, having run Shape Up America.

Larry Kramer continues to pursue his advocacy on behalf of his fellow AIDS victims and to inform and counsel those who seek to understand the illness and its implications for the human race.

Michael Ledeen is the author of *Perilous Statecraft* (1988), a book about the Iran-contra affair. He is the foreign editor of the *American Spectator*, serves as a resident scholar at the American Enterprise Institute, and is a visiting scholar at the Milken Institute in Santa Monica, California.

Suzanne Massie in 1990 published *Pavlovsk: The Life of a Russian Palace*, on which she worked during the Reagan years. In 1991 the Russians made a documentary film about her life, *Better to Light a Candle*. She continues to spend a lot of time in the former Soviet Union, especially in St. Petersburg. She is involved in many civic affairs, including the support of the Hermitage Museum and the Pavlovsk Palace Museum. In 1992 she created the Firebird Foundation, which is dedicated to helping Russian children who suffer from hemophilia. When not traveling, she and her husband, Dr. Seymour Papert of MIT's Media Lab, live in Maine. She is now working on a book about her thirty years of life and work in Russia.

Jack Matlock served as the U.S. ambassador to the Soviet Union from 1988 to 1991. He then became a senior research fellow at Columbia University for two years. Since 1993 he has been the Kathryn and Shelby Collum Davis Professor of the Practice of International Diplomacy at Columbia. His book *Autopsy on an Empire* was published in 1995.

Robert C. McFarlane, the author of *Special Trust* (1994), spends half his time advising developing nations on how to move away from socialism.

Edwin Meese III is a distinguished fellow at the Heritage Foundation and a visiting distinguished fellow at the Hoover Institution. He has also served on the Board of Visitors at the U.S. Military Academy, as well as on numerous corporate boards.

Constantine Menges is a fellow at the American Enterprise Institute and the author of several books, including *Inside the NSC: The President and the National Security Council* (1988) and a book on the future of Germany. Since 1990 he has been a professor of international relations at George Washington University in Washington, D.C., and director of that university's program on transitions to democracy. He also serves as a foreign policy adviser to the Republican National Committee.

Joseph Metcalf III retired from the navy in 1987. He now serves as a consultant on national security affairs, mostly involving weapons systems. Admiral Metcalf has also served on several National Academy of Sciences panels and as secretary of the navy's Research Advisory Committee.

Keith Mitchell left the Grenadian government in 1989 and spent the next several years helping to build a political movement, which won elections held in July 1995, making him Grenada's prime minister.

Langhorne Motley resigned from his position in the Reagan administration in 1985. For the past ten years he has been a principal in a company that consults with U.S. companies on international trade. He is co-chairman of the Ambassadorial Seminar, a two-week briefing run by the State Department for new ambassadors. He also lectures at the National War College.

Richard Murphy has been a senior fellow at the Council on Foreign Relations since 1989 — full-time for three years. He now spends half his time at the council and is also engaged in organizing study groups and private consulting.

Yaacov Nimrodi continues to be a major personality in Israeli life. In the spring of 1996 his daughter was killed while vacationing in the Sinai Desert; a mine — a remnant of a past Israeli-Egyptian conflict — detonated beneath an automobile in which she and other family members were traveling.

Lyn Nofziger was indicted and convicted of violating the Ethics in Government Act. The conviction was eventually reversed. Since leaving the Reagan administration, he has done consulting work and written three Western novels.

Manuel Antonio Noriega, following a protracted military operation by the Bush administration that began on December 20, 1989, surrendered to U.S. authorities on January 3, 1990. He was arraigned the following day in Miami on multiple counts of drug trafficking and conspiracy, according to charges listed in the indictment that had been handed down against him nearly two years earlier. Subsequently convicted and sentenced to forty years' imprisonment, he is incarcerated in the Miami Correctional Institution.

Oliver North, in 1989, following years of legal difficulties related to the Iran-contra affair, established Guardian Technologies International, Inc., in partnership with Joe Fernandez, a former CIA station chief in Costa Rica. The company, which went public in 1996, manufactures life protective equipment for law enforcement and military personnel. Mr. North has also written a newspaper column and a newsletter, both syndicated, and hosts a nationwide radio talk show. In 1992 he ran for the U.S. Senate in Virginia on the Republican Party ticket and was defeated by the incumbent Democratic Party candidate, Charles Robb.

Nimrod Novick, following the end of the Unity government in 1988, returned to private life as a business consultant. He remains an influential adviser to former Labor Party leader Shimon Peres.

Pavel Palezchenko served at the Soviet Foreign Ministry. He interpreted for Soviet General Secretary Gorbachev during U.S.-Soviet summits in Malta in December 1988, and in Washington the following spring. He also served on Gorbachev's staff, and when Gorbachev resigned his presidential post, Mr. Palezchenko joined the former Soviet leader at the foundation bearing his name.

Shimon Peres served as leader of the Labor Party's opposition until 1992, when he became foreign minister in the administration of Prime Minister Yitzhak Rabin. In November 1995, following the assassination of Rabin, Mr. Peres became prime minister. On May 29, 1996, he was defeated in his bid for that post by the Likud Party candidate, Benjamin Netanyahu, but continues to be active in Labor Party affairs.

Richard Perle serves on a number of corporate boards and since May 1987 has been a fellow at the American Enterprise Institute. He has also participated in programs on the Gulf War produced by the British Broadcasting Corporation. His novel *Hard Line*, about the ending of the cold war, was published in 1992.

Giandomenico Picco left the United Nations in 1992 after twenty years of service. Involved at that time in the negotiations to free the hostages still being held in Lebanon, he left Beirut in 1992 with the remaining captives, two German nationals. He then worked for two years for multinational companies before establishing a concern in 1994 that seeks partners for joint economic ventures with emerging nations.

Nicholas Platt served as the U.S. ambassador to Pakistan and since 1992 has been president of the Asia Society in New York City.

John Poindexter says, "I spent the first couple of years in legal battles" in the aftermath of Iran-contra. Later he became the senior scientist at Presearch, where he developed the prototype for a sophisticated video system. With a partner, he created a computer software company, and in January 1996 he became vice president of another company, Syntek, Inc.

Charles Powell left government service and established a new career in the private sector as a director of several large, international companies and of the Westminster Bank, whose international advisory board he chairs. In addition, Sir Charles says, "I do a lot of writing and broadcasting."

Colin L. Powell became chairman of the Joint Chiefs of Staff in the Bush administration, leading the U.S. military forces during the 1991 Gulf War. In 1996 his memoir became an instant bestseller. Later that year, during the 1996 presidential campaign, General Powell was courted by the Republican Party leadership, both as a potential presidential candidate and as presidential candidate Robert Dole's running mate. He declined the Republican Party's overtures but was a well-received speaker at the 1996 Republican National Convention and is now much in demand as a speaker.

Joan Quigley has written a book about her career and her experiences with the Reagans. She lives in San Francisco, where she continues to write about astrology and do astrological consultation.

Kendrick Radix is a practicing lawyer in Grenada, "serving society now, more than ever, and championing the cause of the ordinary person."

Michael A. Radix practices medicine at two locations in Grenada, in Saint George's and on the Grand Anse.

Michael Reagan lives with his wife, Colleen, and their children, Ashley and Cameron, in southern California, where he hosts *The Michael Reagan Talk Show*, heard on more than 120 radio stations in the United States. He serves on the board of the National Association of Radio Talk Show Hosts. Mr. Reagan has written two books and publishes a newsletter, *The Monthly Monitor*. Following the 1994 congressional elections, he was chosen as a "Majority Maker" by the House of Representatives.

Donald T. Regan now lives in Williamsburg, Virginia, where, he says, "Mr. Regan has been minding his own business."

Rozanne L. Ridgway retired from the State Department in June 1989 to become the president of the Atlantic Council. In 1992 she became that group's co-chair, with General Andrew Goodpaster. She also sits on the board of directors of numerous corporations, including Bell Atlantic, Boeing, and Citicorp.

Richard Schifter served as assistant secretary of state for human rights and humanitarian affairs in the Bush administration. Since 1993 he has been a special assistant to the president and counselor for the National Security Council. He is a recipient of the State Department's Distinguished Service Award.

Barry Schweid continues to serve as diplomatic correspondent for the Associated Press. He writes a weekly column on diplomacy that appears in newspapers nationwide and regularly makes radio commentaries as well.

Paul Scoon retired in July 1992 from his position as the governor general of Grenada. He has since served as chairman of the Year of the Family Committee for his local church and chairs the St. John Council, which is responsible for the St. John ambulance brigade. Sir Paul is chairman of fund-raising for one of Grenada's leading educational institutions.

Richard Secord is the author of *Honored and Betrayed*, published in 1992. In 1995 he became president for international operations of CTI (Computerized Thermal Imaging), a small public company dealing with medical diagnostic systems. He has since become president and CEO of that company.

Judy Nir Shalom is a journalist with the Moses family–owned newspaper *Yediot Ahronot* and also hosts a radio program. She has remarried and lives in Ramat Gan, Israel, with her husband, Sylvan Shalom, a Likud member of the Knesset who chairs that body's finance committee; her two sons with Amiram Nir; and her two-year-old twins with Sylvan Shalom, a girl and a boy.

Yitzhak Shamir served as leader of the Likud Party until 1992 and retired from the Knesset in 1996. He maintains an office in Tel Aviv, in the same building where Shimon Peres established his headquarters following his defeat in May 1996 in Israel's presidential elections. Mr. Shamir's autobiography, *Summing Up*, was published in 1994.

Harry Shlaudeman retired in June 1989. He was asked to assist the Bush administration in dealing with the contras, who were then in negotiation with the Sandinistas. At President Bush's request, he became the U.S. ambassador to Nicaragua, remaining at that post for twenty months before retiring once again.

George P. Shultz maintains an office at the Bechtel Corporation, in San Francisco, where he served as executive vice president and vice chairman. He is the author of nine books, including *Turmoil and Triumph: My Years as Secretary of State*, published in 1993, and is a distinguished fellow at the Hoover Institution.

Uri Simhoni, since retiring from the Israel Defense Forces, has become a real estate developer in Israel.

Bernadette Casey Smith and her family live on the North Shore of Long Island.

Abraham Sofaer served the State Department as legal adviser until 1990. He then became a partner in Hughes, Hubbard and Reed, remaining with that law firm until 1994. Judge Sofaer is a distinguished scholar and senior fellow at the Hoover Institution.

Stuart Spencer is involved in lobbying and strategic planning. He advises political candidates and was a consultant to the 1996 presidential campaign of the Republican candidate, Robert Dole.

Abraham Tamir left the Israeli government in 1989. Since then, he has been involved in academia and serves as an adviser on long-range planning to Israel's president, Ezer Weizman.

Sergei Tarasenko resigned from the Soviet Foreign Ministry at the time of Shevardnadze's resignation and is now employed by the Foundation for Realism in Policy. He is also active in the Foreign Policy Association, the first nongovernmental organization of its kind.

Howard Teicher established Teicher Consulting and Representation (TCR), which provides specialized business services to advanced-technology companies in North America, the Pacific Rim, Southwest Asia, and the Middle East. A lecturer and writer, he is also a syndicated columnist for the *Los Angeles Times* and the author of *Twin Pillars to Desert Storm: America's Flawed Vision in the Middle East from Nixon to Bush*.

Edward Teller has served since 1972 as a research fellow at the Hoover Institution. He is also director emeritus of the Lawrence Livermore National Laboratory and a recipient of the Presidential Citizen Medal.

Horst Teltschik left Chancellor Kohl's office at the end of 1990 and worked for two years at the Bertelsmann Foundation. Since 1992, he has been a member of the board of management of BMW.

Cal Thomas writes political commentary in a column distributed by the Los Angeles Times Syndicate that appears in more than 350 newspapers. His political commentary is also heard on 100 radio stations throughout the United States. He is the author of nine books, the most recent of which, *The Things That Matter Most*, was published in 1994.

Victor Hugo Tinoco left the Nicaraguan government to work on the local and neighborhood levels. In 1990 he was elected vice president of the Sandinista Party's Managua branch, and in 1992 he was elected its president. Mr. Tinoco also serves as a national official of the FSLN.

John W. Vessey has retired from the U.S. Army. He and his wife live in Minnesota, in the house they had been building when General Vessey was chosen to become chairman of the Joint Chiefs of Staff.

Lawrence Walsh spent several years writing his official report on the Iran-contra case. His popular treatment of the subject, *Firewall*, was published in 1997.

James Watt lectured at universities for five years after resigning as secretary of the interior. Since then he has established business interests in Wyoming.

Caspar Weinberger served as counsel to Rogers and Wells from 1988 to 1994. Since 1989 he has also been the chairman of *Forbes* magazine. He is the author of *Fighting for Peace* (1990).

Benjamin Weir, since his return to the United States in September 1985 from captivity in Lebanon, has taught at the San Francisco Theological Seminary in California.

John C. Whitehead has served since 1989 as chairman of AEA Investors in New York City. In addition, he is a trustee of Haverford College.

Charles Z. Wick is a board member of both the News Corporation and a foundation named for former British Prime Minister Margaret Thatcher. In addition, he says, "I play classical piano and help my wife, Mary Jane, with her various community endeavors, and with the Reagan Library."

Desima Williams is an assistant professor in the Department of Sociology at Brandeis University.

Margaret Wright lives with her husband, Sir Oliver Wright, in Purley, England, where she maintains her interest in the theater.

Oliver Wright served from 1986 to 1990 as a distinguished visiting professor at the University of South Carolina. From 1989 until 1992, Sir Oliver was president of the German Chamber of Commerce and Industry in London. He serves as a corporate director and lectures at schools and universities.

Schedule of Interviews

NAME	DATE	VENUE
James Abrahamson	10/5/96	Telephone
Elliott Abrams	8/16/95	Washington, D.C.
David Abshire	6/6/96	Washington, D.C.
Martin Anderson	9/26/95	Palo Alto, California
Terry Anderson	11/30/94	New York, New York
Hudson Austin	9/2/95	Grenada
James A. Baker III	1/30/96	Washington, D.C.
Benjamin Ze'ev Begin	8/1/96	Jerusalem, Israel
George Bush	7/18/96	Faxed letter
Adolfo Calero	9/5/95	Managua, Nicaragua
Frank Carlucci	6/5/96	Washington, D.C.
Sophia Casey	8/22/95	Roslyn Harbor, New York
Eugenia Charles	7/16/96	Washington, D.C.
William P. Clark	7/15/96	Telephone
Duane Clarridge	7/1/96	Escondido, California
William J. Crowe Jr.	3/19/96	London, United Kingdom
Arturo Cruz Sr.	9/6/95	Managua, Nicaragua
Nicholas Daniloff	11/16/95	Boston, Massachusetts
Michael Deaver	2/5/96	Washington, D.C.
Miguel D'Escoto	9/5/95	Managua, Nicaragua
Rafi Eitan	9/15/96	Telephone
Jerry Falwell	11/27/95	Lynchburg, Virginia
Gerald R. Ford	4/23/96	New York, New York
Craig Fuller	6/4/96	Washington, D.C.
Roy Furmark	11/1/96	New York, New York
Hans Dietrich Genscher	5/22/96	Bonn, Germany
Gennadi Gerasimov	5/30/95	Allentown, Pennsylvania
Ronald Godwin	10/10/95	Washington, D.C.
Donald Gregg	10/30/96	New York, New York
Eitan Haber	3/25/96	Tel Aviv, Israel
Alexander M. Haig Jr.	1/24/96	Washington, D.C.

NAME	DATE	VENUE
Albert Hakim	7/4/96	Los Gatos, California
Fawn Hall	6/30/96	Beverly Hills, California
Arthur Hartman	4/30/96	New York, New York
Charles Hill	2/13/96	New York, New York
Geoffrey Howe	3/18/96	London, United Kingdom
Max Hugel	8/25/95	Salem, New Hampshire
King Hussein	6/25/95	Amman, Jordan
John Hutton	6/5/96	Bethesda, Maryland
Bernard Ingham	3/18/96	London, United Kingdom
David Jacobsen	8/2/96	Telephone
Craig Johnstone	8/17/95	Washington, D.C.
Yehiel Kadishai	6/28/95	Tel Aviv, Israel
Max Kampelman	2/6/96	Washington, D.C.
Geoffrey Kemp	1/24/96	Washington, D.C.
Adnan Khashoggi	5/23/96	Paris, France
David Kimche	3/28/96	Tel Aviv, Israel
Jeane J. Kirkpatrick	2/8/96	Washington, D.C.
C. Everett Koop	10/22/96	Telephone
Larry Kramer	10/9/96	New York, New York
Michael Ledeen	3/12/96	Washington, D.C.
Suzanne Massie	10/18/96	New York, New York
Jack Matlock	3/1/96	New York, New York
Robert C. McFarlane	10/26/95	Washington, D.C.
Edwin Meese III	1/30/96	Washington, D.C.
	2/5/96	
Constantine Menges	1/23/96	Washington, D.C.
Joseph Metcalf III	8/16/95	Washington, D.C.
Keith Mitchell	9/1/95	Grenada
Langhorne Motley	10/10/95	Washington, D.C.
Richard Murphy	2/1/96	New York, New York
Yaacov Nimrodi	3/26/96	Savyon, Israel
Lyn Nofziger	11/28/95	Washington, D.C.
Manuel Antonio Noriega	8/30/95	Miami, Florida
Oliver North	6/5/96	Sterling, Virginia
Nimrod Novick	5/15/96	Raanana, Israel
Pavel Palezchenko	7/3/95	New York, New York
Shimon Peres	7/29/96	Tel Aviv, Israel
Richard Perle	6/4/96	Chevy Chase, Maryland
Giandomenico Picco	3/6/96	New York, New York
Nicholas Platt	2/27/96	New York, New York
John Poindexter	4/24/96	Rockville, Maryland
Charles Powell	3/15/96	London, United Kingdom
Colin L. Powell	5/30/96	Telephone

NAME	DATE	VENUE
Joan Quigley	9/24/95	San Francisco, California
	9/25/95	
Kendrick Radix	9/3/95	Grenada
Michael A. Radix	9/2/95	Grenada
Michael Reagan	11/19/96	Sherman Oaks, California
Donald T. Regan	7/18/96	Telephone
Rozanne L. Ridgway	2/7/96	Washington, D.C.
Richard Schifter	11/28/95	Washington, D.C.
Barry Schweid	10/26/95	Washington, D.C.
Paul Scoon	9/2/95	Grenada
Richard Secord	7/9/96	Washington, D.C.
Judy Nir Shalom	7/31/96	Ramat Gan, Israel
Yitzhak Shamir	7/2/95	Tel Aviv, Israel
Harry Shlaudeman	1/23/96	Washington, D.C.
George P. Shultz	9/26/95	San Francisco, California
Uri Simhoni	3/27/96	Tel Aviv, Israel
Bernadette Casey Smith	8/22/95	Roslyn Harbor, New York
Abraham Sofaer	9/26/95	Palo Alto, California
Stuart Spencer	6/28/96	San Francisco, California
Abraham Tamir	3/24/96	Ramat Aviv, Israel
Sergei Tarasenko	10/9/96	Telephone
Howard Teicher	7/9/96	Washington, D.C.
Edward Teller	6/28/96	Stanford, California
Horst Teltschik	5/20/96	Munich, Germany
Cal Thomas	7/16/96	Alexandria, Virginia
Victor Hugo Tinoco	9/6/95	Managua, Nicaragua
John W. Vessey	2/8/96	Arlington, Virginia
Lawrence Walsh	11/13/96	Telephone
James Watt	5/28/96	Telephone
Caspar Weinberger	1/10/96	Telephone
Benjamin Weir	7/11/96	Telephone
John C. Whitehead	12/22/95	New York, New York
Charles Z. Wick	7/1/96	Malibu, California
Desima Williams	11/14/95	Cambridge, Massachusetts
Margaret Wright	7/4/95	Purley, United Kingdom
Oliver Wright	7/4/95	Purley, United Kingdom

Bibliographical Note

This book is based on oral interviews. We were, however, greatly aided in our background research by the memoirs of Nancy and Ronald Reagan, as well as by the books of others who were involved in aspects of the Reagan presidency, including Elliott Abrams, Martin Anderson, Michael Deaver, Alexander Haig Jr., Michael Ledeen, Jack Matlock, Edwin Meese III, Constantine Menges, Lyn Nofziger, Peggy Noonan, Oliver North, Joan Quigley, Donald T. Regan, Yitzhak Shamir, Natan Sharansky, David Stockman, Howard and Gayle Teicher, Margaret Thatcher, and Lawrence Walsh. Special mention should be made of George Shultz's *Turmoil and Triumph* (1993).

We also found helpful the books of Steve Albert, Wolf Blitzer, Robert Dallek, Ronnie Dugger, Roy Gutman, Haynes Johnson, Don Oberdorfer, Ze'ev Shiff and Ehud Ya'ari, and Bob Woodward.

We are indebted to *Facts on File* for an accurate record of the Reagan presidency, Peter Kornbluth and Malcolm Byrne's *The Iran-Contra File*, and the *Report of the Congressional Committees Investigating the Iran-Contra Affair*.

Finally, anyone researching Ronald Reagan's career must thank Lou Cannon for his comprehensive trilogy *Ronnie and Jesse* (1969), *Reagan* (1982), and *President Reagan: The Role of a Lifetime* (1990).

Index

Abbas, Abu, 374, 379–80

ABM Treaty, 233, 240

Abortion, 26n, 49, 80

Abrahamson, James, 231–32, 234–35, 237, 239–40, 243–44, 246, 248, 587

Abrams, Elliott, 145, 171, 178, 312, 315–16, 331, 349, 483, 492–93, 515, 532, 534, 536–37, 539, 542, 551, 576, 577, 587

Abshire, David, 71, 230, 240, 245, 247, 329, 449, 515, 523, 539–40, 542, 543, 544–46, 575, 587

Achille Lauro hijacking, 374–80, 376n, 391

Adelist, Ron, 446

Afghanistan invasion, 197, 411

AIDS crisis, 135–43

Akhromeyev, Sergei, 350, 350n, 352, 354, 357–58

Algerian Accords, 466–67

Allen, Charles, 374, 461

Allen, Richard, 25, 30, 42, 66, 75, 77, 83, 86, 92, 103, 115–16, 513

Alvarez, Walter, 456

Alzheimer's disease, 580–85

Ames, Aldrich, 372, 372n

Anderson, John, 3, 35, 132

Anderson, Martin: on administrative style of RR, 97, 107; after RR's presidency, 587; on "belly button" account, 556–57; on Casey and secretary of state appointment, 67; on Casey's brain tumor, 498; on chief of staff for RR's first term, 63; first impressions of RR, 4, 41; on Haig's resignation as secretary of state, 86; on hostages in Lebanon, 394; on intelligence of RR, 100; on international legacy of RR, 570–71; on Iran-contra investigation, 539; on Nancy Reagan, 48; on RR's early presidential ambitions, 4, 5; on personality of RR, 45, 57, 58; on presidential campaign of 1980, 14–17, 31, 36, 38; on Republican vice presidential candidate in 1980, 19–21, 24–25; on "scripting" of RR by key staff, 98–99; on SDI, 246; as supporter of RR, 110; on transition between Carter and Reagan presidencies, 59; on White House staff, 63; on worldview of RR, 147

Anderson, Terry, 390, 392, 393, 393n, 395, 448, 467, 472, 510, 516, 517, 550, 587

Andropov, Yuri, 53, 147, 152, 329

Angleton, James Jesus, 368

Aquino, Corazon, 325–26

Arabs. *See* Iran-contra affair; Middle East; PLO; *and specific countries*

Arafat, Yassir, 209, 211–13, 319, 320–21, 374, 379

Arens, Moshe, 192–93, 192n, 321

Argov, Shlomo, 202

Armacost, Michael, 525

Armitage, Richard, 367

Arms control. *See* Defense policy

Arms sales. *See* Iran-contra affair

Aronson, Bernard, 42

Assad, Hafez al-, 324